Theories of Organizations

Theories of Organizations

FORM, PROCESS, AND TRANSFORMATION

JERALD HAGE
University of Maryland

A Wiley-Interscience Publication

JOHN WILEY & SONS, New York · Chichester · Brisbane · Toronto

Library of Congress Cataloging in Publication Data

Hage, Jerald, 1932–
  Theories of organizations.

  Bibliography: p.
  Includes index.
  1. Organization. I. Title.

HD31.H188   302.3'5   79-26715
ISBN 0-471-33859-1

Printed in the United States of America

10 9 8 7 6 5 4 3

This book is dedicated to Max Weber
who aroused in me a theoretical interest
in organizations and to Jewell Hage who
fostered in me a practical interest with
the hope that I have served both masters
equally well.

Preface

My practical interest in organizations grew out of listening to my father talk about all his problems in attempting to manage a paper company. He created in me a concern about how workers could be made happier and more efficient at the same time. Although it was not always apparent how my dad reconciled these two goals, they certainly became essential ones for me. The difficulty of this feat became clear to me when I spent three years in the Navy, first as legal officer and then as personnel officer.

After leaving the Navy in 1958 I entered the graduate program at Columbia University where I encountered Max Weber's ideas about organizations for the first time. Like many students, I found the complexities of his writings hard to grasp. But that his was a good mind at work there was no doubt. So I made it a practice to read and reread his writings, attempting to assimilate not only the ideas in all of their subtleties but also the analytical thought patterns. For better or for worse, the theoretical issues in this book are largely defined by him. In addition, the ideal type construction he employed is frequently used as well. For these reasons, I have dedicated this book to both Weber and my father, because each in his own way has shaped my mind and made this book what it is.

In my second year at Columbia I had the opportunity to take two courses on organizations, one with Robert K. Merton and the other with Amitai Etzioni. In the former course I read March and Simon (1958) for the first time and discovered that I had a very different perspective from theirs, took my first plunge into the topic of organizational change, and met Koya Azumi, all three important events in my intellectual development. What I, like many students, learned at Columbia was the paradigm of structural-functionalism. But unlike many students, I developed a strong conviction that its real potential lies in social engineering, not a popular view in those days.

Much of my work for the first decade, in the sixties, was an attempt to indicate how one could write structural-functional theories, and more specifically with the objectives of designing organizations that would facilitate innovation. It was only in the seventies that I moved into system analysis and concerns about cybernetic control, specifying the key variables in that system, and finally became concerned with the larger problem of adaptiveness.

In these past twenty years of trying to build some codified knowledge about organizations, I have benefited from knowing a number of people who have enriched me in many ways. I have also been influenced by particular works of individuals, to which I feel an intellectual debt. These works and the individuals who have shaped my ideas are, among others, as follows.

The Aston studies, and especially David Hickson, Derek Pugh, and Bob Hinnings, have made a massive contribution that becomes one of the cornerstones of this book. I also appreciate their allowing me to reanalyze their data. Their separate papers, one on technology, another on role specificity, and a third on the relative power of departments, by David Hickson and colleagues and some as yet unpublished work on the process of decision-making are an essential part of my effort to synthesize the literature.

The work of Peter Blau and of his many students, including Marshall Meyer, Wolf Heydebrand, and Richard Schoenherr, is a key link as well. Although I have had less opportunity to interact with them than with David Hickson, their work represents another foundation upon which this book is built. While they may not like my reinterpretation of their research, the synthesis could not have been made without their very solid contribution to the literature.

Koya Azumi, whose close friendship dates back to Merton's seminar, has also provided several crucial connections in his work on Japanese firms and in the theory that he developed with Phelps Tracy. He kindly reanalyzed his data so that I could check some new hypotheses. Likewise, the work of Cornelius Lammers has helped me a great deal to see a larger picture. Cor carefully reviewed a number of chapters and his insightful comments helped improve the manuscript immeasureably. Both men, one Japanese and the other Dutch, together with the Englishman David Hickson and their colleagues, have advanced the generalizability of organizational research across national boundaries, in books now being published.

Although we spent most of our time arguing when he was at the University of Wisconsin, Charles Perrow and his work on goals and on technology have strongly influenced my thinking. In fact if any single work has helped me to break the mold of linear thought in which I was cast, it was his typology of technology, one of the richest and densest theoretical pieces in the entire literature. Chic moved me back to a renewed appreciation of Weber. He will probably argue with what I have done with his ideas. Nevertheless they served as a fertile irritant to my thinking.

Although I do not know either Paul Lawrence or Jay Lorsch well, their work on contingency theory, and even more important the way in which they thought about the problem, have had a very beneficial effect, reminding me of my commitment to practical concerns.

But perhaps the person who has played this role the most for me is my close friend Pierre-Maire Fourt, a French businessman who has to confront every day the problems of building creative research. He, probably more than anyone else, has helped me to understand the limitations of theories in practical settings, especially my own!

Another man who has done the same thing — and whom I count as a close friend — is Andre Delbecq; he stimulated my thinking the most at the University of Wisconsin when we were there. His many students and above all Andy Van — de Ven made my teaching of organizations, the few times I gave the course, exciting. Again their work, which builds on James Thompson, another typologist, forms still another cornerstone of this book.

James Price, another student from Columbia and a friend, has very carefully criticized and improved my thinking on several occasions. More importantly, his theoretical works on effectiveness and turnover have helped me to revise my own position on these matters.

Finally, I have profited very much from three years' residence in France, where I have made a considerable effort to learn to reason á la française. This means an appreciation for qualitative rather than quantitative research, a preference for political rather than structural-functional paradigms, a more historical and institutional understanding of organizations rather than searches for generalizations, especially a conviction that organizational theory manufactured in the United States will not work in France because things are different, and finally a predilection for ideal-type construction rather than hypothesis formulation. The European Group of Organizational Studies meetings in Europe and a visiting professorship at the École des Mines for one year, thanks to the then Director of Research, Michel Turpin, provided many opportunities for an intellectual confrontation that allowed me to reflect about ways of thinking other than my own.

There are many others who have in various ways influenced me, or whose research studies have proved very important, Richard Hall, the late Joan Woodward, Richard Scott, Gerald Gordon, Arnold Tannenbaum, Richard McCleery (whom I have never met), the late James Thompson, John Child, Hans Pennings, Howard Aldrich, Ken Benson, John Freeman, Jeffrey Pfeffer, Al Kaluzny, James Palumbo, Steve Paulson, and so on. I am particularly grateful to both John Child and Steve Paulson, who helped me reanalyze their work. This allowed for an instantaneous replication that is critical for the development of a science of organizations. Also, Steve Cohn has been most generous in the reanalysis of the shoe industry study. To all these people, I want to express my appreciation for what they have done and my apologies if in various ways I have distorted or failed to understand their contributions.

The federal government has been a long silent partner in these twenty years. They gave Community Hospital a large grant to study physicians' resistance to change, which paid my way through graduate school (1960–63) and allowed me to do my first panel study. Then in 1964–67 and 1968–70, the Vocational Rehabilitation Administration, now the Social Rehabilitation Services made two large grants to Michael Aiken and myself so that we could do another panel study, this time of organizations, to test a number of propositions in the axiomatic theory. This first-hand confrontation with data considerably enriched my thinking.

All the data analysis of the Azumi, Child, and Pugh et al. studies were done by Robert Hanneman, who very carefully helped me to survive why I spent three years of my life in Paris. Without his keeping track of my mail and my research, I could never have completed this book.

Last but not least, the manuscript has been typed several times. The first drafts were done largely by my sister-in-law François Pellerin and our *au pair* Pat Bousse in France. The second and third drafts were also typed in Paris by another sister-in-law, Annie Cottenet, several friends, Suzanne Toche and Marie-Claude Pignet, and a superb professional, Ruby D'Arschott. Because all are French, I especially appreciate their reworking my English. The fourth and final draft was done under the supervision of Gladys Graham in the Department of Sociology at the University of Maryland. Also, Dorothy Bowers, Danielle Morel, Catherine O'Toole, and Joyce Sterling, typed or worked on this manuscript. I appreciate their patience.

JERALD HAGE

"La Bruyere"
Arrigas, France

Contents

Figures   xix

Tables   xxi

Chapter 1   Substantive Issues and Analytical Paradigms   1

1.1.   Substantive Issues: Power, Change, Human Factor, and the Environment, 6

1.2.   Analytical Levels: Micro, Meso, and Macro, 8

    1.2.1.   The Definition of the Meso Analytical Level, 9

    1.2.2.   The Definition of the Macro Analytical Level, 11

    1.2.3.   The Definition of the Micro Analytical Level, 13

1.3.   Analytical Paradigms, 14

1.4.   Analytical Themes: Form, Process, and Transformation, 20

1.5.   Conclusions, 21

Chapter 2   Alternative Forms of Organizational Structure and Function   23

2.1.   Weber's Model of Bureaucracy, 24

    2.1.1.   The Implicit Theory, 25

    2.1.2.   A Critique, 28

2.2   Burns's and Stalker's Mechanical and Organic Models, 29

    2.2.1.   The Implicit Theory, 30

    2.2.2.   A Critique, 33

2.3.   Hage's Axiomatic Theory, 34

      2.3.1.   The Major Hypotheses, 36
      2.3.2.   The Derived Hypotheses, 39
      2.3.3.   A Critique, 46

2.4.   Conclusions, 46

PART ONE   POWER: STRUCTURE, PROCESS, AND SUCCESSION

Chapter 3   Power: The Problem of Centralization or Participation   53

3.1.   A Meso Structural Theory of Power, 57

      3.1.1.   The Major Premise and Hypotheses, 57
      3.1.2.   The Concepts and their Measures, 63
      3.1.3.   The Findings, 68
      3.1.4.   Summary, 82

3.2.   The Distribution of Power Among Hierarchical Levels and Departments, 83

      3.2.1.   Coping with Uncertainty Theory, 87
      3.2.2.   Coalition Theory, 90
      3.2.3.   A Special Problem: The Power of the Board of Trustees, 94
      3.2.4.   A Special Problem: Worker Participation, 98

3.3.   Centralization and Job Autonomy: Meso and Micro Structures, 100

      3.3.1.   Job Autonomy and Its Measure, 102
      3.3.2.   The Findings, 104
      3.3.3.   A Special Problem: Why People Obey Orders, 106
      3.3.4.   A Special Problem: Powerlessness, 107

3.4.   Conclusions, 107

Chapter 4   Processes of Power   109

4.1.   Kinds of Decisions, 109

      4.1.1.   The High Risk, Discontinuous Decision, 110
      4.1.2.   The Major Premise, 114

4.2.   Decision-Making Processes, 116

4.2.1.   Variables for Describing Decision-Making
Processes, 116
4.2.2.   Kinds of Processes, 120

4.3.   Meso-Structure and the Process of Decision Making, 124
4.4.   Conclusions, 129

**Chapter 5   Transformation of Power: Dominant Coalitions and
Succession   130**

5.1.   A Meso-Theory of Structure and Effectiveness, 133

5.1.1.   The Theoretical Definitions of Objectives and
Effectiveness, 133
5.1.2.   The Major Premise and Hypotheses, 137

5.2.   The Dominant Coalition and Its Values, 143
5.3.   Succession and Changes in the Dominant Coalition, 150

5.3.1.   The Causes of Succession, 152
5.3.2.   The Consequences of Succession, 155

5.4.   Conclusions, 158

**PART TWO: CHANGE: STRUCTURE, PROCESS, AND
ADAPTIVENESS**

Chapter 6   Structure and Changes in Outputs   161

6.1.   A Meso Structural Theory of Output and Process Change, 165

6.1.1.   Major Premises and Hypotheses, 165
6.1.2.   The Concepts and Their Measures, 170
6.1.3.   The Findings, 176
6.1.4.   A Special Problem: Values and Innovation, 184

6.2.   Relative Change by Products and Periods, 188

6.2.1.   The Prevalence and Importance of Radical
Innovation, 189
6.2.2.   A Theory of Radical Innovation, 191
6.2.3.   A Theory of Innovation Periods, 197

6.3.   A Micro-Structural Theory of Creativity, 199

        6.3.1.   Major Premises and Hypotheses, 199
        6.3.2.   The Findings, 204

6.4.   Conclusions, 205

Chapter 7   A Process of Change   **207**

7.1.   The Process of Change: Key Stages and Analytical
        Problems, 208

        7.1.1.   Hypotheses about the Evaluation Stage, 212
        7.1.2.   Hypotheses about the Initiation Stage, 217
        7.1.3.   Hypotheses about the Implementation Stage, 220
        7.1.4.   Hypotheses about the Routinization Stage, 226

7.2.   The Causes of Resistance and of Conflict, 229

        7.2.1.   Vested Interest Theory, 230
        7.2.2.   Capacity for Change Theory, 231
        7.2.3.   Cost-Benefit Theory, 234
        7.2.4.   A Special Problem: Client or Customer
                  Resistance, 237

7.3.   Overcoming Resistance to Change, 239

        7.3.1.   Evolution or Revolution? Two Change
                  Strategies, 242
        7.3.2.   The Strategy of a New Division or a New
                  Organization, 244

7.4.   Conclusions, 245

Chapter 8   Transformation of Form: Adaptation   **247**

8.1.   Kinds of Crises and Kinds of Responses, 249

        8.1.1.   The Imbalance Between Performances and the
                  Steering Response, 251
        8.1.2.   The Imbalance Between Inputs and Outputs and
                  the Adjustment Response, 256
        8.1.3.   The Imbalance Between Structure and Performance
                  and the Adaptive Response, 260
                  8.1.3.1.   The Definition of Adaptiveness, 260
                  8.1.3.2.   The Definition of Viable Forms, 263

8.1.3.3. The Definition of Equilibrium and
Disequilibrium, 270

8.2. The Process of Adaptation: Learning the Hard Way, 272

8.2.1. The Lack of a Resource Base and Nonresponsiveness
to Change, 274
8.2.2. The Institutionalization of Success and
Nonresponsiveness to Change, 276
8.2.3. Structure and Nonresponsiveness to Change, 279
8.2.4. Elite Values and Nonresponsiveness to Change, 282
8.2.5. The Hierarchy of Responses and the Choice of a
Wrong Response, 283

8.3. The Dynamics of Transformation, 286
8.4. Conclusions, 289

**PART THREE: THE HUMAN FACTOR: EXIT, VOICE,
AND LOYALTY**

Chapter 9 Exit: Morale and Turnover 293

9.1. A Structural Theory of Collective Effort, 295

9.1.1. The Theoretical Concepts, 295
9.1.2. Premise and Hypotheses, 298
9.1.3. The Findings, 305
9.1.4. A Special Problem: Turnover, 308

9.2. Control and Morale, 309

9.2.1. Basic Premise and Hypotheses, 311
9.2.2. A Special Problem: Social Integration, 315

9.3. The Micro Structure: Work Groups, Job Enlargement, and
Job Enrichment, 316
9.4. Conclusions, 320

Chapter 10 Voices: Conflict and Consensus 321

10.1. The Concepts of Organizational Conflict and Consensus, 323
10.2. A Meso-Structural Theory of Conflict, 328

10.2.1. The Major Premises and Hypotheses, 328
10.2.2. The Findings, 334
10.2.3. A Special Problem: Strikes or Work Stoppages, 339

10.3.   A Micro-Structural Theory of Role Conflict, 344

        10.3.1. Role-Set Theory, 344
        10.3.2. The Findings, 347

10.4.   Conclusions, 349

Chapter 11   Loyalty: Coordination and Control   350

11.1.   A Meso-Structural Theory of Coordination/Control, 351

        11.1.1. The Major Premises, 351
        11.1.2. A Typology of Coordination/Control, 355
        11.1.3. Derived Hypotheses, 359

11.2.   The Findings, 362
11.3.   Transformation of Form: Disequilibrium, 367
11.4.   A Micro Theory of Coordination/Control, 369

        11.4.1. The Premise and Hypotheses, 369
        11.4.2. The Findings, 370
        11.4.3. A Special Problem: Conformity, 374

11.5.   Conclusions, 375

PART FOUR: THE ENVIRONMENT: RESOURCES AND THE TRANSFORMATION OF FORM, STRATEGIES, AND CONSTRAINTS

Chapter 12   Resources and the Choice of Organizational Form   379

12.1.   A Meso Theory of Resources and Structure, 382

        12.1.1. The Theoretical Definitions, 382
        12.1.2. The Impact of Technology, 387
        12.1.3. The Impact of Personnel Size, 390
        12.1.4. The Measures, 394
        12.1.5. The Findings, 396

12.2.   A Meso Theory of Resources, Work-Flow, and Control, 401

        12.2.1. A Typology of Task Scope, Personnel Size, and Work-Flow, 403
        12.2.2. Premises and Hypotheses, 408
        12.2.3. The Findings, 410

12.3.   Growth and the Transformation of Organizational Form, 413

12.4.   Conclusions, 420

Chapter 13   Organizational Strategies of Environmental Control and the
             Choice of Organizational Form   422

13.1.   A Macro Theory of Environmental Constraints and
        Organizational Choice, 425

        13.1.1. The Range of Strategic Choices, 426
        13.1.2. The Range of Environmental Constraints, 437
        13.1.3. The Typology of Environmental Constrairts and
                 Organizational Choices, 442
        13.1.4. A Special Problem: Environmental Constraints on
                 Organizational Autonomy, 451

13.2.   Domination versus Interdependence, 452

        13.2.1. A Macro Theory of Organizational Domination, 452
        13.2.2. The Findings, 458
        13.2.3. A Special Problem: Organizational Exploitation
                 and Corporate Crime, 460

13.3.   Transformation of Networks and Markets by Growth and
        Development, 463

13.4.   Conclusions, 466

Chapter 14   Societal Constraints and the Evolution of Organizational
             Forms   468

14.1.   Societal Constraints and the Evolution of Organizational
        Forms, 470

        14.1.1. Modernization and Organizational Forms, 471
        14.1.2. Industrialization and Organizational Forms, 476
        14.1.3. The Findings, 485

14.2.   The State and Evolution of Forms, 486

14.3.   Organizational Forms and Societal Problems, 490

Appendix A Premises   495

Appendix B Hypotheses   497

Bibliography 508

Author Index 531

Subject Index 541

Figures

1.1 Analytical levels and examples, 12
1.2 A typology of organizational paradigms, 15
1.3 Analytical problems associated with the major themes and perspectives, 19
2.1 Major concepts and hypothesis in Weber's model of bureaucracy, 25
2.2 Burns and Stalker's mechanical and organic models, 31
2.3 Major propositions and corollaries of the Hage theory of structure and function, 40
2.4 A block-recursive model of organization structure and function, 44
2.5 A synthesis of Burns and Stalker's and Hage's theories of organizational form, 47
3.1 Four kinds of power distribution, 85
3.2 The theory of coping with uncertainty, 88
3.3 The path analytical diagram of job autonomy from the Child Study, 103
4.1 The interrelations between decision characteristics, 111
4.2 Definitions of variables describing the process of decision making, 117
4.3 Decision characteristics and decision trajectory, 121
4.4 Social structure and the process of decision making, 125
5.1 A typology of kinds of effectiveness, 135
5.2 A typology of general values, 145
7.1 Different conceptualizations of the process of innovation, 210
7.2 The performance gap and the radicalness of the innovation, 214
7.3 The radicalness of the innovation and the need for resources, 218
7.4 Radical innovation and the extent of conflict, 222
7.5 Radical innovation and its institutionalization, 228
7.6 Strategies for overcoming resistance to change, 239
8.1 Equilibrium problems—steady states and organizational crises, 261
8.2 The characteristics of several organic and mechanical steady states, 264
8.3 The graph of the four ideal-types of steady states, 268

8.4   The standard and revised model of information feedback, 273

9.1   The Hirschman model, 294

9.2   The Price model, 294

9.3   Expanded model of choice of voice versus exit, 295

9.4   Kindred ideas relative to morale, 297

9.5   Meso-structural and the balance of costs and benefits, 302

10.1   The levels and content of conflict, 324

10.2   The consensus-conflict/continuum, 328

10.3   The conceptualization of equilibrium and disequilibrium, 332

10.4   Scatter plot of structure and conflict, from the Hage-Aiken study, 336

10.5   The varieties of conflict, 341

10.6   Special conditions for violent conflict, 343

10.7   The causes of role conflict, 346

11.1   The mechanisms of coordination and of control in the most typical steady states, 356

11.2   Structure, formalization, and communication, 366

12.1   The twin consequences of the growth in knowledge, 385

12.2   The various models of personnel size and structure given different causal structures, 392

12.3   The reanalysis of the Aston studies, 397

12.4   The reanalysis of the Hage-Aiken panel study, 398

12.5   The reanalysis of the Azumi study, 399

12.6   The reanalysis of the Paulson study, 399

12.7   Task scope, personnel size, and work-flow or throughput, 404

12.8   Performance feedback on organizational resources, 414

13.1   The four ideal-types of organizational forms and the hierarchy of strategic choices, 428

13.2   A typology of organizational strategies vis-à-vis demand, 432

13.3   The environmental constraints of task knowledge and available funds and organizational strategies, 443

13.4   The transformation of the market and the larger environment, 464

Tables

3.1 Concentration of Specialists Vis-à-Vis Centralization and Stratification: Secondary Analysis, 64

3.2 Centralization and Stratification, 76

3.3 The Level and Rate of Change in Each Structural Variable, 78

3.4 Levels and Rates of Change in the Structural Variables Taken Together, 81

3.5 The Meso-Structural Determinants of Job Autonomy, 105

3.6 Individual Characteristics and Job Autonomy, 105

5.1 Structure and Organizational Objectives, 142

6.1 The Relationship Between Structure and the Rate of Process Innovation, 177

6.2 The Relationship Between Structure and the Rate of Output Innovation, 178

6.3 The Relationship Between Structure and Process and Output Innovations Combined, 183

6.4 Values, Risk and Innovation, 186

6.5 Values, Structure, and Innovation, 187

9.1 Structural Properties and Morale, 310

9.2 Control and Morale, 312

9.3 Structure, Control, and Morale, 314

10.1 The Structural Causes of Conflict and Consensus, 334

10.2 Meso and Micro Conflict Compared, 347

11.1 Structure, Formalization and Task Visibility, 363

11.2 Studies of Micro-Structure and Coordination Mechanism, 371

Theories of Organizations

Chapter One

Substantive Issues
and Analytical Paradigms

Organizational sociology appears to have reached a critical juncture some twenty years ago after the publication of March and Simon's (1958) seminal work, a convenient bench mark in the development of the field. There has been an incredible amount of new work, both theoretical and empirical. Four different paradigms or perspectives have emerged. Research findings have proliferated. Cross-national studies are common. But generalizations and substantiated theories are few and far between. The field has lost a clear theoretical thrust, and the connections between works are no longer perceived. Certainly much of this is desirable. But at the same time, once in a while there is a need for a new theoretical synthesis that can provide the basis for a new antithesis. Otherwise the dialectic stops. Some efforts have been made to bring together a number of the findings and theories in the field (e.g., see Hall, 1977; Zey-Farrell, 1979; Lammers, 1978) but as yet there has not been a more general organizational theory written in the spirit of March and Simon's work. This is the objective of this work.

To put this current effort in perspective, it is useful to perceive the essential dialectic that has occurred during the past twenty years. The publication of March and Simon (1958) provided a much needed thesis. Their central concepts were derived from psychology and their intellectual concerns were administration. Besides efficiency they added the concept of morale, which they called the motivation to participate. Beyond this Simon noted that individuals tended to satisfy rather than maximize, a principal for which he won the Nobel prize in economics. But the book's concern with the psychological design of organizations spurred many sociologists to suggest an alternative perspective.

During the mid-1960s (Burns and Stalker, 1961; Etzioni, 1961a; Hage, 1965; Thompson, 1967; Perrow, 1967; Price, 1968) this thesis was being challenged by

1

a large number of structural-functional theories largely in the tradition of Weber's model of rational legal bureaucracy. In these theories the organization, not the manager, is the analytical unit. The central concerns are less with design and more with structure and effectiveness, although many acknowledge their debt to March and Simon (especially Burns and Stalker, 1961 and Perrow, 1967). Since these theories were written, few attempts have been made to pull together the many research findings relative to them (except for Etzioni's theory of compliance, 1975, and Hall, 1977). Nor have these variations on the Weberian theme themselves been integrated together. Conceptually each has strong and weak points. Together with the codification of relevant research, they can provide a fruitful synthesis of structural-functional theory.

By the mid 1960s, this paradigm itself was being attacked by a new wave of antitheses. The most prominent have been what might be called the political-value orientation, concerned with coalitions and their goals (Cyert and March, 1963; Stauss et al., 1963; Crozier, 1964; Mouzelis, 1968; Child, 1972a; Karpik, 1972 a and b; Hills and Mahoney, 1978; McNeil, 1978), and a conflict-critical perspective, more pronounced in political sociology than in the studies of organizations (Lammers, 1969; Corwin, 1969 a and b; Lawrence and Lorsch, 1967 a and b; Baldridge, 1971; Benson, 1973, 1975, and 1977; Zald, 1970; Clegg, 1975; Clegg and Dunkerly, 1977; admittedly some of these would feel uncomfortable with the label because they examine conflict while others such as Clegg and Dunkerly, 1977; Benson, 1977; and Goldman, 1977 more consciously adapted a neo-marxist or political economy perspective). There is considerable overlap in these two orientations but, as will be noted later, the former has been more concerned with predicting what organizations will do by knowing what values the managers have and the latter has been more concerned with the larger economic institutions that organizations may serve and how this relates to the state.

The third antithesis to appear might be labeled cybernetic-adaptive (Forrester, 1961; Cangelosi and Dill, 1965; Katz and Kahn, 1966; Buckley, 1967 and 1968; Etzioni, 1968; Miller, 1974; Hage, 1974; Weick, 1976; Hedberg, Nystrom, and Starbuck, 1976); it is distinctive and on another level of abstraction. By being more general, it can unite both rationalistic and humanistic perspectives on organizations (Brown, 1978). At the same time it has been of most interest to those who were tired of the limitations of a structural-functional perspective. In these three new orientations, the assumptions and hypotheses remain as yet vague; these must be specified before their true potential for organizational analysis can be appreciated this is less true with system analysis (Miller, 1975 a and b) than cybernetics (see Hage, 1974 for a discussion of the distinction).

Just as these new theoretical orientations began to emerge, two analytic attacks on the origins of social structure emerged: technology and size. There has been a flood of papers (for technology see Woodward, 1965; Perrow, 1967;

James Thompson, 1967; Hickson et al., 1969; Hage and Aiken, 1969 and their bibliographies; and for size Blau, 1970 a or b, 1972, and 1973; Meyer, 1968 a and b, 1972 a and b, Heydebrand, 1973 a or b; Blau and Schoenherr, 1971 among others). They are variations of structural-functionalism in the sense that their essential analytical thrust deals with the causes of social structure, a logical and consistent development of structural-functionalism rather than a conscious break from it. These two schools have sparked a debate still being fought in the journals (Hickson et al., 1969; Aldrich, 1972; John Freeman, 1973; Miles, Snow, and Pfeffer, 1974; Blau et al., 1976; Tracy and Azumi, 1976; Van de Ven, Delbecq, and Koenig, 1976; Hall, 1977: 127; Dewar and Hage, 1978, etc.), and one that needs to be resolved.

During the past ten years a rich array of theoretical concepts has been added to the literature. Probably the most prominent entry has been that of the environment (Lawrence and Lorsch, 1967 a and b; James Thompson, 1967; Brinkerhoff and Kunz, 1972) which has triggered a variety of studies and conferences (Negandhi, 1975; I.S.A. 1974; Ego, 1976 and 1977; Warner, 1977) exploring the meanings of the concept. This interest developed in two directions, one reflecting the interest in system analysis and cybernetics and the other associated with the growth of a political economy perspective on organizations (see Zald, 1970; Benson, 1977). Beyond this and the kindred ideas of interorganizational relationships (Turk, 1970 and 1973) boundary spanners (Aldrich and Herker, 1977; Leifer and Huber, 1977) and organization-set (Evan, 1966, 1972, 1976; Hirsch, 1972), other new concepts have made a considerable impact: uncertainty (Crozier, 1964; James Thompson, 1967; Lawrence and Lorsch, 1967 a and b; Hickson et al., 1971, etc), succession (Grusky, 1960, 1961, and 1963), strategic choice (Child, 1972a; Warner, ed., 1977), strategies (Mintzberg, 1973 and 1975), coordination (Thompson, 1967; Hage, 1974), and many others. But with some notable exceptions, such as the coping with uncertainty theory of Hickson et al. (1971) and the theoretical work of Hage (1974) and Aldrich (1979) most of these concepts have yet to be integrated into a broader and general organizational theory.

Parallel with the proliferation of new concepts has come an avalanche of research studies, most of them quite good and technically sophisticated (see the past ten years of the *Administrative Science Quarterly*). However, this literature has many inconsistencies and contradictory findings. Most students discover that concepts with the same name have different measures, such as complexity (Hall, 1977; Dewar and Hage, 1978; Zey-Farrel, 1979), technology, and even size (Kimberly, 1976). Other concepts with different names have the same indicators, as for example centralization (Hage and Aiken, 1967) and control (Tannebaum, 1968). Yet, structure and control are not the same (Child, 1972b; Ouchi, 1977) As yet there has not been a careful working through of these various meanings (for an exception see Price, 1972).

The principal objective of this book is to synthesize as much of the previous sociological work of the past two decades as possible around a coherent and systematic thesis. By codifying the existing research, explaining insofar as possible contradictory findings by the nature of their measures or the kind of research design, a new foundation can be built for further advances.

The test of any new thesis is not only how much has been summarized but how many new analytical issues emerge. Throughout the last five years there has been much discussion of the need for process models and process thinking about organizations, with the emergence of some formal statements (John Freeman and Hannan, 1975). But with a few exceptions, there have not as yet been many attempts to develop theories of decision-making (although one is in progress, Hickson, forthcoming), growth and development (the exception is John Freeman and Hannan, 1975), and the like.

The second major objective of this book is to write new hypotheses about a number of the more critical processes that exist in organizations and their environments.

If no one tries to write a general theory of organizations from time to time, there is a danger that the field will remain fragmented into a wide variety of schools and perspectives. Worse yet, given the intellectual disorder and disparity of findings, and the chaos of competing claims and concepts described above, there is the possibility that many will retreat into a kind of historicism in which the world becomes a steady stream of "happenings." Sometimes researchers believe that they necessarily understand something by reporting the correlations without reconciling them with other studies, or that the narrative of what happens is an analysis. Research assumes meaning when it is placed in a larger context. It is easy to write natural histories or to do research, but it is more difficult to find patterns (for techniques on how to find pattern see Hage, 1972). There is a cynicism in those who argue against generalizations of any kind that can prevent further intellectual progress – and worse yet prevent solutions to a number of practical problems. There are organizations where workers are poorly paid (Quinney, 1979). There is a need for radical innovations. Corporate crime does exist. Such problems are only solvable with some set of hypotheses about why workers are exploited, why there is little radical innovation, and why there is corporate crime. Once one knows the whyfors it becomes possible to alter the existing state of affairs. But this means theory, and theory means at least some generalization, however qualified.

One can sympathize, however, with the complaint that theories, whether of ideal-typical format à la Weber or a set of hypotheses à la Blau (1970), irrespective of how sophisticated their equations and how tight their reasoning, are at best a simplification of a very complex reality. But one does not handle complexity by retreating into the simplistic position that everything is different and that unpredictable events occur. Instead one makes one's theories and models more complex. Complexity emerges naturally as an inevitable consequence of reconciling divergent findings, concepts, indicators, perspectives, and assumptions. Each of them is true – but only partly so. By combining them, one not only creates a new thesis but a much more subtle one. But a theory must be, by the nature of the world and our knowledge, a simplification. It is the interaction between our simple ideas and our complex reality that allows for growth in the depth of our analysis. If we retreat into the assertion that all is a stream of history – without pattern – then our understanding can never grow. Intellectual growth, the dialectic, starts with some assertion, however crude. One can thus amend Kant to say:

Intuitions without theories are blind.

But one also agrees with the other part of Kant's couplet:

Theories without data are sterile.

Any new thesis must be grounded not only in the integration of perspectives, concepts, and theories, but most importantly in the reconciling of divergent findings. The divergences in research findings are not an occasion for despair or historicism but an opportunity for learning and scientific advance!

Fortunately at this moment in the development of organizational sociology, there has been a parallel development in theoretical and analytical methods which can aid us in constructing more complex and subtle statements. One methodological advance is theory construction and the other is structured equations. The books and articles on theory construction (Blalock, 1969; Abell, 1971; Gibbs, 1972; Hage, 1972) provide a standard by which the previous efforts can be evaluated and which this present work is attempting to meet. Many of the "theories" cited above consisted primarily of concepts or types with little discussion about how they might be interrelated. There have been few formal attempts to write organizational theory (exceptions are Blau, 1970; Aiken and Hage, 1968; Hage, Aiken, and Marret, 1971) of premises and derived equations. Many of the theories have been quite deficient in explicating precise measures. Since I agree with George Homans (1967) that the essential goal of a theory should be to explain *why* hypotheses are theoretically interesting and believable much attention will be paid to making the premises explicit. However theories must not only be logical but testable and therefore equal attention will be paid to the problem of measures.

Concomitant with the development of theory construction has come a considerably greater sophistication of causal modeling techniques (Blalock, 1971; Heise, 1975; and any of the various issues of *Sociological Methodology* and the journal *Sociological Methods and Research*). Largely confined so far to the work on the status attainment model, they are gradually spreading to other areas of sociology. Causal modeling is a powerful technique for organizing not only one's data, but also one's ideas. So far they have not been employed extensively in organizational analysis. With these new causal techniques has also come a literature on the pooling of time series data (Hannan and Young, 1974), the problems of standardizing on the same denominator, and the analysis of change (Bohrnstedt, 1969) or longitudinal data (Heise, 1970) that allow for considerable sophistication in evaluating causal arguments.

These two methodological developments are really part of the same incessant movement towards much more complex models of the world. In one sense they indicate how far sociology has moved since the publication of March and Simon's thesis in 1958. Organizational sociology, because of these analytical methods, is thus now much more capable of formulating a more sophisticated theory.

To help organize our task, it is useful to spell out several major themes and indicate how organizational paradigms or analytical approaches handle them. Also we must be sensitive to the problem of analytical levels and themes. Where the organization begins and the environment ends is not at all clear and requires careful definitions. The subtitle of form, process, and transformation begs for a clarification. It is not an empty phrase but the core of the analysis.

1.1 SUBSTANTIVE ISSUES: POWER, CHANGE, HUMAN FACTOR, AND THE ENVIRONMENT

The book is divided into four parts, each of which examines a central concern. The first part explores the problem of power, which is probably the single most popular topic in the organizational literature (see indices in Hall, 1977; Zey-Ferrell, 1979, and the various readers). Besides defining what is meant by power and how to measure it, topics include decision types, the basis of coalition formation, problems of control, the management of conflict, processes of decision-making, the relative power of particular departments, organizational autonomy, the participation of the workers, the ability to select goals, problems of succession and leadership, and so forth.

In Part 1, there are three chapters: structure, process, and succession. Each focuses on a different aspect of power and allows us to synthesize the four paradigms as well. But to a lesser extent power is a constant theme throughout the book because it and various measures of power, particularly centralization, are intimately involved in the next three parts as well.

Part 2 focuses on change and its many meanings. Again a division is made into three chapters: structural causes of changes, processes of change, and adaptation. There has been a considerable literature on the subject (see bibliographies in

Zaltman, Duncan, and Holbek, 1973; Hage and Aiken, 1970; Hage and Dewar, 1973; Kaluzny et al., 1972 and 1974; Gordon et al. 1972; Abernathy and Utterback, 1975; Christopher Freeman, 1974; Daft and Becker, 1978). Again we are confronted with the basic issue of what is innovation. Once this is resolved we can broach the issues of the structural causes of innovation and creativity, stages in the process of change, causes of resistances, strategies for overcoming them, kinds of conflict during the change process, the special problem of radical change, the process of adaptation, kinds of crises, and other issues.

Perhaps the best way of conceptualizing the third theme, which I call the human factor (the idea is from James Thompson, 1967, who used the phrase "the variable human"), is to see that it is the perpetual dilemma between human and material costs. On the one hand managerial elites and owners of capital want to drive costs down by means of policies of low wages and uniform tasks. On the other hand workers want to increase their standard of living and have interesting work. There is an inherent conflict of interest between these two perspectives. Hirschman's seminal book on *Exit, Voice, and Loyalty* (1970) is a useful framework, because it suggests that this conflict of interest can be handled by either quitting or fighting. Organizational elites have mechanisms for building loyalty and this leads us into a theory of coördination and control. These provide the basis for the three chapters in Part 3.

The fourth and last theme, the environment, would probably be the one that most would put second on their list of critical ordering terms. But except for the large amount of work on size, and to a lesser extent technology, this area does not, as yet, have as large or coherent a literature as the three others (for a major exception see Aldrich and Pfeffer, 1976). Organizations enter into exchanges with their environment as ways of gaining resources (Parsons, 1956 a and b) and legitimizing their existence. Other organizations compete for scarce resources which leads to problems of oligopoly and cartels, corporate crime, and other social ills (Quinney, 1979; Zeitlin, 1970). Finally the societal context sets limits on how many resources are available, how organizations can compete, and even how many organizations there are (Azumi, 1972). Each of these three views of the environment is set apart as a separate chapter in Part 4.

Included within the discussion is the issue of how technology and personnel size affect the choice of organizational structure. In turn this and the larger environment dictate the choice of strategy. Finally the societal context in conjunction with the twin themes of Chandler (1962, 1977) explain varying rates of change in growth and development.

Clearly these four themes intersect and interlink. Once one knows where the power lies and what determines how much power an occupation has, then how to change the power structure becomes an obvious issue. Change creates turnover and is resisted, which involves a consideration of human costs. Availability of resources in the environment affects all of this, setting limits on organizational autonomy and change, and influencing the choice of exit or voice by the dissatisfied members in the organization. Which control mechanism is selected is determined in part by centralization of power, and the kinds of people hired in the labor markets. During change, implementation makes the issue of human control even more problematic. One could go on for a long time discussing the many ways in which these themes intertwine but this should suffice. Together they order various theories, concepts, and findings, the major task.

1.2 ANALYTICAL LEVELS: MICRO, MESO, AND MACRO

These themes of power, change, the human factor, and the environment can be analyzed at more than one level. Although the first round of theories in the 1960s was primarily concerned with the analysis of the whole organization, the antitheses of the next decade move in part to two other levels, one micro and one macro. The political-value perspective argued for a more micro perspective: the importance of looking at the dominant coalition, and interest groups in general (see Cyert and March, 1963; Child, 1972; and Karpik, 1972 a and b; Hills and Mahoney, 1978 for explicit statements to this effect). In many instances there is a tendency to reduce explanations to psychological mechanisms as in March and Simon (1958). A parallel development was a very large business literature of excellent quality that focused on the group, the department, or hierarchical level (see Lawrence and Lorsch, 1967 a and b; Walton et al., 1969; Hickson et al., 1971; Van de Ven and Delbecq, 1974; Van de Ven, Delbecq, and Koenig, 1976; Mintzberg, 1979, etc.).

In contrast, the conflict-critical perspective moved outside to the environment calling attention to the need for institutional analysis (Benson, 1975) or a political economy perspective (Zald, 1970; Lourenço and Glidewell, 1975). Even the larger society became relevant (Karpik, 1972a). This need to move to the larger environment was already implicit in some of the emerging conflict studies (Corwin, 1969 and 1970; Lammers, 1969; Baldridge, 1971) because the nature of the conflict, especially in violent conflict (Lammers, 1969) or in prolonged and mass conflict (Baldridge, 1971), frequently transcended the simple request for a raise in pay. But perhaps the most critical factor in the emerging interest in the environment grew out of the many society upheavals that occurred — multinational corporations everywhere (Vernon, 1971) but especially in Chile; the mass strike of May, 1968 in France (Seeman, 1975); the turmoil over the Vietnam war in the United States (Hagstrom, 1965); the whole war on poverty, also in the States (Aldrich, 1971 and 1976 a and b); the attempts — and failures — to coordinate care (Benson, 1973; Aiken et al., 1975). All these events made a conflict-critical perspective attractive. They also made the macro level of institutions and societies very visible and relevant. For some, the macro level offered the possibility of explaining the differences between organizations and thus solved the problem of how organizations were the same or different, reconciling divergent findings (clearly the intent of the contingency theory of Lawrence and Lorsch, 1967 a and b). For those solidly planted in the critical perspective, the hope was to learn how to control or change organizations, to prevent their abuses and the like (see Perrow, 1972).

This book is arranged so that all three levels, micro, meso, and macro are considered. While the thrust is primarily on meso and macro theory, the micro work is frequently included as a third section in a number of chapters. Parts 1, 2, and 3 focus on the meso level while Part 4 concerns the macro level. Since these levels can easily be confused some attention must be paid to a careful definition of each of them. An unfortunate recent tendency is for those who prefer to work on one level to deny the phenomenology of the other level. Thus there are some who argue that the level of the group should be studied because there is variation at this level and adequate statements cannot be made at the higher analytical level (Bacharach and Aiken, 1976). The fact that there is variation among the parts does not negate the existence of the whole or even the desirability of studying the whole (see Cormstock and Scott, 1977). This epistomological problem exists at all levels. Thus there is variation among individuals categorized in any way we desire to, as well as among social positions, or jobs (see Rousseau, 1978), groups, levels, organizations, multi-organizations, and environments. Depending upon the problem, it might best be studied at the micro, meso, or macro level. Also, depending upon the problem, how one aggregates the data may require some special procedures if in fact the variation is measurement error. Too often, we assume aggregation is bad because it eliminates variation, but again the issues are at what level is the theoretical problem, and are the data aggregated or disaggregated to this level. The procedures for aggregation should carefully delineate sources of error and how they might be eliminated. The inflation of correlations can occur correctly because error is reduced.

Beyond the question of the appropriate level for analysis, both theoretical and empirical, rests the belief that it is better to work on several levels simultaneously as much as possible. In this way, one becomes sensitized to how each level interpenetrates the other and how each might set limits on the other (for a rare example of this see Lipset, Trow, and Coleman, 1956 and Ritzer, 1976).

1.2.1 The Definition of a Meso Analytical Level

Where does an organization begin? The phenomenological argument of whether units exist at all is useful because it alerts us to the idea that the meaningful boundary may not be found in the name of an organization such as General

Motors or the Federal Government (Brown, 1978; Benson, 1977). Here the most critical distinction is between organization and multi-organization (Bannister, 1970). Although there are a number of qualitative judgements to make, essentially the distinctive characteristic of an organization is the production of products or the provision of services. This separates it from groups or departments [see Azumi and Hage (1972) introduction]. Many organizations produce more than one product or provide more than one service. The analytical task is to decide at what point the difference in products is *large* enough to speak of more than one organization (see Hage, 1974; Chapter 1 for an extended discussion). Consistent with the Katz and Kahn (1966) perspective that organizations have inputs, throughputs, and outputs, we can define the boundaries of each organization around these analytical distinctions. If staff are not interchangeable, if separate budgets are kept, and if different laws and regulations exist we probably have a different production process. Products and services, however, can be classified into families of similarity as we shall see in Chapter 12. Similarity of product implies similarity of production process although here one would also make an obvious distinction as to whether the owners, managers, and workers were the same. But the most critical distinction is operations technology (Hickson, et al., 1969) or throughput. It is the similarity or dissimilarity of technology, of tools, of skills, of know-how that counts. When this occurs within the context of a larger unit, separate divisions are created, as Chandler (1962) noted in his brilliant history and analysis of DuPont, General Motors, and Sears, Roebuck. The same throughput may be produced in many locations: plants, bases, stores, campuses, and the like. Thus for schools, the school district is the relevant unit (Bidwell and Kasarda, 1975). The distinguishing characteristic is the operating technology.

The federal Department of Health, Education and Welfare in the United States is a multi-organization. The Office of Education, the Public Health Service, the Department of Social and Rehabilitation Services, and the Social Security Administration are clearly separate organizations and in many cases already multi-organizations. For example, each Institute of Health is so distinctive that the Institutes are best considered as separate organizations because their staff are not interchangeable, they have separate budgets, and so on. The Veterans Administration administers benefits but also runs hospitals, which in turn have large research units.

Local authorities in Britain contain many administrative departments, each of which is a separate organization yet in the same city or location. One must not be too rigid in deciding whether a concrete unit is one or more organizations. For some problems, a university might be divided into separate departments and for other problems only into separate divisions or colleges. The extent of the differences between inputs and outputs becomes more or less important depending upon the problem at hand. In this sense, I side with the phenomenologists who are sensitive to the difficulty of drawing boundaries and deciding whether this is the same or a different technology. People involved in the situations are more likely to perceive enormous differences, whereas researchers tend to be insensitive to them due to lack of familiarity.

It should be noted that the thrust of the definition is on an essential aspect of system analysis, namely to see organizations as input, throughput, and output systems, first emphasized in Katz and Kahn (1966). The advantage of this perspective is that it calls attention to production processes rather than products per se as the distinctive element. This definition also stresses a technological approach to the study of organizations. However, it does not necessarily argue that there are three or four kinds of technology as Blauner (1964), Woodward (1965), Perrow (1967), and James Thompson (1967) have suggested. Instead it implies that there is an inherent specificity of technique, a knowledge of skills even at the *managerial* level, that makes for the creation of separate organizations, which are usually called divisions when part of a larger structure.

Several more examples are in order. Mental hospitals frequently divide their patients into acute and chronic and house them in different buildings, use different therapeutic methods, and even different staff. The throughput is clearly not the same for these two kinds of mental patients. The military is really four different services, each with its own weapons of war: the army, navy, marines, and air force. Actually the differences between submarines and carriers are so great that one might want to treat them as separate organizations even though there is some interchangeability of personnel at the officer level.

General Motors is an illustration of a multi-organization with one unit producing automobiles, another boats, a third railroad trains, and so forth. Chandler's (1962) analysis of DuPont and the separation of divisions for paints, explosives, and the like is well-known and proof of the need to understand specificity of throughput.

1.2.2   The Definition of a Macro Analytical Level

A formal definition for each analytical level is provided in Figure 1.1. The key point for the macro level is that once one knows the boundaries of the organization, then the environment becomes everything relevant outside that boundary. The most immediate issue is whether the organization is part of some larger multi-organization. As will be noted at other points in this book, there has been a very long-term trend toward ever larger multi-organizations that contain more and more divisions or separate organizations within them and paradoxically at the same time for plant size or agency size within organizations and multiorganizations to become smaller. If one does not see the two levels operating simultaneously then one misses a rather major structural transformation (Chandler, 1962). The growth in the number of organizations within each multi-

Level	Element and definition	Examples
Micro	Social positions: sets of activities with a job title (see Hage, 1972: Chapter 5)	Sociologist, social worker, union representative, foreman
	Groups: Sets of members with shared activities who define themselves as belonging to the same collective (Merton, 1957; Homans, 1950)	Labor unions, professional actions, dominant coalition, peer group, managers, workers
Meso	Organization: Sets of members with a specific objective to produce a product or provide a service, and with a distinctive inputs as in staff, budget, and clientele	School of medicine, cheap car division, naval component of the military, division for chronic schizophrenics, division for paint manufacturing, school district
Macro	Multi-organization: Sets of organizations each with their distinctive input, throughput, and output. Task environment: All organizations that affect either inputs or outputs of a focal organization	Universities, defense departments, mental hospitals, chemical companies

Figure 1.1 Analytical levels and examples.

organization reflects the problem of societal coordination and control. The growth in the smallness and number of different plants and agencies reflects the issue of professional and managerial morale and availability of services and products (see Aiken et al., 1975).

As Azumi (1972) notes there are other organizations in the environment that are essentially concerned with competing not only for sales but for resources of skilled personnel, funds, freedom from regulation, and the like (also see Aldrich, 1979, Chapter 5). Again by focusing on organizations as producing products or providing services (that is, having inputs, throughputs, and outputs) we are led to systematically define which organizations are relevant. Schools, universities, and the like affect availability of particular skills and occupations. Labor unions can affect the size and discipline of the relevant labor force. Professional associations can be very powerful when they determine licensing. Regulatory agencies can control the autonomy of an organization to set prices or to charge fees

(Hirsch, 1975 a and b). The number, variety, and size of competing organizations has long been studied by economists and represents a critical part of the environment and one which we will analyze intensely.

Being a member of a multi-organization is not the only way to achieve coordination. Increasingly there are various kinds of associations that attempt to coordinate and in which organizations are the members (Turk, 1973; Aiken et al., 1975). Some, as in the War On Poverty, were mandated by law. Some have developed in order to gain various economic benefits (as in purchasing associations of hospitals) or to lobby for political benefits (as in various industrial associations). Coalitions of various kinds, while of a temporary nature, are in themselves an important development and an aspect of the macro analytical level.

1.2.3 The Definition of a Micro Analytical Level

Although less time will be spent on micro concerns, this level does offer a very rich potential for relating the individual to the larger social structure of organizations. As indicated in Figure 1.1, a micro, sociological perspective focuses on the position or job, role-relationships (Hage and Marwell, 1968), job performance, and the like. Within each chapter, especially in Parts 1, 2, and 3, there is usually a subsection that focuses on micro issues. For example, in Chapter 3, after an analysis of the structural causes of centralization, there is a consideration of exceptions by department with the theory of Hickson et al. (1971), and an attempt to explicate the political paradigm's concept of coalition, followed by an analysis of job autonomy at the micro level. In Chapter 6, the meso problem of output and process innovation is juxtaposed against the micro issue of creativity. Chapters 9 (on turnover), 10 (on conflict), and 11 (on coordination and control) try to combine both analytical levels. Throughout, the question is whether the same explanation holds at both levels and in what ways the micro analysis indicates exceptions and qualifications to the conclusions of the meso analysis. Both can be done simultaneously and are not contradictory.

There are three analytical levels, each of which sets limitations on the other. They should not be confused; one should avoid the intellectual error of reductionism. Analytical problems at the macro level are not the same as at the micro (Homans, 1961, 1967). Nor should one think that because hypotheses supported at one level are denied at another the other level is nonexistent (Bacharach and Aiken, 1976). Instead special attention should be paid to *why* hypotheses supported at one level are not at another. Frequently the answer may be because some problems and variables are more appropriately studied at that or another level (see Comstock and Scott, 1977). When this is done, one obtains a more complex and subtle comprehension and begins to understand the phenomenology of each level and its emergent properties and problems. For example,

Chapter 3 explores the idea of variation by department and level and Chapter 14 variation by environment. As this is done, the overall theory becomes richer.

1.3 ANALYTICAL PARADIGMS

The word paradigm has been much overused and abused to mean almost everything. I would prefer to define paradigm as an orientation or perspective that contains several key concepts and some basic working assertions about what is important. Well-developed paradigms, as in reinforcement theory in psychology or general equilibrium theory in economics, are characterized by premises and equations that have wide applicability. As yet, organizational sociology does not have such highly specified paradigms. Perhaps perspective is a more apt term.

Sometimes paradigm is used to imply the basic way in which one comprehends reality (Brown, 1978). Here there is a dichotomy between scientific and phenomenological approaches. Sometimes paradigm is used to imply the basic analytical level (Ritzer, 1976). But neither of these was intended by Kuhn, for clearly physics and chemistry have not essentially altered in their way of approaching reality – while new levels have been added on (see Bunge, 1958: Chapter 5). The revolution of paradigms usually occurs when one global theory is replaced by another, as when Einsteinian physics replaced Newtonian. It is these theories, or theory orientations as I choose to call them, that appear to be the more fruitful way of understanding paradigm. However, what makes the discussion of competing theories difficult is that frequently perspectives relative to the same phenomenon disagree as to how reality might be known and what particular level of analysis they are working on. A further complication is that the same methods, such as surveys, may be employed in very different ways depending upon the theoretical orientation.

Thus the distinctions of Brown and Ritzer are suggestive as a way of developing a rough typology of competing perspectives. One basic dimension is whether there is more of an emphasis on generalizing or more of an emphasis on particularizing. One could use the old distinction between nomothetic and ideographic, but instead of this dichotomy it is better to see the essential continuity between an extreme historic emphasis that regards each event as unique and an extreme scientific one where all organizations are perceived to follow general laws irrespective of time and place. These extremes are much less popular today than they were a decade ago in organizational sociology and now one finds various admixtures of general and particular.

Another basic dimension is whether one focuses on the internal workings of the organization, or on the unit and its environment. Substantive issues are frequently major ways in which paradigms differ. They tend to highlight certain variables rather than others and even where they perceive the same phenomenon, they tend to see different aspects. This is all to the good and is why the Hegelian dialectic of thesis, antithesis, and synthesis has substantive force.

As indicated above, there are four basic paradigms which fit into a fourfold typology as outlined in Figure 1.2. These four exist in general sociology as well as in organizational sociology, although their popularity varies (for a definition of three of these perspectives see Hage, 1972: Chapter 7). Structural-functionalism has been extremely important in organizational sociology but largely ignored in the discipline, all of the critiques to the contrary. Similarly until recently a conflict-critical perspective has been largely ignored in organizational sociology although it is popular in the general discipline.

Although frequently not recognized as such, Max Weber in his ideal-type construction of bureaucracy proposed the first structural-functional theory of organizations by asking which form of social organization was the most efficient and why (Gerth and Mills, 1946; Weber, 1947). This is the basic problem of structural-functionalism, often lost to view. Most of the theories developed in the 1960s (Burns and Stalker, 1961; Etzioni, 1961; Hage, 1965; Price, 1968) were in one way or another concerned with what utilities are important and how they might be maximized. However, and this is the irony, Weber was more on the side of particularizing rather than generalizing and put his ideal-types in historical terms (Graham, Gerth and Mills, 1946; McNeil, 1978). In contrast, most of the American organizational sociologists emphasized general variables and hypotheses that transcended cultural space and historical time. For this reason, Chapter 2 starts with Weber and continues with two representative theories within this perspective, Burns and Stalker (1961), and Hage (1965). This is the thesis for the succeeding perspectives, making the historical evolution of thought more visible.

Besides raising questions about what are key structural variables and performances, the problem of effectiveness (Price, 1968), and the like, structural-functionalism has been concerned with change, despite all the critiques to the contrary. The concept of vested interests is a structural one. The stages of

| | Relative emphasis on generalizability | |
Focus:	High	Low
Internal	Structural-functionalism	Power-value
External	Cybernetic-adaptive	Conflict-critical

Figure 1.2   A typology of organizational paradigms.

change have been defined largely in terms of changes in structural variables (see Zaltman, Duncan, and Holbek, 1973). At the same time there is little question that the model of change in structural-functionalism is quite static, postulating a relatively constant rate of innovation as in the organic model (see Burns and Stalker, 1961; Aiken and Hage, 1971).

Similarly, and consistent with many critiques, the problem of what happens to the human being in organizations was largely seen in the positives of morale, consensus (see Georgopoulos and Tannenbaum, 1957; Tannenbaum, 1968; Georgopoulos and Mann, 1962), and conformity or compliance (Etzioni, 1961, although he is aware of the problem of alienation). The biggest weakness in structural-functionalism was its general lack of attention to anything outside the organization. Statements were made about the organization receiving legitimacy but in fact little research was done on this problem (Parsons, 1956 a and b). Only in the late 1960s, when research on technology and size (see Pugh et al., 1969) raised the issue of what caused social structure, was there some attention to the environment. But even then the environment was only there sotto voce, having been implied more than studied. Even Lawrence and Lorsch's (1967 a and b) pioneering work primarily relied upon respondents' perceptions of the environment, rather than on independent measures of the environment per se, which have been since criticized (Aldrich, 1979: 126–132).

The political-value paradigm originated with Cyert and March (1963), who suggested that what organizations do is determined by the dominant coalition. If one knows the coalitation's values – their preferences about utilities or performances – then one can predict what the organization will do. Thus it is quite different from the structural-functional paradigm which uses structure to explain values or goals. This dialectic is employed throughout the book. The power perspective has perhaps been more sensitive to different kinds of decisions, recognizing that high risk and low risk decisions have quite different processes attached to them. The basis of coalitions and the nature of interest groups are important analytical problems.

Although both structural-functionalism and political-value perspectives can have a scientific version and a historical one, their general working assumptions about the nature of organizational reality tend to push them in opposite directions. Structural-functionalism tends to concentrate on the centralization of power and sees this as relatively static, allowing for predictions. This is even true in Weber's work. In contrast, the power-value perspective sees this as constantly changing; therefore prediction becomes problematic (Pfeffer and Salancik, 1974). Structural-functionalism emphasizes what is common, while the political value paradigm prefers what is unique and distinctive. Again, this flows from the assumption that the leaders in power will determine the goals of the organization on the basis of their values.

The two perspectives, however, have a very similar substantive focus and look at many of the same issues. A good comparison between them is to be found in the collection of original articles edited by Warner (1977), where the theme is degree of choice. The concept of strategic choice (Child, 1972a) focuses attention on the debate between these two perspectives.

A political-value view also highlights the different kinds of innovations and the values associated with the process of change. Strategies for overcoming resistance have been one of its contributions. The management of conflict and the choice of coordination and control mechanisms also grow from this perspective, although one could argue that these ideas belong to a structural-functional perspective as well (see Price, 1968; Perrow, 1967; Hage, Aiken and Marrett, 1971 for examples). But in a political-value paradigm the explanation is somewhat different, being postulated as a question of trade-offs between the relinquishing power and at the same time maintaining control (see Child, 1972, and Blau, Heydebrand, and Stauffer, 1966 among others for this viewpoint).

Relative to the environment, the political-value paradigm has made some important contributions. Besides the concern over autonomy which goes back to Selznik (1949), who might be considered the precursor of this school of thought, concepts like strategic choice (Child, 1972; Warner, 1977), strategies of environmental control (James Thompson, 1967; Hage, 1977; McNeil, 1978), and the like at least make one aware of the environment even if they do not focus on the environment directly.

I have made a distinction between the political-value perspective and a conflict-critical one, recognizing that there is much overlap. Yet the distinction seems worth making because there is a noticeable shift in focus. Not only does the latter focus more on conflict as the major topic (see Collins, 1975), in the same way as the dominant coalition tends to be the central idea in the political-value perspective, but in addition much more attention is given to what is wrong and to seeing how things could be (see Goldman and Van Houten, 1977; Heydebrand, 1977), the origin of the second term "critical" (also see Quinney, 1979 and Clegg and Dunkerly, 1977). The dominant coalition is in control, but in a critical perspective one asks what kinds of decisions they do *not* make or what areas are *never* considered. This is enough of a shift that it seems worth recognizing a distinct intellectual species. As we have already noted, the political-value paradigm tends to break the organization up into parts such as groups, coalitions, or departments (not to be confused with the definition of the boundaries of the organization), while the conflict-critical perspective moves more to the macro level of institutional analysis of how the state and the economy interrelate. Political economy falls much more in the latter tradition, although it too is concerned essentially with elites, as in the analysis of boards (Zald, 1967; Zeitlin, 1970 and 1974; Pfeffer, 1972a, 1973b, and 1977), the concern over the industrial military complex (Hanneman, 1974), the critical concern about multinational corporations (Vernon, 1971), and so on.

The essential starting point in a conflict perspective is that there are inherent bases of conflict and frequently, although not necessarily, an economic rather than a political basis for this conflict. Even though each paradigm employs many of the same concepts, there are some nuances in their utilization. For example, in a conflict perspective, the causes of resistance are of more interest than strategies for overcoming them. Furthermore, there is an appreciation for qualitative differences, such as radical innovation, and the difficulties of introducing them. Alienation is a most important topic in the human factor theme area. In this sense, a conflict perspective is more akin to a structural-functional than a political paradigm because so many of the analytical answers lie in structural terms. Such an epistemology is consistent with Marx even if the economic structure is not necessarily seen as the paramount causal force. This is a significant distinction from the political-value paradigm, which tends to break structure down and to view things more in terms of values or goals. Admittedly, these differences in actual work are never as clear as I am making them here.

Perhaps the most distinctive area in this perspective is in the theme of resources and the environment. Concerns about multinational corporations and domination, exploitation, imperialism, and the like are key issues. Human relations techniques are used to manipulate the workers (Tannenbaum et al., 1974: 220). It is here that the differences from a political-value paradigm are the most visible and revealing since the latter tends to take a management perspective as much as does structural-functionalism.

Finally there is a cybernetic-adaptive paradigm. As is quickly apparent from a reading of Figure 1.2, abstractness escalates. This means fewer concepts but also more comprehensive ones, capable of providing the basis for a synthesis of the three other perspectives (see Hedburg, Nystrom, and Starbuck, 1976 and Weick, 1976). Adaptiveness and steering across time, feedback and learning are all key concepts. What determines these are analytical problems that have not received enough attention.

At the same time it is equally certain that the cybernetic-adaptive perspective does not raise the same questions as a conflict-critical one. There are similarities as well as qualitative differences between states of disequilibrium and conflict or organizational crisis. Cybernetics, by its inherent emphasis on the similarity of systems, moves in the direction of generalizing its statements, much more so than even structural-functionalism. A critical perspective tends at times to move in the extreme direction of a phenomenological approach, even more than a political-value perspective. Both share, as is noted in Figure 1.2, a concern for how the organizational unit relates to the larger environment. However, they define the boundaries of the organization in different ways and with different consequences. Cybernetics perceives organizations in terms of their throughput (see Miller, 1975), whereas a critical perspective tends to equate the boundaries organizations take with these defined by their name.

Important perspectives	Power	Change	The human factor	Resources and the environment
Structural-functionalism	Centralization Job autonomy Control Effectiveness	Vested interests Rates of innovation	Morale, turnover Consensus Conformity Productivity	Technology Size
Political-value	Dominant coalition High risk decisions Basis of coalitions Goals	Strategies to overcome resistance Values and the process of change	Management of conflict Coordination mechanisms	Autonomy Strategic choice Strategies of control over the environment
Conflict-critical	Stability of coalitions Conflict in decision-making	Causes of resistance Kinds of conflict in change Radical innovation	Structural causes of conflict Alienation Role conflict	Lack of concern about client/customer needs Exploitation Corporate crime Domination
Cybernetic-adaptive	Kinds of information feedback Energy	Processes of adaptiveness Kinds of disequilibrium	Control feedback Entropy	Growth and development Moving equilibrium Equilfinality

Figure 1.3 Analytical problems associated with the major themes and perspectives.

To summarize these many ideas, Figure 1.3 indicates which paradigms focus on what concepts. Many will feel uncomfortable with the placement of particular issues, especially if they are interested in analytical problems. The institutions and ideas of the researcher and the theorist are always much more complex than their cultural products. Besides summaries such as these are always global and thus at best superficial. But they serve a useful, heuristic purpose. Seldom does one see an attempt to list all of the key concepts and therefore analytical problems in a single perspective. This is only a start and one limited to four themes, which in themselves overlap. However, it does indicate how useful the procedure is. The typology explicates the amount of overlap and the difficulty of making distinctions at the same time as it elucidates the distinctive quality of each orientation. Thus, it serves as a way of codifying the essence of each perspective while goading other theorists and researchers to expand the frontiers of their intellectual perspectives.

It is natural that most organizational theorists have touched upon many of these concerns and will find it difficult to place themselves quite neatly into one of these four boxes. Yet the typology is not intended to classify individuals but particular writings and, beyond this, to give the reader a sense of the scope — and limits — of each perspective rather than a precise shopping list of analytical problems.

1.4 ANALYTICAL THEMES: FORM, PROCESS, AND TRANSFORMATION

The subtitle of the book stresses the words form, process, and transformation to call attention to three different ways of looking at organizations. The word "form" rather than "structure" is employed because four basic ideal-types of organizations are used an an unifying theme. While structure is one aspect and an important one, it is only a small part of the total organization. In particular, considerable time is spent analyzing different kinds of throughput, synthesizing the work of Blauner (1964), Perrow (1976), Van De Ven and Delbecq (1974), and others in Chapter 12 since the throughput is seen as a defining characteristic of the boundaries of the organization. The first chapter of each part gradually builds a steadily more complex typology of organizational form.

"Process" refers to both internal and external processes associated with these basic forms while "transformation" represents the dynamics of how forms themselves are changed. The intellectual debt to biology is apparent and the parallel has already been drawn in system analysis (Miller, 1975). Some attention to process has been paid in the literature, but almost none to the larger issue of what I choose to call dynamics, that is, the alteration or mutation if one permits, of organizational forms.

The word "process" has a large number of meanings, each of which represents quite different aspects of the organization. Among others, the following are considered important:

1. Decision-making.
2. Innovation.
3. Succession.
4. Equilibrium and disequilibrium or adaptation.
5. Coordination and control.
6. Growth and development.

The first two are the most common ones existing in the literature and are usually what is meant by process. Decision-making processes are discussed in Chapter 4 while innovation processes are the focus of Chapter 7. The accent is on the plural because more than one type of process is analyzed in each chapter. Beyond this, two topics frequently included under the rubric of process — conflict and power strategies — are analyzed in Chapters 10 and 13 respectively. *In effect, the second chapter in each part focuses on the more traditional concept of process while the third chapter concerns the more fundamental problems of dynamic change.*

Chapter 5 focuses on the first kind of transformation, namely changes in goals and leaders, that is, the problem of maintaining effectiveness across time given both internal change and upheavals in the environment. Equilibrium, disequilibrium, and adaptation, the foci of Chapter 8, highlight transformation directly. The third chapter in Part 3, Chapter 11, concerns coordination and control processes as a special topic. Its counterpart in Part 4, Chapter 14, returns to the issue of growth and development and how these are affected by the larger society.

To summarize, in each part the first chapter is on form, building a more complex typology, the second chapter is on process, and the third is on dynamic change or transformations of both form and process. Each qualifies the other in various ways; that is, they do represent distinctive styles of organizational analysis.

1.5 CONCLUSIONS

The advantage of making so many distinctions relative to themes, levels, and paradigms is that they can be synthesized where possible, and where not they can create a useful dialectical perspective. They also help the reader make the necessary interconnections between the various chapters. The substantive issues can be and are in many ways synthesized. They have been separated into parts to ensure that topics are covered systematically. In contrast, differences in analytical level help to qualify various findings at one level by insights discovered at another. As much as possible the analytical paradigms or perspectives are synthesized, but throughout the dominant focus is on a cybernetic-adaptive perspective because it appears to be the one most capable of including the others. The analytical themes of form, process, and transformation again are best understood as qualifications to each other. Form does not perfectly predict process or transformation. There are critical qualitative distinctions between these analytical themes as well as fundamental differences between analytical levels, all with their own emergent properties.

We start our dialectic in the next chapter with the essential form of the rational-legal bureaucracy as envisioned by Weber. This perspective represents not only the beginning of structural-functionalism but also the basic insight that a fundamental problem is the transformation of form. Since these concerns are still very much with us, this is a good place to begin.

Chapter Two

Alternative Forms of Organizational Structure and Function

One mark of a good mind is the number of insights that a reader has. If one can come back to work again and again and find new insights, then we have a seminal thinker. This applies to Max Weber and, more importantly, to his work on bureaucracy as a form of rational-legal authority. What is most important for me – though not necessarily for others – is Weber's delineation of three forms of organization, built upon their patterns of authority. One of these forms, rational-legal authority, was favored in the long term evolution of organizational forms because it was more efficient. Finally, he focused on several transformations, most notably that of the routinization of charisma. Here we have a model of thinking that can do much to arrange our ideas and that provides an understanding for our subtitle of form, process, and transformation.

American readers of Weber have tended to emphasize the implicit paradigm of structural-functionalism in Weber's work (see Gouldner, 1956a; Blau, 1955; Merton, 1957 and their summary in March and Simon, 1958; Hage, 1965; Perrow, 1967; Price, 1968; etc.). The Europeans and some of the representatives of the new paradigms in America have been more sensitive to the historical grounding of Weber's ideal types and his general concern about power (Crozier, 1964; Mayntz, 1964; Pugh, 1969; but for an exception see Perrow, 1967). Whereas the first group of scholars has talked about efficiency, the second has emphasized Weber's concerns relative to the potential dangers of bureaucracy. Both perspectives are correct. (Some of the latter school argue against Weber's concern with efficiency, and they are right. He did not emphasize it, being more concerned with power. See Albrow, 1964).

Although cast in historical terms, Weber's (1946) essential reasoning is quite sociological and even more importantly structural: how work is organized determines the amount and quality of product produced or service provided. Weber felt that a strict hierarchy of authority and a reliance on rules would facilitate greater efficiency (for reviews see Hall, 1963b among others). This is an inherently sociological perspective since nothing is said about the personalities of the people who do the work, or whether they find the work interesting. There is little about their aptitude for work, although Weber had some comments about this, too.

A good example of the fruition of Weber's intuition, although it is not juxtaposed against his model of bureaucracy, is Bavelas's famous series of experiments on communication networks shaped in different forms (1946 also see Caplow, 1964: 256–262). The physical arrangement of work (in this case the task was comparing symbols) facilitated the decentralization or centralization of decision-making which, in turn, had certain consequences. The wheel arrangement, which was more decentralized and where everyone could communicate with each other, resulted in fewer messages with more errors but the communicators were happier about their work. The yoke and chain arrangement, which had a stricter hierarchy of authority, accomplished more messages with fewer errors in the same time period but the workers were less happy. Furthermore, these differences hold across a large number of various kinds of personalities, interests, and motives. There are individual and group variations to be sure. But the major differences are between organizational forms, with the most centralized at one end and the most decentralized at the other. The relevance to Weber's work is clear. At least in this simple laboratory experiment, strict hierarchies appear to be more efficient.

Consistent with our desire to emphasize alternative forms and their consequences, we shall review two different theories, both structural-functional, about how the arrangement of work affects performance or utility maximization. The first theory is the mechanical and organic forms developed by Burns and Stalker (1961). The second is the axiomatic theory written by Hage (1965). The former work, created by two Scotsmen, adhered to the ideal-type construction of Weber. The latter, by an American, preferred to emphasize general variables and even implied a long-term evolution towards one end of the continuum. In various ways both works have tried to build upon Weber, explicating his original insights. They are not the only ones to do so but are perhaps most representative of the attempts made. [For some other earlier attempts, most notable would be Litwak (1961), who suggested three types or forms of bureaucracy and ended up with a list not unlike what is suggested later in this book.]

2.1 WEBER'S MODEL OF BUREAUCRACY

Weber's model of bureaucracy, built on the foundation of rational-legal authority, has been reviewed so many times that one hesitates to confront the reader with yet another exegesis. What one can say is that *most of the reviews to date have not made clear the connection between the components of structure and their functional consequences.* Weber himself (Gerth and Mills, 1946; Weber, as translated by Henderson and Parsons, 1947) was not explicit in all cases about how particular aspects of organizational structure lead to specific performances and outputs. The major exception is his discussion of elected versus appointed officials.

Another problem with most of the existing reviews is that they have not made clear the causal mechanisms or the reasons behind the particular implied hypotheses. Yet any review should concentrate on the theoretical rationales because they are the core of the argument (see Hage, 1972; Chapter 4). For these reasons then, I shall emphasize the hypotheses and the probable assumptions behind them.

Various reviewers have done well to indicate some of the errors in Weber's thinking. Weber spent most of his time discussing the structural side and not the functional side. As a result, later theoretical work (Merton, 1957; Selznik, 1949; Gouldner, 1954a; Blau, 1963 but first published in 1955) became concerned with specifying not only some other functional consequences but dysfunctional ones as well, especially for morale. Unfortunately, much of the empirical work has imitated Weber, exploring structure and negating the relationship between structure and performance. (This is not true of the organizational psychologists such as Tannenbaum, 1968; Katz and Kahn, 1966; Seashore and Bowers, 1963).

2.1.1 The Implicit Theory

The implicit causal structure of Weber's model is diagramed in Figure 2.1. Although his discussion begins with the concept of rules (the order of the listing in Figure 2.1 is not the same as in Weber), much of the concern revolves around the problem of power conceived in a variety of ways: the legitimacy of orders, the ability to maintain control and discipline, and the importance of a monocratic

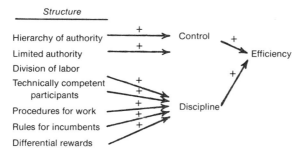

Figure 2.1 Major concepts and hypothesis in Weber's model of bureaucracy.

hierarchy of supervision. Weber merely asserts the superiority of rational-legal authority and does not discuss very much – at least not in the two English translations that are available to us – the reasons why each of these structural components is important for efficiency and control with one major exception: the importance of a strict hierarcy of authority. Here Weber notes that collegiate bodies are unable to maintain discipline and control, and even cites the example of their elimination at the provincial level in Prussia because of the need for quick decisions free of the compromises characteristic of collegial bodies (Weber, 1947: 336).

The argument as to why each of these components facilitates efficiency and stringency of discipline would seem to be as follows: If the official functions are bounded by rules, then these rules prevent caprice upon the part of particular occupants or incumbents. This idea is implicit in much of Weber's discussion of traditional authority. In particular, Weber takes pains to point out the limits imposed on top officials. Also he notes that ministers, kings, and elected officials are not really part of the bureaucratic hierarchy as he defines the boundaries of the administrative staff, although the imposition of limits frequently applies to them as well. Each job is clearly defined and can be learned. The specification of rules and procedures, especially technical ones, provides the standards to which incumbents must conform. They can then be easily supervised and evaluated (Scott, et al., 1967; Dornbusch and Scott, 1974). This is also relevant to item 4, technical specialists, in Figure 2.1. The recording of all acts, decisions, and so forth, serves the same function, making visible what is done so it can be quickly learned, grasped, and repeated. As Weber notes, individual judgment is kept to a minimum. The consequence is a considerable degree of predictability and calculability.

In Figure 2.1 we have listed efficiency and reliability as the major functional performances that are maximized. The separation of offices into clear spheres that are arranged in strict hierarchies makes the responsibilities and authority of each superior and each subordinate perfectly clear. Indeed, it is this hierarchy that gives orders their legitimacy; they come from a superior in the chain of command, therefore they are quickly obeyed. The strict hierarchy also means that each person's work is carefully supervised. Since the superior has both authorities – the right to give orders and to supervise – and the means to enforce them, the subordinate does what he is told. On the other hand, the rights of the superior are carefully bounded as well and the subordinate has formal appeal procedures in case the superior exceeds his limits of power. The theme that runs through almost all of Weber's discussion is the stringency of discipline that is obtained by the structure of bureaucracy as he visualized it. In a sense, a mechanism of control becomes the intervening variable that connects the structure and the performance or function of efficiency.

In Weber's discussion, the importance of the officials' technical qualifications comes across. It becomes crucial in understanding how the individuals occupying the offices possess the knowledge to perform their tasks effectively; knowledge has been gained either through training or experience.

What we have not made apparent is that Weber felt there were other consequences of bureaucracy, problems that have, unfortunately, been largely ignored in organizational sociology. Since there is an emphasis on technical qualifications, Weber felt that bureaucracy would lead both to a leveling of social classes (Weber, 1947: 340), and at the same time an emergence of a plutocracy. This apparent contradiction may be because "social class" in German refers to the prestige rank inherited by the family (as in the aristocracy) rather than the wealth rank per se. Another long-term societal impact that Weber predicted was the emergence of a formalism and an impersonality (Weber, 1947: 340). We will return to these critical issues when we consider the relationship between the environment viewed as society and the organization in Part 4.

Other parts of his theory are of more minor significance in the view of contemporary organizational sociology. They include the separation of ownership of the means of production from administration, and the appropriation of positions by the incumbent. The characteristics of the incumbent are more worth emphasizing because Weber noted a number of factors that in various ways round out his picture of bureaucracy. The incumbent is selected on the basis of technical qualifications. That is, he is appointed and not elected. Likewise, the incumbent can choose to work; he is not physically coerced to do so. The incumbent is paid a fixed salary and subject only to impersonal official obligations. However, the office is his principal means of livelihood and it constitutes a career. Promotion is based upon seniority or achievement or both, but in any case is dependent upon the judgement of superiors. Finally Weber again chooses to emphasize that the bureaucrat is subject to strict and systematic discipline and control (Weber, 1947: 333-334). His is essentially the image of the civil servant.

Throughout Weber's discussion, it is apparent that he intends this form of organizational structure to apply to a wide variety of organizational goals or purposes. He specifically mentions the army, the functions of the state, the modern capitalist corporation, and the church. He even notes that the organizational form is probably more essential in socialist enterprises than in capitalist ones, an insight well supported by research since then (Berliner, 1957; Granick, 1960). Although Weber does limit his discussion to administration per se, it is clear that it can be generalized to other kinds of tasks as well. The principles are general ones, largely although perhaps not completely independent of space and time. Correspondingly, his examples cover many historical empires and epochs.

This then is Weber's model, with more emphasis than he gives on the reasons for the connection between the structural component and the particular functional consequences. The strict chain of command and the careful delineation of rules makes the supervision of work easy and creates the strict discipline that provides efficiency and reliability. Essentially, bureaucracy means a great deal of control over the worker or subordinate. The supervisor has the authority to give orders and the means at his disposal to enforce obedience and punish infraction of rules. Weber does not discuss what these might be but certainly the power of promotion is one of them.

2.1.2   A Critique

One crucial theme in the contemporary literature is the internal contradiction in Weber's model: the conflict between technical qualifications and a strict hierarchy of authority. Parsons (Weber 1947: 55) noted this contradiction in a famous footnote in his translation, but few worked out its implications until Burns and Stalker (1961) began to consider the possibility of other kinds of organizational forms. Internal contradiction was also noted in Blau and Scott (1962). Weber never asked himself how well the various structural components might fit together, perhaps in part because he was concerned with explicating an ideal-type. Here his method is at fault. It is more descriptive than analytical; more concerned with locating characteristics than connecting concepts into hypotheses.

The most common criticism of Weber, his lack of attention to dysfunctions, emerged in the work of both Merton (1940) and Gouldner (1954a). They suggest that one can have too many rules. When this occurs, a rigidity results that in turn leads to lower morale (as observed by Gouldner) or ritualism (as hypothesized by Merton). The Gouldner study is interesting for a variety of reasons. It provides an application of Weber's administrative model to the management of a gypsum plant. Here we have an instance where rules were developed precisely to produce more control; we view the creation of bureaucracy — a rare sight. Finally, Gouldner indicates how morale can be monitored. Low morale results in a positive feedback loop creating more rules that move the organization into disequilibirum. Eventually, this disequilibrium manifests itself in a strike, which is described in Gouldner's second book (1954b).

Another common criticism, though one not shared by everyone, is that Weber felt bureaucracy to be the single dominant form capable of achieving any objective, from fighting wars to fighting fires to fighting sin. Army, state, and church, each needs a bureaucratic administration. The other two forms of authority, which he called traditional and charismatic, were being replaced by the rational-legal authority found in bureaucracy. *This is an important argument, because organizational sociologists tend not to ask about the long-term evolutionary trends and their causes.* Weber did, and his analytical solution is that since bureaucracy is more efficient and reliable than either the traditional or the charismatic form, it is favored in any evolutionary development. Beyond this, the emergence of more complex tasks, the development of a money economy, and the rise of the modern state all contributed in various ways to the need for greater efficiency and the elimination of various obstacles to bureaucracy.

In a sense, of course, Weber allowed for variations on the rational-legal model since he used an ideal-type method. Unfortunately, although many talented sociologists developed names for the many variations observed (see Pugh et al., 1963, for a review of some of these, also Hall, Haas, and Johnson, 1967), none have remained in the literature, presumably because they have not tapped the essential differences between organizational forms. We shall focus on the critical issue of which forms are favored, and why, in Part 4, especially Chapter 14.

In summary, Weber's model admits of no alternative, at least in the long term. It sees neither internal contradictions, as did Marx and Engels (1969) in capitalism, nor dysfunctions. It is important as well that Weber located his analysis in a larger world view and especially in the institutional structures of society. Current adherents of the conflict-critical perspective (see especially McNeil, 1978) are right to note the general neglect of this aspect of Weber's work by American and Anglo-Saxon students. A return to and renewed recognition of this aspect is itself a sign that we must pose these larger questions about form and transformation. They are best broken down into three fundamental issues:

1. What forms are best for which functional performances?
2. What consequences do these forms have for society?
3. How does societal change favor particular forms, and in what evolutionary sequence?

Even if we do not like Weber's answers, let us not forget the questions. They are particularly important today for socialists and capitalists, workers and managers, theoretical sociologists and management consultants. As our own vision becomes greater, and as our world becomes more complicated, we must continue our search for new answers.

2.2 BURNS'S AND STALKER'S MECHANICAL AND ORGANIC MODELS

If Weber's model of bureaucracy largely developed out of his first hand knowledge of army hospitals in Austria and out of historical studies, especially of the Prussian government, Burns and Stalkker learned something from their research in electronics firms. The shift of 50 years, from the Austrian-Hungarian or Germanic Empires to Scottish or English democracies, and from public administration to electronics firms, radically increased the probability that their research would uncover another model than the bureaucratic one. It is important for us to recognize that the organic model, as described below, could not have existed in Germany, Austria-Hungary, Great Britain, or even the United States at the time Weber was writing (see Chandler, 1977 for the history of organizational forms in the United States). The organic model does seem to represent a new organizational form, one that has developed largely since the Second World War and then only in what might be called post-industrial societies (Bell, 1973). (The precursor might be seen in the divisional structure of multi-organizations but, at least in the early 1920s, each division was organized more on a mechanical model.)

The mechanical model of Burns and Stalker shares a number of features with the bureaucratic model. It differs from Weber's bureaucracy in several critical aspects, but the juxtaposition is helpful, giving us a much better understanding of each.

2.2.1 The Implicit Theory

In answering the question of which form is best for what goal, Burns and Stalker perceived two different goals, each requiring a different organizational form or model. However, whereas Weber emphasized efficiency, predictability, calculability of results, etc. (that is, certain functional performances), Burns and Stalker characterize the environment as either stable or unstable. In other words, the problem becomes one of an organizational structure adapting to environmental circumstances, an implicit cybernetic image. There is an implied functional performance in the title of their main work: innovation. Also apparent in the exegesis of their two models is the need to maintain output while the environment is changing. This functional problem is different when the environmental conditions are stable or unstable. To the third question raised in Weber's analysis, how does societal change affect particular forms, Burns and Stalker turn away from the larger societal context and shift to another conceptualization: the immediate product, market, and technological environment. Thus the juxtaposition of their work with Weber's begins to provide us with some feeling for how complex the Weberian questions are, and perhaps some understanding of why they have not yet been answered.

The structural characteristics of the mechanical and organic models and their functional consequences are listed in Figure 2.2, in the same order as in the previous figure, to make comparisons with Weber easier. The mechanical model is very similar to Weber's bureaucratic model, but has been amplified, building in much more information. Where Weber stressed efficiency, Burns and Stalker have emphasized innovation. We must now concern ourselves with two functional performances which appear to be in opposition.

Burns and Stalker note not only the structural differentiation between functional tasks — the offices of Weber — but contrast the kinds of knowledge empha-

Mechanical	Organic
Hierarchical structure of control, authority, and communication	Network structure of control, authority, and communication
A tendency for operations and working behavior to be governed by instructions and decisions issued by superiors	A context of communication that consists of information and advice
The specialized differentiation of functional tasks	The adjustment and continual redefinition of task
Greater importance attached to local rather than cosmopolitan knowledge	Greater importance attached to affiliations and expertise valid to the goal but external to it
The precise definition of rights, obligations, and technical methods attached to a role	The "realistic" nature of the task which is seen as set by the total situation of the concern
A tendency for interaction to be vertical	A lateral rather than a vertical direction of communication
Loyalty to superior	Loyalty to technological progress

Adapted from Burns and Stalker (1961: 125–30).

Figure 2.2 Burns and Stalker's mechanical and organic models.

sized. In the organic form we see a greater emphasis on professional expertise rather than local expertise. In the mechanical model we see that the rules involve rights, obligations, and methods. Burns and Stalker note that the problem of hierarchy implies not only control and authority but also communication. The Bavelas experiments cited above indicate how channels of communication and authority are tied closely together. But we see more clearly that in the mechanical model interaction is vertical and communication involves instructions and decisions. These ideas help explain how the bureaucratic model provides the systematic discipline that creates the efficiency and reliability of results.

In contrast to the mechanical model, the organic form tends to have the opposite characteristics. There is no precise definition of rights or responsibilities. Instead of a hierarchy, there is a network of control, with the *ad hoc* center shifting continually. Communication consists of information and advice, while interaction goes along horizontal lines.

Although we have not included rates and direction of communication as part of the structure, Burns and Stalker make some interesting observations about the kinds of goals that develop in these two different organizational forms. In the mechanical form, the individual tends to become committed only to his narrow specialist concerns, task, or function and thus is concerned about the improvement of technical means, whereas in the organic form the motivation is the improvement of the entire firm. The juxtaposition with Weber is fascinating. The latter emphasized the happy civil servant content with his bureaucratic career; here we see the image of the narrow specialist.

Why does the organic model fit well in an unstable environment, whereas the mechanical model works best in a stable situation? While Burns and Stalker are not explicit about this, their argument might be constructed as follows: Stable conditions permit the separation of work into separate tasks or offices, to use Weber's term. Following an argument of March and Simon (1958: 158-160) who influenced Burns and Stalker, organizations develop programs of action where the rules are precisely specified. Under these circumstances, the bureaucratic mechanisms involved in Weber's model operate with efficiency. It is easier to supervise and to enforce compliance. With a specific program of action, interaction need only follow the chain of command. That is, it is vertical, and moves largely upward with reports and questions. Downward communication need involve only orders and instructions. In other words, the desire or strain is always towards the bureaucratic form, but if conditions are changing all the time, then this form is not viable. The changing circumstances make programs impossible, including, in the extreme, a clear chain of command. Beyond this, there is the implied assumption of team solutions to unique problems, which necessitate lateral interaction in a network of control and an emphasis on consultation and advice. Since there are different abilities, the center of control keeps shifting, depending on the nature of the problem and whose expertise is the greatest. Presumably, team solutions are better because of the difficulty of finding the novel solution to a difficult problem.

The necessity for innovation, that is, the continual production of new products, requires continual creativity. Under these circumstances, the creative spark could come from anyone; thus everyone becomes involved. More importantly, the creative solution is a collective product requiring frank interchanges. This in turn mitigates against hierarchies, rules, supervision, and other characteristics of the mechanical model. For those who worry about sociology losing sight of the individual, here is an organization concerned with maximizing individuality and creativity!

Unlike Weber, Burns and Stalker spend some time noting what could be called the dysfunctions of the organic model. The ambiguity of their situation would seem to create some anxiety on the part of the managers. Here we see one of the dilemmas built into organizational forms. Too many rules can lead to a lowering of morale because of conflict over control. Too few rules can lead to a lowering of morale because of anxiety (see Hickson, 1966, for a further specification of dilemmas of rules found in many different models of organizations).

Like Weber, Burns and Stalker do not ask whether there might be some internal contradictions in the various structural components that they list as defining characteristics. However, one can say that in fact they have at least partially resolved the Weberian contradiction between technical qualifications and a hierarchy of authority by advocating another form. Perhaps all the experts – the scientists, the artists, the professionals – can move from the mechanical to the organic form.

It is also important to note that the mechanical versus organic polarity is a continuum, not a dichotomy. Burns and Stalker observed a variety of intermediate forms that fit well with the intermediate situation found in the stability of the environment, but they did not make clear what these intermediate forms might look like. Still another subtlety is that the multi-organization can have a mechanical form for its stable environment and an organic one for its unstable environment, a theme that becomes important in the work of Lawrence and Lorsch (1967 a and b). However, our authors did not raise questions about the ways in which these two forms are coordinated within the same administrative structure.

If Weber was concerned with the role of the bureaucrat, Burns and Stalker show more feeling for the politics of organizations. Thus, despite an emphasis on structure, the latter provide a sense of process and especially the internal dynamics associated with decision-making; indeed, a process perspective that has only recently been emphasized (see Baldridge, 1971; Pettigrew, 1973; Hedberg, Nystrom, and Starbuck, 1976; Benson, 1977). Burns and Stalker report some of the struggles for power and status after presenting their basic model (see 1961: Chapter V). We also see their concern for process in the discussion of communication and control. Although I have listed them as structural components, mainly because their emphasis is on the idea of hierarchy or network, these concepts are the necessary link between structure and performance, indicating how the structure articulates to ensure conformity – certainly a better understanding than in Weber, where the causal connection is not made clear.

2.2.2 A Critique

Except for the problem of manager anxiety in the organic form, Burns and Stalker do not stress dysfunctions. They have a tendency to see each form as suited to a set of environmental conditions rather than seeing each form as problematic, even within its own environmental niche. This is critical, since it means that the sources of change remain largely external and environmental, rather than deriving from in the malfunctioning of the organization.

Nor do Burns and Stalker make any argument about what is likely to be the dominant form of the future. They specifically avoid any predictions, and argue that there is no one perfect form. It is especially interesting that they did not try to predict what would happen to environmental conditions in the future: would there be a movement towards more or less stability?

In summary, Burns and Stalker's mechanical model in various ways augments and amplifies Weber's bureaucratic model, extending it in needed directions. They added another form to the bureaucratic model which they call the organic form. In the process, they added another interpretation to the concept of environment, namely the immediate technical-market situation. Besides a concern for efficiency, we now also have one for innovation. Again, there is little attention to the problem of internal contradictions.

The underlying argument for the fit between the mechanical form and stable conditions and the organic form and nonstable conditions appears to be twofold. With stability one can program; with nonstability not only can one not program, but innovation requires a team approach where each member is equally important, although the direction shifts from member to member depending upon the task at hand. Here is a line of argument and an organizational form quite different from Weber's conception of bureaucracy and certainly from the Prussian Empire's implementation of this form (see Rosenberg, 1956).

With Burns and Stalker, we can now pose some new questions that enrich our understanding of how form, process, and transformation operate. These issues are:

1. What form is best for the immediate technological and economic market, and what types are there?
2. What political processes are attached to particular forms?

Again, the attractive element of their analysis is the location of form in a technological-economic market place, if not in the larger society and its institutional nexus. It begins to alert us to the necessity of seeing environment as existing on multiple levels just as organizations can be analyzed at different levels. So far, to my knowledge, no one has called attention to the appreciation for process and particularly to the struggles for status and power inherent in their work, in this sense their work has remained very contemporary.

2.3 HAGE'S AXIOMATIC THEORY

Unfortunately the work of Burns and Stalker remained largely unknown in the United States until the mid-1960s. Most organizational sociology here was dominated by the work of Weber and of Barnard, an American capitalist who learned about organizational forms by being president of New Jersey Bell Telephone. On the empirical side, there were a number of isolated case studies, largely in the tradition of Weber's bureaucracy, with little attempt to synthesize (see Price, 1968 for a list of these studies).

About that time, Hage tried to synthesize both Weber and Barnard into a set of interrelated propositions organized in an axiomatic format (Hage, 1965; Barton, 1966; and Hage, 1966) within the explicit paradigm of structural-functionalism. There is, however, a major difference between this theory and the previous models: the concepts are general ones and the hypotheses are made explicit. In other words, the attempt was not to write a set of ideal-types that are historical in nature but to set forth general sociological propositions that could be easily measured and tested. Measures were reported with the theory and then actually employed in subsequent research. Thus it was an example of a more active approach to theory and research (see Hage, forthcoming for an analysis of the effectiveness of this intellectual strategy).

The theory also attempted to codify a number of other theoretical works into a more concise and coherent statement about organizations. Two basic problems existed in the formulations of Weber and Burns and Stalker: the list of functions or performances was too short, and there was a lack of consideration of internal contradictions. Parson's work (1956 a and b) is suggestive of a longer list of functional performances (Nagel, 1961). His functions of adaptiveness, goal achievement, integration, and pattern maintenance suggested the performances of adaptiveness, volume of production, cost efficiency relative to volume of output, and morale or turnover. Each of these seemed necessary for the survival of an organization, although their relative importance varied considerably according to the particular environmental circumstances, goals, and resources available to the organization. The importance of having a list of functional variables can not be stressed too much. *Both the Weberian forms and the Burns and Stalker forms suffer from considering only one or two performances, thus not indicating that there might be dysfunctions as well as functions with each structure.*

In the four performances of innovation, efficiency, quantity of production, and morale, we have two of the performances that interested Weber and Burns and Stalker: efficiency and innovation. Another, morale, was typically discussed by Merton (1957), Gouldner (1954 a and b), and others when they analyzed bureaucratic dysfunctions. Certainly the companion concept, motivation to participate, is a central theme in the work of March and Simon (1958). Finally, the volume of production, or the relative emphasis on quantity versus quality, is implicit in the earlier models, as a careful reading will indicate. These four performances appear to be central to any theory involving how well an organization is doing. It also might be reiterated that the functionalist assumption is that these performances (and others) are necessary for the survival of the organization. If all the workers quit or costs skyrocket; if there is never any product change or worst of all, there is no production whatsoever, then the organization presumedly ceases to exist. But what has been wrong with most functional theory, including these two examples, is that no one has asked what costs might accrue by a single-minded emphasis on either efficiency or innovation – in modern economic terms, there is no cost-benefit analysis. Hage tried to solve this problem by pointing out inherent contradictions and enduring trade-offs between these various performances, which opened the way to power struggles and conflicts, managerial upheavals, and even dissolution.

On the other hand, if Weber and Burns and Stalker do not explicate their models on the performance or output side, their models are quite strong and explicit on the structural side. A number of characteristics are listed and described, as we have seen. In the organizational literature there developed a rapid convergence on the concepts of specialization, centralization, and formalization (Pugh, et al., 1963).

2.3.1 The Major Hypotheses

The axiomatic theory of Hage (1965) takes Weber's model of bureaucracy and translates some of the key ideas into general variables. The concept of hierarchy of authority is translated as the degree of centralization. That is, how many of the decisions of the organization are made only by an elite and how many by the entire membership. Items 3 and 4 in Figure 2.1, which refer to the emphasis on rules, can be translated into the variable degree of formalization, which represents how much the behavior of each job is codified into rules and regulations. Once these translations are made, the essence of Weber's model appears to be summarized by the following hypotheses:

2.1. *The greater the centralization, the greater the volume of production, and vice-versa.*
2.2. *The greater the centralization, the greater the efficiency, and vice-versa.*
2.3. *The greater the centralization, the greater the formalization, and vice-versa.*

The assumption is that centralization not only provides the efficiency that Weber (1947 as translated by Henderson and Parsons) explicitly predicted, but that this could occur only with a relatively higher volume of production. In other words, if efficiency is defined as some cost per unit of production, then normally one lowers costs by increasing the volume of production. The term efficiency has many meanings in the literature; here it should be interpreted as productivity or technical efficiency in the economist's sense of the term. Furthermore, this efficiency is not measured by quality, but only by the quantity of output. If centralization can affect one, it has to influence the other as well. These ideas come through more clearly in the Gerth and Mills (1946) translation, which emphasizes the importance of speed.

We could also add the following hypotheses, which are also part of Weber's model: The greater the formalization, the greater the emphasis on the quantity of production and vice-versa; and the greater the formalization, the greater the efficiency and vice-versa. But these can be derived from and implied in the first three hypotheses. While important in themselves, they are not necessary in an axiomatic format, where an attempt is made to derive as many corollaries from as few axioms as possible (Zetterberg, 1963).

One might also ask if Weber really meant "and vice-versa" in his formulation. Does efficiency cause centralization or formalization? The answer is yes, because of his evolutionary argument. Desires for more efficiency lead to the adoption of more centralization and formalization as in the bureaucratic model because they work better (see Gouldner, 1954a for this feedback).

The hypothesized relationship between centralization and formalization deserves some special comment. The offices are defined by rules and arranged in a hierarchy, indicating that these two components went together in Weber's mind. In fact, as soon as one lists a series of characteristics, all of which have the same hypothesized relationship to the same variable (in this case efficiency), one implies that these components covary more or less; that is, the variables are interrelated. Thus it seems reasonable to argue that Weber would see centralization and formalization as varying, assuming he would accept the idea of variables at all. Certainly strict discipline requires not only the observing supervisor but the specific standards as well, as we have already made clear.

One of the limitations of the axiomatic theory is that it did not always make explicit the arguments about why the hypotheses made any sense. Although Hage does give some reasons, he does not consistently do so. Nor was there any attempt to provide the higher order premises from which these hypotheses could be derived. Besides those already given for Weber's model, one can add that the development of separate tasks in offices or jobs results in a limitation of what has to be known, which in turn makes the development of expertise easier. It also makes supervision easier. Therefore, as decisions become centralized, the elite desire to exercise more and more control, which they do by formalizing rules and procedures. As already stated, formalization makes evaluation possible; without rules judgements about bad job performances become difficult.

Working in the essence of a bureaucratic or mechanical organization, AT & T, Chester I Barnard (1946) worried about the dysfunctions of this form for innovation. He developed a seldom referenced theory about the pathologies of status systems, a key element in Weber's model. Rather than use the term status system, we prefer to discuss stratification as a general variable that can be applied to a wide variety of organizational forms in a quantitative way. Stratification is here defined as the concentration of rewards and the amount of upward mobility. Although Barnard used the term status systems, it is clear that the variable degree of stratification is a correct term for his intent. In a very rare structural-functional theory of status systems, he hypothesized:

2.4.   *The higher the stratification, the lower the morale, and vice-versa.*

2.5.   The higher the stratification, the higher the production, and vice-versa.
2.6.   The higher the stratification, the lower the innovation, and vice-versa.

He stipulated a number of reasons why these particular variables were related. The development of a pyramid of rewards provided a motivation to work hard, which increased production, but since only a few ever made it to the top, there was a lowering of job satisfaction among the much larger number who did not get promoted. He also noted that inevitable injustices occurred, which in turn had the same depressing effect on morale. In other words, Barnard felt that in a system where most are promoted, injustice is less likely to occur and promotion on the basis of friendship rather than ability is less of a problem. It is also probably less likely to occur, since the judgment is made by more people. The problems of nepotism and sycophantism can only flourish with small elites.

Barnard did not include "and vice-versa" in his hypotheses, so we need to justify the addition of these words. As morale declines, there is likely to be an even greater emphasis on the manipulation of rewards as an organizational response. Frequently employers start to use bonus plans or piece rates as a way of solving morale problems. This helps to increase production, but at the cost of greater status differences – in this instance, income – between workers and managers, lowering morale even more. We have the beginnings of a vicious circle. Higher production leads to more emphasis on differences in status and so forth.

What is most interesting is that stratification tends to reduce innovation because subordinates become yes men. Fearful for their promotions, they no longer criticize existing situations. The first step in the adoption of a new program is the recognition of need, which implies a criticism of the past. With the absence of change, those at the top of the status pyramid more and more perceive themselves as deserving remuneration above and beyond what they probably deserve. When new ideas upset the status quo, they may be vetoed by the elite at the top of the status pyramid, another way in which the status system becomes entrenched and solidified.

This largely ignored article by Barnard is especially interesting because it contains a rare structural-functional theory that sees both functions and dysfunctions, positive and negative consequences relative to the survival of the organization. It thus represents a model of what good organizational theory can be and how important it is to recognize multiple consequences, good and bad.

When there are eight variables, one needs seven bi-variate hypotheses connecting the eight variables, to cast the work in an algebraic format. The seventh hypothesis summarizes a part of the theoretical efforts of Victor Thompson (1961 a and b), who published a book in the same year as Burns and Stalker. Like them, he has a good feeling for some of the processes involved in organizations, and especially the problem of conflict. We shall return to some of his other ideas later. But now, we borrow the major cause of organizational conflict and of change: the desire of specialists with technical qualifications to have a share of power. Here is one of those critical internal contradictions, a structural one, summarizing Parsons' doubts about Weber's bureaucratic model. This idea can be captured in the following proposition:

2.7.   The higher the complexity, the lower the centralization, and vice versa.

Hage's definition of complexity is the diversity of different specialists. The emphasis on variety which is missing in both Weber and Burns and Stalker, is yet consistent with them, particularly with Weber's concept that each office is presumedly a specialist. The key is to know how many offices there are. In turn, this has consequences for the distribution of power. A number of reasons for this hypothesis can be given. As individuals with technical qualifications (to use Weber's terms) spend longer and longer periods of training, it becomes more and more difficult for superiors, even with a system of rules, to have the requisite knowledge to supervise and control the work of their subordinates. The greater the variety of disciplines involved, the more this is true. To make decisions, the superior must consult with the relevant experts who, in turn, can withhold information, thus giving them more and more power, which manifests itself in participation in decision-making that is, decentralization (Dalton, 1950). When the system is decentralized, the participants are motivated to learn more about their jobs and to be more open to the hiring of other specialists. Specialists usually develop informal channels of communication that result in the formation coalitions, which in turn fight for a greater share of influence in decision-making. The formation of coalitions, or teams, is one of the best ways of learning, and results in the development of more expertise. In this way decentralized systems facilitate coalition formation, and encourage the gaining of greater expertise.

2.3.2   The Derived Hypotheses

These seven hypotheses connecting eight variables, four of them structural and four of them functional, were then used by Hage in the axiomatic theory to generate 21 more bi-variate hypotheses (listed in Figure 2.3). In order to do this, one must make the assumption that the variables form an interdependent system. If so, then all this procedure does is spell out the implications involved in the original hypotheses. However, in each case, one wants to ascertain whether there are reasons for the plausibility of the particular hypotheses.

This assumption has been criticized by Duncan (1965), Blalock (1969), and Costner and Leik (1971), who argued, largely on statistical grounds, that it is better to have one-directional causality when making theoretical inferences. However, since then the statistical pendulum has swung back. Bailey (1970)

Major Propositions

1. The higher the centralization, the higher the production and vice versa.
2. The higher the formalization, the higher the efficiency and vice versa.
3. The higher the centralization, the higher the formalization and vice versa.
4. The higher the stratification, the lower the morale and vice versa.
5. The higher the stratification, the higher the production and vice versa.
6. The higher the stratification, the lower the innovation and vice versa.
7. The higher the complexity, the lower the centralization and vice versa.

Derived Corollaries

1. The higher the formalization, the higher the production and vice versa.
2. The higher the centralization, the higher the efficiency and vice versa.
3. The lower the morale, the higher the production and vice versa.
4. The lower the morale, the lower the innovation and vice versa.
5. The higher the production, the lower the innovation and vice versa.
6. The higher the complexity, the lower the production and vice versa.
7. The higher the complexity, the lower the formalization and vice versa.
8. The higher the production, the higher the efficiency and vice versa.
9. The higher the stratification, the higher the formalization and vice versa.
10. The higher the efficiency, the lower the complexity and vice versa.
11. The higher the centralization, the lower the morale and vice versa.
12. The higher the centralization, the lower the innovation and vice versa.
13. The higher the stratification, the lower the complexity and vice versa.
14. The higher the complexity, the lower the morale and vice versa.
15. The lower the complexity, the lower the innovation and vice versa.
16. The higher the stratification, the higher the efficiency and vice versa.
17. The higher the efficiency, the lower the morale and vice versa.
18. The higher the efficiency, the lower the innovation and vice versa.
19. The higher the centralization, the higher the stratification and vice versa.
20. The higher the formalization, the lower the morale and vice versa.
21. The higher the formalization, the lower the innovation and vice versa.

Limits Proposition

8. Production imposes limits on complexity, centralization, formalization, stratification, innovation, efficiency, and job satisfaction.

Figure 2.3 Major propositions and corollaries of the Hage theory of structure and function.

noted that in many instances two-directional causality makes more theoretical sense. Currently the cross-lag model of change has become popular (Bohrnstedt, 1969 and Heise, 1970 and 1975), which is precisely this kind of theoretical model. As Hannan and Young (1974) note, this model is popular because it allows for the possibility of feedback models. Now this kind of two-directional interdependent system of variables becomes very attractive as an assumption not only for theory construction but for statistical analysis. But it is necessary to provide theoretical arguments for each causal direction.

Another misconception (Hall, 1977: 46-59) has been that this axiomatic format is a closed system and therefore not open to the environment. This results from a confusion over the logical requirements for algebraic manipulation and the empirical reality of the organization. To manipulate and to synthesize the propositions from Weber, Barnard, and Victor Thompson, we must assume that we have the key variables and that they are interdependent. In no way do we assume that the system is closed to the environment. Just the opposite! Given bivariate relationships, each of the eight variables is allowed to be open to the environment or other variables in some larger system and to reverberate throughout the other seven variables. Thus innovation may increase or production decline or complexity increase or centralization decrease as consequences of environmental disturbances, and then these changes impact on the other seven variables. Thus one argument for two-directional causality is that it allows the variable system to be much more open to external influences. This is also an argument for constructing bi-variate relationships; it allows each variable to have an impact — to represent an avenue of influence. There are disadvantages in bivariate hypotheses, but lack of openness to the environment or lack of flexibility in analytical reasoning are not among them. In fact, it turns out that the disadvantages are really too much openness, too much flexibility, and a certain analytical cumbersomeness. We would like one or two major causal forces that would dominate the system rather than eight equals, each of which can be the first causal change in the chain. In statistical terms, we would prefer a path analytical diagram that creates several paths of causal direction (see Blalock, 1969). This is a more parsimonious and rigorous formulation.

There is, however, one sense in which these eight variables form a closed system vis-à-vis the environment. One must assume there is not some other variable that reverses the hypothesized relationships. This assumption is always made in any theory, regardless of content. As we shall see, at times this is not true, and certain conditions or limits to the hypotheses must be stated. Nor is this assumption quite the same as current contingency theory in organizational sociology. Contingency theory usually takes variables not included here, such as size, technology, or environment, and shows how they affect one or more variables in this system of eight. As yet, almost no one has argued for reversal of relationships under certain combinations of size and technology. (see John Freeman and Hannan, 1975, for one such exciting example).

In summary, for current statistical reasons – the advantages of the cross lag model of change – and for current theoretical reasons – the advantages of an open system – algebraic manipulation of bi-variate relationships appears to be a more sensible procedure today than it did some 15 years ago. In any case, each instance of this must be evaluated on its own. In this particular case, the manipulation of the eight variables led to a number of new insights, and to a program of research on innovation (see Aiken and Hage, 1971, and Hage and Aiken, 1967, 1970).

What is interesting about this procedure is that many of the ideas in the Burns and Stalker model can be derived from these seven major propositions, including the following: the greater the centralization, the less the innovation, and vice versa; the greater the formalization, the less the innovation, and vice versa; and the greater the complexity, the greater the innovation, and vice versa. These hypotheses summarize the major differences between the mechanical and organic models (see Figure 2.2). Again, while centralization and formalization are clearly implied, complexity (that is, the number of specialists) is not. These hypotheses do not capture all of their ideas, however. When we come to the problems of processes involving centralization, control, and communication, we shall need to return to these particular models and find new hypotheses (see Chapter 11). In this theory the concern was with structural-functional relationships and not coordination or control, a usual deficiency of structural-functionalism.

We can now see, however, that both Weber's model and the mechanical model have some dysfunctions, including (besides the several on innovation) the following:

The greater the centralization, the lower the morale, and vice versa.

The greater the formalization, the lower the morale, and vice versa.

The greater the stratification, the lower the morale and vice versa.

The strict discipline that Weber saw does not lead to happy subordinates. A lack of participation in decision-making produces a sense of powerlessness, which lowers morale. The careful delineation of rules has the same result. Conversely, as we have seen in the Gouldner study, lower morale tends to result in attempts to proliferate more rules and centralize decision-making even more. In other words, the normal response is to do the wrong thing! These derivations from the theory are important. They mean that the explicit criticisms of Weber's model made by Merton and Gouldner are at least handled in this new formulation.

The negative relationship between bureaucracy and innovation is a popular theme in the literature. Here the ideas are deduced from the algebraic manipulation of a few central themes of Weber and Barnard. Actually, if one looks at Barnard's article carefully, it becomes clear that centralization is a hidden variable; it comes across in the idea that those at the top of the status pyramid can veto ideas. In other words, centralization and stratification are closely intertwined — another derived hypothesis.

In a similar fashion, the organic model turns out to have dysfunctions as well: The greater the complexity, the less the volume of production; and the greater the complexity, the less the efficiency. Specialists cost money, so that even though they are hired to reduce costs, they actually raise them relative to production volume. Specialists also do not normally emphasize the volume of work but rather its quality. Conversely, concerns about efficiency and quantity of production lead to a lack of hiring of new specialists and a tendency to let them go as concerns about costs mount.

Thus, one consequence of the synthesis of Weber and Barnard, along with the major proposition of Victor Thompson (1961), was to derive the essential features of the organic model. Another consequence was to derive dysfunctions of bureaucracy; performances such as morale and innovation are reduced by the structural characteristics of Weber's model. Likewise, we find dysfunctions associated with the organic model of Burns and Stalker. This is important because these dysfunctions represent mechanisms of change.

Although we have not discussed all of the hypotheses, the reader can note that they could be organized around several themes. This will be done in succeeding parts as we discuss the themes of power, change, and the human factor. At that time, we shall include the theoretical and empirical work that has been written since the axiomatic theory, revising it as need be in the light of current thinking and evidence.

With the advent of path analysis, one might ask if some of the eight variables are more critical than others and also whether the variables can be grouped. Blalock, in his book on theory construction (1969), has suggested that some variables are so highly interrelated and change so quickly that they form a block. In this case, it is useful to separate the variables into four blocks, two structural and two performance (see Figure 2.4). They then illustrate the main interconnections and internal contradictions.

On the structural side there is a bureaucratic block, consisting of centralization, stratification, and formalization, which largely vary together. If one makes the relationship between complexity and this block asymmetrical or one-direction causal, as Costner and Leik (1971) suggest, then the long term evolutionary bias of the theory becomes apparent. This was actually suggested in a long footnote (Hage, 1965: 318). This one-directional arrow corresponds to the common observation that staff are never fired during slumps in demand for either products or services (John Freeman and Hannan, 1975). Usually unskilled labor is let go,

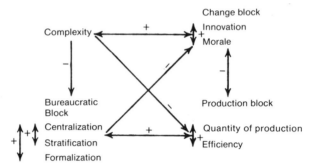

Figure 2.4   A block-recursive model of organization structure and function.

but not skilled or professional-managerial labor, thus maintaining the same score in the variety of occupations. Even if professionals or managers are let go, it is unlikely that all of those in an occupation would be. Out of three social workers or salesmen or system analysts, one might be released, but not all three. Again, the consequence is that the growth in the division of labor tends to be a nonreversible process. In contrast, centralization and the other variables in the block can vary much more depending upon the need for a high volume of production at low cost or the need for innovation and morale. The literature has concentrated on changes in centralization as a solution to problems (Coch and French, 1948; Chandler, 1962; Tannenbaum, 1968, etc.).

On the performance side, there are two production blocks, corresponding to the dilemma of human and material costs and the dilemma between change and continuity of products. These dilemmas help explain much about various kinds of changes in organizational form (that is, the transformation process, and especially the transformation of the bureaucratic block).

The most interesting causal connections are between the two performance blocks, because they illuminate the inherent dilemmas of both mechanical and organic forms. Each of them has dysfunctions and each of them tends to gradually cycle into dissolution. *Buried in functionalist thought is the notion that one needs all the performances in order to survive.* Certainly Parsons' scheme of AGIL contains this simple idea. Likewise, one finds much the same reasoning in the business literature. An organization cannot continue to be effective without innovation, production, efficiency, and morale (see Price, 1968, for a good review of this literature). Thus, even though innovation and efficiency are negatively related and would appear to require opposing kinds of structures organizations must have both of these to survive. The same is true for the relationship between the volume of production and morale. If the workers are too unhappy, they will quit or go out on strike. Again both these variables, while associated with different conditions, are necessary for the maintenance of effectiveness in the organization. This is one reason for the large confusion in the literature on morale and productivity.

To make this explicit one needs an additional hypothesis, a limits proposition, which states that the continued production of products or provision of services requires some morale, innovation, and efficiency. Likewise, we can add the structural variables as well to our production function. This proposition reiterates the concept of dysfunctions, and makes more explicit the functionalist assumption about the necessity for all four performances. Morale cannot be allowed to sink too low, nor can production. The elite of an organization must steer across time, avoiding extreme scores. The practical solutions to these dilemmas we shall explore at length in the third chapter of each part. For example, in Chapter 5, succession of leaders is seen as one mechanism for achieving a balanced emphasis on these four functional performances across time. In contrast, Chapter 8 uses these contradictions as a way of understanding how organizations move into disequilibrium.

Perhaps the most interesting implication of the causal structure combined with the limits proposition is that while there is a long-term trend towards more complexity and greater decentralization, there are many counter-cyclical movements towards greater centralization because of the dilemmas inherent between the two production blocks. These ideas are explored at greater length in Chapter 14.

The causal structure in Figure 2.4 is expressed in a block-recursive form (Blalock, 1969), to make it easier to grasp the two forms or types or organizations, each with their functions and dysfunctions. The original theory, with its 28 hypotheses, is best visualized as a wheel or cobweb in which each variable causally impacts on the other seven. In other words, not all the causal arrows are drawn in Figure 2.4. However, as noted above, it highlights the essential problem of form and transformation.

The limits proposition in Figure 2.4 is represented by a qualification. The two blocks are negatively related only when the organization is in an equilibrium state (see Chapter 8); that is, within a certain range of scores. In disequilibrium, the blocks can be positively related or have no relationship at all. In correlational terms, the size is much closer to zero and the relationships tend to be curvilinear rather than linear. Here the concept of marginal utility works well, because small changes can produce quite striking improvements. Instead of avoiding the criticism of functional theory, the limits proposition, relative to the two performance blocks, provides a dynamic, allowing for the synthesis of structural-functional with political and conflict paradigms. These dilemmas create tensions and conflicts and lead to internal power struggles and the succession of leadership teams. They provide some of the more dramatic moments in the biographies of organizations, whose members are struggling to survive.

Like Weber, Hage perceives an evolutionary bias towards a particular organizational form, namely the organic form, because of the steady increase in the complexity of the division of labor. The organic form is the organization for post-industrial society (Bell, 1973). However, the theory also delineates problems. Unlike Weber, one of the model's most interesting features, is that within organizations one obtains status equality and some measure of freedom only when there is relatively high complexity. Similarly, the organic form demands a movement away from formalism and presumably from that impersonality that concerned Weber. Thus Hage's answers to Weber's questions are quite different from Weber's own.

2.3.3 A Critique

The strengths of this theory are the weaknesses of the others, and vice versa. Although this theory explicitly stipulates dysfunctions and internal contradictions, it does not handle the environment qua society (as did Weber) or qua technique-market nexus (as did Burns and Stalker). Instead, consistent with an open system perspective (Buckley, 1968), the organizational system is seen as free floating and permeable to many outside influences. These influences should be specified.

Although Burns and Stalker saw process as a key element in their study, Hage's theory only hints at the internal power and status struggles. It predicts them as reflected in the causal arrow between complexity and the bureaucratic block, but does not specify the attendant processes.

This theory was most explicitly cast in a structural-functional paradigm where the basic issue was how structure affected the kinds of utilities achieved. However, it avoided all the standard problems of functionalist theory noted by Merton (1957: Chapter 1). Dysfunctions, contradictions, and changes are all built in. There is both long term evolutionary change and cyclical change; there are equilibrium states and disequilibrium ones.

In summary, Hage added two more questions to Weber's list:

1. What are the dysfunctions associated with each form?
2. What are the inherent contradictions?

These questions – or better, their answers – allow us to fill in more of the issue of how forms change and transform themselves. For Weber and Burns and Stalker, the answers lie largely in the environment. Hage put much more emphasis on the organization itself.

2.4 CONCLUSIONS

Since we are interested in synthesizing various theories we can begin here by noting that while Hage reformulated Weber's model into general variables and

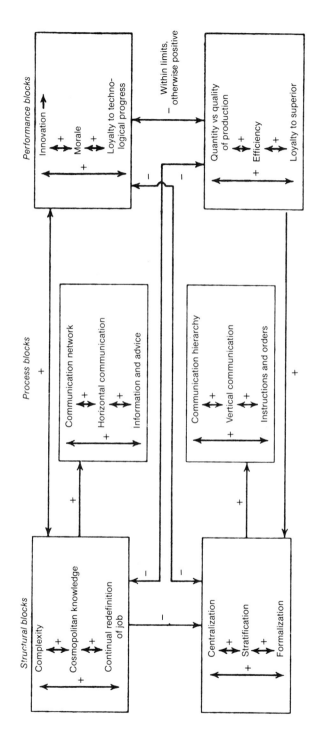

Figure 2.5 A synthesis of Burns and Stalker's and Hage's theories of organizational form.

combined it with a status theory of Barnard, this was done quite independently of the Burns and Stalker work. In Figure 2.5 their work is combined with Hage's to create a much more complex typology of organizational form.

In the structural block containing complexity, Burns and Stalker add two ideas that are quite important: the relative emphasis on cosmopolitan knowledge, and whether or not the job itself is being continually redefined. Here we have the essential image of professional and managerial work, where an occupational specialty may retain the same name but will change constantly because of the growth in knowledge. We have a paradox. On the one hand there is the phenomenological position that it is impossible to define the nature of work because of its subjective experience and because of the fact that change is continuous. On the other hand, the structuralist position that it is possible to define relative enduring entities called jobs and structures. This opposition is captured by recognizing that the label remains the same but the content changes. Furthermore, the speed with which this occurs is itself predictable.

On the performance side, Burns and Stalker add the duality of loyalty to technological progress, and loyalty to superior as goals. Again, these are seen as co-varying with performances as stipulated in Hage's theory. We have here, however, an example of Weber's distinction (Weber, 1947: 115) between *Welt*-rationality and *Zweck*-rationality, or perhaps more precisely between self-interest and altruistic value. What is being suggested here is that some forms of organization generate self-interest and others an interest in larger issues, a topic that is explored at greater length in Chapters 5 and 13.

The major contribution of Burns and Stalker, as we noted, was to add a process perspective, and in particular a set of process variables. These are added as blocks situated between structure and performance. However, they are hypothesized to be primarily determined by the structural blocks. In effect, we have two alternative patterns of control, one with the organic form and one with the mechanical form.

Another way in which a synthesis can be achieved is to combine the issues that each theorist focused on. These issues become the dominant analytical problems for the entire book and explicate the form, process, and transformation trilogy in the subtitle. Relative to form, these issues are:

1. What forms are best for which functional performances?
2. What dysfunctions do these forms have?
3. What internal contradictions do these forms have?

Clearly we want to explore some of the basic processes relative to each form that can be delineated. Finally, relative to transformation, we must ask:

1. What form is best for the immediate technological and market environment?

2. What form fits best within the larger institutional nexus of society?
3. How does societal change favor particular forms, and in what evolutionary sequence?

The last two issues, under the heading of form, help elucidate some of the answers about transformation and are a necessary part of the understanding of how organization and environment fit together.

PART ONE

Power: Structure, Process, and Succession

Chapter Three

Power: The Problem of Centralization or Participation

Many organizational sociologists, like many intellectuals, believe that the most important question about organizations is the problem of power (see indices in any of the books on organizations). Certainly two recurrent themes that have occupied both heads of states and serious journals of opinion have been the theme of participation and that of whether modern organizations — not only multinational corporations but public welfare agencies, schools, hospitals, and so forth — make decisions in the best interests of the nation or its people. Both Ralph Nader and Valéry Giscard d'Estaing agree on the need for more participation, although they may differ about which groups are involved and why. A large number of different kinds of worker participation schemes (see Tannenbaum et al., 1974; Bergman, 1975; Mulder, 1976; Dachler and Welpert, 1978) have been proposed in Europe while a number of different consumer representation ideas are current in North America. Both reflect the present lay concern about the problem of who makes what kinds of decisions. Echoing the popular concern at a professional level, several large multinational research projects are in operation (Hickson, personal communication, Lemmers, personal communication).

In this chapter we shall focus on the question of who participates and why in making basic and fundamental decisions, such as whether to produce a new product like Concorde or fix the price of gasoline, whether to open a plant in Peru or close one in Pennsylvania, whether to hire blacks first or fire women last, and so forth. Behind these decisions lie possibilities that are not even discussed (Perrow, 1972). Currently, the new Marxist literature has pointed out that the *real* decisions, the ones that would make this a better world to live in, are ruled out of the realm of possibility. In manufacturing organizations, it may be safety devices for the workers; in welfare organizations it may be a coordinated delivery system for the multiple handicapped; and in the military it may be a 20% reduction in the budget. The decisions that are not made may be more important than those that are for letting us understand the power of particular groups both within and without the organization.

Who makes strategic decisions (Price, 1968: 61)? This question represents one of the most critical aspects of power, real power; an issue that concerns current researchers. However, another kind of decision, which might be called a work decision, was a major theme in the organizational literature during the sixties (see Blau and Scott, 1962; Hall, 1968; Blauner, 1964; Engel, 1969 and 1970). Usually called the problem of professional autonomy vs bureaucratic control, it is the question of how much freedom the worker has to make his own decisions, such as the choice of therapies, the number of people served, the pace of the assembly line, the time for a coffee break, and so forth. Much of the industrial democracy literature involves this kind of participation (see Emery and Thorsrud, 1976), a concern over worker participation in job decisions, an interest stemming from the early Coch and French (1948) study. It is important to make clear distinctions between worker participation over work-related decisions, and worker participation over strategic decisions, since these are very different kinds of participation with very different mechanisms for implementation. It is not all certain that those groups with a great deal of work autonomy necessarily have a lot to say in the formulation of organizational policies. At one time there were some (Blauner, 1964) who felt that workers were only interested in decisions that immediately affected them, such as the pace of work. We must see whether in fact this is still true, and also how the two kinds of power relate.

So far, we have been speaking of power as if it were a question of decision-making. Yet, the standard definition of power (stemming again from Weber, 1947), that is, one who possesses power gets what he wants despite opposition, would appear to be different (Zey-Ferrel, 1979: 147-150). This definition involves the imagery of power struggles, conflicts, and winner take all. This image can be very useful, because there are indeed major power struggles – from mutinies on ships (Lammers, 1969) to slowdowns in police departments, from fights over community power in school systems to political maneuvers among managers over such fundamental decisions as building a new generation of small cars. But usually the problem of power is handled in a quieter way. Generally, however, patterns of compromise exist and certain kinds of understandings prevail. Votes are traded and spheres of influence are recognized (Coleman, 1974). There are standard patterns of decision-making and a relatively stable distribution of power. The do-or-die fights that cause breakdowns of coalitions are handled in the next chapter.

The regular and routine decisions and the exceptional decisions, although they have different processes attached to them, can be viewed from the perspective of coalition theory. Each interest group, whether consumers or workers, managers or salesmen, has preferences for particular courses of action involved in the decision. In turn, these preferences provide the basis for the formation of coalitions and relatively stable processes of decision making. We need not assume that decision preferences represent naked self-interest: many times they do, but not always. Thus, the word "preferences" appears to be better than "self-interest", since we will want to explore the latter as a separate issue. Decisions about new products or services may have a healthy mixture of what various groups think is best for the organization and best for the interest group because some departments in the organization will be expanding or benefiting as a consequence (Burns and Stalker, 1961: Chapter 5). Just because there is some possibility of self-interest does not necessarily mean that this is the only deciding factor. Also groups do try to enhance preferred utilities or values or ideals, even if there is no direct payoff for them. For example, many – but not all – professionals may approve decisions to improve the quality of service, even when this does not involve an incremental increase in power, status, or salary. For example, physicians may approve of an improvement in the quality of patient care even when it means a *loss* in authority and status (see Hage, 1974: Chapter 5), or when it might result in a net loss for them.

A major issue in discussions of power is whether power is a zero-sum game or not. The structural-functional perspective tends to perceive power as expandable, while the power-value perspective tends to do the opposite. Part of the reason is because the two perspectives look at quite different kinds of decisions. The former focuses on routine and every day decisions where trade-offs and exchanges can occur, while the latter focuses on nonroutine ones involving high risk and where divisibility of action is not possible. The incrementalist literature supports the importance of routine decisions, even about money (Wildavsky and Hammond, 1965; Davis, Dempster, and Wildavsky, 1966).

If one asks what factors affect the sheer number of decisions facing an organization, then at least the following would appear to be critical: the scope of the task, the size of the budget, and the degree of control or regulation either by a multi-organization or a government agency. The impact of these three variables on the total amount of power available to the organization is the focus of Chapter 12. Here we merely note that these variables can expand or contract over time. Regulation can increase or decrease. In the airline industry, the present tendency is toward deregulation. Technologies can be routinized or become more complex. Budgets in real purchasing terms can expand or contract. As these variables change, so does the amount of power.

Beyond this, most routine executive decisions are made in the context of the push and pull of various interest groups. Seldom does one interest group win everything. Budgets are not allocated just to a single department; everyone gets a certain piece of the pie. Talk about increasing worker participation in industry, or public participation in science policy, does not mean less participation for the managers or the scientists. This is a point frequently not understood. Expanding participation does not *necessarily* diminish the power of any one group: it only means that the power is being shared (for a case study of this see Hage, 1974: Chapter 6). Beyond this, as we shall see, we can rather concretely discuss what happens as the power of an organization increases. What this means within the decision-making model of power is that the number of decisions can expand or it can contract. During expansion periods, it will be easier to delegate decisions, to reach compromises, and the like. During contraction periods, when the total sum of power is diminishing, these processes become more difficult.

From the perspective of the managers or administrators, power tends to be seen as more of a zero-sum game. Everyone remembers the decision to build a new product, to adopt a new policy, or to give a 5% raise. What they lose sight of is that these are not the only decisions, and even here there are more sets of decisions than a simple yes or no would imply.

There is therefore really no inherent conflict between a decision-making model of power and older, more traditional definitions. The former makes the latter more concrete and intelligible, to say nothing about how it simplifies the problem of measurement. Decisions are made regularly, while naked power struggles are rare. One must study both, but it is better to begin with who is making decisions about policies and programs before proceeding to the power struggles. This means in some sense focusing on the dull routine decisions rather than on the exciting and emotional ones. Everybody likes a good conflict, but this is unfortunately not the typical state of organizational affairs! Besides, we may only begin to understand why there is a conflict by studying how decisions are made regularly – therein the problem might lie. Beyond this, the determination of decision outcomes is after all the real power question.

To answer this question, we start with a structural theory of power. Which groups have the most power, and why, can be answered in a variety of ways. The structural paradigm is only one of several possibilities. It is, however, a useful place to begin, as many of the other approaches either impact on the social structure of an organization or else are mediated by it. Thus, a political paradigm concerned with which group wins, and why in a particular decision battle must begin with some structural perspective as to how many groups there are and what relative assets they have at their command, which are essentially structural issues.

After a theory about the structural determinants of power has been presented in the first section, a series of qualifications and subtleties are added in the next two sections. The second section tries to understand which departments and levels in an organization might have the most power, given a particular internal distribution of power. It reviews the uncertainty theory of Crozier (1964) and of Hickson et al (1971). The third section integrates the micro theories about job autonomy with the basic structural theory about the determinants of power. Here we can integrate the work decision analytical level with that of strategic decisions. Throughout, the fundamental axioms are made explicit.

3.1. A MESO STRUCTURAL THEORY OF POWER

A very common assumption running through much of the human relations literature is the idea that everyone wants more power (Champion, 1975: 45-50). Indeed, much of the current thrust of worker participation programs is built on this same assumption, namely that workers are unhappy because they are never given enough say, especially relative to decision outcomes that affect their lives. Or, to put things more positively, even if the workers are happy, their morale and productivity will climb if they are allowed more participation in decisions (Tannenbaum, 1968, and Tannenbaum et al., 1974; Pennings, 1976). Certainly there are issues where unions leaders and a proportion of their workers want a more effective say, but it is not immediately clear how much more power they want relative to specific issues. Furthermore, participation schemes may amount to window-dressing, with workers sitting in committees where they have no effective power to make decisions. It remains to be seen whether the German plan, which proposed 50% worker membership on directors boards and which goes the furthest perhaps outside of Sweden or Yugoslavia, really does speak to the needs and the wants of the workers, however popular it is with the Social Democrat party. Among other things, it assumes that the board of directors is relevant. It may well be in Germany, but this is far less certain in the United States. Most interestingly, it is another example of an elite deciding what the needs of the workers are and making the decision for them.

Participation schemes then raise two fundamental practical problems for organizational sociology: how much participation should there be, and how is it actually implemented? Oddly enough, in some ways the first problem is the easier to solve, and it is the one upon which we shall address first.

3.1.1. The Major Premise and Hypotheses

The essential imagery starts with a political model (Cyert and March, 1963), rather than a static structural one. There are a number of different interest groups, usually, although not always, organized around occupations or departments. They do have self-interests: power, prestige, and pay, including fringe benefits and privileges (Maris, 1964). Our question is: how much power, prestige or privilege does any particular interest group want? The answer very logically could vary from none at all, to complete domination of every other group. My premise is

3A   Occupational or other interest groups want the same rank in power, prestige, pay, and privileges as they have in training and skill.

It is most important for us to recognize that this is an assertion about groups and not about individuals. There are always the power hungry among us, but the organizational issue is how much power over strategic decisions the workers, the doctors, or the teachers want. Unskilled workers will want very little, irrespective of what their union leaders will say, while highly skilled workers will want a lot (Allutto and Belasco, 1972; Conway, 1976; Mulder, 1976). The distinction between individual and group is frequently lost to view, and to appreciate it one must take a phenomenological perspective. If Jim Jones wants a raise or a promotion, then he is acting in his own self-interest. If Jim organizes the workers to demand a raise, then we have an example of an interest group. One must look at the nature of the demand, who is making it, and for whom. As one listens to the arguments, usually there is a concept like equal pay implicit in wage demands. Groups compare themselves with other groups. These comparisons are made within institutional spheres. For example, professors at the University of California compare themselves with professors at Harvard University and seldom with managers at Ford Motor Co. Similarly, policemen, firemen, and garbage collectors or sanitation workers tend to compare themselves with comparable groups elsewhere. These comparisons are also made, however, within the context of organizations. It is here that the rankings in terms of education and skill are especially important for shaping expectations relative to pay and fringe benefits.

The example of pay is used because it is more frequently articulated (see Hyman, 1972 on strikes in Britain). But pay is frequently overemphasized as a factor in satisfaction (Fournet, Distefano, and Pryer, 1966: 174). Power may be more critical (Tannebaum, 1968). Various levels of education and skill imply *relative to groups* who have comparable levels of authority and job autonomy. This does not mean that every member expects equal say in decision-making, but rather that the group has a certain expected range or power relative to other groups on a hierarchical axis. Considerable variation between individuals can exist but the group has a central tendency or average as well as a range that allows for a hierarchical ranking.

This assumption does not give us any notion of which of these ranks or dimensions is the most important. Some may say power; others pay and fringe benefits; and some may even say certain rights and responsibilities. The truth of the matter is that the relative importance of particular dimensions will vary according to the historical circumstances of the interest group and its cultural context.

Americans appear to be more concerned with material benefits and the French with power (Ardagh, 1977; Peyrefitte, 1977). But regardless of what *beta* coefficients should be applied and what affects their size, the four dimensions do have relevance in all situations. Furthermore, the problem of the coefficients is best worked out empirically, when enough studies have accumulated for researchers to begin to see consistencies and understand patterns of change in the coefficients. It might be noted in passing that what divides schools of thought is the perceived relative importance of these particular dimensions. The technologist might argue skill and training, the Marxist pay, whereas the student of power would of course see authority as most important. Hall (1977: 191) and others assume that some authority is necessary. Without taking sides with any one of these viewpoints, the assumption attempts to pull the four dimensions and their associated perspectives together.

The most critical dimension in economic organizations is material benefits. In the areas of education, science, and health and welfare, privilege may be the more important dimension. Again, the relative importance of each dimension just means that certain trade-offs are allowed. Thus professionals are given considerable latitude in terms of when they work but much less pay than one would expect on the basis of their education. Those managers who must work long hours on a regular basis are given much more pay than one would expect given their education level. The relative importance of power, pay, and privilege can also vary as a function of societal values. Power is important in the Soviet Union and pay in the United States.

This fundamental axiom gives us the basic reason why complexity or structural differentiation might be negatively related to centralization and stratification. The main theoretical fault with all of the theories presented in the previous chapter is that we are given a set of hypotheses, usually only implicit, but not given the theoretical reasoning that makes them plausible. Here we have a premise that allows us to deduce hypotheses at a lower level and test them in various empirical settings. As we shall see, it can organize a large number of empirical findings.

There are six immediate hypotheses that can be deduced from this one single assumption:

3.1 *The greater the concentration of highly trained and skilled specialists, the greater the decentralization of power in strategic decisions and vice-versa.*

3.2 *The greater the concentration of highly trained and skilled specialists, the greater the destratification of pay and prestige and vice-versa.*

3.3 *The greater the concentration of highly trained and skilled specialists, the greater the equality of rights and responsibilities and vice-versa.*

3.4 *The greater the centralization of power in strategic decisions, the greater the stratification of pay and prestige and vice-versa.*

3.5   *The greater the centralization of power in strategic decisions, the lower the equality of rights and responsibilities and vice-versa.*

3.6   *The greater the stratification of pay and of prestige, the lesser the equality of rights and responsibilities and vice-versa.*

The first three hypotheses stress what might be called the organic equilibrium described by Burns and Stalker (1961), while the second three emphasize the image of a mechanical equilibrium state. All represent a description of the meso-structure of an organization and thus reflect distributions of attributes across social groups. In other words, it is not only the number of groups but the *proportion* of them that have equivalent ranks across each pair of dimensions that form the basis of the hypotheses. If 20% of the groups have high rank on skill, 30% moderate training, and the rest are unskilled, then we would expect the distribution of power on basic strategic decisions to be about the same; that is 20% of the groups will participate all of the time, 30% will have moderate influence, and one-half almost none or very little. Although there is no necessary assumption that there are only three levels or echelons on each dimension, or that the absolute levels are the same, it is a useful way of thinking about the relationship between the ideas in the assumption and the derived equations. Stratification is a measure of the distribution of pay among groups/individuals, while centralization is a measure of the distribution of power over strategic decisions. Like Marx and Engels (1889), we are assuming that a concentration of the former leads to a concentration of the latter but unlike Marx and Engels, vice-versa. The hypotheses are saying that if we know how skill is distributed among the groups, we will then know how power, pay, and privileges are distributed as well.

They also provide a scenario of what happens when a new occupational group enters the hierarchy of authority, pay, and privilege within an organizational structure. They will expect, then demand, and finally if need be, *fight* for their share of these resources. No assumption is made that the redistribution will necessarily occur automatically. Quite the contrary! Power is seldom relinquished without a struggle.

But what makes the struggle usually, though not always, resolvable is the fact that there are three potential compromises available that allow for the renegotiation of the power structure when a new occupational group enters an organization (Strauss, 1963). First, areas of preferred interest can be worked out. As Coleman (1974) and his students have noted (Hernes, 1976), people and occupational groups vary in how much involvement they have in certain decision areas. Thus, purchasing agents (Strauss, 1963) are given top say in their area of competence, the legal staff in theirs, the accountants in theirs, and so forth. There is a frank recognition of spheres of competence and of right to greater say. This might be called compromise by specialization of decision-making. Second, the principle of participation diminishes the intensity of power struggle. It is one thing to take away a group's decision making influence and quite another to ask them to *share* in the decision making (see the very consistent control graphs in Tannenbaum, 1968). This makes compromise much simpler and easier. It might be called compromise by the sharing of decision-making or participation. In one sense, one might argue that there is no compromise at all if one group demands participation where previously it did not have it. But frequently the group wanting participation will demand exclusive power in a certain area. The compromise is to share the power. Third, any increase in the level of organizational autonomy that is the number and variety of decisions provides another easy and interesting compromise. If the number of decision areas and the frequency with which decisions are made within these areas are increasing, then the sharing of power is that much easier, because in a sense there is more power, more spheres of influence, and more decision work to do and to share. This makes the first two compromises both easier and more likely. This is why the assumption of a zero-sum power game is unrealistic, especially for those concerned with a bargaining and coalitional model of an organization.

In other words, the theory suggests that power, pay, and privilege gradually move towards more equality as there is a change in the distribution of specialists. As their concentration increases, then the valued resources should become more equitably distributed over the long haul. The redistribution frequently involves conflict (see Chapter 11). However, the intensity of conflict is diminished when the organization has expanding resources (Hills and Mahoney, 1978). Thus, increases in the level of autonomy and in the per capita budget enable the haves to give to the have-nots, without taking away from the haves. In absolute terms, the haves do not lose power or pay if the organization's resources are increasing, but in relative terms the entire distribution shifts towards a more equalitarian stance. Needless to say, the shift is slow to occur, though it will occur over the long term.

Weber (Gerth and Mills, 1946) has been one of the few individuals to worry about whether bureaucracy would bring about plutocracy or not. The implication of our first assumption is that where there is a low concentration of specialists, power, pay, and privilege will be concentrated as well. That is, there will be little organizational democracy, and plutocracy will prevail. In contrast, where the concentration of specialists is high, organizational democracy and equality are more likely. It depends upon the changes in the larger society (see Chapter 14), and the existence of a mass-college educated population. For me, the question of where and under what conditions members of an organization can have liberty, equality, and fraternity is one of the central problems of sociology.

For those who are interested in industrial democracy or worker participation, the implication of the assumption is that one can give too much participation to the worker — more than he wants. Conway (1976) has shown that some teachers are dissatisfied because they have too much power. In the next section we shall discuss the meaning of participation in various boards and committees but, if the assumption is correct, groups do not want more rank in the participation of strategic decisions than their ranking in skill and training allows. Thus industrial participation plans may have a very different meaning for unskilled workers than for skilled ones. However, if one accepts the idea, which is probably true, that most workers have less power than their rank of skill and training, then various governmental laws requiring more worker participation are at least a step in the right direction, and may reflect the long term power struggle between managers and workers that is only now being resolved. At the same time participation schemes, seen as a panacea for many problems in industry, are unlikely to work uniformly precisely because of the different skill levels involved in different industries and industrial sectors.

For those who are interested in socialism, and for the neo-marxists, the assumption is somewhat gloomy regarding the time when interest groups, including social classes, will fight for a bigger share of the pie. It is not the absolute differences between the haves and have-nots that count. Only when groups — such as women, blacks, teachers, foremen, or middle management — achieve a certain level of skill and expertise do they start demanding a comparable standard of pay and equivalent say in running the organization, and the same set of privileges as other groups with their level of skill and expertise. Thus, the long term struggle for equality depends upon the changes that occur in the level of training and the process of specialization. This brings us to the first most important fact about all modern organizations: the steady increase in the number and variety of specialists. The reasons for this are discussed in Chapters 13 and 14 and lie in the environment. Here it is only important to remember that the concentration of specialists becomes the major driving force for changes towards more liberty and equality.

Equilibrium is achieved structurally when all interest groups have the same rank across four major kinds of dimensions. Disequilibrium at the meso-structural level occurs when one or more groups within an organization do not have consistency in rank. This definition is critical because structural-functionalists always assume that there is equilibrium, and conflict theorists always assume that there is not; but neither ever provide a definition that will facilitate a clear and unambiguous classification of whether or not equilibrium exists (for a rare exception see Caplow, 1964: 116-18). This is what our assumption does. It is also important because since March and Simon (1958) there has not been much attempt to define equilibrium conditions in an organization; yet this concept is fundamental to the development of a number of theoretical concepts and mathematical equations.

Furthermore, by comparing the distributions, or more simply the means, of all groups in an organization, we can define different kinds of disequilibrium and, as we shall see in Chapter 10, different kinds of conflict as well. For example, if there is a discrepancy between the level of skill and training and the level of power, we can have two kinds of disequilibrium. If the former is higher than the latter, we have a power gap, and we would expect conflicts to change the distribution of strategic decision making so as to include the excluded groups. If the latter is higher than the former, we would expect that the groups not exercise their power due to lack of interest and that *de facto* centralization would emerge. The resolution of the disequilibrium can be different depending on its form, and conflict is not the only manifestation of this problem. Apathy is another!

3.1.2. The Concepts and their Measures

Although the concepts in our hypotheses appear straightforward there are a number of issues involved that require some explanation and elaboration. This is particularly important because there exists in the literature a number of concepts that appear to be similar and in fact are not. Centralization is a concept used widely, but its measures differ greatly from one study to the next.

We shall start with our first hypothesis and define its two major concepts.

The concentration of specialists: The level and variety of trained and skilled groups relative to the number of groups in the organization.

This definition is not the same as the concept of complexity used in the previous chapter and found in comtemporary literature (see Hall, 1977: Chapter 5; Zey-Ferrel, 1979: Chapter 6; Azumi and Hage, 1972; Hage and Aiken 1967, 1969, 1970: Price, 1972, Chapter 7), nor is it the same as the concept of structural differentiation as found in the work of Blau (1970, 1972, 1973) and his students (Blau and Schoenherr, 1971; Meyer, 1968 a and b; Heydrebrand, 1973), nor is it the same as the concept of specialisms as found in the work of the Aston group and their colleagues (Pugh *et. al.* 1968; Holdaway, Newberry, Hickson, and Heron, 1975). All of those concepts count in one fashion or another the *number* of specialists within job titles or functions, but in no way do they measure the *proportion*. Indeed, most of Blau's research has focused on the relationship between size and structural differentiation, whereas the premise suggests that at the organizational level the key is the concentration of specialists; that is, the ratio between the number of specialists and the number of persons in the organizations, taking into consideration the extent of their training and skill, which is not always indicated by job title (Dewar and Hage, 1978).

It is worth noting that much of this research has not separated multi-organizations into organizations, and it is therefore very difficult to compute comparable measures of the concentration of specialists. How each of these three research traditions went on to count specialists is also of interest. Blau and his students count job titles, hence there is little weighing by skill level or area of expertise, except insofar as different jobs reflect this. The Aston studies also do not measure level of skill. Furthermore, they count only specialists in staff relative to manufacturing, ignoring the managerial specialists in the line or production side. Yet the thrust of Chandler's (1962) book *Strategy and Structure* and the argument of the technological school (Woodward, 1965; James Thompson, 1967; Perrow, 1967 and 1970), is that managing the production of refrigerators is not the same as managing the production of automobiles (as Ford discovered when it purchased Philco). Finally, Aiken and Hage counted major occupational groups and attempted to measure skill level indirectly by a professional activity measure, but in fact theirs is not a measure of skill or expertise as much as it is of professionalism. So all three research traditions are not exactly what is desired. The errors introduced by these measures have to be estimated when the results of a secondary analysis are reported below. The "concentration of specialists", is employed so that there is no confusion with these existing ideas (such as complexity), and to underline the proportional or distributional nature of the concept.

Little has been said about how to operationalize groups in an organization. What makes this difficult is that the groups can vary in size, from the unskilled workers, perhaps as many as 350,000 on the various assembly-lines of a multi-national automobile company, to three or four highly skilled market researchers with PHDs in psychology working on the motivation problems of consumers in a multinational soap company. Tannenbaum's (1968) approach to measuring the distribution of power is one solution: there are inherent conflicts of interest according to level in the organization. But we need to do more than this. One very simple solution is that every time there is a separate union or professional (or managerial) association, we know we have identified another interest group. Beyond this, different training – both formal and informal – implies different values, interests, and even jargon (for a more extended discussion see Dewar and Hage, 1978). Research in France under the direction of Karpik has emphasized the same basic values about power strategies as one way of distinguishing interest groups. But just as Tannenbaum's measure only emphasizes hierarchical level, the Karpik approach only looks at a few groups, and frequently only one dominant group. Interest groups can coalesce over many different bases and for this reason, the positional procedure is the most appealing. It includes both level and occupational specialties as the bases of interest group formation.

As noted in the introduction to this chapter, the essential thrust in our analysis of the structure of power is the focus on decision making and, more specifically, strategic decisions. Centralization, the standard term employed in the literature, is defined as follows:

The centralization of power: The level and variety of participation in strategic decisions by groups relative to the number of groups in the organization.

The theoretical definition is complex. While more elaborate than Price's (1972: 43) definition of centralization as the concentration of power, it is essentially the same. The definition calls attention to the necessity of measuring a number of different areas as well as the extent of participation in each of them. Again, there is the still unexplored possibility that some areas might be more important than others. Centralization has been conceived largely in distributional terms ever since Tannenbaum's pioneering work on the control graph (see 1968 for the reprint of the major articles and also Price, 1972: 50-55). In many respects his and his colleagues' work is probably the best single approach as it taps influences of various groups over various decision areas. The interest groups are defined by hierarchical level, thus ignoring the very important occupational dimension. Their measure also distinguishes between level of influence, which is important. In contrast, Hage and Aiken (1967a) measured positions defined by both level and occupational group, and by the extent of participation in five major areas of strategic decision making: new programs, policies, promotions, personnel, and budgets (see Price, 1972: 44-47).

Rather than measuring a mean or a slope — and again only Tannenbaum (1968) and his students really emphasized the importance of the slope as well (see Pennings, 1976 for a contemporary example) — the Aston group (Pugh et al., 1968; Child, 1972a) measured the level to which a decision was delegated across a large battery of decisions. This ignores the joint decision-making made across hierarchical levels and with other departments Although level may be the key defining property of an interest group, such as the management versus the workers, it is not at all apparent that there might not be major divisions between occupations on the same authority level. For example, in hospitals the physicians and the administrators have different skills and levels of training (depending of course on the kind of hospital); they occupy the same authority echelons (depending upon how one defines this) but have quite different power, privilege, and pay. The Aston measure does not allow for variation among groups at the same hierarchical level. Likewise, the Blau measures (see Blau and Schoenherr, 1971 and Blau, 1973) are essentially ones of delegation and therefore do not attempt to measure participation or influence over all echelons and departments. Delegation of decisions is still related in certain ways to participation, if we are willing to assume that effective member participation is a certain range probably distributed normally about the point defined as where the decision is made. Thus the department head may "make the decision" but may consult with his subordinates and also his superiors about the decision he makes. There is, however, the distinct possibility that subordinates would perceive that they participate less and have less influence than superiors believe. The latter probably think they delegate more than their subordinates perceive – one reason why an influence or a participation measure may be better – but there is no reason to believe that the rank ordering is wrong even though the extent of participation is not accurately measured.

The definition of centralization combines a structural perspective with a political-value paradigm, but both of these are quite different from a conflict-critical perspective. This latter would put great emphasis on the ownership of the means of production, the presence of monopoly capital, and the fact that a small institutional elite may effectively limit the bounds of decision-making (Quinney, 1979). These bounds are set at the macro level rather than the meso level, at the level of the multinational, multi-organization and the relationships between the state and the economy. These become more of a focus in Chapters 13 and 14. For now, we merely note that these perspectives are operating at different analytical levels and with different definitions of organizational boundaries.

One other paradigmatic point should be made and that is a structural and a political perspective difference in the relative emphasis on process. As was mentioned briefly in the introduction, the bargaining, the exchange, and the sharing or negotiated process of power are present (Bucher, 1970) and explain why the structure of power is relatively stable. We have something akin to the movement of molecules in a solid. There is movement and it is in predictable orbits, but one can still speak of it as a stable solid. The same is true for the structure of power. The processes of decision-making, both stable and unstable, receive extended analysis in the next chapter. Here, I only reiterate the observation that *most processes are attached to structures and maintain these structures*. What is correct for biology is also correct for organizational sociology. While process and structure are frequently in opposition – certainly their phenomenology is different – they have intimate causal connections. (For a contrary perspective see Benson, 1977).

The extent of stratification within organizations has seldom been studied. Indeed, several of the major studies (Whisler, 1964; Palumbo, 1969) have included it as a measure of centralization. The definition is as follows:

The stratification of rewards: The level of pay or remuneration and of fringe benefits of groups relative to the number of groups in the organization.

The intent is to include all forms of remuneration including stock options and profit sharing as well as wages and salaries, but not necessarily prerequisites which belong more to the privileges associated with work. Admittedly, the rug on the office floor is hard to classify; is it a fringe benefit or is it a privilege? To me it appears to be more the latter. More assuredly fringe benefits are such items as number of paid holidays, vacation time, social security, medical insurance and so forth. Indeed, these items are now such an important part of the total pay package that in France the employers share of social security is forty percent of the salary. As for top management, they may receive many forms of payment in kind including paid vacations for wives, housing allotments, and even reduced prices in the local company stores. The military has traditionally provided tax-free articles for its personnel. In the U.S.S.R., top managers are allowed to shop at special stores where only certain kinds of goods are available.

The concept "normative equality" has been created by me to replace formalization, which appears to be a measure of control, as has been pointed out by Child (1973) and as I have myself come to recognize (Hage, 1974). Because professionals or managers do appear concerned about whether they have certain privileges, it does seem wise to include this as a separate structural dimension. It is defined as follows:

The normative equality of rights: The level of responsibilities and of privileges of groups relative to the number of groups in the organization.

It may seem strange to think of responsibilities as a right, or something that people would want, but again interest groups do compare themselves on whether they have "meaningful" work. When the word meaningful is closely examined in this context, one discovers that this concerns their responsibilities. People take pride in having them. Faunce (1958) has indicated that when automation reduces responsibility, then workers become more dissatisfied. Walker (1957) and Mann and Hoffman (1960) have shown the reverse. Much of the literature on intrinsic satisfaction in work implies the importance of responsibilities (Champion, 1975: 205-08). Promotions may mean much more in terms of this definition than even power or pay. Indeed, one way interest groups struggle to get more power is by assuming more responsibilities, precisely so that they become indispensable. Parallel to responsibilities is the idea of privileges. Privilege is a very hard concept to define because it can include so many things. We have already noted that privileges such as office space of a certain size, a secretary, a chauffeur-driven car, and so on can be considered as forms of pay. However, when they represent things or prequisites that the person would not pay for himself if they were not supplied, it seems we are dealing more with privileges, than we are with payments in kind. More typical kinds of privileges are the relative freedom of action, to come and go as we want, to work when we want, and so forth — although here, too, there is some shading into the idea of worker or professional autonomy, which is the micro counterpart to the concept of centralization.

Aspects of normative equality have been included in various discussions of control, such as in the pace of the assembly line (Blau and Scott, 1962); but in general the idea that different interest groups rank relatively high or low in the number of privileges and of responsibilities has not been considered in the organizational literature.

3.1.3. The Findings

The large number of studies on organizational structure allows us to do a secondary analysis and test these hypotheses as directly as possible. As the discussion of the differences between the theoretical concepts defined here and the measures used indicates, however, we can at most only obtain an approximation to what is desired. But it is best to test these hypotheses as closely as we can, because they provide at least some insights into the correctness of our fundamental assumption about the strain towards consistency of rank. In particular, considerable attention will be paid to the Aston studies, the panel study of Hage-Aiken, the Child study, the Azumi study and the Paulson study, since these are large data sets where measures of a similar nature have been employed. These studies are also of special interest because they span the United States, Britain, and Japan. They include a wide variety of public and private organizations, both organizations and multi-organizations.

In the reanalysis of the work of Hage-Aiken, one finds a relatively consistent and high negative relationship between the concentration of specialists (that is, their complexity score divided by log size), and centralization, as measured by the lack of participation in strategic decisions. What is striking is that, despite some massive changes (see Dewar, 1976), particularly in the addition of specialists and the growth in size, the cross-sectional correlation remains relatively constant $r = -.60$. There is a considerable improvement in the size of correlation when one uses their complexity measure standardized on log size. This indicates that the concentration of specialists is the preferred measure. As further confirmation, an examination of the increase in variance indicates an average of 10% across some twenty variables. This range and stability of improvement means that the concentration of specialists is not only a better predictor of decentralization, but is a more fundamental concept. In fact, centralization, which is a proportion, as well as most of the other variables were in fact standardized, although not always in the same way. They therefore do not have the same denominator; variables that have the same denominator have inflated correlations. Once complexity is standardized on size, then its correlation improves because a major source of measurement error has been removed.

A reanalysis of the Paulson (1974) data indicates that when his measure of complexity is divided by size, and when organizations smaller than size 10 are eliminated, the correlation between this measure of the concentration of specialists and centralization is $r = -.28$ (N = 43). This correction of this original study (1974) is non-trivial because when organizations are smaller than size 10, group dynamics replace organizational rules and procedures (see Evers, Bohlen, and Warren, 1976). In the original Hage-Aiken study, which has a sample very similar to that of Paulsen, all of the agencies smaller than 10 were eliminated as well. A study of government agencies found a dramatic shift between agencies size 20 and over, and under 20 (Blau, Stauffer, and Heydebrand, 1966). As further confirmation of the need to be careful about how large the organization is before it should be noted, Evers, Bohlen, and Warren (1976) found that organizational hypotheses about interaction between agencies began to be supported at size 10 but not at smaller sizes. Again, the correction procedure seems justified and indicates that once errors of measurement are eliminated, consistency appears.

The replication of the findings in the Paulsen study (1974), despite some differences in measures, is encouraging because the sample of organizations is quite similar, albeit collected in a different part of the United States. The Hage-Aiken panel study, because it is longitudinal, allows for a test of consistency across time. It does not have a very large number of organizations until the augmented third wave, when the number increases from 16 to 29. In contrast, the Paulsen sample has 43 organizations of size 10 or larger.

Since the concentration measure improves the correlational pattern we have more confidence that the essential argument regarding the proportion of specialists is correct. As high ranking occupations, such as professionals, increase in number, they demand more say in determining policies, budgets, and programs, and this gradually reflects itself in a greater decentralization of power. In contrast, if the organization grows in size but adds low ranking occupational groups, such as the unskilled, then the concentration of specialists *declines*. We would expect the centralization of power to increase as well. This property is another advantage of the concept, concentration of specialists, and its measures. Complexity, structural differentiation, and the like tend to be nonreversible processes. Once a new occupational specialty is added, it is never or seldom subtracted. However, the concentration of specialists can decrease — and precisely as organizations become successful — and shift from batch to mass production or from individualized services to limited mass provision of services (see Chapter 13 for a discussion of this growth process).

Recognizing that the measures are somewhat different in the Aston studies, which were completed on different samples of organizations and at different times, one finds that the correlations are remarkably similar, albeit always less. Since the Aston study did not define organizations relative to their input, throughput, and output, they have not counted specialization in production relative to different kinds of technologies. This is especially true of management specialties. Thus there is an undercount — especially in multi-product firms. In other words, it is a measurement error that can affect not only the magnitude but the relative rank of the organizations in their sample. What is also of interest is that if one uses the role specialization indicator rather than the functional

Table 3.1   Concentration of specialists vis-à-vis centralization and stratification: secondary analysis of Alternative Operationalizations

Concentration of specialists (variety of occupations/log size)			
Hage-Aiken panel study	wave 1	wave 2	wave 3	wave 3A[a]

	wave 1	wave 2	wave 3	wave 3A[a]
Centralization (nonparticipation)	-.60	-.52	-.69	-.58
Stratification (proportion)	-.77	-.56	-.53	-.45
(N)	(16)	(16)	(16)	(29)

Concentration of specialists (variety of specialisms/log size)		
	Pugh et al.	Azumi
Centralization (nondelegation)	-.54	-.01
(N)	(52)	(40)

Concentration of specialists (level of professionalism)			
Hage-Aiken panel study	wave 1	wave 2	wave 3	wave 3A

	wave 1	wave 2	wave 3	wave 3A
Centralization (nonparticipation)	-.74	-.58	-.75	-.52
Stratification (proportion)	-.55	-.59	-.51	-.44
(N)	(16)	(16)	(16)	(29)

Concentration of specialists (no. of job titles/log size)	
Blau and Schoenherr	
Centralization (noninfluence)	-.32
Centralization (nondelegation of budget)	-.20
(N)	(53)

[a]Augumented wave, that is, includes the sixteen organizations reported in the previous wave.

specialization indicator, the results are less striking. Again, *it appears that the key is the variety of different occupational groups rather than the sheer number of specialists.* This is also an argument for considering the interest group level of analysis rather than the individual level.

Perhaps the most striking difference lies between the Aston studies of Pugh et al. (1969) and Child's (1972), one that has received much comment in the literature (Donaldson, 1975; Aldrich, 1972 and 1975; Child, 1975, Mintzberg, 1979). Donaldson improved the consistency of findings by focusing on the plant level but this still leaves aside the question of whether this should be done with all organizations. Some organizations, those with the same inputs, throughputs, and outputs should be analyzed at the level of the headquarters and others should be analyzed at the level of the plant. Thus, although Donaldson has moved part way to resolving the problem, he has not done so completely because the next task is to separate out true organizations from multi-organizations. Whether this would solve all of this inconsistency remains to be seen, but the plant analysis is promising. However, the major problem remains that manager specialists in production are not counted.

In the replication of the Aston instruments on colleges in Canada (Holdaway, Newberry, Hickson, and Heron, 1975), the problem of ignoring the many professionals in the teaching departments becomes striking. Each of these is a different occupation and therefore an interest group. This data has not been reanalyzed as a consequence. Given the weak relationship between functional specialization and centralization, if the concentration of specialists were actually measured, it appears reasonable to expect a negative relationship with centralization.

The difference this can make is also illustrated in a very large study of hospitals (Moch, 1976). Complexity was measured in two ways: the number of medical specialities present and the number of specialized units. Both of these have a negative correlation with centralization ($r = -.41$ and $-.36$ respectively). Presumably if these were divided by size, and the ratio variable correlated with centralization, the negative relationship might become even stronger. Hospitals, very much like colleges, have a number of specialists, professionals, who are usually grouped in separate departments — that is, a functional design. To leave this out of the measure is to miss most of the diversity and also the major variation in skill and expertise. Although the Moch measure is not a proportional measure, its findings are certainly consistent with the other research. It is an important study because of its large size and because it taps a very different kind of organization — general hospitals.

The Blau and Schoenherr (1971) data have also been reanalyzed — that is, their measure of the number of job titles is divided by the logarithm of size. We find essentially the same negative relationship between the concentration of specialists and two measures of centralization, one a measure of lack of influence and the other more specific to the non-delegation of decisions relative to the budget. We would assume that especially in social security agencies, job titles are not quite the same as occupational specialities. Civil service tends to result in a proliferation of grades for pay purposes, and to provide motivation for career personnel, but it does not necessarily mean that there are different occupations. Thus it is possible that there is lesser range among these agencies than is suggested by a count of job titles, which in turn might mean a higher correlation with decentralization if one were to count only occupational specialties and then compute a concentration ratio.

All of the Blau studies (1972) that indicate the large correlation between size and the number of job titles can be reinterpreted in the same way. Generally these studies have found that size is negatively related to the amount of delegation of particular kinds of decisions (see Blau and Schoenherr 1971: Chapter 5). When the number of job titles is divided by logarithm of size we find that it is negatively related to centralization as measured by influence. It seems reasonable to conclude that it is really the presence of specialists more than anything else that accounts for the delegation of responsibilities. In the more detailed analysis of Blau and Schoenherr (1971: 128) one finds this line of reasoning supported in a multiple regression of automation, education, size, number of levels, and staff ratio on the delegation of personnel responsibilities. Automation and education have a positive partial correlation and size a negative one, indicating that experts may account more for decentralization as measured by delegation than size per se.

Likewise Blau's (1973) other major and detailed analysis, a representative sample of universities and colleges, suggests that expertise is associated with greater faculty participation in formulating educational policies, the administrations' influence in appointments, and the senior faculty's appointment authority. Although the multiple regressions sometimes involve measures that appear to be extraneous, such as the geographical location or relative affluence of the college, the importance of faculty qualifications and research emphasis — which are indirect measures of specialization and of skill — have a strong negative correlation with the different aspects of decision-making. In the regressions, size is always included as another variable, so that the impact of faculty expertise is seen as relative to this and other concepts; for example, the impact on the senior faculty to make appointments is .58 and the partial is still .19 when eight other variables are controlled. Log size still has a partial of .30 in the same regression, suggesting that insofar as this is a proxy for the concentration of specialists, then it contributes to decentralization. When one examines the administration's influence in a multiple regression, log size has a partial of −.51. Size is not related to centralization of decisions on educational policy, a domain for the administration and board of trustees. Since this is a study of universities and colleges in the United States, it helps support the contention that if Holdway, Newberry, Hickson, and Heron had measured occupations in teaching and research rather than just those in administration, their results might have been different.

Do we always expect that the concentration of specialists will lead to a decentralization of decision and equality of pay and privilege? Of course not. The clearest piece of *negative* evidence comes from the study of Japanese business firms made by Azumi. Here there is no association between the number of specialisms divided by log size and centralization. Again, part of this may be explained by the lack of measures of specialization by product technology. But another reason may be found in their very different education system. If the

Japanese produce generalists, and if this is reinforced by a systematic rotation through each kind of job activity, then one would expect that there would be less association between the concentration of specialists and centralization, precisely because the generalists who are at the top of the hierarchy are less dependent upon the specialists. Ouchi and Johnson (1978) indicate that Japanese firms do have less task specialization and career mobility. The argument, advanced in part, is that the men at the top cannot know everything: March and Simon's (1958) limit to cognitions assumption. However if the men at the top do know everything then one would expect more centralization and stratification than one would otherwise predict on the basis of the concentration of specialists.

In a case study of Sears-Roebuck and Montgomery Ward, Hyre (1970) found that the latter was more centralized but also had a different pattern of upward mobility. Montgomery Ward rotated managers through all departments and then promoted them, in effect training generalists. Likewise all the military services have used the same technique. The office corps are for the most part generalists, and rotated through all relevant areas as they are promoted upward. They are allowed to specialize somewhat, but in fact their continued promotion is dependent upon the ability to move from one substantive area to another. In France, the *"grandes ecoles,"* despite their specialized titles (mines, army, roads, education, business, and the like), in fact receive a generalist education that places great stress on mathematics, itself a general subject (Peyrefitte, 1976). In part this explains why French organizations are more centralized and also why top management is less receptive to the divisional structure as suggested in Chandler (1962).

If one examines the level of professionalism and accepts the idea that it combines some concept of training and skill, or reflects an emphasis on person specialization (to use the term of Victor Thompson [1961]), then we find in the Hage-Aiken panel study more confirmation of the idea that the higher the level of skill and training, the less the centralization of power and the less the stratification of pay. The relationship between professional training and the degree of centralization is in the predicted direction, but consistently less strong. The four correlations vary between .20 and .30 ($N = 16$). Perhaps the reason for the relative lesser influence of professional training is the importance of continued education or socialization. This is best tapped by examining professional activity. As has been suggested above, professional activity in welfare agencies may be the more direct indication of skill or expertise, just as participation in research for faculty is so important in universities (Blau, 1973).

Measuring the degree of stratification by the proportion of all personnel at the bottom of the hierarchy is at best an indirect indicator of the distribution of pay. The correlation between an income ratio and the proportion of workers at the bottom level in the Hage-Aiken panel study is .59, indicating a reasonably high association. In the third wave, the pattern of correlations vis-à-vis a large number of other variables for these two indicators is essentially exactly the same, giving us some confidence that indeed these are alternative measures of the same phenomenon. The associations between the concentration of specialists and stratification as measured by the proportion of lower participants are the same. The concentration of specialists has a consistently high and negative relationship with stratification (r varies between −.53 and −.77). Professional activity as an alternative indicator for a concentration of specialists has essentially the same pattern (r = −.55, −.59, and −.51) — that is, consistently and strongly negative. Professional training tends to have a positive relationship albeit small. As the concentration of specialists, especially professionally active ones, increases, it is successful in changing the distribution of pay and fringe benefits to more equalitarian standards. Specialists have the skill and expertise not only to do their work but to fight for their salary and wage demands.

These research findings are replicated in a study of 14 public health agencies conducted by Palumbo (1969). He found that professional activity had −.26 correlation with his measure of centralization and −.33 with a stratification measure based on an income ratio. Although the results are not statistically significant, the indicators are quite close to those used in the Hage-Aiken study.

Since structural differentiation (see Blau, 1972) has occupied such an important place in the organizational literature, we must explore it as an alternative measure. On theoretical grounds, one might defend number of levels and number of departments as good proxies for the number of interest groups. Whether they also represent a proportional measure of the concentration of specialists, which is what our axiom focuses on, is much less certain.

Whether one examines vertical or horizontal integration, either defined as absolute terms or relative to log size, there is little or no relationship to the degree of centralization. Only in the first wave of the Hage-Aiken study is there some association between the number of hierarchical levels and the extent of participation in strategic decisions, and then only when standardized on size (r = −.33). This becomes negative in the second wave and zero in the third. Likewise the number of departments starts out being negative and gradually the size of the correlation reduces across the succeeding waves. This is important because it has been argued that with multiple hierarchical levels, there would be delegation of decisions (Meyer, 1968b; Blau, 1968). This is supported only in the first wave of the Hage-Aiken data and then only when standardized on size. Similarly, one might assume that with a greater number of departments there would also be greater participation in strategic decisions, but this does not appear to be the case. Thus, it would seem that structural differentiation is different from the concentration of specialists and it is not as important in predicting the extent of centralization, at least in the Hage-Aiken kind of organizations. At the same time, we must remember that the structural differentiation of the organizations studied by Hage-Aiken is quite different in general from the social security agencies that Blau and Schoenherr (1971) studied and the finance departments that Meyer studied (1968 a and b, 1972 a and b). The latter are more likely to have tall structures because they are largely clerical with semi-professionals, based on civil service and affected by state and federal regulation. Local residential treatment homes, mental hospitals, sheltered workshops, and even welfare agencies are more likely to have professionals and thus more flat structures. The major exceptions within the Hage-Aiken study exactly fit the kind of organizations studied by Blau and his students: nurses in mental hospitals and social workers in public welfare agencies that check on eligibility requirements. In both cases, these were controlled by civil service (county not state) and had deep or tall hierarchies. Thus, before generalizing, it seems necessary to distinguish the kind of organization and its major occupational groups. Why some organizations have tall structures and others flat, a fundamental problem in organizational design, is deferred to Chapter 12 where the throughput is analyzed in some detail.

A more compelling argument might be made for the relationship between vertical and horizontal differentiation and stratification as measured by the proportion of personnel at the bottom of the hierarchy. However, this is not the case. The absolute scores of vertical (number of levels) and horizontal (number of departments) integration tend to be negatively related with stratification, whereas the standardized scores are positively related. The pattern of findings is not consistent across the three waves in the Hage-Aiken study. In contrast, the relationship between the concentration of specialists and the stratification, as measured by distribution, is higher and much more consistent across time. This leads again to the conclusion that it is better to focus on the concentration of specialists rather than complexity or structural differentiation as a key structural concept.

Theoretically, we would expect a stronger relationship between the concentration of specialists and the other structural variables as additional support for the assumption. The former concept much more directly taps the relative rank of skill and training in an organization. Knowing how many hierarchical levels and departments there are does not tell us much about this until we recognize that there are flat patterns, as in universities and hospitals, and tall ones, as in the military services and assembly line manufacturers.

This should not be surprising because both vertical and horizontal differentiation represent physical variables rather than sociological ones. It is somewhat akin to the problem in physics of the difference between the volume of an object and its mass. Analogously, levels and departments tell us something, but the crucial theoretical property is the concentration of specialists. This establishes one of the key dynamics for changes in the distribution of power, pay, and privilege.

Table 3.2 Centralization and stratification

Hage-Aiken panel study	Stratification (proportion of lower participants)			
	Wave 1	Wave 2	Wave 3	Wave 3A[a]
Centralization (nonparticipation)	.64	.60	.56	.45
(N)	(16)	(16)	(16)	(29)

[a]Augumented wave, that is, includes the sixteen organizations reported in the previous column.

The relationship between centralization and stratification is reported in Table 3.2. Again we have relatively consistent findings; the correlation varies between about .45 and .60, depending upon the particular wave or study. In the panel study of Hage-Aiken, the measure is the proportion of lower participants, while in the Palumbo study measures of income ratios (which are more appropriate) are employed. In the third wave of the panel study, an income ratio similar to that of Palumbo (1969) and Whisler (1964) had a correlation of .47 with centralization of strategic decisions.

Still a different way of testing the hypotheses about the relationship between the concentration of specialists and the demands for power, pay, and privilege is to examine instances where a new interest group that involves new occupational specialties is introduced into a social structure. One has additional confidence if one can see changes in the concentration of specialists leading to changes in the centralization of power and the stratification of pay. Then causal order is determined and one understands better the process of structural transformation.

In a study of a community hospital (Hage, 1974: Part 1), a group of physician-teachers entered and attempted to change the distribution of power, pay, and privilege. As specialists, they had higher levels of skill and training than the typical physician who was a general practitioner. The physician-teachers tried to obtain exclusive say over many of the major strategic decisions in the hospital relative to patient care. Finally after a long and bitter series of conflicts, the compromise was a sharing of power. In addition, the physician-teachers and the attending physicians in the hospital battled over the relative pay of the former. Likewise, the former tried to get the latter to assume certain responsibilities in the clinics *that were* those of the attending physicians. The issues of the right to perform operations and the right to supervise patient care became major sources of conflict. This case study of structural transformation illustrates several theoretical points. The movement towards decentralization does not occur automatically, and frequently occurs only because of social conflict. [For a similar finding see the original Dalton (1950) article on staff and line in business organizations, and the McCleery study (1957) of a prison.] The changes require time to work out. Thus part of the lack of a perfect correlation stems from the time lags between changes in the concentration of specialists and changes in other structural variables. The considerable movement towards decentralization of power resulted not in a loss of power but a sharing by the various groups. Again, this finding is strongly buttressed by all of the Tannenbaum (1968) research, which shows that groups (in this instance hierarchically defined) increase their influence without a corresponding decline in the influence by other levels. In this sense, power is not a zero-sum game.

All of this evidence is strong, circumstantial support for the causal nature of our axiom. But these are cross-sectional case studies, except for the case study of Hage, and not direct, measured tests of whether changes in one variable produce changes in another. In Table 3.3. are reported the crosslag correlations first of the concentration of specialists and centralization, then of the extent of professional activity and centralization, then the extent of professional activity and centralization, and finally both the concentration and the extent of professional activity and centralization from the Hage-Aiken panel study. The great advantage of this longitudinal study, even though the N is small, is that it allows for a quite direct test of the causal ordering.

By comparing the auto-correlation of the variable with itself across waves, one obtains some measure of the stability of particular social structures. It is moderately high for centralization; the auto-correlation in a pooled wave design ($N = 32$) is $+.62$. The higher the score the greater the tendency towards less change — that is, little regression toward the mean. These auto-correlations, and especially with centralization, allow us to speak to a certain extent about the debate between the structural-functionalists and the power-value people over the relative fluidity of the power structure. It suggests that there is more movement than the structuralists would admit, but not as much as the process perspective of the "garbage can" model of Cyert and March (1963) implies. The existence of some regression towards the mean is itself quite important because it suggests that decentralization can occur by relatively large amounts that are in one sense "too much" with a corresponding and later correction factor. In contrast the concentration of specialists appears to be even more stable. There is still regression towards the mean but it is much smaller. The auto-correlation is $+.82$. *Instead of thinking about the distribution of power as a static or stable structure, a structure that is continually oscillating as it slowly evolves is more appropriate.* This supports the analogy with molecular movement employed at the beginning of the chapter. The oscillations are represented in part by regression toward the mean, but there is an over-all stability with changes in the distribution of power occurring within a certain range.

The results reported in Table 3.3 indicate that both the level and the rate of change of the independent variable affect changes in the score of the indepen-

Table 3.3 The level and rate of change in each structural variable
Hage-Aiken Panel Study, N = 32[a]

	Independent Variables					Dependent Variables
	ΔConcentration of specialists	Centralization$_{t_1}$	Professionalism	ΔProfessionalism	Centralization$_{t_1}$	Centralization$_{t_2}$
Concentration of specialists$_{t_1}$ −.42	ΔConcentration of specialists −.21	+.42				$R_m = .70$
Concentration of specialists$_{t_1}$ −.28	ΔConcentration of specialists −.29	Professionalism −.29$_{t_1}$	−.43		+.32	Centralization$_{t_2}$ $R_m = .77$
Centralization$_{t_1}$ −.30	ΔCentralization −.21	Concentration of specialists$_{t_1}$ +.70				Concentration of specialists$_{t_2}$ $R_m = .84$
Concentration of specialists$_{t_1}$ −.21	ΔConcentration of specialists −.37	Stratification$_{t_1}$ +.39				Stratification$_{t_2}$ $R_m = .64$
Stratification$_{t_1}$ −.21	ΔStratification −.37	Concentration of specialists$_{t_1}$ .72				Concentration of specialists$_{t_2}$ $R_m = .85$

[a]Pooled time series, that is two waves are pooled at a time; waves 1 and 2, and then waves 2 and 3. Applying statistical tests of significance becomes somewhat difficult because many assume that there is not any independence of time related scores as there is with a cross-sectional sample. The number of degrees of freedom is probably more than 16 but not as high as 32, even not counting the loss due to the inclusion of variables because the time interval is three years and independent events could occur and change the scores.

dent variable. For example, even after controlling for the prior level of centralization, both the concentration of specialists and changes in this variable impact on the subsequent level of centralization, *decreasing it.* Add more specialists to a given size of organization (that is, increase the proportion) and more decentralization results. Why does both level and change rate in the concentration of specialists have an impact on decentralization? One might reason that since:

$$X_{t_1} + \Delta X = X_{t_2}$$

there should be no independent effect for ΔX assuming enough waves or timepoints (Bohrnstedt, 1969). However, in so far as the system is an open one then random impacts provide opportunities for X_{t_1} to vary independently. in one sense, the ratio between the betas of ΔX and X_{t_1} is a crude index of openness of the system (see Buckley, 1967, for a discussion of this concept). In this case, the small number of waves and the time between waves increase the importance of X_{t_1} as opposed to ΔX.

Still another reason why X_{t_1} can have an independent effect is the amount of time needed before a change is observed. The changes in the case study of a community hospital and in the prison study discussed above occurred over a longer time period. The impact of level represents longer term changes which cannot be accounted for by the immediate changes in the rate.

All of the partial correlations reported in Table 3.3 are *conservative* measures of the true strength because in each regression equation the partial of the variable at a previous time point is employed as one of the independent variables. There is no a priori theoretical reason for assuming that centralization (or decentralization) causes itself unless one wants to argue, as Marx and Engels (1969) did, that the rich (or the powerful) get richer (or more powerful), but it does result in focusing on only those changes in the dependent variable, that are not explained by regression toward the mean.

If one measures both the concentration of specialists and the extent of professional activity vis-à-vis the distribution of power, all of these variables – *their levels and their rates* – result in a decrease in centralization. Adding more specialists who are professionally active brings about an even greater shift towards decentralization. This is important because it indicates how one must try to develop multiple indices of education and skill. Past education is perhaps not so important as present education.

In developing any predictions about long term transformations towards particular forms of organizational structure, one must examine whether particular structural variables are stronger than others and whether certain relationships are reversible. If the concentration of specialists leads to a decrease in centralization, does an increase in centralization lead to a decrease in the concentration of specialists? Equilibrium states in the structure of organizations could be achieved by *both kinds of adaptation* in form. Findings relative to this theoretical issue are also reported in Table 3.3. Increasing centralization tends to delimit the concentration of specialists. Although the prior level of the concentration of specialists has a very high partial correlation (r_p = .70), centralization and changes in centralization still have the predicted negative impact. This means that centralization does tend to result in a decrease in the concentralization of specialists. Presumedly this occurs more through growth processes that result in the hiring of unskilled or semi-skilled personnel rather than in actually letting go of trained specialists. This increases the denominator without altering the numerator of this ratio variable. However, in a case study of a community hospital that was centralized (Hage, 1974: Part 1), the more well trained physicians were resigning because power resided in the hands of a few general practioners.

Do changes in the concentration of specialists also lead to changes in the distribution of pay or the basic shape of the status pyramid? (Although these two indicators have similar impact, it is the later measure that is reported in Table 3.3.) The answer is yes. Both level and rate affect the degree of stratification even when controlling for the prior level of this variable. The reverse process occurs as well. A broadening of the status pyramid means a reduction in the concentration of specialists, through the basic process of the addition of new employees at the bottom of the pyramid.

The axiom about the relationship between the ranks of interest groups on education and skill, pay, and privilege does not speak to whether one is willing to accept more power in return for less pay or vice versa. Some might argue that there are trade-offs, as I have suggested above. Does the concentration of specialists still have an impact on stratification when centralization is included in the regression equation? One could imagine that power is the key variable in the struggle for status. The results in Table 3.4 indicate that each structural variable has an independent effect when combined with another. Both centralization and stratification predict the concentration of specialists, just as both stratification and the concentration of specialists predict centralization and the latter two predict stratification. Furthermore, changes in independent variables produce or appear to produce changes in the dependent variables. Although the partials are never very large, it is their consistency that is so striking. This is important because with a limited time period of, say, three years, one can be more confident – when changes in the independent variables produce changes in the dependent variables – that there are causal relationships, an approximation to a laboratory experiment (Donald Campbell and Stanley, 1963).

Since each variable has some independent influence on the other, it suggests that there is some trading off. In some organizations, the members might accept more pay rather than an increase in prestige or power. However, there are clear limits to these exchanges since no one variable dominates the system. Perhaps

Table 3.4 Levels and rates of change in the structural variables taken together
Hage-Aiken Panel Study, N = 32[a]

Independent Variables						Dependent Variables
Centralization$_{t_1}$	ΔCentralization	Stratification$_{t_1}$	ΔStratification	Concentration of specialists$_{t_1}$	Time[b]	Concentration of specialists$_{t_2}$
−.25	−.18	.01	−.25	.77	.49	R_m = .89
Concentration of specialists$_{t_1}$	ΔConcentration of specialists	Stratification$_{t_1}$	ΔStratification	Centralization$_{t_1}$	Time	Centralization$_{t_2}$
−.24	−.18	.29	.31	.37	.19	R_m = .75
Concentration of specialists$_{t_1}$	ΔConcentration of specialists	Centralization$_{t_1}$	ΔCentralization	Stratification$_{t_1}$	Time	Stratification$_{t_2}$
−.13	−.25	.17	.31	.33	−.06	R_m = .83

[a]Pooled time series, see footnote *a* in Table 3.3.
[b]Time is used as a dummy variable to eliminate serial correlation effects and to see if there is a trend.

what is most interesting is that power, at least as measured by centralization, in these organizations does not dominate the systemic system. This means that changes in power do not have to occur before changes in status, or vice versa. Again, there is considerable support for the idea of a relatively fluid structural variable system that tends in the long run towards equilibrium as defined by our basic axiom.

There are other interesting results in this table. First, since each variable has an independent effect, and in both directions, then this finding substantiates the two directional causal nature of at least these structural variables assumed by Hage in his theory summarized in Chapter 2. Second, the independent importance of each variable argues that there are influences on them that need to be considered — that is, they are independent sources of change which in turn have some causal source. There is a cobweb of interrelationships. At least these organizations are open to outside influences, and through these structural variables — a most open system (Buckley, 1967). Third, the relatively high multiple correlation suggests that there are not too many other variables that help explain variation. For example, a 75% of the variance in the concentration of specialists is explained, close to 50% in centralization, and 68% in stratification. Admittedly, part of this is auto-correlation of the variable with itself but it is also a more stringent test of the axiomatic theory vis-à-vis the impact of other structural variables. Fourth, the time variable allows us to measure whether there was some systematic changes in these variables across time that was not captured by changes in the independent variables. Table 3.4 suggests that the concentration of specialists increased and, to a much lesser extent, so did centralization. *This is non-trivial and supports the idea that organizations keep tending to centralize, all other things being equal.*

3.1.4. Summary

What explains the distribution of power in organizations? The very large number of studies suggests that the concentration of specialists does lead to decentralization and destratification. But the reverse is true as well. Increases in centralization and in stratification set limits on the concentration of specialists. This can occur by simply hiring a number of unskilled workers who are given little say and placed at the bottom of the status hierarchy. This is actually the model implied in Blau's formal theory (1970). Although not all studies have employed the same measures, the discrepancies make sense and appear largely consistent with the errors that one would expect. Together these large numbers of studies appear to support the axiom that interest groups feel that equity means approximately equal ranks of skill and expertise, power, pay, and privilege.

This is only a structural explanation and leaves aside many other kinds of variables that can affect the distribution of power. These are considered in succeeding chapters and most centrally in Part 4. One major qualification is implied in the reanalysis of the Japanese data. When the specialists have been trained as generalists, increases in the concentration of specialists are less likely to be translated into decentralization. This has been suggested as a characteristic of some types of organizations such as the military, where promotion policies of systematic rotation allow for training generalists, and in those countries with elite schools, such as Japan and France (Peyrefitte, 1976; Ardagh, 1977).

Another critical qualification is that perhaps not all organizations fall along a mechanical-organic continuum. The theoretical question of what forms exist is usually answered by the idea of either a mechanical or organic form, or else a continuum between these two forms (see Chapter 2). We now need to examine this more closely, by decomposing the power structure into some of its component parts. If we study the different ways in which the interest groups can be added together, then we can discern if there is more than just the mechanical-organic continuum of organizational forms.

3.2. THE DISTRIBUTION OF POWER AMONG HIERARCHICAL LEVELS AND DEPARTMENTS

Recently there has been an interest not only in predicting what the average score or mean would be on some measure of the distribution of power, but in addition trying to predict which department would have the most power. Perrow (1970a) reported on the relative power of sales departments in business organizations and in surgical departments in general hospitals (1965). Other research findings are those of Hall (1962, 1777) and Polumbo (1969). Some (Bacharach and Aiken, 1976) have argued that given the large amount of variation among departments or levels, one should shift from the meso to a micro analytical level. Here there is, however, a confusion. The fact that there is variation is not in question. What is important is that a change in analytical level leads to the recognition of two emergent problems that are worth considering: First, which department has the most power, and second, which level has the most power? Furthermore, one can search for major discontinuities between departments and/or hierarchical levels. This is in some respects a more interesting problem because it allows us to recognize that there are more than two forms of power; that is the mechanical/organic continuum analyzed in the previous section.

Hickson et al., (1971, also see Hinnings et al., 1974) have constructed a theory about the relative power of particular departments. This theory can also be applied to the problem of the relative power of particular hierarchical levels, although in this regard the work of Perrow (1967) is also of some interest.

Surprisingly, the advocates of a political-value paradigm have not developed a theory about coalitions of interest groups. Yet if we start with the image of

organizations as a collection of interest groups (Cyert and March, 1963) —
with different interests, values, and even subcultures — then questions arise:
What are the bases of coalitions? Who are the natural enemies and the natural
friends? The problem becomes even more compelling when it is remembered
that organizations are social collectives designed to accomplish specific objectives. Teamwork and coordination are essential elements. A power-value perspective mitigates against the harmonious image of a structural-functional
perspective.

The theory of uncertainty developed by Hickson et al. (1971) focuses on the
problem of which department is the most powerful. Coalition theory, instead,
focuses on which set of interest groups is likely to be the most powerful. The
former is concerned more with the horizontal distribution of power and the
latter with the vertical axes. These two middle range theories can be synthesized
because they differ only on the basis of how an interest group is defined.

Both uncertainty theory and coalition theory also allow us to focus on another
practical problem. Not only can they provide exceptions and qualifications to
the basic structural theory suggested in the previous section, but they can also
help determine which departments and what levels will have how much power
relative to specific decision issues. We might reason that those departments with
the most skill — physicians in hospitals, professors in universities, and professional managers in manufacturing firms — would have the most departmental
power. Hall (1962) found that the higher the level in a hierarchy the greater the
power, pay, and privilege, which is what one would expect. Palumbo (1969)
found that nurses who had more training than sanitarians (on the average across
a number of organizations), had correspondingly more power and status, despite
being at the same level. Similarly, Bacharach and Aiken (1976) found that size
had a strong relationship to the relative influence of both strategic and work
decisions for both the middle and the lower echelon in 44 public administration
units in Belgium. If we can assume that size is correlated with a variety of specialties (Bacharach and Aiken used the Aston measure but it is inappropriate in
this setting because as in universities, it leaves out a number of relevant occupations in public administration such as firemen, police, various kinds of engineers,
etc.), there is consistency with the previous data. Needless to say, they also
found that the correlation size shifts from level to level. As soon as the multi-
organization or organization (it appears from their report that they were using
town government as the analytical unit) is decomposed into levels or departments, variations in findings are inevitable. For example, hierarchical ranks in
particular are less likely to have as much variation as organizations on variables
like the concentration of specialists and centralization, since these are hardly
randomly distributed among levels and departments. This tends to attenuate
correlational size depending upon the specific index or measure. This is akin to
researchers who break nation- state data into regions and find different patterns.

As soon as one decomposes larger units into smaller ones, the internal variation is reduced, ranges are restricted, and not unexpectedly, patterns of association change. All of these cause changes in the findings. Some have concluded from this that a meso or macro level does not exist. What they have failed to see is that it is a product of dividing their data set in categorical sets without understanding what the categories mean. What Bacharach and Aiken (1976) have failed to do is give us a theory about the purpose of each level or why a particular department should have more power than another. Once these issues are addressed, differences in correlations become predictable and fit into a larger overall pattern.

If we could make the assumption that an overall organizational score on centralization would always be related in the same way to the internal distribution of power among departments and hierarchical levels, then it would not be necessary to study the distribution of power qua distribution. We would know that in a highly centralized organization all effective power resided in a small elite. In a decentralized organization, power would gradually diminish down the hierarchical levels but in a predictable fashion. This point is diagrammed in Figure 3.1. Here we see two typical distributions, both of them continuous. The

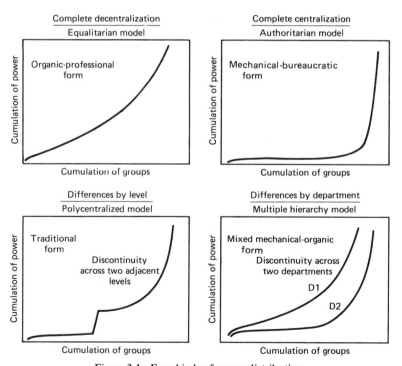

Figure 3.1   Four kinds of power distribution.

one is characteristic of organic organizations and the other of mechanical organizations, to use Burns and Stalker's (1961) terms. We have already reviewed a
large number of research findings that tend to support this. The higher the
correlation between the concentration of specialists and decentralization across a
large number of different studies, the more that one can conclude there is a
single basic continuum. Tannenbaum's (1968) research on control graphs supports the notion that in general, power tends to be distributed continuously
across hierarchical levels.

But while this may be the general pattern, it is by no means the only one.
Figure 3.1 shows two simple kinds of discontinuities in the distribution of
power. The first is discontinuity by herarchical level. This occurs when there is a
polycentralized power structure. Division and department heads may have a
great deal of participation in the strategic decision of the organization, but there
is little participation at lower echelons. The second is discontinuity by department or, more correctly, by hierarchy. Not only do organizations have multiple
levels, but they frequently have several hierarchies that are quite distinct and
separate (Etzioni, 1965). Universities, hospitals, advertising agencies, and other
organizations have both a professional and an administrative hierarchy. One
hierarchy, mixed with various occupations, can have considerably more power
than another. For example, in hospitals the nursing, accounting, personnel,
housekeeping, and similar departments are usually included in the administrative
side while the physicians have their own hierarchical system.

In a seminal article by Perrow (1967: 199) one sees the advancement of the
basic four ideal types of power structure. At one end of the continuum is the
centralized structure and at the other end the decentralized (he uses the term
polycentralized but it is inconsistent with his own analysis). The two off this
main continuum are what interest us. In the polycentralized case, one would
expect more power at the department head level than at either the higher or
lower echelons. Although there is much evidence that the top man has the most
power, there are many cases where, for a variety of reasons, effective power
resides in the hands of the department heads, who in turn do not delegate (see
Boland, 1973 for an example of how small universities are more centralized).
One finds this in traditional universities or colleges both in North America
and Western Europe (for an amusing description of the powerful chairperson
who runs his department like a baron see Caplow and McGee, 1958). As we shall
see in Chapter 12, this is characteristic of organizations that have craftsmen, as
Perrow suggests, and where work-flow is independent or pooled (in Thompson's
[1968] terms). The preferred labels for this type are traditional or craft forms;
they rely upon apprenticeships and their production is produced in small
batches. The classic cases are print shops (Lipset, Trow, and Coleman, 1956).
In this ideal-type there is more centralization of strategic decisions than one
would expect on the basis of the concentration of specialists – in this instance

skilled blue collar workers, but there is also great job autonomy. In people-processing organizations, the examples are primary schools, public welfare agencies, residential treatment homes and other organizations that rely upon the semi-professionals.

In the other situation, which I prefer to called mixed mechanical-organic organizations, we have a situation where some departments have more power than others. This is, as Perrow notes, typical of engineering firms such as electrical, chemical, computer, and other companies that stress both research and mass production. As he notes, the research and development is likely to be decentralized and production is likely to be centralized. Many mental hospitals would fall in this same category, as do large state colleges and perhaps federal hospitals. The production line is frequently automated, or continuous, to use Woodward's term (1965).

As yet, there have not been many tests of the existence of four ideal-types, mainly because the emphasis in large scale research has been on linear analysis, with little attention paid to non-linear combinations. Although some analysis has been done of different levels, much less has been done with different occupations. Beyond this, the decomposing of moderate centralization scores into these kinds of discontinuities has, to my knowledge, not been attempted. Yet, in a recent cross-national review of the literature a consdierable convergence is being found (Lammers, 1978; Lammers and Hickson, 1978: Chapter 22; Azumi et al., forthcoming). Not only is there considerable evidence that there are at least three of these types (what we have called traditional, mechanical, and organic), but they dominate in particular parts of the world as well.

All that this does, however, is say that there are four basic types, two of which form a continuum that Burns and Stalker (1961) have labeled the mechanical-organic forms. We must analyze why there would be discontinuity in the distribution of power among either departments or levels. We must determine the reasons why some departments – even with continuity – have more power than others.

3.2.1. Coping with Uncertainty Theory

The interest in the problem of uncertainty grew out of a study conducted by Crozier (1964) of several highly routinized and nonautonomous organizations in France. He observed that the maintenance engineers in a highly centralized organization were one group or department that had more power than one would expect because they had control over uncertainty. From this it led to the hypothesis that those would could control uncertainty therefore have more power. It might be noted in passing that the maintenance engineers did not have power to make strategic decisions in the tobacco company where they were working. What Crozier actually observed was job autonomy and power to make work decisions. What the maintenance engineers had was power to block decisions affecting their own work — for example, attempts to routinize and program their responses to break-downs. Decisions about where to build plants, the prices of cigarettes, and the hiring and firing of personnel were not made by them but at an elite level (or, more specifically, Paris).

In response to this work, Hickson et al. (1971) and Hinings et al. (1974) developed and tested a contingencies theory of departmental power which is diagrammed in Figure 3.2. Before reporting the research results, the connection between this model and axiom 3A should be made clear. Although the labels are different, there is considerable similarity in thinking about what provides power. Their perspective places much more emphasis on the process of how a department may augment power. The words "centrality of work flows" mean that the department has a set of skills that are important to the organization. This is naturally always relative to a particular organization. The skills of a physician are not very relevant to a paper company who hires him to do physicals or to treat minor accidents, but they are very important to a general hospital. Conversely, machine maintenance is critical to the former kind of manufacturer but not to a hospital where machines represent a subsidiary aspect of treatment and diagnosis (even air conditioning, electric typewriters, and x-ray machines).

Coping effectiveness is the key and most interesting variable in the Hickson et al. model, because it is the demonstration of expertise. Men and women in organizations are almost always pragmatists, and the specialist who can demonstrate that he knows what he is doing gets power. Another variable in the uncertainty theory is centrality or the pervasiveness of work links of any focal department. As we shall see, this tends to be the characteristic of specialist work because it solves coordination and control problems (see Chapter 10).

The origins of several aspects of this theory would appear to lie in an earlier article by Mechanic (1962), who raised the critical question of the circumstances under which people low in the hierarchy might be able to hold their own against

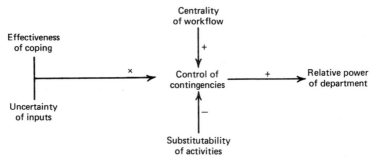

Figure 3.2 The theory of coping with uncertainty.

those with more authority. Mechanic's theory, however, only focuses on the problem of individuals and not that of departments. Yet, although the stress is on the vertical axis of power, many of the same ideas can be applied to the horizontal axis. Like us, Mechanic emphasizes the role of the expert and notes that their replaceability is an important factor. He also insists on the control of what might be called resources, including persons, information, and instrumentalities. What remains unanswered, however, is why the Hickson et al. strategic contingencies model does not consider the relative resources controlled by departments, including the level of training, personnel size, budget size, and autonomy — variables that appear to be so central in coalition theory. Perhaps this stems from the idea that organizational departments have equal votes, an assumption that seems unwarranted. Parallel to the Hickson et al. model, Mechanic notes the importance of centrality.

The theory of Hickson et al. has been called the strategic contingencies theory because the key variable is contingent upon the influence of the environmental constraints, but with a very important nuance. Strategic contingencies here refer to the effective control over inputs of other departments by one department. One extreme would be strict hierarchical control, where one department would control inputs for other departments — that is, their resources. At the other extreme would be strict equality, where each department controls the inputs of the others. One might use the Bavelas imagery of yokes and wheels.

The issue raised in juxtaposing their theory about how departments can increase their power with others needs to be interpreted in several ways. In what sense does a department have the opportunity to increase its success in coping with uncertainty through risk taking? The assumption made in the previous section suggested that the skill and expertise required for a particular task in an organization was largely predetermined. Here the thrust is to suggest a room for maneuver, a useful qualification that moves us closer to a process model. Two accounting departments in two different organizations within the same industry — and therefore having approximately the same tasks and environmental constraints — can have different power positions vis-à-vis marketing and production. One department may cope better with its problems, and may attempt to increase its links with other departments, through, for instance, the establishment of information flow over expenditures. Whether one would in fact discover that the accountants were better trained in the department that coped better remains to be seen. There can be variations in skill and expertise, especially in the sense of coping skill within the same occupation and there are likely to be clustered by level within organizations. One university has a strong French department and another a weak one; their power within their respective universities will vary accordingly (Pfeffer and Salancik, 1974).

A common strategy for augmenting power is to increase responsibilities (normative equality) and thus indispensibility. The great advantage of professional managers is that they possess a set of skills which are then translated into responsibilities, which in turn demonstrate their expertise and their coping skills.

The more similar the training of the specialists in each department within an organization, as in the case of the university, the more important the relative coping success of a particular department becomes in predicting the power of the department, measured in a variety of ways. This was demonstrated in the Pfeffer and Salancik study (1974) of the University of Illinois. The university departments with more power were those that were more successful in getting outside research funds, graduate students, and, to a lesser extent, undergraduates. All departments may have the same rough level of training, but they have clearly different levels of skill and of expertise in gaining money from the instructional budget and outside research funds. In accordance with our assumption, we find that the higher the rank of the department in funds, the higher the rank in power measured in several ways. But note that this can also be interpreted as more effective coping. Effective coping is itself a way of saying more skill and expertise.

Perhaps what these two variables contribute to the most is our recognition that not *any* skill or expertise gains power – only those that contribute to the main objectives of the organization. Also, how well the professionals or the managers perform is itself a critical determinant of power.

The data that Hinnigs et al (1972) collected in Canadian and American breweries and in several divisions of container companies largely support their theory. The ability to cope – or what can be interpreted as expertise – has a correlation of .81 while nonsubstitutability – or what can be considered as skill – has a correlation of .60. A partial correlation analysis indicated that each variable retained its importance when controlling for either of the other variables or for the speed of the work flow.

The coping with uncertainty allows us to understand when the marketing department may be more influential than the production department in a manufacturing organization, or when a language department might be more influential than a social science department in an educational organization. As depicted in Figure 3.2., the overall degree of centralization may be the same but the distribution may be different, because some departments have more power even though they may have equal skill, budgets, and responsibilities. Thus the coping with uncertainty and nonsubstitutability give us some understanding of how departments can maneuver, within the general framework of how they rank on these dimensions, to increase their power and influence over strategic decisions.

3.2.2. Coalition Theory

It is strange that with so many references to Cyert and March's (1963) work and the popularity of an interest group approach to the decision-making process in large organizations so little has been done to advance coalition theory. Yet one of the important issues in this tradition is under what circumstances and in what ways various interest groups coalesce into a power group. The basic of the coalition can vary depending upon the rank of the interest group, especially relative to skill and to expertise.

How many interest groups does an organization have? There are a number of characteristics that can create an interest group, but these can be usefully reduced to four essential themes: occupation, level in the hierarchy of authority and status, similar goals or values, and socially ascribed characteristics such as color, sex, age, and religion. What makes the discussion difficult is that these can be combined in different ways. Thus, all the top managers can be engineers, Catholics, and graduates of a few *"grandes ecoles"* while all the workers can be unskilled, atheists, and dedicated communists (a very typical pattern in French business organizations). When so many social, political, economic, and organizational characteristics hold, there are essentially only two interest groups and two coalitions of interest groups: the haves and the have-nots. Conflict theory works very well and we need not go any further in developing coalitional theory. However, as these axes criss-cross each other (Simmel, 1955), the number of interest groups multiply, and we need to modify Marxian theory somewhat to handle this complexity.

In each concrete situation one would have to count how many interest groups there are. In general, these four bases should cover most situations: the number of different occupational specialists, the number of groups with values relative to strategic choices or preferred performances (organic vs. mechanical, change vs. efficiency, growth vs. stability) the number of major hierarchical levels, and relevant social characteristics. The last two are likely to yield only two or three interest groups. Of these, the first, the number of occupations, gives us the largest number of possible interest groups. The options in strategic choice, the relevant levels, and meaningful social characteristics are relatively few in number. The real problem is how much these criss-cross. Are there members of the same occupation group who belong to different value groups and/or have different social characteristics? Black and white social workers may not mix. Kover (1963) has indicated how, in an advertising agency, each occupational specialty broke into factions that were for or against the reorganization of the structure; he labeled them the careersmen and the craftsmen.

The essential task in building a theory of coalitions is to decide first what are the bases on which coalitions are likely to be built, and second, when do these bases tend to breakdown? This second issue is the focus of analysis in the next chapter, where high risk or crisis decisions are perceived as the usual way for coalitions to dissolve and new ones to form. Here we concentrate on the reasons why coalitions are formed. As we have noted, the literature has identified a number of different bases but in fact these can be reduced to the four ideas mentioned above.

We start our theory with the same phenomenological view of organizations as given in axiom 3A: namely, there are interest groups with various ranks on a number of dimensions.

3B *The greater the proportion of members who have low rank, the more important will be hierarchical levels and social characteristics as the basis of interest group formation.*

3C *The greater the proportion of members who have high rank, the more important will be occupation and value preferences as the basis of interest group formation.*

Essentially these two axioms suggest that as the stratification system of an organization — measured as in Lenski and Lenski (1978) by the number of people in various unskilled, semi-skilled, skilled blue collar, and white collar occupations — shifts from a pyramid to a diamond shape, the bases upon which coalitions can be formed tend to proliferate. The differences between occupations as suggested in the pioneering research of Lawrence and Lorsch (1967 a and b) tend to be much greater than social characteristics. Admittedly, particularly in the United States, differences in ethnic background, race, and religion have tended to fragment the worker-class and prevented the development of class based political parties (see Lenski and Lenski 1978). Still, many unions and organizations have in the past tended to be homogeneous in terms of their social characteristics because of selective recruitment and prejudice upon the part of both workers and managers.

As one moves from a mechanical social structure (that is, low concentration of specialists, high centralization, high stratification, and low normative equality), to an organic social structure (that is, the opposite scores on these four dimensions of social structure) the basis of interest group formation shifts. Why do occupation and value preferences or goals tend to divide those with relatively high levels of education and skill? The reason is that each occupation is itself a subculture. It has its own tools and techniques, its own language (which we perceive as jargon), its own style of work, its peculiar problems, and the like. As Lawrence and Lorsch (1978 a and b) have observed, occupations vary greatly in how fast they receive feedback on their decisions, and therefore in how much uncertainty they live with. In turn, this leads to very different values about risk-taking and even concern about self-interest. As societies modernize and industrailize they develop a large number of values, which can become the basis of what Perrow (1970b: Chapter 5) would call derived goals. Hiring women managers, training blacks, reducing pollution, supporting college scholarship programs, and the like are social values that have become critical in post-industrial United States, and which have their counterparts in Japan and Western Europe. Another way of thinking about this is that as societies become much more complex, there are many more problems upon which individuals and groups can form values, just as there are more occupational specialties designed to solve these problems (for an extension of this argument see Chapter 14).

A wide variety of hypotheses could be deduced from these two assumptions about interest group formation, which the reader can easily do. Our main interest lies in predicting the basis of coalition formation.

3D   The more similar the occupational activities, value preferences, rank level, and social characteristics of the interest groups, the more likely they are to form a coalition.

Although this is a very old idea, it would appear to apply in organizations as well as in the choice of friends — similarity is the key. For example, Kapik (1972b) has suggested that having similar values relative to the strategy of organizations to control their environment is a basis of coalition formation. His team of researchers actually use it to define who is in the coalition, rather than employ it predictively. There is a large literature on consistency theory that need not be reviewed here [see for example Davis's (1963) theoretical formulation, which supports this axiom].

What creates tensions is that in any one situation several of these themes may be operative at the same time. Again, a large literature in cross-cutting statuses can be applied to this problem.

Since as the concentration of specialists increases, the distribution of power becomes more decentralized, we would expect that the formation of coalitions will be either the similarity of activities or the value preferences, that is goals. But since different occupations have different activities, by definition, the concentration of specialists makes coalitions more difficult to form and also more difficult to maintain. The only basis of formation left is agreement about the strategic choices that the organization has and should select (Karpik, 1972b). But this can shift with changes in organizational performances, developments in the market, technological breakthroughs, altered attempts by the government to regulate, and the like. Therefore, values as a basis of coalition tend to be more unstable. As noted in Chapter 1, this is an article of faith within this perspective, but what has been unrecognized is that it flows from a series of changes taking place in the larger society. Furthermore, the emphasis has been on managers and elites rather than workers and have-nots. At the bottom of the hierarchy the bases of coalition — social characteristics including political preferences — are much more stable.

Implicit is a long-term trend towards greater instability of coalitions in organizations, primarily because occupations produce large differences that make stable coalitions difficult and since value preferences are not necessarily stable but contingent.

The concentration of specialists becomes a pivotal variable in the development of coalition theory because:

1. It predicts how many interest groups there are.
2. It predicts the preferred basis of interest group formation.
3. It predicts the applicability of the Coleman model (1974).
4. It predicts the stability of the coalition.

As the concentration of specialists increases, the number of interest groups proliferates and, most importantly, the distinctions between occupations becomes very important, as do preferences regarding the goals and policies of the organization. But since coalitions are usually formed on the basis of some agreement, and since specialization means dissimilarity in activities, value preferences become the dominant basis of coalitions in organic and mixed mechanical-organic organizations. However, agreements about strategic choices are at best fragile coalitions, easily broken apart in the face of changing circumstances or failure relative to some performance (see Chapter 5).

In contrast, mechanical organizations tend to have quite stable coalitions where the haves are quite united against the have-nots. If the haves – in power, pay, and privilege – are also white Anglo-Saxon protestants, while the have-nots are brown Mexican Catholics, then the coalitions are exceptionally stable and the intensity of the conflict – when it occurs – severe. This can be seen in the long-drawn out grape growers-migrant workers strike (although many of the owners are not necessarily white Anglo-Saxon protestants). Under these circumstances the themes of exploitation and domination make a great deal of sense, and ideology unites.

3.2.3. A Special Problem: The Power of the Board of Trustees

Ever since C. Wright Mills' *Power Elite* (1957), it has been popular and fashionable to think that the country is run by a small elite, sitting on the top of the major corporations and banks, running the government and especially the military, and making decisions that benefit their interests and needs. A key in this image is the variety of interlocking directorships (Zeitlin, 1970 and 1974) studies that inevitably show how various businesses, banks, universities, and so forth are tied together. Most of the proposals for reform of industry visualize worker participation on the boards as a meaningful way of ensuring the representation of their interests. But is it?

All of this work assumes that the board, because it is at the apex of the hierarchical structure, has the most power. Mills counted the number of people in the top two echelons of power and assumed that they have the power and that therefore there is an elite. The starting point is a conception that power is distributed downwards uniformly in all organizations. Our previous analysis indicates that this can be incorrect for certain kinds of organizations and can vary enormously even within specific institutional sections. It might be correct for the oil companies and the army, but incorrect for hospitals and welfare agencies.

The essential point is that while the board is at the apex, it does not enjoy great power except under certain stipulated conditions. A discontinuity exists between the executives and the members of the board. Except for appointing or firing the top executive — which can be exercised only rarely — the typical board has little power to make strategic decisions. *What the board does is ratify what the chief executive and his administration propose.*

As always there are exceptions. Some boards are quite powerful most of the time and literally run the organizations. Most boards become powerful during major crises. These exceptions and qualifications need to be spelled out.

The main reason why boards tend not to be very powerful is that they do not have that much knowledge and skill relative to the operation of the organization. They typically meet once a month to listen to the proposals of the president, who is their major source of information. In addition, the work of Mechanic (1962) on the power of lower participants can be applied to many of the boards. Boards have some major control over appointments and firing, but they lack information.

The boards are likely to be most powerful under the following circumstances:

1. When the concentration of specialists within the organization is low.
2. When the concentration of specialists within the board is high.
3. When the organization is highly centralized.
4. When the board members have direct access to people and information within the organization.
5. When the board members work every day.

The themes are variations in skill and expertise and how these affect the capacity of the board to influence or even decide the major outcomes. As the ratio of the board's skill and expertise in running an organization increases relative to those who manage, then it becomes more powerful. But even when this is true, typically the lack of direct access to information and the lack of time spent in the organization have the consequence of reducing the power of the board members, even if they are administrators in another organization, a typical pattern.

One reason why boards appear to be powerful is that they are seen to act in dramatic situations. When the board fires the president of R.C.A., it makes headlines. But once they have exercised this option they cannot repeat it; they must support the man that they select at least for a grace period of several years. During campus crises in the 1960s, the regents of universities became much more powerful because the universities were not functioning well. Since its task is to ensure smooth functioning, a board must exercise much more involvement in major decisions whenever there is manifest failure, such as the calling in of the national guard or the presence of large and persistent financial losses. But evidence of failure is usually lacking because management sees to it that the organization does not fail.

What is the evidence relative to the power of boards? Pfeffer (1972a) reports that in general management controls boards except in the case of inside boards (but of course an inside board is nothing more than management sitting on the board itself). This is not an independent board, but one representing management's policy. Pfeffer asks when is there an outside board. He finds that problems of financing and regulation lead to the creation of outside boards. In other words, the more important the environment, the more critical an outside board is likely to be. The circumstances under which the environment impinges upon the organization, requiring a shift in membership, is left to Part Four. For now, one might note the Burns and Stalker answer: namely, turbulent or changing conditions make the environment more salient.

What does an outside board do? It provides expertise on various external matters, such as government regulation and financing of investment. By studying what kinds of occupations are represented on boards one sees over time how the concerns of management and of administrators have changed. (On the functions of boards see (Aldrich, 1979: 296-303.)

What evidence is there on the relative power of boards? Chandler, in his masterpiece *The Visible Hand* (1977), notes that railroad boards even in the 1850s and 1860s had lost power to the management, in contrast to the textile industry of the 1830s. The size of operations, the complexity of the technology, the intricacies of cooperation and competition, the problems of growth, and so on, plus the lack of daily involvement made the boards go along with management. Interestingly enough, the boards of railroads did not want to expand and grow and it was management that forced this policy on them.

Gordon, Tanon, and Morse (1975), based on a large study of hospitals, found that the power of hospital boards was decreasing over time ($N = 500$), a thesis consistent with a longitudinal study of Perrow in a single hospital (1963). In an unpublished study of community hospitals ($N = 140$), Hage found that the greater the proportion of specialists and the larger the size of the hospital, the less the influence of the board over medical practice as reported by the directors of medical education.

This finding was replicated in a study of universities and colleges by Blau (1973: 164-66). Control over educational policy, which was the kind of decision most likely to be concentrated in the hands of the trustees, was negatively related to the development of power upon the part of the faculty as measured by the percentage of faculty in the senate and the percentage elected on committees, such as policy committees. In contrast, the greater the ratio of administrators to faculty, the more likely power over educational policy is found in the hands of either the administration or the board of trustees. What we have here is the measurement of the power base of the faculty versus the power base of the administration. Unfortunately, the relative power of the administration vis-à-vis the faculty is in part the function of the relative skill of these two interest groups and not the absolute measure of, for example, faculty qualifications.

Although the evidence in general points toward the long term decline in the power of the board, it is also apparent that as either internal conflict or certain environmental crises occur (relative to financing, governmental regulation, and the like), the board's power vis-à-vis management will increase. There is a moving equilibrium with a great deal of oscillation. As with the power structure for the full-time members, there is a waxing and a waning of power. The expertise of the board can shift as well, depending upon circumstances; deregulation may make lawyers less relevant or liquidity shortages, bankers more essential.

Schemes to place workers on boards are not likely to produce great changes, precisely because the workers will seldom be specialists relative to the organization, nor is the board likely to meet often enough to become an important forum. What will be gained? Workers representation will provide the other board members with direct access to information that they would not otherwise have, which can set some limits on management action. It will also mean that in certain strategic decisions – the opening or closing of plants, the scheduling of work shifts, lay-off policies – worker interests will be represented. But these gains can be effected in other ways, such as management union bargaining, joint committees or representatives, and so forth.

Similar proposals to place clients or their representatives on boards are likely to have the same consequence. Unless they have expertise relative to the organization and unless the board really works full-time, the impact is likely to be minimal. This is not to say that they shouldn't be represented, but only to recognize the relative importance of this representation.

The placement on boards of the clients or customers, workers or staff of the organization – or their representatives – can serve an important symbolic function for a particular group, but it would not be much more than a symbol unless the board members have a great deal of skill and expertise relative to the goals of the organization.

If there are to be representatives of various interest groups on a board – and that is the model – it seems desirable to have a clear image of what the various interests in the larger society are. One hears various proposals but seldom a carefully articulated model of interest group representation. One exception is a model proposed by Aiken et al. (1975). They suggested a three estate board with resource controllers, professionals, and clients, or their representatives being the three major interest groups relative to most delivery agencies.

European countries have carried corporatism – which is what this is – much farther, and mandate into law very complex schemes of representation of administrators from central and local government, professionals from various occupational categories, and the like. However, it is not immediately clear that these boards have more power or if in fact the interests of their constituencies are really taken into consideration.

3.2.4   A Special Problem: Worker Participation

If not much power resides at the apex of the organization, then where does power rest? As organizations increase their concentration of specialists and decentralize, the decision-making process breaks down into a series of committees, usually specialized by domain or area. While power does not always reside in these committees, it usually does, and this is where worker and customer/client participation can be most effective. Here, university students have shown the way. In many universities they have demanded, and in some have received, representation on various committees, both at the department and the college level. We have already mentioned how Blau (1973) found that faculty representation in committees and especially the senate was strongly related to less administrative and trustee control over educational policy. Student representation can have the same impact, although there is a need for research on this issue.

In committees – within the limits of expertise and skill – the lower participants, to use Etzioni's term (1961, 1975), can function more effectively and probably have much more impact on the representation of their interests and values. The more decentralized the organization, the more important these committees become and the more typically their recommendations are followed. In Chapter 11 evidence is presented that decentralization and the number of committees are strongly correlated (among other studies, see Hage, Aiken, and Marrett, 1971; Van de Ven and Delbecq, 1974). Beyond this, committees members usually include key decision makers who then are in a position to be influenced and at a vulnerable moment – as alternatives are being considered and options discussed. By the time the decision reaches the board, it is too late to reopen the discussion, and the managers or administrators have probably already committed themselves to a position. Besides, a number of small decisions can add up to a policy perhaps more effectively than any pronouncements by the board.

One of the great advantages of membership in specialized committees is that the latter make the problem of skill or expertise more manageable; education or experience can be specialized. It does not, however, solve the problem completely. Customer or client representation is effective insofar as it has knowledge relative to the decisions being made. If not, then representation becomes primarily an information channel, which in itself is desirable. It does not mean effective power, even though it can provide the appearance of influence.

Those that have followed the logic of the argument will note that as the concentration of specialists increases, the representation of the workers on these committees should increase as well. The same can be said for the clients and customers, albeit at a much slower pace and with perhaps less effectiveness. *If there is greater decentralization, then there is more participation in strategic decisions, including more worker and client or customer participation as well.* Although we are still far from customer representation on organizational decision-making committees in businesses, the axiom does predict that in those organizations where the concentration of specialists is the greatest – such as universities – we are most likely to find customer representation. However, one must admit that the situation of the student is very special, and generalizations from this case must be approached cautiously.

In sum, for those interest groups that want to make their interests felt, the advice differs depending upon the structure of the organization. Board representation is most helpful in mechanical organizations where centralization is the greatest and the concentration of specialists is the least. Naturally, this is also where resistance to this kind of power change will be the greatest. Committee representation is advocated as the organization evolves towards an organic form – that is, where centralization starts declining as a consequence of increased concentration of specialization in the division of labor.

The research on worker participation indicates that representation usually does not mean effective participation (Rasner et al., 1973; Mulder and Wilke, 1970; Mulder, 1976). Participation appears to be more effective when the technology is advanced but this means more well-trained workers (Taylor, 1971). And again it is worth repeating that studies have found individuals – but not groups, to my knowledge – who were dissatisfied with their power (Alutto and Belasco, 1972; Conway, 1976) because they had too much.

The solution to the need for worker participation can now be given: it is complex and there is no simple yes or no. The lower the level of skill or expertise, the less the demand for participation in strategic decisions, irrespective of what various elites, young intellectuals, union leaders, and party members may think is good or desirable for the workers. However, there is one quite important qualification. The skill and expertise demanded on the job may not represent the skill and expertise of the workers. Everywhere in industrialized countries there is a movement towards mass college education (Bell, 1973). This means that many have an occupational skill, such as English or history major, without necessarily being able to utilize this skill in work. These individuals will make demands *as if* they were in occupations with comparable levels of training and expertise. Thus, the long-term trend would appear to be for higher levels of skilled personnel being available even if their training is not directly employed. This implies a long-term trend, even necessity, for greater decentralization, destratification, and normative equality among the members of an organization.

It is also worth examining the consumer and client movements within this same context. These are responses to the same general societal movements that are occurring. As the skill and expertise of the patients, the students, the customers for automobiles, and the customers for computers increase, they, as interest groups (and not as individuals), will demand an ever increasing participation in strategic decisions, in at least those strategic decisions that affect their interests or values (again we need not automatically assume a narrow and selfish self-interest perspective). It may seem strange to think of students of the 1960s as having more skill and expertise than students of the 1950s, but indeed the first television generation and the first Spock generation would appear to have precisely these characteristics. However, the interesting difference is between the activities of the best students at a few elite universities (such as Berkeley, Wisconsin, and Michigan) and the vast majority. There were significant differences in demands for more student power, but these differences seem quite explicable in terms of our fundamental assumption.

Likewise, Nader's Raiders are essentially the better trained and more sophisticated consumers. The consumer movement as reflected in *Consumers Union* has been appealing primarily to a narrow segment of the population, a highly educated and articulate segment that is concerned with the problem of product quality. Similarly, the ability to organize the poor and the needy to push against the welfare bureaucracy would appear to be a consequence of the steadily rising levels of general education. The client is beginning to see his plight more clearly, even if he does not have the expertise to evaluate what the professional is doing. Gross mishandlings and treatments are now recognizable and become the basis for activating the clients through interest groups.

Even physicians are not immune to this rising tide of client expertise. The number of malpractice suits has sky-rocketed. It reflects again the general veracity of our fundamental assumption about when interest groups are likely to demand more power, pay, and privilege. We have concentrated on members of the organization, but the customers and clients follow the same immutable law (see Etzioni's concept of lower participants, 1975: 15).

All of these trends suggest a greater push towards more worker and customer participation in both public and private sector organizations. But if the participation is to be effective it must occur in the context of committees, for this is where the real power lies in at least the organic form.

3.3. CENTRALIZATION AND JOB AUTONOMY:
MESO AND MICRO STRUCTURES

Argyris (1972) criticized structural sociology in organizations for not studying the psychological level — what the individual manager feels and does — and argued that a complete explanation requires the merging of both the micro- and the macro-organizational level of analysis. So far we have concentrated on the structural causes of strategic decisions or organization-wide decisions relative to the policies, programs, personnel, and budget. Little has been said about work decisions made at the level of the job, an area where Blauner (1964) at least has argued there is much more interest. This issue has been labeled in the early organizational literature (Blau and Scott, 1962) the problem of professional autonomy.

Two distinct issues are really being raised by Argyris and should be kept quite separate. The first is: in what sense does the meso-structure determine the micro and vice versa? Concretely, if we know the extent of the centralization of strategic decisions, can we predict how much job autonomy there is? This argument can be extended to include other structural characteristics such as the concentration of specialists. The second issue is: what other variables at the micro-organizational analytical level affect the extent of job autonomy? The identification of these is by far the harder task, because in general this level of analysis has been ignored in organizational sociology, although not in industrial psychology.

Essentially there are two thrusts to our argument. Meso-structural properties will determine at least the outer limits of work autonomy at the job level, and micro-structural properties will help explain at least some of the variations within these limits.

It may appear that the discussion of job autonomy is at the individual level and the data, of course, is based upon individual reports – but in general the referent is a job, not an individual. Frequently, methodologists confuse the way in which the data is collected with the content of the data. There are two separate questions, as follows:

1. How much freedom do you have to make work decisions?
2. In your capacity as director of medical education, how much freedom do you have to make work decisions?

The second question taps the individual while the first taps an occupant of a position. It is true that in most cases the respondent may make no distinction in his or her own mind. But it is equally apparent that individuals can have more than one job in the same organization, and that individual positions of power can be greater or lesser than the average. To add to this theory about the distribution of power relative to work decisions, the article by Mechanic (1962) on the power of lower participants provides some additional situational factors that can help explain variations in work autonomy not attributable to differences in skills or expertise, pay, or prestige. The other major variables that can affect differences in work autonomy are:

1. Average length of time in organization or seniority.
2. Average effort exerted.

As these increase, the job occupants will generally be allowed more work autonomy. Of course, in one sense this reflects greater skill and expertise (length of time in organization) and greater responsibility (effort exerted usually would be correlated with number of responsibilities) but the ideas are different enough to be worth separating.

3.3.1. Job Autonomy and Its Measure

The measurement of power at the micro level is even more difficult than it is at the meso level. The distinction between the bases of power (French and Raven, 1959; Warren, 1968 and 1969), such as expert power, referent power, coercive power, and so forth should be kept separate from some direct measure. These may represent causes, but they are quite different. Likewise, there is a tendency to confuse job codification (Hage and Aiken, 1967) with job autonomy (Bacharach and Aiken, 1976 do this, calling job codification job autonomy). Admittedly, conceptual differences between measures of power and measures of control are hard to draw. For me the big difference is between how many of the work decisions are made by the workers and how often the quantity or quality of their work is checked — which is the idea of supervision — and how tightly regulated these decisions are by rules — which is the concept of formalization. This confusion occurs because of too ready an acceptance of factor analysis as a technique for generating indices, without checking whether the content is really different (Aiken and Hage, 1966 and see Perrow's critique, 1967). The measurement arises in many organizations where work decisions are checked as well as supervised. This same confusion existed in the axiomatic theory of Hage, described in the previous chapter, where formalization, a control variable, was considered to be a structural variable, an error rectified in the work of Child (1972b and 1973c), Tracy and Azumi (1976), Dewar (1976), Zeitz (1976), Bacharach and Aiken (1976), and others. Regulating is the other side of control, but rules sometimes (but not always) reduce the area of work autonomy. There is then an intimate connection between the extent of control and the degree of job autonomy, but we still want to keep them quite separate in our minds.

One intellectual solution is to define autonomy as the power to make work decisions relative to the specific task at hand performed by the worker (Bacharach and Aiken, 1976). This means then that there is a continued focus on the capacity to make decisions, parallel to the focus on centralization as the power to make strategic decisions. In this way, a careful distinction is made between the causes of more or less job autonomy, job autonomy as a measure of power, and various mechanisms of control such as close supervision (how often checked), job codification (how many job prescriptions), and so forth. (These various control measures at the micro level are discussed in Chapter 11).

Another index, the hierarchy of authority, exists in the literature (Aiken and Hage, 1966), but the difficulty with this measure is that the nature of the decisions is not made clear. They could be strategic decisions or work decisions or some mixture of the two. Probably the respondents interpreted them primarily as work decisions. To be more certain, Aiken et al. (1972) developed a battery of what they call work decisions. Although it did represent a separate factor in an orthogonal factor analysis rotation, the correlation between centralization of power over strategic decisions and average job autonomy measured by work decisions remains quite high. In contrast the correlation between hierarchy of authority and work decisions is only -.49. Thus the hierarchy of authority appears to be tapping something different and perhaps closer to the idea of decisions being made by those higher in the chain of command.

Rather than use work decisions, Zeitz (1976) developed an index from a factor analysis of a number of items. The three items were how much responsibility you have in deciding how your job will be carried out, how much freedom you have in deciding exactly how to do your work, and how much authority you have to contact others outside the organization without checking. The last item may be somewhat special, and therefore may not always load on a responsibility factor. This index was then called job autonomy.

Still a different approach, and in many aspects a much better one, is that taken by Child (1973c), who relates another measure of job autonomy which he calls perceived authority not only to centralization, but also to how much questioning of authority there is (see Figure 3.3). He includes the measures of other positional variables as well. This conceptualization is preferable because it not only relates a meso-structural variable with a micro variable in his

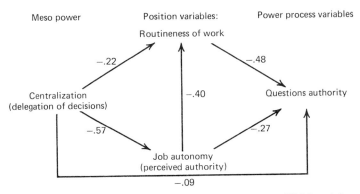

Figure 3.3   The path analytical diagram of job autonomy (Child study).

study of the job autonomy of top management, but it moves in the direction of a process analysis of power by focusing on how much questioning of authority there is. The two studies then provide an excellent juxtaposition, allowing us to synthesize the literature.

More difficult is the definition of the word "job". One could analyze the average job autonomy within an organization and correlate it with other structural properties. Or one could examine the hierarchical level of a job, such as middle management or professional workers. Finally, one could analyze how much job autonomy there is in specific positions, such as nurses or sanitarian workers (Palumbo, 1969), maintenance men (Crozier, 1964), and so forth, making distinctions for both department and hierarchical level. But if one examines the thrust of much of Argyris's criticism and of Mechanic's theory, the emphasis is not on the micro-structural problem of the relative power of a particular social position, occupation, or interest group but instead on the relative power, job autonomy, of particular individuals. We shall focus primarily on the first and the second levels – that is, on meso and micro-structural characteristics – because these remain closest to the thrust of this synthesis. Beyond this, the problems of how to disentangle the proportion of the variance that should be considered as individual differences from the proportion considered as typical positional differences is quite difficult, especially since there are complex aggregation issues involved. For example, the fact that all physicians must have an M.D. might be considered as an individual property, yet it is clearly an occupational one, a task requirement for entry into the position. However, doing a residency is much more likely to reflect individual choice, although it is a requirement for those who would like to be specialists. Just as the level of professional training is subject to various interpretations, so is the level of professional activity. Each profession has a model amount depending upon the skill and expertise levels; as these increase, so presumably does the average professional activity. But there is a considerable variation in participation in these activities among various members of the profession. Thus separating these effects into individual and group (Blau, 1960) influences becomes quite difficult. We shall ignore this problem, accepting the fact that while concentrating on micro factors, we have mixed in some individual aspects as well.

3.3.2. The Findings

Although in one sense one would like to know to what extent the macro-structure determines the micro and vice versa, it will be impossible to answer this question completely. Our starting point is to consider the macro-structural properties as setting the limits within which variations in job autonomy occur. The correlations in the augmented third waves of welfare agencies, mental hospitals, sheltered workshops, and the like are presented in Table 3.5 ($N = 29$).

Table 3.5   The meso-structural determinants of job autonomy

Hage-Aiken panel study	Average job autonomy (work decisions)
Concentration of specialists	.79
Centralization (nonparticipation)	-.77
Stratification (pay scale ratios)	-.42
(N)	(29)

The zero-order correlations at the aggregate level are quite strong. Centralization of strategic decisions has a correlation of -.77, while the concentration of specialists has one of -.79. Neither of these findings are surprising and they are quite consistent.

To shift to the individual level of analysis (N = 548), in a sample of 20 health and welfare agencies in an eastern city, Zeitz (1976: 182) found that his index of job autonomy was related to professional activity, education, participation, hierarchical rank, and age, (see Table 3.6).

At a level specific analysis of work decisions for managers or department heads and those lower in the administrative chain of command in 44 local governments, Bacharach and Aiken (1976) found that size was highly correlated with their measure of work decisions for both the middle and lower echelons. If we can assume that this is correlated with the degree of occupational specialization and, in the case of the middle echelons, their education and experience of the department heads, then we can say this replicates the findings of Zeitz.

What none of these studies has done is look for discontinuities. On the basis of

Table 3.6   Individual characteristics and job autonomy
Zeitz Study

	Job autonomy (index of freedom)
Professional activity	.24
Professional education	.17
Participation	.35
Hierarchical rank	.53
Age	.12
(N)	(548)

the previous section, we might predict centralization and job autonomy co-existing with semi-professionals and skilled craftsmen in traditional organizations. These various studies confirm Mechanic's essential thesis: that control over resources augments the power of lower participants. Although it is an obvious point, power to participate or influence strategic decisions gives one a great deal of latitude in making work decisions or job autonomy. The reverse causal process is also possible, because being an expert and providing evidence of the capacity to function will lead not only to greater job autonomy but to more say in critical decisions. For these reasons professional activity and education are proxies for expertise, albeit not very good ones. A study needs to be done combining the various measures developed by Warren, French and Raven, and others on the basis of power (see Price, 1972) with these measures of strategic and work decisions.

3.3.3. A Special Problem: Why People Obey Orders

It is worth considering why individuals accept the orders of others. The answer is complex. To say that someone is a natural leader is no answer. In fact, leadership studies have indicated that there is considerable variation in characteristics of leaders. One can find all kinds! In one sense, the reason why people obey orders is the reverse of the question of who has power and why.

In an interesting study by Peabody (1962 and 1964), individuals were asked why they obeyed orders. The questions were posed in three different settings: a police department, a welfare office, and an elementary school. One could argue that these were all comparable organizations — in effect public administration and agents of social control. Furthermore, these occupations tend to be semi-professional and somewhat similar in level of training and probable professional activity. The answers of the respondents revealed different reasons why lower participants obey orders. About 40% of the police gave reasons that reflect personal character, and almost the same number said that because the superior occupied a position, he had a legitimate right to do so. In contrast, over 60% of the social workers gave this as the reason, and very few said personal characteristics counted. Finally, almost one half of the school teachers stated competence was the major reason. This research helps substantiate the idea that there are multiple kinds of power structures, which in turn have some distinctive patterns of authority.

Although, I did not refer much to Weber's two other forms of authority in the previous chapter, this research in effect substantiates that there are different reasons for obeying orders. The dominant themes remain those of legitimacy and competence, themes one would associate with rational-legal authority. However, and this is an important point, legitimacy is much more salient in a mechanical organization, and competence in an organic one. The theme of personal qualities was important in Weber's two other types, namely traditional and charismatic. Here we find some respondents answering in these terms.

3.3.4. A Special Problem: Powerlessness

I have suggested that not everyone wants power, and perhaps it would be best to provide some evidence for this. In the first wave of the Hage-Aiken study, the respondents were asked not only how much power they had but how much they wanted. Some reported that they had too much, a finding that has since been replicated in other research studies (Payne, 1970; Conway, 1976). A number reported that they did not want more than they had. Here powerlessness is measured quite directly by the discrepancy between what they have and what they want.

Lawler and Hage (1970) did an intensive analysis of 144 social workers. By concentrating on a single profession, or in this case semi-profession (Etzioni, 1969), the intent was to eliminate the impact of professional characteristics and perhaps of technological ones as well. All of the social workers were employed in organizations and therefore confronted with the same dilemma between bureaucratic constraints and professional autonomy (Blau and Scott, 1962).

Since the amount of additional power desired can be affected by the ceiling of the instrument, the analysis controlled for the actual level of power in a partial correlational analysis. The results were as follows. The higher the level in the organization r_p = .22, the greater the amount of professional activity r_p = .18, and the more desirous of change r_p = .24, the greater the feelings of powerlessness upon the part of social workers. However, the greater the amount of professional training, the less powerlessness r_p = -.22. At least for social workers, upward mobility in the organizational hierarchy does not lead to satiation but instead to a desire for even more power. Certainly the impact of professional activity and the desire for change make sense. More surprising is the notion that training leads to less powerlessness. Does this mean professionals – at least social workers – are socialized to accept their power fate?

We need more analyses in this area, but by determining not only whether groups fight for more power, but also which individuals within groups feel a lack of power we can more adequately test our assumptions. Presumably at the individual level personality characteristics start to play a critical role (Rousseau, 1978). Unfortunately, the Lawler-Hage analyses could not explore this side of the problem.

3.4 CONCLUSIONS

This chapter has begun to make the basic model of two kinds of organizational forms more complex by suggesting that there are really four basic power distributions: the mechanical, the organic, a traditional form, and a mixed mechanical-organic form. The last two kinds of forms are essentially nonlinear combinations of several variables, and more especially the concentration of specialists and the centralization of strategic decisions.

What determines the basic distribution? The central axiom argues that interest groups want equality or consistency in rank across the major dimensions of skill, power, pay, and privilege. It is an inherently sociological premise since this strain towards consistency does not work at the individual level. This central premise also seems largely consistent with the coping with uncertainty theory relative to the power of particular departments. Yet the synthesis of this theory with the Burns and Stalker and Hage structural theories in the previous chapter adds a considerable depth and helps explicate the process by which interest groups increase their power in the inevitable struggle. We have here an internal contradiction in the social structure of organizations: they can not have a high concentration of specialists and a high centralization of power. There are certain qualifications to this, as were noted in this chapter and will be noted again in Chapters 10, 11, and 12 as the basic four forms are fully explicated.

The conclusion of this axiom is essentially pessimistic about workers' participation schemes. Unless they are skilled they are unlikely to have much effective say. But the same axiom seriously questions whether the board is likely to have much say regarding the internal workings of the organizations either.

A major weakness in coalition theory has been an inattention to how interest groups are formed; that is, their basis. Several basic premises are suggested that relate the basis of interest group formation to the distribution of rank in an organization.

The same general explanation for the meso distribution of power appears to work at the micro level with the concept of job autonomy. However, the correlations are smaller, precisely because group dynamics are more likely to be operative. Furthermore there has not been an explicit test of the presence of high job autonomy and high centralization of power in the traditional form. So far all of the research has focused on linear combinations of the variables included in the analysis.

Chapter Four

Processes of Power

The word process can mean many different things. At the most general level, there are two kinds of processes: those that essentially maintain the system and those that result in changes in the system. In this sense one can speak of general processes that apply to all systems (Miller, 1975a). The subtitle, "form, process, and transformation" calls attention to this difference by using the term transformation to mean a change in form, which itself occurs by means of some process. Sometimes the term "adaptation" is employed to describe this change process. This same distinction applies to any discussion of processes associated with centralization. There are homostatic processes that essentially maintain this power structure and there are adaptive processes. In this chapter and in the next we will focus on two basic kinds of power processes: decision-making and succession.

Despite the call for power process studies, there have been relatively few. The work of Pettigrew (1972) and Hickson et al. (forthcoming) are the major exceptions. The former is a descriptive case study, but the latter builds an analytical framework for the analyses of decision-making processes. To help locate processes that might upset the power equilibrium or bring about a break up of the dominant coalition, the first section of this chapter focuses on the high risk decisions that leaders must take from time to time. These decisions have power processes that can bring about at least a qualitative change in the coalition that has power, if not a quantitative change in the degree of centralization. In contrast to these rare major decisions with long term implications are the relatively routine ones. These are much more likely to be predictable and maintain the status quo.

4.1. KINDS OF DECISIONS

In power processes the unit of analysis is an issue about which a decision must be made (Abell, 1975). It may be a trivial one such as whether or not to purchase a Remington-Rand typewriter, or it may be a high risk one such as whether or not to rent an IBM 360 computer. What we want to know is where the issue originates, how it progresses, what groups or individuals are involved, if bargaining or negotiation occurs, how much conflict there is, and naturally what the final decision outcome is. Each of these is a complex analytical problem that requires a number of variables even for simple description.

The best imagery for a decision-making process is that of a trajectory. Although this calls to mind a bullet, a better analogy is of a molecule in a bubble chamber. Ideas follow seemingly random paths, bouncing off of individuals and groups as they progress through some power structure. Upon closer analysis one finds that this movement is not random, but in various ways follows predictable trajectories.

The bulk of organizational decisions are routine ones. Every once in a while a nonroutine decision occurs and its trajectory is quite different (March and Simon, 1958). This qualitative distinction between kinds of decisions which can be quantified is fundamental, because as we focus on a wider variety of decision issues — the trivial as well as the important — we can more easily grasp the kinds of decision-making processes, and which lead to change and which do not. Determining how often a decision issue occurs is relevant for the big or strategic decisions as well as for work decisions. In general, we shall confine ourselves to strategic decisions — that is, decisions about new products or services, about objectives, and about strategies for controlling the environment (McNeil, 1978). It is only these kinds of decisions that are likely to involve the interests and value preferences of relevant interest groups, whether inside or outside the organization.

4.1.1. The High Risk, Discontinuous Decision

A single decision can be quickly characterized by its frequency of occurrence, its costs, its discontinuity with previous issues, and its risk. Risk refers to the predictability of outcome, whereas cost is the investment needed to produce the outcome, and discontinuity is defined as the dissimilarity with previous decision issues. Not unexpectedly these three attributes tend to covary (see Figure 4.1.). For those who would like a broader or more comprehensive list of decision characteristics, the work that has been done on attributes of new programs is very suggestive (Zaltman, Duncan, Holbek, 1973: Chapter 2). Producing a new product or providing a new service implies a new technology, a new staff, equipment and space, and therefore capital. In system terms, there are changes in inputs as well as throughput. Beyond this are considerations of market (and this is true even in the public sector), of competitors, and therefore strategies. This is the nontypical high risk decision. (For a series of case histories of this see Chandler, 1977).

Our main concern will be the analysis of two distinctly different kinds of

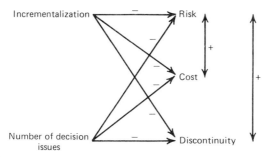

Figure 4.1   The interrelations between decision characteristics.

decisions, high risk and low risk. The high risk decision is not only one where the outcome is uncertain but where cost is high, experience is limited because the decision occurs infrequently, and – usually but not always – there is a considerable discontinuity with previous strategic decisions.

An example of a high risk issue was IBM's decision to build the 360 computer. The outcome of this decision affected almost everyone employed. Furthermore, the capital investment required was so large that if the product was not successful IBM would go bankrupt. What made the decision high risk was the lack of assurance that customers would really want to shift to a new series of computers with all the inevitable start-up costs. In what sense was the decision a discontinuous one? One could argue that IBM had made a comparable decision with the previous generation of computers. It is discontinuous or qualitatively different each time the decision requires a new technology. Furthermore the decision to implement a new process technology (that is, production process) always occurs in the context of a historical situation that has similarities but at the same time remains unique. Each major change in technology is historically specific if for no other reason than that the same problem faces the decision-makers: too soon or too late. Although the general problem is the same, the decision is experienced as unique and qualitatively different precisely because it is time dependent and relative to specific historical circumstances.

In general, the major kind of nonroutine and high risk decision is the production of a new output that at the same time requires a new production process and technological change. Consistent with our definition of organization, which emphasizes the distinctive inputs, throughputs, and outputs that are largely but not completely technological, one could argue that a new organization is created. Because this change process is so important, it receives extended analysis in Chapter 7, where the resistance to radical innovation is considered. Here our concern is with the processes of power and, more specifically, decision making that brought about the new product or service and the attendant inputs and throughputs.

Everyone can remember the success stories, where high risk decisions were the correct ones. But these are more the exception than the rule. Unfortunately, there has been a tendency to ignore failure in the United States, and yet failures provide the greatest opportunities for learning. We tend to forget that more businesses go under than survive. And while many public organizations are maintained despite inefficiencies, there is much more visible failure in this area than one realizes. Most universities offer graduate programs in sociology, but probably less than 20 are worthwhile in the sense of actually attracting good graduate students. The famous Teamsters' study of patient care in the New York City area (Trussel et al., 1961) showed that most hospitals provide poor patient care. The federal government funds many demonstration projects but few become institutionalized as ongoing services. Many organizational sociologists have observed that some organizations are so large that they will not be allowed to fail. Lockheed and the Pennsylvania Railroad are recent examples. However, in many instances we are observing multi-organizations. Within them specific organizations may be discontinued or replaced as the product or service becomes obsolete or fails.

Some interesting examples of high risk decisions relative to new products from the world of business follow. In each case, it was perhaps the right decision but at the wrong time; that is, either too soon or too late. During the 1940s, Hotpoint pioneered an electric stove with the buttons in the back where children could not reach them. The shift to safety as a product quality requires a corresponding change in consumer preference, which came twenty years later. DuPont brought out Corfam after many years of development during the 1960s but finally had to abandon the project, losing 50 million dollars. This is an example of where a multi-organization lets one of its organizations fail or, more correctly, discontinues it. While second guessing is unfair, one wonders if the explosion in leather prices in the 1970s would not have changed the market situation. Also DuPont went after the high priced shoe market rather than the low, and it is in the latter — if the product could be cost effective — that greater inroads might have been made. This decision, much more than Hotpoint's, also illustrates the need to perfect technology. Frequently what makes new products and services risky is the very long time needed to improve the techniques in the throughput process.

The automobile industry is studded with case histories of major product failures and of product successes. In each instance it was the design of a new car for a new kind of person — that is, a new market. at Ford, for example, the successes were the Model T, the Thunderbird, and the Pinto. Its biggest failure was the famous Edsel, which came out at the wrong time. American Motors was successful with the small car as was Volkswagen, of course, but both have had troubles with some of their other cars. Packard shifted the product line downwards, hoping to cash in on the mass automobile market immediately after the Second World War, but instead it lost its reputation for quality and went out of business. Another famous failure was the Kaiser car, a rare failure of an entrepreneur who built jeeps but was unable to make the grade with a consumer product.

Each of these failures illustrates the characteristics of high risk decisions — they are discontinuous and require massive capital investments.

Although the decision to produce a new line of cars does not appear to be a discontinuous one, it is in the sense that it means developing a whole new division within the multi-organization, with new marketing strategies and the like. What Ford wanted to produce with the Edsel was a competitor to Pontiac, but it did not create the necessary divisional structure. One of the biggest problems is the attempt to produce a new throughput with the same staff responsible for producing other products. Frequently not enough change occurs with all the corresponding problems.

This is most noticeable in the cases of Kaiser and Packard. The managerial elite did not recognize that it should have a mass car division separate from its quality car, presumably with separate tools, plant, workers, foremen, managers, and so on. This is a classic example of a discontinuous decision because the market is different but is not recognized as such.

Failures occur in people-processing organizations as well. They are usually not as well publicized because the decisions carry less risk. Normally universities can test student interest with courses, and then only later decide on a separate organization. The University of Wisconsin tried an experimental college and had to close it down after four years (Cremin, 1961). Failure has even happened to Harvard, where its Veterinary School was closed shortly after the beginning of the century. Again, these are examples of multi-organizations that close down an organization that is failing. They also illustrate two different kinds of failures. In the case of the experimental college at Wisconsin it was a radical innovation in line with the more extreme position of progressive educators. In the case of Harvard, it was a program successful elsewhere.

Governments in their various branches have also started a number of programs or services that proved to be either unnecessary or unwise. Again the dramatic mistakes are perhaps most easily seen in the armed services, where the decision to buy certain kinds of weapons is a critical one. A classical example is the United States Navy, which invested heavily before the beginning of the Second World War in a torpedo that did not work (Morrison, 1950). The mistake was not corrected until 1943, by which time a number of American submarines had lost many opportunities to sink Japanese ships and had taken needless risks. Finally they realized that the torpedo did not work in open water (it had been evaluated in bays where there are no waves!).

A review of the many success stories in Fortune magazine can provide examples of where high risk decisions did work. Here I have emphasized the failures so that one will appreciate the nature of risk.

In summary, high risk and discontinuous decisions are dramatic events in the history of an organization. They obviously affect the careers of the individuals involved, and success or failure means succession, the topic of the next chapter, as well as shifts in coalitions. The discontinuity results usually but not always because of the new technology, new market, and therefore new environment that the organization enters when it adopts a new product. Not much risk is involved if the organization can start small, but in certain industries and certain areas of the public sector one can only start big. It is this combination of bigness and newness that makes a decision truly risky.

Those who are familiar with the concept of uncertainty — as in the work of Crozier (1964), James Thompson (1967), Lawrence and Lorsch (1967), Khandwalla (1976), and others — might wonder why I have not employed this term, rather than "risk." The reason is that organizations do vary in having more or less uncertain environments, but the high risk conveys more correctly the sense of gamble. Once a decision is taken there is no turning back. Uncertainty is a more enduring characteristic. These two concepts do have a relationship. Sometimes elites take high risk decisions with the hope of reducing uncertainty. But in general they are different phenomena.

4.1.2. The Major Premise

Consistent with James Thompson (1967) and March and Simon (1958), our fundamental assumption about administrators is that they will try to avoid high risk decisions wherever possible. Sometimes this has been called the desire to reduce uncertainty, but the essential idea is that seldom does the power elite want to expose itself to failure unless it is forced to do so. High risk decisions are broken down into smaller risk decisions wherever possible. This can be labeled the policy of incrementalism (Wildavsky, 1964), a policy that mitigates against radical innovation (see Chapter 7).

The more the decision can be incrementalized, the more the elite can reduce risk, cost, and discontinuity. In fact, examples of high risk, high cost, and discontinuous decisions are rare precisely because incrementalism is so important. In the ten years of the Hage-Aiken study, there was only one example of a decision that was really far-reaching, and that was the creation of a community mental health center. All new outputs began on very small scale, involving little commitment of resources. This is the typical practice of universities, of hospitals, of business, and so on.

The military will make large scale commitments for the purchase of weapons, but almost always after having had considerable experience with a prototype. Likewise business organizations attempt to produce products on a small scale before moving to a mass market. Market research is used extensively to gauge acceptability.

The major exceptions are organizations operating in mass markets or where the initial investment must be quite high. One can not start small in the manufacture of a car except to produce custom built cars. DuPont could not start small with Corfam. The same problem exists with large scale computers. In the public sector, the best examples remain weapons procurement by the military.

Our assumption is:

4A   The dominant coalition will try to reduce risk as much as possible.

Thus even in high risk decisions, steps such as market research, trial runs, and the like are taken to reduce the gamble.

There are organizations and especially multi-organizations that specialize in taking high risk decisions more often than do others. If it is a multi-organization, the diversity of products/services – plus the basic financial base that this implies – reduces somewhat the cost of failure. Learning can also result from the success of having taken a high risk decision that works. One is more willing to take high risks in the future. Therefore, the number of decisions, and especially past high risk ones becomes important. As the amount of risk-taking increases, the importance of any one decision issue diminishes. The experience transcends the immediate. It also makes it easier to incrementalize some high risk decisions. And this leads to the recognition that decisions are best not analyzed in isolation but as sets.

Once we shift our perspective to the set of decisions at the aggregate level, we come to recognize that one of the most important properties is the number of decision issues that there are. Later when we discuss the environment in Chapter 12 we shall observe that this helps to define how much autonomy an organization has. But it has a critical impact on the decision-making process itself. As there are more decisions, more are likely to be delegated. Crozier (1964), in his study of the power of the maintenance engineers, which was based on their control of uncertainty, did not emphasize the fact that the situation in a tobacco plant is characterized by a low number of decision-issues, thus making the ones that remain more salient. As this frequency of decision-making increases, the risk, cost, and the discontinuity decrease. Low risk decisions can be safely delegated downwards.

At the same time that decisions are being delegated, they are likely to be routinized (Blau and Schoenherr, 1971). Formal committees are established, systematic channels are created (and not necessarily hierarchically), and definite procedures of review relative to a certain topic. This routinization has the objective that a variety of viewpoints are considered and that relevant interest groups have a chance to be heard. Routinization of decisions by means of routing slips are designed to assure wider participation. This is also true for the delegation of decisions. Decisions are delegated downwards but superiors are kept informed, especially when the decision may be slightly out of the ordinary. In many instances a decision requires the signature of a superior, although the decision has been effectively made at a lower level. The higher risk decisions are made at higher echelons and the lower risk ones at lower echelons. We normally do not think of risk varying by rank but in fact it does.

This leads naturally to our next problem: what is the decision-making process, and how is this related to the kind of decisions and volume of decisions being made? In part, we have already alluded to some of the characteristics of this process, but we must be more explicit about just how decisions are made.

4.2. DECISION-MAKING PROCESSES

Whether the decision is of high or low risk, it goes through a process. To analyze this process, it might be useful to think of the decision-issue as having a trajectory, one reason for the imagery used in the previous section. This trajectory passes from individual to committee to individual to staff meeting and the like. We need a number of variables to describe this movement through the organization.

4.2.1. Variables for Describing Decision-Making Processes

As the frequency with which a decision-issue increases, the more the trajectory is likely to be routinized (see Figure 4.2 for definitions) and the decision delegated downwards. This practice has been much noted in the literature (see Blau, et al., 1966; Blau and Schoenherr, 1971). The key mechanism is that once the decision is routinized, in effect, it can be programmed, a point made by March and Simon (1958: 100-10). This aspect is analyzed in Chapter 11 where the idea of programming as a means of affecting control is discussed.

The next few variables have been emphasized much less in the literature. Other variables that are helpful for describing the decision-making process are duration of the decision-making process and discussion, which usually tend to be positively related. Low risk decisions occur rapidly, by means of routing slips and memos. High risk decisions lead to an escalation of discussion, some of which may not be task relevant but more designed to handle the anxieties associated with risk taking.

Again, these are ideas consistent with March and Simon's (1958) information search given uncertainty. One way of searching is for continued discussion until all aspects are explored and considered.

Another useful distinction is between the extensity and intensity of participation in the process. The former is the number of interest groups defined by occupation, level, department or other social category involved (Chapter 3), while the latter represents how much effort they expend to affect the decision outcome. Typically these vary together, but not always.

Figure 4.2 Definitions of variables describing the process of decision-making

Characteristics of a single decision trajectory

1. The degree of routinization:	The extent to which specified steps in the process are defined and used
2. The degree of delegation:	Extent to which the bulk of the process occurs at lower echelons
3. The duration:	The length of time between the first proposal and the final decision outcome
4. The intensity of participation:	The amount of effort each interest group expends
5. The amount of discussion:	The amount of time spent considering verbally the decision-issue
6. The extensity of participation:	The number of interest groups involved
7. The amount of information search:	The extent to which the interest groups seek facts relative to decision-issue
8. The stability of coalitions:	The extent of change in the combination
9. The amount of joint creation:	The extent to which the final decision outcome is the product of the ideas of various interest groups and/or individuals
10. The amount of negotiations:	The amount of time spent bargaining
11. The amount of deliberate delay:	The amount of time spent in avoiding a final decision
12. The amount of conflict:	The extent of disagreement among the interest groups
13. The duration of conflict:	The amount of time the disagreement continues

Characteristics of a set of decision trajectories

1. The variety of trajectories:	The amount of overlap in the ways in which decision-issues are processed
2. The variety of origins:	The number of different starting points for the decision-making process

The stability of coalitions or ease with which they change is an extremely revealing property of a decision trajectory. The more stable the combination of interest groups, the more likely there is to be a major conflict with a high risk decision. In fact, as will become clear later, the process that interests us the most is the one attached to high risk decisions because they produce a series of qualitative changes in the form of the power structure – that is, they transform it. High risk decisions typically break up the dominant coalition, fractionizing it along value dimensions (see Chapter 5).

The information search is a major mechanism by which risk, cost and discontinuity are reduced (March and Simon, 1958). Joint creation of a decision-outcome is a property that is perhaps difficult to perceive, because we frequently conceive of decision processes as conflicts between two or more coalitions where one side wins. This is not the usual situation except in high risk decision trajectories. Usually, and even with major decision issues, a creative synthesis emerges from the efforts and discussions of the interest groups. Many strategic decisions are quite complex, allowing considerable room for negotiation and joint creation. The former encourages the latter. In this way, vital interests of particular groups are protected and in all probability the decision outcome will be a more subtle one. Although Coleman (1974) has noted the importance of the trading of votes as a stabilizing mechanism and a way of understanding basic power processes, the possibility for joint creation has not received enough attention. It offers a valuable insight and appears to be what Burns and Stalker (1961) had in mind.

An excellent case study of how trading occurs across decision-issues is the study of Abell (1975) in labor-management relationships. Some decision-issues were more important to labor and others to management. Negotiation occurs most frequently when there are several alternatives that are equally attractive. It is also more common in non zero-sum game decisions, that is, where there is some room to maneuver. Joint creation is found in those situations where even a single solution does not appear self-evident. Again, it is also more characteristic of high risk decisions.

Although in the power-value paradigm the amount of negotiation is emphasized, the use of deliberate delay as a process tactic is as important as negotiation, especially when the interest groups have not had enough time to think through all the alternatives and evaluate which is the best option. One reason why high risk decisions may take so long is not so much the need for discussion, but because people simply need time to make up their minds.

The amount of conflict in decision-making is a complex phenomenon. Here is where ideal-types might be useful because there are a number of conflict style modes. Indeed we have made a distinction between the duration and the amount of conflict in order to classify different modes. The two most typical patterns are long periods of small conflict and short periods of intense conflict; the former is characteristic of decision-making in an organic organization and the latter is characteristic of the processes in a mechanical organization (Burns and Stalker, 1961).

The same variables can be applied to some aggregate of decisions as well. At this level, the image of a graph is very helpful. The points represent the various actors or interest groups. These points can also represent committees as well as informal cliques and individuals. For each decision trajectory we could study the particular pathway that occurred, numbering the links in sequence (I am indebted to Amitai Etzioni for this idea). For example, a basic decision about curriculum form might start with a single person, who discusses it with an interest group. In the discussion the idea is transformed – that is, we have an example of joint creation. Then it might move on to a committee who further transforms the proposal. During this process various relevant interest groups might be consulted. Each step can be seen as a link between the points in our graph. Furthermore, the issue may move back and forth as it is reformulated and shaped.

The purpose of using a graph image is to recognize that there is a way of describing the entire trajectory of either a single decision or a series of them. Consistent with Burns and Stalker (1961), we might use the terms "network" and "hierarchy" to describe trajectories. In a network or wheel situation, the idea moves back and forth between all relevant points. In a hierarchy, the idea moves only in one set pattern. The distinction between the two becomes even more apparent once one studies the aggregate of decisions. Particular decision issues might involve only parts of a wheel or network, but all issues would cover the entire wheel.

One would find a very different pattern for a high risk trajectory than a low risk one. Our hypotheses are:

4.1 The higher the risk, the more likely the trajectory will follow a network pattern.

4.2 The lower the risk, the more likely the trajectory will follow a hierarchical pattern.

A key element in the organic form is the need to develop new products and even technologies. These tend to be more like high risk decisions. The consequence is a complex trajectory, with the decisions moving back and forth.

The origin of a network pattern does not depend only upon the degree of risk. It also depends on the variety of decision-issues. The number of decision-issues tends to lead to more complex trajectories (Hickson et al. forthcoming). The hypothesis is:

4.3 As the number of decision-issues increases, the variety of origins increases and therefore the variety of trajectories and the emergence of the network pattern.

The reasons for this are also consistent with Coleman's process power model (1974). In effect, particular departments or interest groups retain the most power relative to certain decision issues. A relatively stable bargain is struck. Votes are swapped. As issues within a sphere of influence occur, the key actors or cliques participate in the decision making but only the relevant decisions. Only part of a network is activated.

However, if the decision-issues just kept increasing there would soon be an overload. As a consequence, elites tend to group decisions into categories and then develop procedures for handling them. In March and Simon's terms (1958: 158) a program is created that specifies steps of action — the routing slip and the guidelines. This leads to our fourth hypothesis about process:

4.4 *As the number of decision-issues of the same kind increases, the low risk decisions are delegated and routinized, reducing the variety of trajectories and encouraging the emergence of a hierarchical pattern.*

These tendencies tend to counterbalance each other. They also suggest that single decision issues, and especially low risk ones, are likely to be hierarchical. Multiple decision issues and even single ones are more likely to be of the network type. There is a need for research in this area. But the advantages of graph theory are clear. With it one could gain additional insights about the forms of aggregate decision issues.

There are two kinds of variables that have been employed to describe decision issues. The first group deals with the characteristics of the process; the second with the characteristics of the form. The latter emphasizes the aggregate while the former highlights a single decision-making process. We now turn to describing two kinds of power processes, one that maintains the system and the other that upsets the dominant coalition.

4.2.2. Kinds of Processes

Most of our attention will be focused on the qualitatively different, high risk decision. Typically this means the decision to produce a new product that requires a high initial investment. The B-51 bomber, the 360 computer, the Edsel car, and the Corfam shoe are all examples. There is no way in which the risk can be reduced. The process by which these decisions are made can be predicted even if it appears to be a highly unique phenomenon. Surely each of these decisions was quite special. But across them, I suggest, is the following pattern. These kinds of decisions arouse the interest and concern of almost everyone in the organization, even those who do not have formal authority. Even workers will become concerned about jobs, and they might resist the introduction of a new technology. A variety of interest groups are activated (extensity of participation) and they will put forth considerable effort in affecting the decision outcome (intensity of participation). The novelty of the situation leads to considerable information search and extended discussions which are themselves reinforcing. Each new piece of information leads to more discussion, and the discussion encourages information search-up to the point that there is some sense of closure. And since it is a new situation, the stability of the dominant coalition is reduced and typically breaks apart (see Figure 4.3).

The impact of these four variables on conflict is interesting and complex. The activation of various interest groups and their involvement brings out all of the inherent but usually latent conflicts that exist between them. High risk situations make the different interests and values — a topic for the next chapter — apparent, and these differences become the basis of conflict. However, the information search and discussion tend to help manage this conflict (Lawrence and Lorsch, 1967) and reduce it. But since this requires time, the process duration is lengthened. The profile of conflict in high risk decisions varies by the time period.

In the beginning the conflict is likely to be quite high. The dominent coalition falls apart. Eventually, a new one forms and the conflict begins to diminish.

The high risk decision

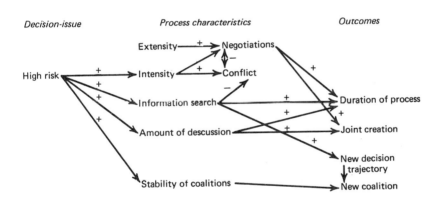

The low risk decision

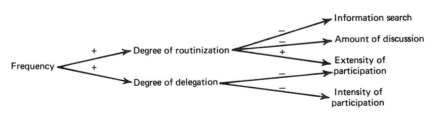

Figure 4.3   Decision characteristics and decision trajectory.

The extent of the conflict also varies depending upon whether the high risk decision is a yes or no proposal or whether it also involves a large amount of work relevant to new technologies, new market strategies, and the like. The yes or no proposals obviously produce the most conflict.

One of the interesting by-products of high risk decisions is that they produce new decision trajectories as various interest groups are activated during the process. The power of particular interest groups or key actors will rise and fall depending upon the decision made. Although idea men frequently can be rejected and are less liked (Bales, 1957), during high risk decision processes their power rises because frequently they become critical in shaping the decision. High risk decisions also tend to produce new coalitions, and for precisely the same reasons. The old trajectories and coalitions are no longer relevant. New ones form around the values and interests involved in the decision. The usual pattern is the formation of two new coalitions, those for the decision and those against. This is most likely when the high risk decision is a simple yes or no proposal: to build a base in Thailand or not, to produce a mini computer or not, to buy a nuclear carrier or not, to offer a program in East Asian studies or not.

If there is a considerable struggle between the opposing factions, the coalition that wins will frequently assume the leadership of the organization if it does not have it already. For example, those in favor of the IBM 360 computer within IBM rose in power and those opposed to it lost power (*Fortune,* 1965). More typically, the relative power of particular individuals will rise or fall depending upon how they have aligned themselves. This is especially true as the results of the decision become known. If successful, they are promoted; if not, they are fired. This is of course one reason why these decisions are called high risk; the uncertainty of outcome is evident. Thus competence of decision makers is being assessed and it leads to either the entrenchment of the decision makers who advocated the correct choice or, their succession by a new elite (see next chapter).

As the decision-issue weaves a new trajectory, a new coalition tends to be formed that cuts across the previous distinctions. It may be stable, but frequently is not, precisely because high risk decisions are usually rare, and the old coalitions are based on more stable lines of division such as hierarchy and occupation. *This then is our first example of the transformation of the power structure: the creation of a new dominant coalition and the creation of a new trajectory of decision-making.* There is no necessary indication that there is a change in the degree of centralization. Sometimes there is and sometimes there is not. The more typical transformation is a qualitative change, the formation of a new dominant coalition or elite. The membership changes but not the phenomenon of elite control.

One of the most important aspects of high risk decisions, as March and Simon (1958) noted long ago, is that there is high information search. As this occurs, new information sources or new specialists are likely to be discovered. For example a consultant might be brought in who calls their attention to various key sources. Once recognized, this source may be used again in the future. A new link in the chain of power is formed and a new trajectory. Not atypically there may be the creation of a new position for a specialist, who proceeds to secure the necessary information relative to the problem at hand.

Social science research has played a key role in the information search that occurs. Forecasting, surveys, market research, advertising research, and so forth have all been attempts to reduce some of the risk involved. Again, our basic premise helps us predict some of the characteristics of unique events – that is, a high risk decision making process.

If high risk decision issues change at least qualitatively the form of power, *the low risk decision has just the opposite effect. It tends to institutionalize the power structure, and in interesting ways.* As decisions are programed and then delegated downward, there is the illusion of power in decision making, but in effect the options are highly controlled. The conflict-critical school is right to point out that real power consists in opening options, considering new alternatives, and the like. The programed decision is not like this.

As the decision issue occurs more and more frequently, then two consequences for the process emerge: the decision-making process is routinized and the decision is delegated. The objective of the former is to ensure information search, discussion, and a certain extent of participation. It may occur by means of a routing slip in which suggestions or advice are solicited, but typically the routinization is done through committees in which the representation of key interest groups is ensured. Although we usually think of the members of an organizational committee as decision-makers, they are also representatives of various interest groups, at least departmental if not also occupational. Typically the members are selected for this reason.

Increasing frequency of occurrence also leads to the delegation of the decision, which is designed to reduce decision overload for the top managers, administrators, professionals, and decision makers. Delegation of decision-making reduces both the extensity and intensity of participation in the decision-making. The decision outcome becomes more and more automatic, and while there may be a formal signature on a piece of paper, in fact the decision is made at a lower level. For example, division officers in the United States Navy typically decide which man can go on leave and when, although technically the executive officer signs the "final" approval and the papers. The right to intervene is always there but seldom exercised. The United States Navy represents the prototype of the mechanical organization. Its concentration of specialists is quite low and its centralization quite high. Yet even here one finds considerable delegation of routine decisions.

The same pattern exists, and even more so, in an organic organization such as a medical school where Bucher (1970: 9) found a blockage on a decision at a higher level only once in some five years. As the concentration of specialists increases, the upper echelons must exercise their power of veto or of disapproval more and more cautiously. The larger number of decision issues in an organic organization allows for a greater sharing of power, the development of spheres of influence, bargaining, and the like. But most of the decisions fall into patterns that become programed and predictable. What differentiates the organic form is that it does have many more decisions and more high risk ones.

The research of Blau (1970b) on the nature of several specific issues does suggest that indeed there may be some support for some of these hypotheses. The delegation of decision to local office managers is very much associated with the standardization and formalization of procedures. Although this is not exactly the same as the routinization of the decision-making process, it implies much the same thing and the argument is analogous.

However, Blau's interpretation is different from ours. He suggests that trivial decisions are delegated downwards, provided the decision outcome is completely controlled. In my opinion this is a too hierarchical view of organizations. Blau is correct for a certain as yet undetermined percentage of cases. More important in my view is the work overload created by too many decisions. It is a relief to give others these decisions. Beyond this, there is the even more important pull factor of subordinates demanding that they be given these responsibilities. But this leads into a discussion of how structure determines the process of decision-making, the topic for the next section. Furthermore, control mechanisms such as those described by Blau may actually not work well in these instances.

How does the delegation and routinization of decisions lead to the institutionalization of the power structure? The main mechanism is that *if individuals are given a little piece of the action, they buy in and accept the entire power structure and all of its decisions.* Blau and Scott (1962) in a seminal insight noted that foremen allow workers to violate some rules so as to gain compliance with a number of other regulations. The same principal applies — and with greater vengeance — to managers and administrators. Give them some decisions to make, even if carefully controlled, and their loyalty and commitment is gained to the whole range of decisions made. Many wonder how power corrupts. This is one of the essential mechanisms by which Richard M. Nixon was able to bring so many along with even illegal decisions.

4.3. MESO-STRUCTURE AND THE PROCESS OF DECISION-MAKING

There are three theoretical observations to be made about the relationship between the structure of an organization and the process of decision-making. The first is that there is no or little relationship between the high risk, infrequent, and discontinuous decision-issues. The second is that there is a great deal of association between the low risk, frequent, and continuous decision-issues. And the third is that the essential imagery of Burns and Stalker (1961) offers us perhaps the best model for synthesizing structure and process relative to decision-making. Each of these points needs to be expanded and justified.

The whole thrust of the argument about the high risk decision is its qualitative difference. This issue cuts across the classic lines of coalitions, even across the basic interests and value preferences of the various interest groups. At this point there may be formed an "old" and a "new" guard. What is especially interesting about these rare decision-issues is that new coalitions are formed about the alternative decision outcomes that are available. The best examples of this lie in the policy study area rather than in organizational studies. An example is the alliance for and against the joining of the common market in Norway. This most uncertain and high risk decision split across all of the traditional cleavages that existed in Norwegian society. Likewise the decision to build the 360 computer at IBM had much the same consequence, cutting across departmental and hierarchical lines, forging new coalitions around the two possibilities: yes or no.

Of the four structural variables discussed in the previous chapter, two appear to be most decisive for setting the tone and style of the process of decision-making: the concentration of specialists and the decentralization of strategic decision-making (see Figure 4.4). The former variable is in some respects the most critical one because it impacts on the major parameters already discussed: the number of decision-issues and the frequency of any one. The concentration of specialists thus helps explain why there is a network pattern in an organic organization. Each specialist monitors a different part of the environment and

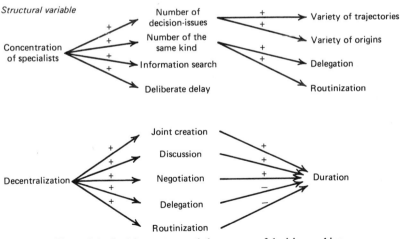

Figure 4.4 Social structure and the process of decision-making.

performance of the organization, bringing in new decision-issues from both sources and especially from the environment. The concentration of specialists thus affects decentralization, the structure of power, but also the attendant processes. As we have seen in the previous chapter, creating new uncertainties and then coping with them effectively is a way for a department or an occupational group to increase its power. The mechanism is the creation of new decisions and especially those with some risk. It is in the self-interest of departments or occupations to increase business. This is best done by finding decision issues — especially high risk ones.

At various places above, we have indicated how the presence of multiple issues allows for a much greater flexibility in the power structure. The trading of votes, the joint creation of decision outcome, the development of spheres of influence all become possible under these circumstances. Conflict may increase but its intensity declines. The key structural variable that impacts on this is the concentration of specialists. The environment is equally important but is discussed in Part Four.

Beyond motivations to augment power, the specialist is motivated to seek out decision issues, because this expands his range of responsibilities (normative equality) and justifies higher salary and fringe benefits (stratification). These structural variables are therefore not irrelevant, but they are of smaller significance. Thus, the expansion of decision issues becomes the major power game of the specialist. The decision-issues faced by the organization grow geometrically.

This discussion can be summarized as:

4.5 The greater the concentration of specialists, the greater the number of decision-issues and number of issues of the same kind.

For exactly the same reasons, the variety of origins and the variety of trajectories increase at the same time. The different origins represent the different specialists posing problems requiring decisions — and usually solutions, that is, the outcomes of decisions as well. The different trajectories emerge as different groups whose interest or values are involved articulate. Indeed, studying decision trajectories would give us a key insight into how coalitions are formed and how these shift from one high risk decision-issue to the next. They are a needed area of research.

Insofar as specialists rely upon their skill and expertise, they will document decision-issues with information (verbal and not necessarily written), and prove their competence by seeking out solutions (Hickson et al., 1971). Indeed, professional managers pride themselves on the well thought out solution; this is the best way of demonstrating their competence and their deserving of another promotion. Thus new decision-issues seldom come without some indicated alternatives and the recommended decision outcome in organizations where the concentration of specialists is high. Beyond this, specialists are members of associations that are continuously producing new knowledge, which both encourages more information search, and defines new issues and new solutions (this is one explanation for why professional activity appears to be so much more strongly related to decentralization than professional training).

But as the concentration of specialists increases, and despite the recognized spheres of influence that are created, the occupational interest group can not win on skill or expertise alone. The greater variety implies other occupations who may know something. This encourages the formation of coalitions and in turn the various other process variables. Votes are bought by participation in the shaping of the decision-outcome, that is in joint creation. Deliberate delay as a tactic is used to allow for persuasion and reflection to build consensus. When dealing with other interest groups, of approximately equal rank and status, one must proceed slowly carefully paying attention to their interests. This helps explain the long decision-making process involved in organizations with a high concentration of specialists.

These ideas are summarized by the following hypotheses:

4.6   *The greater the concentration of specialists, the greater the amount of information search and the amount of deliberate delay.*

The structure of power, decentralization, affects other aspects of the decision-making process. By definition it encourages joint creation. The purpose of allowing multiple groups to affect decision outcomes is usually to create more complex decision outcomes that presumably are better. But the biggest impact of decentralization is on routinization and delegation. The involvement of many interest groups and the consideration of many issues means decision work overloads. The volume is handled by routinization and delegation. This is done in committees. Appointments to committees are based on the representation of various interest groups and spheres of influence, or appropriate specialist knowledge relevant to the decision-outcome. Each committee represents a particular kind of decision area. At the same time decision-issues are also moved down the chain of command as they increase in frequency. Both procedures reduce the decision work load, since not all people can participate actively in all decisions and at the same time, they ensure the representation of vital interests.

The following hypothesis summarizes this argument:

4.7   *The greater the decentralization, the greater the joint creation, delegation, and routinization of the decision-making process.*

Therefore both the concentration of specialists and decentralization tend to reinforce the tendency to delegate and routinize, and explain how more decentralized structures tend to have much more delegation.

One could argue as Blau does (1970b) that delegation is the essence of decentralization, but this does not appear to be the case. Unimportant and routine decisions are delegated downward, as Blau himself has argued. But the real problem in decentralization is whether a greater proportion of the organizational members participate in *strategic* decisions. This is the key to the definition of the concept and of its counterpart, democracy. It is true that delegation contributes to decentralization, but the crux of the problem is the scope of actual participation or influence across hierarchical levels and substantive departments. Committee structures rather than delegation ensure this greater scope, that is extensity of interest group participation.

Organic organizations function much more like representative democracies, as Bucher (1970) has made so clear in her study of a medical school. Members of committees not only represent the interests and values of their group but they are sure to sound out other individuals with the same interests. The members are appointed rather than elected, which is one divergence from representative government. This is not true in all cases. There are organizations where the professionals elect their committee members, as do physicians in hospitals (Hage, 1974) and faculty in many universities (Blau, 1973). This may become increasingly the pattern in professional organizations.

The elaborate committee structure that is the sign of a decentralized power structure encourages the variety of trajectories and of origin points to increase, again helping to explain why organic organization creates much more discussion. This committee structure affords an arena for negotiation. Thus while the concentration of specialists impacts the most on information search and deliberate delay, decentralization affects discussion and negotiation. Our last hypothesis is then:

4.8   *The greater the decentralization, the greater the discussion and the greater the negotiation.*

Again, these process characteristics help explain why decentralized power structures are more stable. Consistent with the participation in power thesis of the human relations perspective (Coch and French, 1948), individual involvement can lead to commitment and acceptance of the status quo. Discussion and negotiation clearly facilitate the institutionalization of the power structure. Perhaps the strongest support for these two kinds of processes lies in a book by Weiss (1956) that contrasted two government agencies, one having much more routine decisions than the other. Needless to say, the extent of specialization and professional activity was much higher in the other situation — that is, where there were less routine decisions. Unfortunately these were work decisions and not strategic decisions. They certainly did not involve high risk. They do, however, *independently* confirm the hierarchical and network process forms, if not the process variable characteristics predicted above.

For a variety of reasons then, low risk decision making stabilizes the power structure. The latter can be decentralized or centralized but as long as delegation and routinization occur, there is a *perceived* participation that may not have much substance but which leads to acceptance of the existing hierarchy and the dominant coalition. In a decentralized structure, where there are even more decisions and delegation, even greater stability exists.

However, the paradox is that there is also a greater fluidity in the dominant coalition in an organic organization, even as the decentralization remains relatively stable. The negotiation that occurs allows for shifting coalitions across decision issues through the trading of votes. As decision issues decline in number, there is a loss of the room to maneuver and the dominant coalition is more fixed and rigid.

4.4. CONCLUSIONS

At the end of Chapter 2 we posed a number of critical issues relative to our basic analytical themes of form, process, and transformation. Some of these issues can now be addressed. Parallel to a centralized form of power structure there is a hierarchical form of decision making. The network form is associated with decentralized power structures. Low risk decisions tend to maintain both kinds of structure. In contrast, high risk decisions lead to a qualitative transformation of the power structure by redefining the dominant coalition. But high risk decisions do not necessarily change the degree of centralization — only the membership in the elite. From a phenomenological perspective this is interesting because it means that there is considerable change in content without much change in form.

On the one hand the argument has been made that when there are high risk decisions, especially if they are costly and discontinuous with previous experience, there is likely to be little relationship between the process and the existing structure. New coalitions are likely to be formed that cut across traditional interest group lines with the adoption of high risk decision. New decision trajectories emerge. Perhaps one of the most important points is that high risk decisions can activate a larger number of people that would not normally be involved, even in a highly centralized organization and if only for a short time period.

In contrast, low risk decisions are more likely to be related to the existing structure of the organization but in a variety of complex ways. Concentration of specialization leads to a proliferation of decision issues, which means work overload. In turn, this is handled by routinization and delegation. This is another way in which one structural variable produces a change in the power structure. This facilitates the transformation of the existing form, and for the various reasons noted above.

In general then decision-making processes maintain the same degree of centralization. Even high risk decisions do not change this, except under special conditions which are discussed in Chapter 7, under the rubric of radical innovations. Whether high or low risk, power processes do have predictable patterns, however much the participants experience them as unique.

Chapter Five

Transformation of Power:
Dominant Coalitions and Succession

The word power is not far removed from the idea of the capacity to determine the goals and actions of others (Weber, 1947; Hall, 1977: 197-98). Indeed, our definition of the term has emphasized decision-making and decision outcomes. One critical class of decision outcomes is the selection of organizational priorities, the objectives that the organization will pursue and with what costs. If we know who has the power, then which courses of action will they choose?

The concept of goal has played an important part in the development of organizational theory (see Etzioni, 1960 and 1961 a and b; James Thompson and McEven, 1958; Perrow, 1961a and 1970b, Chapter 5; Simon, 1964; March, 1965; Warner and Havens, 1967; Price, 1972; Kochan, Cummings and Huber, 1975; Hall, 1977: Chapter 3) and any attempt at a comprehensive theory of organization must consider this idea. Our approach here is to shift the terminology from goals to objectives. Most readers think of goals as attached to individuals. The analytical issue is not what are individual goals – or motives – but rather the organizational objectives that elites in power, the dominant coalition, pursue. As Khandwalla (1977) notes, organizations act as if they pursued goals but it is equally important to recognize that the substance of individual goals and organizational objectives is different.

The essential thrust of our analysis is that once the dominant coalition selects a course of action then that becomes the objective of the organization. The workers may be opposed. The consumers may have different priorities. *The naked reality – the power reality – is that the preferences of the dominant coalition carry the day.* These objectives may represent the special class interests of the owners, they may feather the nest of the managers and administrators, or they may even be sensitive to worker and consumer concerns. But regardless, the dominant coalition's objectives are those of the organization because, by definition, they have the power. The objectives may not be consciously selected and articulated (Mintzberg, Raisinghani, and Théorêt, 1976). Nevertheless, one can chart the behaviors of the organization and determine what the implied goals are. In the literature, and since the work of Perrow (1967 and 1970a), one speaks about operative goals.

Why focus on the dominant coalition? If one can predict its preferences, then one can predict what the organizational objectives are on the assumption that preferences become translated into causes of action. Beyond this, if the dominant coalition fails then it is likely to be replaced. This in turn can lead to a transformation of the power structure not only qualitatively — one elite replaces another — but quantitatively, a change in the degree of centralization. The dominant coalition stays in power as long as it is effective. Once it becomes ineffective, it loses power and is replaced. The new dominant coalition is likely to change objectives to correct the mistakes of the previous one and in so doing may find it necessary to alter the structure and design of the organization.

This simple model of power and success or failure immediately suggests a number of substantive topics in the organizational literature. First, there is the issue of effectiveness. This concept has been the traditional way of speaking about success or failure in the literature. (Seashore and Yuchtman, 1967; Price, 1968; Goodman and Pennings, eds., 1977; John Campbell, 1977). Second, there is the issue of leadership. Again, there is a large literature that essentially supports Fielder's (1967) contingency theory of leadership. Third, there is the issue of succession. Here, one notes changes in leadership that appear to lead to changes in effectiveness and changes that do not (Grusky, 1960, 1961, and 1963).

However, since our focus is more on the meso analytical level than the micro, we will analyze the changes in the dominant coalition rather than the changes in leaders. The issue is the team of leaders — the power elite — rather than a single individual, even though one sees the succession of the new president as the initial event. Furthermore, we are interested in distinguishing between succession that leads to changes in the power structure and processes that do not.

To predict when succession processes produce real changes in the power structure we must have the concept of effectiveness. But this concept appears to mean all things to all people (see Mahoney and Weitzel, 1969; Price, 1968; John Campbell, 1977; Steers, 1975; Seashore and Yuchtman, 1967; Goodman and Pennings, eds., 1977). Some have suggested that the concept be eliminated from the lexicon of organizational research (Hannan and John Freeman, 1977), and others that it is a necessary ordering device (Pfeffer, 1977). However difficult it might be to define and to measure effectiveness, one can not handle the problem of the transformation of power without this concept.

The major reason why this idea has proved hard to grasp is that different organizations achieve success in different ways (Caplow, 1964: 145–48; Steers,

1975; Mahoney and Weitzel, 1969). In what is probably the best work on the subject, Price (1968) notes that effectiveness subsumes some five objectives. Is an organization effective if it achieves only two or three of these objectives? How are these objectives to be weighed? Beyond these conceptual problems both organizational objectives and effectiveness have presented enormous measurement problems (Zald,1963; Donabedian, 1966; Seashore and Yuchtman, 1967; Perrow, 1968, 1970b: Chapter 5; Hannan and John Freeman, 1977). Generally organizational objectives have been defined relative to outputs of one kind or another (Scott, 1977): while effectiveness has been an attempt to cover a much broader category of ideas including processes, performances and outputs (see Price, 1968; Seashore and Yuchtman, 1967; and John Campbell, 1977). In one sense, the goal concept has not been stretched far enough and the effectiveness concept has been made to cover too much.

There is a simple solution to this problem. If we start with the assumption that each social structure is simultaneously effective and ineffective; the dynamic of change in the dominant coalition is established because of this internal contradiction. The basis for power struggles — overemphasis on one or another set of priorities — is provided. And we have an understanding of when succession means a transformation of the power structure and when it does not.

Consistent with the idea that structures encourage the pursuit of certain objectives rather than others, the first section analyses the association between social structure and the kind of effectiveness demonstrated. This returns to the theme of Chapter 2: Do some structures have functions and dysfunctions, and what might these be? The next issue is to explore the values of the power elite and how these might be related to the choice of objectives for the organization. This has been the central assumption of the political-value paradigm, but to my knowledge no one has yet attempted to develop a set of hypotheses about the dominant coalition's values and how they affect objectives. This has to be done to avoid the tautology that the objectives are the values, or vice versa.

It it is a fact that structures have dysfunctions and dominant coalitions prefer to pursue specific objectives because of their value preferences, then the dynamic for change is established. Given failure, the board must replace the dominant coalition with another. Frequently boards recruit new leaders internally, which typically means that the dominant coalition remains in place. Repeated failure leads to a change in the promotion or hiring of the president and then a change in the dominant coalition that manifests itself in a shift in emphasis. Changes in the dominant coalition over time can be viewed as the movement between alternative ways of achieving effectiveness (Grusky, 1962). Once this is recognized, the three sets of ideas — objectives, effectiveness, and leadership succession — can be seen as best analysed together and not separately.

The leadership perspective does bear a relationship to the dominant interest group paradigm but there are some important differences: while admitting that interest groups have preferred values and inherent interests, it relates the choice of leaders to how well they perform. Thus it is a bridge between the structural-functional and political-value perspectives, permitting a synthesis of them. The leadership perspective has tended to emphasize the single man whereas the political-value paradigm focuses on the dominant coalition, or inner circle, to use James Thompson's term (1967). The latter approach seems wiser because seldom do leaders — and especially effective ones — work alone (Gamson and Scotch, 1964). They have allies (Grusky, 1963) and move them up the chain of command as they are promoted (White, 1970).

Again, as in the previous chapter we have an important power process, succession, that can lead to either the maintenance of the power structure or a change in it. Which kind of succession process it is depends upon whom is recruited, and this in turn depends upon the extent of failure and how well it is recognized.

5.1. A MESO-THEORY OF STRUCTURE AND EFFECTIVENESS

5.1.1. The Theoretical Definitions of Objectives and Effectiveness

One of the central tenets of those who advocate participation is that the interests of the workers and of the clients or customers will then be represented. But just what are these interests? Substantively, in any concrete situation one might expect higher wages and lower prices to be the major considerations. But this is to think in terms of interest groups' interests and not necessarily their value preferences — that is, their priorities for the organization. There has been a confusion here. Just because individuals think and because they have their own personal goals does not negate the possibility of individuals having preferences relative to organizations. Clearly in the social conflict over the Vietnam War, different groups were expressing preferences about what the United States should be doing — not what individuals should be doing. Individuals do not declare war, in the normal sense of the term. It is political entities that do. Thus there is the need to recognize that there is a meso level, a level appropriate for organization, about which individuals and groups develop preferences or at least opinions. Individuals have opinions about whether universities should emphasize teaching or research. They also have opinions about whether hospitals should provide quality service or low cost care. Interest groups have been formed to put pressure on business organizations to make their products safer and more ecologically responsible. All these attitudes reflect preferences about the priorities of organizations.

The definition of organizational objective is:

Organization objective: The priorities relative to organizational performances and outputs held by the dominant coalition.

As Perrow (1970b) has indicated, the concept of objective should be much broader than just the operative goals or outputs. For this reason, the term performance is added to the definition. By stipulating that the performances and outputs are organizational ones, one avoids psychological reduction. Here the issue is what the individual prefers for the organization — high profits, quality patient care, or teaching children how to read. He or she may want certain outputs emphasized because they mean a bigger salary. Perrow has suggested that in companies that are operated and controlled by professional managers there is a strong bias towards mergers because this means higher salaries. But while this may be true, one does not want to confuse the managers' desire for higher income as the objective of the organization. This illustrates nicely the difference between the various analytical levels. To obtain higher income, the managers must demonstrate organizational effectiveness, including their own leadership capabilities, and one way of doing this is by growth. The organizational objective is growth, the managers' goal is income, and the means to these ends is the strategy of mergers. The emphasis in the definition is on the plural. Effectiveness can be summed up as the problem of achieving adequate levels on all performances and outputs. Once one accepts the idea that there is a plurality of objectives, then the problems of selection and of effectiveness become apparent. Price (1968) suggests that innovation, morale, and efficiency or productivity — as well as several other concepts — represent effectiveness. Seashore and Yuchtman (1967) argue for the ability to gain resources, and obtain 10 dimensions in a factorial analysis of a large number of specific indicators of performances and resources, including volume of business, production cost, new member productivity, business mix, manpower growth, productivity, and the like. An even longer list of 30 has been compiled by John Campbell (1977); besides those already mentioned he adds profit, accidents, motivation, readiness. Many on his list are best seen as means to achieve particular ends — for example control, planning, consensus, role and norm congruence, managerial interpersonal skills, managerial task skills, and the like. However difficult it is to separate means from ends, it does seem desirable to focus on performances and outputs of the organization rather than the structural, leadership, and process variables that produce or facilitate performances and outputs. If all of these ideas are lumped together, then a whole series of analytical problems are lost. The major theoretical problem is how does control, for example, affect effectiveness, defined by certain performances and/or outputs.

In an exhaustive review of effectiveness studies, Steers (1975) found some 15 different measures or standards. Adaptability-flexibility was used in over half the studies. If one lumps productivity and efficiency together, then again one-half measured this aspect. Satisfaction and employee retention combined together were involved 40% of the time. While the many items mentioned make it appear to be complex, these three dimensions created by collapsing categories do imply more consensus about what are important dimensions than appears at first glance.

Although it is easy to measure profit, there are a number of difficulties in choosing this as the measure of effectiveness. First, it only applies to business organizations and not to nonprofit ones. While the term prestige can be substituted in people-processing organizations that do not have profit goals, the difficulty still remains that all organizations more or less strive for profit or for prestige or some equivalent. This is the functionalist assumption about survival (see Selznik, 1949). All dominant coalitions attempt to survive. What differentiates them is the particular standards they use to demonstrate that they are effective in coping. Profits can be made by cutting costs or by producing new products. It is this difference that we want to capture.

Perrow (1967) has suggested that organizations demonstrate their effectiveness by either producing a quality product or service, or by producing a low cost product or providing a fast efficient service. (See Figure 5.1.) *This recognizes that organizations can be effective in more than one way and that therefore one does need to know the particular objectives of the organization to understand which kind of effectiveness is relevant.* There is a relative emphasis also on innovation or change in outputs. With this other dimension, we have a typology of four ways in which organizations can demonstrate their effectiveness to themselves and to others.

Figure 5.1   A Typology of kinds of effectiveness[a]

Importance of inno-vation vs. efficiency	Importance of quality vs. quantity	
	Quality	Quantity
Low innovation and high efficiency	Craft products and services of moderate cost	Mass produced low cost products or universal services
High innovation and low efficiency	High quality and innovative products and services of high cost	Limited mass production with moderate innovation and moderate low cost

[a] Adapted from Perrow (1967: 202).

Effectiveness: The achievement relative to the priorities of innovation versus cost and quality versus quantity.

Although it is somewhat vacuous to say that effectiveness is achievement vis-à-vis priorities, it becomes meaningful once given content by the four ideal-types of objectives as suggested by Perrow. The main advantage of this scheme is that it can be applied across a wide variety of organizations and environmental contexts. Nor is it limited to capitalist societies. We need no longer worry about what profit is in the USSR. Instead we must determine whether specific organizations are attempting to achieve quantity or quality with a greater or lesser emphasis on innovation or the cutting of costs.

There have been several factor analytical studies, most notably Seashore and Yuchtman (1967) and Campbell et al. (1970), that have developed multiple dimensions of effectiveness. The implication of this research is that indeed there is more than one way of being effective. Although they have developed anywhere from ten to thirty or more factors, in many cases these are based upon variables other than performances and outputs. Both Mahoney and Weitzel (1967) and Duncan (1973) show that different managers use different criteria to measure effectiveness. Finally, Goodman and Pennings (1976) argue that effectiveness must be understood in the context of constraints. The thrust of this argument is again to perceive different criteria because of different constraints.

This definition of effectiveness as essentially based on two dilemmas follows the discussion in Chapter 2. The efficiency versus innovation choice corresponds to the Burns and Stalker forms of mechanical and organic. Aldrich (1979: 22) has also noted that they correspond to open and close models of organization. The quantity versus quality choice represents an important addition. For those familiar with Parsons' AGIL scheme (Parsons, Bales, and Shils, 1953), these two dilemmas do not cover all of the possibilities that one might want to add. I have not included the general dilemma of human versus material costs, a topic reserved for Chapter 9. And perhaps the issue of conflict avoidance or control should be included as well. Again, these are perceived as subsidiary objectives and not as central as the four mentioned above, which are more likely to be related to the maintenance of either profit or prestige (that is, the demonstration of effective leadership).

Nor does the definition include strategies for controlling the larger environment, whether stability or growth. The question remains: how does one achieve growth or stability, by innovation or efficiency, by quality or quantity? Growth and stability as objectives are relevant to the larger environment. These concepts are quite important; they are analyzed in Chapter 13.

5.1.2. The Major Premise and Hypotheses

Weber suggested that centralization would lead to a maximization of efficiency, while Burns and Stalker indicated that decentralization would lead to a maximization of innovation (see Chapter 2). Hage agreed with both, adding that quality would be most likely to be emphasized in the latter kind of organization while quantity would be the priority in Weber's bureaucracy.

Building upon these various ideas, Perrow (1967) went one step farther and suggested that centralization can not only be seen as varying between high and low – but there are two quite different exceptions: polycentralization, and a mixture of centralization and decentralization. The latter occurs in organizations that have different departments, as in research and production. Although his main intellectual thrust is a concern for routine technology, his ideal-types suggest the following hypotheses:

5. 1 *The greater the centralization, the more likely the dominant coalition will choose the objectives of quantity and low cost with little emphasis on innovation, and demonstrate effectiveness in this way.*

5. 2 *If the organization is polycentralized, then the dominant coalition is more likely to choose the objectives of quality and moderate cost with little emphasis on innovation, and demonstrate effectiveness in this way.*

5. 3 *If the organization is mixed centralized-decentralized, the dominant coalition is more likely to choose the objectives of quantity and moderate low cost with some emphasis on innovation, and demonstrate effectiveness in this way.*

The power structures of polycentralization and mixed centralized-decentralized have been defined in Chapter 3. Here their link to the choice of goals and the type of effectiveness being demonstrated is shown.

The great advantage of recognizing these alternative objectives and effectiveness ideal types is that the values of the customers/clients are such that both are important ways for organizations to gain resources from the environment, whether by sale or fee for service. Some customers want cheap and dependable products while others prefer custom-made ones. Some clients want highly individualized attention to be easily available while others want fast service and do not care about the quality as much as they do about the cost. Organizations can make a living both ways because these values co-exist in the larger society even if there are dominant preferences.

These hypotheses should be juxtaposed with the effectiveness theory of Price (1968). In a synthesis of a large number of case studies, he suggests that more effective organizations will have the following characteristics: Except where there is a high degree of complexity, organizations which have a high degree of centralization with respect to tactical decisions are more likely to have a high degree of effectiveness; and organizations with a maximum degree of centralization with respect to strategic decisions are more likely to have a high degree of effectiveness. Thus, Price argues for centralization more than do Perrow and others. The first difficulty is that the particular criterion of effectiveness shifts throughout his discussion. Sometimes it is productivity, sometimes morale, sometimes profit. Which measure one uses will affect the particular conclusion reached. What is being argued here is that some organizations will be perceived as effective if they have high quality and others will also be perceived as effective if they are efficient. If this is true, then the role of centralization may be more complicated than Price indicated in his hypotheses.

Another tradition that has made much of the link between participation in power and the consequences for performance has been the human relations school (Tannenbaum, 1968; Seashore, 1963). They suggest that as the influence of workers increases, their morale is raised, they become better motivated, and in turn will produce more – that is, increasing productivity. Here we have the exact *opposite* hypothesis of Price, who argued for centralization rather than *de*centralization.

Running through some of these hypotheses is a lack of specification of why centralization of the social structure should affect the choice of goals and the kind of effectiveness. With some people arguing for the advantages of centralization and others for the advantages of decentralization, we should be suspicious. There are more dimensions to the social structure than just power, however important that might be. Why should the nature or arrangement of tasks influence the value preferences or priorities of the coalition of interest groups that is dominant? A key component should be the nature of the dominant coalition. The first premise is:

5A   *The greater the diversity of interest groups represented in the dominant coalition, the more complex and varied the choice of priorities will be.*

Interest groups have their special interests, values, skills, and expertise. If we start to aggregate these in some way, such as in a coalition, then there is a much broader range of input which leads to more innovation – a topic for the next chapter – and a more complex view of the product or service. The essence of a concern for quality appears to revolve around two themes – the recognition of many differences such as different customers or clients, and the recognition of multiple attributes of the product or service. This is a more complex view of reality. The spread of participation among divergent interest groups leads to conflict over goals, but the resolution of that conflict is most typically an emphasis on quality and a proliferation of attributes. In the converse situation of high centralization a small and narrow power elite finds it easy to perceive little differentiation in customer needs and wants.

These distinctions between quality and quantity break down into special terms, such as custodial versus rehabilitative or custom made versus mass produced. We find custodial care, a quantity service, in many contexts: mental hospitals, prisons, or residential treatment homes. Likewise there is a difference between custom built cars such as the Rolls Royce and mass produced ones like Plymouth. The terms custom-made usually reflect an emphasis on quality rather than quantity. Implicit in these concepts, too, is a recognition of individual differences — whether needs or tastes. Also implied are standardized versus non-standardized ways of producing the product or providing the service (see Chapter 12).

All other things being equal as decentralization occurs, the dominant coalition becomes more varied. Therefore this premise provides the rationale for much of Perrow's implied hypotheses. However, it makes more sense to derive another hypothesis, to wit:

5. 4   *The greater the concentration of specialists, if they are professionals, the more likely the dominant coalition will choose the objectives of quality and of innovation.*

There are a number of reasons why specialists, especially if they are professionals, will push for new products or services, new technologies, and other kinds of innovations, all of which are discussed in Chapter 6. For now, we note that to recognize the need for a new product or service is to see the environment in a more complex way. As the variety of interest groups increases there is also greater knowledge about the environment. More complex views also lead to the recognition of differences among customers and clients — that is, a need for qualitative distinctions.

If the concentration of specialists are craftsmen, then the emphasis is likely to be on quality but with little consideration for change (Perrow, 1967). And if the concentration of specialists are engineers, then the emphasis is likely to be on quantity or reliability (Perrow, 1970b) and moderate innovation. Artisans rely upon traditional bases of knowledge that change slowly. In contrast, engineers rely upon scientific bases of knowledge that change more rapidly. However, they are less likely to be professionalized and therefore have different objectives.

One way to measure effectiveness is to ask the members which objectives are most emphasized. This approach works when there is an agreed upon set of dimensions that cut across a variety of organizations, requiring the use of words such as quality, efficiency, and innovation.

Building upon Perrow's work, Hage and Aiken (1969) asked respondents to report the objectives emphasized during the past. They were provided a list of dilemmas and asked to choose which had received the greatest attention.

There are some major problems with their measures. Words like quality, and even productivity are subject to alternative interpretations. Many of the criticisms of subjective measures apply to their study. Their work could be improved in several ways. First, one contribution to the literature would be a research study in which respondents reported their definitions of these terms. This could then be used in a follow-up study with more specific questions relative to each reported meaning. This would improve both validity and reliability. Second, the amount of actual effort exerted relative to these objectives would make a useful contribution. For example questions about the amount of time spent discussing each of these goals might give a more accurate picture of their importance in an organization.

Much of the research on goals has concentrated on ones specific to particular organizations, such as their outputs (see Perrow, 1961a; many of the articles in March, 1965; also Kochan, Cummings and Huber, 1974 for a more recent example). Focusing on objectives perceived as general performances rather than specific outputs solves many of the problems. The first set of findings is largely based on case studies. We have already reviewed the work of Burns and Stalker in Chapter 2. Although the review focuses on their ideas and theoretical concepts, it should be remembered that these were induced from a vast amount of experience and thus are partial empirical confirmation of the different ways of establishing effectiveness — especially since all of the cases are within a single industry, the electrical sector. Some companies survived by producing small volume products for different customers and others by producing products for a mass and undifferentiated market — essentially a quality versus efficiency contrast. The organic organizations are decentralized, and the mechanical are centralized.

Price's (1968) case studies are hard to reconsider because they cut across a wide variety of different kinds of organizations — food stores, a truck plant, an electrical company, a mental hospital, and the like. There are few multiple studies of different food stores, electrical companies, and mental hospitals. Most of the cases he reviews involve tactical or work decisions of the store managers, research scientists, and psychiatrists. As has been demonstrated in Chapter 3, professional occupations demand autonomy. But more important is the negative finding that if not given this autonomy, the organization becomes ineffective by various measures. For example, the mental hospital is evaluated as ineffective because of too much centralization. This and his other examples suggest the connection between the structural variables and certain types of effectiveness, but one must make distinctions by effectiveness types. When a mental hospital is under budget and goals constraints (see Pennings and Goodman, 1977), it is forced to adopt efficiency as the relevant standard of effectiveness. Under these circumstances it becomes effective even if the morale of the psychiatrists is low.

Perrow (1967) in his framework reviews a large number of studies that in various ways can be interpreted as supporting some of the hypotheses connecting structure and goals. More directly relevant are the effectiveness studies of Lawrence and Lorsch (1967 a and b). They found that in the plastics companies, whose products were quality and small volume, decentralization was strongly associated with their measures of effectiveness. In the container industry, however, where standardized efficient service is the key, centralization was strongly associated with comparable measures of performance. Here is strong confirmation for the idea that there is more than one kind of effectiveness as measured by product characteristics, but effectiveness can require either centralization or decentralization.

Pennings (1976) shows that stock brokerage firms were more effective if they were more decentralized. But one would assume that the customers, who are mostly upper middle-class, want individualized attention, and that the quality of service is what counts. If so, then decentralized organizations would become more effective relative to sales or turnover or growth measures in this kind of organization. In the same way one must work through the many effectiveness studies, asking which type the organization should be classified as before testing the hypotheses relating centralization and effectiveness.

Another set of findings relating structure to reported objectives is from the Hage-Aiken panel study. In Table 5.1 are the correlations at the level of the organization. In general, the correlations were weaker in the second wave than in the third. This improvement in magnitude is probably a consequence of improved measurement. The wording was changed in the third wave so as to provide much more consistent interpretations of the meanings. The measurement of the relative importance attached to quality versus quantity was not changed because no satisfactory specification of quality across a diversity of organizations was found. However, the hypothesis about the emphasis on efficiency is strongly supported and in both waves. This may reflect a greater consensus on what this term means, at least in the context of these people-processing organizations.

The next chapter analyzes the relationship between the rate of innovation and structure and the reported emphasis on this as objective. As predicted, the concentration of specialists is related positively, albeit weakly, to quality and to

Table 5.1 Structure and organizational objectives
Hage-Aiken panel study

Structural variables	Reported objectives: second wave			
	Qual.	Innov.	Morale	Effec.
Concentration of specialists	.10	.23	.23	−.45
Centralization of power	−.10	−.17	−.33	.33
(N)	(16)			

Structural variables	Reported objectives: third wave			
	Qual.	Innov.	Morale	Effec.
Concentration of specialists	.08	.32	.30	−.47
Centralization of power	−.08	−.18	−.27	.35
(N)	(29)			

innovation, and more strongly and negatively to efficiency. Centralization has an opposite pattern. In general, the change in wording in the third wave improves the pattern of findings. Here, however, centralization appears to be negatively related to efficiency contrary to all of the above hypotheses.

Is there any way to validate these simple questions about objectives? One way is to examine their correlations with measures of performance. Both a job satisfaction battery and an independent count of new programs were correlated with a reported emphasis on morale and innovation respectively. They were related. Since the innovation measure was obtained from an independent source, there is some confirmation. Given the crudity of the measures and the various difficulties noted above, any pattern of findings is amazing.

In summary, these various findings, although largely scattered, support the relationship between structure and choice of objectives and kind of effectiveness. Perrow's typology affords a handle for consolidating a large number of isolated cases. It requires, however, accepting the idea of more than one way for an organization to prove effective and thus receive legitimacy. The nature of the social structure tends to dictate how the dominant coalition views reality. The more the world is perceived as complex — which follows from the presence of many interest groups in the dominant coalition — the more that innovation and quality become the operative objectives. This is reflected in the concentration of specialists and the degree of decentralization. Together these increase the probability that there are a variety of interest groups in the dominant coalition.

When structural-functionalism was first suggested as a paradigm in organizations (Parsons, 1956 a and b, but also Blau, 1955 and Gouldner, 1954a), the importance of values was very much a theme. During the sixties many lost this essential ingredient, and it was Perrow (1967) who most effectively brought back a goal or value perspective, even though he did so in the context of technology. Implicit is that structural-functionalism argues that the origin of values such as organizational objectives lies in the structure. Or as Marx argued, the structure determines the superstructure. Clearly this is not the only view.

5.2. THE DOMINANT COALITION AND ITS VALUES

The other view is that values have an independent origin and one that lies in other aspects of the superstructure or collective attitudes. Not unexpectedly the political-value paradigm differs from structural-functionalism by arguing an independence of the values (for this see Karpik, 1972b; Child, 1972a; and for some of the debate Warner, ed., 1977). While this is probably true, most adherents of this perspective have not asked what the origins of the dominant coalitions values are if they do not lie in the structure of the organization (or environmental context, or technology, or other aspect of the material conditions). While the power-value approach has been advocated as a perspective since Cyert and March (1963), surprisingly few specific hypotheses have been developed. Perhaps the single best hypothesis is that of the late James Thompson (1967), who suggests that regardless of how decentralized the power structure, there will always be an inner circle. This can be seen as a corrective to the ideas advanced above and especially to those which argue that decentralization is a panacea for problems of productivity.

There are at least two separate analytical problems. The first is to predict the ideology or general value system of the dominant coalition. The second is to predict what values in prior socialization tend to shape these value systems or ideologies. Again, the most interesting work is that of Perrow (1967, 1968 and 1970b). He suggests not only the familiar distinction between conservative and liberal ideology, but also the unfamiliar concept of derived goals. This is particularly relevant because one would like to know under what circumstances organizations – and especially multinational corporations – will be friend or foe, concerned with solving social problems or in making a quick profit, a topic that receives special attention in Chapter 13. Up to now workers have been seen as happy or alienated, but not both. Multinational organizations are either good or bad. The real question is why some dominant coalitions have a liberal ideology and others a conservative one. Which managements worry about the social consequences of their policies and which do not?

In this context Perrow's concept of derived goals is helpful. This idea allows us to tackle the problem posed by the conflict-critical perspective — namely, why are certain products never created; why are certain concerns never articulated (Benson, 1977)? The concept of derived goals, although it does not completely avoid the enormous methodological problems posed by thinking about the unthinkable, does at least allow us to ask how much social consciousness the organization has. Does it have a soul? This would actually appear to be the thrust or meaning of the critical school's critique of the power literature in any case. We want to know whether the organization is at least attempting to tackle some of the larger issues that lie outside of its normal domain (James Thompson, 1967).

Perrow answered his theoretical question about the origins of liberal and conservative ideology, and derived goals by looking at technology and the social structure and more specifically the power structure — essentially the same hypotheses given in the previous section. However, consistent with a political-value paradigm, we want to search for answers in the other collective attitudes of the administrators in the dominant coalition.

Another way of approaching the problem of organizational objectives is to see general value orientations that predetermine the choice of objectives. Here the most significant theoretical work on general value orientations has been done by Parsons (1951). Two dimensions from his work appear especially relevant: the relative emphasis on universalism versus particularism, and the relative focus on external versus internal concerns. Together these provide four major kinds of value preferences that can predict the four kinds of objectives, and therefore the kinds of effectiveness. These value dimensions correspond to Parsons' (1951) pattern varieties of particularism versus universalism and self versus other. His other three pattern varieties are not used because they correlate so highly with universalism versus particularism. To my knowledge these have not been much employed in organizational research, yet they offer at minimum a way of tackling the problem of how to predict the objectives of the dominant coalition.

The cross-classification of these general values produces a typology. Within each cell generated by this typology (see Figure 5.2) are found four major objectives that we have been discussing. A particularistic value with external or environmental focus means concretely that there is an interest in quality: making particularistic responses and perceiving a wide variety of customer/client needs. Such organizations are highly responsive and have liberal ideologies.

It is when we contrast two universities or two hospitals or two rubber plants or two furniture manufacturers that we begin to perceive the advantages of the

Figure 5.2 A typology of general values[a]

| | Degree of universalism : | |
Scope of focus	Particularistic	Universalistic
Internal- organizational	Quality, modest cost Little innovation Conservative ideology	Quantity, low cost No innovation Conservative ideology
External- environmental	High quality, high cost High innovation Liberal ideology	Quantity-Quality, moderate cost Moderate innovation Liberal ideology

[a]Adapted from Parsons (1951), where scope of focus is equivalent to the pattern variable of self vs. other orientation and combined with Perrow (1967)

political-value paradigm for making predictions. One university can have an elite concerned with quality but little innovation, and another university a dominant coalition interested in innovation and quality. One would like to make predictions about when one or the other combination of objectives or kinds of effectiveness are selected. The explanation can lie in the general value orientation of the elites.

The hypotheses suggested in Figure 5.2 can be summarized as follows:

5. 5 *The greater the value of particularism in the dominant coalition, the more they will choose quality as an objective.*

5. 6 *The greater the value of the external environment in the dominant coalition, the more they will choose innovation as an objective.*

5. 7 *Given the values of universalism and a focus on the external environment in the dominant coalition, they will choose a combination of quantity-quality and moderate innovation.*

5. 8 *Given the values of particularism and a focus on the internal-organization in the dominant coalition, they will choose a combination of quality with little innovation.*

The scope of focus and the degree of universalism affect not only the choice of objectives, and thus the way in which effectiveness is proved to the larger society from which resources are obtained, but its impact on the ideology of mangement. Consistent with our theoretical reasoning about complexity in the perception of reality, particularistic and environmental orientations lead to a preference for a liberal ideology and a concern about derived goals — objectives other than the operating objectives and narrow concerns about either profit or prestige.

The importance of perceiving factors other than structure that affect the choice of objectives emerges once General Motors is contrasted with Ford, Kodak with Polaroid, and Westinghouse with General Electric. Clearly different ideologies can exist in organizations and multi-organizations with the same technology, markets, and structures.

A conflict-critical perspective calls attention to the importance of the workers and the values of the customers/clients, the two interest groups usually not represented in any dominant coalition. A consideration of their values is likely to give us some insight into what might happen if they were represented in the decision-making process, and if the dominant coalition were more concerned about their values.

Two observations are necessary. First, the values of the workers and customer/clients are likely to be more narrow and specific to their immediate self-interests. Second, their self-interests are not the same. The fundamental cleavage among workers is usefully described by social class position. What middle class workers – white collar workers, professionals, engineers, and so on – want and what working class workers – blue collar, craftsmen, skilled and unskilled workers, etc. – want are not the same thing. The same is true, obviously, for the customers or clients. Although this fundamental conflict of interest has long been noted since Marx and Engels early writings in 1848, its implications for organizational analysis have not been spelled out. They would appear to be applicable for organizational sociology.

As workers, the middle class wants differential pay for competence and performance, whereas the working class views the best standard as the same pay for all. Job autonomy is much less critical for the blue collar worker than it is for the white collar worker. As customers/clients, the middle class wants individualized attention whereas the working class prefers universal availability (see Hage and Hollingsworth, 1977). The former kind of customer prefers choice to cost whereas the latter prefers just the opposite. Running through these values are different standards of social justice. The middle class is likely to say "to each according to his needs" and thus view the desirability of varying kinds of products and or services, losing sight of the fact that not everyone gets something. The working class is likely to say "each should get the same" and thus view standardization as desirable, losing sight of the fact that not everyone will get what they need. For obvious economic reasons costs play a more important part in the calculations of the working class customers, while choice is a predominant utility for middle class customers who can afford to pay more.

With the workers and customers there is a link between the nature of their social class interests and their preferred utilities. These may not be represented in the thinking of dominant coalitions. Middle class managers can pursue the policy of producing standardized products at low cost, meeting working class interests. Clearly they are not doing this for the benefit of the working class but instead as a way of maximizing profits. Furthermore, given a chance to raise prices and lower salaries, they are likely to do so if they have a conservative ideology, as was demonstrated recently by the oil companies. Similarly working class representation in the dominant coalition does not necessarily mean responsiveness to social needs.

A contribution of the conflict-critial perspective has been the idea that one wants to specify not only what organizations do but what they fail to do. An analysis of customer values or preferred utilities is a link in the chain of understanding — and one missing from many power studies.

The explanation of customer and worker preferences returns us to the basic structuralist perspective, or at least to an idea shared by it and the conflict-critical perspective — values are expressions of structural interests. Here we have located the causes in the class structure of the society. One could search for sources of these values/interests other than in their social-economic standing.

Some readers might find it unsatisfying to explain the choice of organizational objectives by emphasizing the general value orientations of particularism versus universalism and internal versus external focus. Are there other sources of these values?

What are the determinants of universalism versus particularism and of an internal versus external focus? Here there is an early literature that can help us pull together a number of different research studies. A large literature revolves around the concept of professionalism (Hall, 1967). Another and smaller literature offers us the idea of cosmopolitanism versus localism (Merton, 1957; Gouldner, 1957, 1958, and 1959).

The dominant coalition will have a certain self-image. This image can be professional — whether manager, engineer, administrator, or whatever — and thus have some commitment to a generalized and admittedly vague set of values, such as belief in public service, belief in self-regulation, and a sense of calling. Or, it may not (Hall, 1967).

This distinction cuts across a large number of different kinds of dominant coalitions. As Perrow (1961a) notes in his hospital study, the modern professional hospital administrator is quite different from the traditional administrator. Which occupation dominates the power elite — whether professional or not — is not the issue. Rather, it is how professional the self-image of the coalition is. Chandler (1962) has used the phrase, "the replacement of family owners by professional managers." Recently (1977) he has documented how first railroad managers, and then those in the large multi-unit organizations created in the 1880s and 1890s, developed a professional ·orientation to their work. The hypothesis is:

5. 9 The greater the professionalism of the dominant coalition, the more likely it is to emphasize particularistic rather than universalistist values.

This hypothesis seems contrary to common sense, and very different from Weber's just bureaucrat who dispenses service even-handedly. Here professionalism refers to the self-image rather than its training (Hall, 1967). Attendance at conferences, presentation and publication of papers, and the reading of journals are all behavioral manifestations of this professionalism.

Our reasoning is that as individuals are trained more and know more, they develop more complex views of the world. Professionalism implies this. As a consequence, the concept of one house, or vitamin pill, or education, or tank for all conditions breaks down. The need for varied responses to the environment becomes apparent. Chandler (1977) notes that the concrete problem faced by a railroad's middle management, of moving many kinds of products over vastly varying distances, produced professionalism in this industry during the nineteenth century.

Once a dominant coalition develops professionalism it is likely to become institutionalized and maintained across time. New managers are socialized to these attitudes and internalize them even if they did not have them before. Once established through processes of selection and socialization, this value becomes inculcated in the perspectives of the dominant conception. Professionalism appears to produce this perception of complexity as part and parcel of its socialization and intellectual dynamic. Note that it is not uncertainty but instead complexity; an appreciation of the variety of things rather than the hazard of things. Again, it is worth repeating Chandler's observation that the sheer variety of demands encourages a more professional orientation.

In general, the level of cosmopolitanism in the dominant coalition affects whether the values are internal or external, organizational or environmental. Several scales of this concept have been developed which tend to mix in professional ideals as well. In Merton's (1957: Chapter 10) original study of *Time* magazine readers, the central idea was the area of interest: local, regional, national, or international. This scope is orthogonal to professionalism. If professionalism produces a more complex view of the world and therefore a more particularistic value framework, then cosmopolitanism represents how much of the world is viewed.

The hypothesis is:

5.10 The greater the cosmopolitanism of the dominant coalition, the greater the emphasis on external rather than internal focus.

There is certain tautology in this last hypothesis. One would want to be careful in choosing the indicators so that in effect not the same ones are being used. Merton defined cosmopolitanism in terms of how much scope there is. One would want to demonstrate that international concerns are associated with an environmental focus in the dominant coalition. The similarity in content is obvious.

More interesting are the corrolaries that can be derived by combing the previous hypotheses (see Hage, 1972: Chapter 2):

5.11 The greater the professionalism in the dominant coalition, the more likely they will choose quality as an objective.

5.12 The greater the cosmopolitanism in the dominant coalition, the more likely they will choose innovation as an objective.

5.13 Given non-professional values and cosmopolitanism in the dominant coalition, they will choose a combination of quantity-quality and moderate innovation as objectives.

5.14 Given professional values and localism in the dominant coalition, they will choose a combination of quality and little innovation as objectives.

The first hypothesis allows us to generate a four-fold typology of power elites or dominant coalition that is independent of substantive occupation or of social class. Most members of the dominant coalition are likely to be upper middle class. What separates and divides different coalitions is their degree of professionalism and cosmopolitanism, whether they are managers or administrators. Changes in either dimension produce one of the other types.

Let us return to the problem first posed at the beginning of this chapter. If we know who the members of the dominant coalition are, can we predict which organizational objectives are likely to be pursued? In other words, how will power be used — to benefit self-interest or to pursue derived goals? Will the organization be cost effective or innovative?

Instead of seeing the answers to these questions as a substitute for those given in the previous section, they should be added together for a more complete perspective of why organizations select particular objectives. An organization can have a dominant coalition with an universal perspective even if the structure is decentralized. It is the combination of structural influence and general value orientations that is needed in future research.

5.3. SUCCESSION AND CHANGES IN THE
DOMINANT COALITION

The theme of power has been discussed from a variety of perspectives and on different analytical levels, and yet little has been said about leadership. The actor has been the dominant coalition. The discussion of power can not be left without at least some analysis of the role of leadership within the context of organizational sociology.

Words like leader, elite, dominant coalition, and other terms describing the apex of a power structure reflect the biases of the various disciplines and paradigms. Psychologists and management specialists prefer to see the importance of the leader, whereas sociologists think in terms of dominant coalitions or power elites, that is, sets of leaders. As a sociologist I prefer to define leadership not as the single great man, although they do exist, but instead as a team. The smart leader has lieutenants that he places into positions close to him (see Gouldner, 1954a; Grusky, 1969). When the leader is promoted so are some members of his team — that is, there is a chain of promotions (White, 1970). The higher up in the hierarchy the promotion occurs, the more this is likely to be the pattern. The dominant coalition can be seen as a set of leaders and of allies working together to achieve the objectives that they have selected.

Beyond the issue of the preferences of different disciplines lies the larger reality of just how important a single leader is. Chandler's (1977) exhaustive study of nineteenth century businesses makes clear over and over again the essential role of middle managers and the particular teams selected. Admittedly some entrepreneurs chose correctly and others did not, but the real point is the emphasis on having several or even many key managers who run the organizations.

In his review of the literature, Hall (1977: 238) argues that leaders are made more constrained than one appreciates. The environmental constraints are discussed in Chapter 13 and the technological and size constraints in Chapter 12. Here we are concerned with the problem of demonstrating effectiveness. Selznik (1949) sees leadership as choosing correct action and this is very much my view. Consistent with our definition of effectiveness, there are four correct actions: innovation, efficiency, quantity, and quality. Clearly in any given environmental-organizational context, the range of choice is limited.

In his research on small groups, Bales found instrumental leaders, expressive leaders, and idea men. In fact, these correspond, admittedly roughly, to different leadership styles. Fiedler (1967 and 1972) has proposed a two-fold contrast somewhat akin to the Bales dichotomy. My view is there there are these four courses of action and that different personalities are more or less successful with each style. One might agree with Hall that perhaps the best example of leadership is the innovator who can also persuade others of the correctness of his vision. These are the entrepreneurs who bring together meaningful ideas, money, and men into some coherent team. There has been a surprising lack of emphasis on this leadership style, perhaps because of its rarity.

Our analytical problem is to understand when the dominant coalition might change. Our thesis is a simple one. The dominant coalition will change when it is perceived to be ineffective. Since coalitions can prove their leadership skills in more than one way, they tend to be relatively stable over time. Succession has tended to focus on changes in the top leaders. This is not necessarily the same as changes in the dominant coalition. If the new leader is promoted from below, he or she is likely to come from the dominant coalition. If he or she is selected from outside the organization, then almost by definition there is a change in the dominant coalition. The new man will try to place his lieutenants in key positions, that is, to create a new team and a new dominant coalition.

Even when promotions are from within, they can reflect the creation of a new dominant coalition. When the board selects an individual who has been in opposition to the prevailing management philosophy the intent is clearly to shift to another way of demonstrating effectiveness (Donaldson and Pugh, 1977). Nor does the new president have to be in actual conflict. Boards will decide that the environmental conditions dictate new ways of demonstrating effectiveness and seek out such a person from the management personnel available. In large organizations enough variety exists that particular individuals can be found.

In the succession literature it has been observed that sometimes new leadership is related to failure and sometimes it is not. The crucial point is that there are many reasons for turnover in the top position — it is not just a function of failure. This is why it is better to focus on the dominant coalition. Leaders come and go, but dominant coalitions remain.

To put the problem in other terms, we want to predict when succession means a change in the dominant coalition and when it does not. The former power process means at minimum a qualitative change in the power structure. The latter power process means the continuity of the power structure across time.

To predict this requires understanding how changeable values and personality characteristics can be. In the previous section, general value orientations were assumed to be relatively stable. The same might be said about personality characteristics. Since this micro assumption is so critical to our analysis, we might make it quite explicit as our second major premise:

5B   The general values and personality characteristics of individuals remain relatively stable across time.

This does not deny the possibility of radical personality change by means of some process such as psychoanalysis, but only that it is rare and unlikely. Nor does this deny the possibility of a certain small incremental change. All the assumption asserts is a consistency in personality and fundamental values for most people most of the time.

Standards of effectiveness alter because of changes in either the internal organization or external environment. If they do, then the dominant coalition must change so as to have a new set of values and a new set of personality characteristics. Insofar as stability tends to be the rule, the only way to shift organizational objectives is to change the nature of the dominant coalition. This is consistent with the idea that different kinds of situations (Fielder, 1967) require different personality characteristics. Not only do new leaders emerge in new situations, but — equally important — leaders with new values and characteristics emerge.

Our basic assumption above is helpful but it does not allow us to make predictions until we can identify the key situations and the personality characteristics needed to handle them. Our previous discussions can now be integrated. If there are different kinds of effectiveness, then these can be used to classify situations. If there are different values associated with these situations, then the appropriateness of the elite's choice of objectives can be predicted.

5.3.1. The Causes of Succession

Much of the discussion of leadership has focused on the style of leadership — whether the leader is supportive or authoritarian. This seems to miss the main point. *What leaders must do, and what dominant coalitions must do, is select the correct course of action as Selznik (1949) has suggested.* Simon (1964) and others have found goal a useful concept since it reflects the direction in which one wants to move, an intended course of action as well as a desired end point.

My perspective is that leadership essentially revolves around the importance of correct decision outcome. If nothing else, leaders should be competent at selecting the correct course of action for the organization and getting others to agree to this choice. If the organization is in a situation where an emphasis on quality and innovation are most likely to improve the chances of survival, then the dominant coalition needs to pursue this objective. However, if the external environmental change, for example, has made costs important, then the coalition or power elite has to shift to a more universal service or mass-produced product cutting costs as much as possible.

But what is the correct course of action? Most studies of the relationship between succession and various measures of effectiveness have found only modest support for the idea that failure leads to turnover in the top management. Part of the difficulty lies with the measures and part with the definition of what is success or failure. This is a very relative concept. Furthermore, the standards for many organizations are not clear. Ignoring for the moment the research on sport teams, which present unique difficulties and are therefore perhaps not very generalizable, the alternative ways of being effective make evaluation complex. If one organization's goal is low cost, then quality does not enter into the evaluation except when some limit is exceeded. If another organization's goal is high quality, then efficiency does not become part of the calculation of success. For these reasons profit measures, growth in sales, and the like (see Seashore and Yuchtman, 1967, for a number of examples) may be totally irrelevant in some organizations, even those with the same technology and environmental context (Lawrence and Lorsch, 1967 a and b). Under these circumstances, sometimes succession occurs for lack of enough cost reduction even when the performance is more efficient than a quality conscious one. Or in some situations, the dominant coalition may change because it does not have a high enough innovation rate in new products. Without knowing the objectives or standards of effectiveness, one cannot make predictions about changes in the dominant coalition. We thus can agree with Goodman and Pennings (1977) that effectiveness is contingent and the contingencies must be known.

We are interested in predicting under what circumstances succession means a change in the dominant coalition – that is, a new coalition with a new set of objectives. To make this prediction we need to have some assumptions about effectiveness.

The first premise is borrowed from Parsons (1956). Organizations must maintain four functions in order to survive and grow in prestige or profit: innovation, quality versus quantity of outputs, cost efficiency, and member motivation to participate (or morale). The second premise is buried in a single sentence in Parsons's writings (Parsons, Bales, and Shils, 1953:182), but was a critical part of Bales's work (1950). He emphasized the incompatability between adaptation and integration – in our terms, innovation versus cost. Furthermore, as we noted above, quality and quantity appear to be in opposition as well. The dynamics of succession, goal change, and effectiveness then unfold within the parameters of these two premises:

5C *To survive, organizations must maintain a minimum level of innovation, efficiency and morale, and a balance between quality and quantity.*

5D *The more that innovation and quality are emphasized, the more difficult it is to maintain a minimum level of quantity and efficiency, and vice versa.*

These premises are saying several things. Continued emphasis on innovation means that eventually costs will become too high. Continued emphasis on quality means there is not enough volume of production. Eventually a very effective dominant coalition is perceived as ineffective because there is a deterioration in the overall capacity of the organization to survive. Here is a typical sequence of events. A dominant coalition emphasizes efficiency; the deterioration in quality will eventually lead to customer resistance, which is manifested in declining sales. The organization has a crisis. Management is replaced. In another and opposite scenario, the dominant coalition overemphasizes quality, the deterioration in efficiency will eventually lead to resource controller resistance, which is manifested in smaller budgets. The organization has a crisis. The administration is replaced. This would be an example of where following bad performance, but one that flowed from overachieving relative to the goals of the organization. This corresponds to Caplow's idea (1964: 126–34) of points of stress. Every organization has them.

Our hypothesis is:

5.15   If the dominant coalition overemphasizes some objectives of the organization, it creates ineffectiveness in others and is replaced.

Admittedly quantifying the prefix "over" is not simple. Furthermore, this hypothesis leaves open the possibility that the dominant coalition may achieve a balance in the objectives, a problem that is analyzed below.

Whether or not a shift in objectives requires a change in the top leader and his/her team depends upon how much adaptability one sees in leaders, their personality characteristics, and their basic value orientations. The more these are perceived as relatively enduring, the more apparent it will be that a shift in objectives requires a change in the power structure – a new dominant coalition. This internal weakness is not the only source or cause of an organizational crisis, that is, a failure in one or more objectives.

The other situation that produces a crisis is a change in the environment that requires a change in organizational goals and standards of effectiveness. The environment can be stable for long time periods, and then suddenly there is a qualitative break. Kuznets-like economic cycles (1967) can predominate for ten or twenty years, favoring one standard of effectiveness, and then change, forcing new standards to be adopted.

The hypothesis is:

5.16   If the standards of effectiveness change, then the dominant coalition will be evaluated as ineffective and will be replaced.

All the hypotheses relative to structural variables and general values and the choice of objectives in the two previous sections can be cited as reasons why the dominant coalition should be replaced with a new one. Major shifts in the environment which necessitate new organizational objectives are rare, but when they occur they can lead to a long period of confusion in the dominant coalition. Typically they will stumble around, attempting to continue to do what they have done previously – it is what they know best – and be unable to cope with the new circumstances. Caplow (1964: 148-54) has discussed the complacency of elites as a basic problem. One sees this in the context of environmental change.

Failure is frequently not recognized. Dominant coalitions can be stable over very long time periods. There are a number of reasons for this, some of which are already implied in the previous hypotheses. Overemphasis may not occur and balance may be more or less achieved. This is most likely to occur when the dominant coalition is large. The hypothesis is:

5.17   *The larger the size of the dominant coalition, the more it will attempt to achieve a balance in its emphasis on objectives.*

One of the advantages of rule by committee is that there is not a single mindedness. Rough edges of ideas are eliminated. Extremes in emphasis are avoided. As we have already noted, the organic forms are likely to have this characteristic because of the high concentration of specialists and low decentralization of power.

Deciding when the dominant coalition is ineffective is not as easy as it sounds. Measuring quality is very difficult; therefore determining the effectiveness of the dominant coalition is difficult. Becker and Gordon (1966) have noted the importance of the visibility of consequences. Also see Becker and Neuhauser (1975).

5.18   *The less visible the effectiveness of the organization, the less change in the dominant coalition.*

Besides the presence or absence of a particular standard, the stringency of that standard counts as well. Failure occurs more or less rapidly depending upon not only the visibility of the standard but the expectation of attainment. Simon's (1958) idea of satisfying rather than maximizing is relevant here. The lower the expectations, the less likelihood of failure. Dominant coalitions thus engage in behavior that tends to make the measure of effectiveness difficult and the probability of being evaluated as successful high.

5.3.2. The Consequences of Succession

A new leader, even when the organization is successful, can change the goal, that is, ways of demonstrating effectiveness. New leaders want to prove themselves. A simple way is to shift slightly the emphasis in objectives. However, a change in objectives is most likely to occur with a change in the power structure, and more specifically in the dominant coalition.

*5.19 When a new dominant coalition emerges, it will tend to emphasize the
opposite objectives of the previous elite.*

When a new leader is appointed by the board, presumably he surveys the needs
of the organization. He may even be appointed with a new designated mission:
to cut costs, improve morale, or stimulate innovation — that is, to change the
goal focus. *The important point is that the new leader's mandate rests on correcting the deficiencies of the previous administration.* If there is some incom-
patibility between objectives, then any new leader starts with a ready-made
problem and an opportunity to prove himself. The previous administration
focuses on innovation and is likely not to have been cost conscious. Then the
new person can put somewhat more emphasis on efficiency. This should be
understood primarily as a variation on the basic theme of effectiveness appropriate for the organization. Unless it is a crisis produced by a shift in the environment or by faulty management, in which case the board will give the new
executive a specific mandate, the problem of correct action becomes one of fine
tuning. Organizations are in a moving equilibrium over time solving the inherent
dilemma posed by premises 5C and 5D. Succession produces slight shifts in goal
emphasis that try not only to maintain a typical effectiveness style, but to
eliminate the worse deficiencies of that style.

The four kinds of objectives represent a future area of research. Are there
personality types more suited to each one of these four ideal-types of effectiveness? Some people appear better equipped to cut costs, while others have a flair
for innovation. Still others are socio-emotional leaders. This means than that not
just anyone can do a specific job. Instead individuals with certain characteristics
are chosen as leaders to do certain jobs. A change in the environment occurs
and the board decides that they must select a new leader. This leads to a change
in the dominant coalition as follows: Boards of directors will announce that
given the current state of the market they need someone who is good at cost-
cutting. They choose the vice-president of finances as the next president. If the
man selected was part of the old coalition, then there is no change, by definition, in the dominant coalition. But equally critical, despite the mandate there
may not be enough change in the emphasis on cost-cutting either. Because the
person selected was a member of the "old guard," he/she has been socialized
into one set of values, and may find it difficult to change his/her patterns of behavior. After a period of time, the board may realize its mistake and seek an out-
sider who can bring about the desired change in goals.

A boards of regents, dismayed over the internal conflict of the university,
will select a president with known socio-emotional skills who can pull administration, faculty, and students together into an effective team. Given the problem, they are most likely to seek candidates from outside the university, who are
not associated with any faction.

Once a new man or woman is appointed, he/she proceeds to appoint his lieutenants, who reflect his/her perception of organizational priorities, to key positions. A new dominant coalition has emerged with a new set of objectives. They may fail and be replaced but the dynamics remain the same. One starts with the appointment of a leader, but it is necessary to see how a team is created across time through key appointments, the reshuffling of appointments to committees, and the like.

The major hint of a shift in organizational strategies comes with the creation of a new dominant coalition. This is almost always true with the appointment of an outside leader. When the new leader is selected from within one must determine whether he/she was previously a member of the existing dominant coalition.

The major dynamic cause is the internal conflict between goals. In one sense it is a no-win situation. Organizations are partially failing most of the time – even though we do not realize it – regardless of what course of action the elite selects. The succession of leaders and their selection of objectives is a continuous search for equilibrium between incompatible functions. The succession of dominant coalitions is like a gigantic phase-movement (Bales, 1953) between, first, an emphasis on production and cost cutting, then quality of product or service, and then innovation and the development of new products or services, to be followed by a consolidation period which in turn leads to new concerns about production, cost-cutting, and so forth.

These premises and the theories of Chapter 2 provide a scheme for classifying leadership situations. It can be done first by knowing the structure of the organization, and second by knowing the areas of previous emphasis or priority. These then classify what style is appropriate and which priorities should be taken. In general, organic organizations tend to be weak in the area of cost-cutting and concerns about expanding production, while mechanical organizations tend to be weak in the area of product innovation and morale. But beyond this, all organizations must rotate their emphasis between these goals if indeed these are all functions necessary for the maintenance of the organization (as Parsons, 1956, has argued) and assuming that: (1) the priorities are somewhat in opposition and (2) the personality characteristics for achieving these goals are also somewhat in opposition.

The model can be made more complex by rating the environment and its impact on the organization. Although environmental changes from stable to unstable – to continue with the Burns and Stalker (1961) idea – are rarer, they do occur. Environmental change requires a change in objectives and ways of demonstrating effectiveness.

This model helps explain the generally weaker relationships between structure and objectives. Given the necessity for all four performances and the alteration in emphasis, the strength of association is reduced.

This section can be closed with a final question: Does leadership make a difference? The answer is yes, provided the set of leaders recognizes the need for balance in priorities over time and correctly identifies current organizational deficiencies — and then chooses the appropriate actions to correct these deficiencies. The theory presented here is designed to aid this process.

Clearly as the concentration of specialists declines and the centralization of power increases, the importance of the top man becomes great. And there have been remarkable men who have built or reshaped organizations — Eliot at Harvard, Jane Addams at Hull House, Sarnoff at RCA., Gilman at Johns Hopkins, Land at Polaroid, and so forth (see Chandler, 1977 for other examples in business). But today it is becoming harder and harder for a single man to so shape an organization. The team approach, the variety of specialists, the complexity of the environment, the need for joint decision-making make the stamp of one man or woman less and less likely. This is the era of the dominant coalition.

5.4. CONCLUSIONS

One process that maintains the structure of an organization is the low risk routine decision. Another process that has the same consequence is succession. Usually succession of leaders means the continuation of the status quo. However, succession in the dominant coalition implies at the minimum a shift in values and therefore in organizational priorities. It is not quite a transformation in form unless there is an extreme crisis, but that problem is left for Chapter 8 where the issue receives extended analysis. Rather, it is a qualitative change, a replacement of one elite by another.

Here we have complicated our typology of forms in two ways: first by recognizing that there are inherent dilemmas or contradictions in achieving all goals simultaneously, and second by recognizing that both the structure and the values of the dominant coalition influence the choice of organizational objectives. In Part Four this model is made more complex when the impact of the environment is considered as well.

The concept of goal or objective is best seen as an intended cause of action for the organization. Effectiveness is seen as being achieved in more than one way. Together these approaches to these concepts suggest how both ideas can be revitalized in the context of sociology.

PART TWO

Change: Structure, Process, and Adaptiveness

Chapter Six

Structure and Changes in Outputs

Change, like power, is a word that has had a wide variety of meanings difficult to encompass in a single definition. Any part of an organization can change: goals, work-flow, structure, location, personnel, technology, finances, etc. Some changes occur quite infrequently, such as the change from custodial to therapeutic goals in a mental hospital (Greenblatt, York, and Brown, 1955), or from revolutionary to evolutionary goals in a political party. Some changes occur almost daily, such as turnover growth in personnel size and alterations of the budget. Some changes appear to be quite important: increased centralization or a dramatic loss of prestige or profit. Some changes appear to be quite trivial: changes in plant layout or organization chart. But even these generalizations are subject to many qualifications because all depend on the magnitude of the social change; that is, how many people are affected — both inside and outside the organization.

A common definition of innovation is a change of idea, practice, or behavior (Zaltman, Duncan, and Holbek, 1973). But if change is everything, it becomes almost nothing. There is no qualitative distinction; no separation of what is meaningful change.

The systematic nature of the organization is better appreciated in social change studies because alterations in one part are frequently interrelated with changes elsewhere. Studies of the introduction of change, and especially of a major alteration, become a way of understanding the causal connections in the organizational system. For example, Woodward (1965) did several case studies of organizations that shifted their technology from batch to mass production, or from the latter to continuous production, and found that the structure altered accordingly — not by design but by necessity. Greenblatt, York, and Brown (1958) observed the consequences of changing the technology for mental patients from custodial care to milieu therapy and discovered that, again, the form of the organization had to be altered. These studies also indicate that by focusing on changes in technology or the production process, we may be locating a significant kind of social change.

Most of the work on change in the last ten years (Zaltman, Duncan, Holbek, 1973; Hage and Dewar, 1973; Moch, 1976; Kalusny et al., 1972; Gordon et al., 1972; Daft and Becker, 1978) has focused on changes in outputs – that is, the creation of new products or services for customers or clients. The researchers have not used this word, but usually their term has been innovation. However, if one examines what is actually studied, it is either new products or services, as in the work of Aiken and Hage (1971) or Dewar and Hage (1973), or new tools or techniques, as in the work of Kalusny et al. (1972), Gordon et al. (1973), or Moch (1976). Daft and Becker (1978) studied what they called technical innovations and administrative innovations. Many of the latter do not affect either input, throughput or output, however. There is a close connection between technological change and program or activity change since new outputs usually but not always imply changes in the inputs and the processes or throughputs of the organization at the same time. Because organizations are input, throughput, and output systems (Katz and Kahn, 1966), it becomes difficult to change one aspect of the production process without changing others.

Technological change is the usual term in the economics literature (Mansfield, 1968; Christopher Freeman, 1974); but again a closer examination indicates that many of these changes are in the basic production process. Again, this literature emphasizes the necessity to distinguish between process and output changes (Freeman, 1974; Abernathy, 1978), which corresponds to the distinction in the sociological literature between new programs and services (which are new outputs), and changes in tools or techniques relative to existing outputs.

In one sense, although it has not been conceptualized as such, output change represents a change in organizational goals, but goal with a small "g." There is a change in product or service but not a change in performance. Frequently, the new products or services are incremental developments that do not appear to be discontinuous to the members of the organization. These are natural developments, given the number of different outputs or product mix of the organization. Thus, the addition of an adoption program for black children in an adoption agency, or the development of a tape deck in a hi-fi electronics company are obvious extensions of these organizations' technology, skill, and expertise. They do not represent major alterations, as they would if the organization moved into a totally different product line: for instance, if the adoption agency added a halfway house for convicts, or the hi-fi electronics firm produced infra-red ray stoves. These would be quite discontinuous changes relative to the existing technology of the organizations. Economists have made much of the desire of managers to employ under-utilized resources as a basic motive for product development, but these innovations utilize the existing personnel and equipment.

One additional general point: Sometimes researchers (Daft and Becker, 1978) prefer to restrict the term innovation for the first time a product or service is offered – for example, the first time a frozen food is produced or the first time a half-way house opens its doors. The difficulty is that these occur quite infrequently. In the next chapter where we analyze radical innovations, some attention is given to these kinds of changes. In this chapter the bulk of the analysis is on changes for the organization.

Our analysis in this chapter is on changes in the production process – that is, changes in either inputs, throughputs, or outputs. In Chapter 8 we focus on changes in the form of the organization – that is, transformation, and especially adaptation. Here the emphasis is on the many incremental changes occurring, whereas in the next chapter, radical innovation is given special attention. This definition potentially leaves out managerial innovation, (Kimberly, 1978) but it is also possible that these may be either changes in throughput or form.

Why limit the concept of organizational innovation to changes in the production process? *First,* these changes have been the dominant focus in this literature. Although called by many names, most of the theoretical conceptualization and research has implicitly had the production process in mind, and this is a good place to begin. *Second,* output changes imply changes in goals, the availability of new products or services, attempted solutions to either real or imagined needs (Hage and Aiken, 1970: Chapter 1). Having television, dishwashers, nuclear energy plants, penicillin, supersonic planes, audio-visual aids, milieux therapy for mental patients, and so forth represent important events not only for the organizations that first produced them but for the larger society as well. In various ways, these changes have touched all of our lives and not necessarily always in positive ways! Even more fundamentally, changes in the production process call attention to the definition of what is an organization. This is consistent with our systems perspective. The addition of a new product or new service may mean the creation of a new organization, depending upon whether it is discontinuous in technology from the existing techniques and skills of the organization. In other words, these changes have a special theoretical relevance.

Third, changes in outputs have been the major practical concern of many governments. The development of new products has been seen as the major way of maintaining the balance of payments, ensuring employment, raising the standard of living, and in a word, surviving in international competition. The government's focus has been primarily on industrial organizations, but they have also been interested in the problem of how to develop new health, education, and welfare programs. (Indeed, most of the research that has been funded has had this set of concerns.)

Fourth, changes in throughputs or outputs relate to the basic issue of the role of technological change. Although economists have been sensitive to this kind of change, organizational sociologists have largely ignored it. Yet it is primarily technological change that necessitates changes in the production process or leads to output changes or both. Again, it is the centrality of this kind of innovation that dictates our interest.

Whether for theoretical or practical reasons, this kind of change is worth our analytical emphasis. It does not cover all kinds of social change but it does represent the majority of changes that do occur in organizations. And in Merton's phrase, this kind of change represents a strategic site for a number of analytical issues.

As with power, the analysis of change is done in three chapters, each concerned with a different analytical problem. This chapter analyzes how the structure of the organization affects the rate of innovation in outputs, throughputs, or inputs. The crux of the analysis builds upon Burns and Stalker, and on Hage's axiomatic theory in Chapter 2, seeing the presence of two basic kinds of organization form. Here no qualitative distinctions are made between major and minor changes; those with low and with high risk. These problems are left to Chapter 7, which analyzes the innovation process. Most of the discussion there focuses on the processes associated with radical innovations. Although there are many ways of classifying innovations, radicalism taps what is a critical dimension which subsumes many others because it implies major changes in the form of the organization as well. Implementing radical change implies a transformation of the structure, that is, adaptation. Here the themes of resistance and conflict become important and, correspondingly, the strategies for overcoming them. Chapter 8 focuses on the basic process of adaptation and the transformation in form that can occur. The concepts of equilibrium and disequilibrium are defined and illustrated. The transformation from one state of equilibrium to another frequently requires passage through one or more states of disequilibrium. In fact, it is usually disequilibrium that leads to a recognition of the need to at least search for a different organizational form.

Within this chapter the main focus is on the structural causes of output innovations. This is a major practical problem: how does one organize to increase innovation? This topic has exercised the minds of various policy makers in the highly industrialized countries (for example, see the special Organization of Economic Cooperation and Development series on industrial innovation). One finds many research projects largely devoted to this question (but where the economists have done most of the applied work to date, see Mansfield, 1968 and Christopher Freeman, 1974 as well as the research programs of the National Science Foundation).

To answer our practical problem of how best to organize, we can begin with the human relations paradigm. Although this approach is usually perceived as a social psychological one (for a good review see Katz and Kahn 1966), there are structural implications in T-groups and other techniques designed to facilitate change. They usually discuss the power structure. Following this early tradition

(Coch and French, 1948) came a structural-functional paradigm, as in the work of Burns and Stalker (1961) and Hage and Aiken (1970). (See also Zaltman, Duncan, and Holbek, 1973.) However, many of these articles and books suffer theoretically because their premises are not clearly stated. Once these assumptions are made explicit, the hypotheses they suggest can be tested vis-à-vis the existing research findings.

The second section focuses on the inevitable qualifications. Not all output and process innovations are the same – some are important and some are trivial. Likewise, not all innovation rates are the same – organizations have periods of rapid changes and periods of consolidation. Once one adds these kinds of qualifications, many of the structural hypotheses are limited in scope. In particular, the theory of elite values, introduced in the previous chapter, must be synthesized with a structural paradigm, creating a more complex theory predicting output and process innovation.

When one shifts to the micro level, the focus is not on output innovation, new products, or services but on work creativity as reflected in patents, papers, or ideas. The assumptions used in the structural theory of output innovation are equally applicable to the micro level and are tested here as well.

A rather critical leitmotif in this chapter is the problem of measurement. Words like change, innovation, and creativity are easy to use but not so easy to operationalize. An essential argument, and one contrary to the literature, is the necessity of standardizing output innovation on ˙organizational size. Although there has been considerable discussion on the meaning of size (see Mansfield 1968; Freeman, 1974: Chapter 6), almost all studies have used crude or raw scores. Yet almost all research has indicated that size is strongly related to innovation. Hence there is a possibility of a tautology. At minimum one would like to find something more interesting than the idea that larger organizations have more innovations. The empirical justification of a particular definition is equally important, especially when a departure from the existing literature is being advocated. Similarly, phrases like "meaningful change" and words like "creativity" require very careful and extended theoretical and empirical analysis, forming one of the major preoccupations of this and the next two chapters.

6.1. A MESO-STRUCTURAL THEORY OF OUTPUT AND PROCESS CHANGE

6.1.1. Major Premises and Hypotheses

The Coch and French study (1948) was a great landmark in the development of the social sciences because it demonstrated how academic ideas could be put to practical use to solve some major problems – in this instance poor morale, labor turnover, and inefficiency. Although its success has not always been repeated (for example see Bowers and Seashore, 1963), this experience as well as others have led to a new paradigm for introducing change into an organization. Summaries are never easy and never accurate, but the essence of the approach might be called the sharing of power. What was distinctive about the Coch and French (1948) study was that the workers were consulted in advance and allowed to make suggestions. A number of these suggestions were then implemented. One can argue that there was at least increased job autonomy in the implementation, if not decentralization. Even more critical was the creation of upward and downward communication that resulted in more feedback, as well as the introduction of change.

The many offshoots of Lewin's work frequently are, implicitly if not explicitly, built around the idea of sharing not only power, but status and privilege as well. Thus the T-groups are really an unstructured stimulus where at least in the beginning there are no rank distinctions among the members. The consequence is a different kind of communication — presumably more horizontal as well — that can lead to a recognition of organizational or personal problems (this technique has also been used in group therapy). This is important, because behind the idea of elimination of rank differences is the notion that there will be more effective communication, which in turn will lead to the awareness of the need for change and perhaps to the desired solution as well. Since the technique of the T-group makes everyone equal, at least initially, we might call the first assumption the equality premise. That is, if we could make everyone equal in rank, in regard to either skill, power, pay, or privilege, then we would have many more changes and ideas about new inputs, throughputs, and outputs.

There seems much truth in this premise and certainly, under various conditions, the sharing of power and of rewards would seem to be a necessary precondition for the recognition of the need for change — namely, the free flow of ideas including criticisms. Our first premise is:

6A   *The greater the equality of rank on skill, power, pay, and privilege, the greater the amount of change implemented.*

Perhaps the best example of the importance of this assumption is when managers or administrators attempt to simulate the sharing of power. This ruse is quickly recognized and the free flow of communication stops. Also the necessity of having equal skill, power, and so forth has been demonstrated time and again in the many studies of representation of various worker groups on governing boards (as cited in Chapter 3). One can try to create equal power but if it is not also accompanied with equality in these other ranks, then the advantages of equal power are quickly diminished.

The reverse of this assumption might be called the vested interest argument, in honor of Veblen, who coined the phrase. The concentration of power and status in the hands of a dominant coalition usually means their use of a veto. Those with power, the power elite, will oppose proposals of change even for new outputs, because change will upset the balance of power and thus affect their position in the hierarchy. Because lower ranking members want promotions, they will be reluctant to advocate change. Both high and low ranking members of an organization have a vested interest in not advocating change when power and status are concentrated. Implicitly, when power is dispersed, the potential loss of power is less, and the responsibility for failure is shared. When a *small* dominant coalition makes all of the strategic decisions, failure lies only on their shoulders and no one else's. Some of these intervening processes have been spelled out by Barnard (1946) and are briefly summarized in the axiomatic theory of Hage in Chapter 2.

The accent is on the word implemented. Wilson (1966) has suggested that many ideas might be initiated but relatively few actually implemented. Recent research (Beyer and Trice, 1978; Daft and Becker, 1978: 39–40) has indicated that there is little difference between the number initiated and the number implemented; they tend to vary together. In any case, we are concerned more with implemented innovations than those suggested.

The dispersion of power and status is not enough to produce and sustain a high rate of output and process innovation. Something more is needed, perhaps the key factor. There may be a great deal of equality, with few differences in skill, and yet there may not be much change because all members of the organization think alike, share the same values, and perceive the world in the same way. Indeed this is precisely why it is better to think in terms of sets of leaders and a dominant coalition rather than leadership. It alerts us to the similarity of perspective that may be necessary for the organization, for a certain time period if not forever. The members may all be part of the same occupation, as in a private psychiatric welfare agency. Or the members may all share the same values, as is typical in many public schools.

The number of different perspectives represented among the organizational members has a considerable impact on input, throughput, and output innovations. What is also necessary, both for the recognition of the need for change and the development of the correct solution, is a diversity of occupational perspectives and organizational values; that is, of interest groups. This flows from the inherent limit to cognitions which, as March and Simon (1958) noted, is a critical aspect of the human condition; but it is equally applicable at the level of an occupation group or other kinds of interest groups formed on the basis of some similarity. Similarity of perspective means, by definition, some limitation of perception and of imagination. At the same time the world – even the organization world – is complex and growing more complex all the time. Some would argue that it is too complex even to comprehend. While this point is perhaps debatable, the necessity for a diversity of perspectives – so that at least some of this complexity is comprehended – would appear to be obvious. With a greater range of perceptions and especially opposite ones, a greater opportunity emerges for a synthesis of various limited perceptions into a concrete proposal for change. Our second premise in our structural theory of change is:

6B   *The greater the diversity of knowledge, the greater the amount of change implemented.*

This assumption might well be called the dialectical assumption, because it is built much more on the notion that change comes from thesis, antithesis, and synthesis. With different occupations, in particular, there are different definitions of problems and of solutions. From this clash of perspectives, interests, and values comes a creative synthesis. This premise calls attention to change frequently involving conflict – at least the conflict of ideas. But also implied are struggles of power; Burns and Stalker (1961) noted that one motivation for innovation was the increased status achieved by the department that gets to implement a new product. We do not see innovation as something that is necessary or even desirable. The motives of the men and women involved might be quite base. Here we are asking what structural conditions encourage or facilitate innovations, not why particular interest groups advocate a new product or service.

The image of the creative scientist in the laboratory or the clever tinkerer in the garage is so much part of our history, and the names of Edison and of Einstein so much part of our education, that we have lost sight of the many major output innovations today which are essentially team products. Teams created the computer, Corfam, and the Concorde. Likewise most committee meetings in organizations involve group decision-making and the decision outcome is a joint product, usually a creative one. The importance of particular individuals may vary considerably but the decision outcome is different when *not* made by a single person. This is especially true when the decision is to create a new output to meet some unmet need. The design and the deliberation will extend over time and involve the efforts of many, as has been spelled out in the analysis of the process of decision-making in Chapter 4. To change the output is to change both inputs and throughputs, which requires many hours, days, and months of experimentation and research (see for example Ronken and Lawrence, 1952). The term research and development, R&D, refers to the long, arduous road from a bright idea to some product or service. As this occurs, no one can speak of anything but a collective product. This difference is also obvious in the education programs of universities. Some are the work of a single professor, but most involve more than one teacher. Some even include team teaching, where students are much more likely to be really creative and exciting, whereas the students trained by a single professor tend to be conformist (which is not always bad, depending on the professor). This is one reason why creative researchers produce noncreative carbon copies.

Admittedly, the importance of the single man is still debated in the litera- ture — and is a topic for the last section of this chapter — but the creative team seems to be a more fruitful avenue of research, especially in those areas where the technology is already sophisticated (Freeman, 1974). When the team is made up of different occupations and thus different technologies, interests, values, and so forth, we are most likely to get our creative solution. Under these circumstances, a dialectic, discussions, dialogues, debate, and even short conflicts occur. It is a nonviolent conflict of ideas, perspectives, and values, rather than a violent conflict based on self-interest and narrowly defined (see Simmel, 1955). But from this conflict of ideas emerges the new output or process that will be more or less successful in meeting some customer or client's need. For this reason the dialectical assumption appears to be an apt name.

These two premises imply the following hypotheses about organizational change:

6. 1 *The greater the concentration of highly trained and skilled specialists, the greater the rate of output innovation.*
6. 2 *The greater the stratification of pay and prestige, the less the rate of output innovation.*
6. 3 *The greater the centralization of power in strategic decisions, the less the rate of output innovation.*
6. 4 *The greater the normative equality of rights and responsibilities, the greater the rate of output innovation.*
6. 5 *The greater the concentration of highly trained and skilled specialists, the greater the rate of process innovation.*
6. 6 *The greater the centralization of power in strategic decisions, the less the rate of process innovation.*
6. 7 *The greater the stratification of pay and prestige, the less the rate of process innovation.*
6. 8 *The greater the quality of rights and responsibilities, the greater the rate of process innovation.*

These statements should include "and vice versa". However, the order is important because implicit in it is the notion that the structure is more likely to be the first effect in some causal sequence. In Chapter 12, the reverse causal sequence becomes important in the discussion of system change through innovation and growth.

We could also create four more hypotheses relative to the rate of input innovation but this does not seem necessary. It is even more difficult to separate clearly input from process than it is to make the distinction between process or throughput and output. What is more important is the realization that the term "change" comprehends a much larger conceptual territory than just new outputs or processes. We are back to the original concern and interest of Zaltman, Duncan, and Holbek (1973), who defined innovation as any new idea, belief, and so on. Additional hypotheses relative to other kinds of change could be derived from these two assumptions. The emphasis is on output and process innovations because of their centrality in the existing empirical literature, their current practical impact, and their theoretical significance as a kind of change that seems important, whether one examines the sociological (Hage and Aiken, 1970), business (Zaltman, Duncan and Holbek, 1973), or economics literatures (Freeman, 1974).

The objective is to keep our analysis restricted to the factors that explain the rate of innovation. But it might be observed in passing that structural change was the focus of Chapter 3, where these same variables were interrelated so as to explain the distribution of power.

These hypotheses suggest that if an innovator wants to find the best possible circumstances for trying a new idea — a new product or service, or else some new technique relative to existing products and services — he should go to what Burns and Stalker (1961) termed an organic organization. There he will find a concentration of specialists, low centralization, low stratification, and high normative equality. In the organic organization, bright ideas will be extended, corrected, and amplified as well as implemented. It isn't only the creation that counts but successful implementation as well, which is most likely to take place where the diversity of knowledge and the similarity of rank make open communication possible and probable. A number of studies have indicated that many new industrial products failed because of a lack of marketing skill, even when there was considerable manufacturing expertise (Freeman, 1974). Similarly, one wonders how many good ideas relative to the provision of human services abort for lack of a successful public relations campaign.

In summary, these two premises 6A and 6B, provide us with a number of hypotheses about input, throughput, and output changes, plus a considerable number about structural change. Although these do not represent all the forms of social change that one would like to study, they certainly include two of the three or four major categories of organizational change. Others are introduced later.

6.1.2. The Concepts and Their Measures

The task is to provide operational definitions for output and process innovations. Separating simple model changes from a really new output is difficult. The operational problem — as always — in this chapter will be to distinguish between a continuous and discontinuous change, a qualitative rather than a quantitative distinction. At best, we can only provide some rough guidelines.

Our first kind of change is defined as follows:

Rate of output innovation: The number of new products or services, relative to the size of the organization, within the course of a year.

There are three essential parts: the first is the word "new", the second is the phrase "relative to the size of the organization", and the third is the word "rate."

The product or service does indeed have to be a new one and not just a model change. Illustrations will make the definition clearer. In the automobile industry, for instance, the production of a new series each year is not normally a change in the output. Essentially it is the same kind of car, whether two-door, four-door, sedan, or coupé; whether longer or shorter, with more or less horsepower, and with greater or less variety of interior finishes and exterior colors. When the manufacturer first decides to produce a station wagon model, however, then we can talk of a new output. Admittedly, the station wagon may be made of many of the same parts, but there is enough change so that the manufacturer and his customers regard the product as a new one, relative to the particular product line previously offered. Similarly, distinctions between Chrysler, Dodge, and Plymouth are large enough so that one can regard these as differences in product. Again, they may have many parts in common, and the technology of production (the throughput) may be quite similar, but the change is great enough, nevertheless, that one can regard it as a new output. The reasons are many. The output appeals to different kinds of customers, in this instance usually on the basis of social class. Therefore, the marketing strategies are quite different. Furthermore in general whereas the technological process is approximately the same, there is considerable difference in the quality, the skill of the workmen, and the time taken to produce the product. There are, of course, a number of subtleties that are not always so easy to resolve. When is the change along some quantitative dimension big enough for us to label the new model a new *product?* Increasing horsepower should not count, but offering a four instead of a six cylinder engine does represent a change. Likewise a diesel versus an internal combustion engine clearly represents a different output.

The same problem of making distinctions exists in service organizations. A sheltered workshop may offer physical rehabilitation programs to stroke, heart attack, and polio patients. Again, in rough outline it is the same technology: namely, some form of physical therapy. Yet the differences are large enough that one would consider the adoption of any of these new groups of clients as a sign that a new service, and therefore a new production process, is being implemented. The parts of the body that need rehabilitation are frequently as different as are the physical exercises. Thus one finds that rehabilitation workers tend to specialize in one or another form of physical disability.

The major defining characteristic for the coding of innovation is that there are either some new activities involved in the production of the product or in the provision of the service, or else that the product or service is at least geared to a different kind of customer or client (Hage and Dewar, 1973). The more these new activities mean change not only in the throughput but also in the staff services relative to the production/provision, the more confident we can be that indeed the organization is innovating. The change does not have to be new for the entire industry or public sector, only for the organization. In some respects, the solution of the symbolic interactionists is applicable. If the members of the organization experience the change as new activities, then indeed it is new (but note the plural in the word members; the perception of a single person could not count).

Naturally it becomes somewhat easier to discuss the distinctions between new outputs within a particular production where the input-throughput-output is the same. It is much more difficult to maintain the same criteria across processes. The development of a more subtle and general measure will have to await future research.

Although these illustrations do not handle all of the ambiguous cases, they provide at least a rough guideline that can aid the researcher until more precise criteria are found. Besides the annual changes that occur in certain products in free-market economies, there are other examples of changes that should not be counted. The addition of new research projects should not be considered as a new output. The first time research occurs as an activity it is a very significant new output, but change in topics for research should not be counted unless they involve demonstration projects that offer new outputs or services. Closely connected to this kind of exception are those products or services that are only offered for a short period of time and not on a continuing basis. Again, as in many research projects, the output is maintained for such a short duration that it does not have a meaningful existence within the context of the organization.

More controversial is the definition of the rate of output innovation relative to the size of the organization. Why should one use a standardized rate rather than a crude rate? Everyone in the literature – including myself – has used crude rates – that is, has counted either all the innovations adopted within a certain time period (Aiken and Hage, 1971), or else has used the number from some list that has been predetermined to be fairly representative (Palumbo, 1969; Gordon et al. 1972; Moch, 1976; Kaluzny et al. 1972; Daft and Becker, 1978). The former procedure is employed more often when the focus is on new outputs; the latter procedure when the interest is in new inputs or processes, such as tools or techniques. Yet both procedures would make the comparison between General Motors and Goodwill Rehabilitation, both of whom have plants scattered across the country, quite impossible.

The need to standardize other kinds of performance has been well recognized. No one would count the number of people that quit their jobs in the course of a year as turnover (Price, 1978). Everyone realizes it must be computed as a rate, which is why it is called this. Likewise, morale scores are averaged, another way of saying that they are standardized on size. Since most research has been done on relatively homogeneous samples, and because it is not immediately obvious what would be the best denominator, the importance of standardizing innovation has not been appreciated. It is precisely when one begins to study different kinds of organizations with different technologies that one becomes sensitized to the importance of size.

Size is proposed here only because it is related to so many other variables. In the future, total assets might prove to be a better denominator. Fortunately, personnel size and total assets are so highly related (Pugh et al. 1969; Child, 1972a; Blau and Schoenheer, 1971) across a wide diversity of organizations that the former can be safely used for the present as an indirect indicator. There are theoretical justifications as well. The imagery of the second premise, 6B, is not that of surplus resources, which is one of the theoretical arguments about why larger organizations may have more innovation (Cyert and March, 1963; Wilson, 1966; Aiken and Hage, 1971), but instead the dialectic between different interest groups, prospectives, values. The key is communication and the conflict of ideas, rather than enough manpower and money to produce a new output. Another reason why financial resources may not be as important as the diversity of knowledge, for which size is a crude proxy, is that organizations whose members clamor for innovation frequently find the needed resources (Aiken and Hage, 1968; Daft and Becker, 1978: 153-54). Conversely, while the concept of slack resources makes a great deal of economic sense, one wonders if in organizations much attention is being paid to the introduction of new outputs because it will provide a better employment of existing resources. Certainly product differentiation may occur for this reason. And available monies may be used to purchase other companies, as occurred with DuPont (Chandler, 1962), and is practiced by multinational corporations (Utterback, 1971).

Despite the theoretical rationale for why the rate of output innovation should be standardized on organization size, is there any empirical justification? The answer is yes. If by standardizing innovation on size there is a systematic improvement in the amount of variance explained across a large number of variables and not only a few, and if this finding is consistent across time (that is, if it replicates) then there is a powerful empirical argument that buttresses the theoretical one. This happens to be the case at least in the Hage-Aiken panel study; the *average* variance explained (R^2) increased some 10%, and consistently so in all three waves. Furthermore, this was even true for variables not involved in the hypotheses and for findings contrary to the hypotheses, providing additional confirmation that the procedure was not arbitrary. The large number of studies reporting strong positive correlations between size and innovation suggest that a similar pattern would emerge in other research.

The third word is rate, for which one needs to count how many changes in outputs there were in a given time or how many from a given list that might be constructed as the external stimulus or state of the art relative to the organization. As soon as one begins to focus on a single new product or service — or even a type — then few of the hypotheses are necessarily correct. All sorts of historical factors can intervene. For example, Daft and Becker (1978) found a somewhat different pattern of findings for college bound innovations versus terminal student innovations in high schools. As soon as one focuses on a particular kind of innovation, the characteristics of the innovation affect the relative importance of several variables (Kaluzny et al., 1972).

The importance of studying changes in inputs, throughputs, and outputs was stressed at the beginning of the chapter. Abernathy and Utterback (1975) have observed that it is necessary to know that products go through three stages, roughly from batch to mass to automated production (to use the terms of Woodward, 1965), or the increasing automaticity of production (to use the term of Hickson et al., 1969). During these stages the relative frequency and kind of innovation will change. In the early small batch stages, the tendency is to emphasize output innovations — that is, product differentiation — while in mass production stage the emphasis is on process innovations. Freeman (1974) argues that the major technological hurdle for many manufacturers is not necessarily the development of a new product, but instead the creation of all the new throughputs — the production technology. Another stumbling block is establishing new procedures for marketing the product. Frequently only a very skilled labor force and management can evolve the appropriate technologies in their respective occupational specialties. Freeman cites the chemical and computer industries as examples.

Even more dramatic examples are provided in Chandler's (1977) definitive study of nineteenth century organizations. For example the invention of the railroad engine required a whole series of process innovations, including methods of construction, railroad tracks, grading, tunneling, and budgeting. The non T-rail came into common use in the 1840s, followed by the development of cams, sandbox, driver wheels, swivel or bogie track, and equalizing beams. The next innovations were passenger cars and different kinds of cars for different kinds of freight: box cars, cattle cars, lumber cars, coal cars, and so on. In turn, a series of organizational innovations became necessary: the development of line and staff, a through bill of lading, and the car accounting office, all to facilitate the exchange of goods between railroad companies. Typically a large number of the innovations occurred in a relatively short interval of twenty years. The growth of the railroad industry in the 1870s and 1880s was the expansion of an existing technology.

Although the industrial examples are easy to see, much of the same can be said for process innovations in education and in government. Progressive education was never successfully implemented on a large scale in the United States prior to the Second World War (Cremin, 1961) because of the difficulty of finding teachers with the appropriate skills, talents, and training. This was also a temporary problem with the new math. Audio-visual aids are still not used in many classrooms for many of the same reasons. Management by objectives, an evaluation process, has been widely adopted in many government agencies, but one wonders how well it is working. In each case, the introduction of a new technology requires not only a specific organizational adaptation of the process but a number of other changes.

A change in output does not necessarily mean a change in process and vice versa. For example, the shift from assembly line manufacturing for automobiles to semi-autonomous work groups (as Volvo did) was a very significant change in the throughput because the work flow was considerably altered (see Chapter 12), but it does not mean that there is any innovation in output. Likewise, one could use fiber glass rather than steel in the manufacturing of the car body components – an enormous technological change. The open classroom (Patton, 1972) may also represent a radical output innovation – as its advocates will argue – but one is more impressed by the many changes in input and process – the technology and processing of grade school students – rather than by the elementary school really adopting a new output. Admittedly this depends on how much one believes that a really different kind of person is socialized by means of the open-classroom. All of the evidence is qualitative but it does tend to support the idea that in fact a more inquiring kind of student is created.

In hospitals radioisotope equipment can be added, which changes the diagnostic process considerably but does not necessarily mean that new kinds of patients are being served or that a new health care program is being implemented. However, the addition of an intensive care unit is more difficult to code. Clearly it is a very significant process change, but it does not necessarily result in the addition of a new kind of output, since it is usually used for patients that hospitals have traditionally handled, such as stroke or cardiac patients.

With these considerations in mind, and with the obvious limitations attached to any illustrations, our definition for this kind of change is:

Rate of process innovation: The number of new processes relative to the size of the organization within the course of the year.

As with the previous definition, "new" is always relative to the organization. All other hospitals may already have intensive care units but if hospital X does not, the unit is counted as new for it. Again, obviously the boundaries of the organization make a great deal of difference in counting the rate and in standardizing it as well. Many of the studies of industrial companies have been at the multi-organization level, as for example DuPont, General Motors, US Steel, and the like.

It would be desirable to have another definition for input innovations, but in fact it becomes very difficult to maintain the distinction between input and throughput whenever there is some new technology. There are enough difficulties in making operational distinctions between process and output innovations without further complicating our measurement task. In practice inputs and processes can be lumped together, until more refined research procedures are developed.

6.1.3. The Findings

We do not have as many studies on the relationship between the characteristics of the social structure and rates of process and of output innovations as we do of organizational structure. However, there are several large studies by Hage and Aiken on output innovations, by Gordon et al. (1972) and Moch (1976) on process innovations, and by Daft and Becker (1978) on both, that allow us to test the plausibility of the structural theory that has been advanced.

In an as yet unpublished study of the American shoe industry by Cohn and Tryn, I found that when one focused on specific technological innovations, such as the use of proportional grading, rise-flow molding thermoplastic box toe machines, automatic needle positing, heat setting, and the like, the relative importance of particular variables changed considerably. However, when these specific innovations are added together, that is, a rate is computed, there is considerable improvement in the amount of variance explained and several measures of the concentration of specialists become the dominant explanation (see Table 6.1). This is a particularly fascinating study because the shoe industry in the United States has declined in the face of foreign competition. New machines have been developed that would make the industry more competitive but they are not being purchased. The results of the Daft and Becker study of high schools are reported below, illustrating the same general point. The impact of the structural variables is not vis-à-vis specific kinds of innovations but across a rate.

In the study of the shoe industry economic explanations about the size of the company or, perhaps more critical, the number of times that the machine manufacturers contacted the shoe manufactures were explored. The multiple regression of ownership, the two measures of the concentration of specialties, personnel size, and the number of visits per year by representatives indicates that size has a strong *negative* partial on innovation standardized ($r_p = -.38$), but the effect of managers per employee remains ($r_p = .42$), and the partial of the specialties/manager, ($r_p = .27$), is slightly larger than the zero order correlation. The number of visits has no influence and ownership only some; the $R_m = .65$. Put differently, what counts is not contacts but whether managers or specialists are monitoring the environment; it is not size or slack resources but instead the concentration of specialists.

Why personnel size is negatively related to innovation standardized will not

Table 6.1   The relationship between structure and the rate of process innovation

Input-process innovations in the shoe industry (Cohn and Taryn, n.d.)

	Innovation Standardized
Concentration of specialists	
Managers/employment	.41
Managerial specialties	.17
(*N*)	(302)

Input-process innovations in hospitals (Moch, 1976)

	Innovation Nonstandardized
Complexity	
Occupational specialists	.67
Functional departmentalization	.66
Centralization	−.43
(*N*)	(386)

be explored here except to point out that this finding is quite consistent with a large number of studies on the relationship of size and innovation. In a large study conducted by Gordon et al. (1972), De Kervasdoué found that the larger hospitals had a diminishing rate of adoption of technological innovations. Utterback reported in an article in *Science* (1971) that the large industrialists, despite having their own R&D departments, purchased 60% of their new products from small companies, usually by purchasing the company and its management. Across three waves and some 15 years of organizational experience, Hage-Aiken found that the logarithm of personnel size was consistently and negatively associated with innovation standardized, the zero-order correlation varying between -.40 and -.50. Some of the reasons for the negative relationship are statistical; that is, the use of size as a denominator in a ratio variable and as a causal variable means a large probability for a negative relationship. But there are theoretical reasons as well. In fact the existing theoretical arguments for the relationship between size and innovation standardized on size would all predict a *positive* correlation. The thrust of slack resources says that as size increases arithmetically, innovation should increase geometrically. Similarily, any argument about economies of scale in research and development would have the same impact. Clearly this and other studies do not support this line of reasoning. The explanation for the negative association is given in Chapter 12; the growth and structural differentiation processes are perceived as having negative feedback effects that tend to dampen innovation in the future.

Although the Moch (1976) study does not compute innovation standardized on size, a path diagram is reported that allows one to infer the probable relationship. The innovations again are technological and in only one area, respiratory disease. The zero order correlations between two measures of complexity — the number of functional specialists and the number of functional departments — are .67 and .66 with the crude rate of process innovation; centralization has a -.43 correlation with this rate. More important, when a multiple regression is performed, where personnel size is assumed to cause specialization and these in turn cause innovations, we have something more like the concentration of specialists and the innovation standardized. Also included is the unique contribution of having an inhalation department in the hospital. The partial correlations with innovation are r_p = .20 for occupational specialists, .18 for functional departmentalization, .18 for personnel size, .24 for the presence of an inhalation therapy department, and -.12 for centralization. The positive partial with size suggests that, if actual ratio variables had been constructed, the partials between concentration of specialties and innovation standardized might have been stronger. The impact of the inhalation therapy department indicates how the presence of a functional unit encourages technological innovation in that area and is in effect another proxy for the concentration of specialists, in this instance specialists relative to the innovations being studied.

In the reanalysis of the Hage-Aiken panel study, one finds that the concentration of specialists has a relatively high and consistent relationship with the rate of output innovation (see Table 6.2). To reduce the spurious correlation caused by the common denominator of log size, the concentration of specialists is computed as the variety of specialties relative to the number interviewed, which has little relationship to the logarithm of personnel size. The correlations between the concentration of specialists and the subsequent rate of output change are .66 and .46 respectively.

Table 6.2   The relationship between structure and the rate of output innovation

Output innovations in mental hospitals, residential treatment, welfare agencies, and sheltered workshops (Hage-Aiken panel study)

	Innovation standardized	
	1964–1966	1967–1969
Concentration of specialists	.66	.46
Professional train	.06	.14
Professional act.	.50	.36
Centralization (nonparticipation)	−.39	−.11
Stratification	−.64	−.00
(N)	(16)	(16)

Table 6.2 (continued)

Output innovation in public health departments (Palumbo, 1969)

	Innovation standardized (proportion of effort expended)
Professionalism	.37
Centralization (lack of influence)	−.63
Stratification (ratio of income)	−.34
(*N*)	(14)

Output innovation in colleges and universities (Blau, 1973)

	Innovation standardized (proportion of new departments)
Complexity	
Number of departments	.35
Mean number of publications	.30
Centralization	
Initiative	−.20
Salary influence	−.18
Policy	−.18
Nonfaculty control of appointments	−.31
(*N*)	(115)

Output innovation in neighborhood centers (Heydebrand and Noell, 1973)

	Innovation standardized (demonstration projects)
Complexity	
Number of branches (locations)	.48
Number of programs (outputs)	.32
Proportion professionals	.32
Size	.25
(*N*)	(122)

One might assume that in this instance the organizations with the high innovation rates in the prior period of time are those with the high innovation rates in subsequent time periods. Indeed, this would be consistent with our understanding that an organization is a system of variables and, furthermore, a system that is in moving equilibrium. As changes occur in the concentration of specialists there are changes in the rate of innovation and vice versa. The correlation of rates of output innovation unstandardized across time are moderately high, that is varying around .50 (using the standardized rate would increase artificially the association because of the relatively similar denominator). But these are not perfect correlations by any means. Furthermore, the correlation between the innovation rate unstandardized in 1961–1963 and 1967–1969, that is, one three-year period removed, is only .29. There was a considerable shifting among organizations during the various time periods. More important, the rate of output innovation in some organizations doubled with the influx of money for the Great Society programs during the Johnson administration. This meant a disturbance in the equilibrium of the organizations in health, education, and welfare, which took a considerable amount of time to dampen.

The crux of the second premise is the diversity of knowledge. Concentration of specialists is one measure of this. Equally important are measures of the level of skill and expertise. The average level of professional training, which tends not to be related to other structural variables, has little impact on the rate of output innovation; the correlations are .06 and .14 in the three waves. Professional activity, which taps more directly the implied argument about the awareness of a more complex world and represents an external communication link with that environment, is even more strongly related to the rate of output innovation, being .50 and .36. In the second period there is a decline, presumably as the flood of welfare dollars in the War on Poverty diminished the importance of organizational variables. For both alternative measures of the diversity of knowledge, there is little difference whether one takes the prior or subsequent innovation period, suggesting two directional causality.

Structural differentiation – that is, the number of departments and of levels – could be a measure of the diversity of knowledge as well (Hall, 1977: Chapter 5). However, both of these variables have weak and consistently negative relationships with the rate of output innovation. Most surprising is that the number of departments, which one might assume to be the most direct measure of diversity of knowledge, has its strongest negative relationship ($r = -.32$ and $-.10$ respectively) in the first time period before the equilibrium of these organizations was disturbed. Structural differentiation appears to be measuring something quite different and again we are led to the conclusion that this variable is not necessarily a substitute for the concentration of specialists, especially when used across a variety of organizational types.

When one examines the impact of centralization on output innovation, a different picture emerges. Instead of a relatively consistent pattern of association, one finds a changing pattern. As predicted in the first time period, centralization of strategic decisions has a negative relationship, $r = -.39$. But in the second time period the relationship diminishes. It becomes positive, albeit really zero in the third wave. How does one explain this? The answer would lie in the relatively large increase in public funds available for many, but not all, of the organizations.

The same can be said for the pattern of associations between the prior innovation rate and stratification, here measured by the proportion of lower participants. In the period of 1964–1966, largely but not completely before the influx of federal funds, the association is as predicted, $r = -.64$ but it disappears during the second time period. This panel study suggests the importance of timing in the pattern of association. If the research happens to occur just as there is some major change in the external environment it can affect the results.

This does not mean that the organizations might not look quite the same after a certain period when the external stimulus stabilizes. In this particular study, many of the associations were returning to the 1964 pattern (Hage, 1978). The changes in the associations reflect the time it takes the various variables to achieve a new equilibrium state, a problem discussed in Chapter 8.

This problem of timing may also explain some of the *negative* findings in other research. For example, a study of junior colleges in 1969 found that the number of specialties was positively related to innovation (neither variable standardized) in outputs as predicted, but also positively related to centralization. Unfortunately, the later variable was based on mail questionnaires with only few being sent and with high refusal rates. Measurement errors could be enormous. If one accepts their results as valid, however, then the reversals might be a function of the large number of programs instituted during the late 1960s. This research is also complicated because the innovations had to be approved by a state board that approved all requests. The board may have tried to achieve balance in program development, allowing those organizations with fewer programs to implement more. These could be organizations with more centralization and leadership concerned about "catching-up"!

The Palumbo study (1969) largely replicates many of the findings in the Hage-Aiken research, although the way in which the output innovation is standardized is quite different. In 14 public health departments, which varied in size from 67 to over 1000 employees, Palumbo measured what percentage of the total time was devoted to 15 new programs (from a list representing programs that professionals in the field had emphasized as being important and new). As can be seen in Table 6.2, those departments with a greater effort in innovative programs were those likely to be less centralized ($r = -.63$), have less stratification of pay ($r = -.34$), and have a higher average level of professional training ($r = .37$).

In his study of universities and colleges, Blau (1973) counted the number of departments in anthropology, biochemistry, biophysics, journalism, linguistics, microbiology, nursing education, statistics, and urban studies, and then computed a ratio to the number of existing departments, so that in one sense there is standardization. This is not the same, though, as standardizing on personnel size or student size; nor is it the same as the rate of innovation within a certain time period. Therefore one would anticipate weaker correlations with the structural variables. The zero-order correlations are reported in Table 6.2. The number of departments, which are usually functionally arranged in universities is a considerable underestimate of the concentration of specialists and has a positive correlation of .35. Various measures of centralization have a negative impact. Blau reports one partial correlational analysis, which unfortunately does not include number of departments or faculty control of appointments, but does include the logarithim of personnel size (faculty). Size still retains a positive association (r_p = .28) and the centralization measures he uses have negative partials (r_p = -.23 for initiative and -.22 for salary). Again, strong support for the idea that centralization discourages the development of new outputs – in this instance new academic disciplines.

In still another study, Heydebrand and Noell (1973) report positive associations between the unstandardized number of demonstration projects (new services), and several different measures of complexity, number of branches, number of outputs, and proportion of professionals. All have moderate correlations with the number of demonstration projects. (They are called R&D by the authors, and therefore there is some question whether they are new outputs or research projects, but the examples provided suggest more the former than the latter – that is, new services and therefore new outputs). Given the very high correlation between size and the number of branches and the number of programs, and yet the low association between size and the crude rate, it seems likely that ratios might improve the correlations between these indicators of complexity, especially if a more direct measure of the concentration of specialists could be found. There was almost no relationship with number of hierarchical levels; it was positive (r = .11), in contrast to the Hage-Aiken study.

Equally interesting is the research in school districts reported by Daft and Becker (1978). The study illustrates the importance of the definition of boundary. In this instance the district is the correct boundary because each high school produces essentially the same output, albeit in different neighborhoods. It is at the district level that the basic decisions are made about program and where resources are allocated. Daft and Becker argue against complexity as a variable (see 1978: 136-43) and instead divide their sample into two kinds of innovations: those for college bound students and those for terminal students. As can be seen in Table 6.3, both complexity and centralization have the predicted associations. Professional training has a strong positive relationship with innovations for college bound students but a negative one with innovations for terminal students. They note that if they had added together the two kinds of innovations, then professional training would not have had any association. But dividing a sample into two parts needs some stronger basis than this. In fact, the general law of science is parsimony. One wants explanations that work for various kinds of innovations. If the innovations had been divided into high and low risk or along some other general attribute this would be desirable, but to partitition on the basis of content is to produce the wrong pattern. It is also interesting that professional training measured in the same way as in the Hage-Aiken study has essentially no pattern across all kinds of innovations.

Table 6.3 The relationship between structure and process and output innovations combined

Process and output innovations in high school districts, Daft and Becker (1978)

	Innovations Unstandardized For:	
	College bound students	Terminal students
	(1968–1972)	(1968–1972)
Professional training	.65	-.31
District size	.41	.54
Complexity	.24	.27
Centralization	-.11	-.33
Pro-change elite values	.47	-.10
(*N*)	(13)	(13)

The positive correlation between size, measured here by number of students, and number of innovations suggests that if innovations were standardized, the correlations with complexity (especially if it is standardized as well), would improve.

Beyond this there is another reason why complexity or the concentration of specialists may be a more critical variable in predicting innovation, and that is its association with the structural variables. Daft and Becker (1978: Table 15) found that complexity was associated with decentralization, as one would expect from Chapter 3. However, their measure of training (which uses only a single indicator, presence of a masters degree) has a negative association. It is this consistency in the overall pattern of findings, rather than just correlation size, that gives more credence to a theory. Thus, even though they argue against complexity, their own data support the importance of the variable. We can only speculate what the concentration of specialists would show, since the data have not been reanalyzed.

In a study designed to test the adequacy of the differentiation-integration thesis of Lawrence and Lorsch (1967), Gabarro (1972) contrasted two urban school systems on the number of new services developed for the Puerto Rican population, which was on the increase in the two districts. From the data presented, it is clear that the school system with the higher innovation rate had a higher concentration of specialists, and this was computed on a per pupil basis.

In summary, what can be said is that for those studies where innovation is standardized on size, the concentration of specialists appears to be a critical variable. Centralization has an impact — a negative one — but its influence is less consistent depending on whether the organization is going through a sudden surge of innovation. *In the Hage-Aiken study, there were a few organizations among the original sixteen, and also among the thirteen added in the third wave, that provide illustrations of how a new dominant coalition can lead to a high innovation rate, even if the decision-making is largely centralized.* A custodial mental hospital appointed a professional interested in making the organization a place of treatment. There were hardly any occupational specialties, and even the nurses were not trained as psychiatric nurses. He systematically introduced a number of new services that were in effect considered normal for this kind of client population. In effect, there was a "catching-up."

The same or a similar pattern occurred in several Catholic agencies that were breaking their ties with Catholic Charities and seeking public funding – again in response to the surge in monies during the War on Poverty. To be eligible for public funds, they had to add both professional staff and a number of new services. This was done largely by decree rather than through discussion and participation. This is the same pattern of "catching up" described above. The organization's dominant coalition recognizes that there is a certain array of services that are expected and proceeds to implement them. But implementation occurs in a centralized power structure. (The use of centralization as a strategy for overcoming resistance is discussed in the next chapter.) In turn, these findings suggest the necessity for finding an alternative explanation for when centralization is positively associated with innovation in products or processes.

6.1.4. A Special Problem: Values and Innovation

The power-value paradigm was suggested in Chapter 5 as an important set of intervening variables in understanding the interrelationship between structure and performance. The essential insight is that if the dominant coalition has a set of values, these can be used to predict which objectives will be pursued. In turn these objectives are translated into courses of action that then have a major impact on performance and one independent of structure. In the analysis of change, we have a special case of the relative importance of values versus structure in determining innovation rates. In this specific case, we would expect dominant coalitions with pro-change values to steer organizations towards higher rates of innovation than one would otherwise expect on the basis of the concentration of specialists and the degree of decentralization. In fact, when centralization is positively related to innovation it may be because of a dominant coalition having these pro-change values.

Most of the attitude studies of change have focused on cosmopolitanism versus localism (Merton, 1957: Chapter 10; also see Rogers, 1962) as an important orientation that facilitates change. But when one examines the questions employed, they frequently represent indirect measures of professionalism and of information search in the environment (the original concept developed out of a study of *Time* readership), and the like. These do tap indirectly individual openness and knowledge about new problems and their solutions but are still perhaps not the best measure. While it appears to be an exception, this research reflects the correctness of our basic premise about diversity of information. It also supports the hypotheses in Chapter 5, which predict a positive association between cosmopolitanism and the objective of innovation.

The correctness of these relationships is demonstrated in the Daft and Becker (1978) study. They found that elite values (the superintendent and school board) relative to innovation had a strong positive correlation with desires for quality ($r = .54$) and with one kind of innovation but not another ($r = .47$ for college bound innovations and $-.10$ for terminal innovations). Interestingly these values had a positive association with centralization, although not a strong one ($r = .32$). Together they suggest that values of the dominant coalition can vary independently of structure, or in fact may even be positively related to centralization. Values for innovation are associated with concerns about quality, as was suggested in the Chapter 5. Finally, the objective of innovation is not always translated into the performance of innovation. Unfortunately Daft and Becker did not determine who the dominant coalition was on the basis of their participation in basic decisions. Instead, they assumed the board had the power. As was suggested in Chapter 3, this needs to be tested. If the dominant coalition among the administrators and teachers, including high school principals, had been measured and if they had pro-innovation values, the pattern of correlations might have been much stronger.

In his study of 115 colleges and universities Blau (1973) found that the proportion of faculty with a strong local allegiance had a negative correlation of $-.30$ with the recency of the creation of a new department, and still retained $r_p = -.23$ when several other variables were controlled, including faculty size and various measures of centralization. Unfortunately, again the number of departments was not included in the multiple regression analysis, although it does have a zero-order correlation of .24. Again one might predict that the ratio of this to faculty size might prove to have a stronger zero and partial correlation with this variable. But the point remains that local allegiance is *negatively* related to his measure of innovation in outputs.

Kaluzny et al. (1972), in their study of innovation in hospitals and public health agencies, found — in a stepwise regression — that generally the cosmopolitanism of the administration or the staff had a high correlation with the amount of process and production innovation among a list of designated innovations (see Table 6.4), even when holding constant degree of risk, change values, and professional training.

What is more relevant is the impact of change values, an attempt to measure the goals of the administration and the staff. This is found to have an important impact in a stepwise regression analysis, except in hospitals where the innovations involve high risk. In this particular instance, it is interesting to observe that

Table 6.4   Values, risk and innovation

Process and product innovations in hospitals and public health departments
(Kaluzny, Veney, and Gentry Study, 1974)

	Hospitals	Public health departments
Low risk:		
Cosmopolitanism of administration	.00	.38
Cosmopolitanism of staff	.34	.45
Professional training	.32	.39
Change values of administration	.22	.32
High risk:		
Cosmopolitanism of administration	.19	.47
Cosmopolitanism of staff	.25	.32
Professional training	.21	.60
Change values of administration	.04	.30
(*N*)	(59)	(23)

the impact remains despite the control for their measures of staff and administrator values which would tap prochange values. This study indicates that the choice of change objectives is related to cosmopolitanism and may in fact be the cause of it. Unfortunately stepwise regression analysis assumes simultaneous causal impact rather than some causal path. Our theoretical argument would be that cosmopolitanism causes a concern about innovation, professionalism causes a concern about quality, and the two together impact on the rate of innovation in an organization.

In another study of the relative effectiveness of values and structure to predict output innovations, Hage and Dewar (1973) found that the values of the elite defined not on the basis of the formal position but instead on the amount of actual participation in all strategic decisions all of the time again affected innovation. the partial correlations reveal that the values of the dominant coalition are critical for explaining the amount of output innovation and represent a quite distinctive force from the key characteristics of social structure (see Table 6.3).

What is especially interesting about both studies is that they suggest that centralization may not have much of a role, and in some circumstances may be even positively related to innovation if there are change values. Under these circumstances, centralization can be positively related to the innovation rate. Thus Corwin (1973) finds in study of the Teacher Corps that more input-process change is introduced into schools when they are centralized and the faculties are political and liberal, and when the university has high quality, suggesting

Table 6.5 Values, structure, and innovation
Output innovation in residential treatment homes, mental hospitals, welfare agencies, etc. (Hage and Dewar, 1973)

	Structural variable	Elite values	R^2
	r_p	r_p	
Complexity			
No. of occupational			
specialties	.57	.71	.59
Professional activity	.58	.75	.60
Centralization	−.37	.70	.48
(N)			(16)

again high change values, although they are not measured directly. The impact of change values coupled with centralization may also help explain the negative findings in the study of junior colleges reported above. How centralization can have a positive effect on innovation is discussed in the next chapter as an example of the revolutionary strategy of change.

Much of this literature can be summarized as:

6. 9 *The greater the emphasis placed on the objective of innovation by the power elite, the greater the innovation rate.*

This hypothesis also helps explain how change agents can affect the amount of innovation in an organization. If they can make the dominant coalition adopt a pro-change value orientation, which then becomes crystallized as an organizational objective, then there is the possibility for a considerable increase in the innovation rate.

Admittedly this hypothesis, which says that people with power do what they will do, is not very interesting. To know that if the dominant coalition has a pro-change value, it is likely to pursue innovation strikes the lay person as the kind of common sense that gives the social sciences a bad name. However, we have tried to make the argument more complex by asking what variables can predict pro-change values as was done in Chapter 5.

Furthermore the measurement of the dominant coalition, which Hage and Dewar defined as those with power (as measured by standard centralization batteries), makes the thesis somewhat more interesting. It is not the top echelons, another common-sense view. In particular, it is not usually the board. Sometimes common sense is right and sometimes it is wrong.

6.2. RELATIVE CHANGE BY PRODUCTS
AND PERIODS

From the discussion of the definitions of new outputs and processes, in the examples that have been provided, it is apparent that not all new outputs and new processes are the same. Some are more "new" than others! The same theme has also emerged from the discussion of strategic decisions, some of which are quite risky or uncertain and others much more routine. One of the more interesting examples of qualitative differences is the concept of the change team which has been introduced into schools or school systems with the expressed purpose of providing a steady and continuous innovation stimulus. Likewise, some manufacturing organizations, such as Texas Instruments, have been concerned with how to institutionalize change and fight against the continuous tendency towards satisficing (March and Simon, 1958) and the avoidance of risk.

Most of the high risk decisions used as examples in Chapter 4 were in fact the introduction of qualitatively different products or services. Chandler's latest analysis of the development of the modern corporation (1977) provides a series of examples which, while appearing obvious once mentioned, indicate that not all innovations are the same. Among others, let us just mention: railroad, telegraph, telephone, sewing machine, refrigeration, automobile, synthetic textiles, and so on. In the area of education, the development of graduate education and of progressive education represent quite qualitative breaks with the past. In health, the tuberculosis sanitarium and the half-way house are examples.

The qualitative distinctions among innovations have been widely recognized in the innovation diffusion literature (Rogers, 1962) where the properties of innovation have been used as a major explanatory force in understanding different speeds of diffusion. Among others, there are initial cost, continuing cost, rate of cost recovery, pay-off, social approval, saving of time, regularity of reward, divisibility for trial, clarity of results, association with existing technology, and so forth (Fleigl et al., 1968, quoted in Zaltman, Duncan, and Holbek, 1973: 34). Likewise a number of authors have proposed other dimensions as well, but the major themes or most critical dimensions would appear to be radicalness, cost, and divisibility. The research of Kaluzny et al. (1972) has demonstrated that many of these dimensions or characteristics are inter-related; they suggest lumping them together under the basic dimension of low versus high risk. And this is much the same as radicalness. The sole advantage of the latter term is that it places the accent on the extent of the innovation rather than the likelihood of its adoption by some organization — the perspective of much of the literature on risk. Zaltman, Duncan, and Holbek (1973) explicitly define risk as radicalness or difference from the existing situation.

6.2.1. The Prevalence and Importance of Radical Innovation

Knight (1967), in particular, has called attention to the importance of radicalness as a major dimension. Radicalness is defined as the creation not only of a new output but also a new input and throughput. It represents a qualitative distinction rather than a quantitative one. Although these are at best questions of judgment, one is struck by the relative unanimity with which people can agree about the larger radical changes that have occurred in the last century. These are the ones that everyone tends to talk about and to remember. For example, the production of a car, plane, radio, television, computer, and so forth represent major departures involving not only new production technologies but a wide variety of other changes, including marketing, logistics or raw materials, and the like (see Chandler, 1977, for an extensive analysis of this). All of them occurred in new organizations which, as we shall see in the next chapter, tend to have been in the past the simplest solution to the problem of overcoming resistance. Equally important are the great breakthroughs in the people processing organizations, although they tend to be less well publicized: vaccination, open-heart surgery, engineering education, open classrooms, half-way houses, and so forth. *Again, and particularly for the older radical innovations, we find that they are developed most often in new organizations with new personnel as well as new processes and outputs.*

How rare is radical innovation? In the 15 years in which Hage and Aiken studied a number of health and welfare organizations, there was only one single innovation that could even begin to qualify as radical: the introduction of community therapy with the complete reorganization of the staff into teams based on geographic areas of the city. This was one change among about one hundred observed or one percent. Hage-Aiken attempted to measure the cost of each new output that was adopted and found that all organizations practiced the principal of divisibility – that is, new services were started on a very small scale. If successful, they were expanded; these executive directors kept their risks minimized as much as possible.

In manufacturing organizations one finds essentially the same pattern. The radical change is rare, almost by definition. Most organizations produce minor changes when they introduce new products. There are exceptions however. The chemical industry has been one where radical change has occurred relatively frequently, and perhaps most importantly, in existing companies (Freeman, 1974). Likewise the computer, electronics, and electrical industries have shown a tendency towards radical change – the production of new products with new technologies – although it may be debated as to how radical a shift has occurred with each new generation of computers or the change from hi-fi to stereo. What is perhaps more critical is the willingness of these corporations to diversify and add entire new product lines, as have General Electric, IBM, Westinghouse, RCA and so forth. These corporations have not only made radical departures from the existing variety of available products, but also discontinuous changes relative to their own product lines. But these are the exceptions that prove the rule. One is more struck by the lack of radical change in most industrial sectors, and especially in the large well established companies such as AT&T, General Motors, General Foods, US Steel, and so forth, where a policy of incrementalism is followed: small changes rather than radical ones, and changes that do not move into divergent new areas relative to existing technology. Many of the radical changes have tended to start in small companies that grow after the products have proved successful on a mass scale: Xerox, Polaroid, Texas Instruments, Hewett-Packard, and so forth.

The same general pattern holds in the area of education. Most of the radical changes of the nineteenth century started in new organizations such as the Rensselaer Institute of Technology (engineering), Johns Hopkins, and the University of Chicago (graduate education). Again there were exceptions, such as at Columbia, Yale, and Harvard Universities, where critical reforms were made in old institutions, (founded in 1754, 1701, and 1636 respectively), affecting graduate education, medical education, and teacher education. The University of California has followed the policy of creating different kinds of education on different campuses, much as DuPont builds new plants for new outputs. These are structural equivalents to new organizations, especially when we realize that these are multi-organizations already.

In many of these examples, it is important to keep quite clear which multi-organizations (such as universities and electrical equipment corporations) are moving into the creation of new and radical departures. Some multinational corporations do not. Sheer size and availability of slack resources does not necessarily mean a strategy of radical innovation (Utterback, 1971). Quite the contrary! We return to this problem in Chapter 13.

Many of these examples also illustrate the other two dimensions that are useful for characterizing process and output innovations: divisibility and cost. Divisibility is important because if it is possible to break an innovation into pieces — the idea of incrementalism, so important in decision-making — then both radicalness and cost are considerably reduced. For example, purchasing a computer does not just involve initial cost but also the addition of soft-ware, the hiring of new specialists such as programmers and key punchers, the retraining of clerks handling information, the redesigning of the accounting inventory and other information systems, and so forth. In this instance we have an innovation that is not easily divided into segments to be adapted piecemeal. The divisibility clearly influences the radicalness as well. If an innovation can be subdivided, absorbed in segments, then its potential for shock to the system of variables is considerably reduced. Indeed, one of the interesting properties of most really radical innovations is that their potential in many areas is usually underestimated. This has been the typical pattern with computers which have usually been adopted by organizations to do one job such as cost accounting. It is only later that other potential uses are recognized and implemented.

Radical innovation is especially interesting because it represents so many special problems of process, including difficulties of implementation, the likelihood of conflict being engendered in the organization, and the lack of immediate acceptance by potential customers or clients externally. Its rarity is due in part to the many almost insurmountable problems involved in the change process, some of which are discussed in the next chapter.

Still another reason for studying radical change is that there are many unmet social needs. If one adopts the model of the perfect society, or even the Great Society, then it is clear that not only are we light years away from utopia but that many of the solutions – even for the problems that are recognized, which says nothing about the ones not recognized – require radical changes on the part of existing organizations such as schools, stores, corporations, cooperatives, and hospitals, or the creation of very new kinds of organizations. Even forgetting some absolutist or ideal standard, the current interest in post-industrial society (Bell, 1973) reflects the recognition that there has been a qualitative change along the quantitative continuum of industrialization. The societal problems that exercised Marx, Weber, and Durkheim have also changed in quality. But have our organizations also transformed themselves? Where are the new outputs for post-industrial society? Beyond this we need to ask what kinds of organizations will provide these new outputs. We seem far removed from the new institutions that are needed.

6.2.2. A Theory of Radical Innovation

Given that radical change for both its rarity and importance – deserves a special theory, then we need to specify the theoretical and operational definitions.

Degree of radicalness: A change in input, process, and output that represents significant departure from existing technologies and their corresponding products or services in the larger society.

The key to radicalness is not only that it is a significant departure from existing technology for the organization but also for the larger society. Daft and Becker (1978) and others have preferred to restrict the term innovation to just this meaning. Here we are concerned with the first one or two organizations that produce the product or provide the service, the leaders in the field. Although a radical change is by definition a qualitative distinction, it also can vary because the significant departure itself can vary in degree.

Indeed, one is struck by the fact that in some industries, such as electronics, computers, precision instruments, and drugs, and in some public administration sectors, such as universities and hospitals, the rate of qualitative change is so fast that the distinction between what is a breakthrough and what is not is no longer easy to draw. One speaks of generations of computers, of the continual increase in the speed of aeroplanes, of new families of drugs, of the evolution from hi-fi to stereo to quadraphonic sound, and so forth. The research of Kaluzny et al. (1972) and of Freeman (1974) allows us to begin to *quantify* the degree of radicalness. Although I have emphasized the qualitative distinction of radicalness, it is a variable that subsumes across several dimensions. We have already suggested high cost and lack of divisibility as critical components. But it is not the only way of proceeding. Besides looking at the degree of change in the inputs, one can study the degree of change in the outputs.

In general, the simplest approach is to quantify some improvement in the performance utility. Quantum leaps then become breakthroughs. For example, the one-half decrease in flight time with the Concorde is quite easily measured. In the case of the shift from black and white to color television we have the addition of a new dimension to the product. With the open classroom the utility may be the sense of self-worth. With many drugs or surgical techniques, such as penicillin or open-heart surgery, the standard is either rate of recovery or extension of life. And so forth. People will disagree on which utilities should be employed in making the judgment of a breakthrough and how much of a quantum leap there must be, but the degree of radicalness is in principal measurable. And since it is measurable, it is also therefore predictable!

One of the reasons to be concerned about the different characteristics of process and output innovations is that one can well imagine that different hypotheses are necessary for different degrees of radicalness. Knight (1967), in a provocative theory of organizational search, has suggested that organizations are not likely to be open to radical innovations unless there is some crisis. He identifies two major kinds: underutilized resources and declining acceptance of the output. Of the two, it is the latter that is much more likely to lead to radical change, not only of new outputs but of the entire organizational structure (such as in community mental health, the example cited earlier from the Hage-Aiken research).

The presence of underutilized resources or slack is applicable to DuPont (Chandler, 1962), General Electric, IBM, and many of the other large companies that have had a history of supporting more radical innovations. Probably the large endowments at Columbia, Yale, and Harvard have facilitated their early movement into new areas and forms of education. It is harder to document cases of considerable failure leading to radical change, although that is always a question of degree. Certainly the continual profit failure of Ford Motor Co. pushed its management into new directions, as did the same phenomenon for

US Steel (Hage and Aiken, 1970), but their new product outputs were hardly radical new technologies but instead incremental changes. Indeed, one is struck more by their lack of attention to performance gap, to use the theory of Zaltman, Duncan, and Holbek (1973). In fact, something is missing from the theory of performance gap, and that is the importance of values in affecting the perceived need for radical innovation.

If one turns to studies that have attempted to measure the innovation properties (see review in Zaltman, Duncan and Holbek, 1973) one is struck by four important points. *First* most of this research has not focused on the kind of radical changes that have been used as examples here. The sheer rarity of this almost forces one into a case study approach. Therefore much of the existing research that has tended to quantify aspects of output innovations may not be relevant to much of the foregoing discussion, and specifically to Knight's thesis. *Second,* what research there is indicates that in various ways the concentration of specialists is important in both high and low risk innovations. In the Kaluzny et al. (1974) research this was tapped by the extent of specialist training and the cosmopolitanism of either the staff or administration (see Table 6.4). While the particular importance of these variables varies, the general pattern remains and confirms that largely irrespective of the extent of risk, cost, and so forth, this variable tends to retain its predicative importance. However, it should be noted that innovation was not standardized on size, although size was included in the multiple regression equation.

Third, and most interesting, the importance of centralization does vary both by kind of organization and risk involved. It would appear that certain kinds of innovations can occur when organizations are centralized. Centralization can be positively related to either innovation or periods of a particular kind precisely because the participation of a large number of individuals in the decision-making process is likely to dampen both the radicalness of the innovation and the speed with which changes are introduced. Decentralization is a stabilizing force which, while it encourages higher rates of innovation, is much less likely to be associated with either radical departures or with large bursts of change when many aspects of an organization are likely to be changed at the same time. This has been implicitly an argument or assumption of the conflict school, and it would appear to be correct under certain stipulated conditions. *Centralized organizations can introduce highly radical innovations if the dominant coalition has positive attitudes towards change and indeed pursues a pro-change policy.*

And this leads to the *fourth* important point, namely the relatively consistent importance of change values (see Table 6.4 and also, Rogers, 1962, although these are community studies). Only in the case of high risk innovations in hospitals does this variable appear less crucial. The combination of the concentration of specialists and positive change values leads to the potentiality for high rates of output innovation or even the possibility of radical change. This can even occur when the organization is somewhat centralized. But while the change values of the dominant coalition diminish the importance of the structural variables such as centralization and stratification, they do not appear to affect the importance of two other variables: one structural, the concentration of specialists, and one functional, the previous rate of output innovation. These two variables plus the values of the dominant coalition in the Hage and Dewar study (1973) accounted for 70% of the variance in the subsequent rate of output innovation. This special issue of how the past affects the present, and how past innovation rates determine the present one, is left until the end of Chapter 12 when the organization is seen as a system of variables, and the positive and negative feedbacks of innovation and growth are analyzed together.

Although none of these studies really focus on radical innovations, they suggest a multivariate hypothesis that might help explain situations where radical innovations could occur:

6.10   *The more committed the dominant coalition is to the introduction of change and the greater the concentration of specialists, the more likely there is to be a radical innovation.*

This may explain the relatively high rate of output innovation and even radical change characteristic of SNCF, the French railroad company, which has pioneered in new high speed transport and many other kinds of change. There has been a long term policy of output innovation on the part of a managerial elite with a higher concentration of specialists than is true of most American railroad companies. This also provides the causal explanation as to when a successful organization, to use Knight's term (1967), engages in slack innovation, when there is both a concentration of specialists and a dominant coalition committed to change. Not all successful organizations engage in slack innovation, only some. The distinguishing characteristic is the power elites' commitment to this organizational objective.

Why would a dominant coalition have values favoring change? In Chapter 5 we suggested that one origin of values relative to organizational innovations is cosmopolitanism. And in this cahpter we have seen that there is some support for this idea. But there can be other reasons for the adoption of innovative objectives. The answer lies in the work of Knight, as elaborated by Zaltman et al. in the concept of performance gap.

Knight's modified cybernetic model emphasizes a crisis in the form of declining demand, availability of funds, or usually both; or else the dominant coalition recognizes that the organization must catch up, requiring a burst of innovation and even perhaps a radical innovation. (We shall ignore the slack funds and underutilized personnel thesis as a source of innovation values.) Performances and availability of resources are being evaluated and found wanting. Frequently the dominant coalition may be changed precisely so that a new era in the life of the organization can be opened, as was argued in the Chapter 5. But this leaves unanswered the determination of the gap in performances. It is not just objective but also subjective. Suppose the dominant coalition may start with a positive attitude towards change. Why are some elites more pro-change than others? Some of the explanation may lie in the organizational and environmental situation, but not all. A better source for the cause of the performance gap lies in the expectations: the higher the standards of performance in the dominant coalition, the more likely it is to advocate change.

The recognition of the need for change is a function of how perfectionist the dominant coalition is. The higher their standards, the less they opt for a satisfying course of action and the more for a maximizing one, contrary to March and Simon (1958). In particular, if they set high standards for output quality, they push more for a major innovation – that is, a radical one. The dominant coalition defines the nature of its crisis and this determines search for a solution.

These ideas can be made more explicate in the following hypothesis:

6.11   The higher the standards of performance relative to outputs, the more likely the dominant coalition will be open to radical innovations.

Participant observation in a community hospital (Hage, 1974: Part One) impressed upon me the realization that two different groups can look upon the same set of facts and see different things – and both are right! One group, the attending physicians, saw *good* quality patient care. Another group, the innovators, saw *poor* quality patient care. Both were right in a relativist sense. What distinguished the two groups were their standards of performance.

Might it not be true that the people most upset with the American participation in the war in Vietnam had in effect higher standards of what it means to be a democracy and about how decisions about going to war are made? What makes Ralph Nader a crusader against the "poor" standards of corporations such as General Motors and its Corvair? Could it not be that he has higher standards – for whatever reasons – than many others?

This may also explain why in the past, radical change has been so much associated with new organizations. It is only present where a small group dedicated to some vision of the future can work together without resistance from others committed to more traditional procedures. The innovators and the dominant coalition are one and the same. The acceptance of centralization under these conditions is also more explicable; it is for the cause of radical innovation. Developing radical innovations requires some of the same discipline that one associates with revolutionary groups. Some of the special devotion to charismatic leaders, who in turn might be quite autocratic, would also fit with this thesis. Stories of some of the great organizational innovators suggest exactly this pattern, Ford being an excellent example. Certainly it corresponds to my own personal experience with the innovators that I have known — very autocratic, and justified always on the basis of the ideals they were pursuing.

In the future, the new organization may become less and less necessary as a strategy for a variety of reasons, the most important being the concentration of specialists. Once this is above a certain as yet undertermined minimum, the organization is in some state of continuous renewal. Another reason is the willingness of many large organizations to create special units where innovators can try out new ideas. This is called venture capital in business schools, but one sees the same pattern in universities where the center or institute provides a considerable flexibility, approximating but not equaling the new organization of the past.

The concept of the multi-organization also helps us to understand how new organizations can be more easily created. If a multi-organization has a number of divisions, each producing its own products and with quite different throughputs, then the creation of a new organization to produce a radically new product or service is more easily undertaken. The risk of failure at this level is reduced because of the presence of many other divisions that can provide the necessary capital and other resources. *It is not so much the availability of slack resources as it is reduction of risk that allows multi-organizations to be innovative.* But the decision is made at the level of the multi-organization, and the decision is usually to create a new organization, whether a division in a business multi-organization, a school in a university, or an agency in HEW or a comparable multi-organization in government.

What causes high standards in some organizations rather than others moves us beyond the focus of this study. Education can have this impact, but more likely it is the movement from one organization to the next, experiencing and recognizing differences, that makes one recognize potential ways of innovating. Once again we are led back by the logic of the evidence to see how important diversity is. Again, we have an understanding why those who read more, travel more, or change jobs more often are likely to be more accepting of change. They are also likely to be more perfectionist. Seeing two different solutions to the same problem usually causes us to recognize that there is a higher ideal better than either, because not only is one better than the other but both are at least partially wrong. This is one reason why when a board makes a rare intervention and wants to shake up an organization, it will bring in an outside man (Helmich and Brown, 1972). But the nature of why elites vary considerably in their standards of performance needs much more descriptive data and should be explored in future research.

In summary, the dominant coalition's values relative to innovation provide a critical exception to the structural theory of process and output change in two ways. When the dominant coalition has positive values towards change, the equality premise appears to be much less predictive. If their values are positive towards innovation and there is also a concentration of specialists, then there would be a greater probability for some radical change to occur. The importance of our second premise does not appear to be diminished when one considers the causal significance of the dominant coalition values.

Relative to the origin of the dominant coalition's choice of innovation as an objective, several new causal arguments have been given. The first is a crisis in the output – a loss or stopping of growth. The second is a crisis in the inputs – a drop or stopping of growth. The third is a change in the dominant coalition. These three explanations are quite highly interrelated and are consistent with the succession model provided in Chapter 5. Throughout all three explanations, the subjective nature of how much innovation as needed or how severe is the crisis should be understood. The concept of performance gap is helpful in this respect.

6.2.3. A Theory of Innovation Periods

There are the roaring twenties and the soaring sixties; periods of historical time when anything seems possible. The availability of funds grows rapidly. The economy is booming (Easterlin, 1968; Flamant and Singer-Kére, 1970). People experiment with alternative life styles. These periods are usually followed by swings to more conservative values and a greater distrust of change – less interest in social experimentation and more concern about the cost of things. There are eras of change and eras of consolidation. In both, the values of the dominant coalition, if not the membership of the dominant coalition, are likely to be affected. The former kind of era requires a dominant coalition with pro-change values in order to exploit the existing market situation. Just the opposite is the case during periods of consolidation. In these times, one wants to phase out unneeded or unwanted products and services, reduce the amount of product differentiation, and the like. Shifts in historical epochs can cause the breakup of the dominant coalition and its replacement by another with a different set of organizational objectives. These eras need to be seen as another kind of qualification to the basic structural theory of process and output innovation. The concept of an innovation era might be defined as follows:

Innovative era: A short time period in which there is an extraordinary number of process and product/service innovations.

For an organization that has been way behind in its rate of innovation, innovation periods are a way of catching-up. Those periods are characteristic not of leaders but of followers, not of pace-setting organizations but old traditional ones that are trying to become relevant. In computing innovation rates, they can unnecessarily give a picture of an innovative organization, as Daft and

Becker (1978) have noted. The best safeguard is to note the date of introduction and the general prevalence.

The cause of an innovation period is almost always the succession of a new dominant coalition as detailed in the previous chapter. The new leadership recognizes that the organization has a performance gap and tries to remedy this with a burst of innovation, but most of the innovations are standard ones.

Illustrations from a panel study made over a 6 year period by Hage and Aiken are of a mental hospital for chronic schizophrenics that needed updating, and of several Catholic agencies who cut their purse strings to Catholic charities when they wanted more money and had to match the current professional standards to receive public funds. These are not organizations that are or will be known for their pace-setting.

In the industrial area there are many examples. Hage and Aiken (1970: Chapter Three) report the case of US Steel which in the 1950s that had fallen behind because of lagging sales due to a lack of product innovation, the case of Ford Motor Car in the 1930s which had the same problem, and the case of a number of tobacco companies which followed a policy of purchasing products other than tobacco and thus became multi-organizations. Clearly, they did so due to a drop in sales following the Surgeon General's report on the relationship between cancer and cigarette smoking.

The theory of the performance gap (Zaltman, Duncan, and Holbek, 1973) or the concept of crisis (Knight, 1967) works exceptionally well in covering these organizations. But the crisis does not produce a radical innovation as much as a frenzy of activity that largely duplicates what already exists. It is not perfectionism or high standards, but rather more realism and finally having at least some standards that motivate the leadership of these organizations.

The qualitative differences between process and output innovations have been recognized, but the distinction between periods of high and low innovation rates has gone unappreciated as yet in the literature. Just as there can be particular innovations that represent a considerable departure from existing outputs there can be change periods that are atypical. This is another critical qualification to the general thesis of a continuum between organic and mechanical organizations given in Chapter 2. While this may be the typical pattern, there can also be eras when organizations have relatively high rates of innovation for whatever reason, followed by a consolidation era when the innovation rate assumes a more normal level relative to the structure and goals of the organization.

A more interesting phenomenon is when whole sets of organizations have innovation periods. These most typically occur when there is some technological breakthrough, such as when a new process technology is developed in the assembly-line production of automobiles or a new product is produced as in computers. This usually triggers off a flood of innovations in many other areas, new forms of organization may be created, and there is spill over into many other areas of the society. Aldrich (1979: 100–102) provides an example of this in the machine tool industry and Chandler (1977) documents the spread of the modern corporation. Schumpter has gone so far as to argue that there are long-term economic cycles created by major product innovations such as the railroad, the automobile, and the airplane. Chandler (1977) has carefully documented all the innovations that occurred in the railroad industry within a relative short period of time. The same can be said for automobiles once the concept of an assemblyline was considered. This is an area that needs much more research.

6.3. A MICRO-STRUCTURAL THEORY OF CREATIVITY

With the exception of the landmark study of Pelz and Andrews (1966), there have been relatively few organizational studies of creativity. In part this may reflect the extreme pessimism about the ability to measure creativity, a pessimism which is not entirely justified. In part, this may reflect the general lack of attention to the micro level of analysis in organizations, which we have already noted. In general the subject of creativity has been confined to the problem of research and development. Creative doctors, lawyers, teachers, managers, and so forth have been ignored. On the worker level, business studies have been more concerned with productivity or efficiency than with worker creativity – that is, the number of new ideas that they suggest. Yet increasing this would appear to be a fruitful research avenue especially for evaluating the effectiveness of semi-autonomous work groups (Emery and Thorsud, n.d.) or of various organizational designs such as the matrix organization. The real meaning of the Coch and French study (1948) is that with more vertical communication downward, the workers have a number of practical suggestions that in the long run may be the most effective way of increasing productivity. Also in line with Maslow's hierarchy of needs (1954), although perhaps not all individuals have needs for self-actualization, a sizeable number like to be creative. One important way of achieving a sense of self – something increasingly important for many men and women and especially the latter – is being creative.

6.3.1. Major Premises and Hypotheses

Traditionally we might assume that creative people have a set of gifts, a certain kind of personality, and other special psychological characteristics, that set them apart. While this may be true, these gifts can be diminished or magnified depending upon the environment in which the individual works. The work group *in which the person is a member* is his most immediate environment and is likely to be quite influential. If the person works alone, then this is an important fact about his environment. The test of the presence of a work group is whether decisions depend not so much on superiors but on peers. One would assume that the individual who makes all of his own decisions would be the more creative individual. But the thrust of the assumption and of this micro-sociological perspective is to suggest that is not the case. Man cannot stand alone. This applies to the problem of creativity as well. It is participation in a peer group, a team, that is most likely to facilitate and foster the individual's creative potential. Ideas need to be bounced off of others. This is most likely to occur in the context of a team — one where there is joint responsibility, joint decision-making, and joint sharing of the rewards, whatever these might be (and money isn't the only one, prestige or fame might be much more relevant).

The most difficult task is to define what creativity is. Frequently the research measures involve counting such things as the number of articles published by scientists. In the work of Pelz and Andrew (1966) judges have been employed to rate the relative contribution of a particular paper or idea.

Work creativity: The number of new ideas or patterns of behavior.

As with innovation, the crux of the problem is to find satisfactory definitions for the word "new". Again, the word new should be kept relative to the work. There is an enormous amount of independent discovery. The fact that others have perhaps had the idea first is not really very important except for Nobel Prize winners. For the rest of us struggling in our jobs, the bright ideas that we have are what counts.

Although the same premises as in the first section of this chapter form the core of the theory, the derived hypotheses are different. For example, the equality premise means that in work groups the creative person is an equal in power status and the like. The stimulus for creativity comes from one's peer group, and this is by definition the group defined as being alike in power, pay, privilege, and of course skill and expertise.

This leads to our first hypothesis:

6.12 *The greater the sharing of work decisions among peers with the same skill and expertise, the greater the creativity.*

The juxtaposition of this hypothesis against the one relative to job autonomy is especially interesting. *Greater and greater job autonomy is not necessarily desirable even relative to the self-actualization of the individual.* This of course, depends upon how one measures job autonomy but certainly the sharing of work decisions is not usually the meaning used; normally it means how much the worker can decide entirely by himself. Here the accent shifts somewhat to how much these decisions are shared with others. The idea is not inconsistent with job autonomy, but because the imagery of the latter does not include the parallel notion of both autonomy to decide and nonautonomy to decide alone, freedom from superior control and nonfreedom from peer control, it seems best not to use the term job autonomy since it might lead to confusion.

This seeming inconsistency with the discussion of job autonomy in Chapter 3 can be easily handled by shifting the operation to how often the individual participates in his work decisions of various kinds and whether his peer group participates as well. This is exactly skin to Tannenbaum's (1968) distinction between total control, which is the influence exercised by each hierarchical level, and the amount of influence of the bottom level, which can be a great deal. Again, there is no inconsistency, provided one does not think of autonomy as a zero-sum problem. The hypothesis could be phrased as a multivariable one; that is, the greater the sharing of work decisions and the greater the job autonomy, the greater the creativity. Then there is no ambiguity.

Hypotheses about the equality of status and privileges can be derived, but the power to make decisions is usually what counts. Although one is continually surprised at distinctions in status or privilege, it can cause depressions and resentments.

Another way of understanding the importance of this hypothesis about the sharing of decisions is that there is a difference between liberty and license. And here we have another argument that explains why the sharing of work decisions is so critical. Not only the bouncing of ideas off each other, but the need for more complex decisions which take into consideration more facets of the problem being tackled, that make the sharing of decision-making important and most particularly relevant to the utility of creativity. Individuals, even very gifted and talented ones, are more likely to make bad decisions without some system of checks and balances provided by peer group control. No control means no check on one's reasoning.

But the sharing must be with individuals that have the same skill and expertise. This is hardly a trivial qualification and is more difficult to ensure precisely because of the vast individual differences in ability. Beyond this, in our age of specialization, and especially at the post-graduate levels, one finds a world of very subtle distinctions and a bewildering array of specializations and interests. The team members must not only have the same skill and expertise but must be concerned with the same task and objective even if their training may be different. It is the level of skill and of expertise, rather than the area of training, that is most critical in this hypothesis.

This is one reason why the emphasis on a group situation in human relations is worth considering. With peers one can have a free exchange of ideas, the critique and even intellectual conflict that leads to some creative sequence of ideas. However, what constitutes a peer group is a subtle distinction that has not always been appreciated. This is one reason why the human relation technique has not worked everywhere, especially in more hierarchically organized societies such as the Latin countries. In Europe, those with diplomas from higher ranking schools would be expected to take the lead. The tradition of equality is much weaker there than in the United States so that the concept of sharing decision-making and even of a peer group is much more alien. Therefore, the dynamics of the group are different.

Micro-sociological hypotheses usually require limits. The human scale is much smaller than the organizational one — at least as far as hypotheses are concerned. Beyond this the "world" of the individual appears to be dominated by normal curves where too much of a good thing is as bad as too little. In contrast, linearity appears to be a good first approximation in the organizational "world". Hypothesis 6.12 above is already qualified. It is not just the sharing of decisions, but the sharing among peers defined on the basis of the similarity of skill and expertise. But then this is the true impact of the equality premise; it is the operation of the several dimensions together that is critical. But the hypothesis when tested requires careful consideration of what these qualifications are.

One condition is the size of the peer group or the number of individuals who share in the decision-making. Two or three colleagues can do wonders. Twenty or thirty destroy much opportunity for self expression.

Thus our hypothesis becomes:

6.13   There is a curvilinear relationship between the sharing of work decisions among peers with the same skill and expertise and individual creativity that is a function of the number of people who participate in the sharing of the work decisions.

The upper limits of improvement in creative performance are very quickly reached. As soon as the peer group becomes larger than five or six persons one can imagine that constraints start emerging by way of the development of power and status distinctions. The iron law of oligarchy rears its ugly head quickly (Michels, 1962)!

Beyond this, much of the small groups literature (Hage, Borgotta, and Bales, 1965) has indicated that the pattern of communication quickly follows the same lines so that one individual, the leader, talks the most, and with each increase in group size there is a smaller and smaller proportional input for the one who talks the least. Indeed, the equation relating group size and the communication distribution is one of those regularities that appears to be well-established in the literature. Under these circumstances information exchange and communication openness quickly disappear. The work is no longer a peer group. One can imagine a large number of psychological reasons why this communication regularity exists and why size in this sense is so important. For now, we only note the difficulty of having more than five equals in a group without some hierarchization occurring.

The second premise, 6B also has several interesting and complex deductions at the micro-sociological level. Again one might want to argue that the diversity in information and skills is important. At the micro level this is the diversity of activities in the task itself performed by the individuals being studied rather than the variety of occupations. More important is a diversity of intellectual perspectives, paradigms, and methodologies that create the true dialectic between thesis and antithesis which can lead to the creative synthesis. Again, the diversity of activities and of perspectives increases the probability that there is some check and balance on the creative thought processes, leading to a complex perception of the problem to be solved, regardless of its content.

These ideas can be summarized into two very simple hypotheses:

6.14 *The greater the diversity of activities performed by the individual, the greater his creativity.*

6.15 *The greater the diversity of perspectives entertained by the individual or by his work group, the greater his or their creativity.*

The second hypothesis is nothing more than a formal statement of the essential Hegelian insight. Individuals can entertain several paradigms at the same time, allowing the clash of perspectives, perceptions, and deductions to stimulate and formulate new insights. This whole book is nothing but an exercise in that. But it is difficult for any individual to remain equally committed to more than one paradigm. All of us feel more comfortable with one perspective. Finally, eclecticism is not a true perspective or intellectual stance, but at the level of the peer group it is much easier to work and to live with individuals who have the same perspective. The eternal dilemma! The solution lies, obviously, in recognizing the benefits of having colleagues who disagree with us. Provided that we can listen as well as talk, exchange rather than convert, and recognize the contribution of each, there is the possibility for true creativity and I might add not incidentally, self-actualization as well.

As with hypothesis 6.13, these two have limits. There is an upper limit in both activity and paradigms diversity that is quickly reached. Beyond three or four dialectics comes an aimless search which is not synthesis or creativity. The dialectic was never phrased in terms of three theses and ten antitheses — and for good reason. True synthesis is only possible with some commitment to a point of view and then the willingness to entertain the opposite idea.

The formulations are:

6.16 *There is a curvilinear relationship between the diversity of activities performed by the individual and the individual's creativity.*

6.17 *There is a curvilinear relationship between the diversity of perspectives entertained by the individual or by his work group and the individual's creativity.*

Several different activities or paradigms are stimulating, but five or six become chaos. Large amounts of diversity are possible at the meso-structural level but not at the level of the occupant of a social position, the individual. Too much diversity produces more complexity than can effectively be integrated in the mind.

These three hypotheses provide a way of understanding how the micro environment of the individual can be structured to facilitate creativity. The emphasis is on participation in a peer group defined by equality in power and skill, and at the same time diversity of activities and of perspectives, limited to five or six members -- a very special set of circumstances. One can quickly appreciate that many teams or work groups do not have these characteristics. Typically there is one person in charge: a doctor, a foreman, a group leader, a teacher, or the like. The leaderless group is a rarity.

Although essentially the same hypotheses have been derived from premises 6A and 6B at the mico level as at the meso analytical level, there is a critical difference. Most of these at the mico level are curvilinear rather than linear. The phenomenon at this level is inherently different and not to be confused with that of another analytical level. In fact, it is why separate hypotheses must be derived.

6.3.2. The Findings

Many of the ideas for these hypotheses come from the work of Pelz and Andrews (1966), whose carefully completed research study is largely devoid of theory.

In the various findings that they report, perhaps the most striking is the association between amount of time spent in research and both productivity and peer evaluations of creativity. Those who spend *less* than 100% of their time in research were *more* productive and creative. This was not dependent upon the nature of the second activity, whether teaching or administration. It did not depend upon the institutional location. But it did depend on the combination of activities. This is a very powerful argument for the importance of diversity.

A careful examination of their data suggests that the maximum given in both productivity and quality – as rated by peer judges – was achieved at between 60 and 70% time in research. This suggests that while a combination of activities is important, there still must be a central thrust. Equal time is not a correct solution.

Also relevant is their finding that those individuals who talked to people who had different perspectives than their own were most likely to be creative. The curvilinear notion of this finding was strongly demonstrated.

The other critical finding is that increasing autonomy leads to greater creativity, until the point is reached where the individual has total freedom. Under these circumstances creativity declines. Again powerful support for the notion that work decisions are best shared with peers.

We need many research studies as carefully done as this one before we can begin to specify the inflection points in the equations. The parallels in findings between this work and the meso-structural literature gives us some confidence that they will be replicated.

In a very different research study on the open classroom, Patton (1972) found support for several of these hypotheses. What is significant about the open classroom is that it is designed to produce creative children; that is, the output is a child capable of greater self-actualization. In the state of Nebraska, the New School had trained interns who were then placed in various school districts. Patton measured both a process innovation, the diversity of teaching materials, and in one sense an output innovation, the extent of individualized instruction within the classroom. He found that the decentralization of decision-making between teacher and child had a correlation of .94 with individualization of instruction and .71 with diversification of teaching materials in the 24 classrooms that he researched, most of which were located in separate school districts. It would interesting to have a follow-up study on whether the children were themselves more creative.

In a study of hospitals with psychiatric in-patient services, Rosengren (1967) found essentially the same pattern. In those hospitals where staff were allowed to have much greater variety in their work and were not restricted to a narrow specialization, the hospitals reported much more innovative treatments. Although this may be a research study more appropriate for the meso level, it demonstrates this same link between variety of work activities and variety of performance outputs found in Pelz and Andrew's research.

6.4. CONCLUSIONS

The theme throughout this chapter has been primarily the importance of diversity. Whether in occupations or perspectives, sources of information or paradigms, diversity generally produces creativity. At the individual level, a little goes a long way. At the organizational level, more than a little is needed to have any impact on performance. But here too diversity can create problems of coordination which are discussed in Chapter 12.

But diversity functions best when placed in a context of equality. This is not always true, but frequently is. The major exceptions are during periods when organizations have bursts of innovation and when radical innovations are introduced.

Essentially a structural paradigm has been synthesized with a power-value paradigm. The structural conditions can produce high or low innovation rates depending upon whether it is a combination of high concentration of specialists with a low concentration or the reverse. But the values of the dominant coalition make a difference as well. A synthesis of these two perspectives allows us considerable predictive power.

One origin of pro-change values lies in general cosmopolitanism and professionalism as outlined in the previous chapter and supported in various research findings here. Another origin lies in a performance gap that indicates organizational failure. This can occur in either the outputs or inputs, declining sales or the fall off of available funds, but in either instance leads to a greater interest in innovation as a way of suriving. Shifts in pro-change values also occur with the succession of one dominant coalition by another.

Chapter Seven

A Process of Change

Radical innovation requires a special set of circumstances before it is introduced. And while it is rare – and even more infrequently studied [the few case studies almost occurred by accident; see McCleery (1957); Greenblatt, York, and Brown (1955), and probably the one exception, Hage (1974: Part One)] radical innovation is a strategic research problem. As we study the introduction of a significant and discontinuous change, we find out exactly how the system functions. Radical innovation causes a disequilibrium. How the dominant coalition copes with the problem is instructive not only relative to their skill, but to the more fundamental and basic nature of the power structure of the organization. Radical innovations are always high risk decisions and therefore consistent with our argument in Chapter 4, they upset the dominant coalition. There is an inevitable struggle for power. When sociologists speak about change involving conflict, it is usually the introduction of a radical innovation that they have in mind. The lower participants are likely to resist the introduction of radical innovation, and one major practical problem is how to overcome this resistance. Finally, radical innovation usually involves some transformation of the organizational form. Therefore it is a process that leads to change *of* the system and just not change *in* the system.

Although a process perspective has been largely absent in organization research, the one area where it has received some attention is in studies of change (see Hage and Aiken, 1970; Zaltman, Duncan, and Holbek, 1973). Much of the intellectual effort has been concentrated on the defining stages and not enough on the creation of hypotheses. Questions that should be asked in any acceptable stage theory include: when is an organization more likely to adopt a radical innovation and when is it not; how much conflict is generated and why; is the change institutionalized or not; and so forth. Only recently has someone (Zaltman, Duncan, and Holbek, 1973) called attention to resistance to change as an analytical problem. Most other analytical issues have been ignored.

The preoccupation with stages in the organizational change process stems from the literature on the diffusion of change (see Rogers, 1962), where the imagery proved useful. But as is typical of most stage "theory" it is quite difficult to determine when a particular stage exists and why the stage is of analytical interest. To avoid these pitfalls, each stage in this chapter is defined as the activation of different variables and causal chains, an unfolding of resistance and conflict. The main theoretical justification for stage "theory" is the need for multi-variable hypothesis. Consistent with a process perspective, one would expect hypotheses during particular stages – that is, a specific set of organizational conditions – to be the reverse of what one might hypothesize during more "normal" conditions.

The ways in which meso-structure and the change process interrelate are quite complex, and at best we can only begin to sketch what some of these causal connections might be. In Chapter 4, the process of making a decision to adopt a new output is an example of a strategic decision and indeed tends to be the most frequent example of the high risk decision. In this chapter the focus is on the consequences of making the kinds of decisions that are generated during the process of initiating and implementing an innovation.

If there is a second theme in the change literature, it is the problem of how one overcomes resistance to change. The causes of this resistance are given in the second section while the strategy for overcoming resistance is the topic of the third section. There are three implicit themes in the literature that explain why individuals or groups are likely to resist innovation. Parallel to these one can find at least two strategies for dealing with resistance. The major contribution of the human relations approach to the study of organizations has been the evolutionary strategy for overcoming resistance to change. The disadvantages of this approach have been somewhat ignored, as have the advantages of a frank revolutionary perspective.

7.1. THE PROCESS OF CHANGE: KEY STAGES AND ANALYTICAL PROBLEMS

One reason there has been more attention paid to the defining of stages in the process of change than to the process of decision making is that the former process takes much longer and is much more visible, with periods of overt conflict and passive resistance. Targets are set and not met. Interpersonal strain grows and tensions mount. A number of studies (Hage and Aiken, 1970: Chapter 3) have made clear that most conflicts and resistances occur only at certain times in the change process. Therefore, distinctions between time periods during the process are worthwhile.

Although the terms vary considerably and different authors choose to accent one or two of the stages rather than others (see Figure 7.1), I continue to prefer the following four names:

1. Evaluation.
2. Initiation.
3. Implementation.
4. Routinization.

Preference for these particular names rests on theoretical grounds. There is a close affinity with the four functional problems of a social system and the group process work (Parsons, Bales and Shils, 1953). Evaluation refers to the pattern-maintenance functional problem — how successful the organization is in maintaining its relative position in terms of either prestige, profit, or market penetration, or whatever the performance standard is. It is during this stage that the analytical problem of the recognition of a performance gap is posed and that radical innovation may be selected as an option. In turn, this decision is affected by a whole series of variables, only some of which have been alluded to in the previous chapter.

Initiation is the adaptive functional problem. Here the critical issue is the search for resources and their availability. Radical innovations frequently fail because of inadequate funding or the inability to find the right kind of personnel, a problem not only of skills but of personality characteristics.

The goal achievement functional problem is the implementation stage. The innovation has an objective, namely, the reduction of the performance gap. But it is also a means to this end. The more radical the innovation, the more the way in which things were done in the past must be changed and the more likely this is to be resisted.

Finally the routinization stage refers to the integration problem. On the one hand, dominant coalitions must decide whether to retain or reject the innovation. On the other hand, special procedures must be routinized. There is a need to reintegrate the organization.

Why tie the stages into the four functional problems? Smelser (1959) has already indicated that it is useful to see change processes move through the different phases where a particular functional problem becomes paramount. I have found this quite helpful in organizing the sequence of events involved in the process of change, although I have not used the seven step model of Smelser. The central idea that each stage concerns a new functional problem is an important insight and allows one to add content to stage theory.

There are other reasons why I continue to prefer the terms as originally employed. I prefer the term evaluation because of its close connection to a cybernetic paradigm, a point emphasized by Zaltman, Duncan, and Holbek (1973:

Figure 7.1 Different conceptualizations of the process of innovation[a]

Hage and Aiken (1970)	Zaltman et al. (1973)	Milo (1971)	Shepard (1967)
Evaluation	Initiation stage	Conceptualization	Idea generator
	Knowledge awareness sub-stage		
Initiation	Formation of attitudes sub-stage	Tentative adoption	Adoption
	Decision sub-stage	Resource getting	
Implementation	Implementation stage	Implementation	Implementation
	Initial		
Routinization	Continual	Institutionalization	

[a]Zaltman, Duncan, and Holbek (1973: 62).

55-56) in their discussion of performance gap — a significant analytical insight. In their terms, this is the knowledge-awareness substage. This is the essence of the evaluation stage: a recognition of some failure and the search for a solution. Equally important is the evaluation of various means to remedy the failure; the solution adopted must diminish the performance gap.

The initiation stage might be more accurately labeled the resource gaining stage. Most models of the process of change have tended to ignore this problem, yet it is a major reason why radical innovations may not be implemented — not enough funds, personnel, and autonomy. For example, in a study of a hosptial (Hage, 1974: Part One), although the dominant coalition decided to initiate a new medical education program to change the existing education and treatment processes, it was up to the innovator to secure funding from foundations, to recruit personnel willing to participate, and to seek the necessary approval from various departments in the hospital where the team members of the new medical education program were to work.

Almost everyone has agreed that the next stage should be called implementation. This phase starts with the first attempts to manufacture the new output or to provide the new service. The word "attempts" is carefully chosen. The more radical the change, the longer this stage lasts because frequently the first trials fail. One must continue to redesign the new output (see Mann and Hoffman, 1960; McCleery, 1957). Many innovations die aborning because of unwillingness to continue to develop the necessary technology to make the new product viable. In this sense the word development is an apt name since so much of the effect is expended in specifying the throughput. In manufacturing, this is sometimes done in what is called a pilot plant. What makes radical innovation of special interest is the necessity to redesign the entire organization. The changes in throughput have implications for the form of the organization. Typically the radical innovation requires not only a restructuring of the power structure, with a change in the nature of the dominant coalition, but a reshaping of almost everything else as well. During the implementation period, conflict and resistance are usually the greatest, since implementation requires changes in the relative power, status, and salaries of the existing personnel. Their behavior changes are frequently resisted, at least passively.

The last stage, routinization, might be labeled institutionalization, to use Milo's term. This stage begins with the decision either to keep the new output or to discontinue it. Like the evaluation stage, there is a period of reflection about whether the perceived performance gap has been eliminated, but unlike the evaluation stage, the costs are much more well known. Regardless of whether the decision is go or no go — and typically it is no go — there is a period of restabilization as the new unit is incorporated into the existing structure or eliminated. What may cause some confusion is a decision to alter somewhat the existing innovation, that is, to have another trial period. Radical changes may go through a number of trials before the throughput is routinized. These reruns are part of the implementation stage. Routinization focuses primarily on the decision to maintain the innovation or not. However, a decision to replace one innovation with anotner would mean the start of another cycle, that is, the stage of evaluation, the stage of initiation, and so on.

Stages can collapse altogether or be truncated, but there is seldom a movement back and forth. The terms evaluation, initiation, implementation, and routinization label events in any change process that must occur in the stipulated order.

Needless to say organizations can have several of these processes in operation simultaneously. However, only one radical innovation is likely to be tried in a given period. The change process can be speeded up or slowed down depending upon a number of factors, the most critical being the radicalness of the change: the more radical the change, the more prolonged and difficult the implementation period and the greater the conflict and resistance by the members of the organization.

7.1.1. Hypotheses about the Evaluation Stage

The key dependent variable is the extent of the performance gap (Zaltman, Duncan, and Holbek, 1973). Consistent with Knight's (1967) theory of crisis, a large performance gap can induce a willingness on the part of the dominant coalition to adopt a radical innovation. But this then begs the question of what produces a performance gap. In formulating hypotheses about what affects this gap, we are creating a cybernetic theory. As we noted in Chapter 1, this paradigm tends to be more of a model than an explicit theory, or if there are hypotheses they tend to be more descriptive than analytical (see Miller, 1975a for examples). The essential imagery is information feedback and the selection of some course of action. Although these ideas are central, little work has been done on when there is information feedback and why a specific remedy is selected.

Our central insight is that there is seldom information about a performance gap in many organizations. One can easily agree with the neo-Marxist critique about the relative absence of cnange, and especially radical change. But one can not so easily agree with their answer: class interests or vested interests, especially economic ones, would suffer if radical change were instituted. The reasons for the lack of radical innovation are more complex than this. They revolve around the lack of information relative to various performances and especially to the performance of innovation.

Since we are in a capitalist economy, we tend to think of profits as the measure of success. The analog for public service organizations is some vague prestige measure. But, as was argued in Chapter 5, these are not the critical performances. The ones that concern us more are the quantity versus quality of product produced or service provided, the cost of same, the innovation rate, and the level of turnover or some other measure of the motivation to participate. These and various mixtures of these determine overall effectiveness (see Price, 1968).

The first issue in the evaluation stage is, then, are there measures of each of these four functional dimensions and especially the first three dichotomies: quantity versus quality, cost versus innovation rate and human versus material costs. In the previous chapter the stress was put on values that would affect whether or not a radical innovation is likely to be adopted. Here the emphasis is on the inherent problem of getting information feedback, a difficulty which relates to the nature of measuring performance gaps.

The most typical reason for the lack of information about a performance gap is lack of a measure. For example, suppose the objective is to produce creative students. Creative students become very difficult to measure because there are no acceptable standards. How does one measure creativity? Although the measures discussed in the previous chapter are available for research institutes, there is less agreement about what might be adequate measurement for students (for one attempt, see Getzels and Jackson, 1959). The first line of defense against innovation is the statement, "It can't be measured." Quality education, quality patient care, and quality customer service are in fact hard to measure because there is little agreement about acceptable indicators. With no measurement, there is naturally no performance gap. What a comfortable position to be in! One need never fail because there is no reckoning. While this is most easily understood in the provision of services, it is also relevant to products. Even with products, one of the differentiating characteristics is the quality of service provided with the product.

Teachers resist measuring quality teaching, physicians circumvent the requirements of the American Hospital Association, and most professionals define job autonomy as *not* being evaluated. The origin of this resistance to evaluation lies in the self-interest of escaping control. A major source of professional power lies in being able to control the evaluation of performance.

Although job evaluations of professionals are rare, evaluations of whole organizations have been even more rare. How often do we collect statistics on the effectiveness of particular colleges, hospitals, welfare agencies, police departments, fire departments, and the like?

Lack of measurement does not, however, mean lack of failure. Insofar as the various functional performances are interrelated, then inattention to the innovation rate gradually has an adverse impact on other performances (see Hage and Aiken, 1970: Chapter Three for examples).

In Figure 7.2 are causal chains that spell out the consequences that flow from infrequent measurement. The less frequent the measurement, the greater the gap becomes before it is detected. If the performance gap relative to a particular variable becomes quite great, it is likely to start affecting other performances as

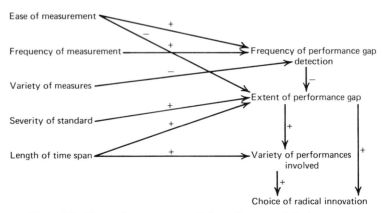

Figure 7.2   The performance gap and the radicalness of the innovation.

well. For example, there may be no measures of labor turnover, but if it continues to increase, then eventually productivity will decline, and if costs rise, sales will probably fall. The corporation is on the way to dissolution. At some point the failure is recognized. Observe that the issue is not what the organization does, that is, its actual performance, but rather the recognition or perception of failure by responsible parties, whether elites or followers. The major *"raison d'être"* of measures is to allow for finer discrimination and quicker detection. They diminish misperception and wishful thinking. It is also true, however, that quanitification can lead to an overzealous concern for only those things that are measurable, as Blau (1955) demonstrated in his study of performance records in a welfare agency. But despite these pathologies of quantification, they can lead to self-corrective action that in itself can produce a more innovative atmosphere.

Most people-processing organizations find themselves in the situation of not having agreed upon measures for their outputs. This is one of the main reasons why they are so conservative and why the rate of new outputs is low. In a large study of hospitals, Gordon et al. (1972) demonstrated that those with more visibility of performance tended to have much higher rates of process innovation.

Parsons and Smelser (1956), in their study of the economic sector of society, have argued that it is the most adaptive one. In fact, universities and research centers are more likely to be adaptive (see Bell, 1973) because they produce new knowledge and, therefore, the rate of technological change and the amount of technological knowledge increases. Those companies with environments of fast product change are forced to innovate (see Chapter 13). Some business organizations are innovative and keep developing new outputs, others are not. Two organizations, whether organic or mechanic, can have the same level of concentration of specialists, but if one of them does not measure its rate of innovation, the consequence is a lower rate of output innovation in the organization.

Health care has become much more dominated by technology than education because the output — improvement in the patient — is more apparent and easily perceived, even if not measured. No wonder we have so many different kinds of pain-killing drugs — pain is an easily detected problem. But failure to produce creative students is not as easily measured. The consequence is a less developed pedagogy or variety of technological tools for teaching creativity than there are for curing cancer, which is also an intractable problem. But note the different sums of money allocated to the two problems. Death by cancer is more visible, and it becomes a major research target of the society. This visibility of failure may explain one of the reasons why educational organizations tend to be resistant, and especially to radical innovations, whereas health organizations are more quick to try radical treatments.

Since efficiency — cost per student, cost per automobile, cost per patient — is simple to quantify, this frequently becomes the dominant performance. The real conservative bias against radical innovation stems more from a concern about costs. An expensive product is resisted on this basis alone.

The variety of performance standards is an important indicator of an organization. If only a few performances are measured, performance gaps will be detected less frequently and the innovation rate will be slower. When there are only a few performances, cost and quantity of production — such as number of clients handled or number of products produced — are the most typical standards. As the number of performance measures increases innovation rate and quality are more likely to be monitored, and if they are, there is a better chance for a higher innovation rate.

Some business organizations are now concerned about the rate at which they develop new products, recognizing that this may be the most sensitive performance of all for future survival (Hage and Aiken, 1970: Chapter 3). One now finds in the annual reports to the stockholders information about the expected product life and the number of new products introduced. This is especially true for multi-organizations where the visibility of this phenomenon is almost forced upon the top management that coordinates the separate divisions producing different products. Increasing the variety of standards thus becomes a major way of making organizations more adaptive to their internal and external problems.

Another variable affecting the detection of a performance gap is the severity of standard. Although March and Simon (1958) argued for the long term tendency towards satisfying rather than maximizing, probably the distinctive characteristic of the innovator in an organization is a perfectionism that leads to the demand for a greater effort and thus the search for new ideas, and new processes and outputs. Whether the innovator — the one who proposes a solution for a particular performance gap — is able to convince the dominant coalition of the need for innovation depands upon a number of factors. If not, then the organization remains in the evaluation stage until the performance gap grows large enough to be detected by others. There is a suggestion in the literature that innovators move between organizations until they find one that is congenial to their ideas.

In the previous chapter, the importance of values relative to change was stressed as a variable that could influence the likely rate of innovation. What seems even more important is the severity of standard used to measure especially the rate of innovation and the quality of product production or service provided.

Another variable that affects the content of information feedback is the duration of the time period used in measurement. A long time perspective increases sensitivity to the need to prepare for future events and to detect environmental change more quickly. Some corporations are interested in the quick profit, not recognizing that today's success may mean tomorrow's failure. The more the dominant coalition asks how well the product meets not only today's needs but also tomorrow's, the more they recognize the importance of a continuous evaluation of product life. The same is true for services. Although future events can not always be anticipated, long-range planning can at least increase the likelihood of appreciating more qualitative factors that need to be taken into consideration. Today's rehabilitated prisoner becomes tomorrow's recidivist. Today's fad is tomorrow's ennui. Long time perspectives make us much more aware of costs as well as benefits, and give us a much more realistic appraisal of the organization. The presence of a five-year plan is indicative of concern about where the department is going and what it is doing.

Unfortunately, the consequences of particular innovations unfold at different rates, with some becoming visible rapidly and others slowly. The major problem facing most organizations is to adopt a time perspective long enough to facilitate both short and long term evaluation. Some organizations have solved this problem by having separate units involved in operations and long range planning. The continual movement toward accountability (Bell, 1973; Perrow, 1970b: Chapter 5) is forcing organizations to adopt performance measures and to do long term planning. As both of these things occur, there is an assumption in cybernetics towards chaos or disorganization. Within the context of organizations, this gets translated into the idea of the tendency for them to move towards failure. One cause of this is now apparent. The dominant coalition fails to measure performance and, more particularly, its innovation rate.

Figure 7.2 provides a number of hypotheses about why failure goes undetected. They can be summarized as:

7. 1   *The greater the ease of measurement, the more frequent the measurement and the greater the variety of measures, then the greater the frequency with which performance gaps are detected.*
7. 2   *The more frequent the measurement and the more frequently that performance gaps are detected, the smaller the extent of the performance gap.*

7. 3   *The more severe the standard and the longer the time span, the greater the extent of the performance gap detected.*

7. 4   *The greater the extent of the performance gap and the longer the time span, the greater the number of performances on which gaps are detected.*

7. 5   *The greater the number of performances on which gaps are detected and the greater the extent of the performance gap, the more likely the choice of a radical innovation.*

There are two implications of these causal chains about information feedback. As organizations move towards greater accountability, a prediction of Bell (1973) for post-industrial society, they are likely to adopt a relatively constant and planned rate of innovation (and of product balance). This implies more innovation but less radical innovation.

These hypotheses are consistent with and help explicate Knight's (1967) prediction that organizations that experience crisis are most likely to adopt radical innovations. If all of these conditions — difficulty in measuring outputs, infrequent measurement, low standards, short time perspectives, and so on — are met, the organization is likely to slide towards massive failure, which becomes a major crisis of survival. Under these circumstances, as Knight (1967) has suggested, the organization is ready for radical change. Then the organization's dominant coalition engages in a far ranging search for ideas as described in Chapter 4, typical of high risk decisions.

This search has received more attention in some of the other stage "theories," particularly those of Milo (1971) and Shepard (1967) as quoted in Zaltman, Duncan, and Holbek, 1973 (See Figure 7.1.) They considered the evaluation stage as the problem of conceptualization and of idea generation, which are critical elements. Future research needs to consider what factors affect the kind of conceptualization or the variety of solutions generated. For example, one standard pattern for organizations in crises is to seek an outside person who then is allowed to develop solutions (Helmich and Brown, 1972). This man or woman then creates a new dominant coalition, which has a set of pro-change values.

Another area for future research is the history of the development of particular radical innovations. Ideas have origins at least in analogs. How the technology of the throughput is conceived and developed makes for a rich area of investigation.

7.1.2. Hypotheses about the Initiation Stage

Given both an organizational crisis and the need for a radical solution, the board of trustees, governors, or supervisors is likely to intervene and play a role at least in the change of leadership. This is one of their few responsibilities; they are most likely to exercise it given a crisis. Radical innovation almost inevitably involves new technologies and requires new occupational specialties. Finding people willing to take the risk, live with the uncertainty, and capable of developing the process technology is itself another stumbling block. For example, Cremin (1960) concludes in his long and definitive history of progressive education that most attempts failed because the staff could not be found which could handle the implied technology. The reason is clear. In fact, the technology had not been well-developed. Dewey had several bright ideas and some noble ideals but not enough of the former to achieve the latter.

If many radical innovations are never adopted in the evaluation stage because of the tendency for dominant coalitions to satisfy rather than to maximize as March and Simon (1958) argued twenty years ago, those selected are not likely to get off the ground because of lack of resources (see Figure 7.3).

The role of resources is one reason why the slack resource hypothesis is attractive. Multi-organizations have available to them large amounts of money that can be invested in radical innovations. But are they? The chemical, computer, and electrical giant corporations have had a history of financing radical innovations, as Freeman (1974) notes in his book. But this might be due to institutional factors rather than anything else, and they may be the exception rather than the rule when it comes to multi-organizations.

Beyond this, the most critical element in a radical innovation is the technology. It is one thing to decide to produce a pill to cure cancer and quite another to have the capacity to do it. Cremin's study of progressive education can be applied not only to many other radical innovations in education, but also in industry. The real problem is technological. And this means not only developing the necessary throughput but also finding the people with the right skills to handle the new technology. Frequently the new personnel must themselves invent many new techniques so that the production process becomes a viable one. Except for the economists, there has been little attention paid to the problem of the necessity for a new throughput or to the many problems involved in its development in the organizational literature on change (see Hage and Aiken, 1970, and Zaltman, Duncan, and Holbek, 1973 for examples).

The necessity of finding the personnel with the special qualifications may send the dominant coalition into a long search. In a study of a community hospital that adopted a radical output innovation of medical education (Hage, 1974: Part One), two years were spent gradually assembling five people willing to participate in the experiment.

The development of technology requires patience, skill, and a special set of

Figure 7.3   The radicalness of the innovation and the need for resources.

personality attributes that can fulfill this job description. The individuals involved in the development of the new processes and outputs will have to have a great deal of persistance in order to last through the frustrations of the many trials. Finding these kinds of people is not easy. Gilman (1906), when he was establishing Johns Hopkins University, traveled all over the United States to locate faculty and students for the first real graduate school in this country. In business organizations, especially the chemical industry, one starts with a pilot plant that has new personnel with special training. Likewise, the United States Navy uses special, hand-picked personnel to man its first ships that are radical departures from existing ships, such as the first guided missile cruisers and nuclear submarines. Note that the former is a new output and process and the latter just a new process innovation.

The need for new personnel thus flows from two sources. Insofar as the choice of a radical solution is dictated by a failure of the previous management/ administration, there is usually a need to replace the dominant coalition. The choice of a radical innovation diminishes considerably the likelihood that there are the necessary personnel that can handle the new output because by definition there is a discontinuity with the existing technologies.

Usually, one must search for new funds as well, because the traditional financial sources in at least the people-processing organizations are unlikely to be willing to support radical innovations. It is a mistake to try innovations without adequate financial support, as has been the case with many experiments with the open university. As Weber noted long ago, charismatic movements, which are much like the development of radical new processes and outputs, cannot survive long on altruism; they need a solid financial basis. The search for new funding sources thus becomes a critical aspect of the initiation stage. Again, the crisis nature of radical change in organization means that surplus or slack funds are unlikely to be available unless the organization is part of a multi-organization that can then direct funds into a new adventure. Since banks are generally very conservative about supporting radical changes, it becomes difficult even for manufacturing organizations to find the necessary funds to support entirely new endeavors. Again, the board can play a critical role here in helping to secure the necessary financing of radical change.

The management literature speaks of the entrepreneurial spirit as being very important. And it is at this stage – the initiation stage – that this blend of characteristics is most critical. Finding the right people, the needed cash, and obtaining the go-ahead from the board are difficult tasks. What has *not* been stressed is the importance of entrepreneurial activity in nonprofit organizations, especially with regard to radical innovation. It is essentially the same set of skills, and yet to my knowledge the concept of entrepreneur has not been employed in public administration.

Typically radical innovations require the development of new occupations.

Consistent with Daft and Becker (1978: 5), we can define a radical innovation as new not only for the organization but also for an entire institutional sector. When this is the case, one must find or even create new occupational specialties at all levels of the organization. One needs new artisans and marketing specialists, new foremen and new personnel managers, and so forth. But since these do not exist, the new specialists must be invented.

A good feeling for how this occurs is obtained in Chandler's (1977) discussion of the new middle managers in the railroads. Most of them were engineers by training and had to learn how to become managers. The necessity for this re-training and the need for a new set of skills even in management has been demonstrated over and over again each time a new technology is either added to an organization or invented. Thus, McNamara's Whiz Kids were not successful in managing Philco even though they had been at Ford. DuPont (Chandler, 1962 discovered that it had to create a divisional structure to accommodate the different kinds of technologies that had been added on through purchases at the end of the First World War.

The concept of a technological imperative (Woodward, 1965; Perrow, 1967; and James Thompson, 1967) becomes most interesting when juxtaposed with the problem of radical innovation.

These ideas can be summarized as follows:

7. 6   *The more radical the innovation, the greater the need for new personnel, funds, and technologies.*

This hypothesis verges on a tautology. It is inherent in radical innovations that there are new technologies or throughputs. What makes the hypothesis interesting is the implication about whether or not the dominant coalition actually seeks to develop the new technology, or seeks new personnel who can do so. This is the key ingredient in entrepreneurical spirit and, Hall (1977: 240) agrees, distinguishes the leader from someone who only has power. This hypothesis also proves interesting as a bridge to the causal chain during the next stage. Insofar as new personnel who have new skills are sought, the potential for conflict increases.

7.1.3. Hypotheses about the Implementation Stage

The full implication of the impact of a radical innovation on the social structure of an organization is felt only during the implementation stage. This stage starts once the funding, personnel, and technologies have been selected. Or to put it in other terms, once the organization actually tries to produce a new output, the existing personnel will encounter the frustration of being new and will begin to resist. All the tensions and conflict inherent in social change appear. The initiation stage is characterized by vision and high ideals. How else can the entrepreneur obtain his resources? The implementation stage is characterized by the opposite — dirty politics and disillusionment.

The major hypotheses relative to this stage are diagrammed in Figure 7.4. The more radical the solution adopted in the evaluation stage, the more difficult this trial period becomes. This is because as the number of new personnel and new occupations increases, the behavior changes required from existing membership become greater. Even the job descriptions of various existing occupations are altered. The new specialists will also demand a change in the power and status structure. This triggers a series of power and status conflicts. Role conflicts will be engendered by the new personnel as there is an attempt to develop a new throughput. The expectations of the new people about what others should be doing will inevitably be different from those of the existing personnel. This will create interpersonnel tension.

If the radical innovation is introduced by a new dominant coalition, then the conflict can be even more intense. The decision to produce a new output usually does not result in all the required personnel being recruited from outside. Some are recruited from within, and it may be necessary to restrain them or to alter their behavior. This will be resented. Beyond this, the new outsiders and the old insiders will probably have different values. Certainly the members of the new occupations will have new jargon and new ways of thinking that will present a number of communication blocks and produce a lack of interest in cooperation. These can also create conflict and resistance independent of resistance to change. A dramatic illustration of this is the change from custodial to therapeutic goals (Greenblatt, York, and Brown, 1955). The behavior of the attendants and nurses — not just that of the psychiatrists — had to alter to implement this new technology, which represented a radical departure in mental treatment.

Another concrete example is the study of prisons by McCleery (1957) of the introduction of rehabilitation services. The guards were violently opposed and resisted the change not only passively but actively. Here the power and status of the guards was decreased, whereas in milieu therapy the power and status of the attendants and nurses was increased. Therefore, the extent of conflict and its content were different in the two cases. The two cases also illustrate the clash of values in one organization and the consensus in the other. This had a great deal to do with the quite different levels of conflict. The staff in the mental hospitals were aware of the lack of rehabilitation, and agreed on the need for it. The guards in the prison were not aware of recidivism and did not agree that rehabilitation would make a difference.

One of the practical implications is that insofar as organizations can create entirely new units, such as pilot plants, new college campuses, or separate de-

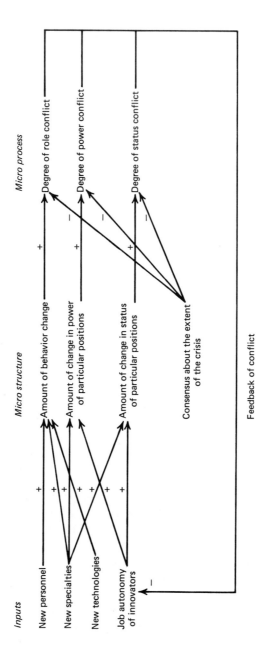

Figure 7.4 Radical innovation and the extent of conflict.

222

partments (Ronken and Lawrence, 1952) with new personnel, many of the problems of implementation are reduced in magnitude. But even then, new organizations physically close to the multi-organization can have difficulties. The experimental college (1928-1932) at the University of Wisconsin, while its own personnel had all been especially recruited, was a constant target for the more traditional faculty who disagreed with its objectives — developing the whole person who would be creative — and its method of high interaction between faculty and students who lived together (Cremin, 1961). This innovation was killed by the administration.

The arrival of new personnel and of new occupations always means a new organizational chart. Where the new positions will be slotted inevitably produces some conflict. A particularly striking example of this is the study of a community hospital that added a radical medical education program (Hage, 1974: Part 1). The determination of the power and status rank of the new physician-educators created two years of conflict until finally a new power and status structure was negotiated. The new production unit may be placed relatively high in the hierarchy with the hope that this will solve these problems (Ronken and Lawrence, 1953), but usually it does not. In either case, there is usually a new dominant coalition created as a consequence. The existing power and status structure are reconstituted — but only after a long, drawn out battle (Mann and Williams, 1960)!

The new personnel require some autonomy to develop the throughput. This places them directly in conflict with existing lines of supervision. Decentralization of the power structure can give the necessary flexibility at the operating level where the new technological processes are being developed. Generally the reverse is likely. Typically, the organization's dominant coalition attempts to centralize the operation and practices close supervision (for example, see Ronken and Lawrence, 1952). Even if the innovators are given a great deal of job autonomy, the conflicts that they generate are likely to lead to attempts by the dominant coalition to centralize. In turn, the innovators will resist this.

A conceptual distinction can be made between resistance and conflict. They might be defined as follows:

Resistance: An unwillingness to cooperate with change.

Conflict: An overt disagreement about the change.

Passive noncooperation, which is what I mean by resistance, can be as deadly as conflict. The development of a new throughput, the working out of all the necessary details, the discovery of new techniques and new procedures, can not be accomplished by a small group but requires the active participation and involvement of everyone.

There is one thing that alleviates resistance and conflict: the agreement or consensus about the extent or depth of the crisis facing the organization. The greatest conflicts are engendered when a group of innovators perceive a performance gap, but this is not shared or agreed upon by the others in the organization. For example, in a community hospital (Hage, 1974: Part 1), the physician-educators perceived poor quality patient care, while many of the physicians on the staff perceived good quality patient care. Different assessments of output can generate very intense conflicts indeed, as any faculty member who has complained about the quality of teaching knows. Frequently, the rank and file do not share the same standards — otherwise they would be innovators — and thus do not perceive the same performance gap. Again, we return to the necessity of crisis as a way of obtaining the kind of consensus needed for a radical innovation.

When the performance is efficiency or quantity of production, then there can be widespread recognition that something drastic has to be done to keep costs down or restore profits because the measures are more clear-cut and easy to make. When there is consensus about failure there is a mandate for change that is usually accepted by the rank and file. Given a crisis, a new dominant coalition is likely to be formed and this, too, will go a long way toward facilitating the introduction of a radical innovation.

Role conflict has been widely studied in organizations (Gross, Mason, McEachern, 1958; Kahn et al., 1964) but its relevance to change processes has perhaps not been appreciated as much as it should be. Status and power conflicts are more dramatic and more easily remembered but usually of shorter duration. In contrast, role conflicts are less sharp but more enduring. They should be of most concern to the dominant coalition. Admittedly the pure role conflict without power conflict, and vice versa, is difficult to imagine. New responsibilities imply new power prerogatives, and changed patterns of action and interaction mean new status distinctions. Nevertheless the daily difficulty during implementation is creating new behavior and interaction patterns as each person learns his new job relative to the throughput (Hage, 1974: Chapters 4 and 5; Mann and Williams, 1960; Mann and Hoffmann, 1960).

Since radical innovations mean new inputs, throughputs, and outputs, the role definitions of many people are touched even if this is not appreciated. Because new techniques must be developed, it is impossible to provide a job description. Considerable experimentation is necessary. Thus Mann and Williams (1960) report all the role conflicts engendered by the addition of a computer, admittedly not a very radical innovation but a major one nevertheless. Just what the nurses and attendants were to do in milieu therapy was not at all clear when it was first tried (Greenblatt, York, and Brown, 1956). Nor is the job prescription for a teacher in an open classroom exactly concrete, as Patton reports in his study (1972).

Another reason why role conflicts are the more typical symptom of the change process is that they are based on expectations by definition. Change, and especially radical innovation, brings great expectations – liberté, égalité, fraternité – about what can be done. The new output solves mankind's problems and makes a tidy profit as well. This is especially true of the innovators and for the dominant coalition (which may or may not be the same people). They expect that the radical innovation will work on the first trial. Nothing is less certain! With failure comes frustration and conflict over who is not doing his job correctly. This is the source of much of the frustration reported in the change literature (see Mann and Williams, 1960; Walker, 1957; Hage and Aiken, 1970; Hage, 1974: Part 1, Patton, 1972) – too high expectations of the innovators that becomes translated into unreal demands for behavior change upon the part of others in the organization. This is frequently compounded by very clear expectations about some performance standard and less clear expectations about how this is to be achieved. Thus the membership of the organization is caught in something like a double bind – a very precise goal and a very imprecise means to achieve it. The hypotheses diagrammed in Figure 7.4 can be summarized as follows:

7. 7 *The more new technology, personnel and specialties, the greater the behavior change of the membership.*

7. 8 *The more new occupational specialties and the job autonomy of the innovators, the greater the change in power and status of particular positions.*

7. 9 *The more behavior change in positions and relationships, the more role conflict.*

7.10 *The more change in the power and status of particular positions, the greater the power and status conflict.*

7.11 *The more role, power, and status conflict, the less the job autonomy of the innovators.*

7.12 *The greater the consensus about the performance gap, the less the role, power, and status conflict.*

The feedback of conflict on the job autonomy of the innovators, usually results in a reduction of their freedom to maneuver. In turn, this tends to reduce the radicalness of the innovation by reducing attempts to change the behavior of others involved in the throughput. The consequence is a movement towards a more traditional technology rather than the development of a new one.

For example, teachers trying to operate in an open classroom (Patten, 1972) experienced conflict with parents, and responded by reducing the extent of the "openness" of the classroom. In a community hospital, the innovators stopped attempting to change the behavior of the physicians and introduce other changes after several dramatic episodes of conflict (Hage, 1974: Part 1). The prison guards were able to effectively undermine the rehabilitation changes introduced by resistance (McCleery, 1957). Unfortunately, we lack many case studies of change processes, especially ones that span three or more years, so that we do not know the extent of conflict and of resistance engendered.

7.1.4. Hypotheses about the Routinization Stage

If the conflict becomes too great and the cooperation too little, the innovation may be aborted without a fair trial. Some of the new personnel may be let go. Or more usually the innovators begin to scale down their demands and expectations for behavior change, which gradually leads to more cooperation. This allows for a concretizing of what each person's job is to be, and the working out of new expectations. These are the first steps towards routinization, which means the acceptance or rejection of the innovation by the power elite and its consolidation. and yet it may be very decisive in the go-no go decision regarding a radical innovation.

If a crisis has precipitated the choice of a radical innovation, then the time span for evaluation is likely to be short. Paradoxically, every expensive innovations increase the time span. The greater the sunk costs, the greater the reluctance of the dominant coalition to admit that it made a mistake.

The judgment of success or failure is partially affected by how long the dominate coalition waits before it evaluates. *The quicker the judgment is made, the more likely negative costs will outweigh the positive benefits.* The reasons for this are as follows. The first part of the implementation stage tends to be dominated by conflict rather than cooperation, and this stage may last several years. Management perceives mostly a cost rather than a gain – in this case a human cost – which may also make itself felt in declining productivity, higher turnover, and lower production, depending upon the extent of the conflict and resistance. Not only relative to material costs but for others as well, the balance sheet is at first negative and only later is more likely to be positive.

In the case of the prison McCleery (1957) studied, the administration stood completely by the innovation, but the costs outweighed the benefits: guard conflict, prison riots, external and negative publicity. In a community hospital, Hage (1974) found that the administration noted the physician conflict, intern and resident rebellion, and high cost of the medical education program, but did not note the improvement in quality care or even in medical education. But, then, how much visibility is there of rehabilitation or quality care, except in the long term, and maybe never. The ease of measurement not only affects whether organizational elites recognize the need for change but it also affects the institutionalization of a particular radical change.

The nonmeasurability reduces visibility of benefits, which may reduce the probabilities of an innovation being accepted and then institutionalized. Thus, one wonders if many of the radical innovations that were either rejected or never institutionalized – such as the experimental college at the University of Wisconsin and other experiments in progressive education (Cremin, 1961) – died primarily because positive benefits were difficult to prove by measurement or quantification. This in turn also affects the diffusion of radical innovations. If their success is hard to demonstrate, then these are unlikely to diffuse and change the larger society. For this reason, most health innovations diffuse very rapidly, and most education innovations very slowly.

This same case of demonstrating "a just noticeable difference" to use the psychologists' term affects client or customer acceptance. It is why black-and-white television diffused rapidly, but color very slowly; why each improvement in airplane speed has tended to be accepted rapidly, but not the improvements in train travel; why stereos replaced hi-fi somewhat rapidly but quadrophonic sound will probably never be widely accepted, and so forth. The more radical the innovation, the longer it takes to make the innovation viable. Furthermore, there is likely to be market resistance upon the part of clients or customers, unless there is a quantum leap or qualitative benefit that is clearly visible. This becomes especially important in people-processing organizations because of the difficulty of demonstrating benefits while costs are visible. Physicians complained that their patients did not like to be used as teaching cases in the community hospital, but did not report better care. The old convicts were opposed to the rehabilitation program because they lost status and power and did not see the recidivism rates of those who had been in the rehabilitation programs.

There are essentially two factors that would appear to counterbalance the negative balance sheet. The first is the sheer cost of the investment. As this increases, it becomes harder and harder for management to admit mistakes. There is, then, a vested interest upon management's part to retain the innovation. Usually one discusses vested interests as being opposed to change but here the same logic works in reverse. More positive is the influence of the time horizon of the management/administration. The longer the duration of their temporal horizon, the more they perceive the negative consequences of the innovation as temporary, and make the decision to retain the innovation as an investment for the future. The evaluation of costs and benefits in five years can be quite different. It does not mean that this assessment is correct, but only that it is more likely to be accurate when the facts and figures have accumulated for several years.

Once the decision to either accept or reject the radical innovation is made, the cycle is largely completed. We are concerned with why a dominant coalition might institutionalize the innovation or reject it.

The hypotheses are:

7.13   *The greater the consensus about the performance gap, the less the extent of conflict, and the extent of costs and the more the extent of benefits perceived, the more likely the decision to institutionalize the innovation.*

7.14 *The greater the consensus about the performance gap, the greater the duration of the time span for experimentation.*

7.15 *The greater the cost of the innovation, the greater the duration of the time span and the extent of costs perceived.*

7.16 *The greater the measurability of benefits and of costs, the greater the number of benefits and of costs perceived and the more likely the decision to institutionalize the innovation.*

As can be seen in Figure 7.5., the cost of innovation has a curious impact on the decision to institutionalize the radical output. On the one hand, it obviously affects the cost side of any cost-benefit analysis that the dominant coalition does. On the other hand, it increases the willingness of the coalition to wait out the trial period. In fact, as sunk costs increase the dominant coalition almost becomes committed to perceiving success even in the light of failure. This was exactly the problem of the Edsel and of Corfom.

It should be remembered that the radical innovation may not reduce the performance gap. Just because it is radically new or different does not make it good or desirable. We tend to forget all those failures. This is one reason why, in the discussion of high risk decisions in Chapter 4, I included a number that did not turn out well. Many of those involved radical innovations relative to their market at that time. Being ahead of one's time does apply with radical innovations.

By analyzing each stage in a change process as centered around a problem, we begin to understand a large number of reasons why radical innovation is so rare. Some of the more critical reasons are:

1. Dominant coalitions seldom perceive enough of a performance gap to explore or to seek out a radical innovation.
2. There are frequently not enough resources available and especially personnel to develop the new throughput, to invent the technology.
3. Radical innovations generate both conflict and resistance, which tends to make them less radical.
4. Evaluation of the innovation occurs too soon during the trial period so that the benefits have not had a chance to appear.

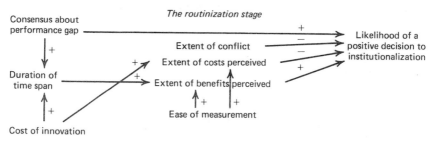

Figure 7.5 Radical innovation and its institutionalization.

At each stage, there is another pitfall that prevents the full development of a radical innovation.

7.2. THE CAUSES OF RESISTANCE AND OF CONFLICT

Although the greatest conflict usually occurs during the implementation stage, resistance to new ideas is a continual organizational problem. Whether in the evaluation stage, when the dominant coalition refuses to perceive a performance gap because they have lower standards, or in the initiation stage, when resource controllers are fearful because the remedy is a radical departure from contemporary ideas, or in the routinization stage, when the unwillingness to have another trial is manifest, resistance to new ideas is a leitmotif. Typically, one thinks of the dominant coalition as the major stumbling block. In fact, it is more likely to be the rank and file and the customers or clients who are most resistant to change.

As is clear from the discussion of the various stages, resistance can take many forms and guises, from mental blocking to physical conflict (see Zaltman, Duncan, and Holbek, 1973). Its most typical variety is non-cooperation, which we have defined as resistance.

The concept of mental blocking is usually applied at the individual level, but it can exist at the group level by an occupational denial of a problem. When the famous Teamsters' study of patient care by Trussel et al. (1959) was published, indicating bad patient care in a number of hospitals, the American Medical Association said that it was ridiculous because *all* physicians provide good patient care. Academic departments in universities may claim they are one of the best in the nation, but do not measure their citations in the scientific indexes. The examples are endless. The general point is that most people are unwilling to admit failure and therefore accept the need for some change.

What are the major causes of resistance to change? If this can be determined, then one can explore strategies to overcome these resistances, reduce conflict, and ensure cooperation. There are essentially three different theories or explanations: the vested interest theory, the capacity for change theory, and the cost-benefit theory. Each of these involves a quite different conceptualization of why interest groups resist radical innovation. And each is partially applicable some of the time, completely accurate some of the time, and irrelevant some of the time. Each implies a different strategy for overcoming resistance. Usually in any concrete situation these three models will be combined in various proportions, thus requiring some integrated change strategy for overcoming resistance. *All three theories operate at the level of an interest group and may not be applicable to specific individuals.* This is not a trivial point because it is easier to understand why groups might resist than why particular individuals might. In all three themes, the assumption is made that there is some micro-impact, that is, in some way an interest group variously defined is affected.

7.2.1. Vested Interest Theory

It was Veblen who coined the famous term "vested interest" as an explanation for why a dominant coalition would veto change ideas. This thinking was also very much a part of Barnard's (1946) understanding of why status systems tend to resist the development of new ideas, as described in Chapter 2. These will disturb the distribution of power, status, and privilege, and those with the most to lose will be most opposed to the introduction of new ideas. Like any theory about human nature, this is true at some times and not others. The theory becomes more complex when one stipulates *when* vested interests are operative. Consistent with the axiomatic theory of Hage, which synthesized the work of Barnard and of Weber, vested interests of the dominant coalition are operative precisely when the dominant coalition is small and narrow. The hypotheses are:

7.17   *The more centralized the organization, the more that the dominant coali-tion will resist radical change because of their vested interests.*

7.18   *The more stratified the organization, the more that the dominant coali-tion will resist radical change because of their vested interests.*

7.19   *The less the normative equality of the organization, the more that the dominant coalition will resist radical change because of their vested in-terests.*

7.20   *The deeper the crisis facing the organization, the less the dominant coali-tion will resist radical change because of their vested interests.*

The theme that those who have do not want to give it up is especially compelling precisely when they have a lot. Essentially the hypotheses are saying that when power and status elites represent a small group with great gaps in power, privi-lege, and prestige between them and lower participants, — status schisms, to use Caplow's term (1964) — they are more threatened by the possibility of change. The findings of the previous chapter all tend to partially support these hypothe-ses. Vested interest theory is a special case of our equality premise, 6A.

The addition of new outputs also usually means the introduction of new spe-cialists who will in various ways demand some power and status. This is what makes the fourth hypothesis so interesting and allows us to predict a sharp — and sudden — reversal in the opposition of the dominant coalition. If they do perceive that they might lose all — that is, the organization is about to go under — then their resistance to a radical innovation proposed by some innovator becomes transformed into willing acceptance, but the reason is the same — their own self-interest. Thus, we see the management of DuPont reversing their stand on centralization in the light of continual falling profits (Chandler, 1962). Furthermore, this sudden or abrupt about-face is a discontinuous one. A slight further drop in profits or loss of patients will send the management or administration in the direction of radical solutions which they previously would have found unacceptable.

This helps explain some of the negative findings about the association between centralization and innovation rate reported in the previous chapter. The "catch-up" phenomenon observed in a very traditional mental hospital and in various Catholic agencies changing their goals, while not radical innovation, does represent an example of a similar phenomenon, the dominant coalition making a major effort to innovate because of a deep crisis.

At various points, we have observed that a crisis frequently leads to a change in the dominant coalition. The new coalition can and does develop a vested interest in seeing to it that a radical innovation works. Vested interest in innovation has *not* been discussed in the literature and yet is very much present, especially when there has been a succession with a mandate for change.

7.2.2. Capacity for Change Theory

If vested interest theory has a narrow conception of what people and especially of what elite self-interest is, the capacity for change approach — as represented in books like Toffler's *Future Shock* (1970) — has an equally narrow accent: on people's tolerance of change per se, irrespective of content or self-interest. Scales have been developed to see how much change individuals can absorb, with more points for dramatic changes such as divorce, death of spouse or child, loss of job, change of job, and the like. As yet, scales have not been created to measure how much change in behavior occurs on the job given a radical innovation.

At the micro level, one obtains some feeling for how technological innovation, most typically the introduction of automated throughput, can alter the job descriptions of all of the workers in a number of case studies (see Walker, 1957; Mann and Hoffman, 1960; Mann and Williams, 1960). In each instance, the machines eliminated much of the routine work, and the remaining activities in different positions were combined into new jobs that required much more thinking and much less manual labor. Woodword (1965) generalized this finding by indicating that qualitative shifts in technology required quite different behavior patterns. Even management had to change patterns of interaction.

Groups can work in a context in which a lot of change occurs or in a context in which little occurs. In the former situation, they develop coping mechanisms for handling change; in the latter they develop a preference for stability. How much of this represents socialization and how much self-selection may be hard to say, but clearly the individuals who work in a context where new products or services are continually being developed have learned how to cope with the problems described above.

Hage (1974) found that those medical departments with the greatest amount of previous change were most likely to accept the radical change of a physician-teacher working in the department. In a predictive study of innovation of programs and services, Hage and Dewar (1973) found that previous history of innovation combined with values favoring change and complexity (variety of occupation specialties) together accounted for 70% of the variance. These partials imply much more than may appear at first glance. Each of these variables has a critical implication. Despite the presence of such controls as pro-change values in the dominant coalition and the impact of the diversity of perspectives in complexity, the previous history of change still contributed to the amount of variance explained, that is, there is a significant partial correlation. This means, *sheer experience with innovation develops a capacity for tolerance, which is independent of the two major explanations for varying rates of innovation outlined in the previous chapter.* Thus, the reaction of the entire membership is an important causal explanation as well. Further, the Kaluzny et al. (1974) study indicates that both high and low risk innovations correlate highly with overall innovation rate, suggesting that there are not even qualitative differences (admittedly their list of innovations does not include real radical innovations as they are defined in this chapter). While this idea can be trivialized as organizations doing in the present what they have done in the past, this evidence supports the capacity for change thesis. People become socialized to accept the problems of the implementation stage, to live with the conflicts, and to handle them, perhaps relying upon special mechanisms as in the Lawrence and Lorsch (1967 a and b) study of the plastics industry.

It is a standard axiom that past behavior is a good predictor of future behavior in most of the social sciences. This typically bores people, and simultaneously not enough is done to explain why. In this instance, the essential argument lies in socialization, or the learning of coping mechanisms.

The reverse side of this argument is that there is a tradition in every organization, and tradition produces its own need for stability and continuity. Usually this argument is invoked in the literature in underdeveloped countries, but it has also been critical in the diffusion of innovation literature (Rogers, 1962). Notice that typically vested interest theory is applied to the power, status, and privilege elites whereas usually capacity for change is a statement about the membership – the lower participants. However, dominant coalitions can change or be bound by tradition, just as the rank and file have their own vested interests. In any concrete situation, these motivations for resistance are found in various mixtures; it is difficult to distinguish how much resistance results from fear of power or status loss, from how much resistance results from fear of the unknown. Sometimes one can determine the relative importance of various causes of resistance by asking individuals why they evaluate a particular innovation as good or bad. In a panel study of physicians resistance to a radical innovation, I found support for both these models of motivation (Hage, 1974: Part 1).

Most of the change scales at the individual level conceptualize change as (Mann and Williams, 1960; Mann and Hoffman, 1960; Walker, 1957; Toffler, 1970) stressful. And many of their indicators, such as loss of spouse or child or divorce, have in them a particular kind of stress that does not have much counterpart at either the micro or meso organizational level of analysis. It would be incorrect to assume that change is necessarily stressful. Radical innovation might be, but even this can vary enormously among individuals. It is this variation that interests us and requires explanation.

What most people resist — elites, lower participants, resource controllers, and customers/clients — is *change* in the *rate of change*. In mathematical terms, it is the points of inflection that hurt; the accelerations or decelerations in the continual change that become stressful. The intelligent manager or administrator slowly increases or decreases the rate at which new outputs are introduced. With radical new innovations, this option or strategy is usually closed. Since radical innovation necessitates a lot of behavior change, it is by definition stressful and therefore likely to be resisted.

Under what circumstances can organizational members tolerate changes?

7.21 *The greater the experience with role behavior change in the past, the less members will resist radical change.*

7.22 *The greater the experience with different perspectives, paradigms, schools of thought, and so on, the less members will resist radical change.*

7.23 *The greater their experience with different cultures, languages and social groups, and so on, the less members will resist radical change.*

7.24 *The sharper the increase in the rate of change, the greater the resistance to any change.*

The essential theme uniting the first three hypotheses is that variety breeds a taste or a tolerance for more variety. Under certain experiential histories, radicalness loses its sharp edge and fear disappears or at least dissipates. It is a very common finding in the change literature that people who travel widely, read more, and have broader concerns tend to be more favorably disposed to change (Rogers, 1962). Likewise creativity appears to be higher in those who know two languages, although this is far from a definitive finding. The various findings relative to professional training, professional activism, and cosmopolitanism, reported in the previous chapter, all support this. These hypotheses are special instances of our second premise, 6B.

What most effectively sets limits is accelerations in the rate of innovation. It is this that most people find stressful. Steady introduction of new products breeds tolerance and coping mechanisms, but a sudden and large jump creates an anomic situation and resistance starts to grow — rapidly (Dewar, 1976). Radically new outputs and technologies imply this. Usually when they are introduced, many other kinds of changes are occurring at the same time. It is only an impression, but radical innovations are much more likely to be tried in periods when there is a great deal of change occurring in the society. The 1960s was such an era in the history of the United States, and we had many new kinds of organizations and institutional patterns — from the open university to the open marriage, from communes to venture capital, from half-way houses of various kinds to the open classroom. Some worked, some failed, but they could emerge more easily in a context where there was already a fast rate of innovation as in the many new disciplines, products, social welfare programs, medical treatments, and the like being invented during this time period.

7.2.3. Cost-Benefit Theory

The third model of resistance is less general than the first two and much more complex. It postulates rational men computing what the balance of gains and losses is relative to both their values and interests. If one knows what the consequences of the change are relative to various costs and benefits, then one can predict a priori what the reaction of the members of the organization will be to a particular change. This is familiar to most readers as exchange theory (Homans, 1961), and it can be applied to the problem of resistance to change as well.

The values may not be economic ones, nor need they be other than self-interest. As Maris (1964) notes, managers can be driven by desires for prestige just as can academics. Rational men and women can decide to maximize worker morale and reduce alienation and then evaluate the consequences of various innovations for achieving this objective.

However, when applied to the problem of evaluating innovations, there is always a double calculus. The individual member is weighing on the one hand what the costs and benefits are to him, and on the other hand what the costs and benefits are to the organization. The interesting question is: when do members resist innovations that benefit the organization, and when do they accept innovations that cost them? In these latter situations self-interest theory breaks down, and in the former situations it works very well. The real problem — and this is the problem with exchange theory — is to predict the weights attached to particular costs and benefits, and especially when they might vary for the member and for the organization.

The first assumption is that losses in status, power, or privilege, and changes in role behavior are perceived as costs by all members. The two theories above provide some explanation of how much weight to assign to these costs. In other words, when organizations are centralized, the dominant coalition weighs the costs of a loss of power heavily. When organizational members have not had much experience with role behavior change, then these costs become great. What lessens these costs is the potential gain for the organization vis-à-vis its various performances. Note that implicit in any change is some potential benefit for the organization — improvement in product quality, increased sales, reduction of costs, better worker morale, and the like. The second assumption is that gains in benefits for the organization in any of its performances, if perceived, are benefits for the individual as well. As was suggested in Chapter 3, members have not only self-interests but preferred values relative to the objectives or performances of the organization.

The real problem, then, is what determines the relative importance of individual costs and organizational benefits for individual members? Rather than see individuals or groups always operating from a motive of self-interest or high ideals, as Weber did (1947: the specific distinction between *Zweck* and *Wert* rationality), it might be more useful to determine when groups are most likely to adopt one or the other stance vis-à-vis a radical innovation. The answers at the meso level of the organization have been suggested in Chapter 5; organizations with a high concentration of specialists and decentralizations will tend to emphasize innovation and quality while those with the opposite set of characteristics will prefer stability and quantity. Relative to radical innovations that improve quality, they are likely to be resisted by members in organizations that have few specialists and are centralized. At the micro or individual level, the following hypotheses can be formulated:

7.25 *The more standardized is the work-flow or throughput, the more important are losses of status and of power.*

7.26 *The more professionalized is the work-flow or throughput, the more important are gains of improved job performance, and especially as regards quality.*

7.27 *The more standardized the work-flow or throughput, the more important are the costs of efficiency and of production.*

7.28 *The more professionalized is the work-flow or throughput, the more important are benefits of quality and of improved organizational prestige.*

Innovations, especially radical ones, have a large number of costs for the individual. They also affect the costs and benefits of the organization. Consistent with what determines the objectives of an organization, professionalization and standardization have opposite kinds of effects on group preferences. Some hypothetical answers are: Professionalized work forces like being the technological and service leaders, the first in ideas and quality of service, and are willing to pay the costs for this.

Routinized work forces will accept more readily technological innovations that improve production and increase market share or the dominance the organization has. The replacement of the assembly line by automated technology is not necessarily resisted, as long as there are no major reductions in the labor force size or other obvious individual costs (see Mann and Hoffman, 1960; Walker, 1957). Likewise, management – given routinization of the work flow – is likely to be especially interested in production maximizing technology, even radical departures from the existing one. These would help explain exceptions to the hypotheses in Chapter 6.

The next step is to know which of these various utilities are enhanced by a particular innovation, especially a radical one. McCleery's prison study (1957) can be reinterpreted as change to produce a quality output; that is, no recidivism. For the guard and prisoner elite, the rehabilitation program meant a loss of power and status. It meant a role behavior change for all of them. Finally, given their routinized work flow, the introduction of a rehabilitation program meant a reduction in the efficient handling of the prisoners. Prison riots and conflict became great as the authoritarian system of control broke down. The cost benefit analysis for the guards was all costs and no benefits. They resisted, and bitterly so, involving the governor and the legislature. Note that in these extreme cases, all three models of explanation are applicable. To analyze the conflict only in terms of vested interests is to do a disservice to the guards.

Less extreme is the study of resistance to a medical education program designed to improve the quality of patient care in a community hospital (Hage, 1974). Again, this was a relatively radical departure for this kind of hospital. Those departments that had previously experienced more change accepted the innovations more readily. Those elites with the most power and status resisted. But most interestingly, the physicians who were more professionalized, who read more, and had greater experience working in team situations were most likely to accept the changes because of the benefits for the hospital, even though they perceived costs for themselves. In contrast physicians who had a more routinized work flow, and worked in more authoritarian work situations were resistant to the change, even though they perceived benefits for the hospital, because of the costs for themselves (Hage, 1974: Chapter 5). *Here we see consensus about the individual costs and the collective benefits, but the weights assigned are very different depending on the working situations and professional styles.*

Therefore, if one knows something about the characteristics of the organization, one can begin to estimate what the causes of resistance are. In general, for radical innovation all three models apply, which is why it is so rare. Elites resist because it upsets the balance of power. Lower participants resist because it is too stressful. All members resist if the innovation maximizes quality and yet the work flow is relatively routinized or the reverse. Professionals resist any attempt to increase the quantity of work – that is, numbers of students, patients, or customers handled.

These three theories make three slightly different predictions about the introduction of radical innovation given certain specific conditions. Given a crisis and a new dominant coalition only vested interest theory really explains acceptance of a radical innovation, and especially if it involves the introduction of new output. Without a crisis, capacity for change theory explains acceptance in general. The cost-benefit approach cross-cuts the two theories by explaining acceptance depending upon the nature of the work and the nature of the innovation.

7.2.4. A Special Problem: Client or Customer Resistance

Sometimes radical critiques of organizational management assume that the real problem is that either organizations are manufacturing products that the people do not need, or they refuse to provide products that people really do need because it would not help their profits. While there is some truth in this, the answer is not quite this simple. Equally apparent is customer or client resistance to various things they "need."

Hotpoint developed buttons on the back of the stove for the safety of children, but mothers did not like the discomfort of reaching over the stove. Safety belts were installed in cars, but only information campaigns and laws have forced drivers to wear them. These are resistances only confined to discomfort vis-à-vis safety.

It is also interesting to observe the impact of the consumer movement in this context – a movement designed to measure quality and cost and assess the relative balance. Again one is impressed by its lack of impact except in certain areas where costs are quite visible, as in pollution or safety. Here some advance has been made by Nader's Raiders, especially relative to automobiles.

In each of these examples, the customers are clearly doing cost-benefit analysis. The increased costs are weighed against the gain, and this affects market response. The state of the economy can obviously determine marginal utilities relative to various benefits, but beyond this there are several observations that can be made. When a new quality is created, it is likely to win widespread approval and only cost will affect its rate of diffusion. Thus television, hi-fi, and air travel spread as rapidly as the standard of living would allow. However, improvements in quality are not likely to be so readily accepted, especially if they drive up costs as in color TV and stereo. Improvements in efficiency are usually easy to demonstrate. The Concorde, by cutting travel time in half, hits an important note in the system of customer values. The success of prepackaged foods, automatic dishwashers, little snowplows, and so forth, is that they save time, and efficiency is a highly valued customer utility.

Do the same principles apply to services, especially in the area of health, education, and welfare? They certainly do. Many innovations have waited a long time until there was much customer enthusiasm, usually because no one could really see a difference. Engineering schools such as Rensselear Polytechnic Institute languished until the Civil War in the United States when people discovered that it was useful to know how to build bridges. Graduate education à la the German model was very slow to develop in the United States, yet now it is a critical element in our entire educational system.

In contrast, the new math and Operation Headstart were relatively successful. In the case of Headstart, parents were happy about the participation in the education of their children. In the case of the new math, children did appear to learn a new way of thinking. In both innovations, the effectiveness of the teachers left much to be desired but the two innovations did have some visible consequences. In Headstart, increased status and power for parents was an important benefit. The new math was a more ambiguous innovation. In both instances these educational innovations were pushed by a sense of crisis, one regarding the USSR and the other regarding the child from a disadvantaged home.

Improvements in quality are quite hard to detect; thus many desirable services diffuse slowly throughout the country and the world. Few of the evaluation studies in education have had much impact. The history of new welfare programs is very much the same story. Supplying them does not mean there is a demand for them. Generally, they diffuse slowly through the population. Of course, there are many reasons for this — lack of awareness, unwillingness to accept welfare (which is an important psychic cost), and so forth. But this does underscore the essential observation the service area has all the same problems of creating demand and trying to overcome resistance. The recognition of these difficulties has led to some of the same mechanisms as used by manufacturing concerns: advertising on television (for welfare and drug rehabilitation programs), finding special kinds of welfare workers who can communicate better, developing outreach programs in local communities, and so forth.

In general, the problem of customer and client resistance is greater than has been appreciated, and has been largely ignored in the resistance to change literature. The same essential values appear to be operating. Quality, efficiency, status, and power are critical utilities that are likely to tip the cost-benefit analysis strongly. *The development of new qualities, once these are visible —* here is the critical difference between products and services — *are most likely to be accepted, but improvements in quality are less likely to be accepted precisely because they are less visible.* Improvements in efficiency — the saving of time and money — are likely to be accepted quickly. Services that diminish feelings of status or of power as in welfare are likely to be resisted. These ideas are not new; what has been done is to organize them into a few basic principals that can be applied to any change situation for the purposes of predicting the extent of resistance.

Meeting needs of people is not as easy as it may seem. The needs are not necessarily recognized, and the clients and customers have their own style of resistance. They are as much of the problem as the vested interests of elites and the lack of change capacity upon the part of the membership.

7.3. OVERCOMING RESISTANCE TO CHANGE

What can be done to overcome resistance to change? Are there any strategies that can be employed? And under which circumstances should what strategy be employed? Essentially there are three ways of overcoming resistances, but these are not parallel to the causes of resistance. Two are well-known: evolutionary strategies or incrementalism and revolutionary strategies. The third is usually the most successful one, but it is not normally discussed as a change of strategy: the creation of a new organizational unit such as a separate college or a pilot plant.

The first two strategies are listed in Figure 7.6. Each has a certain contradiction in it relative to the problem of radical innovations. Incrementalism is unlikely to ever implement the entire innovation, that is, in the process of using various human relations techniques the radicalness is vitiated. An all or nothing strategy is likely to create so much resistance that the innovation dies aborning.

Figure 7.6 Strategies for overcoming resistance to change

Element in strategy	Increase centralization or revolution	Decrease centralization or evolution
Discussions with those affected	No	Yes
Participation in decisions by those affected	No	Yes
Speed of change	Fast	Slow
Collective values stressed	Yes	Yes
Costs stressed	No	Yes
Change conceived as permanent	Yes	No
Conflict in implementation	High	Low
Amount of change actually implemented	Low sometimes high[a]	Low

[a]Depends upon the extent of the crisis.

The first strategy provides all the cooperation, but essentially people agree to do very little. The second strategy provides little cooperation, so that the working out of all the necessary detail is not done and the radical idea is not given a fair chance in a realistic experiment. These strategies do, however, have certain situations where they are ideal. This will be explicated later on.

But before we do, we should see how the two basic strategies speak to the various causes of resistance. The evolutionary strategy is best represented by human relations techniques as exemplified in the famous Coch and French study (1948). What has not been appreciated in this tradition is that allowing people to discuss the change to be made must also involve their participation in its shaping, a sharing of power. Otherwise it becomes manipulative and is recognized as such. Once power is shared, then very quickly the radical plan is whittled down to size. In contrast, if there is no participation in planning and development, the purity of the idea can be maintained. The sharing of power is usually done at some cost to the dominant coalition. They must give up some power. Remember we have repeatedly stressed the importance of developing new techniques at the operating level, which requires the active cooperation of the membership. In a revolutionary model, one frankly runs roughshod over the concerns of vested interestes – if one can. Obviously, the ability to use the revolutionary model is usually denied. Only a major crisis provides this mandate. This latter technique, which goes by another name – increased centralization (Zaltman, Duncan, and Holbek, 1973) – has a simple appeal. But it ignores the necessity of having many people cooperate in the development of the throughput.

Besides manipulating the distribution of power, the two strategies also manipulate time. The revolutionary strategy tries to accomplish a lot fast. The motto is the first 100 days. The evolutionary approach takes a very long time of five to ten years. Typically the evolutionary models advocate change as an experiment. Temporary members are therefore more willing to tolerate role behavior change under these circumstances. This temporary and piecemeal approach is also the price to be paid for sharing the planning with those affected by the change and whose cooperation is necessary for its success. In contrast, in the revolutionary model, one attempts to implement the entire program and push it as a permanent solution. Needless to say one can see how this increases resistance. The thinking here is that the new output is all of a piece and cannot be broken down into segments. Many radical innovations can *not* be broken down into separate pieces.

Finally, in the two strategies the sales pitch of the dominant coalition is different. In the evolutionary one, the values of the participants are emphasized and costs are frankly anticipated. This builds a great deal of trust, but its price again is frequently the vitiation of various aspects of the program because they are seen as too costly. In contrast, the revolutionary strategy emphasizes the collective values and ignores the individual costs, attempting to arouse altruistic values and a sense of sacrifice. This is essentially the strategy of charismatic leaders.

Needless to say one seldom finds a pure type. These various elements are mixed and they can change over time. Frequently innovators start with an evolutionary perspective, but as they perceive the problems with this strategy they become more enamoured with the revolutionary strategy. Thus do innovators evolve towards authoritarianism! It is the resistance to change that leads them down this pathway paved with good intentions.

An excellent example of the evolutionary perspective and its problems is found in a study by Hage (1974: Chapter 4). To gain initial acceptance of a new medical education program, the innovator held meetings with both the informal and formal leaders and the rank and file physicians in each department. The first step in the program was to reach an agreement that they accept full-time teachers in their clinical service, one each for surgery, pediatrics, and obstetrics-gynecology. Human relations techniques were employed. However, the price was that the full-time teacher was stripped of any authority or status. The surgical full-time teacher was not allowed to operate. The obstetrics-gynecology teacher was restricted in the number of private patients he could have. Both had to hold teaching rounds with an attending physician, and so forth. Because of these compromises, the further implementation of the program was prevented.

In this situation, the hospital elite did not perceive themselves to be in a major crisis, only a minor one – the inability to attract interns and residents. There was no mandate for a revolutionary change, especially since the innovator was not a member of the hospital's dominant coalition, which was made up of surgeons.

The major problem with implementing changes piecemeal is that usually many of the parts are never implemented. This is exactly what happened in this hospital. Many aspects of the plan were never instituted, and as a consequence the experimental stimulus was at best a half a loaf. More critically the implementation of the various activities was not the same in the four major clinical services so that one clinical department, surgery, had few aspects of the ideal program.

This study also illustrates the use of the revolutionary approach to a certain extent. Tired of constant negotiation and bargaining and frustrated by the lack of progress, the investors abandon the human relations techniques and in the second year practices were instituted without prior consultation and discussion. The consequence was an explosion of conflict and the effective blocking of further change. By the end of the second year, the innovators had ceased to be such and were concerned about their ability to retain their positions.

McCleery's prison study (1957) implies that if the critical interest group and power block – in this case, the guards – is not consulted, a major conflict can result. Although one does not think of the reforms of the rehabilitators as a revolution, in point of fact most of the changes were made by fiat, without allowing the guards to participate in the planning. The guard concerns about custody were not considered. But if the guards had participated would they have accepted the proposed changes? Since these changes affected their cost-benefits so negatively, it seems unlikely. Instead, they would have tried to block many elements of the rehabilitation program. This is the main problem with an evolutionary strategy. It can not really change the cost-benefit consequences without altering the proposal, and this is exactly what happens in discussions.

The two strategies have, therefore, an inherent weakness that increases the probability that radical innovation will *not* occur. In the case of the evolutionary approach, the price of gaining acceptance in the initiation stage is that not much is implemented. In the case of the revolutionary approach, the ignoring of acceptance in the initiation stage lends to heightened conflict. Again not much is implemented. One loses with either strategy.

7.3.1. Evolution or Revolution?
Two Change Strategies

If we use as a shorthand the Burns-Stalker model of organic versus mechanical organizations, we can specify under what circumstances each strategy may be most appropriate. If the organization has an organic structure, then an evolutionary or incremental approach is the most appropriate one. If the concentration of specialists is high and the power structure is decentralized, an attempt at using a revolutionary approach is almost by definition impossible. Since power is shared, there is no opportunity for a leader to be autocratic. Likewise, a high concentration of specialists means that resistance and conflict would be exceptionally high if someone tried to ram through a radical innovation.

Incrementalism as a stragegy can work if the innovator has great patience and can remain in his position for a long time. Charles Eliot, the president, built up Harvard over a 45 year period, between 1867 and 1909 (James, 1930). Whenever opposition developed to his ideas or those of others, he would drop the matter, wait a year, and then bring the matter up again. In Harvard the faculty expected to participate and Eliot had no other choice. But the price was few radical changes. Usually these were pioneered at other colleges. Perhaps the most critical indigenous change was the development of electives and the movement away from a fixed undergraduate curriculum.

The key to a successful policy of incrementalism is that the innovator must be in a position to affect recruitment and gradually change the balance of power in the dominant coalition. And this is exactly what Eliot did. He systematically recruited men with fresh ideas and deliberately added new occupational specialties to the faculty. Fortunately for him, and this is another condition for the success of an incremental policy, Harvard had a considerable surplus of endowment funds. Thus, Eliot could rapidly expand the faculty size, which he did; it doubled in the space of three years. The old guard found themselves outnumbered, making the introduction of new ideas in the process of incrementalism possible. It thus is possible for a whole series of small changes to add up to a qualitatively different and radical innovation.

But it would be wrong to believe that rapid expansion of the personnel size of the organization will mean more openness to radical change. The key is new occupational specialties and people with a pro-change value set. Eliot obtained innovators – a team that really made the difference and gradually built Harvard up. And this is a critical point: it is *not* just one man but instead his capacity to select a team of innovators that will result in the success of an incrementalist strategy for an organization.

In general, however, incrementalism as a strategy does not work for radical innovation. The innovators become discouraged, fatigued by the struggle. They begin to accept the dominant values in the organization, and accept the half-a-loaf approach to radical change. *Thus the conclusion is that while organic organizations have higher rates of innovation, they do not necessarily produce radical change because the incrementalism strategy tends to mitigate against radical innovations.*

In contrast, a revolutionary strategy works well in a centralized organization – provided that there is some crisis. What was missing in the McCleery study of the prison was consensus that there was a crisis that would justify the introduction of rehabilitation as opposed to custodial goals. If the prison riots had occurred during what McCleery called the authoritarian regime, that is, before the introduction of the rehabilitation program, then there would have been a mandate to try something new, even something radical.

Mechanical organizations are contexts in which a radical change strategy is possible for other reasons. First, the low concentration of specialists means fewer demands in the actual planning and development. Second, the high concentration of power means that, assuming an individual innovator is in the elite, he has considerable power to begin a sweeping alteration of the structure. Third, mechanical organizations – by their very nature – are prone to crises and thus present mandates for some radical change from time to time. This will be discussed further in the next section.

Thus we are led to a curious paradox – namely that mechanical organizations, which have low rates of change, are also places where radical innovation can occur, because they are more likely to have crises as well as a structure that is more tolerant of dictatorial practices.

But despite this it would be a mistake to underestimate the powerful resistances that can be generated to radical change even in a mechanical organization in a crisis. Again, the rarity of radical change is not just a function of the difficulty of thinking about discontinuous ideas but of accepting them, or being able to see their existential necessity. While crises make various interest groups more open to considering radical solutions, the potential clash with their self-interests –and values or desired goals – for the organizations has a countervailing effect on their enthusiasm for the selected solution. Everyone agrees now about the energy crisis but the consensus on how to alleviate it is nil.

In general, my position is a pessimistic one: neither strategy is likely to produce radical innovation because each has an internal contradition, even among the best of circumstances. With incrementalism, patience and forebearance are likely to wear out and the human relation techniques delimit the radicalness. With the all or nothing approach, resistance is so great even if there is a crisis that there is not enough cooperation to develop an effective throughput. The autocratic innovator cannot do all the work himself or solve all of the technical problems himself. He needs the cooperation of the staff in the context of the organization. But the inherent logic of his personality and of the revolutionary strategy mitigate against the seeking of cooperation so that the vision is never completed and remains flawed – flawed in both execution and in performance.

Is there no hope? Is there no strategy that would allow for radical innovation? There does seem to be another alternative.

7.3.2. The Strategy of a New Division or a
New Organization

The difficulties of introducing radical innovation are so great, whether one uses evolutionary or revolutionary strategies, that the best approach would appear to be to create a new unit in which new personnel are recruited and which has its own source of resources and enough time to work through the implementation stage. One advantage is that one can recruit personnel on the basis of their commitment to the innovation, by-passing the problem of resistance. There are no vested interests in the new unit, no dominant coalition that has to be persuaded, unless the new unit begins to create too many problems for other organizations in the same multi-organization. In general, they are enough removed from the new unit's operation (although the independence allowed to separate divisions does vary; see Mintzberg 1979: 419).

Given the fact that most organizations, and especially the larger ones, are part of multi-organizations, this is a very viable strategy. The dominant actors in the major sectors of the society are multi-organizations, as are both local and national governments. Similarly most state universities fall into this kind of organization. Only hospitals and farms in the United States – and even here there are many exceptions – are still largely separate organizations unattached to multi-organizations. This, however, is not the case for hospitals in Britain and in France, where most hospitals belong to the Ministry of Health.

It is surprising that this strategy has not been discussed because it is used all of the time. Thus DuPont, like many other companies, creates a separate pilot plant to develop the technology relative to some radically new output, whether nylon, rayon, Corfam, and so forth. The University of California has created separate campuses with quite distinct styles such as Irvine, Santa Barbara, UCLA, and so on, which allow for the working out of alternatives to the standard education program. In England, when the open university idea had finally come of age, a separate organization for it was created. In the United States, the war on poverty was put in a new agency, the Office of Economic Opportunity. Would these innovations have been as effective – and as radical – if they had been made part of existing organizations? The answer is probably not.

The strategy of creating a new unit or of a new organization is indeed the best one for any radical change. It allows for the development of a dedicated band of true believers who can work out the mechanics of the technology without having to make concessions to existing staff with more traditional conceptions and beliefs.

This strategy will still require a quasi-charismatic leader who knows how to work with others and inspire them. A good example of this is John Gilman, the first president of Johns Hopkins, who made the first graduate school in the United States work (Gilman, 1906) and who had the ability to recruit top innovators in various fields and keep them involved as a group in the process of creating a new form of education.

Thus to create the radical new prison (McCleery, 1957) that really rehabilitates it would have been better to start out with a new plant, prison guards carefully chosen to be rehabilitators, and a dedicated staff. Even the prisoners would have to be carefully selected. The new medical education program (Hage, 1974: Part 1) would have been best developed in a new community hospital where there was some control over the selection of attending physicians. Likewise in the Ronken and Lawrence (1952) study we have an example of where the new product line worked well until it was integrated into the existing production line and then problems started.

Karpik (1972a) has suggested that most innovation in the future will come in small companies. We now see some of the reasons why this may be so. But, it is possible to imagine small companies as divisions – provided that they do have autonomy – within a larger multi-organization. Under these circumstances one can see large companies still pursuing successfully a policy of radical innovation.

Admittedly the choice of a new division is not always an option for innovators but it does represent the best way of giving a radical innovation a fair experiment and a good chance of succeeding.

7.4. CONCLUSIONS

The major theme through this chapter, and one consistent with a process perspective, has been what produces a qualitatively different kind of innovation, a radical change. Our answers have, in part, been consistent with the ideas expressed in the previous section and in part have provided exceptions.

Both a cybernetic perspective and a value perspective are helpful in understanding why there is so little radical innovation. Values affect the severity of standard. How feedback occurs influences whether a gap is detected or not. But the relationship between feedback and crisis is actually quite complex and tends to be curvilinear. Frequent measurement reduces the probability of a crisis that would lead to the choice of radical innovation.

Once a radical innovation is adapted, there is a chain of events that makes this change process quite interesting. There is likely to be a shift in the dominant coalition, a period of social conflict, and a transformation of the form of the organization, at least its social structure. This is a process that leads to both qualitative and quantitative change of the system.

The major problem is resistance. There are three reasons for resistance and each is relevant. Any concrete radical innovation involves resistance because self-interests are negatively affected, because there is little capacity for change, and because the particular benefits for the organization are not highly valued. Either the strategy of evolution or of revolution works very well in radical innovations because the piecemeal approach mitigates against them and because the fiat approach tends to generate too much conflict. The best — but expensive — solution is to implement a radical innovation in a new organization designed for this purpose.

Chapter Eight

Transformation of Form: Adaptation

The beginnings of a theory about the transformation of form were laid down in Chapter 5. There it was suggested that every organizational form has an inherent contradiction relative to functional performances. Some dominant coalitions tend to overemphasize innovation and ignore efficiency. Some dominant coalitions become too concerned about the volume of production and not enough about quality. The gradual recognition of this — usually by the board — leads to a succession and a new dominant coalition. In Chapter 6, we added the idea that organizational performance may be so bad that a crisis exists, which makes the existing or — more likely — new dominant coalition open to radical innovation. But this is not the only response to a crisis. Another kind of response is a transformation of the entire system, from one kind of form to another, from one set of characteristics to another. These changes, system changes, are the most interesting ones, because they produce the most enduring and far reaching kinds of changes.

The purpose of this chapter is to specify the kinds of crises and the responses that are possible. Only in some cases does the response mean a transformation of the system. Without understanding the kind of crisis, we can not evaluate whether the response is appropriate. Specification of the forms allows us to define states of equilibrium and of disequilibrium.

Many have criticized the system concept since it is built upon the assumption of equilibrium. But one can as easily criticize the concept of nonsystem because it denies the possibility of disequilibrium. What critics have failed to recognize is that conflict requires some sense of what is a normal state of affairs. Similarly, if one can define the approximate equilibrium states or steady states of the system, then all other combinations define disequilibrium states. Fortunately we need not specify all of the variables that define the system in order to have some moderate level of predictive utility (Ashby, 1956). If we can delineate a few of the major characteristics, then we can begin to identify the most common steady states. These then represent viable organizational forms.

Nor does the assumption of a system negate the idea of equifinality. Quite the contrary. The possibility that there is more than one typical steady state moves system analyses away from mechanistic models that most social scientists find too crude today even as heuristics. It accords with the recent intellectual developments relative to strategic choice (Child, 1972a; Warner (Ed.), 1977; and Chapter 13), that suggests that there are alternatives. Concepts like equilibrium, disequilibrium, and equifinality eschew the principle of total randomness. Not all alternatives, combinations, or causal sequences are viable. The different pathways by which an organizational system can move from one steady state to another, the transformation of form, is the key analytical focus of the book. The essential process by which this occurs is adaptiveness.

Perhaps the hardest concept to define is adaptiveness, since the word has been employed to mean so many ideas. Secretaries develop new filing systems, a worker in the assembly line puts a viable idea in the suggestion box, a university president develops a strategy of expansion, a research team finds a new way of treating cancer patients. Each of these can be perceived as adaptive; some are trivial and others are not. The concept of crisis allows us to focus on the more critical kinds of adaptive responses. And in fact, we will usually restrict the meaning to a transformation of form. This was the original intent in traditional functional analysis, although seldom achieved.

In the first section, three kinds of crisis are defined. These provide meaning to the concept of disequilibrium and add substance to the concept of social system. The critics of functionalism are correct; to assume a system is always in equilibrium is to miss the most important analytical issue in the study of social change. It is the dialectic between equilibrium and disequilibrium that helps us to predict transformation of form. Perhaps the most interesting problems in the adaptive process are the nonresponsiveness of dominant coalitions and their choice of incorrect responses when they finally do take action. The adaptation process usually starts with organizations which are unaware of environmental change until it has made a massive impact on organizational performance. In the previous two chapters we have identified a number of variables that affect whether or not the dominant coalition gets the message, and whether or not it tries to respond to new circumstances. But the process by which organizations cope, listen to feedback, select responses, and learn has not been specified in the literature. This is the subject of the second section.

The theory in this chapter adds substance to the cybernetic or systems paradigm. Too often, the open system's model has been left quite vague and ill-defined (see for example Katz and Kohn, 1966). There is a need to have testable hypotheses about when organizational systems change, why, and in what directions.

8.1. KINDS OF CRISES AND KINDS OF RESPONSES

There are many organizational crises, both objective and subjective, as any administrator or manager will testify. But if we confine our attention to what most managers and administrators worry about — that is, how well they are doing — then there would appear to be three ideal-typical situations: imbalances in the amount of performances achieved (see Caplow, 1964: 116-18 for the concept of points of stress), imbalances between inputs and outputs, and imbalances between structure and performance. In each instance, the dominant coalitions are concerned about performances and outputs, which is their way of demonstrating effectiveness. The difficult problem for them is that the cause of inadequate performance can lie in three quite disparate areas. Herein lies the test of managerial excellence and the reason why organizations appear to be run less than rationally! These situations are easily confounded.

Again, this concern about performances is consistent with our definition of organizations as input, throughput, and output systems. They are designed to *produce,* as Parsons (1956 a and b) noted long ago. This specific objective means that the dominant coalition is evaluated on how well they achieve. Likewise, they measure their own effectiveness in this way. This is one of the sole responsibilities of boards, and one that is likely to be exercised.

The term imbalance is used to stress the notion, consistent with its usage in biological and physical science, that equilibrium is a balance between opposing forces. In fact, it is this idea that is so attractive. Whether structural-functionalist, political-value adherent, or conflict enthusiast, the notion of opposing forces or of necessary and contradictory goals is an attractive one. What distinguishes the social sciences from the natural sciences is that the equilibrium point is more difficult to specify because the opposing forces are so much more complex. The equilibrium point is easy to overshoot or undershoot. For the truth of the matter is, most dominant coalitions do not know when they have achieved equilibrium because they tend to think in terms of the pursuit of a single goal rather than multiple objectives that are in opposition. Gradually, however, cost-benefit analysis and mini-max solutions are changing this mental set.

Once objectives that are incompatible are defined it becomes easy to understand how a performance crisis emerges. The resolution comes in identifying the causes of the bad performance. Sales may be falling but the reasons could be many — poor quality, high cost, obsolescence. Each of these requires a different remedy.

The first crisis, an imbalance in performances, is essentially resolved by steering between the dilemmas that exist, and this suggests an apt name for it: steering. The second crisis, an imbalance between inputs and outputs, is usually resolved by adjusting the amount of resources utilized, and this we can call the adjustment process. The third crisis is the transformation of form, or the change from one steady state to another. This is the adaptive process and the one that most concerns us in this chapter.

For management specialists, the steering and adjustment processes are probably the most interesting and form the core of many courses. How to balance performances and adjust the amount of resources relative to output are the daily decisions of most managers and administrators. For the organizational sociologist raised in the tradition of Weber, it is the adaptive process — correcting the imbalance between structure and performance — that is most relevant. The quintessential sociological problem is how best to design a team to achieve a particular utility. Organizational design has had a long tradition in management courses but is different from the question of which organizational form is best and why — the classic sociological problem. Furthermore, the way in which management and sociological researchers and theorists have focused on the problem of organizational design is quite different. The former have worked more on the concrete issues of unit size, span of control, and job satisfaction. The latter are concerned about the more abstract issues of centralization, innovation, and technology. The social psychologists have touched on both sets of issues (see Tannenbaum, 1968; Seashore and Bowers, 1963; Katz and Kahn, 1966; etc.).

There is little point in discussing organizational crises and states of disequilibrium without making apparent several existential assumptions regarding the environment:

1. Environmental change is inevitable.
2. Environmental change is not constant nor continuous.

Burns and Stalker (1961) noted the stability of environments. But even the most stable of environments does have some change, usually discontinuous, from time to time. These changes in turn affect organizational performances and outputs requiring either steering, adjustment, or adaptiveness upon the part of management or administration. Indeed, it is the interplay between these assumptions that makes life difficult for dominant coalitions. It is fine to construct an organic organization designed for constant innovation to meet environmental changes, but what does this mean when the environment is not changing? Conversely, when change does come to mechanical organizations where managers are used to stability, it is a shock (Biggart, 1977). The unpredictability of environment changes — that is, shifts in the speed with which various kinds of change occur — causes many headaches and explains the succession of dominant coalitions. Why and in what ways environments change is discussed at length in Part 4 of this book. For now we only observe that technological change and consumer taste shifts can occur in many unpredictable ways. The task for the dominant coalition to detect the crisis and respond to it — correctly. At best we can only give rough guidelines, but this we can do.

8.1.1. The Imbalance Between Performances and the Steering Response

In Chapter 5 we noted that there are four functional areas that need to be emphasized simultaneously, but that these tend to be dilemmas because they are somewhat in opposition. It is hard to maximize the quantity of production and at the same time introduce new products or services increasing innovation. Thus organizations tend to have phases — to borrow a term from Bales (1951) — which also correspond to the succession of dominant coalitions and their preferred objectives.

At any one moment the more that certain performances are being pursued, the less that others can be emphasized. For example, an organization may typically have a period when a number of new products are introduced, then a concern about the production volume, followed by attempts to cut costs, and this in turn may require a period of morale building. If so, this would exactly parallel the phase movement in small groups (Bales, 1951). This orderly sequence appears unlikely, and one can imagine that there are as many permutations. Furthermore, organizations can emphasize several of these performance areas simultaneously by means of specialization and departmentalization. The production department worries about production volume and cost, the R & D department is responsible for the development of new products, personnel is concerned about worker motivation, and so forth. But in general, even with team leadership and decentralization, it is difficult to pursue all four functional areas and their subgoals simultaneously.

Typically environmental change necessitates shifts in priorities. Prior to the energy crisis automobile buyers wanted cars that would give them status; afterwards they looked for economy. The dominant coalitions have been more or less successful in adapting to these changes in priorities among their customers. During periods when customers or clients want individualized products or services, organizations need to emphasize innovation and quality. When customers or clients are cost conscious, these organizations have to stress efficiency. During the 1960s the public demanded expansion in government services, especially in health and in education. During the 1970s Proposition 13 made government economy the top priority for all public agencies. Management tends to be judged by its relative performance, that is, relative to that of similar organizations — what Evan (1966) would call the organization-set — and this is largely environmentally determined.

The first kind of organizational crisis — imbalance between the four functional performance areas — can occur at anytime. It can result from too much innovation so that costs get out of hand, as happened with General Motors and DuPont immediately after the First World War (Chandler, 1962). It can be from too much cost cutting and not enough innovation, as happened with US Steel in the 1950s, or NCR and A&P in the 1970s (see Hage and Aiken, 1970: Chapter 3; *Fortune,* June, 1975: 114 et seq.).

With four functional variables – which in turn can be sub-divided into still more – there are already six possible combinations, just treating each objective or performance as either-or. If one starts specifying a number of ranges along each variable, then the various possible combinations start growing exponentially. At present we do not know enough to specify what these ranges would be. This is a strategic area for future research. But what we can do is specify at least three common dilemmas that all managers and administrators face. The equilibrium point between the opposing priorities is different depending upon the kind of organization, the nature of its environment, the various inputs, and a number of other variables. But regardless, the dilemma of too much of one performance or too little of another is eternally present!

An extended illustration of these dynamics is perhaps necessary. With the War on Poverty, suddenly large sums of money became available for welfare organizations (Dewar, 1976). Many of the programs required matching funds so there was an expansion of state funds as well. This led to a very rapid expansion in the number of new programs in some health and welfare organizations and the expansion of their existing programs in others. The War on Poverty illustrates how environments can place a greater stress on innovation. There was agitation for the addition of new services. Community organization became a popular mechanism. At the same time, the enrichment of the environment meant that existing programs could be radically expanded. Many but not all public and private agencies steered – that is, shifted their priorities – towards innovation and growth.

Some organizations experienced rapid change with the addition of new programs and others rapid growth in output. Of the two processes, the former caused greater disequilibrium precisely because it meant a growth in the concentration of specialists. The speed with which this occurred did not allow enough time for the other system variables to change also. A drop in efficiency led the dominant coalitions to try to control the organization through heightened supervision and rule observation. Morale declined for both reasons, in part a response to the rapid speed of change and the accelerated growth, and in part to the necessity for greater control measures, especially those that restricted job autonomy.

This short history of health and welfare organizations in the period of 1964–1969 illustrates how environmental changes require organizational elites to shift their priorities. But as they do, disequilibrium is likely to occur and balance is difficult to achieve.

The *first* dilemma is the correct balance between the quality and the quantity of production (Hage, 1965). The standards that define quality are themselves shifting. Perhaps the most striking illustration of how standards of quality can suddenly shift is the sharp rise in malpractice suits against physicians in the United States during the 1960s. Likewise, bright students at the better universities – Berkeley, Michigan, Wisconsin – began complaining, and rightly so, about the quality of teaching, forcing the professionals to be more concerned about this objective. Even tastes and preferences relative to the *importance* of quality are more or less continuously altering as well.

If the quality of service is a frequent complaint about public organizations, the quality of the product is a complaint against most private organizations. Nader's Raiders have helped bring about major legislation that has provided much more consumer protection. The continual recall of cars and tires is not a sign of lower quality so much as a demand for higher quality that is actually being met.

The costs involved with too much concern about quality are becoming apparent. Management must strike a balance between the quality of the product or service and the quantity that is provided. And since environmental change regarding both standards and tastes is an ever present possibility, finding an equilibrium point does not mean that one can be assured it will remain the same for very long.

In the public service area, administrators would like to deny that they do anything else but provide high quality for everyone but this is objectively not true. Universities vary considerably in the quality of education and the number of students processed. Public welfare agencies tend to be overwhelmed by the number of clients they must service; they have enormous difficulties in maintaining quality. One advantage of the private sector in the United States is that it can refuse students, clients, or patients, attempting to maintain some standards of quality. This is most visible in admissions to Ivy League schools but is found in many areas. Perhaps the most dramatic example of the difficulty of maintaining quality during a period of growth is the illustration of state universities during the 1960s.

The *second* dilemma focuses on the relative emphasis on change versus stability of products and services (Perrow, 1967). If business organizations change too slowly, they can lose their market to competitors. (We are assuming here that organizations have some autonomy and that these are not natural monopolies as in the military; see the discussion of environments where this is not the case in Chapter 13.) If they change too rapidly the same thing can happen. The problem exists also for hospitals and universities, welfare agencies and associations. Patients, students, and clients do shop around for certain kinds of services and if they do not find them will go elsewhere. Again, an equilibrium exists between change and stability – although it is quite different in public or private, and product or service organizations; there is a correct balance for each.

The example above of the War on Poverty illustrates how environments create a mood of change. As we noted in the previous chapter, there are change periods, when rates of innovation become the dominant way of evaluating an organization's performance. There are not only cost leaders but pace setters relative to the tempo of innovation. The major historical periods for this in the United States have been roughly every other decade — for example the 1920s, 1940s, 1960s. — followed by a decade of consolidation and more stability. These swings are associated with periods of economic boom and also of considerable war effort. In fact, much of the technological explosion since the Second World War has its origins first in that war, and second in the cold war with the USSR.

Beyond the cyclical tendency between innovation and consolidation periods there is a long-term trend towards faster and faster rates of innovation and less and less emphasis on stability (Toffler, 1970). Product lives are becoming shorter (Mansfield, 1968). Zero budget analysis in government is becoming more popular. Long range planning is more common (Schonfeld, 1966). All these facts suggest increasing concern by dominant coalitions with their innovation rate, which implies a simple solution. One can increase expenditures on R&D. But one can speed too much, innovate too rapidly, and not develop an adequate stability. The example of the health and welfare agencies above is one illustration of what can happen.

The *third* dilemma revolves around the balance between human and material costs. High motivation and high productivity are not always related, as a number of studies have indicated (see Chapter 9). Keeping turnover down and efficiency up, eliminating alienation and cutting costs, are seldom reconcilable. The test of managerial skill is the finding of this equilibrium point. Nor is the problem a static one. Standards of exploitation change. Workers' consciousness rises. Appropriate safety standards of twenty years ago are now considered barbaric. The length of the work week has shortened and the number of vacation days has lengthened. Our standards of efficiency have therefore considerably altered. Pay scales in general have risen faster than productivity (Brown and Browne, 1968). All these environmental changes have meant a moving equilibrium point between human and material costs, with the accent more and more on the former rather than the latter. Much of this has been made possible by mechanization and automation which are often denounced. But regardless of whether good or bad, the key point is that efficiency is not a static standard and costs are a problem for every dominant coalition.

The same swings associated with innovation tend to be associated *in reverse* with a concern about efficiency. In the United States, the 1930s, 1950s, and 1970s have been decades of cost consciousness rather than concern about working conditions. When the environment dictates a particular value, whether cost consciousness or worker morale, dominant coalitions must also shift in order to maintain legitimacy with both resource controllers and their rank and file.

Each of these pairs is truly a dilemma. Too much quantity and not enough quality or the reverse will cause the company to go out of business. Too much stability or too much consciousness and the workers will strike or have slow-downs. Too little and the resource controllers or customers will stop providing funds.

The effectiveness equilibrium problem can be made more complex by adding other performance dilemmas. However, these three dilemmas allow us to see several ideal-type steady states. All three dilemmas represent rather consistent organizational strains and are standards by which management or administration tend to be judged. As we have noted in the previous chapter, the more frequently the horn of each dilemma is measured, the more sensitive management is to the need for some organizational change. But these standards or dilemmas move beyond the question of whether there is a need for a new output or process change to the relative balance among priorities of the organization, a more subtle analytical problem.

What are some typical steady states? There are two major states, each of which has several subtypes. The first might be called the quality-change steady state and the second the quantity-stable steady state. Over the long term, organizations develop preferences. Some are concerned more about the quality of their product or service than the size of the market or the number of clients. Others worry more about the latter than the former. These two ideal types are what Burns and Stalker (1961) had in mind when they examined the electronics industry. The mechanical organizations were concerned about the production volume and maintaining stability so as to minimize costs. The organic organizations were concerned about the creation of new products to meet quite particularistic needs.

Once these kinds of performances become institutionalized, they are diffi-cult to change because it would require a transformation of the entire system, a shift from a mechanical to an organic form or vice versa. Instead, dominant coalitions are more concerned with finding the right balance. An important variation on each of these two steady states is the organization that produces a quality product or service but where the technology does not change very often. Examples include home builders who make custom built houses for a limited market, small quality furniture manufacturers, perfume manufacturers, employment agencies (although recently there have been a large number of technological changes here), and the like. Likewise, there are organizations that produce goods for large markets but where the tempo of environmental change is quite fast. For example, the electrical and the chemical manufacturers tend to represent examples of organizations that are more likely to emphasize quan-tity and change at the same time. Among service organizations, community hospitals must serve large numbers of patients and at the same time be con-cerned about a relatively high rate of technological change, at least since the end of the Second World War.

With only these two dilemmas, we have four steady states. These represent

ways in which managers and administrators can demonstrate effectiveness. Again
it is important to recognize that there is not one single kind of effectiveness but
instead a variety of ways in which organizations can justify their existence to
resource controllers and gain legitimacy.

If we add the third dilemma between material and human costs we can create
more steady states, but instead it seems preferable to define the nature of the
organizational crisis that organizations in each steady state tend to face. With
effectiveness the crisis is usually "too much of a good thing"! Caplow (1964:
148-54) has noted the complacency of elites, which stems in part from ignoring
other performances. Organizations in the quality-change steady state are likely
to overemphasize these performances and be especially vulnerable in an environment that shifts towards stability and quantity. The reverse is the weakness of the organizations that emphasize the opposite priorities.

Unfortunately successive studies have not examined the four functional problems simultaneously, and therefore the relationship between leadership change
and priority shift has not been directly tested. What one can say is that turnover
is more frequent in complex environments (Caplow, 1964: 196), which implies
the need for different leadership styles and coalitions.

In summary, there are at least four steady states in achieving balance in performances. Disequilibrium is usually an overemphasis on the most typical
priorities brought about by a shift in customer or client preferences. Reequilibration is achieved through the process of succession. Leaders steer between the
opposing priorities across time, attempting to maintain the equilibrium point
most appropriate for the organization given its environmental situation (see
Chapters 12 and 13).

Given the failure of most typologies, one might question the advantages of
trying anew. What distinguishes the typology that is explicited here and in chapters 3, 5, 12, and 13 is that it is built around basic dilemmas that are found in all
organizations, although the relative importance of each performance varies.
Equally important, the definition of some of the viable systems requires nonlinear combinations of variables. This was the true inspiration of Weber's methodology of ideal-types. Also, the typology to be constructed involves variables
of organizational structure, technology and size, environmental constraints,
kinds of throughput, and so forth. In some instances these variables have no
association whatsoever, making them perfect candidates for the generation of
a typology. The attempt is to construct the major features of the entire system.
As this is done, a number of theoretical works are synthesized.

8.1.2. The Imbalance Between Inputs and Outputs
and the Adjustment Response

The Cobb-Douglas production function is well known in economics. And despite
the similarity of concerns between management schools and economics, the

organizational literature has not really tried to apply these ideas in the organizational context despite the popularity of the input, throughout, and output model or definition of an organization (Katz and Kahn, 1966; James Thompson, 1967). For example, any discussion of the trade-offs between labor investment and machine investment is in point of fact a discussion of the balance in inputs vis-à-vis outputs with cost being a major consideration. The discussion of trade-offs can be extended to include other inputs or resources as well, including knowledge and even that intangible, power.

Probably the main reason why production functions have not been much employed in organizational analysis is the relative difficulty in measuring the outputs that many sociologists tend to be interested in, such as education, health, and welfare. Even in the business sector product quality has posed numerous problems for the consumer movement (see any issue of *Consumer's Guide*). Ideally one would want some unambiguous measure of value added.

The recent development of cost benefit analysis in the public sector, however, is changing this, even if the studies primarily reduce all measures to dollars and cents. Gradually measures are being developed (Weisbrod, 1964; any issue of *Policy Studies*) of inputs and outputs. Sociologists would think differently than economists and especially about which ones are most important. On the input side, the factors of production are:

1. Knowledge, and more specifically the skill or training of the labor force and the automaticity of the machine system, including tools.
2. Power, and more specifically the autonomy of the organization to do what it wants and especially to set prices or fees, choose clients, and to compete without regulation.
3. Money, and more specifically capital investment.
4. Labor, or size of the work force as distinct from skill levels.

The distinction between the size of the labor force and its skill or training as human capital is increasingly common in economics (Denniston, 1969). Typically the decision to replace men with machines means reducing the size of the labor force. It may or may not mean any change in the skill levels involved. The adoption of an assembly line throughput technology may mean lower skill levels are needed, while the movement to automation usually implies higher skill levels (Blauner, 1964; Walker, 1957; Woodward, 1965).

Unlike the economists, we can ignore land as not really being a factor of production. But we cannot ignore power as they do. The struggle between the teachers and the community school board in New York City, the many discussions of Soviet dissenters, the debate about the multinational corporation, the complaints of welfare clients and students in the 1960s makes apparent how much organizational autonomy is a factor in the production function. The equilibrium point is another matter, and more difficult to determine. Much of the present debate over free enterprise and government regulation really revolves around the issue of just how much autonomy can be allowed to organizations. This is a key research area that requires investigation.

Organizational sociologists have tended to ignore capital investment and its significance for the organization. As we shall see, however, this becomes an important way of distinguishing organizational environments (see Chapter 13). Part of the swing in the relative emphasis on innovation versus efficiency is due to the ready availability of funds or the richness versus leanness of the environment (Azumi, 1972; Khandwalla, 1977; Aldrich, 1979: 63 et seq.).

How delicate the balance between inputs and outputs can be is illustrated in Becker and Neuhauser (1976: 18). They cite the example that a reduction in the labor of 8000 employees meant a 5% reduction in prices. This in turn resulted in an 18% gain in sales, with presumably a much greater gain in productivity. While the gains are not always so dramatic, the marginal utilities on price are such that small shifts can produce large gains. This occurred in a retail chain where cost was the major utility of the customer.

Instead of arguing that there is a single production function, it appears advisable to recognize that there are several ideal-typical situations. The first would be the mass produced product: rubber tires, low priced automobiles, cement, glass, and so on. Although we do not think of people-processing organizations in the same way, they are universalistic bureaucracies, such as the welfare agencies that dispense funds. Custodial mental hospitals and prisons (Goffman, 1961) or total institutions are similar examples. The second production function would be the custom-made or individualized service such as quality universities, *haute couture,* sheltered workshops, custom-made cars, and university hospitals. We can also imagine several variations to these two, depending upon the market size or number of potential clients. For each of these steady states, the right mix of personnel size, skill, training, capital investment, and autonomy to produce the output is unknown and problematic.

Each of these four inputs represents a dilemma for the management or administration of an organization. Regardless of whether the output is mass produced or custom made, with batch production or some form of continuous automation, the question is how big a labor force is needed, how much training or skill, what capital investment, and how much autonomy. There are optimal combinations relative to each of these kinds of productions. With too much training costs will sky-rocket. With too little investment, the inputs that are available might be wasted, a frequent problem in government grants for demonstration projects (Aiken et al., 1975).

Much more thought can be given to the problem of effective utilization of capital investment relative to clients in the public sector. Many universities tend not to teach in the evenings. Schools could be used as welfare agencies during the late afternoons and early evenings. Just as stores are gradually moving to being open 24 hours a day and plants have been working three shifts for some time, many more uses could be found for public buildings. Much more productive use can be made of the plant investment in the public sector.

Although we do not think of organizational autonomy as a problem, and especially relative to a production function, the optimal balance here is an everyday issue. Berliner's (1957) study of Russian factories is an example of how little autonomy was counter-productive and some relaxation of the rules was allowed so as to achieve more production. Antitrust legislation and the importance of maintaining competition in free market economies are the reverse problem. Give organizations too much autonomy — as is perhaps the case at present with multinational corporations — and we have neither the products we need nor the prices we can afford, nor the maximum of reasonable working conditions, as the history of labor legislation can testify.

Disequilibrium comes most typically when there is an excess of one or more inputs relative to the output being achieved. They are most easily recognized when there are sudden changes in the environment. The most typical situation is falling demand. What does one do with the excess labor force, capital investment, and the like? Typically where the product is mass-produced there are wide scale layoffs. However, when the product is custom-made there are not. It has been a widely observed phenomenon that staff size tends not to decline during economic recessions. Presumably the greater the skill and training of the labor force, the more reluctant one is to let them go because of the high start-up costs in their hiring. The size or scale of the labor force makes a difference as well.

Again it is important to note these are the responses of some firms in some capitalist economies. where the economy is totally coordinated the problems of booms and of busts are much less likely to occur. In the Third World, excess employment is maintained because of welfare considerations (Prethus, 1961).

The problem of adjusting the size of the labor force becomes even greater when labor contracts or other considerations such as worker morale make the costs of doing so too great. Indeed the long term trend has made the reduction of the labor force in the face of falling demand less and less an option. In turn, this explains why increasingly inflation can grow in times of unemployment. Of course, automatic salary increases have a similar impact.

Although we do not think of rapidly rising demand as a problem, it creates a serious difficulty as well. Where does one find the manpower or the capital to meet the increased clients or customers? This was the real crisis in higher education during the 1960s. This involved not only wages rising too rapidly as universities kept outbidding each other for rare skills, but too much power for the professors relative to job autonomy so that student concerns were lost to view. Too-rapid increases can mean a waste of resources as well. The speed with which an organization grows is usually not conceived of as a problem, but it is. Managers or administrators are reluctant to turn away customers and clients, but in the period of rapidly expanding demand this may be the only way of maintaining effectiveness equilibrium. The familiar signs of this are a lowering of standards. Thus staff qualifications decline when there are shortages of staff, the typical problem in rapid growth environments. Wage costs, as already noted, may go up too fast, and so forth.

Besides changes in the amount of demand for a product or service, another very typical change to which organizations may have to adjust is a shift from a market emphasizing cost to one emphasizing quality or the reverse. This requires an adjustment in the balance of inputs, typically from an unskilled to a skilled labor force, from less to more capital investment, and perhaps a reduction in the size of the labor force. And it may require a change in the amount of organizational autonomy also. As we shall see, the problem can be complicated because a real radical shift from producing a quality product to a mass-produced one requires more than just an adjustment of some changes in the mix of the inputs, but perhaps a fundamental change in the structure of the organization.

Here there are probably many more than four ideal-type productive functions. In Figure 8.1, we have listed four that parallel the issues of technology and personnel size – that is, the relative skill level and size of the labor force. Since these two variables receive extended discussion in Chapter 12, we need not explore the issue here except to observe that these represent quite distinct production functions and should not be confonded. Capital investment has complex relations with these. Organizational autonomy can be perceived as a variation with these four basic kinds.

Given a crisis of either too much or too little demand, the dominant coalition typically adjusts its organization's inputs in the ways that have been described. Much more research needs to be done on what might be more appropriate and humane adjustment responses than hiring people and letting them go in recessions and depressions. Here automation may play a decisive role in the future.

8.1.3. The Imbalance Between Structure and Performance and the Adaptive Response

The two previous imbalances did not require much change of the system. Reequilibration is achieved by means of a shift in priorities or an alteration of inputs. Essentially these are processes that help maintain the existing organizational form. This third crisis is of more interest because it is a transformation process, that is, a change of the system rather than a change within the system.

8.1.3.1. The Definition of Adaptiveness. What complicates the discussion of adaptiveness is that implicit in this concept, which is borrowed from biology, is the notion that the response is a correct one. In other words, something adaptive

Figure 8.1 Equilibrium problems—steady states and organizational crises

---

The problem of the equilibrium point for over-all effectiveness: balance in performance.

Dilemmas
  Quality vs. quantity of production
  Change vs. stability
  Human vs. material costs
Steady states
  Quality-change
  Quality-stability
  Quantity-stability
  Quantity-change

The problem of the equilibrium point for the production function: balances in inputs and output.

Dilemmas
  Small vs. large labor force
  Unskilled vs. skilled labor force
  Small vs. large capital investment
  Small vs. large organizational autonomy
Steady states
  Highly skilled, small labor force
  Unskilled, very large labor force
  Moderately skilled, moderately small labor force
  Skilled and unskilled, moderately large labor force

The problem of the equilibrium point for organizational design: balances in structures and performances.

Dilemmas
  Concentration of specialists vs. centralization
  Concentration of specialists vs. stratification
  Stratification vs. decentralization
Steady states
  Organic-professional
  Traditional—craft
  Mechanic-bureaucratic
  Organic-mechanic

---

for an organization helps it to survive, increase prestige or profits, adjust to a changing world, and the like. This is unfortunate because what might be a correct response in one situation is not in another. Organizational elites fumble, frequently make the wrong decisions, and pursue the wrong strategies before finally hitting upon one that is right. Worse yet, the standard of success may be very misleading. NCR had sales increasing at the rate of 12% per annum in the 1960s but its market share was declining (*Fortune,* 1975: 114 et seq.).

For me, the heart of the matter is that adaptiveness is a particular kind of response to a particular kind of situation. There are many situations and many responses, in fact too many to list or even to identify. The best that can be done is to limit the definition to *one* major situation, a crisis of form. The definition is:

Adaptiveness: The alteration and transformation of the form so as to survive better in the environment.

Sterring and adjustment processes are not this and therefore not adaptive. I have labeled each as a distinct category so that adaptiveness can be more easily defined and labeled. Usually discussions of adaptiveness would consider steering and adjustment processes as adaptive as well. However, these two processes are system maintaining, whereas we are most interested in the transformation of the system and especially one that changes the form not only qualitatively but quantitatively. Alterations of the dominant coalitions are most typically the former rather than the latter. The shift from a mechanical to an organic form would be an example; that is, a change from one steady state to another. The definitions of equilibrium states or steady states and their counterpart – disequilibrium – is then the next task. What are viable forms? Each time that we can specify a relationship between a structural variable and a performance variable we also identify an equilibrium problem. There are marginal utilities operating relative to each structural-functional hypothesis. The exact equilibrium point will vary depending upon environmental and resource conditions, but there is some balance point that maximizes that particular performance. This was the original thrust of the work of Taylor and others: Finding the structure that would maximize efficiency. However, Taylor and the early industrial engineers had a very narrow conception of efficiency. It was to divide tasks into very narrow units and simplify physical movement as much as possible. The essential imagery is that of the assembly line. Little was said about managers or administrators. In contrast, the emphasis since the end of the Second World War has been on the managerial side, as it was with Weber and his model of rational-legal authority.

By the time of organization X and organization Y (McGregor, 1960), everyone appreciated that there were perhaps two utilities to be maximized. Similarly

Burns and Stalker's (1961) organic and mechanical structures are designed to maximize innovation or technical efficiency respectively.

8.1.3.2. The Definition of Viable Forms.
Poor performance can be a function not only of imbalance between performances as between inputs and outputs but also between structure and performance. Following Burns and Stalker (1961), we can suggest that there are two major compatible forms or arrangements, which they have called the organic and the mechanical. The variables are listed in Figure 8.2. The pure organic or professional organization has a design of high concentration of specialists and is low in centralization so as to achieve the performances of quality and change. Examples of output are custom-made products and individualized services, as found in many universities, research institutes, law firms, architectural firms, instrument manufacturers, and the like (Hage and Aiken, Chapter 2). Lawrence and Lorsch's (1967 a and b) study of plastic firms provide another concrete example. Nor should we forget divisions of multi-organizations that produce highly sophisticated equipment almost for individual order. Nuclear power plant divisions are one example; the divisions that produce gigantic computers tailor-made to specialized needs are another. High quality mental hospitals, family therapy, rehabilitation homes, half-way houses, and the like are other examples in the service sector.

In contrast the pure mechanical-bureaucratic organizational design has the opposite set of characteristics. The steady state relative to performances tends to be quantity and stability rather than quality and change. The outputs are mass products and standardized services. Examples are tobacco, rubber, automobile, sewing machine, and cement manufacturers and heavy industry in general. Again, we are speaking of particular divisions in multi-organizations.

In the public sector, the military services best fit this organizational pattern. Crozier's (1964) work is an excellent illustration of two publicly owned organizations in France, a service organization and a tobacco factory. The container industry in the Lawrence and Lorsch (1967 a and b) research is another example. Railroads, large chain retailers and – a recent addition – the fast food industry are other illustrations where this form can be found.

There are at least two important variations on these forms. The first might be called the traditional organizational form. The workers are craftsmen – that is, skilled – and the organization produces small batches of quality products. The priority is stability rather than change. There is a moderate amount of concentration of specialists, but not as high as in the pure organic form and the organization tends to be much more centralized and stratified. Because the workers or teachers or staff are craftsmen or artisans or semi-professionals rather than full professionals, there is a willingness to accept more centralization than one would otherwise expect, given the concentration of specialists. They do not have

Figure 8.2 The characteristics of several organic and mechanical steady states

Pure organic (professional)	Traditional craft
Structural variables: High concentration of highly skilled specialists, professional degrees	Structural variables: Moderate concentration of specialists, typically craft
Low centralization	High centralization
Low stratification	High stratification
High normative equality	Low normative equality
Performance variables: Quality-change	Performance variables: Quality-stability
Custom made products, individualized or particularized service	Batch production, artisan service

Pure mechanic (bureaucratic)	Mechanic-organic
Structural variables: Low concentration of specialists	Structural variables: Moderately high concentration of specialists, engineers
High centralization	Centralized and decentralized
High stratification	Stratified and destratified
Low normative equality	Both low and high normative equality
Performance variables: Quantity-stability	Performance variables: Quantity-change
Mass-produced product, standard services	Automated production, moderately standardized product coupled with highly individualized service

much formal education but do have a lot of apprenticeship or on-the-job train-ing. As a consequence they are socialized into certain modes of traditional authority, and because they take pride in their work there is a great deal of self-control, eliminating the need for supervision. As indicated in Chapter 12, these organizations also tend to be small. The lack of constant change implies that strategic decisions are likely to be few and far between. Here one would expect to find centralization of strategic decisions combined with job autonomy for the craftsmen or semi-professionals. Examples are moderate and high priced furniture manufacturers, the garment makers, police departments, elementary schools, and the like. Perhaps the most interesting observation about this kind of organization is that change tends to be associated more with swings in taste upon the part of the customer or client. While this is easy to see in the case of the shoe, clothing, and housing industries, it is even true for organizations such as police departments and elementary schools. There are swings in public demand for what needs to be protected and what needs to be taught. Traditional organizations are a strategic site for research because they can evolve in so many ways depending upon the nature of the environmental change (see Chapter 14).

Somewhere between the traditional and mechanical forms there is a gray area of mixtures of the two that illustrate the basic typology of forms and at the same time the range of possibilities. Most furniture manufacturers are small, but there are a few that mass produce low cost furniture. These organizations look like the mechanical form, or are much closer to it in many ways. There are still differences, however. Most automobile companies are large but some are small, producing almost a custom built car for a very special niche in the market. These organizations, which may be divisions in multi-organizations, look very much like traditional forms. The sense of craftsmanship is a critical element. But note that these seeming exceptions illustrate the basic point about the equilibrium of structure and performance. Clothing manufacturers may mass produce and be concerned about selling low cost suits but they must adopt the mechanical form. Likewise cigarettes are mass produced by machines but cigars are not, to take an example in the tobacco industry. Because of this, these companies have a more traditional, artisan-based organization. This is one reason why it is necessary to define organizations on the basis of their throughput and its similarity. This is technologically specific and there are great variations even within the same common sense classification.

Another important form is the mixed breed, part organic and part mechanic. By this I mean more than the observation that research and development may be designed organically and production be built on mechanical principals, although this is the most typical arrangement (Lawrence and Lorsch, 1967). More critical is the relative importance of these departments for the growth of the organization. Many companies can have research and development, but they differ enormously in size, staff, and operating budget both in absolute terms and in relative ones. Likewise, production departments can vary considerably along the same dimensions. What concerns us here are organizations where both departments are large and critical to the survival of the organization. Examples where research budgets are large and the R&D is a critical part of the organization are the drug companies, the computer industry, the airplane industry, the electrical equipment industry, and by and large the chemical industry.

Since so many of these companies are multi-organizations, the analytical level can frequently become confused. My focus is on the division with a distinctive throughput. It may be nylon or paints or explosives or fertilizers, to take examples from the chemical industry. It may be main frame computers, minicomputers, typewriters, or soft-ware, to take an illustration from the computer industry. But regardless of the division and its specific technology and marketing characteristics, the research is likely to be large and based on organic principals while the production is likely to be large and based on more mechanical principals.

Many of these multi-organizations have a basic research division at the main headquarters that explores its own desires. This may not be the best way of organizing research, treating it as a staff function, at the multi-organizational level. Instead it may be more appropriate to have separate research units for each major division in the company. A basic research unit that is separate from the production units creates coordination problems (Lawrence and Lorsch, 1967).

Another mixed arrangement is for some product lines to be mechanical and others organic. Under these circumstances one finds both highly skilled and semi-skilled, centralized and decentralized, and the like. There are two distinct hierarchies. This is especially likely in the chemical, electrical, and computer industries. The examples in public service organizations are less common mainly because they are not allowed, at least in the United States, to become very large. The Ministry of Education in France, the Veterans Administration in the United States, and the Health Service in Britain are illustrations. However, large scale professional organizations organized on a nation-wide basis are the prototypes in the public sector. The European Social Security system tends to be organized this way.

The French have created regional hospitals for very difficult cases that are relatively rare, city hospitals for the typical health problems, and small rural hospitals which can only handle a limited range of medical needs. Patients are sent to the hospital nearest them, depending upon the level of expertise needed and the kind of equipment. Research is separated very much from hospitals, performed in many laboratories. In fact the French have been trying to integrate research and hospital care more than is done at present.

If craftsmen and artisans are the kind of specialists that one finds in traditional organizations, the mixed mechanical-organic form tends to have a special occupational category: engineers (Perrow, 1967). Engineering is different from most professions, including management specialties, in placing more emphasis on what they have learned than on continual learning (there are many exceptions on both sides of the classification scheme). The consequence is that they are more willing to accept higher levels of centralization than one might otherwise expect. Typically the research may be done by PhDs but the production and marketing, including many aspects of product design, are handled by engineers.

The best way to visualize these few basic forms is as clusters in a two-dimensional space defined by centralization and the concentration of specialists. The space could be made much more complicated by adding other structural variables, most especially stratification and normative equality.

In Chapter 3, we noted a basic tendency for the concentration of specializations to have a negative impact on the degree of centralization. This tendency is represented by the main diagonal with mechanic-bureaucratic forms at one end and organic-professional forms at the other end of the continuum. The important point is that this is a continuum with a considerable range. The automotive divisions and armies are at one extreme and art galleries and advertising firms are at the other. *The first and most fundamental transformation process is the movement along the diagonal of mechanical versus organic.*

The causes of this are discussed in Chapters 13 and 14. Here one might observe that as the concentration of specialists increases, decentralization decreases. At some quantitative point, we have a new form.

The two other forms fall off this main diagonal. They are important because they actually represent a large number of different kinds of public and private organizations. Consistent with our discussion in Chapter 3, they have not only more centralization than one would otherwise expect but their power structures have discontinuities in them. In traditional organizations, the craftsmen have considerable autonomy. These are organizations where the correlation between job autonomy and centralization may actually be positive. The discontinuity exists therefore between hierarchical levels. In mixed mechanical-organic organizations, the engineers accept more centralization than one might otherwise expect given their professional training. But as suggested above, engineers are not the same as most other professionals. Beyond this, there tends to be a discontinuity between the hierarchy in production and in research, which is why it is called a mixed form. These are organizations where one would expect a lower correlation between the concentration of specialists and centralization.

Within these viable ranges of the combinations of variables one finds some interesting hybrids that can add some complexity to our discussion of organizational forms. We have already noted the high volume traditional kind of organization that has evolved towards the mechanical model, and the high quality mechanical kind of organization that has a much more traditional structure. But there are other combinations as well. There are organizations that are half way between a mechanical and a mixed mechanical-organic form. In these change is much more important. Actually the current situation in the automobile industry is a case in point. The need for pollution-free low gasoline consumption cars has made research and product design engineers much more important than they would normally be.

Somewhere between the organic and the mixed mechanical-organic professional lies another gray zone. These are organizations, which while committed to change, are much more sensitive to the balance between quality and quantity. The pocket calculator industry might be a current example.

Probably the rarest organizational forms or steady states are those where both the concentration of specialists and centralization are low. These can exist, but only under a very special set of circumstances. They are usually very small organizations with less than twenty members, and therefore they approximate a group more than an organization. Privately-owned family businesses would be one example. Small private social work agencies where everyone is in the same occupation and usually highly trained is another. Technically the concentration of specialists might score low, but in reality we have an elite high quality agency. Other modern examples are half-way houses and group homes. Again, the small size and the affective relationships involved in the task lead to much more decentralization than one might expect.

The whole question of defining viable forms or equilibrium states, as has been done in Figure 8.3, becomes much more complex as soon as one increases the number of variables defining the organizational system. Throughout we have *oversimplified* for the purposes of exposition and clarity by concentrating on the major dialectic between the concentration of specialists and the centralization of power. Little attention has been paid to the additional variations produced by the structural variables of stratification and normative equality. Yet we know that in certain organizations status and privilege can become much more important than power as dimensions of design. In Chapter 3, we noted that different trade-offs exist. So in certain kinds of organizations, stratification or normative equality might be more important than centralization.

What is the evidence that in fact these four basic forms, where two form a continuum, are the major kinds? The large amount of evidence presented in Chapters 3 and 6 indicates that there is indeed a basic tendency for centralization and the concentration of specialists to be negatively related and for the latter variable to be highly related to innovation rates. The higher the associa-

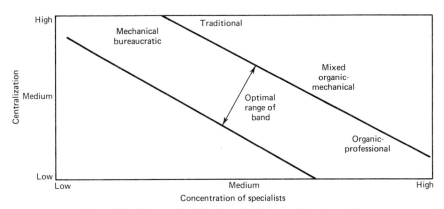

Figure 8.3 The graph of the four ideal-types of steady states.

tion between these variables, that is, the more the correlations approach 1.00, the more that one can argue that there is only one continuum as described by Burns and Stalker (1961) and as theoretically delineated by Hage (1965): the mechanical-bureaucratic and organic-professional. Since many of the studies indicate ranges of .50 to .70, depending upon the kind of throughput and the size of the sample, this suggests that the basic continuum is the dominant axis, but there are enough exceptions so that one must look for other forms.

Unfortunately, as yet there has been no direct test of the typology being proposed. One would have to revisit the organizations in each of the many studies I have reanalyzed, recode them according to type, and then test whether they have the basic characteristics predicted here. Beyond this, many of the business organizations in the Aston, Child, and Azumi studies are multi-organizations. One would have to focus on each of the distinctive throughputs. Finally, one would have to look at relative rates of success within each kind of throughput, as did Woodward (1965) and Lawrence and Lorsch (1967 a and b), to really check the causal link between structure and organizational performance.

An interesting example of this is provided in the research of Child on airline companies (Warner, Ed., 1977); he found that the organic variety and the mechanical variety as we have defined them did function well, whereas the mixture of the two did not. Airline companies have a choice as to whether they want to emphasize quality service or low cost. Thus both ideal-types can be found in this sector.

There are other pieces of evidence that in fact these basic forms are equilibrium states, viable combinations of variables scores. In Chapter 10 some evidence is presented that indicates that as one moves away from the continuum drawn in Figure 8.3, conflict grows. This is circumstantial evidence that there are equilibrium states; if there is not the right combination, then conflict emerges. The signs of disequilibrium not only manifest themselves in poor performance but also in the emergence of internal conflict. Obviously, the two have some relationship.

In summary, there are more than four forms or equilibrium states. The continuum between low concentration of specialists combined with high centralization and high concentration of specialists with low centralization represents as many states as there are distinctive measurable scores. One could easily specify some twenty different steady states corresponding to each increase of 5% in the concentration of specialists, or each decrease of 5% in the centralization of decision making. Given time lags and the like, we can also assume that a certain range of scatter is entirely viable.

There are two other forms: traditional and mechanic-organic. Typically they represent special conditions such as the presence of craft or the separation of specialists and nonspecialists into different but equally important departments and hierarchies.

There are various hybrids that lie between each of these forms. The traditional organization that emphasizes production volume and the mechanical organization that produces a limited quality product is in between these two basic forms. Likewise there are several hybrids that are interstitial between the organic-professional and the mixed mechanic-organic.

Additional characteristics of each of these four basic forms are discussed in other chapters as we touch upon technology, size, capital, autonomy, mechanisms of coordination and control, and strategies of growth. In particular, Chapter 12 explores in considerable detail the production process or throughput associated with each type.

8.1.3.3. The Definition of Equilibrium and Disequilibrium. The essential thesis of this monograph is that the two major causes of transformation are technological development and market demand. How these impact on the structural characteristics of the organization will be discussed in Chapters 12 and 13. For now, let us assume that there is an increase in the concentration of specialists. The reasons for this may be many: product development because of a successful R&D effort, of increased education of the labor force, of the development of new occupations that are employed, and of the impact of new machines on the throughput (Chandler, 1977). Usually the degree of centralization does not change. At some point, tensions build up creating manifest conflict. This problem can then lead to a transformation of the form of the organization towards the organic or the mixed mechanical-organic, depending upon the initial starting point.

Another scenario is the dominant coalitions decision to increase centralization. This may come slowly with the growth in personnel size and a lack of delegation. Or it may come rapidly with a crisis such as the introduction of a radical innovation. Again, there may be conflict unless the concentration of specialists is reduced by the hiring of less skilled workers. Here we have a movement towards the mechanical or a mixed mechanical-organic, again depending upon the starting point.

These ideas are developed much more later. The crucial argument is that the transformation of form starts by the change of *one* system variable. In turn, this creates disequilibrium, which is manifested in conflict or failure to achieve objectives. These events force the dominant coalition to break up, to be replaced, or to cope. Once the variables are changed, we can say there is a new steady state.

These hypothesized ideal-types or organizational forms allow us to define in an unambiguous way the concept of equilibrium.

Equilibrium: A balance in performances, between outputs and inputs, and between structure and performance.

The concept of equilibrium has not been taken seriously and yet offers enormous potential for organizational analysis. Yet, Homan's original analysis (1950) of equilibrium for small groups offered many insights. Caplow (1964: 116-18) built on this relative to several variables somewhat akin to Homan's original theory of interaction, sentiment, and activities. Similarly, Bales (1951), another expert in small groups, argued the basic equilibrium problem between adaptiveness and integration. Yet, with the exception of Caplow (1964), these ideas have not been especially pushed in the study of organizations, despite the popularity of the open-systems framework (see Hall, 1977; Zey-Ferrel, 1979; Aldrich, 1979).

The steady states for each of the four types of organizations have been carefully detailed in Figure 8.2 so that one can test reasonably well whether in fact this is equilibrium. Given the many dilemmas in performance, and the difficulty of determining the exact balance in these many variables, it is natural for organizations to be frequently in disequilibrium.

Contrary to the functionalists, I am more impressed by the imbalances and the lack of equilibrium. Because we have not done much research on this issue, we tend to lose sight of how much failure there is.

It follows from our discussion that disequilibrium can be defined as well.

Disequilibrium: An imbalance in performances, between outputs and inputs, and between structure and performance.

This is, of course, a tautology, but then all definitions are. We have raised it above the ordinary by specifying — within broad limits — what the specific imbalances in Figure 8.1 are. They are built around the dilemmas that adhere.

Instead of assuming equilibrium, we should concentrate our research efforts on examples of disequilibrium. By examining what new dominant coalitions do to achieve equilibrium, we will be able to more clearly define the precise range of balance in each of these many variables and in fact to test the central underlying assumptions: that there are viable equilibrium states.

What has not been made clear is that each balance or equilibrium point is relative to the technology and the environmental situation. What is viable at one time point is not at another. What works for one kind of throughput does not for another. There are families of resemblance but that is all one can say.

These definitions of dilemmas and kinds of organizational crises allow us to add meaning to the general framework of system analysis and cybernetics (for a more detailed discussion of this, see Hage, 1974: Chapters 1 and 2). Concepts like steady states now have some meaning. There appear to be four basic ones, two which form a linear combination of variables, and two which are nonlinear and are possible because of certain specific kinds of occupations and distributions of power.

8.2. THE PROCESS OF ADAPTATION:
LEARNING THE HARD WAY

One of the standard criticisms of organizational science, especially the early work by Taylor, is that it assumes a rational man. Everyone realizes that man, even collective men including the dominant coalition, is not rational. (But note that collectives tend to be much more rational than single individuals and that is a significant point!) This leaves unspecified in what ways a policy or decision is not rational. What is rational in the short run is not in the long term and vice versa. Any discussion of adaptation has to confront this essential problem of the meaning of rationality, a problem recognized by Weber (1947).

We will assume that except in certain instances the management or administration of the organization will not knowingly put the organization out of existence. There is a struggle to survive. It is true that there are speculators who are not interested in anything but money. Ever since James Fisk (see Chandler, 1977) this has been a phenomenon. But these men are the exception and not the rule. More typically managers and administrators want to make their organizations successful.

If we make this assumption, we begin to understand how men can act rationally from their perspective and still the organization can fail. This is very consistent with Weber's implied position on the matter. For him the crucial question was the participants' perception of the relationship between means and ends. If it was rational for them, then it was rational. The same applies to discussions about managers and administrators. It is plausible to give the dominant coalition credit for trying to do the right thing — as they see it — and at the same time appreciate that they are usually pursuing the wrong objective. These two ideas are not at all inconsistent and may go a long way towards eliminating critiques of rational assumption (James Thompson, 1967).

Thus I will assume that at least in the short term frequently the management will do the wrong thing, pursue an incorrect strategy. There is an unfolding or learning process, which needs to be studied (Cangelosi and Dill, 1965). Just as strategies unfold over time (Mintzberg, Raisinghani, and Theoret, 1976) so do structures (Chandler, 1962 and 1977). The equilibrium is constantly sought but seldom found. This process that Cadwallder (1959) has described has been studied by Cangelosi and Dill, (1965). Gradually those organizations that do not make fatal errors — and many do — learn how to adapt to the changing world correctly until the next upheaval occurs.

Before we too quickly criticize people for being bad managers, let us recognize that there are quite definite limits to knowledge and to cognition (March and Simon, 1958). If we were placed in the same position we might do much worse. Since there is little consensus among management specialists or organizational sociologists about what is correct design, how can we criticize organizational leaders for how they design their systems? In fact, much of our knowledge is built on hindsight collected by observing the mistakes of others, mistakes that we would not have anticipated. Here we are concerned with explicating the reasons why managers or administrators, thinking that they are correct, frequently make mistakes that endanger the existence of the organization, making its survival problematic. This is the process by which organizations learn how to adapt, and more specifically to change the system of variables as necessary to meet new environmental circumstances. Throughout, the emphasis is on the process of adaptation rather than the process of steering and adjustment – that is, the changing of the structure to alter performance.

One of the major difficulties with a cybernetic perspective is that the adherents seldom raise the question of when organizations are more adaptive and why. Nowhere in the otherwise seminal works of Ashby (1956) and Buckley (1968) are there any hints about what makes for feedback and what makes for choice or response. The conflict critics are correct in that there is too ready an assumption that leaders monitor performances and make the necessary corrections. *The more interesting aspect of a cybernetic paradigm is the examination of why the management or administration watches some performances rather than others and chooses certain lines of action in preference to others.* We have already explored some aspects of this in Chapters 5, 6, and 7.

In exploring why there is differential responsiveness, both a structural perspective and a political-value perspective offer insights, as diagramed in Figure 8.4. Instead of assuming there is information feedback, one wants to ask how

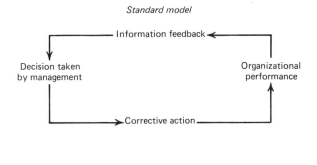

Standard model

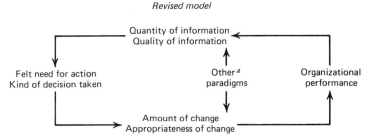

Revised model

Figure 8.4 The standard and revised model of information feedback.

much information there is and of what quality. The latter concept is somewhat akin to the concept of noise in that bad information is sometimes worse than none. One can have a great deal of information of relatively poor quality, a problem that occurs frequently in market research studies. Many educational need studies are based solely on demographic projections. Both the quality and quantity of information feedback affect the felt need for correct action and the kind of decision taken. While the concept of noise has been a critical idea in the cybernetics paradigm, much less attention has been paid to predicting when noise occurs, that is the conditions that affect the quality of information feedback.

Likewise instead of speaking about corrective action, it seems wiser to predict how much change occurs – again our essential concern about radical innovation – and whether the change is appropriate or not. The latter point seems too trivial and yet is so often ignored. Later we shall explore how dominant coalitions experiment with a small amount of change, find that this is not enough, and gradually increase the amount until the response is a correct one – correct in the sense that it produces the desired improvement in the organizational performance. This illustrates the trial and error experimentation found in dominant coalitions. It is a particular kind of rationality, given lack of knowledge about the cause and effect of organizational design.

Our essential task is to explain what affects the quantity and quality of information feedback, and the amount of change and its appropriateness for altering the performances of the organization. A large number of different variables affect the cybernetic feedback process.

8.2.1. The Lack of a Resource Base and Nonresponsiveness to Change

The most common reason for a lack of a responsiveness is a lack of resources. There is not enough people or money. Except in the multi-organizations, there are few people who worry about the long term policy implications of the organizations' current strategy and structure. A Harvard study of small businesses (Childerson, 1956) noted that many of them do not survive the succession crisis precisely because the manager must worry about everything, from day-to-day operations to long-term policy. The latter is ignored and contingencies are not considered. The first upheaval – whether internal such as the sickness of the manager or external such as the sickness of sales – leads to the demise of the organization.

Even relatively large organizations can have insufficient resource bases for studying the environment if they are constantly operating with a shortage of funds as is the case with public welfare agencies, large city general hospitsls, and county mental hospitals at least in the United States. The case loads are so large and the funds so inadequate that there is not enough slack to hire specialists who would spend time monitoring the environment and planning for the future. The sheer struggle to provide at least a minimum of service becomes all consuming. Who in prisons is taking time to estimate future demand and what are future technologies? Naturally some prison administrations are, but they are the exception. In this instance the large mixed mechanic-organic structure of organizations like the Ministry of Education or of Health in Britain and in France can be more adaptive despite their greater centralization. They have enough resources to set aside planning units in which specialists attempt to anticipate future needs and monitor changes in the environments.

Not all public organizations are starved for resources. Certainly the military has allocated a good chunk of its budget for monitoring its environment, developing new technologies, and making long range contingency plans. Although we do not normally think of the army or the navy in the avant-garde, they are in the sense that they have large amounts of resources for information feedback and planning. This does not mean that they do not have any problem of rigidity or failure to adapt their structures. The United States Army showed little capacity to reorientate itself towards the problem of guerilla warfare in Vietnam, just as the British Army failed to do the same thing two centuries earlier in the American colonies. Lack of resources is not the reason for nonadaptiveness in these instances.

Equally apparent is that even when organizations have adequate resources – staff, funds, and unit autonomy – they may not allocate these to environmental monitoring and long-range planning. Although the data are not clear it appears that one reason for the greater success of the Japanese firms is that they spend much more time studying their markets in different countries, maintaining large data banks, and attempting to predict changes in these environments.

A rather special kind of resource is knowledge about what to do. It is one thing to speak about having money enough to pay staff to worry about long range planning in a changing world and still another thing to have enough knowledge about how to do this. The truth of the matter is that we do not yet know much about how to predict future change and especially technological change. The current interest in futurology is in part mankind's attempt to come to grips with this problem, as is the development of planning in Western Europe (Shonfield, 1965). They are attempts to add predictability and in turn make organizations and even nation states more responsive to environmental change. As more and more people are assigned these tasks, a technology will develop and gradually permeate at least the larger and wealthier organizations.

We will make this a basic premise about the nature of organizations, to wit:

8A   *The greater the resource base, the greater the capacity for information feedback and the more likely that eventually the right action is selected.*

A number of specific hypotheses can be deduced from this fundamental assumption. Multi-organizations have much better capacities of survival precisely because their resource bases are so much greater. However, at this level, organizations are eliminated and/or replaced. Unfortunately, because most of the familiar names are multi-organizations, we are unaware of these deaths because they occur at a divisional level.

While much of this may seem to reduce to the very simplistic notion that big organizations survive, a little more is being said. As knowledge grows, the survival rate of organizations will increase and it will be increasingly possible for small organizations to adapt. Managers can take degrees at business schools, hospital and education administrators have their special programs, even welfare administration courses are being developed. In these degree programs, courses, and special training sessions, managers and administrators are learning the importance of long-range planning, problems in policy formation (e.g., Mintzberg, 1973), and the necessity to monitor the environment. But, regardless, the lack of resources is an obvious reason for why organizational systems find it difficult to change from one equilibrium state to another.

Another implication is that with small resources, the dominant coalition finds it easier to make steering and adjustment responses rather than adaptive responses to environmental change. In particular, to move from an organic-professional form to a mixed mechanical-organic form requires an enormous infusion of capital and a transformation of form. Polaroid, Xerox, and Texas Instruments are well-known success stories. Less well-known are the failures.

Venture capital has provided in some cases a happy marriage (Uttal, *Fortune,* April 1977: 166 et seq.). The multinational corporation provides the needed capital and in many cases even more needed staff services, knowledge about the market, and the like. The small organic-professional organization provides an opportunity for diversification of product lines and growth.

8.2.2. The Institutionalization of Success and Nonresponsiveness to Change

The second most important reason why relatively successful organizations do the wrong thing is that they have learned what a successful, viable form is and find it difficult to change from what was a previously successful model. Thus the management of Dupont (Chandler, 1962) finds a highly centralized organization is perfect for manufacturing explosives and finds the idea of shifting to a more decentralized divisional structure – that is, a mixed mechanical-organic equilibrium state, designed around the different technologies of paints, chemicals, and so forth – absurd. Similarly, Henry Ford did so well making all the decisions relative to the Model T, who would suggest that maybe increasingly in a more complex world he should share decisions with a professional management, something that did not really occur until after his death and the ascent of McNamara and his Whiz kids.

An example of an extremely successful operation was the U.S. Post Office. It represented the extreme of a mechanical form with an assembly-line operation performed by task specialists. But the success alone led to an enormous overload. The system collapsed because the old technology could not handle the rapidly expanding volume of throughput. The attempt to automate the throughput has been a continuous problem of adaptation and even after ten years of effort, one can argue that equilibrium has not yet been achieved (Biggart, 1977).

How success can be pursued until the organization dies is illustrated in the histories of *Life, Look,* and the *Saturday Evening Post.* They kept expanding circulation, driving up the cost of advertising. There are maximum limits to economies of scale that have not been sufficiently appreciated by many companies, which if not realized soon enough, create diseconomies and the failure of the companies.

Successful forms in one country can be inappropriately applied in another. McKenzie, the management consultant firm, has noted that a divisional structure works well in one country such as the United States, and he has tried to sell this same form in France, failing to recognize that a divisional structure works better in a country with specialized professional management and a tradition of decentralization, than in countries with generalists (graduates of the Grandes Écoles) and a tradition of centralization (Peyrefitte, 1976). The key point is that successful organizations tend to be copied (Chandler, 1977; Aldrich, 1979). What works at General Electric is mimicked by other companies. It may work for DuPont but would it necessarily for the U.S. Army or the University of California? (Actually I believe the answer is yes for the first and no for the second comparison.) Thus success leads to institutionalization of organizational form and structure that might be appropriate in some circumstances but not all.

Centralization can provide considerable control in a mechanical structure and it is possible for a single man with vision to achieve remarkable success. The success then institutionalizes the correctness of the man's vision and at the same time institutionalizes extreme centralization. The greater the previous success of the entrepreneur and the longer its duration, the more difficult it will be to change when new circumstances present themselves. Thus we find the imprints of men like Armour or Sloan (General Motors) or Avery (Montgomery Ward) remain long after their demise. And the more successful the particular system then put in place, the more difficult it becomes to change it. Practice becomes tradition and tradition becomes sacrosanct. In this context, it is interesting to note how the charismatic leader can be more of a handicap than an advantage. Especially if money is available and the basis of loyalty does not rest on ideology alone (admittedly an important element of Weber's charismatic leadership), charismatic leaders remain in power too long because of their very success and make life most difficult for future managers and administrators.

Although it is more difficult to find examples, the same problems can exist with organizations that find an organic professional structure produces a high innovation rate and in turn this leads to success in the market place. The typical situation is a company that starts small and has to grow fast, such as Xerox and Polaroid. Here the stumbling block is moving to a mixed mechanical-organic form.

An interesting example of this was the acquisition policy of Luckman when he was president of Lever Brothers, a division of one of the first multinational corporations, Unilever Ltd. (British). Recognizing after the Second World War that growth would depend upon the development of new products, he started buying up small companies and expanding the product line. There was naturally a rapid drop in profits and he was sacked. Later Unilever realized enormous profits from his enterprising wisdom but probably gave him little credit, since the time lag between acquisition of a new company and successful integration of its structure and realization of better profits is probably five years or more. This is beyond the time span of most boards' vision.

The key point here is that leaders may try to change the system but find that the board and the staff remain with the old values and standards and will resist. Clearly Luckman in this case moved too fast.

The typical example today are the conglomerates that find that rapid growth can be achieved by the acquisition of other companies but are also discovering that this policy does not necessarily work well during times of economic recession. During these periods products and various occupational specialities should be eliminated, but since previous success was built on them, it becomes difficult to let them go. A particular striking example of this was one sheltered workshop that lost a major contract representing a third of its budget. Not a single program was discontinued – the "product line" was not cut back – and consequently the same variety of occupational specialities was maintained. Instead, staff were let go. Observe that the response was one of adjustment rather than adaptiveness.

It is of course understandable that there is a reluctance to discontinue product lines or programs and their corresponding key staff in the face of falling demand. These represent a legitimacy of the organization, a *raison d'être*. It is the hardest thing for staff to face the fact that something they do is no longer needed. Eliminating products or services is only done reluctantly by management or administration and frequently too late. How often does a university close down an academic department because of its poor quality or because there is no longer a need? Hope for a future demand springs eternal.

Part of the problem here is that it is easier for administrators to think in terms of centralization than of concentration of specialists. Some organizational variables are easier to recognize rather than others. Power is much more readily understood than is change or the importance of knowledge in an organizational context.

Thus in summary the second reason for nonadaptiveness is not that management is stupid, but quite the contrary: they learn their lesson too well. The organiational leaders have learned one form works well and find it difficult to transform the system, whether from mechanical to organic or vice versa. As a corollary, successful products of the past are assumed always to be needed in the future and this means maintaining the variety of skills or occupations needed to produce them, if not maintaining the staff size. Only continued failure forces them to unlearn the previous lesson.

This argument can be summarized in the following hypothesis:

8.1   The longer the period of success with one form, the more difficult it is to transform the system.

Part of the reason for this institutionalization of success is the socialization of the existing personnel. Most typically successful transformation of the form requires wholesale elimination of the previous management or administration — brutal, but perhaps necessary. In universities with tenure rules and government agencies with civil service rules, there is a built-in block that makes organizational renewal difficult.

It is true that both of these principles developed as a way of reducing the intrusion of the political process either by destroying academic freedom or by creating a spoils system. But there is a need to rethink these principles, restricting them somewhat so that organizations can replace part of their staff, precisely so as to respond to new environmental circumstances.

8.2.3. Structure and the Nonresponsiveness to Change

Lack of resources means that organizations do not have enough information, and what they have is of such poor quality that they do not get the message, frequently going under. In contrast, the past success of an organization means it is difficult for the leadership to see the necessity for transformation. But inherent in organizational forms are their own seeds of destruction. This is more true for some organizational forms rather than others. In particular, the mechanical-bureaucratic form has built into it a number of characteristics that reduce the quantity and quality of information feedback.

Our hypothesis is:

8.2   The greater the concentration of specialists, the greater the amount of information and the better its quality.

The most distinctive characteristic of specialists, especially those that have been formally trained, is the reliance on a technology or a knowledge built on the fundamental importance of information. Although Weber stressed record keeping and competitive examinations as two critical aspects of a bureaucracy, administration — whether public or private — is geared much more to the need to gather information and process it. Whether police, army, welfare bureau, electrical manufacturer, hospital or the like, the natural outgrowth of technology is a demand for information that is compiled in a record or dossier. In turn, these become the basis of statistical records of performance as Blau (1955) has shown in his classic study.

The more specialists there are, the more different performances are being monitored and therefore the better the quality of information as well. The sheer variety of performances by itself means that corrective action is taken much sooner and before a real organizational crisis has developed. Multiple measures imply a sensitivity to both long and short term goals and therefore both costs and benefits of particular actions, as we argued in Chapter 7.

It is in the interest of the specialists to establish records and monitor organizational performances, as we have already observed, because this is the way they augment their power (Chapter 3). Control of information is not the only reason. Performances linked to the occupational specialty are *raison d'être*, a legitimation of their necessity. When specialists demonstrate that they cope effectively, they can increase their rewards. This requires documentation. Thus the growth of specialists means a growth in the variety and quality of information feedback.

It is also true that it is in the self-interest of specialists to prevent measurement of their performance. Thus the establishment of performance measures is frequently a struggle for power. But it is a futile struggle. Accountability is increasingly a demand made upon all (Bell, 1973; Ways, *Fortune,* May 1974: 193 et seq.). To resist it is to increase not only political pressures but also the likelihood of failure or — worse yet — lack of recognition of success.

The quality of information feedback is enhanced by the power struggle that is part and parcel of organizational life. Part of the struggle for power manifests itself in the challenging of information provided by a particular department relative to its or some other department's performance and contribution to organizational performances. To make a mistake in reporting organizational performance is to leave oneself in a highly vulnerable position.

Obviously the process and the content of the power struggle over the establishment of organizational records relative to performance is affected by the distribution of power in the organization, that is, the degree of centralization. The more that power is concentrated in the hands of an elite, the less information feedback there will be.

Our second hypothesis is:

8.3 The greater the degree of centralization, the less the amount of information and the poorer its quality.

There are a large number of studies that have indicated that centralization stifles the upward flow of information from subordinates (Hage, 1974). Equally critical is that the subordinates in a centralized situation are motivated to diminish the number of performance measures, just as in a decentralized situation the reverse is true. When power is decentralized, the competition for relative department advantage can unfold (Burns and Stalker, 1961; Hickson et al., 1971; and Hinings et. al. 1974).

The concentration of specialists and centralization not only affect information feedback — quantity and quality — but the amount of change and its appropriateness. We have already discussed how these two variables affect the choice of a radical change such as the adoption of a new program. Specialists constantly monitor their environment, reporting new technological breakthroughs and thus the need for change. But these are usually small incremental changes. Over a long time period they can add up to a significant qualitative change in the organizational system but this goes unnoticed because of its evolutionary nature.

Put in other terms, organic organizations usually have moderate amounts of change, and mechanical organizations very little. In times of crisis *both* may do the inappropriate thing. The organic organization may not shift its structure towards the mechanical and the mechanical will not shift its structure towards the organic. A high concentration of specialists will find it difficult to recommend centralization of power and the layoffs of staff, the discontinuation of certain products, and the like. A centralized organization — that is, a small dominant coalition — will find it difficult to see the necessity of decentralizing and adding a number of new occupational specialties relative to new products or services. Both organizational structures have their inherent weaknesses and blind spots.

Woodward (1965) has provided us with three case studies indicating how a fundamental change in technology appeared to require a change in form. In each instance, it took time and effort. The demise of Packard Motor Co. was probably due to the inability to shift from an essentially artisan factory with a traditional structure to a mechanical-bureaucratic mass production. Consistent with the recommendation in the previous chapter, it would have been better to create a new plant and organization that would mass produce cars rather than expand an existing plant. The same is true for the United States Post Office that shifted to automated handling.

The mixed structures are in some respects perhaps better balanced in their performances, but they too have their vulnerabilities. A traditional system will find it difficult to evolve towards an organic-professional or a mechanical structure. And a mixed organic-mechanical will have the same inflexibility. Some classic examples of this are the movement of the very traditional food industry into the high technological food processing era. Most frozen foods companies started as separate and small organizations and only later were bought up by the large food companies. The half-way houses emerged quite independently of the mental hospitals as did the group homes quite independently of the residential treatment centers. All of the evidence relative to the need for new organizations to implement radical innovations in the larger society indicates how difficult it is for organizations, even multiorganizations, to alter their structures (or the structure of a division).

All of which is to say that once an equilibrium state is found and established, it leads to an *idée fixe* about how the organization should function. While organic organizations frequently have high rates of change they infrequently question their system and advocate a movement towards one of the other steady states. To question the form is in effect to advocate a revolution and the crisis has to be enormous before this is done. But this is essentially the argument given in the subsection on the institutionalization of success.

8.2.4. Elite Values and Nonresponsiveness to Change

It is a paradox but if the elite values are favorable towards change then they are likely to be nonresponsive to any change that requires a diminishment of change. Just as certain forms represent particular equilibrium states, they also tend to be characterized by specific values relative to which performances should be maximized. These have been depicted in Figure 8.2. The organic form has a dominant coalition emphasizing quality and change. The mechanical form the reverse. The traditional form has elites that prefer the objects of quality and stability and the organic-mechanic has a dominant coalition that prefers quantity and change. In other words, the elite values are objects that are congruent with the performances likely to be maximized by the form.

But the fit between form and elite values is not perfect, to say the least. If it were, there would be no need for alternative paradigms. The "goodness of fit" has been explored in Chapters 5 and 7. But there are some additional points that need to be made. A key element in Chapter 5 is the stress on the professionalization of managers and administrators. The more professional they become, the more likely they are to escape the many pitfalls that we have listed above. In particular, the professional manager and administrator is likely to stress long-term planning and see the necessity for altering the structural system relative to different environmental conditions. Thus the hypothesis is:

8.4   *The greater the elite value placed on long term planning, the greater the demands for information, both quantity and quality.*

This is a difficult hypothesis to demonstrate or even illustrate because the experience with organizational planning is still quite limited. But inevitably long-term planning sensitizes management to the unpredictability of the environment, to the need to phase out products, and more critically to change the entire system of variables depending upon the nature of the environment. All of these occur because of the exponential increase in information that planning requires.

Given the rise of the multi-organization in both business (Chandler, 1977) and government, long-term planning is now frequently a function of the staff at general headquarters. This is especially true in conglomerates that place a great emphasis on profitability of their divisions (Martin, *Fortune,* April 1976: 118 et seq.).

The importance of the standard used to evaluate the organizational performance was stressed in Figure 7.2 as a critical one in deciding how big the performance gap is. The head of Burroughs felt that a growth rate in revenue should *never* exceed 15% per annum (Uttal, *Fortune,* January 1977: 94 et seq.) in a corporation because of the problems of adapting to fast growth. Fast growth rates can also conceal the declining market share especially in time of inflation. The best measure remains percent of market share.

8.5 *The higher the standards of performance of the elites, the more likely they are to see the need for a large change.*

Again it does not necessarily mean that the change is an appropriate one but only that need for a radical change is perceived. Perfectionism produces the desire for revolution as we have noted previously, teaching can become perversive if it really does install a pursuit of excellence and recognition of unmet needs among professionals, but this is not always the case.

In Chapter 5, the relationship between professionals and the pursuit of values of particularism and of external focus were stressed — that is, the essential uniqueness of each individual and his many needs. Clearly this concern for quality, which is quite independent of the context of the profession — accountant, physician, librarian, social worker, sales manager — leads to the perception of the constant need for change and is part of the meaning of setting high standards.

8.2.5. The Hierarchy of Responses and the Choice of a Wrong Response

The final reason why organizations are not adaptive is because the adaptive response is almost always the last choice the management or administration or board will make. If the organization is not doing well, typically the reason will be seen as bad management and the president will be replaced — that is, there is a succession. There may be several replacements before the correct response is found.

Typically a new dominant coalition, depending upon how it is chosen, will shift goal emphasis, but this may not be enough. For example, the new management might put more emphasis on innovation. They may increase the number of new products or services or improve the quality of what is provided. But they cannot make radical changes without a considerable alteration of the form, which typically they do not do. Performances can be improved within limits just by different emphasis. If management spends more time discussing the need for efficiency, everyone gradually becomes cost conscious. But this will not produce great swings unless the form is transformed as well.

Since the administration is perceived as responsible for the performances of an organization, it is natural for the board to change the top leadership when performances are disappointing for several years in a row. And this response may be the correct one. Indeed, what is needed may be a new set of priorities, a steering between the dilemmas of effectiveness. Previous experience has taught boards that this *is* one reason for bad organizational performance, but it is not the only one.

If the organization continues to do poorly, then the next succession move is to install an outside man. The second response in the learning hierarchy is tried. This will be an input adjustment. Staff will be let go or hired depending upon the circumstances. Capital investments will be reduced or expanded. An emphasis will or will not be placed on skilled labor, and so forth. While this can have a considerable impact on the outputs, it still may not represent what really is needed.

An important point is that adjustments usually have more effect than the steering response. Letting one half of the staff go, or hiring a group of management whiz kids, or speeding up capital investment does have a significant impact on output and, to a lesser extent, performances. It implies more change than the steering response. But if the causes of the bad performance do not lie in the balance of inputs, then this response will fail as well.

Again there will be another succession of leaders; typically someone at this point will be brought from outside and given a mandate for radical change and/or system change. But note that what has happened is a learning experience. At first a steering response did not work; then came an adjustment response. If this still does not work, then comes an adaptive response, namely a systemic change, which may or may not coincide with some radical program change, depending upon the direction in which the organization is moving. By this time the organization may have gone out of existence! This is learning the hard way. But there are so many reasons why organizational elites do not recognize the necessity for system change, the latter comes only with massive and *repeated* failure.

The themes of steering and adjustment dominate all discussions of change. Even radical critiques advocate replacing one dominant coalition by another — for example, replacing a capitalist elite with a socialist elite in major corporations or a combined worker-management elite in the current discussions of worker participation. In some respects, the latter may represent more change if in fact it means more decentralization. Seldom are there any discussions about the desired organizational form. Yet this may be the real way of achieving *liberté, fraternité,* and *égalité.* For this the organic-professional model may be the desired one.

Typically the politics in western democracies have been dominated by these different approaches to problems. Conservative or right-of-center parties typically advocate a change in priorities or values as a solution. Liberals or left-of-center parties typically advocate a change in inputs – more money or staff. Seldom does either party want a change in the structure of organizations. In this sense the current discussion about worker participation is a new and interesting trend. Repeated failure in the society by certain organizations leads to the recognition of the necessity for a radical new program, such as Headstart or some of the War on Poverty programs, or the changes in the voting system that occurred in the United States during the Progressive era (Hofstadter, 1955) or the social contract attempts in Britain and so forth.

The hierarchy of responses then is quite clear. *First* comes steering or a shift in priorities from innovation to efficiency or quality to quantity. This should be understood as minor and subtle alterations in goal empahsis. *Second* comes adjusting or a shift in inputs such as the size of labor force, the skill level, the capital investment level and perhaps even the degree of organizational autonomy. Although these changes are more substantial, again they usually do not involve deliberate changes in organizational form. *Third* comes adapting or a transformation from one equilibrium state to another. These are more fundamental changes and therefore more difficult to make. Each of these responses to a problem can be accompanied, and usually is, by a change in the dominant coalition.

What makes this a hierarchy of responses is the fact that each represents a more profound form of social change. Each can be the correct response to the same problem of ineffectiveness. The organization may not be doing well either because there is the wrong accent on priorities or because of the wrong mixture of inputs or because of the wrong structure. Naturally the first choice is the simplest solution, the one that requires the least pain. Only as the elite recognizes that one response does not work, does it choose the more severe remedy.

Understanding how organizations handle information feedback, then, requires an appreciation of why so frequently management or administration makes mistakes. It is difficult to know which set of causes for poor performance is responsible, without a complex theory of organizational system. It is a little like new parents dealing with a baby's cry. First they try food and then a diaper change and finally they consider the possibility of something serious such as illness. Modern management is perhaps not in such a primitive state but almost. It is for this reason that organizational theories must attempt to codify the typical crises and the typical responses. Only then can we begin to speak of adaptiveness in any intelligent way.

8.3. THE DYNAMICS OF TRANSFORMATION

We started our discussion of change in Chapter 6 with the focus on the adoption of new programs and technologies — new outputs and throughputs. This represents the simplest way for an organization to remain viable. As new techniques relative to its technology are developed, it adopts them. New models replace old ones by means of some form of incremental change. In the short run there is little system change. The organizational form is in one or another steady state. All have some rate of innovation; they vary only in the quantity of process and output innovations. As long as the larger environment remains the same, whether stable or dynamic, simple or complex, smooth or turbulent, there is little reason to change (Terreberry, 1968; Emery, Marek and Trist, 1965).

What are some of the causes of the transformation of form? *The first and most common reason why organizations may have to transform is the tendency for all organizational elites to loose their élan:* call it complacency of elites (Caplow, 1964) or whatever. Organizational elites even in a situation of equilibrium vis-á-vis their environment obey the law of entropy in cybernetics: the tendency towards failure. Even when there is an equilibrium point or balance between performances and between outputs and inputs, there will be a tendency for organizations to become less organized or less well integrated. Concretely this means that some variables in the system might change without others altering. There is a tendency with success for the power structure to become more centralized. Or various incremental changes in other characteristics will lead to an upset of the equilibrium.

If we accept the idea that environments seldom remain static, then a number of small incremental changes gradually lead to a qualitative change in the environmental context of the focal organization. A number of these are discussed in Chapters 12, 13 and 14, but among others we might note:

1. Increasing levels of education leading to greater demands for quality products
2. Shorter product lives
3. Improved technology for the throughput resulting in greater efficiencies
4. Rising levels of expectation relative to participation in basic decisions
5. Rising standards of living

Each of these very long term evolutionary trends represents after a period of time a distinct, qualitatively different environment that requires some adaptation of the organizational form, at least along the basic mechanic organic continuum. *Thus a second and very common reason for transformation is long-term evolutionary trends.* If the environment shifts from one emphasizing stability to one requiring constant change, then the organization form — if it is to survive — must also change, and in the direction that facilitates the achievement of these utilities. A stable environment, as Burns and Stalker (1961) have demonstrated, works best vis-à-vis a mechanical bureaucratic organization, and a dynamic environment would appear to require an organic-professional organization. *Thus a third but less common reason for transformation is a sharp and significant change in the environment.* As was suggested in Chapter 7, there are cycles when cost becomes more important and others when innovation is the preferred utility.

Nor is the adaptation simply one of moving from mechanical to organic or back again. Traditional organizations may have to shift to mechanical structures if they start mass-producing products. This is what Packard failed to do. Mechanical organizations may have to shift to mixed-organic. This appears to have been the problem with U.S Steel (Hage and Aiken, 1970: chapter 3). Many multi-organizations that are essentially mechanical and mixed mechanical-organic organizations seem unable to exploit small markets that require a separate division that is organic-professional, although the role of venture capital may change this. Nor are these problems operative only in the economic organizations.

Sheltered workshops have had trouble moving from traditional to organic structures. The history (Greenblatt, York, and Brown, 1956) of the shift from custodian to therapeutic goals is also a history of the problems of prisons, mental hospitals, and residential treatment homes adapting their structures from traditional or mechanic to organic-professional or mixed mechanic-organic depending upon the personnel size, technology, and other environmental conditions.

Still a fourth reason for transformation is the addition of a radical new product or technology. It does not always mean a transformation but frequently it does. For example, the addition of a medical education program in a community hospital resulted in a shifts from a mechanical to a more organic form (Hage, 1974: Part 1). The creation of a therapeutic milieu in a mental hospital — a radical new technology — had the same consequence (Greenblatt, York, and Brown, 1955).

Additions of automated technology in industry produce the same results, as has been shown in the case studies of Woodward (1965). Perrow's review of studies (1967) vis-à-vis the role of technology also contains a number of examples where a radical change produced a shift or required a transformation of the system (see Chapter 12 for an explication of technology and throughput).

Organizations that compete must also make changes if one of their competitors adopts a radical innovation. Otherwise they will lose their customers or clients and move towards dissolution. Thus radical innovation has far reaching consequences on an entire set of organizations.

Typically the radical innovation develops in a new industry or sector rather than the traditional one. Or perhaps it would be better to say that it creates a new industry. But regardless, the impact is far-reaching and requires adaptation on the part of many organizations.

What is the process of transformation? The simplest way of describing it is as a sequence of variable changes defining the form. For example, when the prison studied by McCleery (1957) added new specialists, the systems concentration of specialists increased. This meant a system change but there was no decentralization. A state of disequilibrium was created. Eventually decentralization did occur, but before equilibrium was established, the power of the guards had to be restricted.

In the hospital study by Hage (1974), the concentration of specialists increased. This produced a state of disequilibrium that manifested itself in a series of power, status, and role conflicts. Gradually the power structure moved to a more decentralized form and a new dominant coalition was created. The objectives of quality patient care and education became more important.

Thus one very typical sequence is the increase in the concentration of specialists, followed by a period of disequilibrium in which conflict occurs, then followed by decentralization. Reequilibration is achieved usually by a power struggle between the "new" and "old" guard. The transformation of form does not occur easily or smoothly.

Quite a different sequence occurs with the increasing centralization of power. In a study of an advertising agency, Kover (1963) reports that many of the staff quit because they lost power and especially job autonomy. Again, we have a sign of disequilibrium, this time in a move to much higher levels of turnover. Then reequilibrium is achieved, usually by a reduction in the concentration of specialists because the people who leave are those with better or more training or who are more likely to be professionals, as Kover notes.

We could make the sequence of changes more complex by adding other variables. Instead, I have chosen to oversimplify for the purpose of indicating that the process of adaptation passes through disequilibrium states. The dominant coalition must make errors and learn. Other variables are not changed automatically, but instead as part of a response to either conflict or turnover or some other sign of discontent – a point explored in greater depth in the next part. Conceptually the process is best analyzed as changes in variables.

We can now begin to see more clearly what an adaptive response is. If there is too much concentration of specialists relative to centralization, then it is letting some of the specialists go. If there is too much centralization relative to the concentration of specialists, then it is to decentralize. But note that for each problem, the alternative is equally viable. What distinguishes these two situations is the appropriate choice relative to the environmental state. To know if the response is to correct one or not – truly adaptive in the sense of successful – we need to know what is the preferred utility in the environment, the general availability of resources, and why the particular organizational form is in disequilibrium. This is why the concept of adaptiveness has not been researched. It requires a theory of environmental change and of system dynamics, states of equilibrium and of disequilibrium, of correct and incorrect responses. As yet we have not provided a theory about the fit between the form of the organization and the environment. This is done in Part 4.

Since, as yet, we do not have well-substantiated theories about all of this, it is understandable that dominant coalitions frequently make the wrong decision given a discontinuous or qualitative change in the nature of the environment and thus the preferred utilities that the organization must maximize. In the previous section a large number of reasons have been given for wrong choice. But through the process of learning organizational elites gradually find the right response for their given situation.

8.4. CONCLUSIONS

The focus has been not on equilibrium but on disequilibrium because this is the usual triggering mechanism for some kind of systemic change. Likewise, the analysis is not on the smooth running of a cybernetic machine – information feedback, correct decision, improved performance – but on the typical malfunctioning, misinformation, incorrect decision, and organizational crisis. These are part and parcel of the cybernetic perspective, albeit not frequently emphasized. Both the structure and the values of the elites help explain why the organizational system runs with fits and starts, jerks and conflicts. And this is where analytical attention is likely to bring the biggest payoff; the explanation of why information feedback does not occur and why wrong action choice is selected.

The three kinds of crises – imbalance in performances, imbalances between resources and outputs, and imbalances in structure – provide us with a rough guide to the many ways in which "bad management" can happen. We have only begun to identify some of the ways in which responses can be made and some of the reasons why incorrect response is so frequent.

In this chapter, we have gone a long way towards the construction of a typology of equilibrium states. Unlike most others, this typology involves a large number of variables, some of which are combined in non-linear ways. We have placed a great deal of emphasis on concentration of specialists and centralization but stratification and normative equality can be easily added. The major drawing force is the need to demonstrate effectiveness and the inherent dilemmas involved in doing so. Worse yet, yesterday's success is today's failure. Change is a constraint but never in direction or speed. Therefore, the search for equilibrium is continuous.

PART THREE

The Human Factor: Exit, Voice and Loyalty

Chapter Nine

Exit: Morale and Turnover

Organizations are not machines, however much we use this conceptual imagery. The presence of human beings adds a number of additional analytical issues. James Thompson (1967) referred to this as the human factor. Besides the performances of innovation and efficiency, there is the concern about the motivation of the members. If they quit, then the organization incurs additional costs. The relationship between morale and productivity is a complex one and still one that is not completely understood. Some assume that high morale leads to high productivity as in an excellent combat unit. Some assume that routinization of work produces both low morale and high productivity as in assembly-line plants. As yet, the proper balance between reducing human costs and material costs has perhaps escaped us.

Ideally I would prefer some concept that represented how hard people worked to achieve the goals of the organization. The real crux of the issue is effort and hard work. Perhaps the term "collective effort" is the needed label. This concept would be behavioral rather than attitudinal as in morale or job satisfaction. Furthermore, this idea does not focus on the extreme end of the continuum, namely, exit or turnover or what March and Simon (1958) called the motivation to participate.

Unfortunately, most of the research has looked at job satisfaction or turnover. As a consequence we will develop theories relative to these ideas, but note that the real issue might be collective effort.

To provide a framework for Part 3, I would like to build upon the conceptual scheme of Hirschman (1970) (see Figure 9.1). In a seminal book, he asked under what circumstances do people quit and under what circumstances do people fight to change their existing situation. He observed that in some countries, such as the United States, exit or quitting is the most typical response whereas in other societies, such as in Western Europe and especially the Latin countries, voice is the more common response. Both exit and voice, he argued, need to be understood against the backdrop of loyalty which has a complex

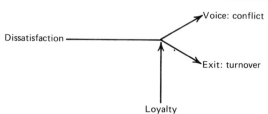

Figure 9.1 The Hirschman model.

relationship to both of these ideas. Exit, loyalty, and voice are helpful for organizing the literature on what might be called the human factor; they call attention to the idea of *alternative* responses to the same phenomenon. What has been
wrong previously in the literature is the assumption that there is a single option
given dissatisfaction.

In another recently published theory, Price (1977) looks at the relationship
between satisfaction and turnover as moderated by opportunities, building upon
the work of March and simon (1958). There is a great similarity between these
two models, yet they are saying some different things. While opportunity might
be perceived as a cognate idea with loyalty, their causes are quite dissimilar. Opportunities lie in the larger environment and are a function of labor markets.
Loyalties adhere in what the organization is doing for the individual and more
specifically in the mechanisms of coordination and control.

In Figure 9.2, I have stressed the term dissatisfaction because I suspect that
there is a U-shaped curve relating satisfaction and turnover. We know that the
higher the rank of the occupation, the greater the satisfaction and yet many
high rank occupations – engineers, professionals, and managers – have opportunities to move, given the nature of their labor markets (Caplow, 1954). As a
consequence, in high rank occupations, high satisfaction and turnover are associated. In low rank occupations, low satisfaction and turnover are more likely to
be associated. In both Figures 9.1 and 9.2, I have focused on low satisfaction –
that is, dissatisfaction – as the key, given some empirical evidence that there are
really two separate factors rather than a continuum. Besides this, it is more
likely to be dissatisfaction that leads to voice rather than exit as a viable option.

Figure 9.2 The Price model.

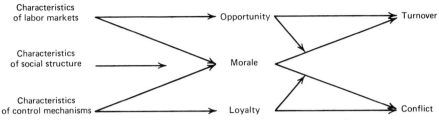

Figure 9.3 **Expanded model of choice of voice versus exit.**

Both exit and voice are costs for the organization, especially if they go beyond a certain threshold, a level somewhat hard to determine. Moderate amounts of turnover and conflict can be beneficial, as has been argued in the literature (Price, 1977; Coser, 1956). But as these variables cross a certain threshold, they drive down efficiency. Therefore, organizational elites must be concerned about the well-being of their workers up to at least some minimal level. This then focuses on the dilemma between efficiency and effort, between material and human costs.

Both models, that is Hirshman's and Price's, can be combined as they are in Figure 9.3. Together they provide an expanded framework. What is missing from this framework is the specification of the basic assumptions implied in the two models and the detailing of the specific variables and especially the characteristics of the social structure.

This chapter looks at the relationship between structure and job satisfaction and how this can be translated into turnover. Chapter 10 will consider how structure affects conflict, and Chapter 11 how structure influences control and coordination mechanisms for building loyalty. Together the three chapters fill out the synthesis of Hirschman and Price, and provide a coherent perspective on the entire problem of how dissatisfaction leads to either exit or voice.

9.1. A STRUCTURAL THEORY OF COLLECTIVE EFFORT

9.1.1. The Theoretical Concepts

The simplest definition of morale is to say that it represents the collective satisfaction of the members in the organization *about their organization.* Price (1972: 156) uses the phrase "positive affective orientation towards membership" which is perhaps a much better way of stating the definition. Implied is the idea that the members want to belong and are either happy or unhappy with their organization. In this sense, it is somewhat akin to the notion of group cohesion, although this has particular behavioral components that are not part of the usual meaning of morale.

The difficulty with this definition is that this can be measured by 1001 items. Indeed, as one examines the various job satisfaction batteries (see Price, 1972; Kallenberg, 1977) which are frequently the way in which morale is measured, one is struck by the bewildering array of items. Most studies of morale or of job satisfaction have, in fact, found in factor analysis that there are multiple dimensions, each of which refers to various aspects of the organization (see Price, 1972; Aiken and Hage, 1966; Kallenberg, 1977; etc.). Since there are so many ways in which we can be satisfied, we must limit our attention to a few.

A large number of the studies have not limited the range of possible sources of activities to just certain characteristics of the organization. Beyond this, since organizational systems contain so many variables, any one of which could be a source of satisfaction (or dissatisfaction), I believe it is better to say let us talk only about satisfaction as it relates to critical aspects of the organization. Following Price (1978) we might focus in particular on the following:

1. Characteristics of the social structure, including micro variables (Rousseau, 1978).
2. Coordination/control mechanisms.
3. Social integration.

In turn, these could be further subdivided depending upon the particular concerns of the researcher. At least this would make more apparent what is satisfaction with the organization and what is not. The *content* must be collective in nature, especially if morale is defined as a collective rather than an individual property.

Is morale the same as effort? This is probably the biggest confusion in the literature (see Figure 9.4). Most industrial psychologists have assumed organizations with higher morale will have higher productivity, be more interested in their jobs, and work harder; that is, be more motivated (Tannenbaum, 1968; Coch and French, 1958; Champion, 1975: 45–50). Essentially, the line of reasoning is this:

$$morale = motivation = productivity.$$

But as with powerlessness and other kindred concepts, we must recognize that we have essentially a hypothesis. Probably much of the confusion in the literature would be removed if both morale and effort were measured quite separately. Price (1972: 157) defines motivation as the degree to which the members of a social system are willing to work, and this is what I mean by collective effort. The difference between these two ideas becomes much more clear when one compares the items used in batteries designed to measure them.

Figure 9.4 Kindred ideas relative to morale

Level	Concept Term		
Micro	Job satisfaction	Motivation to participate	Motivation to work
Meso	Morale	Turnover	Collective effort

Clearly, we have some overlap in meaning. Ideally, it would be nice to have both sets of indicators (or some subset, because 15 to 20 items or even 10 to 15 is too many) employed in the same study to ascertain whether they represent the same scale and whether they have the same predictive power vis-à-vis variables such as productivity. Perhaps one has to have the two in combination, but I believe that most sociologists who are not explaining individual differences prefer to measure collective effort. It is the main concern. The concept of collective effort is more consistent with Parsons' (1953) essential insight that one of the great functional problems of all social systems is to maintain motivation and control the interpersonal tensions that arise from cooperative effort. What has confused people is the naive assumption that individual and collective effort or motivation are the same. Collective effort is more than the sum of individual motivation. Very ambitious individuals work at cross-purposes. Collective effort means a team effort, an esprit de corps, to achieve collective goals. It is interesting to observe that some of the people who have the most difficulty understanding this simple distinction are those who are personally ambitious.

Is motivation to work the same as March and Simon's (1958) concept of motivation to participate? No. Their concept is the same as turnover. Their choice of terms is unfortuante. How hard one works in the organization is another matter. In other words, how motivated the membership is to work *hard,* to *struggle* against obstacles, and *to achieve* as a team rather than as a series of stars. This appears to be quite different from the decision to stay or to quit or the collective dimension of this, which is turnover.

Is morale the same as job satisfaction or the satisfaction with employees, and so on? Yes, but there are a number of subtleties. Morale is the collective counterpart of job satisfaction. But then is job satisfaction an individual or a positional matter? Kallenberg (1977) and others suggest it is both. Of course, there are individual differences and needs that influence the degree of satisfaction. But a more fundamental question is, should individual differences be eliminated in the measurement? If one follows the logic of the desire to measure morale as a collective satisfaction with the organization rather than an individual satisfaction with the meeting of one's own needs, then the answer is clearly that individual differences should be eliminated.

Starting with this premise, Aiken and Hage (1966) solved the problem by averaging scores of respondents in the same job or social position and then aggregating across positions to represent the entire social structure. This eliminates individual differences that are the product of psychological needs, and creates a mean that more nearly approximates the satisfaction with the position. However, they failed to carry their logic to its natural outcome and include items whose content is collective rather than individually oriented.

One would like to know the collective attitude about the satisfaction of the members with their organization. This is not the same as the sum of various individual satisfaction scores. The progress of the organization and the progress of the individual in his career are not identical, although there is a relationship. Satisfaction with the distribution of power implies something different from the satisfaction with one's own power; again there is a shift from a meso to an individual level. An inspection of the items typically used in satisfaction batteries indicates that they are usually referring to the individual situation and not the collective.

So much work has been done with individual satisfaction items that we must infer morale from them. But at least we can insist upon aggregation procedures that eliminate individual differences. Unfortuantely, there have been few studies that have adopted this perspective.

My own preference is for a concept called collective effort, which can be defined as follows:

Collective effort: The effort exerted by the members of the organization to achieve *its* goals.

The key term is effort and it is something more than the number of hours that one works, but also how hard one works and with what efficiency and effectiveness. When hypotheses are developed about productivity, probably it is this way of thinking about morale that is involved. However, even this is complicated by the fact that members can be strongly motivated to achieve quality or strongly motivated to achieve efficiency. Thus, finally, effort must be related back to the goals or objectives of the organization.

In summary, it seems useful to make very careful distinctions between attitudes such as morale and behavior such as effort. A distinction between individual, micro, and meso analysis is fundamental and is the biggest error in the literature (Rousseau, 1978). This is not to say that individual differences are unimportant, but only to say the problem is not a sociological one.

9.1.2. Premise and Hypotheses

Most of the imagery of motivation and of satisfaction has been constructed at the individual level. March and Simon's (1958) model of the costs and benefits of participating in the organization is an excellent example. A collective sense of morale is somehow absent. But because most of the work has been done by industrial psychologists, this is understandable. The imagery of collective motivation is complex and a difficult one to grasp. It evokes concepts like the group mind, from which most people shy away. This then creates problems for creating a theory that links the meso level of the organization with the individual. In what way do various abstract variables such as concentration of specialists relate to motivation? This is our analytical problem.

Since most of the work has been done on the individual level, this is a good place to begin. What are the typical costs and benefits that affect a worker's motivation? Morin (1976), in summarizing much of the literature, suggests that they are as follows:

Benefits	Costs
Interesting work	Monotony and fatigue
Job autonomy	Close supervision, control
Salary	Insecurity of employment
Social integration	Hostility and isolation

These have been rearranged, and in some cases the defining terms rather than the captions have been used for the purpose of parallel construction. Hostility towards others and social isolation, which was not in the original formulation, has been added as the logical counterpart to the benefit of having affective relationships.

When anyone proposes a list of costs and benefits or, more broadly, relative universal needs, it is important to consider what might be left out. Except for the cost of fatigue, not much emphasis is placed on what might be called the physical dimensions of the quality of the work environment such as pollution, noise, heat, toxins, and the like. The desire is to focus on the structural factors that affect collective morale. More critical, in my opinion, is the omission of what I would call privileges and responsibilities. People take pride in having certain privileges such as not having to come to work at 8 A.M. or punching a clock. This is one reason why flexible work hours are rapidly becoming a very important mechanism for improving professional and semi-professional morale. Equally, and even more important, people need a sense of responsibility. It can frequently be a more important psychic reward than material benefits. Indeed, it is one of the reasons why the military can obtain such devotion from the enlisted ranks of noncommissioned officers and higher. They are made to feel responsible and this proves to be a great motivating force.

The nature of social relationships, or what Aiken and Hage (1966) called expressive satisfaction, is on a different plane than the other three, which are instrumental in nature. For this reason, it will be dealt with separately. Various studies of alienation and especially those based upon satisfaction scales have suggested that social integration can override a whole series of negative features including poor pay, powerlessness, and uninteresting work (see Blauner, 1964; Fullan, 1970). There is also some suggestion in the literature that indicates that organizations that are concerned about both social structure and integration achieve a strong collective effort (Ouchi and Johnson, 1978 state this for Japanese organizations).

If we can relate general structural characteristics to these psychological costs and benefits, then we can begin to understand how the meso structure affects morale. Industrial psychologists would call this "climate" and a close inspection of the items suggests that they are tapping the social structure of the organization plus various control and coordination mechanisms. The overarching theory is essentially that of March and Simon's, namely, a cost-benefit model that assumes in effect:

9A   Individuals attempt to maximize benefits and reduce costs.

But to make this theory dynamic and to be sensitive to the critique of capitalistic organizations — which, however, can be generalized to all organizations — we need another assumption about what the organization is attempting to do. It is:

9B   Organizations attempt to maximize benefits and reduce costs.

Now we have the internal dialectic, a kind of class war if you will. Since greater control reduces material costs, organizations attempt to reduce them by holding salaries down. When they routinize work and standardize production processes, they are reducing interest in work. Likewise, concerns about efficiency will lead to close supervision and a restriction of job autonomy. At the same time, the dominant coalitions cannot exceed certain limits because then the human costs for the individuals involved will be too great, either because of exit (turnover) or voice (conflict). These limits vary in each of the four equilibrium states discussed in the previous chapter.

Beyond this, some organizations care more about human costs than material costs, morale more than technical efficiency. There are two foolish intellectual positions to take: the cynical one, that all organizations are heartless and concerned with the maximization of profit (the naive Marxist position), and the optimistic one that all organizations try to do their best and are concerned about their workers (the naive structural-functional position). Nor do organizations lie in between the two. Quite the contrary. Some organizations exploit and others do not, but this is a topic for Chapter 13.

I have very carefully employed the term organization and not the words elite or leadership to emphasize that, regardless of decentralization or centralization, democratic or elitist, there is some organizational imperative to maximize productive benefits and minimize material costs (Caplow, 1964: 262–65, one of the few to really emphasize the equilibrium problem involved). Regardless of the equilibrium state – whether quality or quantity, as discussed in the previous chapter – there are limits to how high material costs can spiral upwards and how fast this can occur in any historical period. The concepts of an efficient organization or the limits of material costs vary greatly in the different equilibrium states, but limits do exist and are quite real.

Thus organizations and their membership, including the elites, do have an inherent conflict of interest. What is best for the collective – the organization and the larger society – is not best for the individual. Organizations are asked to produce the best medical care, education, material goods, external security, and the like, at little cost. Furthermore, they are asked to give individualized service and products conveniently located. But these are not free because the workers are unwilling to give their work free of charge. We all want interesting work with job autonomy and high pay, even though the relative importance of particular benefits and costs varies considerably from situation to situation, personality to personality, and the like (see Alutto and Belasco, 1972 and Conway, 1976 for workers who have too much participation).

A balance must be struck between meeting the needs of the larger society and meeting the needs of the workers and managers or professionals. This is a most complex moving equilibrium problem because the needs are continuously changing. Fortunately, we can standardize this by observing that these remain *relatively* constant. What people expect is a function of the larger societal context. They expect pay, but what is a fair wage changes with time. However, the hierarchy of salaries remains quite constant. The same is the case for power and privilege.

To provide some substance to the premise about maximizing benefits and minimizing costs, we need to stipulate what benefits and costs are within the context of work. To do this, we must also avoid the problem of the specific and quite different needs of individuals. Each of us prefers a somewhat different kind of work but we are alike in wanting interesting work. Likewise people vary in their power needs but most want some job autonomy. Concern about salaries, or perhaps better their feelings about unequal pay (which is a more subtle point), and feelings of insecurity about employment are also basic. The desires for privileges and responsibilities would also appear to be relatively universal. This, then, leads to the following assumption:

9C *All individuals consider as benefits interesting work, job autonomy, salary equity, and social integration, and as costs monotonous work, close supervision, insecure employment, and social isolation.*

These assumptions seem quite simplistic but they are necessary if we are to develop a theory about how the social structure affects morale.

One difference here is that needs are not seen as a hierarchy but instead as covering certain domains. Nor are we covering all the possible areas but instead focusing on those most relevant to the social structure of the organization. Intrinsically interesting work is as varied as there are different jobs, which Marx does not recognize in his alienation thesis.

The hypothesis diagramed in Figure 9.5 relates the structural variables and the likely *average* individual attitude. This reflects the major overriding characteristic of national job satisfaction studies. The higher the status or prestige of the occupation, the higher the *average* job satisfaction. But then the higher the status, the higher the power, privilege, and the more likely the average person has interesting and nonroutine work. In one sense, this general finding supports the above assumption.

The concentration of specialists is hypothesized to have the following impact on collective morale:

9. 1   *The greater the concentration of specialists, the greater the average interest in work and the less the monotony and routineness.*

The distinctive thing is that most people who are specialists can choose their work and do so on the basis of interest. Furthermore, the work that they do — professional or managerial — is difficult to routinize for reasons that are suggested in Chapter 12. In brief, the growth of knowledge makes work more and

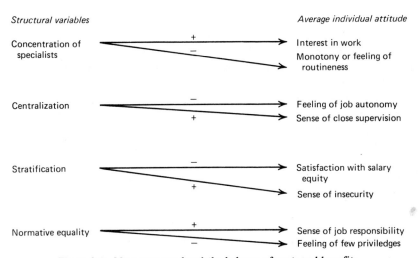

Figure 9.5   Meso-structural and the balance of costs and benefits.

more complex, thus encouraging specialization and diminishing routinization. The same can be said for skilled laborers. Usually they too have some work choice, albeit the range may be more limited. As a consequence, they find their work more interesting. Unskilled labor frequently does not have choice; here motivation problems are the greatest.

What evidence is there for this hypothesis? Actually some direct tests of the relationship between concentration of specialists and job satisfaction are presented in the next subsection. For now we may only note that skill level and reports of job satisfaction and interest in the work are highly correlated in national samples (Morse, 1953). While this may be due to many reasons, the choice of occupation and the intrinsic interest that more complex and less routine tasks appear to have would seem to be a crucial element in the explanation for this consistent finding. More educated workers (Faunce, 1958) disliked jobs with less responsibility during automation.

On the debit side, in organizations that rely on unskilled labor, the production line is arranged on the principal of minute tasks that are highly repetitive. The problems of monotony are great (Blauner, 1964).

A high concentration of specialists means by definition that most of the work force is either professional and managerial or craftsmen and artisans. A low concentration of specialists means unskilled labor. The former ideal-type is likely to have people who have chosen their occupation for its interest, and the latter to have individuals who have had much less choice. The former organization is likely to have complex tasks with great variety and the latter simple tasks with great repetitiveness. In the one, in the extreme, there is all cost and little benefit and in the other situation are many benefits and smaller costs on the average. Naturally, most organizations have mixtures not only of unskilled, skilled, and professional-managerial workers but, in addition, mixtures of routine and nonroutine work, simple and complex tasks.

Participation in decision-making, or giving some control to the workers, has been seen as the great panacea for providing more benefits and less costs. But most participation schemes, such as worker membership on the board of directors, do not really address the costs and benefits of close supervision and job autonomy. Worker representation can lead to the recognition of these hierarchical problems, as we noted in Chapter 3, but in the short run decentralization as we have defined it is more likely to be associated with the lack of close supervision and the presence of job autonomy. And it should be noted that the emphasis is placed on the words "feelings" and "sense" in the following hypothesis:

9. 2   *The greater the centralization, the less the feelings of job autonomy and the greater the sense of close supervision.*

Essentially Chapter 3 has given all the behavioral evidence for this. The only point to make here is that if one accepts the cost-benefit model, then this implies something about collective effort and morale.

There are two approaches in discussions of salary that need to be separated. On the one hand, there is the absolute pay level and sometimes an assumption that individuals want to maximize theirs, and on the other hand the relative pay level and a sense of equity. I believe most individuals and certainly occupational groups think in terms of the latter and even within quite narrow limits such as the pay scales within the organization. There is a collective sense of pay hierarchy and appropriate distances between particular echelons. If this is so, then stratification can affect this in the following ways:

9. 3 The greater the stratification, the greater the salary inequalities and the greater the employment insecurity.

Exactly as Marx and Engels (Feuer, 1969) argued, as stratification increases, workers' pay tends to decline relative to rewards to the elite. This creates inequity. Beyond this, organizations characterized by great differences in salary echelons tend to be organizations that let workers go in times of economic crisis, which produces enormous insecurities about employment. This is probably one of the major reasons why labor history is different in certain countries of Europe and the United States, During the great depression, French workers were not dismissed. Instead, everyone reduced their hours by some 20%, on the average (until the sit-down strikes of 1936, when business organizations adopted a different policy). Thus, even with great stratification, there can be either a small or large economic insecurity depending upon custom in the society. But it is critical to note that workers still accept a pay hierarchy. What is not accepted is when the differences between echelons become too large *and especially between adjacent levels.* The unskilled workers watch the wages of the skilled workers and not the bonus plans of top management.

Privileges become especially important when pay scales are fixed by means of social contracts or an automatic scale. The importance of privilege grows accordingly and represents one of the major rewards for motivating workers. For the military, where pay scales are totally fixed and untouchable, permission to have weekends off or to take leave is a major control mechanism.

This then leads to a fourth hypothesis:

9. 4 The greater the normative equality, the greater the privilege equity and the greater the sense of doing responsible work.

Admittedly people can have too many responsibilities but it is because they have not shifted some downward or shared them with others. Characteristically this occurs in an organization that is too centralized.

If we return to Figure 9.3, it can be seen that all we have focused on are characteristics of the social structure and how it impacts on morale. We have not considered completely the role of coordination and c ntral mechanisms and their impact on morale, a topic for the next section.

But how does this theory about morale relate to collective effort? It doesn't unless we are willing to assume that there is a relationship between morale and collective motivation. Unfortunately, collective effort has been ignored and not researched.

In particular, the human relations advocates and, most notable, Tannenbaum (1968) have argued that a sharing of power — decentralization — would improve morale and thereby productivity. But much of the research findings (Mintzberg, 1979) suggest that one can alienate the workers and still have high productivity. Thus we are left without a clear idea of the causal connection between morale and effort. The problem is, in part, ideological. Will workers work without some control mechanisms? Morale without control may not be enough, just as control without morale may not work either. The problem is the correct mix. What we can say is that relationship is probably very complex.

In summary, our hypotheses are:

9. 5   *The greater the concentration of specialists, the greater the job satisfaction.*
9. 6   *The greater the centralization, the less the job satisfaction.*
9. 7   *The greater the stratification, the less the satisfaction with salary.*
9. 8   *The greater the normative equality, the more the satisfaction with privileges and responsibilities.*

We have, in effect, built in as intervening variables some assumptions about interest in work, salary equity, pleasant work relationships, and the like, so that the connection between an organization wide-property, the individual situation, and then the collective summation of attitudes is made clear. It is important that we accept, however, that these needs are relatively universal.

Throughout this discussion the emphasis has been placed on the worker's satisfaction. Little has been said about the needs of management, or administration, or elites. Broadly their satisfactions are high. One could use these same variables to explain why. However, on the individual level, one can find quite deep dissatisfactions among those who lost out on the last promotion or who have slightly less pay than someone else in the department or where, in order to rise in the hierarchy, a person works day and night. Our concern is with averages, especially relative to each occupation and level in the organization.

9.1.3. The Findings

Table 9.1 reports the relationship between collective properties of structure and collective attitudes about job satisfaction and satisfaction with social relationships for the Hage-Aiken study. The relationships are quite strong in the first

Table 9.1 Structural properties and morale
Hage-Aiken panel study

Zero order correlations

Structural properties	Wave 1		Wave 2		Wave 3		Wave 3A	
	Job satisfaction	Expressive satisfaction	Job satisfaction	Expressive satisfaction	Job satisfaction	Expressive satisfaction	Job satisfaction	Expressive satisfaction
Concentration of specialists	.76	.64	.21	.15	.49	.76	.48	.61
Centralization (non-particip.)	-.56	-.29	-.19	-.10	-.67	-.70	-.55	-.48
Stratification (income ratio)[b]					-.48	-.39		
(N)	(16)	(16)	(16)	(16)	(16)	(16)	(29)	(29)

Multiple regressions[a]

Independent variables → *Dependent variable*

						Dependent variable
Job satisfaction$_{t_1}$ .29	Concentration of of specialists$_{t_1}$ .20	Centralization$_{t_1}$ -.38	ΔConcentration of specialists .36	ΔCentralization -.32	Time -.32	Job satisfaction$_{t_2}$ $R_m = .64$
Expressive satisfaction$_{t_1}$ .43	Concentration of specialists$_{t_1}$ .07	Centralization$_{t_1}$ -.13	ΔConcentration of specialists .38	ΔCentralization -.19	Time -.53	Expressive satisfaction$_{t_2}$ $R_m = .70$

[a] Pooled time series data, $N = 32$.
[b] only measured in original 16 organizations in third wave with accuracy.

wave, become weak in the second wave, and again stronger in the third wave, reflecting the disequilibrium that these organizations experienced as described in the previous chapter.

When one looks at the combined impact of the concentration of specialists and of centralization, one begins to appreciate the importance of seeing morale as a multidimensional problem affected by the entire structure as well as the performances of the organization. Job satisfaction retains a moderate positive auto-correlation, that is, organizations that have high morale tend to maintain it. However, the partial for the concentration of specialists becomes negative, indicating that the biggest drop occurs in the most organic organizations which experienced the highest innovation rates. However, increases in the concentration of specialists are positively associated with the later levels of job satisfaction. Both the prior level and the rate of change in centralization have the predictive negative effect on job satisfaction. In other words, not only does centralization depress morale in these kinds of organizations, but increases in centralization have the same impact. This is a very powerful support for the Tannenbaum thesis relating power to morale. It must be remembered that these are organic-professional organizations for the most part and therefore the findings might not be generalizable to the other three types of organizations.

Finally, the negative correlation of time with subsequent level of job satisfaction means that in general morale as measured by this index went down. As is shown in the next section, most of this was because of changes in the mechanisms of control.

Expressive satisfaction illustrates essentially the same pattern except here the prior level and time account for more of the variation. The higher partial correlation of prior level means that the rank order of these agencies tended to remain much more stable. The higher negative partial correlation of time with subsequent level implies that the general decline was a function of variables other than the levels and rates of change in centralization and concentration of specialists. Again the answer lies in the increased use of control mechanisms that are highly resented by professionals and particularly affect the nature of social relationships in an organization, as we have measured it.

This more dynamic analysis provides striking support for the idea that there are a number of variables that affect morale and that they need to be considered in conjunction. And while, in general, job satisfaction and expressive satisfaction are highly correlated (the r varies between .60 and .85 across the three waves), their causes are not the same, at least in this particular longitudinal study. Job satisfaction is more sensitive to the power structure and, as we shall see, expressive satisfaction is more affected by the control mechanisms that are employed.

Seashore and Bowers (as reported in Price, 1967: 84–86) conducted an experiment and raised the level of participation from almost no influence to some influence or from very highly centralized to highly centralized and there was also some improvement in morale. But what this study makes quite clear is the need to distinguish not only the existing level but the magnitude of change before one can assess the relative importance of power, or any other variable for that matter.

This might eliminate the present controversy over the relationship between morale and productivity. Most of the studies indicate some relationship but what is striking is that the association is always weaker, even when positive, than the relationship between centralization and productivity, or centralization and morale, suggesting that perhaps the association is a spurious one altogether. *Centralization, through its impact on the choice of control mechanisms, leads to lower costs but at the same time lower morale.* However, the levels and the rates of change are critical here, as are the impacts of other structure and control variables.

In a study of stock brokerages, Pennings (1973) found that decentralization, whether measured by the total amount of influence exercised by each group on each other (that is, Tannenbaum's measure of control), or by a participation index were positively related to an index of morale that combined job satisfaction and expressive satisfaction. In a much earlier study, Smith and Ari (1964) reported that in 32 delivery stations of the same company scattered across a number of metropolitan areas, total influence, which is very much like participation, had a correlation of .72 with their measure of morale.

Here is an illustration of how morale and decentralization are more strongly associated than the relationship between either of these variables and productivity, supporting the spurious relationship between morale and productivity, especially if one were to include consensus, their intervening explanation.

In general, decentralization is positively related to morale, but there are exceptions. In a study of metropolitan governments in Belgium, Aiken et al. (1972) did not find a relationship. It is not clear whether they studied multiorganizations rather than organizations. Furthermore, the study is confined to administration and civil service. Therefore, most of the workers are white-collar clerical help. The organizations may function much more as traditional or mechanical-bureaucratic. Under these circumstances centralization may be positively related to morale because within this group of organizations, more centralized organizations are more effective. What is unclear, if one compares these Belgian organizations or local government administrations with comparable ones in Britain or the United States, is whether the relationship would hold. Certainly societal expectations about centralization may make an enormous difference relative to the impact of this variable on morale.

We have already noted that the effective organizations, depending upon how this is measured, can be both centralized or decentralized, depending upon the values of other variables in equilibrium. This means that under these circumstances, morale can be positively related to centralization, that is, if the concentration of specialists is high. However, if compared to other equilibrium states, one would expect to see a lower absolute level of morale.

What is even more critical is that most studies have only examined the impact of power and not all the structural variables, each one of which relates to a different need. The importance of particular needs will vary from organization to organization and from time to time, depending upon the nature of the membership and its expectations. I could not agree more with those who desire to move away from one-factor theories of morale but also one-factor research studies (Rousseau, 1978). Professionals are probably more concerned about power than pay, while unskilled workers may have the exact opposite set of priorities. To study these different needs in isolation is to miss what may be the most critical variables.

In summary, there is a lot of research supporting the general notion that as workers receive more interesting work, higher job autonomy, more pay, and more privileges, they are more satisfied with their jobs. The social structure of the organization impacts quite directly on the average levels in an organization. What is unknown is whether morale is associated with collective effort or productivity. To make matters more complex, productivity is not necessarily the most important goal of an organization.

Most experimental research has left unclear the precise relationship between the social structure and morale, and for several reasons. Usually only one variable is changed and usually the organization is viewed as having only one equilibrium state. As yet, the idea of four ideal-types, some of which have moderate levels of satisfaction and quite high productivity, has not been researched. There is, however, a general finding that *within* kinds of organizations, more decentralized ones tend to have higher morale even though they might not have higher productivity.

9.1.4. A Special Problem: Turnover

If we return to our basic framework which relates satisfaction to turnover, then we need to ask how these two variables interrelate. Is low satisfaction translated into high turnover? In a recently published review of a large number of turnover studies, Price (1977) shows that essentially the same structural variables help explain why people quit. However, turnover can only occur when, in fact, there are alternatives. And this happens to be quite a distinctive quality of the United States. In many European countries, there are fewer opportunities for job mobility. In part, this is a tradition and, in part, family obligations and the desire to remain in the same area have considerably reduced job mobility. As Hirschman (1970) notes in his book, Americans are much more likely to exercise exit rather than voice as a means of expressing dissatisfaction.

What needs to be done is to add some theory of the labor markets. Professionals and managers usually have many opportunities to move. The more rare the particular skill and therefore the fewer people capable of providing it, the greater the opportunity to better one's pay, privilege, and power. Here high satisfaction and turnover are positively related. Unskilled workers, except in times of labor shortages, face the exact opposite set of circumstances, namely, few opportunities to change jobs. Under this set of environmental constraints, low job satisfaction and turnover are related. But this is exit out of desperation rather than exit to better one's situation. The professional is pulled by opportunities elsewhere while the unskilled worker is pushed by the characteristics of the social structure.

What is most striking in Price's admirable review of the literature is that in the aggregate, skill level or type of occupation explains turnover much more than do characteristics of the social structure. Demand and supply theory would appear to be more critical than organizational variables in relating satisfaction or morale with turnover. Unfortunately organizational sociologists have ignored labor market theory (see Caplow, 1954 for one exception), but in this context it not only directly affects turnover but also influences the nature of the association between morale and turnover. As one moves up skill level, opportunities increase – that is, demand increases while supply decreases. This makes for more turnover but it also makes for more satisfied workers.

Another critical factor in job turnover is the nature of the job contract. Civil service or other special arrangements, in effect, reduce turnover rates. This also applies to the military occupations, the foreign service, and academia. Turnover can be measured, but is tied to special restrictions on mobility. In these occupations, turnover tends to be quite low after the first contract.

If one does hold constant the characteristics of the labor marker, and therefore opportunities, there is considerable support for the central thrust of Figure 9.3. Characteristics of the social structure affect morale. In particular, as the concentration of specialists declines and centralization increase, morale declines and this is translated into higher rates of turnover.

9.2. CONTROL AND MORALE

A structural theory of how organizations build loyalty by means of coordination and control mechanisms is elaborated in Chapter 11. Here our concern is with a more narrow set of factors, namely the relationship between the choice of control mechanism and its impact on morale and, implicitly, turnover and collective effort. In the previous section, it was suggested that job autonomy was a relatively universal desire. However, many of the studies reported in the literature measured not this but either influence, as in the Tannenbaum tradition (1968; Pennings, 1976), or participation, as in the Hage-Aiken panel study.

Price (1977), in his review of turnover, reports that both factors have an influence. While we know that centralization and job autonomy are related, the association is not perfect (see Chapter 3) and one of the ideal equilibrium steady states predicts that they should be positively rather than negatively related (most typically in the traditional state as in primary schools, print shops, small construction firms, tradtional police departments, libraries, and the like).

9.2.1. Basic Premise and Hypotheses

We will start with a very simple assumption that comes out of the work of many industrial relations studies – namely, that workers prefer mechanisms that imply trust rather than ones that imply distrust. Concretely this means that mechanisms that create the image of being watched (what is referred to as surveillance), will lower morale. More indirect control measures such as job descriptions are less likely to have this impact.

Our premise is:

9D   *The more that the control mechanism indicate a basic trust, the more likely it will be accepted.*

From this the basic hypotheses that can be derived are:

9. 9   *The greater the task visibility, the lower the morale.*
9.10   *The greater the formalization, if it does not restrict job autonomy, the higher the morale.*
9.11   *The higher the level of communication, the greater the morale.*

Table 9.2 shows the relationship between various control mechanisms that refer to formalization and task visibility among professionals in the Azumi ($N = 40$) and Hage-Aiken panels ($N = 16$ or 29). Formalization appears to have only a small negative impact on job satisfaction or morale in health welfare agencies. The pattern for expression satisfaction (not shown) is about the same. In the Azumi study of Japanese factories, job codification has a positive relationship with an overall measure of morale, and role specificity has an even stronger one. If one examines the indicator of the presence of the rules manual in the Hage-Aiken study, it tends to have almost a zero-order association except in the third wave. Formalization does not necessarily reduce morale. But clearly close supervision or an emphasis on task visibility does.

At least for these organizations, increasing visibility by close supervision and strictness of following general rules is not conducive for high morale. This corresponds to a large literature on the desires for job autonomy by professionals (starting with Blau and Scott, 1962; see also Engel, 1969 and 1970; Hall, 1977).

Table 9.2 Control and morale

Hage-Aiken panel study

Control mechanisms	Job satisfaction			
	Wave 1	Wave 2	Wave 3	Wave 3A
Formalization				
Rules manual	–.10	.06	–.35	[b]
Job description	[a]	–.26	–.22	[b]
Job codification	–.16	–.34	–.23	–.19
Task visibility				
Rule observation	–.66	–.33	–.58	–.55
Closeness of sup.	–.41	–.52	–.39	–.47
(N)	(16)	(16)	(16)	(29)

Azumi study

Control mechanisms

Formalization	Morale
Role specificity	+.42
Job codification	+.24
Task visibility	
Rule observation	–.10
Closeness of sup.	–.62
(N)	(40)

[a] Not included in the first wave.
[b] Missing questions.

What is striking is that it has the *same* strong negative relationship in Japanese factories as among professionals and semiprofessionals in the health and welfare organizations in the United States.

That there is a dialectic between morale and efficiency, at least as a goal, can be appreciated from the self reports of the members of the organizations interviewed in the Hage-Aiken study during the second and third waves. For example, in the second wave, the correlation between efficiency as the most important goal vis-à-vis innovation and morale and the various measures of formalization and task visibility are: $r = .62$ for job codification, $r = .15$ for rules manual, $r = .88$ for job specificity, $r = .59$ for rule observation, $r = .60$ for closeness of supervision. This pattern is replicated in the third wave even with a change in wording of the question regarding the goals of the organization (cost was substituted for the word efficiency). Or to put it in other terms, the relationship between a reported emphasis on efficiency as a goal and job satisfaction as a measure of morale is -.50 in the third wave (N = 16) and -.61 in the second wave. At least for these organizations the dialectic between human costs and material costs is a clear one and control mechanisms affect this quite directly.

But one may argue that perhaps it is more the presence of structural variables that cause the scores on morale rather than the impact of control variables. [This is actually a problem in the Lawrence and Lorsch (1976b) study; on the basis of the evidence presented one could reasonably conclude that the reason for low success in each industry is not enough differentiation vis-à-vis the environment, except for the container industry, see page 103.] The multiple regressions are reported in Table 9.3, the pooled data of the Hage-Aiken study.

Here we find that increases in job codification lead to a decline in morale even when either concentration of specialists or centralization is controlled. The impact of formalization is greater on expressive satisfaction indicating that the supervisor is perceived as the reason for the restriction on the nature of the work (not shown). In most of the comparisons both the structural variable and the control variable have an equal impact on job or expressive satisfaction. It is also important to observe that at least in this study changes have a greater impact on the level of subsequent satisfaction than do the levels of either structural or control variables. For example, the rate of change in the concentration of specialists has a partial .45 with both job satisfaction and with expressive satisfaction. The prior rate of change in job codification has a partial of -.32 with job satisfaction and -.48 with expressive satisfaction. When the impact of rule observation and of closeness of supervision (data not included) is examined, one finds essentially the same pattern of findings. The change rate tends to be a better predictor. One might expect morale which, after all, is a collective *attitude* to be more responsive to changes. It is the break in what we are used to that we find disquieting. It is the disturbance, the discontinuity with what was before, that upsets the members of the organization the most.

Both control mechanisms and structure have an impact on the level of morale after controlling for the prior level of job or expressive satisfaction. Thus there is some support for the idea that professionals do have expectations about the appropriate control system for an organization with an organic form.

An extensive review of a number of turnover studies by Price (1977) indicates that organizations with higher levels of communication tend to have lower levels of turnover. Again communication is quite different from task visibility as a mechanism of control. It assumes that the error is one of inadequate information rather than deliberate error. Communication itself builds trust, especially if it is a two-way channel, allowing for feedback to occur which can, in turn, enhance morale. (See Chapter 11 for a discussion of how communication acts as a control mechanism.)

Table 9.3 Structure, control, and morale[a]
Hage-Aiken panel study, $N = 32$

Independent variables						Dependent variable
Concentration of specialists$_{t_1}$ .03	ΔConcentration of specialists .45	Job codification$_{t_1}$ .05	ΔJob codification -.32	Job satisfaction$_{t_1}$ .33	Time -.48	Job satisfaction$_{t_2}$ $R_m = .61$
Concentration of specialists$_{t_1}$ .04	ΔConcentration of specialists .44	Rule observation$_{t_1}$ -.36	ΔRule observation -.16	Job satisfaction$_{b_1}$ .09	Time -.33	Job satisfaction$_{t_2}$ $R_m = .63$
Centralization$_{t_1}$ -.25	ΔCentralization -.33	Job codification$_{t_1}$ .06	ΔJob codification -.27	Job satisfaction$_{t_1}$ .34	Time -.30	Job satisfaction$_{t_2}$ $R_m = .57$
Centralization$_{t_1}$ -.29	ΔCentralization -.27	Rule observation$_{t_1}$ -.31	ΔRule observation -.12	Job satisfaction$_{t_1}$ .11	Time -.09	Job satisfaction$_{t_2}$ $R_m = .57$

[a]Pooled time series data

9.2.3. A Special Problem: Social Integration

Although research has indicated that individuals do not necessarily choose their friends from the work place, this does not diminish the importance of affective or expressive social relationships. Ever since the wiring bank room studies at Western Electric (Roethisberger and Dickson, 1939), the importance of social relationships has been appreciated. Whether or not workers actually form groups in a strict sense of the term as depicted in Homans's (1950) classic analysis is perhaps debatable. Instead it seems more accurate to say that all workers need some form of *Gemeinschaft* (Turner, 1955) on the job, not just within their family and friendship relationships, but in their instrumental ones as well. Again, Caplow (1964: 123), building upon the work of Homans's has been one of the few to emphasize this aspect.

In Figure 9.3, social integration has not been included as a variable affecting choice of voice and exit, and yet it would appear to be central. I suspect that social integration affects morale and loyalty both, while being perhaps relatively unaffected by either the characteristics of the social structure or the coordination/ control mechanisms. It thus is an entirely different dimension than these instrumental ones.

Typically dominant coalitions worry about work, pay, power, and the like but do not spend much time in building a sense of *Gemeinschaft*, a solidarity or cohesion among the members that is based on something more solid than bonus plans and interdependence of work.

In my opinion this is the real hidden and unrecognized variable in the calculus of individual costs and benefits: is there enough affect and an absence of hostility in the social relationships found in the organization? Is it a friendly place to work (which is not the same as saying that one makes friends on the job)? Are the people cooperative? Is there a minimum of interpersonal conflict or hostility (which is not the same as organizational conflict, see Chapter 10)? Having a warm or *gemütlich* setting, I suspect, is much more critical in affecting worker satisfaction than has been appreciated in the organizational literature. It flows from a basic human need, well articulated by Simmel (1955) who stated that we all need human interaction but at the same time we develop hostilities towards others.

This dilemma exists in organizations as much as in groups. People must work together to achieve not only organizational goals but their own ambitions. This means having to work with others. The quality of this relationship — whether cooperative or competitive, whether friendly or hostile — affects a person's satisfaction.

Another way in conceptualizing the need for social relationships is to take a Durkheimian (1933) perspective that individuals require social integration in expressive groups and not just in instrumental ones. Insofar as the organization's characteristics affect the building up or tearing down of integration, one can imagine a considerable impact on morale and, presumably, turnover.

There are several small pieces of evidence to indicate that social integration may be decisive. Blauner (1964) found that textile workers who objectively had quite bad working conditions were relatively satisfied. They were integrated into a community, and this set of needs appeared to be more important. There is a growing literature on the family corporation (Ouchi and Johnson, 1978) which suggests that organizations that are concerned about the worker's family and their needs build much greater loyalty and have higher morale. An example is IBM. This appears to be a pattern for Japanese factories as well.

In his review of turnover Price (1977: 70–73) found that social integration into primary groups reduces turnover. He cites one study by Van de Merwe and Miller that suggests integration is more important than pay. Unfortunately, there have been few studies that have tried to separate out the relative importance of each of these variables: structural, control, and integrative factors.

9.3. THE MICRO STRUCTURE: WORK GROUPS, JOB ENLARGEMENT, AND JOB ENRICHMENT

At the level of micro structure, there are the job or the work position, the interpersonal relationships, and naturally job satisfaction and job performance. Many of the same hypotheses about the meso structure and morale can be derived and applied at this level as well. The reason for carefully linking microstructural properties with the costs of benefits of work is to make the derivations of these micro hypotheses more apparent. The concentration of specialists is paralleled by the idea of the variety of work activities. In the literature, the latter idea is frequently referred to as job enlargement. Closely akin to this is job enrichment, which means making the activities more interesting ones; in particular trying to add more responsibilities and authority. Thus, job enlargement is a quantitative distinction – how many activities are added, while job enrichment is more qualitative – adding responsibilities as well as activities. In Chapter 3 we already noted the parallelism between the centralization of power and job autonomy.

The long term concern about productivity and various indicators of morale such as absenteeism and turnover has led to a large amount of research at the micro level. Nor has all research been motivated by the desire for more profits. Some researchers have been genuinely concerned with the human costs of unsatisfying work (Walker, 1950).

Perhaps the best example is the idea of semi-autonomous work groups (Emery and Thorsrud, 1964 and 1969). There are some subtle differences between the development of semiautonomous work groups and the whole thrust of the participation movement, although their objectives are very much alike. In general, various schemes of participation refer to the representation of the workers in various policy-making committees or on the board. In contrast, semi-autonomos work groups refer to making of immediate work decisions. Blauner (1964) has suggested that the workers are more interested in the latter than the former except when the former involves the latter. The policy decision to close down a plant would be most important to them. But except for these decisions involving "life and death", most workers are concerned about their pace of work, the noise level, the number of minutes for coffee breaks, the decisions about when to start and to stop work, and so forth.

If this reasoning is correct, then in most instances the best way to improve job satisfaction is to start at the bottom of the hierarchy rather than the top. Of course, the problem is that centralized organizations are unlikely to start the processes of job enlargement or enrichment and the development of semi-autonomous work groups without some prodding from the government. Decentralized organizations are more likely to begin this procedure on their own.

Although the results are anything but clear, the studies do support the notion that job enlargement and the development of greater job autonomy in various ways improves worker satisfaction, but not necessarily efficiency. It has an impact on the latter in extreme situations when turnover has gotten so high or the problem of strikes is so great that any concern for the workers is likely to manifest itself in greater productivity.

Emery and Thorsrud (1964) and also the Swedish reports on Volvo (Morin, 1976) have very carefully emphasized that semi-autonomous work groups are an alternative way of organizing work *not* for the objective of increasing productivity but instead for the purpose of providing greater work satisfaction. *The objective is to hold constant material costs and reduce human costs.*

Unfortunately the Americans have not always understood this. As a consequence they have used job enlargement or enrichment more as a means to increase productivity, rather than to reflect a concern with human benefits. There is also a tendency to confuse which variables are most important. One is improving the variety of work and the other is giving more work autonomy. The advantage of semi-autonomous work groups is that they tend to do both – when properly implemented. In other words, the workers become responsible for their own job design, which means job enrichment at the same time. There is another advantage that is quite important, and that is the movement away from the assembly line to the group also means that social relationships are encouraged and facilitated. In turn this means greater expressive satisfaction. This actually may be the single most important fact about semi-autonomous work groups. They facilitate social interaction and thus speak to the needs for affect and for social integration.

What the Norwegian and Swedish literature has not stressed enough is that the creation of work group is a very powerful means of social control. Indeed, this may be the reason why they are so effective in reducing absenteeism and turnover. One becomes committed to the group norms (Homans, 1950) and will not violate them. Social integration is the hidden variable.

The example of Volvo is a case in point. The introduction of semi-autonomous work groups in place of the assembly line in a rural plant at Kalmar did result in a reduction of absenteeism from 20% to 8% relative to other Volvo plants (Morin, 1976: 128). This reduction may not be due to job enlargement or enrichment, which in fact did not occur, but instead might be due to the more satisfying social relationships and the control of group norms. But it did require an increased investment of 10%; thus it would be wrong to speak about greater efficiency. Also it is important to remember that in Scandinavia there is considerable consensus and a great deal of cooperation between the labor unions and management.

In France, various companies have tried to attack bits and pieces of the overall problem and have even established semi-autonomous work groups (Morin, 1976), but as yet the results of this effort are unknown. In general, the labor unions are opposed to these experiments, in part because it reduces their control and in part because their ideology is nationalization and control of strategic decisions. In France, the Scandinavian kind of labor-management cooperation is unthinkable.

Oddly enough some of the best literature on job enlargement or enrichment is frequently not cited because it occurred by "accident", that is it was unplanned. A study of a steel factory (Walker, 1957) and another of a new power plant (Mann and Hoffman, 1960) both quite independently verified that increased automation had considerably altered the occupational structure. Especially in the new automated power plant, a large number of narrow scope jobs were eliminated and most particularly those activities that were most routine and monotonous. New and much more complex jobs were created. In addition, the new work flow allowed the workers to talk together and to control their pace of work. Automation in the power plant created jobs very much like those described by Blauner (1964) in the chemical industry. The semi-automated production line eliminated much of the routine work and created more complex jobs with the remaining nonroutine tasks. Besides this a new microphone system in the steel plant allowed the workers to talk to each other constantly, something that previously had not been possible because of the noise level (this was not the reason that management installed the microphone, however, but an unintended consequence). The workers could control the pace of the production line. Indeed they had to because of the possibility of accidents. In both of these detailed case studies, the same workers were involved in the old and the new production systems. And despite the necessary job retraining, both job and expressive satisfaction were much higher.

Although the literature on job enrichment does not emphasize the theme of responsibility very much, what is striking in both these case studies is that the workers had more responsibilities and responded quite favorably to this.

These case studies suggest several key points, however, about the problem of increasing job satisfaction. *First,* just adding nonroutine activities without eliminating monotonous work may not improve job satisfaction much. We return to the basic point that there are both costs and benefits relative to each dimension of work satisfaction. Increasing variety does not necessarily mean a reduction in monotony or repetitive tasks. A job enrichment scheme that moves from doing one operation 10,000 times a day to four operations each 2500 times a day is an increase in variety but not a decrease in monotony. *Second,* control over the pace of the work and more critically the rhythm of work is very important. *Third,* work flows that allow workers to interact, whether face-to-face or through some mechanical communication system are critical benefits as well because they allow for more social integration. *Fourth,* a growth in responsibility is very important and its importance is probably underestimated.

But if organizations are to create semi-autonomous work groups, then it seems desirable to start with greater automation of the work flow process so that the more monotonous, repetitive tasks are eliminated and more complex jobs with greater variety of tasks can be created. This is obviously not politically feasible during times of unemployment but becomes quite possible when there is rapid expansion. Greater automation is also the best single solution to solving the dilemma between human and material costs, as I shall argue in Chapter 12, since mechanization eliminates routine while it increases productivity.

Which of these attributes – interesting work, job autonomy, increased responsibilities or satisfying work relationships – is the most important? Some (Maslow, 1954) have argued that there is a hierarchy of needs and perhaps there is. What is more striking is that workers appear to need all of these things, and therefore it is best to attempt to provide all dimensions simultaneously. In this sense, unless semiautonomous work groups do, they can fail because they speak to only part of the problem of satisfaction. A recent study (Shepard and Herrick, 1972) of blue collar work satisfaction suggests that the importance of interesting work, job autonomy and responsible work, has not been appreciated enough. Again, the authors are not saying that economic incentives are unimportant, but that they have been overstressed. This study also supports the notion that instead of seeing a hierarchy of needs, it is better to see that there are multiple needs that must be balanced.

The Shepard and Herrick study also speaks to the problem of whether needs are changing as a function of time. They found that the younger and less authoritarian workers were more likely to be dissatisfied with jobs that had little variety and few responsibilities. In Chapter 14, I will suggest some of the causes for these changing needs.

In summary, there is much in the literature to indicate that essentially the same four or five work satisfaction dimensions apply at the micro level. Most proposals to improve job satisfaction imply changing only one or two dimensions and not all of them. In particular, job enlargement or enrichment is unlikely to work unless it eliminates repetitive tasks at the same time that the variety is increased. More promising are semi-autonomous work groups, especially because they tend to affect more than one dimension of worker satisfaction. But again, if, for whatever reasons, as they implement the changes they do not influence more than one dimension, then the impact on satisfaction is not likely to be large. In order to understand why different results are obtained in different plants and offices, one must study how many dimensions of work were changed and to what extent. As has been suggested, the importance of automation is not to be underestimated. The machines can be designed to eliminate the routine, repetitive tasks, leaving the more interesting ones to be done by humans. With this kind of change, one can really do job design in the context of semi-autonomous work groups.

9.4. CONCLUSIONS

The consistent theme throughout this chapter is that there are multiple needs, not just one or two, which must be met if the morale of the organization and especially collective effort is to be positively influenced. In this chapter we have explored how characteristics of the social structure and control mechanisms affect morale and how characteristics of labor markets affect both opportunity and morale. To be consistent we have restricted the dimensions of morale largely to these categories of variables.

Individual differences are a worthwhile topic but not the focus of this chapter. Instead we are concerned about average needs for interesting work, job autonomy, equity in pay, and a sense of a responsible job, that is what is appropriate for occupations. We are led to note that there may not be a hierarchy as such but more a plurality of needs, and that the need for social integration may be much greater than previously recognized.

How structure and control impact on morale and turnover or the option of exit are clear within the framework presented. And the evidence generally supports the hypotheses. What is less clear is how this translates into collective effort and productivity. There is evidence to indicate that one may achieve a great deal of productivity with quite high levels of turnover. Morale may translate into effort without much impact on productivity. There are two hidden variables: integration and technology. Without somehow accounting for these, it will be difficult to advance much in this area.

In the next chapter, the option of voice is studied, as we move away from the more traditional concerns of the literature — morale and productivity — to the more nontraditional ones, conflict and loyalty.

Chapter Ten

Voices: Conflict and Consensus

Exit is in some way the easy way out. One can leave all the problems behind and seek a better situation. The mobility of the middle classes may help explain why they have higher job satisfaction on the average than the working class, who objectively have less. They have the financial reserves to allow them to change jobs, and many more options. Voice is the harder pathway. It frequently requires organization, whether in unions or professional associations (Hyman, 1972). Strikes are costly and sometimes even violent (for example see the beautiful film *Harlan County, U.S.A.*). Even less stringent voices than strikes have their personnel costs in psychic energy and fatigue. It is these less dramatic and more common forms of voice that we shall analyze in this chapter.

Organizational researchers and theorists have increasingly come to agree with Pondy's (1967) argument that a good organizational theory should include the concept of conflict as one of its essential ideas. More and more one finds in the literature attempts either to build conflict into some theory (Corwin, 1969; Schmidt and Kochan, 1972) or at least to attempt to do research on conflict (see special issue of *ASQ,* December, 1969; Darkenwald, 1971) or both. Neither of these tasks is necessarily easy. Conflict presents a large number of conceptual and operational difficulties, some of which have already been noted in the literature (Pondy, 1967 and 1969a; Schmidt and Kochan, 1972). To build a theory of conflict, especially one integrated with current organizational models (Azumi and Hage, 1972: Chapter 3), is not easy because there is disagreement in the literature as to whether conflict represents a state of organizational disequilibrium or not (Pondy, 1967). In contrast to conflict, consensus has been more widely studied (see Smith, 1966; although called conflict it reviews a number of studies of consensus; Smith and Ari, 1964; Price, 1968 and 1972). Here, too, there remain certain questions about how one might measure this theoretical concept.

Yet, a theory of conflict should be a theory of consensus and vice versa. Both are needed to counter-balance an undue emphasis on theories of exit. Voice is just as important in understanding the human factor in organizations as is exit. Beyond this voice comes in two forms: agreement and disagreement, consensus and conflict. Here most of the emphasis is placed on the latter because it is what Hirschman (1970) had in mind.

One of the essential difficulties is to find a good operational measure or index of indicators for conflict and consensus, especially one that is sensitive enough to detect conflict before it increases in intensity so that there are overt acts. Violence, the usual meaning of societal conflict (Gurr, 1970; Hibbs, 1973), is seldom applicable in organizations. It does occur (Lammers, 1969) but is relatively rare. Thus, one desideratum is that the operational definition be subtle enough to detect more common forms or kinds of conflict, especially those likely to occur in an organizational context. Here the work of Corwin (1969 and 1970) has made an important contribution. Another difficulty is to separate out a wide variety of meanings associated with this concept — role conflict, consensus, competition, and kindred ideas. Their interrelations should be made explicit and, if possible, unambiguous. Still, a third difficulty, but one that has received less attention in the literature, is to make a distinction between organizational or meso conflicts, micro conflict, and interpersonal conflict, all of which can be easily confused. Much of the imagery of conflict (see Schmidt and Kochan, 1972; Pondy, 1967) has been cast in individual terms. Yet, there is no assurance that the causes are necessarily the same for these three analytical levels. This distinction seems particularly important given the pattern of Corwin's findings (1969 and 1970); the size of the correlation alters depending upon the measure. Once one finds a satisfactory solution to the problem of how to measure and define conflict, this should provide an equally viable solution for the concept of consensus since these two ideas are much more closely connected than is suggested by the debate between the advocates of structural-functionalism and the conflict-critical approach.

Finally, there is a considerable problem as to whether one focuses on horizontal, professional-managerial, line-staff conflict, vertical or manager-worker, or have-have-not conflict. Here the accent is very much in the former rather than the latter. The definition emphasizes conflict about ends and means rather than wages and work rules. Hopefully the same theory can explain both, but the crux of the analysis is on the general kinds of conflict reported in the organizational literature rather than the industrial relations literature.

The definitions for these concepts are suggested in the first section. The essential solutions lie *first* in recognizing the difference between a meso and micro level, between group and role conflict, and *second* in appreciating that consensus and conflict can occur in odd mixtures and combinations. It is wrong to assume that consensus and conflict are in exact antithesis even if they are the poles of a continuum. Rather, the problem is to know what the proportion is of each. As the degree of conflict increases, however, there is a qualitative change.

Theoretically, there is a disagreement as to whether or not conflict represents a state of disequilibrium (contrast March and Simon, 1958 with White, 1961). Consistent with the discussion in Chapters 8 and 9, the theory advanced in the second section argues that there are states of equilibrium and of disequilibrium, and the relative degree of conflict supports the notion of what are desired states. All of this also relates to the essential question of equity, at least at the occupational level if not at the level of the individual. In order to understand when the people will fight — exercise their voice, in the words of Hirschman (1970) — we need to predict the sense of injustice or their sense of equity. It is not necessary to know what this is for the individual, which is much more difficult to determine. Every group or occupation has individuals who feel unjustly treated regardless of their power, pay, and privilege, just as there are individuals who will always accept the bottom rung docilely. *The real issue is when blacks or women or physicians or welfare clients or students become conscious of a systematic wrong and fight in the name of the group or occupation or class.* It is at this point that we can speak of social conflict in a quite different sense from individual or interpersonal conflict or even role conflict.

Finally, the special problems of role conflict is considered in the third section. Much more empirical work exists on this topic than on conflict at the meso level. Yet surprisingly the theory has not advanced much beyond the formulation of Merton (1957). These empirical results need to be organized into some new propositions about the causes of this kind of conflict.

10.1. THE CONCEPTS OF ORGANIZATIONAL CONFLICT AND CONSENSUS

As Schmidt and Kochan (1972) have noted, the concept of conflict contains a great deal of ambiguity. They suggest that any good definition should avoid three problems: value-laden terms, such as "breaches," "breakdowns," "antagonistic struggles"; a confusion with either causes or consequences; and a confusion with the idea of competition. Central to the concept of organizational conflict is the idea that the phenomenon must be relatively widespread in an organization, with both organizational causes and consequences. In any organization there are a number of personality conflicts or even conflicts within specific interpersonal relationships. The causes of these adhere less in the basic organizational structure or performance and more in the personality of the people who are involved. In Corwin's terms (1969: 512), we are primarily interested in measuring what he called major incidents, that is, ones involving a substantial segment of the organization. This distinction might not seem necessary, except that a careful inspection of his findings indicates a number of reversals as one moves from what he calls disputes to heated discussions to major incidents. This suggests either that the causes are different at the micro and meso levels, or that the causes of different intensities of conflicts are different, or both. In either case, it becomes important to distinguish what is being measured.

Thus, one crucial theme in our proposed definition is that the conflict is social rather than personal. Meso-conflict or organizational conflict can be defined as conflict between groups, whereas role conflict can be defined as conflict between social positions, and interpersonal conflict as conflict between individuals (see Figure 10.1). Thus where Ego reports conflict with Alter, the question remains is Alter perceived as a person, Mr. Janus, or as the occupant of a position, such as the boss's secretary (see Mechanic, 1962), or as an occupant of a larger social group: namely all workers that belong to the union. Admittedly, in any concrete case, Ego might perceive the problem as interpersonal when in fact the situation is structural either at the micro or meso level. This is one reason why one must interview some representative sample of the membership of the organization. As more and more respondents report conflict, we are more and more sure that the conflict is indeed a general one involving different social groups.

The *content* varies between each of these analytical levels as well. At the meso-level the problem is conflict about organizational means and ends – that is, the policies of the organization. Here it is useful to distinguish between horizontal and vertical conflict – that is, disagreements about power and policy between interest groups at the same level, and disagreements about wages and fringe benefits between interest groups at different levels (the haves and the have-nots). In contrast, micro or role conflict (Gross, Mason, and McEachern, 1958; Merton, 1957: Chapter 9) is conflict about the role performance (Kahn, et al., 1964). At the individual or interpersonal level the content of conflict is individual behavior – we do not like something someone else is doing. The prob-

Figure 10.1   The levels and content of conflict

Level	Definition	Content
Meso	Disagreements between groups	Organization means and ends
Horizontal	Groups are departments, occupations	Most typically power and policy
Vertical	Groups are levels in the hierarchy	Most typically salaries and wages
Micro	Disagreements between occupants of positions	Job performance or behavior
Individual	Disagreements between persons	Individual behavior

lem of separating what is positional from personal behavior is not always easy. Again, the key is how many people in the same position are having the same conflict. If all medical students have problems with the head nurse, or if all the superintendents have difficulty with the principals in their district, or if all vice-presidents have problems with the assistant to the president, and so on, then we are clearly at a role-conflict level rather than an interpersonal one. In the analysis of conflict over decisions discussed in Chapter 4, we most typically have horizontal conflict. However, in the analysis of conflict during the process of social change (Chapter 7) both kinds are represented. Usually the meso conflict occurs in the early stages and the micro conflict during the implementation stage.

But what is the meaning of the word conflict? As I have already noted, we want to measure this at a lower level of intensity than violence. The solution to these problems is to focus on conflict as disagreement. This seems implicit in Corwin's work. It appears to be the sine qua non of at least organizational, if not societal, conflict. And disagreement seems the very essence of what Hirschman (1970) means by voice. Once we tell someone, say the foreman, we do not like what is being done, we have begun to express our objections. Members of organizations frequently have disagreements about politics or rules or salaries (Lawrence and Lorsch, 1967a; Walton et al., 1969 a and b). Indeed, the current view in management courses is that this is quite healthy for organizations. To suppress disagreements is to prevent opportunities for finding out how the organization can be better managed. This is consistent with my view as well as the set of ideas expressed in Chapter 5. If one accepts the idea that different sets of leaders do have value preferences relative to organizational performances, then the stage is set for at least horizontal conflict over such issues as innovation versus efficiency, quality versus quantity, and human versus material costs. No easy solutions to these dilemmas exist and they make the substance of good battles and struggles for power. As we have noted on many occasions, the high risk decision and the radical innovation draw out feuds between interest groups, break up existing coalitions, and create new ones.

Noncooperation is the second step in some intensity of conflict. But at the prior level are the basic disagreements regarding organizational policies and programs and the methods by which they are achieved. These are likely to be much more ubiquitous than the functionalists have suggested. It is true that disagreements reflect what might be called normative conflict, that is, conflict within the rules. But conflict outside the rules, such as burning plants and hitting police, is rare in the organizational context. At the same time, if we can delineate probable causes for conflict involving nonviolent disagreements, there is no necessary reason to assume that these same causes might not explain the more violent and rare conflict forms. This may appear inconsistent with a previous suggestion that there is a necessity to distinguish between personal and group conflict because the causes are different. But the context changes. In more intense conflicts there is not a shift in context but a change in intensity of feeling about the wrongs and the grievances. Here qualitative and quantitative distinctions blend together. Rarely does horizontal conflict as defined in Figure 10.1 involve violence, whereas vertical conflict can reach this level of intensity. The reason is simple. As Simmel (1955) remarked long ago, and as has been well substantiated in the empirical literature, cross-cutting status sets dampen conflict. This applies to line-staff conflict and to battles about new products but seldom occurs in the war between managers and workers, except where workers eventually become managers or owners. Thus industrial conflict is quite different in traditional industry such as in print shops, small construction firms, and furniture makers where the owner may be a former craftsman than in the mechanical organizations where there is a large status schism between management and workers (Caplow, 1964: 280-85).

The nature of the disagreements can be many and varied. This implies at least several indicators, each one representing a particular kind of conflict. Pondy (1967) has suggested that there are bargaining, bureaucratic, and system models of conflict. These might be seen as kinds of conflict. More critical is the idea that if the conflict is organizational, then the content must represent disagreements about what the organization is doing or how it is being done. Again, the point is banal but frequently missed. *Phenomenologically, organizational conflict usually centers around organizational means or ends or both.* How the structure is arranged, how much control is exerted, what the organizational policies are, and how these are implemented are illustrations. Thus, Schmidt and Kochan (1972), by focusing on incompatible goals of individuals in an organization, have looked at a source of individual or interpersonal tension. Here our focus is more on social conflict between groups about either their self-interests *qua* groups and/or their values relative to the performances of the organization.

Given the suggested opposition between quantity and quality, innovation and efficiency, and other functional performances, these become the natural basis for conflict over ends. Inherent dilemmas mean inherent disagreements and natural antagonisms. They give rise to a dialectic that is perhaps never really solved. If so, the conflict over goals in organizations is existential. It can never be completely resolved. Note that it is a functional problem that leads us to recognize that conflict is always present. Multiple ends can never be completely realized.

Conflicts over means are equally important, and more familiar. We expect conflicts over salaries. And certainly there are many struggles for power, especially during processes involving high risk decisions. Stratification and centralization are means employed to achieve organizational ends, as we noted in Chapter 2. Here vertical conflict — between those within the dominant coalition and those without, between the haves and the have-nots — is more likely. Equally important are fights about rules and regulations, the bureaucratic red tape. In part a means of organizational control to ensure conformity, in part a way of limiting the autonomy of workers and supervisors, in part a method for ensuring universalistic treatment or handling, they can form a fertile ground for conflict. As Blauner (1964) has noted, workers frequently desire some say about the pace and conditions of work. These, too, can lead to disagreements. In fact, wildcat strikes are more likely to occur over these issues than they are over wages.

Our theoretical definition thus becomes:

Organizational conflict: Disagreement between the members about organizational means or ends or both.

This means-ends distinction is similar to the normative and value conflict ideas of Smelser (1963) but appears to be at once more general and more relevant, at least within an organizational setting. With this definition one can begin to see how this concept differs from some ideas that are usually combined or appear to be cognate. Competition between various interest groups for scarce resources (Burns and Stalker, 1961: Chapter 7) may be a cause of disagreements about organizational means or ends, but it is not in itself a kind of organizational conflict as we have defined it.

Role conflict, which is normally defined as conflict over expectations (Kahn et al., 1964), is not included within this conception of organizational or meso conflict. This concept is defined and discussed at length in the third section of this chapter.

Conflict is only one way of exercising voice. As we have already suggested, consensus is the other, equally important one. Indeed, much of the debate between functionalists and conflict theorists has been over the relative importance of these two ideas, with functionalists suggesting that consensus is a normal state of affairs, and conflict theorists arguing for the ubiquity of conflict. The theoretical definition is:

Organizational consensus: Agreements between members about organizational means or ends or both.

While agreements and disagreements lie along the same continuum, they are not exactly opposites of each other. As is suggested in Figure 10.2, consensus and conflict can be mixed together and usually are. A certain proportion of the membership will always be in disagreement and a certain proportion will always be in agreement. Beyond this, the content of conflict and of consensus can be quite different. Members might agree about goals but not the means used to achieve them. Or they might agree about what the goals are, but not about their relative priorities. And so forth. Typically, disagreements about new policies, programs, or changes in the structure of the organization are this admixture

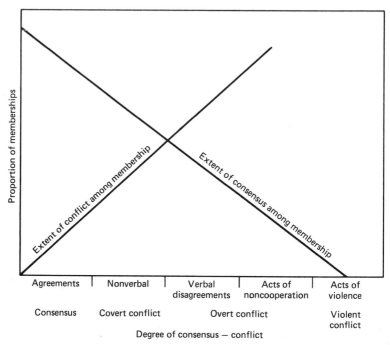

Figure 10.2 The consensus-conflict/continuum.

of consensus and of conflict. It is important to note in the figure that the amount of conflict must be in some way standardized on the number of organizational members or size of the organization. This is the best single way of ensuring that in fact we are tapping social or meso conflict, rather than some kind of role or interpersonal conflict.

10.2. A MESO-STRUCTURAL THEORY OF CONFLICT

10.2.1. The Major Premises and Hypotheses

In his pioneering study of conflict, Corwin (1969 and 1970) developed the following hypotheses about the causes of conflict:

1. The greater the degree of differentiation or of complexity, the greater the degree of conflict.
2. The greater the participation of the membership in decisions, the greater the degree of conflict.
3. The greater the emphasis on rules, the greater the degree of conflict.

The first hypothesis is the familiar idea that as one creates different specialties or separates groups into different departments, by necessity one generates the conditions for antagonisms and disagreements. Occupations and specialties have different norms, values, and the like. They use different technologies and perceive the world in different ways. These problems have been aptly demonstrated in the work of Lawrence and Lorsch (1967), and Walton, Dutton and Cafferty (1969). The rivalries between staff and line (Dalton, 1950) have long been recognized. But the major error in all of this work is the failure to recognize that this perhaps is just a function of size. One wants also to keep quite distinct in one's mind the differences between the role conflict of occupations interacting and widespread major incidents involving a number of different groups or occupations or even whole strata. Line-staff conflict could be nothing more than role conflict — that is, different expectations about what each other should be doing. This is not the same content as disagreements about organizational means and ends, although the one can shade into the other.

The second hypothesis is in some respects more interesting because it is in direct opposition to Tannenbaum's thesis of what produces consensus. He argued (1968) that by sharing power one creates consensus. Of course, much of the problem reflects a very different definition of conflict and of consensus. Sharing power does create greater visibility of the power structure but not necessarily agreement about how power is distributed. But, one must ask, will greater participation result in the resolving of the inherent conflict of interests among various occupational groups, each maneuvering for a greater share of power vis-à-vis each other? Probably not, but at least it will keep it in muted form. In other words, greater participation does set an arena in which negotiation and bargaining as discussed in Chapter 4 can take place. This *in time* can make the conflict of interest more visible but it does not eliminate the problem. Instead one can agree with the literature that speaks about conflict being managed rather than eliminated (Lawrence and Lorsch, 1967a; Walton et al., 1969b).

One does not want to pass too quickly over this hypothesis because buried in it are some of the most treasured beliefs of many Americans, including academics. The deep commitment to democracy in this country is in part based on the idea that with decentralization of power, opposing interests can be gradually reconciled and compromises found. This fundamental assumption about the potential of democracy tends to be taken for granted by many schools of thought. The conflict-critical perspective is more apt to see enduring clashes between the haves and the have-nots and to question whether democracy might not be a sham, a cover-up, for the best interests of the owners and managers of power.

The emphasis on rules refers more to a particular control mechanism and therefore is in some respects different from the two previous hypotheses that refer to structural characteristic. Again, one would expect that the kind of control mechanism used or abused could created conflict, but again only under certain conditions. Teachers might respond one way and factory workers another.

The difficulty with all of these hypotheses is their lack of a relative or comparative context. Will the same amount of differentiation, participation, or control create the same amount of conflict in *all* organizations? This seems unlikely. Again, we are led to ask under what circumstances people become aware of their identity as some interest group or *realize that they are* the have-nots. It is precisely here that contingency theory might be most attractive.

The first assumption in Chapter 3, 3A was:

> Occupational or other interest groups want the same rank in power, prestige, pay, and privileges as they have in training and skill.

This provides the expected basis of equity. In Chapter 5, another assumption was:

> The greater the diversity of interest groups represented in the selection of priorities, the more complex and varied will the choice of priorities be.

Together these assumptions suggest that when an organization has a high concentration of specialists, the equilibrium state should be decentralization, with the goals of quality, innovation, and morale rather than efficiency and quantity. The various other combinations, representing other forms of equilibrium states, have been already discussed. Deviations from these equilibrium states provide the basis for predicting when conflict is likely to be greater. If our theory about how structure and performances fit together is correct, then we can predict that when the concentration of specialists and centralization are both high or when centralization is high and innovation is pursued as the desired priority there will be conflict.

This then means that the derived hypotheses about causes of conflict are:

10. 1   The greater the discrepancy between the extent of the concentration of specialists and the predicted level of decentralization, the greater the conflict and the less the consensus.

10. 2   The greater the discrepancy between the extent of the concentration of specialists and the predicted level of destratification, the greater the conflict and the less the consensus.

10. 3   The greater the discrepancy between the extent of the concentration of specialists and the predicted level of normative equality, the greater the conflict and the less the consensus.

10. 4   The greater the discrepancy between the extent of the concentration of specialists and the predicted level of emphasis on the goal of quality versus quantity, the greater the conflict and the less the consensus.

10. 5 The greater the discrepancy between the extent of the concentration of specialists and the predicted level of emphasis on the goal of change versus stability, the greater the conflict and the less the consensus.

All these hypotheses should be qualified for the nature of the specialists to take into account traditional and mixed mechanic-organic equilibrium states. To repeat a point that is elaborated in Chapters 8 and 12, artisans and craftsmen accept more centralization of strategic decisions if they have job autonomy. Engineers, whether they are hired as salesmen, managers, or in their technical specialty, do the same.

Given the distinctive characteristics of the four major forms, we could deduce specific kinds of hypotheses about when conflict is likely in each circumstance but these qualifications do not appear necessary at this juncture. Likewise we have noted that during a crisis centralization might be more acceptable than it otherwise would be. Again, this qualification should be kept in mind.

Equilibrium and disequilibrium can be understood in several senses. In Chapter 8, these are defined as combinations of variables that appear viable or not. *Here it is being suggested that nonviable combinations are likely to manifest themselves in voice or conflict.* Disagreements and grievances flow from the discrepant combinations of variables. In this sense conflict represents disequilibrium. Even here there are a number of complications. As is argued below, the complete absence of conflict is also a sign of disequilibrium, and an "unhealthy" state of organizational affairs. These hypotheses leave unanswered a critical problem: what is the *predicted* level of decentralization, destratification, normative quality and the like? How important this can be is indicated in Figure 10.3. Suppose we can assume that one unit of change in the concentration of specialists should produce one unit of change in the degree of decentralization. Then it is apparent that one can have too much decentralization as well as not enough. This raises some interesting questions. Does too much decentralization produce conflict? In Chapter 3, I have already suggested that the workers may not want more power. What happens if they get it? What meaning can the words "too much" have, or must value-free sociology avoid terms like this?

Obviously the ratio of coefficients between each of the variables describing the equilibrium makes a great deal of difference in defining the threshold of "too much" decentralization or destratification or the like. In Figure 10.3., the difference score assumes a ratio of coefficients of one and an intercept of zero. If the ratio remains one but the intercept becomes .20 — that is, there always a need for some centralization and complete participation is impossible — then the difference score with the numbers provided would always be positive, (a state of consensus), and never negative (a state of conflict). A higher intercept can also represent different equilibrium states. Consistent with the four forms is the presence of more than one regression slope for the relationships between the

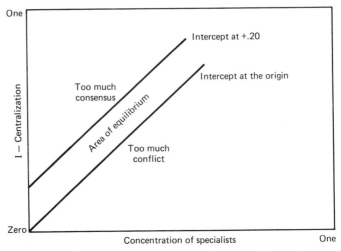

Figure 10.3   The conceptualization of equilibrium and disequilibrium.

ratio between the concentration of specialists and the centralization of power, or at the minimum, certain ranges in which the variables can vary independently.

More complex is the problem of whether a positive difference score, meaning much consensus and little conflict, is a desirable state of affairs. Just as we can speak about an equilibrium state with respect to structural and performance variables, we can do the same for various process variables. It is not immediately clear that an absence of all conflict is desirable. In fact, the change and innovation literature has usually emphasized the necessity for conflict. But in that context, change is being viewed as process, and the assumption is that resistance will have to be overcome (see Chapter 7). More relevant is the conflict that occurs as part of the process of making a decision to adopt a radically new product. One can imagine that if there is too much consensus, then this kind of conflict will be avoided. Therefore I opt for the idea that some mixture of consensus and conflict is desirable. *An absence of all disagreement implies a state of disequilibrium just as much as an absence of all agreement does.* Concretely this means so much emphasis on agreement that no dissenting ideas are allowed. This is quite often the case in academic departments where faculty with different ideas about the discipline or politics or even sex are not recruited. The result is an impoverishment of the intellectual atmosphere.

The conflict theorists (Coser, 1956) are right to criticize the consensus theorists for valuing consensus a little too much. Therefore, as a conjecture in Figure 10.3, I have suggested that on either side of the equilibrium defined by the relationship between the concentration of specialists and decentralization lie two kinds of disequilibrium, one characterized by too much consensus and the other by too much conflict.

Both kinds of voice are predictable. Too much consensus comes, paradoxically, from too much decentralization relative to the concentration of specialists. What happens in these circumstances is that there is an overemphasis on individual rather than group or class interests. Much of Chapter 3 is built on the divergence of views between groups. Some of these divergencies are covered over in an extremely decentralized organization where everyone participates all the time in decision-making. Under these circumstances, the importance of getting along becomes paramount and innovation is likely to diminish. Too much conflict occurs from too little decentralization or democracy relative to the concentration of specialists. What happens in this context is that there is constant group conflict over the distribution of power and the goals of the organizations. Here innovation can not flourish either but for very different reasons. So much time is spent in argument, antagonistic acrimonious debates, and cabals that little, if anything, is accomplished.

If we shift from horizontal conflict to vertical conflict, then too much conflict is seen in those industries that tend to be dominated by frequent and long strikes. Or the problem is more typical of specific organizations that institutionalize conflict and thus have a history of episodic conflicts over one problem or another.

The correct mixture between consensus and conflict or voices of agreement and disagreement, is impossible to determine without research into their impact on at least several performances, and especially the dialectic between innovation and efficiency. One suspects that the relationship is not only complex but marginally elastic. That is, small changes in this mixture can produce large changes in organizational performances.

What causes an organization to move into disequilibrium as defined here? This is a very different kind of transformation process, one involving the movement from a stable form into an unstable one. A number of the answers have already been provided in various chapters. Focusing only on the relationships between the structural variables, a rapid change in the concentration of specialists causes disequilibrium, which in time can cause conflict. Equally apparent, however, is that a very rapid decentralization of the organization would produce another kind of disequilibrium — too much consensus — if the above line of reasoning is correct. Throughout, the reader can add the other variables included in the hypothesis given above, as well as the qualifications relative to the kinds of specialists or generalists involved.

This leaves unanswered what produces these kinds of rapid changes. Typically they are responses to events in the environment — discontinuous changes in the level of technology that required a considerable increase in the concentration of specialists, a sudden growth in demand necessitating the rapid hiring of more personnel, or an infusion of funds as we saw in the War on Poverty, which in turn can create either kind of response (as we have seen in Chapter 8). Government attempts to regulate can have a considerable impact on the internal distribution of power as well.

What are absent are the various control mechanisms that in one way or another may make either voice or exit costly. The problem of control is left until the next chapter. For now, I only note that voice and exit are not necessarily options, depending upon the control mechanisms that are available. In fact voice, as manifested especially in strikes, is a luxury affordable only in a few postindustrial and democratic societies.

10.2.2. The Findings

Building upon the work of Corwin, it is worth examining whether structural differentiation and participation affect rates of conflict and consensus in health and welfare agencies. These data are reported in Table 10.1. The three measures of structural differentiation available in the Hage and Aiken study (1972) either are negatively related to their measures of general conflict or have no relationship at all. If one can say that these organizations are very much like the schools studied by Corwin then the conclusion is clear; there is more conflict in larger organizations but less on a rate or proportional basis, that is, the number of incidents per member. The one exception is conflict over salaries. As the

Table 10.1 The structural causes of conflict and consensus
Hage-Aiken panel study (1972) N = 29

Structural variables	General[a] conflict	Conflict salaries	General[a] consensus	Consensus salaries
Concentration of specialists	−.55	.27	.37	−.21
Number of levels	−.11	−.01	−.02	−.30
Number of departments	−.00	−.22	.23	−.17
Centralization	−.52	−.40	−.48	−.08
Stratification (proportion of lower participants)	.19	.20	−.16	−.01

[a] Composed of three indicators, one about decision making, another about priorities among goals, and a third about rules.

concentration of specialists increases, there is a tendency for disagreements over this area to grow.

What is especially interesting about this pattern of findings is that the concentration of specialists, which is a proportional measure, has a strong negative relationship with conflict ($r = -.55$) but only a moderate positive one with consensus ($r = +.37$), that is, not in all cases is consensus the exact reversal of conflict. In this instance, the potential for conflict to grow with the addition of specialists is retained or even magnified since it expresses the proportion. At best, one might expect no relationship at all. Instead, one finds a strong negative one. This finding appears to be counter-intuitive, especially given the literature on staff-line conflict (Victor Thompson 1961a; Dalton, 1950), but perhaps illustrates best another literature; given differentiation, integrative mechanisms are developed that manage conflict (Lawrence and Lorsch, 1967 a and b). It also lends support to the thesis that by making disagreements visible – by making latent conflict manifest – the members confront it and diffuse it.

There is another interpretation of this result. Durkheim (1933: 278), in a rarely noted passage, suggests that as the division of labor progresses (concentration of specialists) the frequency of the conflict increases but its intensity diminishes. Simmel (1955) made a similar argument about the relationship between frequency and intensity of conflict. Since the measure developed by Hage and Aiken do not measure these minor disagreements, but instead what Corwin (1969) would call major incidents, we find conflict negatively related.

In 16 of the 29 organizations of the Hage-Aiken study, the respondents were asked to name the incidents, state how many staff were involved, and how long these episodes lasted. The original intent of these questions was to measure conflict intensity. In general, neither question worked but they did tend to confirm that major incidents were being tapped. This is because most of the respondents reported chronic conditions that endured for a year or more and that engaged many members of the organization. Respondents frequently mentioned that the disagreements were occurring all the time and sometimes lasted for several years. Thus in general, what was tapped were continuing difficulties. At the same time, major short term incidents – if dramatic – were remembered. For example, in one public welfare agency an activist who was interested in starting a client union was fired. This incident was widely reported by respondents in that organization. All of this suggests that the presence of a concentration of specialists leads to the reduction of organizational conflict as measured by these questions, but not necessarily to the reduction of more minor forms of conflict that are on the micro or interpersonal levels.

How inconsistent is this finding with those of Corwin (1969 and 1970)? It is much less than would appear at first glance. Major incidents, the measure in Corwin's works that most closely approximates that used in the Hage-Aiken study, has a very different pattern of correlations from his other measures. With the exception of a lack of specialization measure, which is not the same as the concentration of specialists, the other measures of structural differentiation had little or no relationship with major incidents.

The measures of centralization reported in Table 10.1 are strongly related to the presence of conflict and the absence of consensus. This exactly parallels Corwin's findings, where participation in the authority system was associated with a reduction in major conflicts ($r = -.38$, $N = 28$). In contrast, however, Corwin found that this was positively associated with the number of disputes ($r = .39$, $N = 28$). Here we have confirmation for the Durkheimian thesis and consistency with the Hage-Aiken study. As the frequency of conflict increases, its intensity declines. This occurs by making latent conflicts manifest through greater participation in the authority system – that is, decentralization. Corwin's measure of participation involved both work and educational policy decisions, and this is comparable to the definition of both job autonomy and centralization as defined in Chapter 3. Corwin's third hypothesis relative to control measures is discussed in the next chapter, where the consequences of various control mechanisms are considered.

One might conclude from this that the more participation the better, but this may not be the case. Instead, it is worth examining whether the real point is not the amount of participation relative to the concentration of specialists. This is diagrammed in Figure 10.4. The results are quite interesting and suggest that this

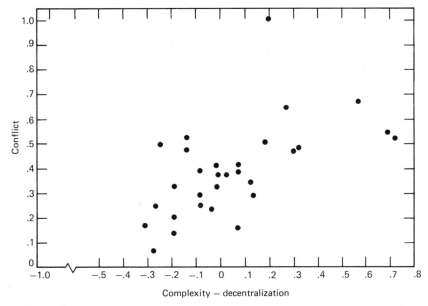

Figure 10.4 Scatter plot of structure and conflict, Hage-Aiken panel study N = 29.

might be a worthwhile approach to explore in future research. In this graph, the assumption is made that the parametric ratio between X and Y is one. Actually the spread of points suggests that, at least for this group of organizations, this is not a bad approximation. What is even more surprising is that one half of the organizations cluster around ±.10. This is strong evidence for the idea that there is an equilibrium state, and one that represents a certain mixture of conflict and consensus. The one exception is a religious organization where there was a struggle for control between the priests and the professionals which was not captured well by the measures that Hage and Aiken employed.

Another possible interpretation is that centralization almost always lags behind changes in the concentration of specialists and therefore in fact organizations are seldom in equilibrium. The best test of this would be whether organizations that have negative discrepancy scores had other problems, such as too slow an innovation rate or too high a cost relative to the output. If so, then it would be another argument that in fact organizations with a negative discrepancy score had decentralized too much. Certainly the organizations with high conflict have low morale ($r = -.64$ for job satisfaction and $r = -.64$ for expressive satisfaction, $N = 29$). Nor is this just a function of the impact on either the concentration of specialists or the centralization where the zero-order correlations are *less* than this. The conflict, independent of its structural causes, is contributing to the lowered morale. This all argues that there can be too little decentralization, at least relative to the concentration of specialists, if not necessarily too much. The best test of the latter idea requires the examination of cost figures, rates of innovation, and other performance criteria.

What is the correlation between the discrepancy score and conflict. The formula for expressing this is as follows:

$$[X - (1 - Y)] = Z$$

where X = concentration of specialists
Y = centralization or other structural variable
Z = consensus/conflict index

None of the parameters are specified but as the discrepancy increases, one might expect conflict to grow nonlinearly rather than linearly. The linear correlation is $r = +.58$ — that is, as the discrepancy grows, the correlation with conflict increases. If one examines the partial of this discrepancy vis-à-vis first the concentration of specialists and then centralization, it remains the stronger of the two and especially with participation in strategic decisions. It is not greater decentralization but instead greater decentralization relative to the concentration of specialists (the partials are $r_p = .02$ for centralization and $r_p = .36$ for the discrepancy score). When the concentration of specialists is the other variable, the discrepancy score is still the stronger partial. Here the problem is that the correlation between the discrepancy score and the concentration of specialists is so high ($r = .96$) that one almost has no difference. The greater the concentration of specialists, the greater the discrepancy. Although with this high a degree of multi-collinearity one must be careful in interpreting the results, the pattern is a consistent one and suggests the following process relative to disequilibrium.

The growth in the concentration of specialists is not followed quickly by a change towards greater decentralization. The consequence is mounting conflict, and eventually a rearrangement of the structure towards greater decentralization. It is primarily conflict that forces the dominant coalition to share power with the new specialists. This process is substantiated by a case study of a community hospital over a four-year time period (Hage, 1974: Part 1). There was a considerable increase in the number of medical specialists who tried to increase their power vis-à-vis the dominant elite (primarily general practitioners). The ensuing struggle of power resulted in some extreme forms of conflict. There was screaming in meetings. Doctors threatened the hospital with a lawsuit, and the entire pediatric service walked out at one point. At the end of two tumultuous years, a new power structure emerged, which was much more decentralized. The major winners were the administrators, who profited from the power struggle within the medical profession.

In summary all these various bits and pieces of evidence indicate that the concept of equilibrium does appear to be a meaningful one within the context of organizational research. The tendency for the discrepancy score to vary between $\pm .10$, the relationship between conflict and the discrepancy scores, and the relationship between conflict and morale all suggest that there are ranges beyond which variable scores can not go without manifestations of discontent. The costs of too much conflict are clear. What have not been established are the costs of too little conflict or too much consensus. There is some evidence for this in the Hage-Aiken study, but it needs to be explored with greater precision in future research.

What is less clear is the precise parametric structure of the equations. While there is some evidence that the *betas* might be one, there is less evidence about whether the intercept or *alpha* should be at the point of origin or at some other value. This intercept has interesting theoretical implications. The best way of establishing this requires determining whether "too much" consensus can exist. The logic is always the same. Disequilibrium states are classified as such on the basis of undesirable performances occurring, or even curvilinear associations. Beyond this, there is a need to explore the possibility of other equilibrium states besides the general continuum between the mechanic-bureaucratic and the organic-professional. Both the Corwin and Hage-Aiken studies reflect organizations in the latter mold. The other kinds need to be studied as well. Some of the negative findings might be explained by the presence of other kinds of organizations, where power might be more centralized and still be acceptable.

So far we have only viewed the problem of equilibrium from the standpoint of the structural variables and their configuration. The relationship between the emphasis on particular performances and conflict exists, but at best it only circumstantially supports the idea that the equilibrium state for the organizations that largely fit the organic model involves an emphasis on morale and new programs. As can be seen, there are moderate correlations between the relative emphasis (note, this is not the same as job satisfaction but reports the perceived priority of the management) on morale ($r = -.29$ with conflict) and efficiency ($r = .38$ with conflict). One would expect these correlations to be smaller for several reasons. Each performance priority is measured by a ranking among the four alternatives; thus there is essentially only one item. Consistent with the argument in Chapter 5, one would expect that all performances must be emphasized at some time point for maintenance of effectiveness, thus reducing the size of the correlation among them. When a discrepancy score is computed between the concentration of specialists and the relative emphasis on efficiency in this study, there is little association with conflict. This may reflect the inadequacies of the measurement more than of the hypotheses.

10.2.3. A Special Problem: Strikes or Work Stoppages

The term "act of noncooperation" is perhaps better than either "strike" or "work stoppage" because there are many situations where strikes and even work stoppages are illegal. But police or postal workers can start rigorously enforcing all of the existing regulations and in effect stop work quite effectively, as postal workers have demonstrated in Britain and the police have in various communities in the United States. One suspects that in socialist countries where strikes are forbidden slowdowns are more common than press reports indicate. In any case, while these more extreme forms of conflict are rare, they hold a great deal of fascination. The measures described above only look at very low or moderate levels of conflict; they do not tap more extreme forms of conflict such as strikes, work stoppages, and especially the presence of violence. It is worth studying acts of noncooperation as a special problem precisely because there can be qualitative changes along the continuum of the intensity of conflict. Although I have suggested that the causes remain the same, this is at best only an assertion.

As Lammers (1969) notes, more extreme forms of conflict can frequently take on the pattern of protest movements – they become concerned with fundamental complaints relative to the larger society (macro conflict). But then the question is, will the model advanced above explain these more extreme forms of conflict? Since the data available are at best fragmentary, only some conjectures can be offered.

The first and most important point is that the reason for the strikes can be different – that is, there can be economic, political, and social reasons (Lammers, 1969). The measure of conflict used by Hage and Aiken tap all these various areas. Extreme forms of conflict may involve a number of issues, but this does not mean that there are not relatively constant themes present in particular countries or in certain institutional spheres (such as in business firms as opposed to public administration). The Hage-Aiken data were collected in welfare agencies, mental hospitals, and sheltered workshops in the United States. In this context, salary conflicts did not correlate with the others. One would expect a different pattern of inter-item correlations in other institutional settings and in other countries.

Second, the theory should work as well in handling these forms of conflict, although the equation might have to be written as follows:

$$[X - (1 - Y)]^2 = \tan Z$$

where X = concentration of specialists
  Y = structural variable in state of equilibrium with X
  Z = consenses/conflict intensity including noncooperation and violence

The above equation states that as the discrepancy increases, the tendency to have conflict grows exponentially and actually fits a tangent curve because of the tendency for conflict to explode once it gets beyond a certain threshold. Also for conflict to reach these upper levels of intensity, it is usually necessary for the normal control mechanisms described in the next chapter to break down. Again, once this happens there tends to be a rapid escalation in the conflict, usually because previously conflict has been suppressed due to the effectiveness of control mechanisms. The expression $(1 - Y)$ is used to represent decentralization, destratification, and the like. All variables have been scaled to the metric of zero to one. This equation relating structure and performance is somewhat different. For example, innovation is positively associated with the concentration of specialists. Then the equation becomes:

$$(X - P)^2 = \tan Z$$

where X = concentration of specialists
  P = performance variable positively associated with concentration of specialists
  Z = consenses/conflict intensity

Again all variables must be scaled between 0 and 1. Since the discussion of equilibrium states noted the opposition between the concentration of specialists and the centralization, I prefer to use the term (1 – centralization) to represent decentralization or the expected state of affairs given a certain level in the concentration of specialists. This also emphasizes the idea that there is central tendency or strain toward centralization (see Chapter 12). By the same logic one would construct equations involving stratification, normative equality, innovation, efficiency, and the like. But of these various discrepancy or disequilibrium scores one would expect the impact to be strongest in the relationship between the structural variables and less with disequilibrium in the performances, since the latter all have a positive relationship with effectiveness.

When is violence pursued? Here interestingly enough, one of Merton's (1957, Chapter 4) middle range theories can be applied. In his discussion of anomie, Merton suggests that there are essentially five responses: conformity, ritualism, innovation, retreatism, and rebellion. Although this is applied to the problem of the blockage of institutionalized goals and more specifically the goal of upward mobility – "success" in the United States – it is suggestive in the context of organizational conflict as well. Within this context the issue is whether or not one accepts the idea of having group conflict and whether or not one accepts the normative channels for handling it. The cross-classification of the possibilities, as done in Figure 10.5, provides us with the following conflict classes:

1. Normative conflict where one agrees to disagree but within the rules of the game, as in strikes.
2. Ritual conflict where one does not really disagree and does this in a highly patterned way, as in one-day strikes.

Figure 10.5   The varieties of conflict

Willingness to use established means	Willingness to express social conflict	
	Low	High
Low	Retreatism as in turnover and apathy	Non-normative conflict as in violence
High	Ritualistic conflict	Normative conflict

Adapted from Merton (1957: Chapter 4). The fifth category, which was rebellion in his scheme, does not logically exist here because unwillingness to express social conflict is the same as replacing conflict with another goal, presumably consensus.

3. Non-normative conflict where the rules of the game are no longer relevant, as in violence or in wildcat strikes.
4. Retreatism, or where one refuses to have even ritual conflict.

Ritual conflict is the dominant form in France and Italy. One is impressed with the real unwillingness to have long drawn out strikes. In a sense, everyone agrees not to have conflict so elaborate rituals are developed. In contrast, Britain is plagued by non-normative conflict and especially the wildcat strike. The United States, in contrast, has both more normative conflict and more retreatism.

Our basic assumption is that non-normative conflict, and most especially violence, is used only as a last resort. Thus the most violent strikes tend to be union recognition strikes because the presence of a union usually establishes normative channels for handling conflicts between managers and workers. When managers refuse union recognition they are refusing a basic mechanism for handling conflict. Non-normative conflict also occurs where there is a breakdown in the relationship between the leaders of the unions and the rank and file. This is the case of wildcat strikes.

Beyond this there must be a build up of a large number of grievances and complaints. To produce more violent forms of conflict, a more extreme state of disequilibrium is needed, not only large discrepancies in power but also in pay and privilege. Thus one would sum across all the bi-variate relationships describing the organization system as follows:

$$\sum_{1}^{l} [X - (1 - Y)]^2 = \tan Z$$

where l equal's number of different structural variables

But the key is likely to be extreme centralization and the consequences this has for a number of organizational policies. Many of these are discussed at various places in the next three chapters.

Essentially violent conflict occurs in the context of relatively centralized companies that in various ways are exploitative. The hypotheses are diagramed in Figure 10.6. The organization that continually moves toward greater and greater centralization and stratification is likely to try to drive costs down. Power is concentrated in the hands of a small elite. This may be the owners or managers, who give all of the rewards to themselves, increasing stratification. As a mechanism of control, there is a heavy emphasis on rules. There is a constant drive for profit maximization, which translates into a concern about costs. The reduction in costs is achieved by reducing wages and spending little for good working conditions.

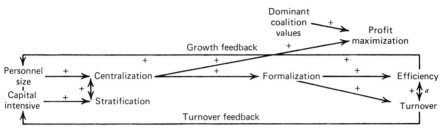

a Complex relationship but largely negative.

Figure 10.6   Special conditions for violent conflict.

This is nothing more than a mechanical organization, especially when located in a sector where there are few competitors and oligopoly prevails (see Chapter 13). Optimal size is large but technological sophistication tends to be small and the rate of technological change is slow. Product life is long. Typically this is the assembly-line form of technology as exemplified in the automobile industry (see Blauner, 1964). This technology requires unskilled labor who tend to be unionized.

It might be hard to argue whether unions are the cause or effect of strikes but certainly the mechanical organization – and especially one committed to profit maximization – has a set of conditions that has given rise to the growth of large unions, which parallel the large corporations.

Too often Marx's theories are either accepted or rejected. It would be more accurate to qualify them so as to predict when they apply and when they do not. Essentially Marx described mechanical organizations. These exist in a given market situation or technological context, and have an inner logic in their structure that drives them towards profit maximization. However, this value is not totally determined by the material conditions. Companies within the same industry can vary on this dimension. When Marx's material conditions apply, we would expect vertical conflict and even violent conflict. However, most typically violence occurs over the issue of union recognition.

Implicit in all of this is the notion that more extreme forms of conflict such as strikes or other work stoppages involve not only struggles for pay but struggles for power and privilege (Lammers, 1969: 559). A careful study of violent strikes suggests that they occur where there are larger problems in the society – sharp class divisions, authoritarian governments, or the like. Under these circumstances, the nature of the struggle moves towards a power contest. In fact, this is the striking characteristic of French strikes and, more broadly, the general strike. For the latter to occur, the adverse organizational conditions must be widespread.

10.3. A MICRO-STRUCTURAL THEORY OF ROLE CONFLICT

10.3.1. Role-Set Theory

If one can generalize from the Corwin and Hage-Aiken findings, and if the general insights of Durkheim appear to be correct, then one would expect that with increasing concentration of specialists or the expansion of the division of labor, there will be a general decline in the rate of at least horizontal conflict. This does not necessarily mean the elimination of vertical conflict. Overly centralized mechanical organizations are still very much with us. Fights over union recognition still occur as anyone familiar with the grape picker struggles knows. But in general, the decline in the intensity of conflict should occur as its frequency increases. Changes in the frequency of conflict may also lead to a qualitative change – a shift in the content or kind of conflict.

The central thrust of this section is that increases in specialization are likely to represent a shift from meso or social conflict to micro or role conflict. Cross-cutting status sets may not only dampen basic and violent conflict between the haves and the have-nots but they can augment and make more painful the many disagreements about who should do what to whom. As groups coalesce into coalitions relative to some contested issue, role conflict disappears. In contrast, as the issues multiply, it becomes increasingly more difficult for coalitions to remain stable. Surely the opportunities for role conflict are many more than the standard bones of contention in either vertical or horizontal conflict.

The major theoretical statement on role conflict was first made by Merton (1957, Chapter 9). It is worth reviewing here. He started with a simple observation: that occupants of positions have role-sets defined by the roles they play vis-à-vis others. Since these role partners occupy different positions in the social structure, they have different values and behavioral expectations. As an illustration, the foreman interacts with the workers and with lower management, frequently with secretaries and shipping clerks, and almost always with supply personnel (for one interesting account of a foreman caught in the middle, see Ronken and Lawrence, 1952). For Merton, this role-set conflict was existential, a structural given. The accent is on conflicts of expectations about what the occupant should do. For example, in the classic study of superintendents by Gross, Mason, and McEachern (1958), questions were asked of teachers and of board members about their expectations as to what superintendents should do. Expectations are preferred norms or rules of conduct upon the part of the occupant of a social position. Merton did not raise the theoretical question about the causes of varying amounts of role conflict. Instead he reviewed the various mechanisms that might reduce it and he suggested the following hypotheses:

1. The less involvement of the role partners, the less the role conflict.
2. The greater the difference in power of the role partners, the less the role conflict.
3. The less the visibility of actions of the occupants, the less the role conflict.

One can in effect take these mechanisms that reduce role conflict and indicate how structural variables might affect their presence or absence and, even more critical, their magnitude.

Before we do, it is important to note that Merton did not mention what are probably the two most obvious characteristics of role-sets: their sheer size and complexity or variety of occupations. Many role-sets have few role partners — the movie usher interacts only with customers, the manager, and perhaps the ticket seller. Other role-sets, and especially those in organic organizations, are quite large. Public university deans have as role partners the other deans, the chancellor, the various vice-chancellors, the president of the university system, the vice-presidents in the central administration, the department chairmen within the college or school, the committee members of various committees relative to university administration, the faculty, the secretaries, the students, and so forth. Furthermore, it might be quite relevant to make distinctions by specialty within the faculty and the student body since each requires different handling. As the role-set grows in size, one expects a much greater variety of occupations. Attached to each occupation are values and interests, beliefs and prejudices, technological skills and environmental problems. The great beauty of the work by Lawrence and Lorsch (1967 a and b) is the clarity with which they demonstrated this within the context of manufacturing. Even with simple notions of professional values, Hall's work (1967) indicates the enormous variations there are. Besides the sheer size of the role-set, its complexity can be measured. By this is meant nothing more than the variety of activities the incumbent or the average occupant must perform vis-à-vis his role partners.

The problem of role conflict takes on added interest in an organizational context because under these circumstances some of Merton's mechanisms no longer apply. The structure of the organization usually reduces differential visibility and, to a lesser extent, involvement. Differences in power are given.

As the concentration of specialists increases, all other things being equal, the average size of the role-set in the organization increases, the variety of occupations expands, and so does the involvement of the role partners, probably for all the reasons given in Chapter 9 (see Figure 10.7). Together these facts explain why role conflict might be on the increase. The hypothesis is:

10. 6 *The greater the concentration of specialists, the greater the variety of occupations, the larger the size of the role-set, and the greater the involvement of the role partners and therefore the greater the role conflict.*

The causes of role conflict

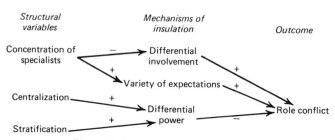

Figure 10.7 The causes of role conflict.

In complex organizations, the specialists are in effect professionals or managers and they have a considerable stake in their expertise and also in their careers. Thus the situation is ready-made for conflict about the job definitions of role partners. A very good special case of this would be the coping with uncertainty theory of Hickson et al. (1971) described in Chapter 3. In the struggle for departmental power, one tries to control the job definitions of other departments.

Both centralization and stratification are listed as affecting differences in power among the various role partners in Figure 10.6. As decentralization occurs and as equality in pay increases, differences in power and status diminish by definition. This, in turn, leads to greater role conflict. The hypothesis is:

10. 7   *The greater the centralization and the stratification (that is, the difference in powers and rewards), the less the role conflict.*

Again, in Chapter 9 a series of arguments were presented that as participation increases or as centralization is reduced, the motivation of those included within the power structure increases considerably. If this is so — and there is much evidence to support this contention — we would expect greater involvement as well. In turn, this increases the potential for role conflict, following Merton's explicit argument.

In organic organizations one would expect a considerable amount of role conflict. In contrast, in mechanical organizations there should be little role conflict. To use the terms of Burns and Stalker, the network of authority with a shifting center in the organic form only adds to the ambiguity of expectations, whereas the strict hierarchy with clear jurisdictions in the mechanical organization resolves many of the potential sources of role conflict.

Merton's mechanism of visibility of conflicting demands is analyzed in the next chapter as part of the problem of control and of coordination. In general, in organic organizations these conflicts are more likely to be visible.

10.3.2. The Findings

Most of the research on role conflict has not examined the larger structural variables so that it is difficult to test the specific hypotheses advanced above. For example, the single most important study of role conflict (Kahn et al., 1964) focused primarily on the psychological costs of this for the individual: lower job satisfaction, higher job-related tensions, and less liking for those creating the pressure. Depending on personality, those experiencing role conflict as they measure it tended to retreat from interaction.

What the research did establish was the general and widespread nature of role conflict. Clearly one of the causes of role conflict was role ambiguity, which might be viewed as the opposite of role formalization or specification. However, the Kahn et al. study focused much more on the hierarchical arrangements that produce role conflict (for example, a foreman caught in the middle between workers and managers).

The research of Gross et al. (1958), while another landmark in this area, does not focus on causes of conflict in expectations, nor does it examine some of the many mechanisms that might help reduce this kind of stress. This is a general problem in this literature. Many studies indicate that role conflict exists, but few focus on either causes or integrative mechanisms.

The research of Corwin (1969) can be reinterpreted. He used one measure that at least approximates the idea of role conflict. When interviewing, his staff recorded all complaints and disputes, which in turn were called incidents. While this confronts both meso and micro conflict, the pattern of correlations is quite different from all incidents and major incidents. In the former, Corwin's hypotheses, which are quite similar to those advanced above, work quite well. These findings are reported in Table 10.2. Here organizational complexity, which is measured by the number of specialists and the number of levels of authority, has a strong relationship to all incidents. One might expect that this relationship would rise if all incidents were confined to complaints. Size reflects the same

Table 10.2 Meso and micro conflict compared
Corwin's Study (1969) N = 28

	All incidents (role conflict)	Major incidents (meso-conflict)
Complexity	.33	.10
Centralization (nonparticipation)	−.17	+.38
Size	.38	.04

relationship, which makes one wonder what the proportion of specialists to size would indicate. But perhaps the most striking confirmation is that centralization decreases all incidents while augmenting major incidents. Greater participation in decision-making makes the conflicting demands surface, and they are more likely to be "complaints." Again, one might anticipate that the differences between these two levels would become even greater if the category of all incidents were purified of the major incident. Needless to say, complaints may not necessarily include conflict about what the occupants should be doing but they are suggestive of the nature of role conflict — "I don't like what you are doing" — much more than the comparison of attitudes on a number of issues as in the Gross, et al. study (1958).

Another way of examining the problem of role conflict is to study interdepartmental conflict. While not always the same as role conflict, it is very close. The essence of the conflict is that sales wants production to provide instant delivery while production wants sales to keep orders flowing at a constant rate. The credit department wants only AAA credit rated customers as in Dun and Bradstreet while sales wants to sell to anyone who wants to buy. And so on. Although interdepartmental conflict has not really been studied extensively, there are a few studies that are suggestive.

Although the study does not present quantifiable data, Price's (1968: 57–59) review of Caplow and McGee's university study reports considerable conflict between departments. While this reflects perhaps the absence of a clear authority structure, power being allowed to lodge where it may, it also represents the consequences of a more decentralized power structure. Under these conditions, each department fights to define and set limits on what other departments can or can not do, especially in regard to the offering of new courses, the hiring of new teachers, and the like.

More explicit is the work of Lawrence and Lorsch (1967 a and b). In effect they argue that the greater the differentiation between departments, the greater the need for integration mechanisms, that is, the conflict between departments becomes greater in their absence. Although they do not present data about the concentration of specialists in the plastics or the container industry, it seems reasonable to infer scores since, in fact, the former industry has both basic and applied research departments and the latter does not. Certainly the addition of basic research adds a group of specialists with values that tend to be quite different from those in production and marketing. Their study also indicates the necessity for the various departments with greater differentiation to work together to solve problems. In other terms, the more successful organization developed mechanisms for handling the conflicts between departments.

Another Harvard Business School study of interdepartmental conflict (Walton et al., 1969b) provides some direct tests of Merton's hypothesis about mechanisms that can reduce role conflict. Salience, or what Merton would label involvement, was highly related to conflict with departmental relationships (r = .85, N = 10), as was dependence (r = .85). Although dependence implies a difference of power, it must also be recognized that all of these departments — commercial, plant, traffic, marketing, plant engineering — need each other, although they vary in relative dependence. One department's ignorance of another had a strong negative correlation (r = -.73), suggesting that lack of visibility does reduce conflict. The conflict of interests (which is another way of saying that different departments have different interests) was also strongly correlated with interdepartmental conflict (r = .91). But this is the basic point: as one proliferates positions, one creates different interests and values which, as Lawrence and Lorsch (1967 a and b) have so persuasively argued, must be brought back together again.

How one arranges occupations into departments can make a difference perhaps on the extent of role conflict. All of the above examples arranged departments according to occupation. But regardless of arrangement at some level, the differences in occupations become relevant. Occupations under a system of functional departmentalization are more likely to organize and act as a group, sharing similar attitudes and the like. Product or client departmentalization might reduce the conflict somewhat,will not eliminate it.

10.4. CONCLUSIONS

The exercise of voice can occur at two levels. One concerns what the organization is doing. This is the level that Hirschman (1970) had in mind, what the occupants of a particular occupation or department are doing. The meso level of conflict, the former case, is caused, in part, by disequilibrium in the structure. The presence of conflict substantiates the usefulness of the concept. This is not a trivial finding since disequilibrium has been so suspect. Yet it offers a way of studying conflict and understanding its causes. At the meso level, the other source of conflict, but one that appears more muted, is the conflict over goals and priorities. This has been the one of most interest in the political-value approach to organizations and would appear to be essentially given if one accepts the idea of the performance dilemma involved in achieving effectiveness. Yet, despite this interest, there has been surprisingly little research on this problem.

Chapter Eleven

Loyalty: Coordination and Control

While the members of the organization are expressing their exit by turnover, absenteeism, and psychological withdrawal and their voice by disagreements, noncooperation, and even violence, the organization – the dominant coalition – is hardly a passive bystander. The power elite has a number of mechanisms of control that can be employed to suppress either exit or voice. Hirschman (1970) emphasized loyalty. This is one way in which elites try to encourage members to choose voice over exit, and even to speak in more muted tones, but it is not the only way. The other and more typical approach is sheer coercion, either in its positive aspect of rewards or its negative one of punishment. This is the larger reality of organizations: their mechanisms of control.

Perhaps the most difficult aspect of the human factor in organizations is teamwork. As Lawrence and Lorsch (1967 a and b) observe, as soon as there is a differentiation of tasks, there is a need to integrate them into a coherent assembly so as to produce the product or provide the service. The different ways of solving this problem have implications for the building of loyalty among the members.

The juxtaposition of loyalty vis-à-vis coordination and control may seem strange, and yet the connection informs. Traditionally organizational sociologists have worried about how to control workers and managers on the underlying assumption that this was the essential problem. The concept of loyalty puts the accent on the positive and involves more the idea of motivation. The real task is to build a commitment to the objectives of the organization and loyalty to its members. In this sense, the term control is only one side of the issue.

Coordination and control have typically been employed to handle two different analytical problems (see Hage, 1974: Chapters 1 and 2). Coordination is the task of integrating each part of the organization so that it contributes to the overall objective. Coordination involves the reduction of conflict and duplication, and typically is the essence of the managerial function. Control is more

350

concerned with the meeting of a standard. If coordination brings together the different departments of the organization, control is concerned with how well each department does its set of tasks. Control implies evaluation; coordination implies integration.

In cybernetics (see Ashby, 1956), the control function is generalized to cover all equilibrium seeking behavior. All of the three processes described in Chapter 8 – steering, adjustment, and adaptiveness – could be and indeed are cybernetic control processes. Here control, as is traditional in sociology, is employed in the more limited sense of how the evaluation of performance occurs.

In fact, here we focus less on the actual processes of coordination and control and more on the mechanisms used to effect them. In this sense, we are analyzing how organizations build loyalty or commitment or motivate their members to work together to achieve some common purpose.

11.1. A MESO-STRUCTURAL THEORY OF COORDINATION/CONTROL

11.1.1. The Major Premises

In several publications (Hage, Aiken, and Marrett, 1971; Hage, 1974), Hage has advanced a formal theory of coordination and control which starts with the following major premises:

11A   All organizations need coordination and control.

11B   There are two basic mechanisms for achieving coordination and control: programming with an emphasis on sanctions, and feedback with an emphasis on socialization.

11C   The greater the diversity of organizational structure, the greater the emphasis on coordination and control by means of feedback and socialization.

11D   The greater the difference in rank in the organizational structure, the greater the emphasis on coordination and control by means of programing and sanctions.

Essentially this theory sees the organizational structure and its basic characteristics determining which set of mechanisms is likely to be selected. In all organizations there is a mixture. The precise proportion depends upon the relative importance of diversity and of rank difference. The first assumption is an article of faith in all of the literature on control. All agree that coordination and control are essential. While this may appear to be a functional premise, there is no necessary assumption that coordination is successfully achieved. Nothing is less certain. The great contribution of both Lawrence and Lorsch (1967 a and b) and of those who worked with Etzioni's compliance theory (1975) is to indicate how difficult it is to fulfill these needs.

The second assumption, following March and Simon (1958) and James Thompson (1967), is that coordination can be achieved in two basic ways: First, the activities of each job occupant can be programed and then a system of rewards and punishment can be utilized to insure conformity to the basic organizational scheme. A clear blueprint of action would make departure from the plan immediately obvious, and a system of rewards would provide the force behind the basic plan. Standards would leave little ambiguity about whom to punish and whom to reward. Second, organizations can rely more upon continuous flows of information (feedback or mutual adjustment) as a method for coordinating the organization. Under this system, errors, when detected, are often seen as a problem of improper socialization or training; one method of correcting this situation is through the provision of new information. Also implied in this approach is that pressure comes not so much from formal sanctions, in the strict sense of the term, as from peer pressures and inner standards of quality developed through socialization.

The first approach relies upon external control, or self-control. Thus, two basic processes to achieve coordination can be distinguished: feedback and programing. In practice, most organizations apply some mixture of both mechanisms. The most important question is the specification of the organizational circumstances under which one or the other of these mechanisms is emphasized. March and Simon (1958) made few suggestions about the structural concomitants of these mechanisms of coordination, although they do suggest that task uncertainty may affect the choice.

The relationship to loyalty is clear. Rewards or positive sanctions build commitment to the organization and motivate people to work hard to achieve their tasks, while programing pulls together disparate activities into a comprehensive whole. But feedback also has a motivating effect. When we are integrated in a team, or better yet a group, *and we are receiving approval from a peer,* we have probably the most powerful motivating force there is. Indeed, social integration can build stronger loyalties than rewards can. The importance of the group for our own sense of self-worth and is perhaps the distinctive sociological contribution to the literature on motivation and conformity. We have already suggested this in Chapter 9.

What causes some organizations, or their dominant coalitions, to coordinate through feedback and others to opt for programing? Why do some organizations build loyalty through social integration and others by means of pay systems?

The theme that seems to run through the work of Lawrence and Lorsch (1967 a and b) and James Thompson (1967) is that greater task complexity forces organizations to rely much more on the use of feedback as a mechanism of coordination. Although Perrow primarily focused on the relationship between the routineness of technology and what he calls task structure (1967: 199–200), the point remains that by simple substitution one arrives at the idea that centralization increases the probability of a greater emphasis on plans.

On the control side, Price (1967), in his emphasis on sanctions and communication, suggests two mechanisms of control. Etzioni (1961, 1975) widens this to three and Warren (1969 a and b) to four, although these can be seen as matters of degree along the basic duality between positive and negative sanctions (such as rewards and punishments) and positive and negative socialization. This seems to be implied in Warren's ideas of legitimate and referent power bases: the negative sanction is that one must do something because it is the best thing to do. Both are forms of self-control in Parson's sense of the term, but they differ in the amount of self-interest involved. Or to follow Etzioni, one can speak of the negative as fear of peer disapproval and response to group pressure, and the positive as loyalty to a higher ideal.

There are two major *structural* factors that appear to influence the patterns of coordination/control: diversity and the distribution of rank. These are basic axes of organization structure that Victor Thompson (1961) and others have noted. As the diversity of an organization increases, it becomes more difficult to plan a successful blueprint for the organization. As the variety of tasks in an organization increases, the number of potential connections among parts increases (a point frequently made, see Caplow, 1964: 29–36) even more rapidly. The articulation of organizational parts by a set of predetermined rules becomes more complicated. Moreover, the application of sanctions becomes more difficult because each of the jobs may require a different set of standards. The dominant coalitions are likely to be forced to rely more upon feedback mechanisms than upon rigidly programed mechanisms of communication. This whole process is further intensified if the nature of most jobs in the structure is complex and involves a variety of activities, as is the case in the professions. Here, we suggest that the variety of tasks as well as the degree of uncertainty are important determinants of the volume of communications (March and Simon, 1958; James Thompson, 1967; Perrow, 1967; Hage and Aiken, 1969) and of an emphasis on continuing education.

The importance of the interconnection between parts is quite striking in the work of Lawrence and Lorsch (1967b), who demonstrated that as the complexity of the environment increases, the need for relationships between the separate departments increases exponentially. The task interdependence between departments becomes quite complex as the number of departments increases. [However, this is different from the coordination of separate divisions, each with its own environment, inputs, and outputs (see Chapter 14); chiefly because the divisions do not need each other for the achievement of some task. They may compete for resources, but the accent is on competition and not coordination in the sense in which we have been talking about it.]

In addition, differences in power, status, and privilege among job occupants in an organization are likely to inhibit the rate of feedback information. As social distance between organizational levels increases, the free flow of information is reduced (Barnard, 1946). Similarly, the threat of sanctions from the top discourages the frank discussion of problems. Thus organizational decision-makers are unlikely to learn of problems until a crisis has developed, as Blau and Scott (1962) have suggested and as Barnard (1946) explicitly argued.

The degree of organizational diversity propels the organization toward attempts to coordinate through information feedback, while privilege, status, and power differences propel the organization towards attempts to coordinate through programing. Together they influence the probabilities of the adoption of either programing or feedback or, more precisely, the particular combination, since each of these factors can be operative at the same time. Organizational elites attempt to program some interaction in the form of regular reports. Even where they have made a conscious decision to rely only upon a feedback mechanism of coordination, there will always be some feeble attempts to rationalize parts of the organization. What is critical here is the differential emphasis on coordination through feedback and coordination through planning or blueprints.

Not only do these two axes of organizational structure affect the way in which the organization is coordinated, but they also affect which mechanisms of control are likely to be employed. Socialization becomes critical because it is the way in which professionals, managers, engineers, and the like learn to master complex tasks – training, in the sense of Etzioni (1975). But even more important is the necessity for continuous education. Complex tasks always require new information. Errors are easy to make and therefore easily forgiven. Presumably the problem of motivation is handled by means of anticipatory socialization (Merton, 1957) because control is internalized. As power, privilege, and status differences increase, the members of dominant coalition increasingly look upon those below them in the power hierarchy and the status pyramid as having to be made to conform to their dictates. Dominant coalitions appear to be perpetually preoccupied with getting *others* to do their bidding. This is one reason why men interested in power are so preoccupied with studying strategies of power. Besides, insofar as there are fewer and fewer people in the elite, proportionally speaking, it is easier for the dominant coalition to apply either rewards or punishments. The more that high rank people are concerned about members with little power, the easier it is to justify the use of coercion. This is precisely the tragedy of totalitarian states; there are no checks or balances on the abuses of power. To a much lesser extent, the same problem exists in organizations. There can be abuses of power, status, and privilege vis-à-vis those at the bottom of the hierarchy.

Beyond this, these abstract premises imply more than just what is said. It is the fit between this theory and previous work that makes more apparent how the many theories can be combined and synthesized within this single one.

It is useful to start with Lawrence and Lorsch (1967 a and b). Clearly their concept of differentiation is cognate with the idea of diversity, the latter being only a more abstract version of the former. In contrast, their idea of social integration appears to be less similar to the notion of socialization or feedback. But insofar as the volume of communication is a measure of both the socialization and feedback, then many of their mechanisms are the ways in which communication is facilitated: departments as integrators, men who act as go-betweens, the use of confrontation, and so on are all methods by which communication is increased.

The Thompsonian concepts of mutual adjustment, plans, and standardization are also similar. As he suggests, increases in diversity (he uses the word complexity) lead to a shift from standardization (which would be the extreme of programing) to the use of plans (which is a more mild form of the same pattern), to mutual adjustment (which is the same as feedback, as has already been noted).

11.1.2. A Typology of Coordination/Control

Perrow's work (1967) on routine technology suggests the four steady states of coordination/control. A number of these lie along the continuum between greater reliance on programing to the greater reliance on feedback. In addition there are several nonobvious combinations that are worth delineating because they represent the control side of the stable states described in Chapter 8. These are listed in Figure 11.1, the most common mechanisms of coordination/control. Perrow (1967 and 1970a) suggests that in the mechanical-bureaucratic steady states, plans will be used relative to all sections of the organization. Here it seems better to follow the suggestion of Thompson and argue that one would expect the extreme in programing and the most profound use of rules, that is, high formalization. At the other end of this continuum is the organic-professional organization where feedback occurs everywhere. It is worth reiterating that between these two extreme ideal-types there are a number of stable steady-states that represent mixtures of planning and of feedback.

Quite different is the traditional equilibrium pattern, or the one that Perrow felt typified craft industries. He suggests that planning is done in the technical support department while feedback is used in the production department. One would expect formalization to be quite low because of the historic tradition and the importance of custom. This is one reason why I call it traditional industry.

Another nonlinear combination of the basic control mechanisms is found in the mixed organic-mechanical steady state which, as Perrow notes, is frequently represented by firms that place a heavy emphasis on engineering, such as in computer, electronic, electrical, chemical and, to a lesser extent, metallurgy industries. Feedback is used in the organic departments, including basic and applied

Figure 11.1 The mechanisms of coordination and of control in the most typical steady states

	Steady States:			
Mechanisms:	Traditional	Mechanical	Mechanic–Organic	Organic–Professional
Coordination				
Goal Objectives	Quality and stability	Quantity and stability	Quantity and change	Quality and change
Major Mechanism	Plans	Programs	Feedback and plans	Feedback
Formalization	Moderate but unwritten (customs)	High and written	Moderate and written	Low and unwritten
Communication volume	Medium	Low	Medium	High
Vertical communication	Multiple hierarchies up	Single hierarchies but upward only	Single hierarchies both up and down	Multiple hierarchies, up and down
Horizontal communication	Some and most likely at bottom	Very little	Some at top and within some departments	All levels or network
Number of committees	Few	Few	Many	Many
Control				
Major Mechanism	Rewards/artisan socialization	Rewards/punishments	Rewards/Pre-job socialization	Professional socialization and continuous
Peer approval	Important	Not important	Mixed	Important
Use of sanctions	Somewhat	A great deal	Moderate	Very little
Task visibility	Moderate	High	Moderate	Low
Attitude conformity	Moderate	Low	Moderate	High

research, as well as in staff specialties such as marketing, advertising, legal, and so on, (what Perrow calls the technical support areas), but planning is employed in the production departments. Here one would anticipate a moderate level of formalization.

The traditional and mixed organic-mechanical equilibrium states have moderate communication volume with perhaps the latter having a higher amount. But the way in which it is distributed is quite different. Price (1968) makes a critical distinction between horizontal and vertical communication, but in the latter case one also wants to distinguish between upward and downward channels. Furthermore, horizontal almost by definition means (or should mean) communication between departments so as to tap the crucial meaning of coordination. The same is not true of vertical communication, which can occur within or between departments. One can also distinguish between scheduled and unscheduled communications within each of these categories. These are not exactly substitutes for each other. Those organizations with more scheduled communication also tended to have more unscheduled (see Hage, 1974: Chapter 7). The former tends to involve coordination of the departments; the latter tends to focus more on coordination of the work-flow process – the throughput (Katz and Kahn, 1966).

In an extensive analysis of unscheduled communication channels Hage found (1974: Chapter 10) that there were indeed four ideal-types of vertical and horizontal communication as suggested by Perrow's typology. The network pattern consists of both horizontal and vertical channels where communication is downward as well as up. This is what Burns and Stalker (1961) would expect to find in an organic organization. At the other extreme is the vertical hierarchy within departments where the dominant flow is upward. This corresponds to the mechanical form. But another pattern found in health and welfare organizations was multiple vertical hierarchies with few horizontal channels except at the bottom of the hierarchy. One would expect this pattern in traditional forms of social organization. In the mixed mechanical-organic form one would predict network patterns to exist within some departments and vertical hierarchical patterns in others, but with strong horizontal channels at the top of the organizations, the organic-professional and organic-mechanical having the most.

Just as there are a variety of mechanisms of coordination implied in the concepts of feedback and of programing, there are a number of terms that can be deduced from the ideas of socialization and rewards. The most common examples of the latter are the various pay systems such as piece-rates, bonus plans, profit sharing, and the like. More interesting and much less emphasized are the various ways in which socialization is used to control worker behavior.

In organic-professional organizations, or normative organizations in Etzioni's termination, one would expect much less reliance on rewards and more on the use of continuous socialization. Here an important analytical distinction is necessary. Etzioni (1975: 245 et seq.) notes that socialization is the requisite orientation for satisfactory functioning in roles. He makes a distinction between instrumental and expressive socialization, or what might be called training and education. However, the key idea in the term "continuous" socialization is the constant training needed to remain abreast of current developments. Given occupations where knowledge is growing constantly, training must be continuous. This is quite different from on the job training for workers in traditional organizations, or anticipatory socialization such as in military academies, teachers' colleges, or engineering schools that are more concerned with teaching a given set of skills. These periods of apprenticeship, whether for crafts or for semiprofessions, are not the same as the postgraduate socialization that must continue in the case of medicine, law, and most academic professions.

Price (1968), in his study of organizational effectiveness, notes the relative importance of secondary versus primary control. While in general it is likely that control is most effective in hierarchical relationships if the relationship is mainly instrumental, rather than instrumental and expressive, the peer group can be a powerful mechanism of control. Much of the negative evidence on the efficacy of peer groups comes from studies of rate-busting norms. Or as Price (1968) indicates in his review of the Blau study (1955), there is a tendency not to apply negative sanctions, such as punishments, when deviant behavior is found. However, the disapproval of peers or colleagues can be an even more powerful sanction than material rewards and punishments. Whether there is an actual peer group or not is perhaps not the question. What is important is whether the approval or disapproval of colleagues or peers is relevant to the conformity of the members.

What is suggested in Figure 11.1 is that organizations based on more hierarchical arrangements control workers through secondary relationships, but in the organic-professional form and, to a lesser extent, the traditional form, the importance of colleague or peer approval can be a critical element. These relationships are perhaps not primary ones in the sense in which Price uses the term, that is friendships, but they are certainly more expressive than instrumental. This could also be called a concern with esteem, which Price includes under sanctions. But consistent with Etzioni, a qualitative distinction should be made between material rewards (such as remuneration) and nonmaterial ones (such as esteem). Now the relevance of peer groups for the problem of conformity can be clarified.

In organizations that rely heavily on materialistic rewards, such as piece rates or bonuses, a peer group, if it exists, is likely to be *against* the management's attempts to manipulate the workers for the purpose of better efficiency. In contrast, in organizations where nonmaterial rewards are more important there will not be a rate-busting norm but instead a prevailing concern for quality.

Likewise grade sanctions, as Price calls them, are more likely to be found in some types of organization than others. Again we would expect them to be most extensive in the mechanic-bureaucratic organizations where status differences are the greatest. They exist everywhere but are most common in highly centralized and stratified organizations. They are most typical in military organizations, organizations that rely upon the civil service, and organizations where labor unions represent unskilled workers.

It is much more difficult to know in which organizations collective versus individual sanctions are employed. These sanctions appear to cut across the ideal-types described in Figure 11.1. For example, some of the most outstanding examples of organic-professional organizations – manufacturers of precision instruments, research centers, universities, law firms, general hospitals, and the like – are built frequently on some mixture of individual and collective reward systems. Many mechanical-bureaucratic organizations, such as assembly-line manufacturers, use exactly the same method, with one system for the workers and another for the managers.

Finally, the work of Warren and Etzioni is relevant because it does state, in fact, that there are alternative mechanisms. Some organizations rely upon material punishment and even physical force, although this is rare in the treatment of employees. Some organizations put the emphasis on material rewards, others use esteem or prestige, and still others rely upon socialization. The value of Etzioni's (1975) work in particular is the considerable strength it provides to the assertion that this variety exists.

Equally relevant is the work of Warren (1968 and 1969), who emphasized concepts such as task visibility and attitude conformity. These ideas, which can almost be conceived as opposites, are of interest because they refer to some of the processes involved in controlling worker behavior. If the dominant coalition is concerned about conformity, they monitor closely the work of the various individuals. If they are not, they rely more upon a commitment or loyalty, which Warren would call attitude conformity.

Feedback is not quite the same as task visibility in Warren's sense. Rather, feedback is concerned with detecting difficulties. Task visibility implies someone always watching. How feedback occurs without this continual close supervision is exemplified in a detailed study of physician control (see Hage, 1974: Part One).

Again, our typology of four kinds of coordination and control indicates how task visibility and attitude conformity are combined in various ways.

11.1.3. Derived Hypotheses

Implicit in the synthesis of these different writers is a large number of hypotheses that can be derived from these four basic premises. Figure 11.1 essentially contains ten dependent variables. The major linear hypotheses are:

11. 1 The greater the concentration of specialists, the greater the volume of unscheduled and scheduled communications.

11. 2 The greater the concentration of specialists, the greater the volume of vertical and of horizontal unscheduled communication.

11. 3 The greater the concentration of specialists, the greater the emphasis on training and education.

11. 4 The greater the concentration of specialists, the greater the emphasis on peer approval and attitude conformity.

The concentration of specialists is only one subconcept included under the concept of diversity. One could also add the number of departments, the variety of occupations, and so forth.

The volume of communication is the best indication of feedback but the direction is important as well. In an intensive analysis of communication channels, Hage (1974) found that increases in volume mean changes in direction from vertical to horizontal, from upward to downward.

11. 5 The greater the degree of centralization, the greater the degree of formalization.

11. 6 The greater the degree of stratification, the greater the degree of formalization.

11. 7 The greater the degree of normative equality, the less the degree of formalization.

11. 8 The greater the degree of centralization, the greater the use of rewards and punishments and the more grades in the reward system there will be.

11. 9 The greater the degree of stratification, the greater the use of rewards and punishments and the more grades in the reward system there will be.

11.10 The greater the degree of normative equality, the less the use of rewards and punishment and the more grades there will be.

11.11 The greater the degree of centralization, the greater the task visibility.

11.12 The greater the degree of stratification, the greater the task visibility.

11.13 The greater the degree of normative equality, the less the task visibility.

Centralization, stratification, and normative equality represent different ways in which differences in rank can occur. Therefore, each of them can be linked to the variables of coordination — formalization, task visibility, and the use of material rewards and even punishments.

Perhaps what are more interesting are some of the multivariate hypotheses that are implied in Figure 11.1 and which derive from the synthesis of these many authors and their ideas.

The first four hypotheses deal with the special circumstances of what might be called traditional organizations — that is, when the concentration of specialists is moderate but centralization is high and where the specialists are at the same time craftsmen or semi-professionals:

11.14 Given a moderate level in the concentration of specialists – where the specialists are craftsmen – and centralization, then the vertical communication is both upward and downward and within and between departments.

11.15 Given a moderate level in the concentration of specialists – where specialists are craftsmen – and centralization, there is little horizontal communication and what occurs is at the bottom of the hierarchy relative to the throughput.

11.16 Given a moderate level in the concentration of specialists – where the specialists are craftsmen – and centralization, then control is via a mixture of rewards with artisan socialization with peer approval being important.

11.17 Given a moderate level in the concentration of specialists – where the specialists are craftsmen – and centralization, there is little scheduled communication and little formalization but instead a reliance on customs.

The distinctive coordination and control characteristics flow from the combination of a concern for quality and the relative stability that occurs. There is thus a reliance upon internal control through training either by apprenticeships or else in special schools. There is little reliance on scheduled meetings, job descriptions, or any other form of formalization. Custom, tradition, artisan standards, and the sense of craftsmanship provide the impulse to control behavior. Coordination is unscheduled, occurring when there is a problem. This explains why there is so much vertical unscheduled communication both up and down, and very little horizontal communication. At the same time there is a system of graded sanctions, but not a very steep one. Rewards are used to motivate, but much less so than in either mechanical or mixed mechanical-organic organizations. Peer approval is probably a much more important motivator. It is not unusual for this organization to have been started by the craftsmen themselves. Thus there is a much more informal atmosphere about these organizations, with much less emphasis on status distinctions. Likewise, people processing organizations – primary schools, libraries, and traditional welfare agencies – are run by individuals who have had the same training and have risen through the ranks.

The other steady state that is off the main continuum between mechanical and organic equilibrium is the mixed mechanic-organic. Here the problem of producing large quantities at the same time that the pace of change is important results in a number of modifications in the mechanisms of coordination/control as follows:

11.18 Given a moderate level in the concentration of specialists – where the specialists are engineers – and centralization, then vertical communication is both up and down but within departments and not between.

11.19 Given a moderate level in the concentration of specialists – where the specialists are engineers – and centralization, then there is hori-

zontal communication usually at the top echelons and within particular departments.

11.20 *Given a moderate level in the concentration of specialists – where the specialists are engineers – and centralization, then there is a lot of scheduled communication and of formalization but again primarily in particular departments.*

11.21 *Given a moderate level in the concentration of specialists – where the specialists are engineers – and centralization, control is via a mixture of rewards and of professional socialization and where peer approval is only somewhat important.*

These organizations tend to be much more formal in their patterns of communication and in their planning. Even change is planned.

Similarly, control rests on a more formal system of sanctions, with peer approval being less important than one would expect given the presence of engineers and the importance of professional associations. This flows from the fact that the knowledge is applied. The origin of the greater formalization and the greater reliance in rewards lies in the much larger size of these organizations (see Chapter 12) because products and services are provided in reasonably large quantities.

One could go on to specify additional hypotheses, but these 21 cover most of the major characteristics of the coordination/control system. Just as in Chapter 8, there were essentially four major equilibrium states specified involving the structure arrangements and organizational priorities, now we can observe that each of these states has a characteristic coordination and control system as well.

11.2. THE FINDINGS

Research relative to our proposed theory of coordination/control might be divided into several sections, according to which premise – or at best which derived hypotheses – one wants to study. First, is there a plurality of mechanisms? Second, are particular mechanisms associated with specific structural arrangements? These are all parts of the intellectual puzzle. Unfortunately most research studies have confronted only one or a few parts without necessarily fitting the pieces together into a coherent picture.

Perhaps the most distinctive characteristic of the literature has been the demonstration of the wide variety of different mechanisms of coordination and of control. Price (1968) and Etzioni (1975) have documented this amply, and it need not be repeated. What is less certain is the appropriateness of the control mechanism relative to the structure of the organization. Except for Lawrence and Lorsch (1967 a and b), this aspect has tended to be ignored. Price (1968) related the presence of particular mechanisms, but did not study whether some were more appropriate for particular kinds of organizations than others.

Given the large literature on the importance of uncertainty (James Thompson, 1967; Hall, 1977), it is desirable to explore the impact of structure in the choice of coordination and control mechanisms by controlling for this phenomenon. In a study of Japanese factories, uncertainty is estimated by operating variability. Log size is controlled as well, because size can increase the amount of bureaucratization considerably. In the Hage-Aiken panel study, task scope, which also is a rough indicator of uncertainty, is controlled along with innovation rate, log size, and professional activity. In other words all the variables that might have an independent impact on task visibility and formalization have been controlled.

Table 11.1 reports the findings from the studies of Azumi and Hage and

Table 11.1   Structure, formalization and task visibility

Azumi Study (1976)

Structural Variables[a]	Task Visibility		Formalization		
	Closeness of supervision	Rule observation[b]	Job codif.	Job spec.	Rule spec.
Concentration of specialists[c]	–.31	.15	–.08	–.16	.38
Centralization	.01	–.24	.26	.19	.17
(N)	(40)				

Hage-Aiken Panel Study

Structural Variables[a]	Closeness of supervision	Rule observation	Job codif.	Job spec.[d]	Rules manual
Concentration of specialists	–.05	–.21	–.19	–.01	.16
Centralization	.32	.14	.15	.31	.15
Stratification	.05	–.05	–.09	.14	.13
(N)	(61)	(61)	(61)	(45)	(61)

[a]With various measures of both technology and size held constant. In the Azumi study, operating variability, and log size are controlled. In the Hage-Aiken study, professional activity, log size, task scope, and innovation are controlled.
[b]Only one indicator.
[c]Functional specialism divided by log size.
[d]These items added in the second wave.

Aiken. In the two studies, the concentration of specialists, admittedly measured in different ways, tends to have a small negative impact on the visibility even when a number of variables measuring personnel size and uncertainty are controlled. In the American health and welfare agencies, centralization appears to have a stronger positive impact on task visibility than it would appear to have in Japanese factories. In the former study, the two indices, although developed in a factor analysis, appear to have the same causes. In the Japanese case, they appear to behave more independently. However, because of some small changes in the wording in the Azumi study and the presence of only one indicator for rule observation, this is not certain.

When one shifts to the various measures of formalization, two important observations should be made. Job codification and specificity are reported by the members of the organization and therefore represent not only what is written but what is unwritten, that is, customs. Role specificity and rules manuals are only written. The former measures are much more sensitive to supervisory behavior even if they tend not to correlate highly with task visibility.

In both studies, the concentration of specialists appears to diminish slightly the *perceived* emphasis on rules but is positively associated with the presence of written documents. Centralization also tends to have a positive relationship with all the various measures of formalization, although the partial correlations are not strong ones (but given the number of control variables, *any* association becomes of interest).

These findings are largely replicated in other studies using the Aston measures. The partial correlation between centralization and role specificity is .18 and between the centralization of specialists .24 in the original study (Pugh et al., 1968, $N = 52$), again with controls for both operating variability and personnel size. A major exception is the Child study ($N = 80$), which shows a negative partial with the concentration of specialists ($r_p = -.08$). However, one of the differences in the Child sample is a larger number of multi-organizations as noted in a commentary by Donaldson Child, and Aldrich (1975), which in turn might explain some of these differences. In fact, it is surprising how much uniformity there is, given the different ways in which the samples are drawn and the inconsistencies in the analytical unit.

When the panel study of Hage and Aiken is analyzed to see if changes in the amount of centralization, concentration of specialists, and of stratification help explain changes in the amount of job codification, rule observation, and closeness of supervision, one finds that indeed this is the case. Although almost all of the partials are small ones, they are in the predicted direction. This provides some additional confirmation that, in fact, there is a causal connection between the structural variables and the choice of either task visibility or formalization or both. The analysis also indicates that each of the structural variables is having an impact at the same time.

None of these studies directly test the nonlinear relationship between the concentration of specialists, centralization, and formalization. Inasmuch as the definition of formalization in the Aston inventory puts an accent on written documents, one would expect some organizations to have little formalization because they rely upon tradition, and a number to have a large amount, or greater than expected amount. This idea is suggested in their typology of organizations (Pugh, Hickson, and Hinings, 1969).

There are also theoretical reasons why these various measures of formalization and task visibility do not produce quite the same results. The specialists themselves develop operating procedures, such as standardized forms for a travel request, rather than tight confining regulations, such as requiring everyone to be at work at 8 AM, which is a job description. The Aston measures really tap the former much more than the latter idea. Specialists develop procedures for handling events that occur frequently, but do not necessarily develop tight, detailed job descriptions that program and specify the work of each position. As the concentration of specialists increases, one would expect a greater and greater emphasis on procedures rather than rules. Admittedly this is a sharp distinction, but one that does seem relevant in large, formal organizations and it helps explain the reasons why job codification à la Hall and role specificity à la Hickson have different patterns of findings. The more that the measures emphasize written as opposed to unwritten manuals, job descriptions, and the like, the more one would assume that this would have a positive relationship with the number of specialists, especially in larger organizations (Zey-Ferrell, 1979: 206 also notes the necessity to look at both the existence and the enforcement of rules).

An extensive analysis of the impact of structure on communication has already been reported in Hage (1974: Part 2) and need not be repeated here. The essential summary of the findings is as follows:

1. Complexity, another measure of diversity, was strongly associated with horizontal communications and especially upward ones.
2. Centralization was associated with less communication and vertical communication but especially downward.
3. Stratification was associated with less communication and vertical communication but especially downward.
4. Formalization and communication tended to be opposite mechanisms of control and of coordination.

As we have already noted there is a lot of evidence in this study that supports the notion of a fourfold typology for building loyalty or maintaining conformity.

In a reanalysis of the Paulson data (see Figure 11.2), where only those organizations of size 10 and above are included in the analysis, and only significant

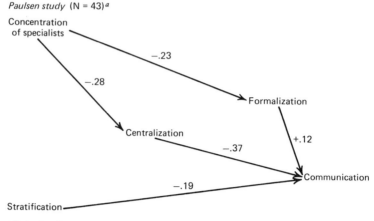

Paulsen study (N = 43)[a]

[a] Only significant paths are reported and only organizations of size 10
and more.

Figure 11.2 Structure, formalization, and communication.

paths are reported, one obtains relatively strong support for the idea that the stratification here measured as in the Hage-Aiken study, and centralization reduced the reliance on communications. The concentration of specialists also increases the use of communications, but mainly through its negative impact on centralization. Insignificant paths have been eliminated. In this particular analysis, centralization was deliberately treated as an intervening variable rather than another independent structural variable in order to simplify the path diagram.

Again this is partial evidence for the likelihood of formalization to be greaater in larger organizations, and for it to be combined sometimes with communication in these circumstances.

Summarizing the general thrust of all these findings, one can observe the following: As formalization emphasizes the restriction in job latitude, the relationship with the structural variables as predicted is stronger. The concentration of specialists leads to the development of written documents that appear to emphasize procedures more than job descriptions, but in any case specialists, like bureaucrats, emphasize paper work.

The more critical impact of the concentration of specialists is to add horizontal channels of communication. Not only is this demonstrated in the Hage (1974: Part Two) reanalysis of 16 health and welfare organizations, but several case studies show the *process* by which it occurs. In the first part of the book, the description of Community Hospital indicates how horizontal channels were added. The McCleery (1957) study of a prison can be interpreted in the same way.

The Lawrence and Lorsch studies (1967 a and b) support these hypotheses as well. Their measures of differentiation all suggest greater concentration of specialists at the managerial level, even when the entire labor force is included. Likewise, there is a tendency for these organizations to have much more integration. Their measures of this are the presence of integrators with the intermediate in a middle position; this suggests a higher communication volume and especially horizontally (1967a: 138).

All these studies focus on communication qua feedback or formalization qua procedures or role specificity, and various indicators of task visibility. They say little about the use of rewards and punishments or the use of socialization as control mechanisms. In other words, much of the multiorganizational research has relied upon some attempts to measure coordination mechanisms (although frequently at the micro level, as in measures of job description and rules manual and the like) rather than the more conventional pay systems.

11.3. TRANSFORMATION OF FORM: DISEQUILIBRIUM

Three different kinds of disequilibrium were discussed in Chapter 8. What happens to the control mechanisms when – for whatever reasons – an organization or a set of organizations move into a state of disequilibrium? The answer is that typically the dominant coalition attempts to handle the difficulties by increasing formalization and task visibility, which in turn makes things worse (for example, see Gouldner, 1954a).

The first kind of disequilibrium, an overemphasis on a performance, can be illustrated in the Hage-Aiken panel study. Given the availability of federal and state funds for welfare during the War on Poverty, a number of agencies added new services rapidly, resulting in a doubling of the innovation rate in some organizations. This overemphasis on one end of the dialectic between innovation and efficiency meant not only a decline in efficiency, presumably beyond acceptable limits, but also a decline in morale.

Although in the first wave the prior innovation rate has a positive impact on morale, in succeeding waves the relationship becomes negative. The correlations are: +.59, −.35, −.21 with job satisfaction in three waves but +.25 in the augmented wave, and $r = +.31, −.29, +.21$ with expressive satisfaction in three waves but +.41 in the augmented wave. The spurt in innovation rate created a condition of disequilibrium. This "great leap forward" required a shift in the variable system, something that cannot be done overnight.

Given the decline in efficiency, the dominant coalition attempted to solve this imbalance in performances by tighter controls, which in turn had the consequences of starting a vicious cycle as in the bureaucratic process described by Gouldner (1954a). The lower morale, in turn, leads to even tighter control.

Again, we have an example where the "rational" manager is tempted to do — and does — the wrong thing. The most striking example of this is the relationship between the prior rate of innovation standardized and the closeness of supervision. The innovation rate for the 1961–1963 period has a -.02 association with this measure in 1964. The innovation rate in the next period, which on the average nearly doubled, was a +.72 association with closeness of supervision in 1967. The rate in the third period (augmented sample) was approximately what it was in the first period; the zero-order correlation with closeness of supervision in 1970 is again nearly zero, -.06. The very strong positive correlation during the period of the "burst" of innovation with closeness of supervision indicates how control is increased. The cost was, as we have seen, lowered morale. Presumably the benefit was greater productivity or better cost control. Certainly the members perceived efficiency as a top priority during this period. Furthermore, as suggested in Chapter 7, the innovation process generates conflict. Dominant coalitions attempt to control this through closer supervision. Although greater tast visibility is an understandable and even seemingly "rational" response by the power elite, it is not a solution. The workers will feel as though they are losing autonomy and, in fact, they are. A more appropriate control is to heighten communication.

This specific longitudinal study indicates how helpful a cybernetic perspective is — as long as one does not assume that the correct action is selected after the feedback of information. With the concept of information feedback we can distinguish stages in the process of adaptation. The first is marked by the rapid change in several variables, in this instance, concentration of specialists and innovation rate. The first feedback occurs; an imbalance in performances is detected. Then the first response is made, the most typical one being heightened bureaucratic control. The second feedback occurs, an even greater imbalance is recognized, with declining morale. A second response is made, this time more likely evolving more appropriate controls. The sequence of responses may not be this, but by knowing some of the key variables in the system and using information feedback as a way to hone our perception on the process of adaptation of the structure, one has a convenient method for studying the most typical responses and their triggering signals.

We could predict that rapid increases in the concentration of specialists are unlikely to be matched by corresponding changes in centralization, stratification, and normative equility. This creates new tensions and conflicts, which also increase the likelihood of formalization and task visibility being increased as an attempt to solve these problems. Since the data in the Hage-Aiken panel study was not collected every year, a more precise test cannot be made of these various feedbacks and responses, but the panel data suggests that this was the process of adaptation (see Dewar, 1976).

We need many more panel studies of different kinds of organizations before we can be sure that this process of adaptation is accurately described. Certainly the analytical problem of how organizations change from one steady state to another, and the role that control mechanisms play in this, has been recognized as a crucial one in the theoretical literature (Buckley, 1967).

11.4. A MICRO THEORY OF COORDINATION/CONTROL

Most of the research described above refers to the control and coordination of the entire organization, with a special accent on managers and professionals. Are there special control mechanisms for the production process itself? Blau and Scott (1962) suggested that technology such as in the assembly line could act as a powerful control.

One of the key units in micro control is the work group at the production level. In this area we have a reasonably well-developed theory about coordination/control by Van de Ven, Delbecq, and Koenig (1976). They started with the work of James Thompson which, as we noted, saw three kinds of work flow: pooled, sequential, and reciprocal. They recognized that these ideas might actually be more easily applied to a work group analysis.

11.4.1. The Premise and Hypotheses

The central premise in the theory of Van de Ven, Delbecq, and Koenig (1976) revolves around the idea of uncertainty. Essentially their premise is that as uncertainty increases, coordination must occur by feedback. They hypothesize that as uncertainty increases, there is:

1. Less emphasis on rules and schedules.
2. More emphasis on unscheduled communication, both vertical and horizontal, both individual and group.
3. More emphasis on scheduled group communication.

They employ essentially the same dependent variables. How similar is the idea of task uncertainty to that of the diversity of work? Their measures are excellent ones and provide an insight into the nature of the variable. They include items on the amount of knowledge, the number of insolvable problems, the amount of time spent thinking, the variety of cases, and the like. It seems that these are measures of what might be called task complexity, or the variety of activities involved. Thus it would appear to be a micro counterpart to the concept of the concentration of specialists.

At the same time, their measures really combine two ideas that I would prefer to keep quite distinct. The variety of clients, problems, and cases, to use their wording, is better as an input to work. What is done, such as the difficulty of the task, the variety of activities, and the like, represents the work itself. At this micro level it becomes almost impossible to make a clear distinction between input and position, the technology and the nature of the work. These blend into each other.

Consistent with James Thompson (1967), they also measured what might be called task work-flow. They called it interdependence. In one sense it is, because they specify four ideal-types along the dimension of greater interdependence: *independent, sequential, reciprocal,* and *team.* These would correspond to the four ideal-types suggested in Figure 11.1, with *independent* being typically found in organizations with small batch production (in Woodward's terms), *sequential* of course fitting the case of the assembly line, while *reciprocal* is more likely to be found in the automated production or continuous process. Finally, *team* is characteristic of the work in organic-professional organizations. They hypothesize that increasing interdependence in work-flow should result in:

1. Small increases in planning and scheduling.
2. Moderate increases in unscheduled individual and group meetings.
3. Large increases in scheduled group meetings.

In effect, one sees this as additive. Every work unit needs plans and schedules. The theoretical question is, what happens as interdependence increases. Van de Venn et al. respond, consistent with the Thompsonian theory, that both un-scheduled and scheduled meetings at both the group and individual levels are added as additional mechanisms.

What is task independence? Is it a technological variable or is it a structural variable? Task interdependence describes the nature of the throughput process, and is a characteristic of work-flow. It mixes technology and size, and therefore should perhaps be left until the next chapter when these variables are introduced. It is included here because it allows us to study coordination/control systems.

11.4.2. The Findings

In a study of 191 work units in a state employment agency, Ven de Ven, Delbecq, and Koenig (1976) found more evidence that there are alternative coordination mechanisms. The use of rules and procedures was highly correlated with the use of plans and schedules ($r = .49$), moderately correlated with the use of vertical unscheduled communication ($r = .31$), and negatively related to the use of horizontal unscheduled group meetings ($r = -.22$ and $-.33$). Essentially the same pattern holds for plans and schedules.

The variable that had the most inconsistent pattern (and one would expect this given the research at the meso-level) is vertical communications. It has little association with horizontal (r = .13) and with scheduled and unscheduled group meetings (r = .17 and .02). In their research, no distinction was made between upward and downward, which would presumably explain when vertical would be associated with plans and rules (upward) and when vertical would be correlated with horizontal and committee communication (downward). The correlations are reported in Table 11.2.

Consistent with the analysis in the previous section, as task complexity increases, the reliance on rules and plans decreases and the importance of horizontal unscheduled and group meetings, whether scheduled or unscheduled increases.

Table 11.2   Studies of micro-structure and coordination mechanisms

Van de Ven, Delbecq and Koenig study (1976)

| | | | Communication | | | |
| | | | Person | | Group | |
	Rules	Plans	Vertical	Hori-zontal	Unsched-uled	Sched-uled
Task complexity	−.46	−.36	.04	.52	.64	.59
(N = 191 groups but in one unemployment agency)						

Bacharach and Aiken study (1976)

| | | | | Communication | |
	Job Cod-ification	Rule Ob-servation	Upward	Down-ward	Hori-zontal
Division heads					
Power-strategic	.28	.09	.36	.55	.52
Power-work	.34	.12	.12	.35	.33
Lower subordin.					
Power-strategic	.19	.08	.23	.53	.37
Power-work	.21	.08	.12	.36	.24
(N = 44 local governments for each level)					

Zeitz study (1976)

	Formalization
Professional activity	.03
Education	−.16
Rank	−.02
Participation	−.02
Job autonomy	−.21
(N = 548 individuals)	

Diversity of task also leads to the choice of feedback as the mechanism of coordination at the micro or work unit level. When the importance of this variable is considered in a multiple regression analysis, holding constant the impact of the process variable, work-flow, and work unit size, the relationships remain almost completely unchanged. These other two variables add little to the explanation except for two instances. Greater interdependence does increase significantly the number of scheduled meetings, and size does increase significantly the emphasis on plans and schedules (Van de Ven, Delbecq, and Koenig, 1976: 328) but we shall return to these findings in the next chapter.

More evident at this point is their evidence relative to four ideal-types of coordination/control systems. We find that rules and plans are used to a great extent in both independent and sequential work-flows or what we would assume is the pattern for traditional and mechanical organizations. This appears to support the hypothesis about less formalization in traditional organizations (see Figure 11.1), but since they asked whether there were either formally or informally understood policies and procedures for coordination work, this may not be the case. The word "informally" characterizes the traditional ideal-types. Furthermore, policies and procedures are quite different from highly specified role prescriptions. We have the amusing irony that their measure is better for the meso level and the ones reported in the previous section appear more appropriate for the micro level.

Given this qualification, rules and procedures are used extensively in the traditional and mechanical forms, and less extensively in the mixed mechanic-organic form based on a reciprocal work flow and the organic-professional based on a team work flow. Vertical unscheduled communication is found in all four forms. But since they did not separate downward from upward vertical communication, this is to be expected.

Unscheduled meetings of three or more are used slightly more in independent than sequential work-flows but are very important in reciprocal and team work-flows. The same is true for scheduled meetings. Horizontal unscheduled meetings increase again in the latter two cases.

Thus there is some evidence for four ideal-types. If additional distinctions had been made between upward and downward, and if quantity in volume of communication had been measured, then the differences between these four kinds of work groups might have been even greater. Task complexity would appear to be a critical variable. Unfortunately they did not measure power or status differences in work units, so it is not possible to see if hypotheses about rank also apply at the micro level.

Additional support that the meso-theory of coordination/control applies at the micro level as well is found in a study by Bacharach and Aiken (1976) in Belgium local governments. They examined separately the division head level and their subordinates but only in the area of public administration. The correlations are also reported in Table 11.2. They may have misconceptualized the analytical unit. Since what they call department heads report to the mayors it seems more appropriate to think of these as division heads of separate organizations. Their conceptualization would appear to make the police, fire department, schools, welfare agencies, and every other governmental unit part of the same organization. This seems unwise since they involve separate technologies, civil service systems, and the like. However, since they do not report more detail, we are unsure.

However, if they indeed have confused organizations, then many of their findings would make sense. One would not expect any relationship between the power of the executive office of a public agency to have any association necessarily with the distribution of power below him. Indeed, they report that the greater the job codification of the lower subordinates and the greater the observation of rules that they report, the greater the power of the division heads as they perceive it.

This is not too surprising. One would suspect that the head of a centralization structure would perceive that he had more power than would the head of a decentralized structure.

In these organizations we find at each level — and we must remember that the lower echelon really collapses at least several levels — that both job codification and communications are associated with higher power in decentralized structures. Since those are organizations of local government, presumably involving civil service, where one would assume that the administrations are semi-professional and the workers are clerks, this mixture is less surprising. In a study of public health offices where essentially the same occupations are involved, Palumbo (1969) did a separate analysis for nurses and for sanitarians. As one would expect, the correlations between various measures of structure and control are different. The correlation between professionalism and formalization is -.07 for the nurses and -.25 for the sanitarians. The corresponding correlations for centralization and formalization are .36 and .63. In general, the relationships are stronger for those that have more restricted work. In another interpretation, as the status of the profession or its rank in the organization increases, one would expect the relationship to become weaker because one is more likely to find a mixture of controls. Here in the local government study, we find another example where a formalization indicator, in this case job cofification, is positively related to decentralization. The other measures — task visibility and rule observation — have much weaker associations reflecting the general tendency for more centralized organizations to rely upon formalization but especially on task visibility.

In an individual level of analysis ($N = 548$) of the semi-professional and professional staff that answered mail questionnaires in twenty welfare agencies in an eastern city of the United States, Zeitz (1976) found that it was primarily job autonomy and education that had a negative relationship with the amount of perceived formalization. When Zeitz examined the relationship between various measures of formalization at each hierarchical level – department heads (N = 86), intermediate supervisors (N = 139), and nonsupervisory staff (N = 323) – he found that it was a job specificity index that was most consistently negatively related to reports of participation in decisions rather than either formal documents or perceived formalization. Again this repeats an earlier finding at the meso level: the closer one moves towards a strict delimitation of the job, rather than just written documents of procedures, the more likely one is to find that the hypothesis that centralization and formalization are positively related holds. The same analysis held for job autonomy (1976: 185–86).

Together these studies indicate that many of the same hypotheses hold at the micro level. The sheer presence of documents as in a role specificity index or even job codification can be present with more decentralization. The crucial issue is a measure of how constrained the job descriptions are, or how specific the procedures. Task visibility appears to be an important control mechanism as well. Task complexity tends to have a strong impact on the choice of control mechanisms. Only one of these research studies really conceptualized work groups, and it is in this study that one finds the clearest pattern of findings. The others focus on analytical units – either levels or individuals – that might not be appropriate.

11.4.3. A Special Problem: Conformity

Ideally we would like more research findings on the combination of coordination and control mechanisms employed, and their effectiveness in achieving conformity. At the meso level, the end result of coordination is effectiveness, where effectiveness can mean different things. At the micro level, the real issue in conformity. The objective of both coordination and control is that each job is done and done correctly.

Why have sociologists emphasized conformity to norms rather than motivation or loyalty? Clearly the bias is much more towards behavior than attitudes. Perhaps the answer lies in the central starting point for sociology – membership in groups. Here conformity to norms is more critical than motivation. But it represents somewhat the same idea, although not completely.

One might assume that since one has measured control, then by definition there is conformity. But this ignores the whole issue of whether the control is an appropriate one or not. In the previous section it was suggested, on the basis of a longitudinal study of health and welfare agencies, that many of the agencies responded bureaucratically by increasing formalization and task visibility, and that is not necessarily the correct thing to do. Therefore, it is worth measuring not only how much control occurs but also how much conformity.

So far probably the best study of conformity is by Warren (1968 and 1969), who compares the conformity of teachers with their principals. He wisely divides the issue of conformity into two components: behavior and attitudes. Subordinates can conform but not like it, or agree but find that the flesh is weak. Coercive power or punishment was most effective in producing behavioral conformity, with rewards being the second most effective. However, the use of expert power, legitimate power, and referent power all produce a combination of attitudinal and behavioral conformity. In particular, expert and referent power can be seen as somewhat equivalent to the idea of socialization, or what Etzioni (1975) would call normative compliance. Warren reports that this is related, and strongly so, to attitudinal conformity. Because his research involves teachers, we would hypothesize that they would respond more to socialization by means of expertise and reference to the larger good as effective control mechanisms. Warren did find differences in this relatively homogeneous sample by level of professionalism. As this increased, principals used coercive power less, and expert and referent power more, as we would expect. These schools relied more on committees and thus scheduled communications as well.

In a study of 20 sheltered workshops, medical clinics, welfare services, and other agencies involving mental retardation, Zeitz (1976) measured conformity with two questions of a general nature. To one the respondent states that organizational goals are more important than professional ones. To the other, the respondent states that organizational procedures should be strictly adhered to. Hierarchical rank had a correlation of .26 and participation a correlation of .29 (N = 548) with this index of conformity. Professional activity was also positively related (r = .15) but education was not (r = -.17). This, of course, indicates what is wrong with this measure. As the status of the professional increases and he/she becomes more autonomous, the higher good may require going against organizational procedures. However, the study does demonstrate that professional activity and decentralization lead to a kind of self-control, to use Parson's (1951) term. It is interesting to note that an impersonal mechanism — formalization — has only some relationship at the individual level (r = .27) with conformity, demonstrating that one must measure control and conformity quite separately.

11.5. CONCLUSIONS

In general there is considerable support for the idea that there are a variety of organizational coordination mechanisms, ranging from the development of plans and rules — including quite detailed specification of programs — to the proliferation of committees and communication channels. Most organizations use mixtures of these and there is some evidence that there are some nonlinear combinations as well, since custom can replace rules and because the same volume of communication can be distributed vertically or horizontally. Similarly there is a considerable variety of control mechanisms although these have not been studied as extensively. What is most lacking is a study of how these two fit together and in turn how effective they are in achieving coordination and control as measured by effectiveness and conformity. The few studies that have been done at each level suggest that the link is there, but is hardly automatic.

At the meso level, the impact of the concentration of specialists and of centralization on the development of communication channels appears well substantiated. What is less well documented is the role of formalization. Part of the confusion of findings relates to the wide variety of measures. The creation of procedures and the existence of written documents appear positively related to the concentration of specialists and to centralization. The tight specification of the job, delimiting its range of activities, appears negatively related to the concentration of specialists and positively related to centralization. Close supervision, rule observation, and mechanisms designed to increase task visibility appear related to centralization. As yet, a good study of the detailed program discussed by March and Simon (1958) is yet to be done.

The Environment: Resources and the Transformation of Form, Strategies, and Constraints

Chapter Twelve

Resources and the Choice of Organizational Form

In the previous three sections, the organizational system has been conceived somewhat as though it were independent and free from external influences. The impact of the environment has been mentioned in passing, but these external influences on organizational structure and performances have not been systematically elucidated. Nor has the effect of the organization on its environment been considered. As Chandler (1977) remarks in recent book, the visible hand of management has replaced the invisible hand of the market. In this, the fourth and last part of the book, these interchanges are explored.

Perhaps the easiest conceptualization of how the environment and the organization interrelate is to think about how the environment affects the input-throughput-output system (Katz and Kahn, 1966). Organizations produce specific products and services that more or less meet the needs and/or desires of the population (Parsons, 1956a). This is what legitimates their existence. Therefore, one way in which the environment affects organizations is by demand for their products or services. This demand may be determined in the marketplace, in the office of a planner, or in the headquarters of another organization but regardless, it affects the continued existence of the organization. Organizations also receive inputs from the environment, and these affect how organizations function as well. In this chapter, the resources of knowledge, wealth, and power are considered necessary inputs for the production of any output.

The three separate kinds of organizational crises — ignoring for the moment the special cases of conflict and the breakdown of control — are maintaining balance between performances, maintaining balance between inputs and outputs, and maintaining balance between organizational structure and performance. These are most often triggered by environmental changes. In Chapter 8, environmental change was simply an assumption. Now we need to be more explicit about how and in what ways the environment does change. Essentially discontinuous changes in technology/knowledge, autonomy, or product demand are the most common.

Cigarette consumption had been steadily rising until the various medical reports (1960-1975) cast doubt on the advisibility of smoking. Governments had been trying to regulate smoking. Under these circumstance a static market — steadily rising sales — suddenly become dynamic, with fluctuating demand and uncertainty about whether the demand would continue to increase. The railroads were in the same situation for almost a century (1840-1939), until the advent of the mass-produced car and bus gradually altered their market situation. The examples of where dynamic markets become static are harder to find but usually represent the beginning of the development of the technology (Abernathy, 1978), as in the early history of the automobile (1900-1930), refrigerator (1930-1950), dishwasher (1945-1955), and the like.

The current regulation of pollution has had a far reaching impact on many businesses. Where are environmental changes most likely to occur? It is the gaining of resources that has the most direct impacts on organizations beyond supply and demand. How and in what quantities do resources dictate the choice of organizational form? *Changes in the quality of resources, or enough quantitative change so that there is a qualitative one, are one major reason for transformation of form.*

Two resources have been extensively studied but they have not usually been conceived of as resources. These are technology, which is the knowledge input, and personnel size, which is the labor input. Perhaps the most striking intellectual developments during the past ten years have been these two schools, each of which sees their input as the decisive causal force. Personnel size is easy to measure, strongly correlated with budget (see Pugh, et al., 1969a; Kimberly, 1976), and can be studied for relatively small sums of money. The consequence has been a very large literature (see Blau, 1972 and Kimberly, 1976 for bibliography). Technology has proved to be much more difficult to measure (see discussions of Woodward, 1965: Appendix; Perrow, 1970) and to conceptualize (Hickson et al., 1969; Van de Ven, Delbecq and Koenig, 1976, Zey-Ferrell, 1979: 108-118). There have therefore been far fewer studies (see above references and bibliography in Hage and Aiken, 1969; Dewar and Hage, 1978).

Both size and technology have been associated with various theories that represent in certain respects the main intellectual achievements in the study of organizations during the past decade. James Thompson (1967) developed a theory of work-flow and its impact on coordination, strategy, and design. Perrow proposed a set of ideal-types built around the concept of the routineness of technology. Although the contingency theory of Lawrence and Lorsch (1967 a and b) might not be considered a technological theory, in fact it is. Finally Blau

(1970a, 1972, 1973) has written a formal theory explicating the impact of size on structural differentiation. There have been no lack of ideas, hypotheses, and even formal theory, in this area of organizational sociology. There is even a debate about the relative importance of size and technology (see Hickson et al. 1969; Hall, 1977; Aldrich, 1972; Blau et al. 1976), but because of confused indicators and concepts it has not made much headway.

All of these various theories, however, were primarily raising an old question: What determines organizational form? Few really argued that technology and size were the major links between the task environment and the organization. Yet of course it is implicit in the work of all of them. Pugh et al. (1963) called these variables "context," recognizing that they established the constraints for organizations. Lawrence and Lorsch (1967 a and b) went further and noted that technology environmentally determined how fast feedback about success or failure could occur. Blau and Schoenherr (1971) recognized the link between personnel size and demand. However, the conceptualization on the environmental side of how much knowledge, demand, and power was available has not been explored enough.

This would appear to be the right time to synthesize these input theories into a more comprehensive theory of how organizational resources affect the structure and coordination of the system, and to test this theory against the findings of the major research studies. For this reason I have reanalyzed (or the researchers were kind enough to do it for me) the data sets of Pugh et al., Hage-Aiken, Child, Azumi, and Paulson, attempting to use approximately the same measures for the same idea. Furthermore, the various studies of Blau (1970a, 1972, 1973) can also be reinterpreted, albeit with less success because there are fewer common measures.

Another reason why it is time to reconstruct the theories relative to size and technology by adding autonomy is that each of these studies has tended to examine different structural variables. Studies of personnel size have focused on job titles, levels, departments, or various measures of structural differentiation (see Blau, 1970, 1972, 1973), where technology has tended to focus on power (Perrow, 1967; Hage and Aiken, 1969). This is not to say that Blau and his students have been unconcerned with the issue of power (Zald, 1970; Blau and Schoenherr, 1971; Meyer, 1968a and b). They have looked at delegation and the like, but this has not been their main thrust. They both have looked at span of control because this can be a measure of both aspects. What will be suggested is that perhaps the procedure should be reversed. *Technology becomes more important for its impact on at least the concentration of specialists, and personnel size might be much more relevant for the analysis of centralization* (John Freeman, 1973).

It is also strange that few theories of organizational autonomy have been developed. Selznik's famous case study, *T.V.A. and the Grass Roots Democracy*

(1949) has been present for a long time. But few have followed in its pathway. The recent moves towards government regulation have shown how important independence or latitude are. And as interest increases in the concept of organizational choice (see Warner, Ed., 1977), invariably the question of independence emerges. The relationship between the autonomy of organization and its internal distribution of power is not clear. One can make the case – and there is some evidence to support it – that organizations with more autonomy are also more centralized (Pennings, 1973). Any thesis about the impact of technology and size is incomplete without some attempt to include organizational autonomy as another organizational resource. It is especially strange that although centralization or the distribution of power has been the single most important structural characteristic, power as input or resource, the total amount of available power has been ignored as a critical environmental constraint.

12.1. A MESO THEORY OF RESOURCES AND STRUCTURE

12.1.1. The Theoretical Definitions

In a trail-blazing research study, Woodward (1965) showed that the data collected in industrial firms in England during the late 1950s was ordered by the simple recognition of different kinds of *machine* technology: small batch, assembly line or mass production, and continuous process. Quite independently and a year earlier, Blauner (1964) found that the same distinctions were helpful in classifying American industry. These studies viewed technology more as process throughput than as input, however (see Appendix in Woodward, 1965). Working with these studies and many others, Perrow summarized an enormous but descriptive literature when he suggested that the real variable was the relative routines of technology. While his conclusions were similar to James Thompson's (1967), he recognized that technological routine has essentially two components: how analyzable were the technical problems and how many exceptions occurred. He then used these to create a technological typology that was used to classify not only industrial firms but people-processing organizations as well into essentially four ideal-types for each. We employed this scheme repeatedly throughout the book to help define the most common equilibrium states and forms.

However, the question remains whether routineness is the most critical technological dimension. About the same time as Perrow published his theoretical article on technology, Lefton and Rosengren (1966) suggested that the best way of predicting the complexity of people-processing organizations was to focus on what they called the latitude and longitude of client treatment. This concept might better be called task scope: how many different aspects, how intensively, and for how long does the organization handle them? This is the dimension that I shall use to order the many seemingly disparate findings. Its counterpart in economic organizations is product-mix.

The first advantage of the term task scope is that it calls more attention to the problem of how much knowledge is needed to complete the task. Technology means both machines *and* knowledge, as noted by Hickson et al. (1969) in their extensive review of the concept. If one focuses exclusively on the machines and tools, the nuts and bolts of the operations, then the impact of technology is likely to be limited. If, however, one focuses on the amount of knowledge involved in the production of a product or the provision of a service, then there is a very different analysis. One could use the term "task complexity," but it implies perhaps only one product. This is one of the limitations of the word routineness as well. For this reason, I prefer to restrict task complexity to the micro level (Van de Venn, Delbecq and Koenig, 1976). One can have both routine and nonroutine products and services. The more critical question is how many are there and how much knowledge does each product/service utilize? Our definition is then:

Task scope: The amount and variety of knowledge employed by the organization in its production of goods or provision of services.

If we go back to Chapter 1 and the definition of an organization as distinct from a multi-organization, it will be remembered that it was done on the basis of the similarity of inputs. One critical input is of course the technology, and here is meant not the process technology such as the assembly line but the content or knowledge input. Both medical students and law students are trained at Columbia University but the content or knowledge is quite dissimilar. The divisions for the manufacture of cars, trains, motor boats, buses, and refrigerators in General Motors have different contexts and therefore are different organizations relative to this input. What is striking in this case is that the amount of knowledge and its variety varies considerably, with much more with medical students than law students, much more with trains than refrigerators. And this leads to an important definition:

Amount of knowledge in the environment: The number and variety of journals published relative to the production of products or provision of services.

This does not represent all the relevant information. There are many artisan skills involved in the production of goods and services, but most typically these states of the art are relatively low. Traditional and mechanical organizations tend to have this kind of knowledge base. So the definition does focus on determining what are technologically intensive industries and service areas. The judgement is best made outside the organization rather than by its members, but in any case journals provide a rough guideline to the state of the art, which is the environmental context.

Kimberly (1976), in a recent review, has noted the large variety of different terms and indicators that are employed to measure the size of the organization. For this reason, the term "personnel size" seems more appropriate than just the word "size" because it calls attention to that aspect of size which represents an input, the labor factor of production in economic terms. This in turn suggests the following definition:

Personnel size: The amount and variety of people who work to produce the products or provide the services of the organization.

Determining who is working to produce the products is not always easy. The clients/customers are not part of the personnel size normally. In sheltered workshops clients are increasingly hired to work as part of their therapy. This is a borderline case but one where the clients are also members. In universities, graduate students and even sometimes undergraduates are hired. Here there is no doubt which are clients and which are workers. The students are not hired to learn but instead to teach or to do research, which is quite different. Nor would be various associations that may provide resources to the organization — such as state legislatures relative to universities, or county boards relative to welfare agencies — be considered as personnel. Chrysler manufactures cars. The dealers who sell and repair them are not part of the organization any more than the suppliers of finished products that Chrysler purchases, if one accepts the definition of Chrysler as producing cars (among other products). Admittedly at times the boundaries may be hard to draw but the desired meaning is clear. Suppliers and customers do not count, but volunteers who actually do some work do. More difficult to classify are organizations that have a separate legal status, but who have complex legal relationships with some supplier, such as automobile dealers.

Again if we consider our definition of the organization, we can begin to draw boundaries between organizations by noting the interchangeability of personnel. Insofar as workers or staff can not be easily shifted from one situation to the next, we have a test of where the boundary lies even when it is part of a larger structure. Naval officers and seamen are not shifted to the U.S. Army even though they are part of the same defense system. Guards in prisons do not get transferred to mental hospitals even though they may be part of the same state government. Automobile dealers do not shift into the automobile headquarters even when the agency is owned by the manufacturer. It is clear that the knowledge inputs and labor inputs overlap to a certain extent because the inability to transfer individuals is in part a function of their training, skills, expertise, and the like. Note, this is technologically given or determined and is what is meant by a division of labor.

Relative to the labor input in the size of the labor force. This environmental characteristic is defined as:

Amount of labor in the environment: The number and variety of people who could work relative to the production of goods or provision of services.

Caplow (1954: Chapter 7) developed a typology of labor markets that has not to my knowledge been exploited. The central idea is that the size of these markets does vary enormously, and this environmental characteristic affects how organizations adjust to imbalances in the production function.

We could systematically build in the wealth input or the size of the operating budget and its parallel concept, the availability of financing, but at this stage in the development of theories about resources and the environment, it seems enough to assume that personnel size and operating budget are strongly correlated (Pugh et al. 1969a). In other words, the economic distinction between capital intensive and labor intensive is not that relevant (although it will become increasingly so).

How does the amount of knowledge and the size of the available labor force affect organizations? The growth in knowledge has two processes: complexity and simplification as in mechanization and automation. The interrelation as suggested by Lawrence and Lorsch (1967b: 235) is given in Figure 12.1. As knowledge grows about how to produce a particular output, part of this knowledge can be routinized into machines. Thus the relationship between the needed labor force and the state of the art is a complex one. At certain time points the routinization of the work may be far enough advanced so that one can rely upon a largely unskilled labor force. At other times, the routinization may be so com-

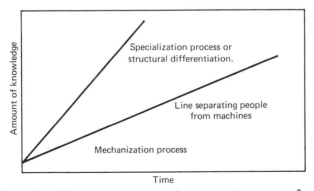

Figure 12.1   The twin consequences of the growth in knowledge[a].

plete that unskilled labor can be replaced by machines. The remaining work, which is nonroutine, is then done by skilled labor. Some argue that the movement from small batch to assembly-line to automated production is the normal machine evolution (see Abernathy, 1978). There is evidence to support this in a number of research studies (Walker, 1957; Mann and Williams, 1960; Woodward, 1965). Concomitantly, *the total knowledge relative to the production of products is growing.* Furthermore, the part of the knowledge performed by the labor force is growing even faster, which means more complex tasks.

For example, at one time cars were largely constructed of steel. Now a wide variety of different materials are employed including aluminum, plastic, glass fiber, and the like. The motor was previously a simple affair to repair and now requires a trained mechanic. Computers for cars are now becoming commonplace. Concomitantly the consumer is no longer a single man who smokes Marlboro cigarettes; he and she have differentiated needs and tastes. Together this has produced a variety of cars each of which now requires a much more complex technology.

In sheltered workshops the same growth in knowledge has occurred, which has resulted in knowing more about how to handle the unemployable, but in turn the unemployed have been differentiated into a variety of clients. Call this product mix or task scope, but there have been both qualitative and quantitative changes. *The growth of knowledge means not only the recognition of new solutions to old problems but the recognition of new problems.* It is this more than anything else that increases the task scope, with all the consequences to be spelled out below.

How much of the production is handled by machines? In what stage of technological evolution does the process of manufacturing affect the quantity and quality of the labor force needed to produce the products or provide the services? Beyond this, the relative wealth of the society will impact on two critical factors that affect optimal size: the cost trade-offs between machines and labor and the demand for the product. Together these affect what is probable optimal personnel size, an optimum that changes with the per capita wealth and also with the growth of knowledge, both of which determine the machine-man trade-off. Because these processes occur in the larger society at such very slow rates, however, they tend to be ignored.

There is a long-term growth in knowledge and the size of the labor force, but there are sudden and discontinuous changes which affect the organizations involved. A new technology that is competitive with existing ones is the most likely discontinuous environmental change. The second most likely is a shift from a shortage to a surplus, or the reverse, in the size of the available labor force. These two basic variables also relate to the two views of Aldrich (1979: Chapter 5) that organizations have resource dependences and also need information.

As yet little has been said about the autonomy of the organization to do what it wants. Power is a resource as well (see Selznek, 1949), although a very difficult one to measure or even to conceptualize. For this reason, variables like financial size or operating budget become the proxy for organizational autonomy. There are two aspects to the problem that need to be captured in any definition. One is the limitation on strategic decisions made by outsiders. Banks may veto certain capital investment plans. State legislators may control the salary increases. Regulatory agencies may set a whole series of restrictions on what the organization can and can not do (Aldrich, 1979: 186–88). Laws may make certain corporate practices like price-fixing illegal, limit certain business strategies of domination such as monopoly, or require certain personnel practices such as collective bargaining, equal opportunity, union representation, and the like. This refers to the usual connotation of autonomy – in what sense are strategic decisions made inside the organization and how limited is the choice among range of options.

But there is another dimension to the concept of autonomy, especially if we think of this as an input, a power resource for the organization. This meaning might be called the number of different strategic decisions that are made. With this we use a zero-sum conceptualization of organization autonomy. What is striking about multinational corporations is the sheer range of decisions that they make. It is not only a decision to build a plant, but the fact that this decision comes up many times, that really bespeaks their power. These two ideas can be and are frequently confused with aggregate assets, and these assets are at best an indirect indicator of power. The critical element is the wide range of decisions that they make, and this is precisely what makes multinational corporations potentially so dangerous.

Putting together these two ideas suggests the following theoretical definition for organizational autonomy:

Organizational autonomy: The amount and variety of strategic decisions made by the members of the organization.

An organization with few decisions to make would have little autonomy; an organization with a large number of decisions has much more power. Again in various ways knowledge can affect the number of decisions that must be made. Similarily, growth in personnel size also suggests the proliferation of decisions but this may be more the effect than the cause of organizational autonomy. But it is for these reasons that the concepts must be considered together. Only then can their relative importance be determined.

12.1.2. The Impact of Technology

Although Perrow (1967) presented a typology of task structure, the essential linear and multivariate hypotheses are that the routineness of technology will lead to centralization. Distinctions are made relative to the power of line and staff given certain combinations of the two dimensions – the analyzability of problems and the number of exceptions – but the thrust of the discussion is primarily power. There has been some evidence to support this idea (Hage and Aiken, 1969) and some evidence against it (Mohr, 1971), although the latter study shifted from the meso to the micro level by focusing on managers.

When one shifts to the concept of task scope however, the key structural variable would appear to be the concentration of specialists. As the variety of knowledges (or technologies) increases, more and more specialists are needed. At the individual level, there is a limit to cognition (March and Simon, 1958). As knowledge expands, it is broken into disciplines which in turn are mastered by specialists, a process quite different from task specialization (Dewar and Hage, 1978). In the larger sociological literature, this process has been referred to as structural differentiation (Parsons, 1966). And while perhaps too much emphasis has been previously placed on the separation into functions, the creation of new occupations is the real critical structural change and one that occurs almost entirely within the context of organizations. The growth in task scope requires a proliferation of specialists. Since this same growth is, in general, replacing routinized work with machines, it affects the ratio of skilled to unskilled labor. Not only does the variety of specialists increase but the proportion grows as well.

The term structural differentiation is so important that it is worth providing a separate definition for it:

Structural differentiation: The creation of new occupational specialties.

Victor Thompson (1961a and b) make a distinction between task specialization and person specialization. Task specialization occurs along the assembly line and is not the same as the development of new professional or managerial specialties. *The growth in new specialties – the development of new professions – is the single most important aspect of structural differentiation relative to the organization, and yet this has not been studied.* Machines and tools have received more attention than expertise and skills.

Contrary to Durkheim (1933) it is not size that creates this differentiation but instead the growth of knowledge. Most of the new occupations are in areas where there are large research projects. Most of the new occupational specialties are found in universities at the graduate level. *It is at the end of the education process where the most structural differentiation occurs because it is here where the most knowledge is accumulated.*

What is difficult to say in any concrete case is how much the task scope is a function of knowledge, the state of the art, and how much it is a function of organizational policy. The answer to this is influenced by the variety of organizations considered. If only those of one kind — retail stores, radio-isotope manufacturers, motion picture companies, or halfway-houses for prisons convicts — are considered, one is struck by the differences due to policy. Some organizations pursue a strategy of attracting a variety of customers/clients and attempting to offer them individual attentions. Others prefer a more delimited or specialized task, a more standardized product or service. But as soon as one makes comparisons across *kinds* of organizations as defined by their outputs, then one is struck more by the great differences in knowledge bases and the similarity of organizations with the same task. For this reason contingency theory has a tendency to restrict the meaning of the environment to those organizations of the same kind. However, a wider perspective, namely that of the larger society, makes it easier to measure and perceive task scope. The first hypothesis is:

12. 1   The greater the task scope, the greater the concentration of specialists.

Essentially the argument is that as the knowledge input increases there must be greater diversity in the social structure to handle this complexity. If one accepts the idea that there are limits to cognition, then the simplest procedure is to create branches of knowledge as the total sum accumulates. The countervailing trend is to maintain a place for the generalist, which is what France, Japan, Britain, and some other countries have tried to do. As the product mix relative to any technology grows however — different kinds of special education students, different kinds of photo copy equipment, different kinds of mental illness — then it becomes essential to have individuals who know more about each kind. Special sales personnel, special workers, special professions, and the like proliferate.

From a power-value perspective, we can now explain why the stability of coalitions varies. The number of different interest groups increases and the coalitions tend to collapse. As the task scope increases, the number of interest groups also increase. The basis of coalition is less and less likely to be hierarchical rank — managers against workers. The political situation becomes more fluid and seemingly "less predictable", as suggested in the Cyert and March (1963) formulation.

12. 2   The greater the task scope, the greater the number of interest groups.
12. 3   The greater the task scope, the more likely the coalition will be unstable.

These three hypotheses can be deduced from a single premise, which is:

12A   The greater the knowledge input, the greater the diversity of social structure.

Whether the proportion of specialists, number of interest groups, or the durability of the coalition, knowledge as a resource inevitably makes the structure more differentiated and political processes more interesting. Some of the implications of the growth in knowledge in the larger society are spelled out in Chapter 14. This fluidity has made the political paradigm so popular (Cyert and March, 1963), but what has been missed is that the seemingly greater chaos of very complex structures is built on a different social basis of organization: the organic-professional or teamwork model. There is much more order than appears at first glance in this fluidity and instability.

We made several assumptions about the proportion of members with low or high rank and the likely nature of the interest groups and coalitions that will exist inside the organization in Part 1. The degree of task-scope inevitably affects what proportion of the members will be of high rank and therefore the basis of coalition formation and the like. If these ideas are combined, the following additional hypothesis can be deduced.

12. 4   *The greater the task scope, the more likely the basis of the coalition will be occupations and values – that is, preferences about organizational performances and utilities.*
12. 5   *The greater the task scope, the greater the number of decision-issues.*

It will be remembered that this leads to a kind of routinization of the decision-making process and a strategy of incrementalism – dividing decisions into small ones that can be handled more effectively. The other implications can be deduced by substituting task-scope for the concentration of specialists, although not in all cases does task-scope have an independent effect. Its major influence is on the number of decision-issues and to a lesser extent the frequency with which they occur.

We could derive a large number of other hypotheses that causally relate technology and the choice of organizational form. The main issue is that as task scope increases, the organization form is shifted from a mechanical to an organic form. The long term trend of the growth in knowledge thus has some major implications about how organizations are structured. But contingency theory is built on more than one environmental factor, just as the production process has more than one input.

12.1.3. The Impact of Personnel Size

If the major impact of technology, conceptualized as task-scope or variety of technologies, is on the specialists rather than on centralization, then the impact of personnel size is primarily on the other structural variables. The essential argument stems from Michel, and is his iron law of oligarchy (1962), updated by James Thompson (1967) and his theses of the inner circle. These ideas can be generalized into another premise about organizations, to wit:

12B   The greater the number of resources other than knowledge, the more likely these are to be concentrated in the hands of an elite.

The distinction between resources other than knowledge and knowledge is a familiar one in the literature and is akin to the Katz and Kahn (1966) separation of energy from information. Typically, when the word resource is employed in the literature it means power, funds, status, and the like and seldom knowledge or skill.

From this premise, which might be called the Marxist premise, since it is a central element in Marx's theory of capitalism, a large number of hypotheses can be derived. Starting with personnel size, the following ideas can be derived if one is willing to accept the above premise:

12. 6   The greater the personnel size, the greater the centralization.
12. 7   The greater the personnel size, the greater the stratification.
12. 8   The greater the personnel size, the less the normative equality.

For those familiar with the research findings in a number of studies, these hypotheses appear to be dead wrong. One of the most consistent findings is that personnel size and centralization are *negatively* related. Bigger organizations are more democratic.

Past research has been so absorbed by proving the relationship between size and structural differentiation (see Blau, 1970a, 1972, and 1973; Blau and Schoenherr, 1971; Meyer, 1968 a and b; Heydebrand, 1973 a and b, etc.) that the general *negative* correlations between size and centralization have been perceived as the consequence of personnel size rather than the concentration of specialtists. As soon as one conceptualizes specialization as a proportion rather than the sheer number of job titles, and as a proportion of professionals and managers with skills and expertise rather than the number of levels and of departments, than the interrelationship between size and the concentration of specialists changes. Likewise, so does the relationship between personnel size and centralization. Previously personnel is seen as an exogenous variable that decreases centralization and increases structural differentiation. Now it becomes more sensible to argue the reverse. The concentration of specialization diminishes centralization, as we have shown in Chapter 3 and personnel size increases it.

Two critical factors affect the interpretation of the very large amount of evidence that shows that personnel size is negatively related to centralization. First, many studies have used delegation to lower levels as a measure of decentralization rather than the proportion who participates. Second, none of the studies have explored simultaneously the impact of organizational autonomy since large organizations also tend to be powerful ones, free or more free to make their own decisions and with many more decisions to make. Personnel size may show a negative path coefficient vis-à-vis centralization when in fact it should be positive. These alternative causal paths are diagramed in Figure 12.2. to make clear the alternative arguments.

Essentially my argument is that growth in personnel size leads to greater concentration of powers in the hands of elites but this is masked by two countervailing tendencies. Organizations with large task-scope have many more decision issues which leads to the hiring of more specialists to handle them and leads to

Model 1: The usual analysis

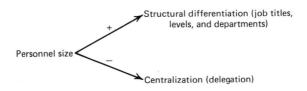

Model 2: The causal structure with the concentration of specialists

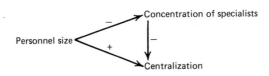

Model 3: The causal structure with task scope, personnel size and organizational autonomy

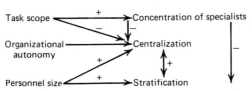

Figure 12.2 The various models of personnel size and structure given different causal structures.

greater decentralization because there are too many decision issues to be handled. More important, the concentration of specialists is the major reason for the movement towards decentralization typical of large organizations. These negative paths between task-scope and the concentration of specialists and centralization on the one hand, are usually stronger than the positive paths between this variable and personnel size and organizational autonomy. Therefore, personnel size appears to be negatively associated with centralization, if task scope and the concentration of specialists are not included in the path analysis.

These alternative influences create a complex dialectic. On the one hand the growth in personnel size, operating budget, and autonomy leads to the concentration of the resources in the hands of an elite as Marx argued. On the other hand the growth in knowledge, the broadening of the tasks or objectives of the organization, means the introduction of new technologies handled by specialists who fight to redistribute power, pay, and privilege internally. In effect, the ratio of the relationship between task-scope and personnel size tells us about where the organizational's structure is.

If we return to the fundamental problem of what produces transformation, we have some more specific answers. There can be periods when the organization is small in size and has a broad task scope. Then we would predict the organization has an organic-professional structure that is high complexity and low centralization. But suppose one of the products becomes popular and appeals to a mass market. Then the growth in personnel size might be matched by a transformation to a mixed mechanical-organic form with centralization and stratification high in the production department, at least relative to the particular product. This is the history of Polaroid or Xerox. Or conversely, a new technological breakthrough occurs and there is a rapid growth in knowledge in a particular area that previously had been traditional. A good example is the development of fast frozen foods which has considerably changed the food processing area. The more successful firms are moving in the direction of the mixed mechanical-organic.

Growth in the size of the labor force impacts on organizational size and budget, while growth in knowledge impacts on the task-scope. Discontinuous changes can occur in either area but are most likely in the latter input into organizations. A discontinuous change in either area would mean the need for a change from one equilibrium state to another. Furthermore, while the more typical adaptation of the system of variables is from mechanical to mixed mechanical-organic, or from traditional to mechanic to mixed mechanical-organic as Abernathy and Utterback (1975) argue, in fact the principle of equifinality is very much in operation. There is movement from any one of the four equilibrium states or forms to any one of the others.

A question mark is placed by the path between organizational autonomy and centralization in Model 3 of Figure 12.2. The premise suggests that powerful organizations will be centralized, and I believe this to be the case. But one can also argue that a greater number of decision issues will result in more decentralization because of overload. My own belief is that elites will always try to make all decisions; that James Thompson's hypothesis of the inner circle is correct. If the decisions occur frequently they will be routinized in the form of manuals, policy directives, and the like, as Blau (Zald, ed., 1970) and his colleagues (Meyer, 1968 a and b) have shown. Decisions are only delegated downward when they can only be made at a lower level or when they are completely formalized. This is one reason why separate measures for both organizational autonomy and centralization are so critical. If centralization is not measured by participation, and autonomy by the number of strategic decisions made within the organization, then some misinterpretations are possible.

Given the premise, and believing in the power of deductive logic, the following hypotheses can be deduced:

12. 9   *The greater the organizational autonomy, the greater the centralization.*
12.10   *The greater the organizational autonomy, the greater the stratification.*
12.11   *The greater the organizational autonomy, the less normative equality.*

Again one does not get very far without keeping quite distinct the boundaries of the organization. In multi-organizations such as Dow Chemical, Remington Rand, or General Dynamics, the boundary between organizations with separate inputs is at the division level. In local governments financial decisions may be made at the level of the county board of supervisors, which also makes decisions for the parks division, the welfare division, and other kinds of organizations with distinct throughputs. In fact, in both cases these respective boards ratify the decisions already made. There is some competition between divisions for money but operational decisions are usually made at the divisional level. However, Mintzberg, (1979) suggests that this is not necessarily true.

It is clear that these variables will also therefore affect the political process involved in decision-making. But it is perhaps best to see their influences mediated by the changes in the structure. In particular, growth in personnel size means a tendency towards the division of the membership along hierarchical lines into classes or strata, the workers and the managers or the professionals and the administrators.

12.1.4.   The Measures

Both task-scope and personnel size would appear to be simple to operationalize but in fact have a number of complexities. The major stumbling block with task-scope is to find some measure that works across a wide range of organizations, those with products and those with services. Perhaps the best work has been done with a factor called operational variability in the research of Pugh et al. (1969). They conceptualized this as providing nonstandardized products. Unfortunately, in their classification they conceptualized teaching, transport, and retailing as being standardized services. This may or may not be so. Since England has largely pioneered with the open classroom in primary schools, where a great deal of energy is spent on recognizing individual differences, the classification of the local educational authority as low task-scope may be quite incorrect.

In a different attempt, Dewar and Hage (1978), building on the work of Lefton and Rosengren (1966), combined several trichotomies, the first measuring the average period of each client visit, the second measuring the number of different clients or outputs. The two indicators had a .36 correlation, which in fact demonstrates the point made by Lefton and Rosengren that these are somewhat different dimensions. Finally, a scale of routineness was added in as well. This scale correlated highly with the idea of client latitude and longitude. An inspection of the scatter plot indicates that variation between kinds of organizations was greater than variation within, giving some face validity to the measure. But clearly it is too crude, and much refinement is required. Yet, it is somewhat akin to the measure developed by Pugh et al.

The crucial theme running through both measures is the idea of how many different distinctions, in terms of either customers or clients, are being made and, in the case of the Dewar and Hage index, with what intensiveness is the technology applied. The rule of thumb is that with more distinctions and more intensiveness, there is more knowledge being applied. Note that both measures have only an indirect association with knowledge input. However, a more direct indicator of knowledge input such as counting the number of disciplines relevant to the work of the organization, would probably strike the reader as tautological in its association with the concentration of specialists.

Personnel size and its operational definition has been somewhat more standardized. There is general agreement that part-time workers should be given a weight of 1/2 and that volunteers might be given a weight of 1/10 since they seldom work for more than a few hours. These corrections are important because they can considerably alter the personnel size of particular organizations, especially people-processing ones. Usually a logarithmic transformation is then made on the assumption that increasingly large increments of growth in the size of the work force are needed to produce equivalent changes in whatever might be the dependent variable. This is well substantiated relative to a large number of different research studies (Blau, 1970a, 1972, 1973; Pugh et al., 1968) and also makes good theoretical sense.

As yet there is no satisfactory measure of organizational autonomy. Perhaps the best measure would be to take a standard list of decision areas, especially strategic ones, and then determine how much influence a standard list of interest groups, competitors, customers or clients, regulatory organizations, resource controllers, and the like have on these decision areas. This would then be qualified by the number of decisions to be made in each area.

This explains the question mark placed by the path between autonomy and centralization. The usual measure looks at whether the board makes the decision and does not also consider whether the board is part of the organization or not. Influence measures are more subtle and, most important, they lead us more directly into a discussion of outside interest groups, an area that has been largely ignored. Hopefully, the new work being done from a political economy perspective will begin to examine the influence of various interests on the autonomy of organizations and multi-organizations.

12.1.5. The Findings

In the reanalysis of the Aston studies (see Figure 12.3), one finds that task-scope as measured by operating variability does have a positive relationship with the concentration of specialists in both the Pugh et al. and Child studies of English firms. In the original Pugh et al. study task-scope has a nonsignificant but negative path to centralization as suggested. In the Child study this causal link is stronger $r_p = -.22$.

The log of personnel size was not allowed to affect the concentration of specialists as the most conservative test of the hypotheses regarding this variable. In both studies, log size has a negative association with centralization, with the path coefficient being much stronger in the Child study. In the Child study the organizations tended to be larger and there were more multi-organizations included in the analysis (Donaldson, Aldrich and Child, 1975), so that part of the explanation might lie in the nature of the research design. One would expect that if organizational autonomy had been measured by the influence of groups outside the organization, rather than their measures of autonomy or dependence (Pugh et al. 1969a), the sign of the path coefficient between size and centralization might change. The reanalysis of the Hage-Aiken data, with all three waves pooled ($N = 61$), presents a similar picture (Figure 12.4). Task-scope has a strong positive path coefficient with the concentration of specialists ($p = .46$) and a negative one ($p = -.20$) with centralization. In contrasting the three studies it is useful to remember that multi-organizations were divided into organizations in the Hage-Aiken panel study. As a result, and also because these are people-processing organizations, the range of personnel size was from 10 to 600 (the largest organization was a mental hospital). Log size here does not have a significant path with centralization but has a large and negative one with stratification. It seems reasonable to believe that some of the large and negative path coefficients between log size and centralization in the Child data are because multiple-organizations and organizations are mixed together. Certainly the range on size is much, much greater.

Pugh et. al. (1968) (N = 52)

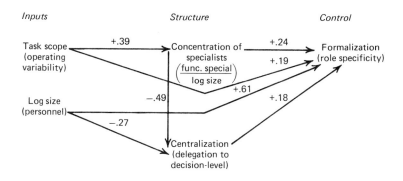

Child (1972) (N = 80)

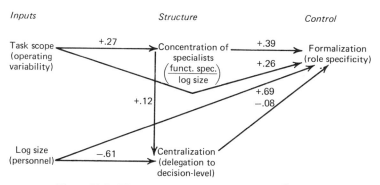

Figure 12.3 The reanalysis of the Aston studies.[a]

Task-scope impacts in the Hage-Aiken study on both the concentration of specialists and professional activity. Innovation rate or change in task-scope (see Dewar and Hage, 1978), impacts only on concentration of specialists. In turn, both of these variables have a negative association with centralization, as does task-scope. If one leaves out professional activity and innovation rate, *then* a significant negative path between log size and centralization appears. In other words, there is good evidence that when professional activity or training is left out, and if not all specialists are counted, and the like, log size begins to become a proxy for these missing technological and structural aspects. Larger organizations have more specialists, as all of the Blau research shows (1970, 1972, and 1973), and they tend to be more professionally active. Given that the concentration of specialists is negatively related to centralization, we have an ex-

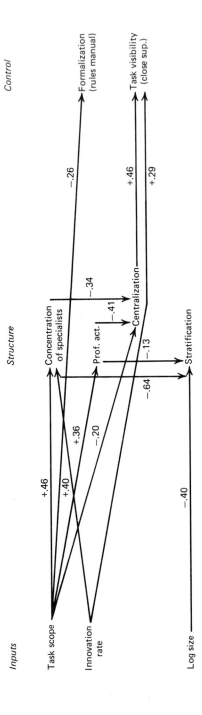

Inputs   *Structure*   *Control*

Task scope

Innovation rate

Log size

Concentration of specialists

Prof. act.

Centralization

Stratification

Formalization (rules manual)

Task visibility (close sup.)

+.46
+.40
+.36
−.20
−.40
−.64
−.13
−.34
−.41
−.26
+.46
+.29

Figure 12.4 The reanalysis of the Hage-Aiken panel study.[a]

[a] Only significant paths are drawn.

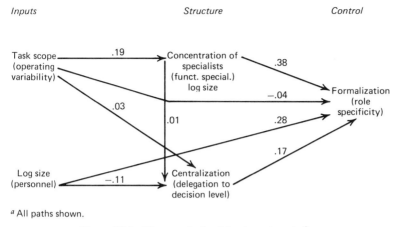

Figure 12.5   The reanalysis of the Azumi study.[a]

planation for the very large number of findings relating log size negatively to centralization. Task-scope, professional activity and similar variables have not been included in the analysis.

In the Azumi study (see Figure 12.5), the coefficients are somewhat weaker but the path diagram is essentially the same as in the other Aston studies, namely task-scope impacts on the concentration of specialists. The relationship between log personnel size and centralization is weak albeit negative. In Chapter 3, I noted a number of reasons why the concentration of specialists does not have much relationship with centralization, in at least this study of Japanese firms. Here in particular the absence of a professionalism measure might be the explanation.

Although the operational indicator of task-scope in the Paulson study (see Figure 12.6) is even weaker than those used by Dewar and Hage, there is surprising confirmation of the results obtained in this study of wealth and welfare agencies. Task-scope has a primary impact on the concentration of specialists

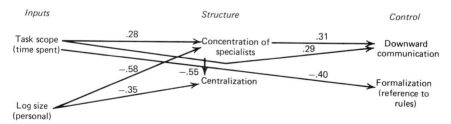

Figure 12.6   The reanalysis of the Paulson study.[a]

and in turn it is this variable that has an impact on centralization. Log size has, again, a negative correlation with centralization but there is little or no relationship with stratification, which is not included in the diagram, although it was in the analysis. Without measures of professional activity or training in this study, however, it is difficult to know whether or not the logarithm of size is becoming a proxy for missing variables.

When one examines the various studies of personnel size and decentralization done by Blau (1970a, 1972, and 1973) and his students (Blau and Schoenherr, 1971; Meyer, 1968 a and b), one is struck by the probability that in a number of these cases it is not personnel size but instead the concentration of specialists and professions in particular that is the major variable. But since there is no measure of the task-scope it becomes difficult to determine if this might not be a better explanation for the *proportion* of specialists as distinct from the sheer number. Their strategy of examining organizations of one kind naturally eliminates the impact of any technology measure such as task-scope. (They have used measures like computers, see Blau and Schoenherr, 1971). If they were to pool their samples of finance departments, work employment agencies, and universities, and include a task-scope measure, very different results might obtain.

The intercorrelation between task scope and the log of personnel size is remarkably consistent at about -.10, indicating that these two variables do vary quite independently and therefore form the basis of a typology about the causes of social structure.

What do all of these studies say about the great debate on the relative importance of technology or personnel size in shaping the structure of the organization? *First,* task scope clearly does have an impact on the concentration of specialists and even the likelihood of more professionalized occupations. If one simply uses a raw count of the number of different occupation specialties rather than a proportion, the impact of task scope is less strong – again underlining the importance of theoretical definitions and the completeness of their measurement (Hage, 1972: Chapter 3). This is consistent across a wide diversity of samples and even measures of this kind of technological variable. This, however does not contradict the findings of Hickson et al. (1969) and Blau et al. (1976) that machine technology does not have much of an impact; it only indicates anew the need for theory to select the right technological variable – task-scope.

Second, once one uses a proportional measure such as the concentration of specialists, log size almost always has a negative relationship, precisely because as Blau has shown many times (1972), with the growth in personnel size the addition of new specialties is likely to proceed at a slower pace. Therefore the real issue is, for which structural variable does personnel size become most important? Despite the large number of studies – including these path diagrams – that indicate a negative relationship between log size and centralization, there is still some evidence to suggest that, in fact, this is because the full impact of the concentration of specialists and how professional they are has not been measured. However, one would want much more research before rejecting this consistent finding.

Third, whether or not log size eventually has a positive or a negative relationship with centralization, clearly one would want to include this variable as a major exogenous factor in any analysis of social structure. The low intercorrelation between technology and size makes them ideal candidates for a typology of organizational systems.

Fourth, the rate of change in task-scope, measured by the number of new programs, does appear to have important feedback effects on the social structures of the organization. Growth in size appears to be less important. However, since these findings are based solely on the Hage-Aiken study, there is a need for more panel studies that in various ways replicate and refine the measures that are employed.

Fifth, the addition of these two exogenous variables does not really change the relationship between the concentration of specialists and centralization. In most of the studies, the former variable retains its negative relationship with centralization.

Given the great diversity in the measures and the generally poor metrics, except for log personnel size, one is amazed more by the similarity of findings than by the many differences in path coefficients. These are in part a function of different kinds of organizations, different kinds of societies, and finally different eras or time periods. Beyond this, the importance of log size may finally rest on its superior metric — as does money — rather than its superior causal force. Counting people produces few errors; measuring power produces many errors. As yet the measurement of task-scope is crude and leaves much to be desired. But these findings at least suggest that it is a factor which dictates the choice of organizational form.

Another reason why it may still be worth while to stick with the hypotheses in this chapter rather than some of the adverse findings is that none of these studies has developed an adequate measure of autonomy. As a consequence, the true impact of both task-scope and personnel size may be over-estimated because it includes some of the influence of unmeasured variables and, more particularly, autonomy. Although task-scope and personnel size have little relationship, one might expect that bigger organizations are also more powerful. Ergo, the negative relationship between personnel size and centralization may disappear once there is a good, sound metric for organization autonomy.

12.2. A MESO THEORY OF RESOURCES, WORK FLOW, AND CONTROL

Although I do not think it is worth using measures of automation or work-flow integration as measures of technology for exploring the relationship between the social structure and the inputs of an organization, I do not want to lose sight of the throughput as a major focus of analysis. This is probably why the concept of technology appears so attractive. One can clearly see the differences between a cement manufacturer and a can manufacturer, or between a custodial prison and a custodial mental hospital (not withstanding Goffman, 1961), to say nothing about the differences between people-processing organizations and product-making ones. The throughputs in terms of content are quite different and this, probably more than anything else, excited the interest in technology as the explanatory variable. This simple elementary fact requires analysis.

In Chapter 11, we noted that a certain part of the control problem centered on the production process. The impact of the inputs of task-scope and personnel size on coordination and control have to be explored as well.

If one examines the original theories about technology, one is struck that most of them really conceptualized the production process and then related this to the choice of control or coordination mechanisms. James Thompson's (1967) theory or typology was long-linked, mediating, and intensive. He discussed kinds of interdependence, again a measure of workflow, but did not make a connection between these and his previous three ideal-types. He suggests that pooled interdependence uses plans, sequential uses schedules, and reciprocal uses mutual adjustment or feedback. Building upon this idea, as we have seen in the previous chapter, Van de Ven, Delbecq, and Koenig (1976) note that there are essentially four kinds of work-flow, which they relate to the difficulty and variability of the task, or what I would call complexity.

In his theory of routine technology Perrow (1967) used four ideal-types, which in turn are explicitly related to the nature of the coordination mechanisms employed. Routine technology is in some ways a description of the production process — literally how much variation in the work-flow there is. However Perrow, in his analysis of the meaning of this concept, really moves in the direction of a description of a knowledge input. This is not accidental, reflecting the very close association between technology as input and technology as process, and is one reason we did not separate them in Part 2 in our discussion of process change. Again, as in James Thompson's work, Perrow perceives the nature of the production process as determining the choice of coordination mechanisms.

Attempting to quantify Woodward's typology, Hickson et al. (1969) developed a continuity production scale that considerably refines her work and suggests a way of combining these various typologies into a more comprehensive one on task-scope and the nature of the work-flow process of throughput.

This intellectual interest in interdependence, work-flow, and the like stems from the recognition of the industrial relations experts and before them, Homans (1950), that somehow the ecological arrangement of machines or of work directly affects interaction patterns, visibility, and therefore at least how much and in what ways people are controlled. Earlier, Blau and Scott (1962) suggested that control and coordination could occur in the machines themselves, as in the pace of the assembly line (also see Blauner, 1964 on this point). But while the insight was readily accepted, quantifiable variables and testable hypotheses were a long time developing. In this respect the theoretical work of Perrow (1967) and the empirical work of Van de Ven, Delbecq, and Koenig (1976) represent major breakthroughs because they provide a theoretical handle on how knowledge as an input shapes the work organizational process or throughput and, through these, mechanisms of coordination/control.

The many studies on the span of control, administrative intensity, and formalization have been concerned with how personnel size affects coordination and control. Much of the theoretical speculation about the two indicators of structural differentiation — job titles and the number of levels and departments — has revolved around the need for coordination (Blau, 1970: Meyer, 1968 a and b). From this has flowed the concepts of flat and tall structures as defined by the ratio between these.

12.2.1. A Typology of Task Scope, Personnel Size, and Work-Flow

Instead of debating whether personnel size or technology is more powerful in predicting coordination/control, it might be much more fruitful to cross-classify these two continua and construct a typology. It may not be either personnel size or task scope, but instead a particular combination of these two variables that determine the mix of coordination and control (Aldrich, 1972). Figure 12.7 shows the association between particular scores on the dimensions of task-scope and personnel size and the work-flow or throughput.

Hall (1972: 119) suggests that size leads to increasing complexity, by which he means more departments and levels, if the technology is routine. Actually, this might be interpreted to mean that personnel size leads to more levels in particular, especially if the task-scope is low. The problem of departments and divisions is complicated by many problems of standardized measure. If the departments are defined solely on the basis of who reports to the executive director or president, then this limits the role of technology (see Dewar and Hage, 1978). All other things being equal, one would expect personnel size to determine the number levels more and task-scope to impact more on the number of departments — especially if functionally defined.

Given both small task scope and small size, a pooled work-flow is also likely with production continuity being somewhat limited. The nature of the technology should be seen as essentially simple, but involving many exceptions. The raw material is perceived as highly stable or relatively uniform. As we have already noted in Chapters 8 and 9, this is characteristic of traditional industry where craft work abounds or else traditional public administration such as in

Figure 12.7   Task scope, personnel size, and work-flow or throughput

Task Scope	Personnel Size	
	Small	Large
Small	Simple problems with many exceptions[c]	Simple problems with few exceptions[c]
	Pooled work-flow[a]	Sequential work-flow[a]
	Production continuity scale of I and IV on Hickson et al.[b] scale	Production continuity of V, VI and VIII on Hickson[b] et al. scale
	Small batch production[e]	Mass production[e]
	Moderately flat structure with[d] few departments	Tall structure with few departments
Large	Complex problems with many exceptions[c]	Complex problems with few exceptions[c]
	Team work-flow[a]	Reciprocal work-flow[a]
	Production continuity II and III on Hickson et al. scale[b]	Production continuity VIII, IX, and X on Hickson et al. scale[b]
	Small batch production	Continuous production[e]
	Flat structure with many departments	Moderately tall structure with many departments

[a] Van de Ven, Delbecq, and Koenig, 1976
[b] Hickson et al. 1969
[c] Perrow, 1967, 1970
[d] Blau and Schoenherr, 1971; Meyer, 1968 a and b
[e] Woodward, 1965; Blauner, 1964

police and fire departments. Elementary schools are another good example of people-processing organizations, although this can vary considerably depending upon the level of professionalization.

Those familiar with the work of Perrow (1967 and 1970a) will note that some changes have been made in his classification scheme, which has inspired this typology. It is not that the analytical problems are unanalyzable; it is more that the tasks are relatively simple, and do not require large inputs of knowledge. This, of course, can change sometimes quite suddenly as it does in some of the traditional crafts and industries. But until recently the body of knowledge has been small — a repository of slowly accumulated experience. In other words, the critical technology variable is not so much the amount of search that Perrow emphasized but the fund of knowledge and its relative size.

The work-flow arrangement, the small batch production, the simple problems, and the like suggest a relatively flat structure with a few departments, each one representing a different craft or skill needed in the production of the work. Cause and effect here are hard to determine. This is why the items are placed in a typology of ideal-types about throughput. These characteristics tend to covary.

More familiar is the sequential work-flow or assembly line that mass produces relatively standardized products. Again, intellectual problems are simple, there are few exceptions, and the raw material is stable. One would expect a very tall structure with few departments. The distinctive resource characteristics are the large personnel size coupled with the small task-scope. In people-processing organizations, custodial prisons, mental hospitals (Goffman, 1961), and residential treatment centers (Street, Vinter, and Perrow, 1966) are examples, although they seldom reach very large size. The military services are the best illustration. Here the much larger size coupled with low task-scope produces wide spans of control as Woodward (1965) and Hickson et al. (1969) have demonstrated. The theory of Blau (1970a, 1972) regarding structural differentiation works quite well with the creation of a number of hierarchical levels that separate the worker from top management. Note that when a manager accepts the use of a universal prescription, for example span of control – should be between five and seven, considerable inefficiency can result.

At the other extreme are team work-flow processes, to use the category developed by Van de Ven, Delbecq, and Koenig (1976), where there is small batch production but of a complex nature. In the production continuity scale of Hickson et al. (1969) they distinguish between simple and complex small batch processes, which I have separated into two different cells according to the level of task-scope. Ideally, their scale at each level of production continuity might be checked to be sure that the task complexity is not being confounded with automation. Certainly one can imagine different levels of task-scope and job complexity involved in the production of a computer on an assembly-line or the making of electricity in an automated power plant, but perhaps this separation is not possible at this level of instrumentation. In team work-flow processes the problems are complex and there are many exceptions. Aerospace, instrumentation, pocket calculators, and radio isotopes are examples in industry. Sheltered workshops, general hospitals, and elite psychiatric hospitals are examples in public administration. The pyramid is likely to be a flat structure, with many departments housing the many specialties.

The reciprocal work flow is likely to exist when there is both large task-scope and large size, typically when there is considerable mechanization. There are complex problems but there are also few exceptions and the raw material is perceived as relatively stable. Here we would expect moderately tall structures with many departments. in industry the chemical, computer, camera, and photo-copy manufacturers are well-known examples. In public administration the most common kinds are likely to be those organizations that attempt to do rehabilitation but at the same time have security problems, such as mental hospitals, re-habilitative prisons, residential treatment homes, and the like. But in public administration, as we have noted previously, it is difficult to find good examples in the United States because the personnel size tends to be small. As soon as we shift to large scale organizations that have multiple units and divisions it becomes easier. The Ministry of Education in France is a good example (although how one decides where to draw the boundary makes a difference). The Veterans Administration Hospital division would be one of the best examples in the United States. It has a relatively large research division but at the same time does a considerable amount of patient care of a more routine nature. Nursing homes may very well be another example if they move in the direction of two departments, one for seriously ill patients and the other for the more routine cases.

Implicit in this typology of throughput are several causal hypotheses that are worth making explicit:

12.12   *Given simple tasks, with many exceptions, and if the size of the work force is small, then the most efficient arrangement is low mechanization with a pooled work-flow housed in a moderately flat structure.*

12.13   *Given simple tasks, as the number of exceptions decreases and the size of the work force increases, then it becomes easier to mechanize and arrange personnel sequentially, housed in a tall structure.*

12.14   *Given complex tasks, as the number of exceptions decreases and as the size of the work force increases, then one must automate and have very high production continuity, with personnel arranged reciprocally and housed in a tall structure but with many departments.*

12.15   *Given complex tasks, as the number of exceptions increases and as the size of the work force decreases, then automation is impossible, and the most efficient arrangement is a team housed in a flat structure having many departments.*

Note the difficulty of really separating the causal sequences. Does large size lead to production continuity — which is after all a technological change — or does the lack of this prevent large size? The variables do combine in different steady states that remain constant for long time periods as Stinchcombe (1965) has demonstrated. Not much advance has been made in the production continuity of automobiles since Henry Ford perfected the assembly line for the production of the Model T. This is not to say that there have not been a number of process innovations over the past half-century that have resulted in a faster production line. But there has not been the leap into the world of automation that everyone expected in the 1950s. Two interesting developments are currently taking place. Automation with robots is being experimented with and the team approach in semi-autonomous work groups, as we noted in Chapter 9. But these are the first qualitative leaps since 1916–1920 when the basic idea of the assembly-line was developed.

Really significant changes in the production continuity of a throughput occur rarely, and when they do it is easy to date their entry. The assembly-line technique largely dominated the development of many kinds of organizations for the period of 1910–1930 (Chandler, 1977). We now appear to have the beginning of the age of automation with the spread of computers, robots, and continuous flow production processes. This will require another half-century of development and modification.

Implicit as well are economic hypotheses about the trade-offs between capital investment in machines and in labor (see Chapter 8), although again one is impressed more by the stability of the work-flow during the past century in many kinds of organizations than by the laws of supply and demand. One must have the machines before one can invest in them!

The work-flow or production process is finally determined by both technology and personnel size. In the latter case, the variable again stands in part for the demand or number of customers/clients and in part for what may be the most optimal physical arrangement of plant and equipment. *The production process, while largely technologically determined by its content, is also shaped and housed by economies of scale.* This is determined in part by size and in part by task scope. They are co-determinant and it is most difficult to argue supremacy of one or the other.

The typology of throughput considerably extends our description of organizational forms, bringing in the many issues related to organizational design. They also indicate how complex are organizational systems. In Figure 12.7 we have added another five variables to the four ideal-type organizational forms and in particular considerably extended the discussion of technology.

How does this typology compare with that developed by Mintzberg (1979) in his recently published book *The Structuring of Organizations*? There are a number of similarities. His simple structure we have called traditional and his machine bureaucracy is the same. However, his professional bureaucracy is sometimes what is here labeled as the traditional form and sometimes what is called the organic-professional. The difference lies in how much standardization of skills there is. With crafts and semi-professionals this is the case but they work in traditional settings. With professionals and PhDs, this is not the case and we have what we have called the organic-professional. His adhocracy would fit this cell as well. His divisional form, I would argue, is a multi-organization and therefore on a different analytical level with a different set of problems. Indeed, his discussion revolves around the problem of capital markets, which indicates at this level that institutional factors become more critical.

A critical difference between the typologies is the much greater stress I give to technology than does Mintzberg, who puts more emphasis on age and size. Beyond this, his discussion of technology is largely limited to the machines and their regulation rather than including the skills of the workforce.

12.2.2. Premises and Hypotheses

But how do these work processes relate to coordination/control? Beyond this, how do personnel size and task scope affect the choice of mechanisms? Personnel size, which means the frequency with which certain events occur, and certainly personnel events – hiring, promotion, the expression of grievances, trips – lead to a much greater formalization. Documents, whether rules manual, job descriptions, or the like, are promulgated. Task-scope has exactly the opposite impact. Its consequence is to see so many distinctions that programming no longer makes much sense. Thus personnel size and task scope have directly opposite impacts on the choice of coordination/control mechanisms.

Here we have a parallel to the problem of decision-making, the subject of Chapter 4. Rare decisions are never programed, but frequently made decisions are delegated and routinized. Task-scope, which means making more distinctions among clients and customers, also means more and more infrequent cases. Personnel size – insofar as it is a proxy for case load – means the opposite.

A theory relating task scope and personnel size to the use of rules and procedures has been developed by Tracy and Azumi (1976) and tested on 44 Japanese factories. Reviewing the large literature, they suggest that what they call task variability is negatively related to formalization but positively related to administrative intensity; they interrupt this essentially as attempts to affect coordination, which reflects a greater reliance on communication as a mechanism. They used sales volume but this is a proxy for personnel size and in any event represents a measure of how frequently cases occur. Similarly, administrative intensity is at best an indirect measure for the volume of communication.

Despite these qualifications there is strong support for their hypotheses. Task scope is positively related to the presence of communication and the absence of formalization. In contrast, personnel size – as measured by sales volume – has the exact opposite pattern. Their analysis included the production continuity scale of Hickson et al. (1969). However, since they have not reclassified this scale (as is done in Figure 12.7), it is a little bit difficult to interpret the findings, except to note that production is positively related to communication and negatively to formalization, although the latter is a weak path. Most interesting is that these two alternatives have no relationship suggesting that they can be mixed in combinations as argued in Chapter 11. However, this study does not control for the impact for structure.

The hypotheses, which can be deduced from premise 11C – that diversity requires the emphasis on feedback and socialization – are as follows:

12.16   *The greater the task scope, the greater the communication volume.*
12.17   *The greater the personnel size, the greater the emphasis on formalization and task visibility.*

*12.18   Given small task scope and personnel size, there is an emphasis on verti-
         cal communication both up and down.*
*12.19   Given large task scope and personnel size, there is an emphasis on hori-
         zontal communication at the top.*

These last two hypotheses make more sense when one examines the character of
the throughput described in Figure 12.7 and the hypotheses describing this.
Pooled work-flow found in traditional organizations makes coordination essentially quite simple. The many exceptions, however, require a vertical flow of unscheduled communication. The small personnel size which is, of course, part of
the small batch production means little formalization. In the previous section,
we noted that the organizations in this ideal-type tend to have customs and
traditions rather than documents and job descriptions. Coordination and control
are simplified given the moderately flat structure and the absence of many
departments.

Reciprocal work-flow is a characteristic of a situation where there are complex
problems but few exceptions. There is a need for horizontal coordination at
the top. The production part of the organization tends to be standardized
whereas the research and development and other staff functions are not. Most of
the coordination problems occur at the managerial-engineering level (Woodward,
1965; Lawrence and Lorsch, 1967a and b) because the tasks are complex. Once
solutions are found, the absence of exceptions allows for a relatively smooth,
standardized production monitored by skill workers. Blauner's (1964) description
of the petro-chemical industry gives one an excellent feeling for this. The advent
of automation and standardized production as opposed to the reliance on either
pooled work-flow or the assembly line can be seen in the studies of a power
plant (Mann and Hoffman, 1960) and of a steel plant (Walker, 1958).

But why should we expect the two resource variables of task-scope and of
personnel size to have an independent effect on coordination/control, even with
structure held constant in multiple regression analysis? The reason is that these
variables affect the throughput, and this has an independent relationship with
coordination control (Hickson et al., 1969; Blau et al., 1976). The work-flow is
the major process to be coordinated; the behavior of workers in this process is
perhaps the most critical one to be controlled. Therefore, one expects both
personnel size and task-scope to affect measures of coordination and control
beyond their indirect influence through social structure. (This is an opposite
position to what I maintained previously, see Hage, Aiken, and Marrett, 1971;
and Hage, 1974, but the evidence has convinced me that I was wrong.)

The production process is after all the most important part of the organization,
since it defines the boundaries of the organization and its mission in the large
society. Furthermore if technology is conceived of as something more than
operations technology, to use the term of Hickson et al. (1969), then it affects

managerial and administrative processes as well. In business schools, management professors (Delbecq, 1976) argue that process affects structure. My own position is somewhat the reverse. But clearly the task-scope and personnel size affect not only the social structure as described in Chapters 2, 3, 6, and 8, but the production and the managerial processes as well. In turn these have an independent influence on the choice of coordination/control mechanisms.

Another argument for their independent influences is simply that we are talking about different coordination tasks which themselves have different causes and solutions. In his analysis of communication patterns Hage (1974) found that treatment or production meetings were not correlated with the social structural variables of complexity and centralization. They represent a different content — the task obviously of coordinating production — and this is determined by the nature of this process: pooled, sequential, reciprocal, team, and the like. In contrast, social structural variables as analyzed in the previous section handle the integration problems produced by diversity or structural differentiation. Since our measures of coordination/control do not separate by content, this obviously confounds the effects of structural and work-flow coordination/control mechanisms. If one could measure the content of different conversations and committee meetings, I suspect one would discover that there are certain kinds of group meetings for the coordination and control of work-flow or throughput and others for the integration of the social structure.

In summary, the causal structure being suggested is this very simple two-step process:

This is another way in which exceptions and qualifications to the theory of social structure can be handled, and it represents still another kind of process analysis.

12.2.3. The Findings

To reduce the number of figures, the control and coordination mechanisms have been included in Figures 12.3–12.6. The following conclusions can be drawn. Hypothesis 12.17 appears well supported by the data in these various studies. Even when structure is held constant, log size has a powerful impact on role specificity in the Aston studies. It is also related to the presence of a rules manual in the Hage-Aiken study. The path coefficient is smaller but we would expect this given the absence of other measures of documents and the much more restricted personnel size range of organizations in their panel study. If one substitutes job specificity in the path diagram, then the relationship between log size is even stronger (r_p = +.37, N = 45). Similarly in the Azumi study (Figure 12.5) — even when structure is controlled — log size retains an impact on role specificity, the Aston measure. When only statistically significant paths are drawn in the Paulson study (see Figure 12.6), there is no direct path between log size and formalization. However, if one relaxes the criterion of significance from .05 to .25, then a positive and direct path appears (r_p = +.31, N = 49).

Although there have been fewer studies of task visibility, essentially the same pattern emerges. Log size has a positive and direct path with rule observation (see Figure 12.4). It does not with close supervision, however, mainly because many of the changes in task visibility are a response to the rapid increase in innovation (the direct path is r_p = +.29, N = 61). The Azumi research is the one study where log size does *not* appear to be related to task visibility as measured by either closeness of supervision or by rule observation. In contrast, the emphasis appears to be on regulations and rules. Thus log size — when the concentration of specialists, centralization, and task-scope are all held constant — has a path coefficient of +.42 with job codification, +.22 with role specificity, and +.42 with the complete formalization scale of the Aston inventory. Does this mean that formalization works more effectively in Japanese companies than in American ones? This is probably the case, but also it must be remembered that there are differences in personnel size between the two samples. The Hage-Aiken sample contains essentially the organic-professional ideal-type where restrictions on formalization are probably greater in any case.

In Chapter 2, the theories of Weber, Burns and Stalker, and Hage hypothesized that formalization and centralization were positively related. Now this hypothesis needs to be changed. *Personnel size appears to have a strong independent effect on the development of the formalization of rules and procedures* (Zey-Ferrell, 1979: 221). Blau and Schoenherr (1971), Child (1972), and others have seen the development of rules as a way of protecting subordinates when they delegate decisions. This certainly occurs but seems most likely in mechanical and mixed mechanical-organic organizations. Sometimes formalization will have a positive association with centralization, as in the organizations studied by Hage-Aiken, which are organic-professional or traditional (but few of the latter). Sometimes formalization will have a weaker association, as perhaps in the mixed mechanic-organic. Personnel size tends to override the impact of centralization. In general, once one controls for this variable, task-scope, and the concentration of specialists, weak positive paths remain. The major exception is the Child study (see Figure 12.3), which has a weak negative path (r_p = −.08). For example, in the pooled time series of the Hage-Aiken panel research, centralization still retains weak *positive* paths with all the measures of formalization and task visibility, even when one holds constant seven variables. Centralization has a coefficient of +.20 with rules manual, +.44 with close supervision, +.16 with rule observation, and +.20 with job codification ($N = 61$). If one restricts the analysis to the last two waves pooled, when additional measures of formalization and task visibility were added, essentially the same pattern emerges. Centralization — and with the same seven controls — has positive coefficients of +.24 with job descriptions, +.14 with rules manual, +.26 with close supervision, +.24 with job specificity, +.21 with job codification, and +.05 with rule observation. Although path coefficients are smaller in the Azumi research, essentially the same pattern emerges. Only rule observation retains a sizeable *negative* path coefficient with centralization ($r_p = -.24$), but this is a single item indicator unlike the index in the Hage-Aiken panel study. *Centralization does appear to have an impact on formalization, but size is the more important determinant.*

In a very different research study Glisson (1978) argued that the routinization of work should be treated as a dependent variable. He largely replicated the earlier findings of Hage and Aiken (1969), finding that centralization had .48 correlation with the specification of work processes, and hierarchy of authority had a .85 correlation ($N = 30$ and where averages of members' responses are employed). It is difficult to determine what is cause and effect, and one can argue that centralization leads to standardization as much as the idea that routine work creates centralization. Indeed, the temporal thrust of Chandler's (1977) work and especially on the railroad industry suggests that centralization leads to standardization. This is one reason why task scope appears to be more of an input than does the routine of work, which reflects the standardization of tasks. Unfortunately, size was not included in Glisson's research.

In a brilliant separation of the micro and meso levels, Comstock and Scott (1977) showed that predictability of tasks leads to lower staff qualifications and more task specialization, as on the assembly-line. Predictability of workflow leads to more centralization and standardization. Again, the causal ordering may be challenged but the association is clear. There were no controls for personnel size.

Although the evidence is less clear, the same can be said for the volume of communication. Especially if one studies unscheduled personnel communication one is likely to find that task-scope, through its affect on the production process, influences the volume of communication and the arrangement of the communication network. Thus Hage (1974: Chapter 9) found that routineness of technology had an independent effect on unscheduled communication at the lower echelons. In the reanalysis of the Paulson study, one finds that both the concentration of specialists and task-scope affect the volume of superordinates conversing with subordinates. Similarly, the research of Van de Ven, Delbecq, and Koenig (1976) at the work group level found that personnel size has some impact on the choice of control mechanisms, even after controlling for task complexity and the type of work-flow.

What remains to be done is to explore more systematically the nonlinear combinations of task-scope and personnel size to see if in fact hypotheses 12.18 and 12.19 are correct. This would also require a much more intensive analysis of communication patterns as is done in the work of Van de Ven, Delbecq, and Koenig (1976) at the micro level and in Hage (1974) at the meso-level. The necessity for dividing multi-organizations into organizations so that more consistent measures of task-scope and personnel size could be found should be equally apparent and may go a long ways towards clearing up the inconsistencies that still exist.

12.3. GROWTH AND THE TRANSFORMATION OF ORGANIZATIONAL FORM

Perhaps the most simple of all of the transformation processes occurs through the process of growth. There are essentially at least two major kinds of growth processes: growth in knowledge, which we will call development or the process of structural differentiation, and growth in personnel size, the more typical one. At various points, we have touched upon examples of the qualitative shifts in forms that occur when one or both variables change quantitatively. Now the series of system changes can be predicted and explicated. The theoretical analysis of task-scope and personnel size, particularly in the Tracy-Azumi theory and the Blau theory (1970a), indicates how these variables allow for the growth of the organization, either by representing lower costs or by creating more innovation. The influences on performances may not be direct but they are there. *To synthesize the arguments of the previous ten chapters, task-scope increases the concentration of specialists which in turn affects the innovation rate. Personnel size would appear at the minimum to lead to much greater formalization and task visibility which in turn lowers costs.* Both of these performances, which as we have noted are somewhat in opposition to each other, change the environmental context – the market situation – of the organization, propelling the organization into a growth cycle either by the development of new products/services which generates greater sales or by lower competitive prices/fees which has the same consequence. *As long as the organization has a competitive edge, either because of the novelty of its product/service or because of its price, growth continues.* This can be the consequence of the visible hand of management as Chandler argued (1977), or else just the superiority of product but in either case the growth in sales or in clients means at the minimum more personnel. Beyond this, continued technological improvement may require constant increase in task scope, a steady proliferation of product lines.

How does growth affect task scope and personnel size? These two variables – along with the as yet not understood organizational autonomy – push the organizational system towards more innovation and efficiency but, in turn, these performances have positive feedbacks on task scope and personnel size (see Figure 12.8).

An *increase* in the innovation rate means almost by definition an increase in task scope and the concentration of specialists. In the Hage-Aiken longitudinal research, prior innovation rate had a path coefficient of .40 with the concentration of specialists even when task scope is controlled. Adding more outputs, the definition of innovation, broadens the range of products and services. Adding new process technologies implies the same because it suggests a greater intensity as well as new specialists, for example, quality control engineers. Both of these imply new occupation specialists. If size remains relatively constant, the concentration of specialists increases.

But personnel size is unlikely to remain constant because innovation implies a growth in demand for the products or services. More outputs also mean more customers or clients which in turn mean larger personnel size. How much growth translates into personnel size depends on the potential size of the demand, a problem explored in the next chapter, but more critically on whether or not the demand is for the same kind of product or service. When standardized workflow, and the mass market both increase, then growth means primarily expansion in size – more employees, more factories or plant sites, and the like. This in turn has an impact on centralization. Admittedly the evidence for this is quite weak but I suggest that if we used participation measures rather than delegation ones, and if we had measures for every year on these variables, this is what would happen. At least we can say that increases in personnel size lead

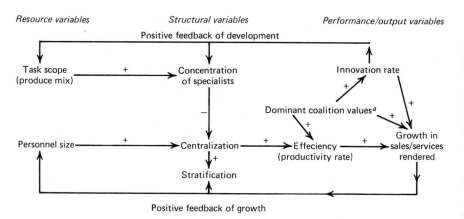

ᵃIt is unlikely that the power elite will emphasize all three values simultaneously; the research issue is which is dominant.

Figure 12.8 Performance feedback on organizational resources.

to a much greater formalization and task visibility, which in turn mean more efficiency.

The diagram in Figure 12.8 is quite simplified, leaving out the production process and the coordination/control variables, and other aspects of the work-flow. For now, we have simplified the dialectic between innovation and cost, which seems the one best supported in the literature.

Since our two exogeneous variables – task scope and personnel size – have a quite different impact (Pugh et al., 1969; Hage-Aiken, Tracy and Azumi, 1976; Paulson, 1974) and yet have no association, they provide two ways in which the transformation of form can occur.

Note that the causes of the process can lie in the values of the dominant coalition, in the structure of the organization, or in the larger environment. In the latter cause, there are again several alternatives. In this chapter, we stress the availability of knowledge and of demand. In the next chapter, the accent is more on the competitive context.

How are the four equilibrium states reached? What are the pathways to each form? Does equifinality operate? The relative availability of the particular resource determines whether the organization evolves and toward which form or steady state. If both personnel size and task scope remain small, there is little growth; the form remains traditional. These are situations where little technical advance is made and where demand is geared very much to individualized products or services. Small batches are produced by craftsmen and artisans. One would expect the dominant coalition to emphasize the goals of quality and stability. Private social work agencies, elementary schools, small furniture manufacturers, clothes makers who place an emphasis on fashion, are all typical of this ideal-type.

But suppose there is a succession in the dominant coalition. A greater emphasis is placed on efficiency, cost cutting, and the like as mechanisms for handling competition. The objective is to increase sales and reach a more mass market. Then the organization starts evolving very rapidly towards a mechanical steady state. Centralization of decision-making and stratification of the status system develop as the organization grows in personnel size. Growth will stop at the point that the efficiency of the organization achieves some equilibrium with demand and the competitive price/fee in the market context. The problem of competitive fee also exists in public administration – although somewhat removed – by means of taxes relative to services rendered.

Thus one reason for a change in the steady state from traditional to mechanical is the emergence of a new set of leaders who push the organization to be more efficient. Some examples of this might be urban school systems, especially during their growth period, the development of mass furniture or clothing manufacturers, and the social security system. But to be effective, the new leaders frequently have to make at least some process innovations so as to lower costs and committedly they must develop mass marketing and transportation systems as did, for example, Robert Hall, who applied supermarket techniques to clothing retail stores.

The more likely reason, however for a transformation of the form in traditional industry and public administration is a major breakthrough in the production process that allows for assembly-line production. It is for this reason more than any other that we celebrate Henry Ford. He gave us the assembly line. And this principle has been applied to many other areas of industry, especially where optimal size is large. But even when optimal size is small, as in convenience foods such as McDonald's, one sees the advantages of the task specialization and assembly line type of production of hamburgers. Why did McDonald's become so successful in the 1960s, when White Tower and Wimpies were less so in the 1930s and 1940s? Both applied essentially the same principals of task specialization. Part of the explanation lies in a sudden and dramatic shift in demand for convenience foods, with price being the major determinant of competitive edge.

It is perhaps more interesting to make predictions about which industries are likely to move from traditional to mechanical steady states because of a quantum leap in the mechanization of the production processes – a radical process change. Chandler's *The Visible Hand* (1977) describes this process in one major industrial sector after another and its impact on the growth of large scale firms. In particular, he details the development of the railroad industry as the first large mechanical organization, followed by retailers, office machine manufacturers, cigarette makers, meat packers, sewing machine makers, and so on. Nor is this process stopped. There are sudden technological breakthroughs and then a whole industry or segment of it starts producing at much higher volume, developing a mechanical organization out of necessity. The development of prefabricated housing and apartment building in the construction industry is a contemporary example.

A very different scenario is the evolution towards the organic-professional equilibrium form. An example of this is where a new group of leaders decides to place a great emphasis on innovation. There is growth, but the biggest change is the expansion of task-scope and the increase in the concentration of specialists. A recent illustration is the food companies reported in Lawrence and Lorsch (1967). Here new technologies of processing (frozen foods) have been implemented and many new outputs are being created – from TV dinners to gourmet meals for quite varying customers. Again while one can see this dynamic as a consequence of entrepreneurs or innovative leadership, a crucial element is the development of knowledge that creates a greater task scope. Technology is more likely to be the explanation for the transformation from a traditional to an organic-professional steady state. Also, a concern for individualized service, meeting small, specialized, or segmented markets accounts for this evolution.

In both of these dynamic explanations the transformation process occurs quite slowly. At some point there is a recognition of a new form or steady-state. The dramatic breakthroughs are few and far between. The more typical causal sequence is an evolutionary one. *Personnel size dominates the change from traditional to mechanical, and technology dominates the movement from a traditional to an organic-professional form.* Both are growth processes but they are qualitatively different. Again, the trigger for them can be either internal or external.

One sees a number of traditional people-processing organizations moving towards the professional-organic as a consequence of the growth in knowledge. Elementary schools have added specialists in remedial reading, social studies, sports, art, music, and the like. In Maryland, different elementary schools have specialized in different programs and children are bussed according to the program they want.

Police forces are becoming professionalized. A recent and illuminating example of this occurred in Madison, Wisconsin when a new police chief was brought in. He tried to change the form of the organization into a professional-organic model. This produced major conflicts and even court cases but eventually the organization was changed. Here is a concrete example of how the transformation frequently involves conflict as a necessary stage. Crime detection is becoming quite scientific. Riot control is a new specialty and meter maids a new task specialty. The computer is more and more an aid in crime control.

Technology is also changing many traditional family agencies. Although we do not think of it as such, the new sex therapy clinics represent knowledge, perhaps misguided (see May, 1969), but technology nevertheless. Social welfare agencies have moved towards family therapy, specialized adoption services, and the like.

Finally organizations can move directly from a traditional to a mechanical-organic state by having simultaneous growth as a consequence of innovation and of lower costs. This appears to have been the pathway for the chemical and computer industries.

We can now define the concept of equifinality as follows:

Equifinality: The existence of alternative sequences in the adoptive process from one form to another.

Organizations that are large and have broad scope, the mixed mechanical-organic, can reach this form by very different pathways. One normal sequence, much emphasized in the literature, is the increase in production continuity and automation is the movement from traditional (small personnel size, small task scope) to mechanical (large size, small scope) to mixed mechanical-organic (large size, large scope). This has been true for many product manufacturers (see Abernathy, 1976). Another sequence is obviously from traditional to organic – professional to mixed mechanical-organic. This is more typical for some people-processing organizations. *Organizations may be created with one of these forms depending upon the environment, a topic for the next chapter, and may move to any other form.*

Changes in the larger environment can influence which of these sequences between equilibrium states is most likely at any particular time. For now the main point is that there is not an inevitable sequence from mechanical to organic nor from traditional to mechanic. Organizations depending upon dominant coalition values, internal structure, and environmental context will move back and forth between these four forms. This is the major thesis. *Permanence of a steady state is unlikely, not only because of disequilibrium but also because of the inevitability of environmental change.* Stinchcombe (1965) has emphasized the long term continuity of throughputs in his provocative article and his thesis is much supported by the definitive research of Chandler (1977). But since the end of the Second World War, there has been a considerable acceleration in the rate of technological change and in population, which in turn has meant the creation of new whole kinds of organizations as well as many kinds of transformations (Toffler, 1970; Aldrich, 1979).

For example, the panel study of Hage-Aiken indicates how the Great Society period upset the equilibrium of a number of welfare agencies. Both task scope and innovation rates in the prior time period were analyzed. Here we can analyze how much impact innovation rate, holding constant task scope, can have on the concentration of specialists as predicted in Figure 12.8. Given the very crude measure of task scope developed by Dewar and Hage (1978) there is unfortunately no change in this variable; it is a constant. However, we can examine the combined impact of these two variables on the concentration of specialists. Both have positive and significant path coefficients. Only task scope has a significant and negative path to centralization. Most of the impact of both task scope and innovation is on the twin variables of the concentration of specialists and professional activity. In turn these variables move the organization not only towards greater decentralization but toward less formalization and emphasis on task visibility, and thus lower efficiency. We thus see the evolution of many welfare agencies along the continuum towards the professional-organic form. Furthermore, we also can predict the sequence of events or the stages in this evolution. During the process and depending upon the speed with which it occurs, many signs of disequilibrium can occur as suggested in Chapters 5, 8, and 10.

Perhaps the most interesting consequence of technology is the creation of new organizations. In the third wave of the Hage-Aiken panel study, a number of organizations were added. In most cases, these had not existed prior to 1963, when the original sample had been drawn. A new treatment center for alcoholics had been started. The mental hospitals had shifted to community care. A number of group homes as half-way houses for mental patients had been created. Likewise another kind of group home for juvenile delinquents had emerged. The traditional county welfare agencies were being reorganized according to function rather than client. Nursing homes were spreading rapidly and being combined in various ways with other kinds of agencies. The popular press concentrates so much on laser beams, radio-isotopes, and other kinds of business technology, that we lose sight of the dramatic changes occurring in the public sector people-processing agencies.

Environments not only facilitate the availability of resources such as technological development and personnel growth, but set limits on the extent of the growth that is possible. In Chapter 6, we noted that there are periods of sudden and discontinuous shifts in customer preferences from innovation in products to cost reduction, or vice versa. An excellent illustration in the 1970s is the concern about the efficiency of higher education and of medical care. Here the constant cycle of innovation begetting task scope begetting innovation has created a growing crisis, a cost crisis.

Furthermore if the innovation rate accelerates too much then the attempts to exert more control via task visibility lower morale even more, resulting in an even greater decline in productivity. At this point some vicious cycle might set in. As we have seen in Chapter 8, this appeared to have happened in many of the organizations in the panel study of Hage-Aiken. Growth in size lowered morale, in part because of the impact on expressive relationships but also because of the impact on control mechanisms. These were designed to handle new personnel with military efficiency.

Therefore, disequilibrium awaits managers and administrators regardless of whether they take the pathway of growth by means of output innovation or cost-cutting or both. One concrete problem is the balance between innovation and efficiency. Another is the balance between morale or turnover and efficiency. Finally, there is the balance of inputs and outputs. Rapid changes in the availability of resources, which are translated into rapid expansion of task-scope or personnel size or both, create still more disequilibrium problems. One change in the system of variables requires a search for a new equilibrium.

Elsewhere we have analyzed the conflict produced by too high a concentration of specialists relative to centralization (see Chapter 10). Now we have one of the causal reasons for this dynamic problem. Too rapid a growth in task-scope is the explanation. The concentration of specialists expands but the centralization of power remains the same. Conflict grows until the structural variables are brought into balance.

But a fast growth in personnel size without the addition of new specialists means a sharp decline in the concentration of specialists. Here the problem is the reverse: increases in centralization and in the development of formalization and task visibility as control mechanisms are not fast enough. Under these circumstances we have not conflict, but organizational anomie marked by little conformity, social integration, and the like. Again we have a manifestation of a serve form of disequilibrium that if uncorrected can lead to the dissolution of the organization.

There are two growth processes. One is technological development, which can be invented within the organization or outside it. The other is the more traditional idea of growth. These mixtures in various amounts push and pull the organization from one form to another. Those are multiple pathways. Furthermore adaptation is not as easy, as we have seen in Chapter 8. Imbalances and disequilibrium occur before a new steady state is reached.

12.4. CONCLUSIONS

At various points in the previous chapters we have alluded to the influence of the environment. Although the bulk of the analysis has been on the internal causes of change in organizational form, in this part, the focus is on the external factors that shape the form of the organization. For simplicity's sake, these have been reduced to three: knowledge or technology, autonomy, and personnel size. Only two of these have been extensively researched and autonomy deserves much more attention than it has received.

Contrary to the literature, technology is perceived as pulling the organization towards the organic-professional form, and personnel size as pushing the form in the opposite direction – towards the mechanical-bureaucratic form. The two variables together begin to generate the essential four ideal-types since they have little relation to each other.

Consistent with the discussion in Parts 1, 2, and 3, these two variables not only influence the shape of the social structure, but the process of decision-making, the rate of innovation and of efficiency, the overall growth rate, and the basis of coordination and control. In one sense these might be considered as internal variables affecting the pace and nature of growth in the organization. They represent the transformation process across time as quantitative changes become qualitative ones, and there is a movement from one stable steady state to the next. But in another sense, these are constraints imposed by the larger environment and this side of the environment – organizational exchange is discussed in Chapter 13. Here, clearly, these three variables – if we now add autonomy – represent resources that exist in the environment and are specific to various sectors (Aldrich, 1979).

The impact of technology may be more pervasive in the long run since we have defined organizations as essentially input, throughput, and output sytems. In particular the throughput or work-flow is technologically given. Organizations can invent new process techniques and skills but these are usually variations on the theme of the state of the art. The whole issue of how size articulates with technology is discussed in the next chapter.

Throughout the previous chapters we have built a steadily more complex model of four organizational forms. Here we have added the three input variables and have extensively analyzed the kinds of general throughput there are. Two basic processes, but both of them the kind that lead to transformation, have also been added: structural differentiation, or the growth in task scope, and the concentration of specialists and the iron law of oligarchy, or the growth in personnel size and centralization of strategic decisions. Together these two processes force organizations into transformations. But the principle of equifinality very much operates. Depending upon when changes occur in either scope or personnel size, organizations evolve in different ways towards various steady states.

Organizational Strategies of Environmental Control and the Choice of Organizational Form

The organization has been conceived largely as an independent actor, concerned with its own problems of pursuing effectiveness in whatever way this is defined, trying to manage conflict and maintain morale, moving in and out of equilibrium. At various points (such as in Chapters 5, 8, and 9) there is a hint of the impact of the environment but it has not been fully discussed. The addition of the available knowledge, size of the available labor force, and organizational autonomy present a set of constraints on the dominant coalition of the organization and its choices regarding how it will pursue effectiveness and what constitutes the meaning of effectiveness. In Chapter 2, I noted that Burns and Stalker suggested that a mechanical form was appropriate in a stable environment and an organic form in an unstable one. Left unanswered is the question, can the dominant coalition choose to be effective in one or the other environment, or in fact are they constrained to pursue certain strategies vis-à-vis their competitors?

We have here an excellent analytical issue: How much does the environment determine the organization and how much does the organization shape the environment? That there is an interaction or exchange, there is little doubt. Furthermore, various individuals can see that the answers can be different depending upon the kind of organization. On the one hand there are multinational corporations and on the other hand there are local schools. We have the defense department and the community hospital. Here we need to distinguish again between the multi-organization and the organization. At the same time we must realize that the essential choice of strategy to control the environment may be made at the level of the multi-organization.

This question of how the organization impacts on the environment has already received two answers. Child (1972a), in a famous article that has led to several conferences (see Warner, Ed., 1977), considered the term strategic choice in opposition to the contingency model of Lawrence and Lorsch (1967). In the latter, the organization is contingent upon the characteristics of the environment, particularly its complexity. This variable, which is largely technological, constrains the organization's decision-makers to pursue certain goals such as research and innovation as a means of surviving. The concept of strategic choice is the reverse idea; dominant coalitions can choose different kinds of structure or organizational forms. Thus Child would argue that irrespective of the environment one will find both mechanical and organic forms in the same industry or public administrative sector. In recent research on five international airlines, Child (Warner, 1977) discovered that mechanical and organic forms were equally effective as measured by profit ratios, turnover, and the like. However, he found that airlines that combined mixtures of mechanical and organic structures were ineffective.

This focus of this chapter is the dialectic between these two assertions about environmental dominance. Can organizations choose their strategies, and can the environments constrain organizational choices? This phrasing, however, is too broad. There are actually not only choices about the nature of the social structure but also choices about control mechanisms, performances, and the like. Likewise, the environment is too subtle to be described by a single variable whether complex (Lawrence and Lorsch, 1967), turbulent (Terreberry, 1968), or stable (Burns and Stalker, 1961). The real intellectual tasks are to determine what the choices are and when they can be exercised, and to determine what the environmental contingencies are and how forcibly they weigh upon the decisions of the dominant coalition. *The thesis of the chapter is that sometimes there is a great deal of strategic choice and at other times a great deal of environmental constraint.*

There are multiple strategic choices and multiple constraints. Unfortuantely, the ones that have been previously emphasized, such as uncertainty, are perhaps not the ones most critical for understanding the extent of strategic choice the part of the power elite. Furthermore in various ways the past work, at least in organizational sociology, has tended to overemphasize the inputs of an organization such as technology and personnel size, and has ignored the outputs and, beyond this, the market context. The real battle over organizational domain (Meyer, 1975) is who has what share of the market — whether customers or clients. This may be set by law, as in the national monopoly of the armed services — although even there is competition — or by a few market context as in farm products. Most typically the market is neither totally free nor regulated. Contingencies and choices revolve around not only the available knowledge, labor force, and power but the nature of this market context, the number of competitors, and the rules of competition.

More recently Chandler (1977), in *The Visible Hand,* has given us a remarkable survey of the growth of both large scale mechanical and of the mixed mechanical-organic organizations during the century roughly bracketed by the 1850s to the 1950s. What is clear in this work is that the technology of mass production is specific to various industries. Each industrial sector moved a certain ways towards monopoly or oligopoly but in many instances this movement was stopped, not by government regulation – but by the problems of optimal size. One finds the number of large firms consistent across a number of countries (Aldrich, 1979: 154, 185). These two characteristics of the environment, extent of technological knowledge and optimal size, provide a framework for understanding how the environment can constrain the choices of the dominant coalition. Chandler's interest is primarily the development of the modern corporation and the divisional structure in particular. In the previous chapter we studied how task scope and personnel size dictate the form, whether private or public. Here we need to see how strategies vis-à-vis the environment – particularly attempts to control the competition – lead to the growth of organizations, and in turn how these choices themselves are dictated by the larger environmental context.

The first section stipulates the variety of constraints and choices and a typology that unites these two sets of ideas. Inherent in the reasoning is that strategic choice varies in its scope as well as its content, depending upon the precise nature of the environmental constraints. Once this is done, the second section focuses on the special problem of domination versus cooperation. Under what circumstances do organizations, and not just multinational corporations but schools, welfare agencies, military services, and the like, exploit and when do they attempt to aid the societies in which they are located? The conflict-critical image of the greedy capitalist is in part correct – but it depends on the nature of the organization and the environment in which it functions. The interdependence of organizations (Turk, 1970, 1973; Aiken et al., 1975) and the nature of their networks has become a popular topic in sociology (Aldrich, 1979: Chapters 11 and 12). Again there is a need for a theory that combines these different perspectives. Finally, the third section integrates these two theories or typologies with the variables in the organizational system of Chapter 12. Both external and internal contradictions become clear and we have another answer to the fundamental problem of what causes transformation.

Many dimensions have been suggested as a way of characterizing environments, uncertainty being the most popular. Aldrich (1979: 63–73) has suggested environmental capacity, homogeneity-heterogeneity, stability-instability, concentration-dispersion, and turbulence. Mintzberg (1979: 268–73) has suggested also stability plus complexity, market diversity, and hostility. Which of these are most important and why needs to be discussed. In various ways they are interrelated.

Perhaps the freshest approach to the problem of how to conceptualize the environment is Mintzberg's (1979: 222) brief discussion of four intermediate variables: comprehensibility of the work, predictability of the work, diversity of the work, and speed of response. Here one has four characteristics of the technical-market complex that in turn allow us to connect more directly environmental variables and organizational characteristics. In the previous chapter we have stressed task scope and personnel size, along with autonomy, as key inputs or resources that are available. Now we need to determine what environmental factors affect these and how these four characteristics identified by Mintzberg articulate.

Throughout the analysis, the emphasis is on the institutional differences between different kinds of common-sense classifications of organizations. An attempt is being made to indicate the major ways in which glass companies are analogous to tire manufactures, and in what ways one glass company is different from another. The dialectic between organizations alike and unalike, to use the title of the book by Lammers and Hickson (1978), is the essence of the chapter. My feeling is that environmental constraints and strategic choices offer the easiest way of understanding these institutional differences and of predicting organizational behavior. The other macro level — the society — is saved for Chapter 14.

13.1. A MACRO THEORY OF ENVIRONMENTAL CONSTRAINTS AND ORGANIZATIONAL CHOICE

Any theory about the functioning of organization in an environmental context must start with the simple assumption that the organization's dominant coalition is interested in some kind of survival. Some organizations are concerned with profit or its equivalent in a socialist economy, which is usually a production quota. Organizations, especially in the public sector, may be more concerned about prestige. Regardless of the measuring stick of performance, there has to be some desire to survive. Companies may be sold, hospitals may close their doors, but in general these are the exceptions that prove the rule. As we have already noted in our discussion of effectiveness in Chapter 5, the selling of a company by an entrepreneur interested in maximizing profit does not mean that this is the goal of the management. One must separate the goals of private individuals, whether capitalists or socialists, who can dictate what the organization will do irrespective of its top management. Many multi-organizations are continually selling and buying companies. This is especially true for certain conglomerates that are essentially holding companies concerned with purchasing companies to making quick profits and then selling them after their assets have been absorbed one way or another. If the boundary of the organization is kept distinct — and the management of the company being sold may not have much choice in the matter, even may attempt to prevent these kinds of take-overs —

then the assumption of survival becomes clearer. Many local welfare agencies, hospitals, and schools are part of a multi-organization called local government. Their administrators may be forced to pursue policies that they would prefer not to (see Lipset, 1960). Our focus is not on the multi-organizational level, familiar names such as Unilever Ltd., Dutch Shell Petroleum, Westinghouse, Volkswagen, Sony, Phillips, General Motors, Texaco, and the like but instead on the divisional or even generic product level that has a distinctive input-throughput-output.

At this level, our assumption remains that the managers or administrators are motivated to keep the organization functioning in its environment. They may be concerned only with satisfying, as March and Simon (1958) assume, or they may be interested in maximizing their goals. Their self-evaluation may be based on profits, prestige, or competitive performance, but some goal or standard exists. Admittedly as Becker and Neuhauser (1976) and Becker and Gordon (1966) have suggested, the visibility of performance makes a great deal of difference in how the organization is structured and how often evaluation occurs. But there is some vague, ill-defined evaluation nevertheless.

13.1.1. The Range of Strategic Choices

If one makes the existential assumption that the dominant coalition at the organizational level is interested in survival and at the maximum holding its own, then what are its choices? Each chapter in this book has analyzed a strategic choice range and its determinants. Organizational leaders can "choose" to be centralized or decentralized, to emphasize efficiency or to maximize innovation, to have happy workers or to pay the costs of conflict, to coordinate by communication or by task visibility, and so forth. But presumably — and this is the central idea of all the theories — these various choices do not vary at random. *Once a "choice" is made in one area, say to have broad task scope, then the "choices" are largely fixed in the other parts of the system.* That is, the dominant coalition "chooses" a high concentration of specialists, low centralization, high volume of communication, high innovation rate, and the like. This does not mean that in reality one finds no exceptions. Data on these exceptions have been reported. But what is crucial is that when other choices are made, difficulties or pathologies emerge. In Chapter 10, conflict was seen as caused by certain combinations of variables — "wrong choices" — on these variables. At various points, ineffectiveness has been demonstrated to flow from wrong combinations of particular variables. Over time and through the information feedback process, manager and administrators learn what are compatible choices. Higher conflict and ineffectiveness cannot be maintained forever. Either they are corrected or eventually there is a succession or the organization ceases to exist.

If this is so, then the next issue is to discover or determine the hierarchy of strategic choices. Where do organization leaders start, assuming that there is a starting point? Consistent with the analysis throughout, it is best to view the environment from the vantage point of four ideal-types or organizational forms.

The first and most important strategic choice for each organization is its stance vis-à-vis its potential clientele, what might be simply called its market objectives (see Figure 13.1). Even here, we quickly perceive that many organizations may not have autonomy to select the business volume. The county welfare department may be forced to take all people who are eligible for their services. Local elementary schools are frequently cited as an example of an organization that has little choice. But does the management of the local grocery store have any more autonomy? They are bound to accept any customer that walks in the door. Conversely, and despite the legal limitations placed on public controlled organizations and economic limitations placed on small private organizations, the managers/administrators have much more choice than may appear at first glance to manipulate the demand size for their product/service. Similarily, the managers/administrators of large organizations in multinational corporations or in national systems of education and of health may have much less choice than would appear at first glance. They may be evaluated on their rates of growth or of efficiency with targeted production/service quotas.

Regardless of the amount of choice available, it is easy to perceive at least four kinds of market objectives: Segmented or specialized, mass, limited mass and highly specialized. The basis of specialization may be by territory or by kind of customer/client or both. Local elementary schools specialize not only on the basis of territory, which is obvious, but – depending upon current laws – by the kind of learning disability as well. Usually, special education is handled in separate schools. Glassware can be made for an exclusive rich clientele that is international, as in the Steuben division of Corning Glass, or it may be made in regional plants designed to meet local needs and tastes. Hospitals in France are organized on the basis of the difficulty and frequency of illnesses into small local ones to handle simple illnesses, to large local ones in medium size cities which handle more complex cases, to regional centers that handle the most difficult and rare medical cases. The latter have the most expensive equipment and best trained staff.

The next choice in the hierarchy represents the means used to achieve the market objectives. A consistent theme in this book as been the relative importance of innovation versus efficiency and quantity versus quality. There is also the variation on these four choices, of the relative importance of human versus material costs – the subject of Part 3 – that can provide further subdivisions. But in the emphasis on performances that are inherently in opposition, the problem of output has not received the attention it deserves. Quantity versus quality is a statement about output, but from the perspective of the market there is a more critical analytical distinction: growth versus stability.

In turn, the means to achieve these objectives are at the minimum threefold:

Figure 13.1 The four ideal-types of organizational forms and the hierarchy of strategic choices

		Organizational forms:		
Strategic choices:	Traditional steady-state	Mechanical-bureaucratic steady-state	Mixed mechanical-organic steady-state	Organic-professional steady-state
Ends				
Market objective	Segmented, specialized	Mass market	Limited mass	Highly specialized
Performances	Quality, stability, moderate concern for efficiency	Quantity, growth, efficiency	Quantity, growth, innovation	Quality, stability, innovation
Means				
Structure	Moderate concentration of specialists (crafts, or semi-professionals) Centralized Stratified	Low concentration of specialists (unskilled) Highly centralized Highly stratified	Moderate concentration of specialists (engineers or civil service) Centralized Stratified	High concentration specialists (professionals) Decentralized Destratified
Inputs	Simple tasks with many exceptions Small to medium personnel size	Simple tasks with few exceptions Large personnel size	Complex tasks with few exceptions Moderate personnel size	Complex tasks with many exceptions Small to medium personnel size

the arrangement of the social structure, the inputs, and the nature of the throughput or production process (see Figure 13.1). The typical equilibrium or steady states for the social structure and the inputs are repeated here. The throughput is detailed in Figure 12.5, including the design of the structure, and needs not be repeated here. Likewise, the special problems of coordination/ control are excluded since they are less relevant and have been outlined in Figure 11.1.

The hypotheses suggested in the previous chapters are that once the dominant coalition pick their market objectives and/or the performance goals there is not much strategic choice left. Consistent with the arguments made throughout, the dominant coalition is forced to make compatible decisions or suffer the consequences. Frequently bad decisions are made, but through the process of learning — the adaptation process — the compatible elements are discovered and the system of organizational variables moves from disequilibrium into equilibrium. The reward is greater effectiveness and reduced conflict. Even these choices may be largely determined, the topic for the subsection of this chapter. But for now let us assume that these choices are in fact available to the organization's management or administrators. Then their structure, inputs and throughputs, coordination/control mechanisms must fall within certain ranges on the variables that have been specified in Chapters 3, 6, 9, and 12.

The crux of the matter is the dominant coalition's strategic choices for its demand — mass or specialized, limited or segmented — and how it achieves this — by innovating or cost cutting, growth or stability. Even here one begins to see how in fact the institutional setting and market context may begin to determine even this choice. In what sense does an organizational elite choose a mass market? This is at least in part a function of how much demand there is. The demand may be determined by need, taste, pocket book, or government law but there is some vaguely defined market, bounded by these four variables. They affect the size and shape of the potential demand. Unfortuantely, organizational sociologists have not thought through the determinants of demand and how this dictates the market objectives of the organization. Dominant coalitions can influence the demand size within certain limits, but these are in themselves dictated by the aforementioned factors.

The first critical decision is the relative emphasis on growth versus stability of demand. It is important that this be perceived as a variable. There is a world of difference between the company interested in growing faster than the demand — that is, increasing its penetration of the market — and those interested simply in maintaining growth parallel to changes in demand and those interested in even less ambitious goals such as the maintenance of some level of sales or production quota or turnover of receipts, if we think of the public administration sector. In one sense, this dimension taps how aggressive the organizational elite intends to be vis-à-vis competition. Although March and Simon (1958) speak of satisfying rather than maximizing, this is a continuum with enormous range. In fact, this is precisely what one wants to explain: the degree of emphasis placed on growth.

Singer had continual growing sales but a steadily declining share of the market during the post-Second World War period. The same has been true for NCR. All the American automobile companies allowed European and Japanese cars to increase their share of the market from 10% to nearly 16% before there was even an attempt to offer a small car. All of these are examples of where companies have accepted moderate growth levels and have not been concerned about market share – until they started to fail dramatically. Indeed, this story can be repeated in almost every major industrial sector in the United States, and is one of the reasons for the balance of payments problems in the 1970s. American companies have been willing to satisfy rather than maximize.

Growth might appear to be irrelevant for the public administrative sector, but this is not true. The growth limits might appear to be greater but there are still quite striking relative differences. Police chiefs can increase business by reporting crimes because there is much latitude in the enforcement of laws (less so with fire departments, which is why they are different). Military services have hardly been passive in their push for more armaments. Since the last decade, this has been one of the fastest growing businesses after energy. The variations in universities are quite clear. Harvard pursued a policy of actually reducing undergraduate enrollment during the 1960s whereas some state universities argued for separate and competitive organizations, and still others tried to create large multi-organizations interested in growth at all costs.

One of the interesting aspects about a choice of maximal growth is how hard the dominant coalition actually tries to enlarge the existing demand. Demand can potentially be enlarged by cutting costs; that is, making efficiency an objective of the organization. Repeatedly in the history of various products we have seen the marginal elasticities operating with rigor. Reduce the price and the market can change from highly specialized to mass market. Chandler (1977) details a number of case histories of this. The efficiency gains in railroading drove rates down and the volume increased rapidly. Singer produced a low cost machine and provided good repair service and quickly captured most of the world market – indeed the company made a profit every year for a century including all depressions. Ford and his assembly line drove down the price of the automobile so that the rising middle class could afford it. Volkswagen did the same with the Beatle. Recently pocket calculators have dropped drastically in price and the volume of sales has soared.

Size of demand is not the same as size of need. Unfortunately, the unpopularity of functionalism has led us to ignore the concept of need and yet if we are to predict how much change in price affects consumption, we require some conceptualization of need or at least unmet desire, which is not quite the same thing. One wonders if some of the products sold really meet needs, but that is a question for another book.

Companies and agencies attempt to influence governments to pass laws that will pay for certain services or purchase certain products. Pollution control laws have led to the rise of a whole new industry. Bicultural education and special education have greatly expanded in areas where previously little visible demand appeared to exist. Although the state enacts the legislation, it frequently does so at the behest of special interest groups and various organizations that stand to gain from the effort. The most striking example is the industrial-military complex and the annual debate over weapons development (Hanneman, 1974).

Demand can also be created by adding new qualities to existing products or services or by creating new products or services – by a policy of innovation. This can take many forms. In some instances, it is simply quality control. In some instances it reflects a distinct advantage in quality. For example, Proctor and Gamble (Vanderwicken, *Fortune,* July 1974: 75 et seq.) will test and perfect a product for as much as ten years before marketing it, and then it will only market a product that will dominate the market. The market share is maintained by adding improvements once or twice a year so that the "old" product always seems "new," just as the automobile companies change their models annually for the same reason.

Many manufacturing companies increase their sales service as a way of adding a qualitative edge to their products. Indeed, increasing this becomes one of the major ways of increasing demand or market share. There have been many examples of organizations generating more turnover in sales/receipts or volume by adding on markets through the strategy of research and development. This is most noticeable in universities (even though one thinks more quickly about the role of research in the drug and chemical business), where an amazing number of new departments have been added, usually because the research focus of a group gradually leads to the recognition of the need to train individuals.

The second critical decision is whether the accent will be placed on the exploitation of existing markets or the creation of new ones. Again we have a variable with a considerable range and much nuance. Some corporations follow the policy of product differentiation with the same technology. The cigarette companies have created a variety of brands to fit a variety of personalities, as have the automobile companies. More innovative is the attempt to manufacture new products that require new technologies, more characteristic of the chemical, electronic, and computer industries. DuPont and IBM are the most famous examples of this corporate policy. But RCA went from broadcasting to development of radios and record players and even computers. Unilever, Ltd. started with soaps, and added a large number of different kinds of household products including chocolate, coffee, and toothpaste. This is the better-known strategy of diversification.

Public administration kinds of organizations can be very aggressive vis-à-vis their environments. The simplest way of expanding client revenues is to develop new outputs that appeal to new clients, which in turn can justify a budget increase, and the addition of more personnel. Thus universities keep creating not only new courses but new departments and implicitly occupational specialities. A rather brilliant example of this was the development of the extension service at the University of Wisconsin, which offered special services, such as information, and developed special courses for adults, including one and two week refresher seminars. Hospitals have generally resisted any attempt to specialize, insisting that they can treat all kinds of patients. Only long-term medical care has been effectively moved to specialized hospitals and thus new organizations (mental hospitals, TB sanitariums, convalescent homes, nursing homes, etc.), except in countries like France, where hospitals have less autonomy. There the rate of specializations is controlled and the addition of new techniques is determined by the Ministry of Health and the Social Security Administration. The typology of strategic choices for generating more demand upon the part of customers/clients is shown in Figure 13.2.

Perhaps James Thompson's (1967) work on the alternative strategies is the most well-known, but it has only two of the six choices listed: horizontal integration and diversification. Both of these strategies might be characterized as the aggressive mode (Maniha and Perrow, 1965), or style of organization-environmental control (control, of course, in the cybernetic sense of the term, see Ashby, 1956) which is an interesting observation. Perhaps our theories are too much influenced by a capitalist notion – an American perspective of inevitable and always desirable growth – that only recently has been challenged. Note that the aggressive mode is the least exercised, although admittedly the most visible (Chandler, 1977) because it has been used by *all* multinational

Figure 13.2   A typology of organizational strategies vis-a-vis demand

Decision to:	Decision to:	
	Maintain demand:	*Increase Demand:*
Maintain product/ service	Product/service protection via price-fixing, territorial arrangements, cartels, etc.	Horizontal integration monopoly or oligopoly
Create variations on existing products/ services	Product/service specialization (same technology)	Product/service differentiation (same technology)
Create entirely new products/services	Product/service replacement (new technology)	Product/service diversification (new technologies)

corporations. The other four strategic choices have been largely ignored, yet they have within them some very relevant strategies such as product specialization and product replacement.

Given the current discussion about the limits of growth (Meadows, et al., 1972), the more interesting strategies involve those that maintain demand vis-à-vis a segment of the market such as product protection, product/service specialization, and of course product replacement.

Perhaps some illustrations of these policies or strategies are in order. About ten years ago the American government charged, and proved in court, that a number of electrical companies had been involved in price fixing. This strategy is best labeled product protection, which should not be confused with the Thompsonian idea of the protection of the core technology. In fact, product protection as a corporate strategy is employed where it is difficult to add distinct qualities to the output and where the possibilities for demand growth appear limited. Thus one finds the use of cartels in the diamond industry, and the tendency is strong in all mining operations. The device of territorial arrangements is frequently employed by the major retail firms. Recently a secret agreement, which divided the electrical market, between the two major electrical products companies in France, Thompson and Schneider, was revealed. The practice of product protection is much more common in Europe than in the United States (where the anti-trust laws are at least applied, if not with much vigor). Why? Because Europeans want stability more than growth.

Chandler (1977) details attempt after attempt on the part of either boards or management in various industries in the nineteenth century to create trusts. Since that period is usually considered the hey-day of trusts and monopoly capital in the history of the United States, it is perhaps surprising that most of these trusts fell apart *without* government intervention. The reason is simple. The much larger market and the rapid growth in demand characteristic of the United States during the latter part of the nineteenth century encouraged growth policies, which mitigated against protective trusts. This was a period when maximization rather than satisfying was the rule.

Local schools, welfare agencies, and the like, practice various devices that maintain demand, precisely because demand is limited by the availability of funds. Territorial arrangements are most often used with schools, but waiting lists are a mechanism for preventing growth in some public organizations. For example many French public bureaucracies are able to obtain high efficiency and control demand by the simple device of long waiting lists for various services. Many people give up, and those applications that are finally processed are done so slowly that future efforts are discouraged. In the United States private welfare agencies, at least those in the United Fund, have followed both strategies: limited case load and specialization in clients. The Jewish agencies take only Jews, the Catholic agencies only Catholics, and so forth.

Niche creation is a viable strategy. Here niche is not used in the sense of a population of organizations of the same kind (see Aldrich, 1979: 28), but rather of what do small organizations do vis-à-vis large ones that use the same technology and that may dominate the industry or sector. Development of a special product that fits a limited need but does not compete directly with products of major or dominant companies – if there happen to be any – is another way of maintaining demand. Examples are Control Data in the computer industry, American Motors in the automotive industry, Universal Studios and American Independent in the film making industry, and so forth. Niche creation is also a very common strategy for many retail stores. The management caters to the special needs of the local customers. This is what keeps many family businesses alive.

Again we do not think of public agencies following a policy of niche creation, but in fact most of them must cater to the local community and fit its specialized needs. Whether police, fire, school, or park service, most departments in local governments follow the policy of catering to local demand. Indeed, this is the standard argument as to why governments should be decentralized.

Product replacement may appear to be a strange strategy, but it is becoming increasingly common as the product/service lifetime grows shorter and shorter (Mansfield, 1968), Studebaker started out in the 1850s making covered wagons. When the automobile came along it replaced one product technology with another. After the Second World War, it followed the strategy of niche creation, and to a lesser extent horizontal integration, when it purchased Packard. Both strategies failed and Studebaker tried product replacement again, closing down its automobile plants and concentrating its business on air conditioning. Here is where the distinction between multi-organization and organization is so crucial. As we shall see in the next section, there are forces that have been driving both private and public organizations into the multi-organization form, or divisional structure, to employ Chandler's (1962) term. Whole organizations can be let go and the multi-organization continues to survive.

Cigarette companies have moved into food products. Mobil Oil has bought Montgomery Ward. Exxon (Uttal, *Fortune,* April 1977: 166 et seq.) has invested venture capital in many small highly specialized companies. W. R. Grace has gotten out of shipping and become largely a holding company. The Japanese holding companies have been particularly adept at product replacement, moving out of textiles into more profitable endeavors. The multi-organization has the maximum flexibility, especially insofar as slack funds are invested in those organizations or divisions that have the greatest growth potential (see Martin, *Fortune,* April 1976: 118 et seq. for the sample of the Beatrice Food Co. and O'Hanlon, *Fortune,* June, 1975: 114 et seq. for another example).

Many American multinational corporations have currently been selling their more traditional divisions in Europe as the sales of cheaper products from various underdeveloped countries penetrates this market. Conversely the Europeans have been buying a number of American companies, taking advantage of the cheap dollar and the general lack of competitiveness, to diversify their risk. Korvettes was recently purchased by the French, and A&P Food Co., one of the largest food retail chains, by the Germans. Not to be outdone, the British have purchased Howard Johnsons.

The strategy of product/service replacement is not usually discussed in public administration and yet one of the most famous organizational studies, that of Sills (1957), deals with the case of the National Polio Foundation. The growth in medical technology led to the development of a vaccine that largely eliminated the disease, and moved the issue to public health departments. Sheltered workshops first dealt with the unemployed, then moved to the physically handicapped (Kimberly, 1976), and then to the psychologically handicapped (mental illness and retardation). Now there is a consideration of the socially handicapped — if that is the right word — in the current programs for ex-prison convicts and the like. Of course not all of this has been service replacement. Some of this reflects a growth policy. Orphanages overloaded with customers in the nineteenth century have shifted to taking care of children with emotional problems or have become residential treatment homes (Street, Vinter, and Perrow, 1966). T.B. sanitariums are now handling problem children in France. These are clear examples of product replacement but in people-processing organizations.

How articulate or conscious are these strategies? Despite all the images of organizations and their leadership as rational, probably few have articulate strategies until some environmental crisis occurs and the management/administration finds itself forced to think about survival and search for alternatives. In several research studies Mintzberg (1973 and 1978) has indicated that many organizations do *not* have a conscious articulated strategy vis-à-vis the environment. The dominant coalitions muddle through, making probably many wrong decisions, steering to use the cybernetic concept; but gradually by the force of events and of facts they developed some conscious strategy vis-à-vis the environment. Rational strategies only appear in textbooks and classrooms — never in boardrooms or in corporate plans — although this is perhaps less true today than it was in the nineteenth century.

Throughout our discussion of strategic choice one must remember that these choices are usually made only once at some critical hisotrical moment and then played out over a very long time span. Chandler (1977) documents this nicely for a number of companies and whole industries. Railroads tried trusts, found them wanting, and grew into about seven major groupings. Shipping, however — given the nature of the technology — never became anywhere as near as oligopolistic. In contrast, Singer Sewing Machines developed a strategy in the 1850s that allowed it to dominate more than 70% of the market for a century. The development of a new machine technology in cigarette manufacture meant only a few companies could supply the entire world. The ones who succeeded were those who practiced the principles of mechanical-bureaucratic organizations better and more efficiently. Similarily, business machines, electrical equipment manufacturers, agricultural equipment, meat packers, and retail chains were largely created in the latter half of the nineteenth century. Once they developed a successful mass-produced product or provided a mass service, a few companies came to dominate. *The number of successful companies is in part a function of the technology.*

This does not mean that there have not been critical moments when various successful companies have been forced to change their strategy. Ford Motor had to do so in the 1940s, US Steel in the 1950s, Singer and all of the cigarette manufacturers in the 1960s, all of the energy companies and NCR in the 1970s, and so forth. Times do change and the most successful companies tend to be the least adaptive, as we argued in Chapter 8.

Once a company chooses to produce a standardized product such as telephone equipment it cannot shift overnight to another product. Mental hospitals don't become general hospitals, and vice versa. In this sense, at the operating level of the production process or throughput, there is a strong technological fix. The same is true for the organization's strategy vis-à-vis the environment. The market strategy of selling a mass-produced product at low cost is a choice usually made at the early stages of a company's history, or at the historical moment when the potential for demand becomes great. The decision is *not* repeatedly made. It is institutionalized into the system and acted out by succeeding generations of members. The dominant coalitions are socialized into the rules of the game. To change marketing strategy from innovation to efficiency, from stability to growth, from quantity to quality or the reverse is to change the rules of the game. Most unlikely. A very rare kind of decision and one of very high risk. In Chapter 4 we noted a number of examples of where the dominant coalition did try a new strategy — and failed. We need not repeat the examples here.

This does not mean that there are not shifts in relative emphasis. It goes without saying that if the general economy slows down, the dominant coalition may be less interested in pursuing a policy of growth and may become more concerned with simple maintenance of its market position. During these moments price-fixing or territorial arrangements might become attractive. Similarly, conglomerates tend not to purchase companies or even sell them during recessions. Again during these times, one considers closing out unprofitable lines of business by simply dissolving them. There are undulations in corporate strategy just as there are movements in the relative emphasis on which performances are important in demonstrating effectiveness. Indeed, these undulations are themselves in part environmentally determined. But over the long haul, one can see that there are fairly consistent market strategies. As we shall see, these are institutionally determined.

Another qualification is that there are several different strategies pursued in multi-organizations at the same time, one choice for one division and another for another. In public welfare, family therapy and child care are placed in divisions separated from the income maintenance and medical care. Chronic and acute mental illness are handled with different technologies, and housed in separate divisions. We have already observed that special education typically occurs in separate schools. High and low priced cars are always built in separate divisions. The different producing and marketing problems of explosives and paints forced DuPont to shift to a divisional structure (Chandler, 1962). This can occur even within the same division if it does not cover more than one process technology or kind of market.

There is considerable range of variation within each ideal type. Horizontal integration can be either the ruthless pursuit of monopoly – as practiced by Standard Oil under the direction of Rockefeller, US Steel under the direction of Morgan, and other industries directed by the robber barons, a strategy common in the United States during the latter part of the nineteenth century – or the continuation of oligopoly as practiced by General Motors, IBM, CBS, J. Reynolds Tobacco, and other industries controlled by antitrust legislation. Furthermore, what constitutes an oligopoly can vary considerably; some mangers will feel secure if they have 50% of the market, others need only 20% or even 10% to have effective control over their environment. For example General Motors, which is in a position to eliminate all competition in the automobile industry in the United States – if it wanted to and if the government were willing to allow this to happen – has systematically tried to *prevent* its penetration of the market from getting larger than about 55%. The consequence has been a larger profit sales ratio than is characteristic of the entire industry. Here we see the pivotal role that organizational autonomy plays. If the larger society rules out certain strategies then the choice is even more constrained.

13.1.2. The Range of Environmental Constraints

In our discussion of task scope in the previous chapter, considerable emphasis was placed on task complexity and the number of exceptions. This seems to be the theme that underlies Perrow's work (1967; 1970) more than routineness and is central to that of Van de Ven, Delbecq, and Koenig (1976). This also appears to be the real theme of Lawrence and Lorsch's (1967 a and b) seminal work. The many references they give in their bibliographies appear to be adequately classified by task complexity or technological sophistication rather than by routineness *per se,* although one can note subtle nuances in their discussions. The size or range of task scope is constrained by the amount of task or technological knowledge relative to the production of the product or the provision of the service as we have already noted in the previous chapter. *Organizations*

are environmentally dependent on the amount of task knowledge that exists.
As this grows, task scope tends to grow both extensively and intensively. Increasing knowledge means more journals filled with more pages that contain
more ideas. The mass of medical journals overwhelms and staggers the imagination. The same can be said for business organizations that depend on physics
and chemistry. This growing knowledge means more distinctions in customers/
clients and more applied ideas as how their needs can be met. Although the importance of environmental complexity (Mintzberg, 1979: 268) or technological
sophistication has been recognized by a number of authors (Lawrence and
Lorsch, 1967; Woodward, 1965; Duncan, 1972), the theoretical linkage with the
choice of system type has not been made as precise as it might be.

The reasoning usually used is that the uncertainty of the technological market
segment of the environment puts a heavy premium on the expertise of researchers. Instead, it would appear that the complexity or difficulty of their
task flows from the amount of knowledge there is. In the previous chapter, we
noted that the greater the amount of knowledge, the greater the task scope. But
here we need to specify the impact of knowledge on the nature of the demand.

*13. 1   The greater the technical knowledge, the more likely the demand is to be
specialized and limited in scope.*

The essential theme of complexity in knowledge is the awareness of more or
more distinctions. In turn this means that the market is not perceived in terms of
a mass but instead as a wide variety of different kinds of clients or customers.
Thus market diversity is technologically given (Mintzberg, 1979: 268).

Another kind of impact that the growth of knowledge has and one apparent
in our discussion of task scope is that there is a greater diversity of work. Knowing more means that one can do many many more things — offer more products
and services. It is perhaps an obvious point but one that needs to be stressed.
The hypothesis is:

*13. 2   The greater the technical knowledge, the greater the diversity of work
and therefore the larger the task scope.*

Most people have a negative image of technology but the paradox is that in
many cases it allows for much more individualized treatment. The point of
numbers in the computer is to allow for more individualized attention to those
who need it. The most striking examples of this are the attempts at individualized instruction and medical treatment. Robots and other machines are developed to take over unpleasant work — providing service and meeting specialized
needs. Increasingly companies sell not products but service. This is precisely
most common in the technologically intensive areas.

The impact of the growth in knowledge or demand is perhaps easiest to perceive in the public sector. The proliferation of courses in education, disease entities in medical treatment, and the distinction among kinds of family therapy needs are all technologically determined. One must have the knowledge to recognize that there are kinds of students, patients, or clients. The point is a simple one but frequently not considered.

Concomitant with a large amount of technological knowledge, is usually a relatively rapid rate of product or service creation. Expanding knowledge shortens product life, making it increasing important for an organization's decision-makers to emphasize innovation as a performance goal. The hypothesis is:

13. 3 The greater the growth rate in technical knowledge, the shorter the product life.

Mansfield's (1968) review of the evidence on product life is not conclusive, but many believe that product lives are in general getting much shorter. It is this that seems the best approximation to turbulence (Terreberry, 1968). Shorter product lives are especially the case in those industries dominated by large R&D budgets such as weapons, computers, drugs, photocopiers, certain chemical products, and the like. On the people-processing side, the dramatic case is medical care and hospitals in particular.

Clearly product life means a great deal to a corporation. The shorter it is, the more the company must expand its innovation rate to maintain its competitive edge. This is most striking in the drug industry (Robertson, *Fortune,* March 1976: 134) but is also characteristic of specific companies that were built on research such as Polaroid (Ardtz, *Fortune,* January 1974: 82 et seq.), Xerox (Ardtz, *Fortune,* September 1974: 116 et seq.), and IBM. In general, as knowledge increases the rate of product innovation does as well.

The impact of shorter product lives on management including researchers is to increase the need for fast responses. If one does not quickly exploit the new idea and capture 50% of the market, then there is not much point in entering into production. This leads to a fourth hypothesis:

13. 4 The greater the growth rate in technical knowledge, the faster the needed reasponse rate.

Two of Mintzberg's (1979: 222) suggested intervening variables — diversity of work and speed of response — are now included in our discussion of the connection of technical knowledge to the specific organization. Part of the experience of future shock (Toffler, 1970) relates to this dynamic of growth requiring faster responses on the part of organizations.

The second major constraint is largely economic and is best expressed in terms of potential demand and its impact on operating budget and personnel size. This may be determined in the market place by the laws of supply and demand or in the legislature by the laws of the balance of power between the working and middle classes (see Hage and Hanneman, 1979), but in either instance there is some goal of available customers/clients that represent cash sales or fees for service for which various organizations are competing. This in turn affects their operating budgets, personnel size, and the like. The hypothesis is:

13. 5   The greater the potential demand, the greater the average personnel size.

This really is nothing more than the traditional economist's argument about economies of scale. Given large demand, then large scale organization is possible. The organization's decision-makers find it more efficient to hire their own specialists in various areas as Blau (1970a) has hypothesized. This relates to environmental capacity (Aldrich, 1979: 63) because it means more resources.

Closely related to potential demand is predictability of demand. Much more than uncertainty, this variable really affects the optimal size. Clearly, as demand becomes unpredictable, organizational elites cut back in size. The hypothesis is:

13. 6   The less the predictability of potential demand, the smaller the average personnel size.

But potential demand is not the only economic factor that dictates certain aspects of the organizational system – in this case its size. It also affects the choice of a performance utility – in this case, the importance of efficiency.

13. 7   The greater the potential demand, the greater the importance of efficiency.

The logic underneath economies of scale is the necessity of emphasizing price or cost of operation. Presumedly the more important that quality becomes and the more the size of the market is limited – which are in part the same statement since, as I suggested in Chapter 8, quality means individualization of products and services – the less and less critical efficiency or cost becomes. Price changes produce little change in demand, neither increasing nor diminishing it. In contrast, with quite standard products that everyone wants, price can make an enormous difference. Customers do shop around. The competitive situation is quite intense. Publicly owned Renault in France finds that the large demand for cheap cars makes cost one of the decisive factors. However, very expensive cars such as the Matra sports car made by privately owned Simca (Chrysler in France) are fairly inelastic in price. Small changes will have little or no effect on the demand.

These dynamics of demand size and the importance of efficiency also operate with public organizations, whether economic, political, educational, health, or the like. Primary schools have for a long time been dominated by efficiency concerns. In contrast universities with a very small demand *in the past* have been more concerned with quality, and efficiency has not been a major concern. This does not mean in all of these examples that efficiency has been of no concern or the only concern but that in the hierarchy of values it is sometimes first and sometimes last, which is a different statement. It is a matter of emphasis.

There is a very peculiar way in which technology and demand interact that is specific to each technical market sector or task environment. Chandler's (1977) study of the growth of the modern corporation indicates how sudden breakthroughs in the process of mechanization dramatically alter the price of a particular product or service, making it available for all. These breakthroughs are major discontinuous events and they usually are associated with either the invention of a new product or the creation of a new process technology that alters the volume of production, as in the case of the cigarette machine, the assembly line for the car, and the mechanization of machine manufacturing more generally. Xerography is a contemporary example of a process invention that radically cut costs. The computer is another.

What has driven up the standard of living has been largely the growth in productivity. Most of these gains are provided by machines, although economies of scale and managerial effectiveness can have an impact as well.

The amount of technical knowledge and the demand size thus in various ways subsume a number of dimensions that have been proposed for describing the environment. The amount of knowledge affects turbulence, increasing it, because of shorter product lives, and the need for faster responses. It leads to more complexity and greater product-diversity. Large demand means large environmental capacity and also implies greater stability in that demand as well – that is, predictability.

We have said nothing about uncertainty. There are a number of problems of measuring this (Aldrich, 1979: 126-132). Although I feel member measures of internal properties are important, still one desires measures other than perceptions for the external environment. One can agree with Mintzberg (1979: 224-226) that the real issue is how both contingencies and perceptions of them affect organizational structure.

Although the amount of knowledge and the demand size do not represent all the environmental dimensions that one wants, they do seem to predict to a number of internal resources and objectives that have been identified as important. They also escape some of the measurement difficulties associated with uncertainty. Three of the four dimensions suggested by Mintzberg (1979: 222) have been included as well.

The third major constraint is political but is perhaps best expressed by the variable of available power. What characterizes the concept of the free market is not so much the idea of price competition, which is what economists like to talk about, but instead available power, the freedom to do anything without controls from someone else. It is not easy to quantify this concept of available power but one can at least state, relative to a particular kind of institution, how much the organizations are allowed to choose the volume of work, the nature of their operating budget, the personnel qualifications, and the like. It is therefore the exact counterpart to organizational autonomy and is usually different for each kind of organization. The hypothesis is simply:

13. 8   The greater the available power, the greater the organizational autonomy.

This is largely a truism and therefore like the two others perhaps not very insightful.

What makes the hypothesis more interesting is the quantification of the available power. The sheer difficulty of this makes the issue worth some extended effort. One needs to identify all of the relevant interest groups and determine how much power they have. For example, the power of the consumer movement has clearly increased in the United States with some dramatic results especially vis-à-vis the automobile manufacturers. Likewise the development of community boards, usually somewhat toothless, is at least an attempt to bring underrepresented interest groups such as blacks into various HEW organizations. The American government has been adding both carrots and sticks as a way of inducing organizations of all kinds to change their policies on everything from hiring to firing, from pollution control to investment rate. The governments in Western Europe and in Japan have proceeded much farther down this road. But how much carrots and sticks really limit the autonomy of organizations is another issue, one that is discussed again in the next chapter. Cooperative relationships between institutional sectors have the possibility of augmenting the autonomy even more than it may be restricted by providing more resources and more environmental stability. More interesting is the impact of available power on the choice of strategies, which is discussed below.

13.1.3. The Typology of Environmental Constraints and Organizational Choices

We have suggested that knowledge and economic constraints dictate the inputs of task scope and personnel size and the relative importance of innovation rate and efficiency as utilities to be emphasized by the dominant coalition. Ignoring for the moment the role of power constraints on the system, these two variables — technological knowledge and potential demand — can be cross-classified to create a typology of organizational constraints that allows us to predict what are the right choices of marketing strategies (see Figure 13.3).

Figure 13.3 The environmental constraints of task knowledge and potential demand and organizational strategies

Task knowledge[b] (level of complexity, number of exceptions, rate of change)	Potential demand (level of personnel size, operating budget)[a]		
	Small	Medium	Large
Low	Product/service protection	Mixture of protection/horizontal integration	Horizontal integration
Medium	Product/service specialization	Mixture of specialization and differentiation	Product/service differentiation
High	Product/service replacement	Mixture of replacement and diversification	Product/service diversification

[a]This assumes that personnel size and operating budget covary. This is less and less true and therefore produces additional variations in strategies of environmental control. Rough guide lines are for each organization or division: 10–99 employees is small, 100–999 is medium, 1000–9999 is large, and 10,000–99,999 is very large.

[b]This assumes that complexity, number of exceptions, and rate of change covary, which is not always the case. Rough guide lines are the percentage of sales or turnover or employee time engaged in research. Under 1% is low, 1–9% is medium, 10% or more is high.

443

13.1.3.1. The Environment of Large Demand and Low Task Knowledge. If technological sophistication is low, then so is the rate of technological change as well. Typically these industries and public sectors are fixed technologically at a particular point (Stinchcombe, 1965). There may be a rapid period of development of the output and then a very long period in which improvements in the process technology occur but at a relatively slow rate. The railroad and telegraph in the middle of the nineteenth century are examples. Essentially the technology of the former was perfected in the 1840s (Chandler, 1977: 82). The major innovation in the latter was fixed even before 1850 (Chandler, 1977: 247). This was followed by the manufacturing of the sewing machine by machine in the 1850s. The cigarette-making machine was invented in 1881 and led to the rapid concentration of this industry. Match, soap, and film making by machines were all largely perfected during the same decade. At about the same time, machines for processing grains and canning food were developed as well.

In the 1890s meat packing, oil refining, office machines, elevators, and linotype manufacturing all followed the same pathway to concentration. In this century, tire and automobile manufacturing are the most well-known examples. If potential demand is large, and especially when the investment needed for optimal size is quite great, then the most appropriate strategy is *horizontal integration.* The company or companies will attempt to approach the upper limit of monopoly by eliminating competition. This upper limit is set by the available power given in antitrust legislation and other government regulations.

Here we may quote from Chandler (1977: 347)

The largest manufacturing firms, whether they grew large through merger or internal expansion, were clustered in industries with characteristics similar to those in which the integrated enterprise first appeared in the 1880s and 1890s. . . . The large industrial enterprise continued to flourish when it used capital-intensive, energy-consuming, continuous or large batch production technology to produce for mass markets. It flourished when its markets were large enough and its consumers numerous enough and varied enough to require complex scheduling of high volume flows and specialized storage and shipping facilities or when the marketing of its products in volume required the specialized services of demonstration, installation, after-sales service and repair and consumer credit. It remained successful because administrative coordination continued to reduce costs and to maintain barriers to entry.

In other words, optimal size is large and costs can be reduced by means of machine intensive technology and large scale operation. Furthermore, Chandler here does not emphasize another point: the technology remains largely static. Small improvements are made, management is perfected, machines do improve but the essential advantage lies with the company that first puts together machines, administrative coordination, and marketing strategy.

Aldrich 1979: 149–51) quoting Caves (1972) notes that the economy of scale *prevents* new companies from being formed. Once a few large companies control most of the market, then it is nearly impossible for a new large company to be created. Small companies may practice niche specialization vis-à-vis the large ones but this means specialized markets of small size.

Today most of the successful companies of the nineteenth century are still with us, although some have become multi-organizations or divisions in multi-organizations. Singer, Western Union, the major railroads, Kodak, Otis, Standard Oil, Armour, Swift, Wilson, Anheuser Busch, Schlitz, Quaker Oats, Heinz, Bordens, Libby's, Coca-Cola, California Packing (Del Monte brands), Pillsbury Flour, National Biscuit, American Tobacco, Campbell's Soup, Proctor and Gamble, Diamond Match, and so on are all examples. Furthermore, although these are all American examples, their European counterparts – and in the same industries – have done the same: Unilever, I.G. Farben, Imperial Tobacco, Imperical Chemical, British Motors, Peugot, Critoën, Thompson, Phillips, Nestlé, the major Japanese holding companies and so forth.

We have already noted that these organizations have the mechanical form as described by Burns and Stalker (1961), with the rational-legal bureaucracy among their managers as described by Weber. The demand is determined by price advantage so the logic of the operation is to perfect the standardization of the production process and to keep costs as low as possible. Low wages are one policy of this kind of organizational system. What innovations there are are of a process nature and these occur rarely.

Given price advantage, the mechanical organization can drive all of their competitors to the wall. *Typically this is done by producing at faster speed rather than simply producing a large volume.* For example, Henry Ford's assembly-line dropped labor time making a car – the Model T – from 12 hours and 8 minutes to 2 hours and 35 minutes in the fall of 1913. By the spring of 1914, the plant in Highland Park was producing 1000 cars a day and the average labor time was reduced to 1 hour and 33 minutes (Chandler, 1977: 280).

The high speed of throughput and the resulting lower cost gave John D. Rockefeller his initial advantage in the competitive battles of the American petroleum industry. In the 1860s increased size of the still, intensified use of energy, and improved design of the refineries dropped the price per barrel from 6¢ to 3¢ (Chandler; 1977: 256).

High speed machines in cigarette manufacturing dropped the cost per pack to one-fifth of what it had been. The same advantages occurred in all of the examples and industries cited above. Gradually, all of the competition is eliminated or absorbed. The environment consists of several large companies or a single dominant one. This happened in each of these industries. Standard Oil largely controlled the petroleum refining sector until it was broken up in 1911. Singer had 70% of the world market by the turn of the century. Essentially four meat packers accounted for this sector, while US Steel, which was founded in 1907 but with Carnegie as the major element, controlled over half of that industry. We have monopoly capital in its most stark form.

The managerial elites achieve efficiency by routinization of the technology, standardization of the product, use of unskilled and relatively cheap labor, the maintenance of high production and thus the avoidance of innovation in products, and so forth.

Crozier's research on a French public bureaucracy (1964) indicates that the problem of high volume production is not limited to manufacturing. Chandler (1977) reports the development of retail stores such as Sears, Roebuck, A&P Food Co., Montgomery Ward, and the like. In all these instances, the same standardized service is being provided to a mass who needs it or wants it.

The dictates of optimal size are also clearly operating. *By comparing the limits to monopoly growth in particular industries one discovers where the limits of technology and of coordination exist.* Western Union controlled all telegraphs, but the railroads never became one single corporation or trust. Shipping, which has an even smaller potential for high volume throughput than railroads, remains even less concentrated. Singer built the perfect sewing machine but more complex machines with more limited markets did not become as concentrated.

13.1.3.2. The Environment of Small Demand and of Low Task Knowledge.

As soon as potential demand is small there is room for other strategies and especially that of product specialization – provided we continue to speak about a relatively standard product that does not require much technological sophistication. The furniture, clothing, and house construction industries are all good examples. There are a large number of medium to small companies that turn out quality products for certain tastes within the public; they develop a product line and this becomes their niche within the larger market. Note that this is a successful strategy in those industries where fashion or taste are to a certain extent dominant. At the same time, there are moderately large companies that produce standardized clothes, furniture, or houses at low cost that fall more in the middle of the continuum and approximate more the mechanical form but with many traditional elements.

Why are these large companies unable to drive out all of their competitors, even though they pursue the strategy of horizontal integration? The answer is that when the initial investments needed are small, businesses can be easily started. Almost any mason can start as a contractor. The same is true for the cabinetmaker, the tailor, and other artisans. Insofar as they have some flair for design and for business, they do not need large capital investments or large demand. There are not scale economies operating as a barrier (Aldrich, 1979: 149-51). These can appeal to a small, limited, and highly specialized market. It may even be nationwide but it is still small. If the small manufacturer has a successful line, then the large manufacturer must develop a competing product. This can not be done. There are too many tastes; even the large manufacturer must accept a certain segment of the market, but a large one nevertheless.

This cell in the typology is populated with traditional organizations. The niche in the environment is usually provided by a distinctive quality, taste or service. Typically in public administration there are territorial arrangements such as school districts or client specialization such as in religious agencies that handle only those of their own faith. The Catholic, Lutheran, and Jewish religions in the United States built their own organizations to take care of their own: schools, hospitals, welfare agencies in the nineteenth century, and nursing homes, old age homes, sheltered workshops, resident treatment homes in the twentieth century. Only the costly public services such as university education, mental hospitals, TB sanitariums, and the like have been largely in the public sector. But even here there has been an amazing amount of segmentation of demand by religion and by social class, with the private sector especially trying to meet limited markets.

In this ideal-type we can begin to say that in fact there is some strategic choice available to the management or administration. They can choose to emphasize quality and remain small in size and budget, with an emphasis on craftsmanship, or push in the direction of more mass production, growing in size and budget with a more mechanical structure. But there is a limit to the potential demand that prevents the organization from pursuing horizontal integration to its logical limit. The economies of large scale do not operate; demand relative to taste is inherently limited. Price does not dictate nearly as much.

13.1.3.3. The Environment of Large Demand and of High Task Knowledge.

A very different environmental situation exists when the product/service represents a high level of technological sophistication and the potential demand is great. The electrical, metallurgical, and computer industries are all examples (see Freeman, 1974). More difficult to classify is the chemical industry, which has companies of all sizes. On the one hand there are chemical companies such as drug manufacturers that have a highly specialized technology and markets and on the other hand, synthetic textiles manufactures and other mass products that are also technologically intensive but have enormous demand potential. It is the latter kinds of companies that are the main concern here. What is distinctive about these industries is that they have generally followed the policy of product diversification.

The rate of technological change and the availability of slack funds and research personnel make the development and exploitation of new technologies a more effective means to employ underutilized resources. Conversely, to achieve a monopoly position when there is a high rate of technology change is best done by constant innovation. The competitive advantage is always with the firm that is first with the new product. With the constant rate of technological change, stability is achieved by having a wide variety of products and technologies that have different demand curves and product-lives. These firms, which are likely to make large profits when they bring out new products that are quite successful, have both slack funds and slack personnel, including research personnel, that they can utilize in the manufacturing of new products, even ones requiring new technologies. The successful companies in this sector all maintain large research departments, although they also purchase small companies and patents in order to maintain their technological competitive position (Utterback, 1971). Furthermore, since the rate of process innovation is as high as output innovation the major mechanism of competition becomes not so much a price-war but product improvement or the development of new qualities. An interesting example has been the movement from hi-fi to stereo to cassette to quadraphonic sound in the record industry. Here clearly the major competitors have followed the principal of growth by means of product innovation.

The large task scope thus becomes both cause and effect. It pushes the organiztion to invent more and at the same time to specialize in a particular kind of output innovation, one which has very large potential demand. The logic of this technological drive is to move towards the multi-organization and the divisional structure. The constant emphasis on research leads to disparate technologies, which in turn must be placed in separate divisions. Westinghouse has 125 divisions that produce some 8000 products. By starting in a more complex technology — electrical — rather than a less complex one such as car manufacturing, Westinghouse ends up today being quite different from Ford Motor Co. Likewise one can contrast General Electric and General Motors. I.G. Farben, Dow Chemical, Imperical Chemical, and other companies have pursued the policy of product diversification but mainly for those products that have very large demand. When their research teams develop products that have small demand, at that point the researchers may set up their own companies, sometimes with backing from the former employer. But to my knowledge there has not been much venture capital in this kind of environmental setting.

In the area of public administration as we have already noted there are fewer examples. The U.S. Public Health Service is one illustration. Frequently their research is oriented to the large demand areas such as heart disease, cancer, mental illness, rehabilitation of the physically and psychologically handicapped, and the like. Similarily the concentration of most research in France in one organization, Centre Nationale de Recherche Scientifique, a division of the Ministry of Education, led to the focusing of research on large demand, prestige projects which are highly visible.

One can study when technology increases to the point where there is some take-off point, and organizations are transformed from a mechanical to a mixed mechanical-organic form. Business machines have moved into the age of computers. IBM was the first to exploit the potential and also the first to decentralize and put a high emphasis on education. Since then everyone has been trying to catch up but with little success.

In some respects the most intriguing organizations are those that have more moderate demand and yet are technologically sophisticated; they tend to be average size companies that have very large R&D departments. They spend more on research and product development. As the potential demand size decreases one finds the companies following the strategy of product replacement instead of product diversification. Examples are Polaroid cameras, photocopy equipment, drug manufacturers, film makers (MGM is the exception), airplane manufacturers, and the like. Some of these have been purchased by conglomerates, but the companies themselves have not pursued policies of product diversification.

13.1.3.4. The Environment of Small Demand and of High Task Knowledge. As demand decreases, in some respects it would appear that there is more choice, yet paradoxically we find less being exercised. High technological change requires product replacement as the standard policy. This can be seen in the electronic pocket calculator, and specialized machine industries such as robot manufacturers. The real question is why they do not pursue a strategy of product diversification that would provide greater stability given their environmental constraints? Other examples of this quadrant of our typology are companies that provide radio-isotopes, precision instruments, and small batch products based on chemistry, physics, and biology.

Here we would expect product replacement to be the dominant strategy. Why? The combination of the short product life and the small demand means that the companies replace one product with another. If they can get extra funds, they have the option or choice of product diversification, which then allows them to eventually achieve some stability vis-à-vis their markets. In fact, the industries that are presently located in this cell will probably gradually move into the next one if eventually large demand develops for a product. The most conspicuous cases have been Textron and Xerox because transistors and photocopy equipment suddenly developed large markets.

What is striking about companies in this ideal-type is that frequently their research strategy is one of developing products/services with small potential demand. Occasionally a product with great potential is developed, but in these cases the managers or inventors may choose to sell it with patent royalties to a multi-organization that pursues the policy of product diversification because it does not have the financial resources, personnel size, technical skill, and so on to produce for mass market, even a somewhat limited one.

Karpik (1972) suggests that in modern capitalism this quadrant is the one associated with the highest rates of innovation. Then in turn, when companies in this cell produce a product with potential for a mass market, they are likely to be purchased by a firm in one of the other quadrants and most typically, the high technology and high demand cell. It is this cell that helps explain Utterback's (1971) finding that large companies even with R&D departments buy their patents elsewhere.

In public administration the classic cases are university hospitals and universities. These remain medium or small in size. New courses and diplomas are developed constantly. We tend to lose sight of the fact that certain fields once quite popular can largely disappear. How many students major in Latin or Greek? Anthropology has not grown much in demand and civil engineering has declined enormously. However, biological engineering is a hot new field, as is management in public administration. Product lives apply in universities as well. In hospitals more striking is the disappearance of certain diseases and the emergence of others, sometimes requiring a change not only in medical specialty but also in the disappearance and emergence of organizations. The TB sanitarium has been replaced by the nursing home. Smallpox no longer exists but cancer is present everywhere, resulting in the gradual elimination of isolation wards and their replacement by intensive care units.

In summary, environmental constraints of task knowledge and potential demand dictate the most likely goals and the nature of the system inputs. Together they suggest what is the most appropriate market strategy as well. Given large task scope, small personnel size, and the goals of high innovation and high quality, then organizations that find themselves with these inputs and performance choices are most likely to pursue product replacement. As their personnel size grows as a function of demand, product diversification becomes more attractive and their innovation rate concentrates on products with large potential demand — products or services that are more quantity oriented, more standardized.

Given little task-scope and small personnel size, and the goals of low innovation and high quality, these organizations are more interested in niche creation through product specialization. As potential demand increases, and their personnel size grows, quantity replaces quality as an operating goal, and the market strategy is that of either product differentiation or horizontal integration.

The processes of change can be handled thus quite easily. Demand can decline, and task knowledge can grow with the resulting consequences for organizations in these environments. In the next chapter, some long-term predictions about the evolution of organizations are made on the basis of what is likely to occur given changes in these environmental constraints.

Where both task scope and personnel size are medium, product specialization becomes the appropriate strategy for the small firm, while the large firm can pursue to a limited extent the strategy of horizontal integration. Thus we find both mechanical and organic structures that are successful. This is the true middle of our typology and is perhaps best represented by the aircraft manufacturing industry and the like.These kinds of firms and their strategies tend not to be studied as often. Yet, they reflect one of the more interesting segments of the typology.

The argument running through this whole discussion is that in general there is not much strategic choice. *Given certain constraints that determine the resources and performances of the organization, then there are appropriate marketing strategies.* Perhaps the best area for maneuver revolves around the relative emphasis on growth, or the decision to maintain or increase potential demand. This in turn affects the relative importance of the various goals given a certain task scope and personnel size.

13.1.4. The Special Problem: Environmental Constraints on Organizational Autonomy

Implicit has been a third set of variables, namely the relative degree of autonomy allowed organizations to set prices, form cartels, purchase other organizations, and so forth. In general, I have assumed that these options are not open. In fact, they are to varying degrees, and more so in Great Britain and France than the United States. The governments in these countries have actually encouraged mergers and the development of oligopoly as a mechanism for competing better in international markets. Note that the hypotheses allow us to predict where these strategies are most likely to be followed. *Also if our reasoning is correct, as these choices are increasingly limited by governments, product specialization and differentiation should become more popular strategies for particular firms in specific industrial and public contexts.*

This can be stated as a general rule:

13A *Given the lack of choice of the most appropriate stragegy for controlling the environment, the next closest one in the typology of strategies will be selected.*

Therefore the availability of power in the environment tends to cut across technological and economic considerations, providing another kind of constraint. Although the literature has tended to emphasize the importance of laws prohibiting price fixing, cartels, antitrust legislation and the like, little has been said about the very large power constraints on public administration organizations. Public schools, welfare agencies, police and fire departments, mental hospitals, and the like frequently find little power available in the local communities, and their autonomy seriously constrained. This in fact may be one of the most striking differences between economic and political organizations broadly conceived. The latter do not have complete control over price or fee for service (although more than is realized). They frequently have little control over staff salaries, and only somewhat more over selection of clients — as we have already mentioned — since the potential demand is often stipulated by law, and so is therefore the marketing strategy. Either territorial arrangements or monopoly may be mandated by legislation. The private sector exists in health, welfare, and education but it tends to be small. Typically the strategy followed by private hospitals, agencies, and schools has been niche creation, providing distinctive services with limited demand.

As soon as the task scope and/or potential demand grows we find that public people-processing organizations tend to have more autonomy and there is more power available or fewer constraints are exercised. Universities, large general hospitals, and the major branches of the federal and state and even local governments function much more independently.

These three constraints then — technological, economic, and political — bear down on organizations in varying degrees, determining the nature of their three inputs — task-scope, personnel size, and organizational autonomy and their goals relative to performances and outputs — innovation rate, efficiency, and growth. In turn these constrain the marketing strategies for stimulating demand and make one or another of the four forms in Figure 13.1 appropriate. Deviations by admixtures of elements should result in internal conflict or ineffectiveness or both. There is some room to choose especially relative to the desire to grow or not, but once this strategic choice is made, most others in the hierarchy are predetermined.

13.2. DOMINATION VERSUS INTERDEPENDENCE

13.2.1. A Macro Theory of Organizational Domination

A growing area in environmental research is the study of interorganizational relationships (Negandhi, 1971 and 1975). It started with the original study of Levine and White (1961) which noted that organizations are connected by exchanges. Not much was done with this idea until Aiken and Hage (1968) developed a theory of interdependence between organizations. This theory essentially saw the scarcity of financial resources pushing organizations into cooperative arrangements with other organizations against their desires to maintain autonomy. The push for this came from the structure, namely a high concentration of specialists (they used the term complexity) which in turn meant a demand for new outputs and therefore a need for resources to support them. However, the organizations that they studied were health and welfare organizations and therefore presumably not operating with the logic of the profit motive (but with the logic of the prestige motive which is not much different). Schmidt and Kochan (1977) have since suggested these two approaches, exchange and resource dependence, as the two basic models.

Since then a number of studies have begun to call attention to the problem of the multinational corporation (Vernon, 1971) and the problem not of interdependence but instead of domination. Some definitions of these theoretical ideas are in order:

Strategy of domination: The dominant coalition attempts to make its organization the most powerful organization vis-à-vis organizations involved in exchanges and in competition.

Strategy of interdependence: The dominant coalition attempts to make its organization an equal power vis-à-vis organizations involved in exchanges and in competition.

Both ideas involve the question of autonomy and presume that organizations attempt to protect their independence. But again there is a difference between trying to maximize and to satisfy. Whether or not customers or clients are organized into separate organizations does make a difference in how the dominant coalition of a focal organization will respond to them. Since the customers or clients are usually not organizations, the usual focus of the strategy is with competitors and suppliers. However, when the customer is an organization such as the United States Army, U.S. Rubber, or A&P Food Company, then the same problem exists: how best to create either domination or interdependence.

Pfeffer (1975) has suggested that mergers are an example of interdependence, but if organizational identity is lost it is hard to speak of the organization being an equal power, although within the context of a multi-organization it may still have a distinct status. For example, if a large bank purchases a small bank and merges its operations, there is no longer a distinctive set of inputs, the technology is the same, and the staffs are interchangeable. In contrast when Mobil Oil purchases Montgomery Ward, this is not the case. Here merger does not mean the elimination of an organization, but instead reflects a policy of product diversification. There is a distinct difference in technology, personnel are not interchangeable, and the organization may have some autonomy within the multi-organizational structure (Chandler, 1962). Therefore each merger situation must be analyzed.

Keeping in mind our definition or organization, it is at this level that one studies policies regarding domination of interdependence. For example, does Philco, a division of Ford Motor Co., try to maintain equity vis-à-vis its competitors or dominate them? Does the electric typewriter division of IBM strive towards controlling the whole market or is it satisfied with a share? Does Harvard's Medical School try to dominate its competitors or does it strive for equality?

The thesis of Lenin regarding economic imperialism has taken on new meaning with the behavior of the American copper companies in Chili. Essentially he argued that the logic of capitalism, an idea originally to be found in the *Communist Manifesto,* was to propel organizations to seek ever larger markets and to pay ever lower wages until a minimum was reached that would be just above starvation. The driving principal is the maximization of profit. The means are cheaper products, which necessitate a more efficient operation, which in turn means the gradual domination of the national markets by a few companies. In turn if the major economic decisions are made by the people in other countries there is a form of economic imperialism. The national markets are no longer controlled internally but externally. There is plenty of evidence to support this thesis when one looks at the histories of Standard Oil, Singer, American Tobacco, and the like.

The increasing governmental concern with the movement of funds across international boundaries, their exchanges into different currencies, the creation of jobs in some countries rather than others has made the problem of the multinational corporation a major topic of research and study, polemics and apologies.

Consistent with a critical perspective, we want to ask under what circumstances large organizations will attempt to exploit, and be a problem for the larger society. But instead of assuming that all multinational corporations are bad, one wants to pose this as a question for research. In other words, not all multinational corporations attempt to obtain the maximum profit. Some have little interest in derived goals (see Chapter 5), that is, concerns relevant to the larger society, including social concerns such as minority employment, currency stability, and the like and others do not.

March and Simon (1958) have suggested that the dominant coalition (actually they use the term individuals) attempts to satisfy rather than maximize. Marx has argued the opposite relative to capitalism. Its internal contradiction results in a series of booms and busts with an inevitable increasing concentration of economic power. Who is right? Is capitalism the real problem?

Implicit in the hypotheses advanced in the previous section, we have some ideas about when organizations will attempt to maximize profit or prestige and when they will merely satisfice, that is pursue strategies of domination or interdependence. My essential argument is that some organizations do operate as Lenin and Marx would predict, but not all organizations. Some companies exploit their workers and the larger society and others do not. What would seem to separate the two situations is the nature of their environment, which determines their competitive situation, and the relative importance as a result of cost efficiency. The major hypotheses about when they attempt to cooperate are:

13. 9   The larger the average size of the organization, the greater the potential for growth, the less the level of task knowledge, and the less the growth in this, the greater the emphasis on efficiency and growth, and therefore the more the dominant coalition will attempt to dominate its environment and eliminate competitors.

13.10   The smaller the average size of the organization, the less the potential for growth, the higher the level of task knowledge and the less the growth in this, the greater the emphasis on innovation and quality, and therefore the more the dominant coalition will attempt to achieve equality and accept competitors.

13.11   The more that the dominant coalition emphasizes efficiency and growth, the more likely it is to attempt to dominate its environment and to eliminate its competitors.

13.12   The more that the dominant coalition emphasizes innovation and quality, the more likely it is to attempt to achieve equality and live with competitors.

Another characteristic of organizational environments that affects the choice of a domination or interdependence strategy is the number of competitors (and their strategies as well).

13.13   The fewer the number of competitors there are and the larger they are, the more likely that a dominant coalition will choose a policy of domination.

It is perhaps this last characteristic that makes a capitalist economy quite distinctive. In public administration natural monopolies may be enforced that eliminate competition or certainly diminish it. Thus there is only one police department, one fire department, and the like. When privately owned organizations are allowed to compete, usually they are given a special niche or they create one for themselves. For example, most private schools in the United States, especially at the primary level, have appealed to particular populations, whether religious, racial, or social class. There are special police organizations that guard banks and do detective work but not any allowed to control riots or traffic. Private hospitals run for profit have not been very successful in the United States, although they have been in France primarily because they have been allowed in areas where the public hospital is absent. In the United States in the hospital area, there is too much competition at the local level.

But the fact that the government owns various manufacturers or commercial enterprises does not mean that the laws of competition do not apply. In France, the governments own three national banks but they are required to compete against each other. In contrast, in the USSR there is one bank centrally controlled. Again, one must keep quite distinct not only whether or not there is public ownership but more critically whether there are competitors and what their relative size is.

The problem of maximization stems from the logic of low cost versus the major mechanism of growth within the context of a competitive situation of a few large organizations. It is this more than profit per se that pushes companies into attempts to dominate their environment and therefore to use almost any means to achieve this goal. We have seen in the previous chapter that efficiency is achieved through standardization, and this means routinization of work. The breakdown of work into small tasks, performed by unskilled labor as on the assembly line, becomes possible. Wages are kept low unless there are unions. The organizations will attempt to prevent unionization and it is in this environmental context where the most violent strikes are likely to occur (for a documentary on this problem see *Harlan County, U.S.A.*).

But the logic of growth through efficient production is not the only logic of action (Karpik, 1972) that exists. Quite different are small organizations in relatively stable environments where technological development is occurring rapidly. This is the context that Aiken and Hage (1968) examined in their study of health and welfare organizations. Quality is much more likely to lead to cooperative relationships between organizations because the concern is more with how well products are produced or services provided than with growth per se.

Consistent with a political-value paradigm, organizations in the same structural circumstances can pursue somewhat different strategies. Organizations that are controlled by elites concerned with growth, and growth at almost any price, are very different from organizations that are controlled by elites who want innovation and quality. In these two sets of causes, the environmental structure is likely to be the stronger determinant but elite values certainly do play a role if not a decisive one.

If there are differences between economic organizations concerned with profit and public administration organizations that are concerned with prestige it is likely to revolve around the key words "efficiency" and "growth." Most schools, welfare agencies, hospitals, military units, and police and fire departments are natural monopolies or close to it. Under these circumstances, the problem of growth is not fixed by efficiency or the reduction of costs, or necessarily by innovation either, although the latter may result in more growth. Thus schools have generated more business by developing special education, sheltered workshops by moving into handling the emotionally disturbed and the mentally handicapped, universities by offering new degree programs and courses, police and fire departments by adding on functions, and so forth. But this growth dictated by the strategy of innovation occurs in a relatively noncompetitive market context. As the organizations get larger and as they compete with other large organizations price may become a method for growth, as has occurred in the national marketplace of universities (Caplow and McGee, 1958), but even here quality, innovation, and state policies of quasi-monopoly may count more. If they do, then the strategy of interdependence counts more as well. Thus one finds large competitive universities entering into interdependent arrangements. The Big Ten have allowed for the exchange of students between graduate programs. The big three Ivy League universities tried to establish a common medical library, but this failed. What is interesting is that Harvard, Yale, and Columbia are in more direct competition with each other than with the Big Ten universities or the latter with each other. Similarly hospitals in the same city have entered into common purchase plans. But they have not usually agreed on specialization among various kinds of domain (James Thompson, 1967) and therefore niche specialization relative to domains. But even here the forces of competition are not by means of price but quality and innovation. In fact, frequently the hospital competes for the physician — and thereby his patients — by purchasing the latest medical equipment, which in turn pushes up costs rapidly. In the same way universities compete for faculty by giving them the opportunity to develop certain programs and the equipment to do so. The crux of competition occurs in the market place over personnel, and the operating mechanism is prestige (Caplow and McGee, 1958). These mechanisms can operate in a totally centralized delivery system such as the national system of education like the one in France. Most professors dream of being in Paris, and because of this Paris can compete for the best men. To retain their best people the other universities have to offer various inducements of one kind or the other.

Perhaps the most interesting aspect about the consequences of these two strategies are the kinds of interorganizational relationships that they produce. The strategy of domination generates conflict; that of interdependence, cooperation. Here it is difficult to separate cause and effect. Hypothesis 13.13 argues for the degree of conflict on the basis of the number of competitors and their size producing a strategy of domination. The best defense is an offense in this kind of environment. Although these observations are perhaps somewhat elementary, it is worth making them as separate hypotheses because they call attention to the interplay between the kind of interorganizational relationships and kind of organizational strategy vis-à-vis them.

13.14 *The greater the degree of conflict in interorganizational relationships, the more likely the dominant coalition will choose a policy of domination and vice versa.*

13.15 *The greater the degree of cooperation in interorganizational relationships, the more likely the dominant coalition will choose a policy of interdependence and vice versa.*

These hypotheses help explain why in non-domain areas all organizations are more willing to engage in cooperative gestures such as joint purchase agreements or joint research and the like. Once the subject of domain is broached, however, the conflict increases, with the result that a policy of domination appears more reasonable. Exchanges of goods and services lie halfway in between, being neither nondomain or domain activities of the organization. And in these areas one finds more of a mixture of interdependence and domination.

These hypotheses then fill out the relationships between the organizational system and its environment, a topic that we began in the previous chapter. On the one hand, the context of task knowledge and the average size of the organization push the organization into adopting particular strategies for controlling the environment. One strategy deals with policies of growth, the subject of the previous section. Another strategy deals with the nature of the interorganizational relationships, which in turn establish another kind of environmental context, a typical way of doing business, which is another constraint on the organization. Together they unite the two different ways in which the environment has been conceptualized with the various paradigms that have been employed to analyze organizations.

13.2.2. The Findings

Unfortunately, most of the existing research has concentrated on health and welfare organizations where the competition tends to be much more controlled by means of mechanisms of natural domain monopolies, niche creation or service specialization, and task interdependence (see Aiken et al., 1975 for a series of examples of the latter). Furthermore, these organizations are characterized by a concern for quality and innovation.

The specific hypotheses advanced above have not been tested in the literature but a number of inferences relative to them can be made. In an article by Aiken and Hage (1968), we find that complexity and innovation rates have quite high correlations with the number of joint programs — their measure of interdependence ($r = .87$ and $.74$ respectively, $N = 16$). These findings were largely replicated in a study of health and welfare organizations in another city, this time in the eastern part of the United States (Zeitz, 1976).

Perhaps more interesting is the research by Klenglan, Warren, Winkelpleck, and Paulson (1976) that demonstrates that the theory works with social services but the strength of the relationship varies by the nature of geographical reference, working best at the local level and not so well at the state level. This suggests that when organizations, even people-processing ones, enter a national arena where competition becomes a more important factor, the desires for domination rather than interdependence become greater. We are also dealing with larger organizations whose goals are somewhat different. This is even true of an organization that has units at the local, state, and federal levels. As one moves up this political hierarchy, the task shifts and as it does, the environment context shifts as well. Providing services at the local level and competing for funds at the national level represent two quite different tasks, one encouraging interdependence and the other a strategy of domination.

Equally provocative is the research by Pfeffer and Nowak (1976). This demonstrates that businss organizations in capitalist societies such as the United States do engage in joint ventures. A good example is the commitment by Ford and Socony to try and develop a pollution-free gasoline, a joint venture of $20 million.

Equally relevant is the membership on boards. This provides another way of helping to create links between organizations, at least at the level of resource controllers. In Chapter 3, I argued that in general the board did not have much power. In part this is because its function is institutional (Parsons, 1956), building bridges between different sectors of the society, depending upon the needs of the organization. Many of the concerns about interlocking directorates (Zeitlin, 1974; Aldrich, 1979: 343-48) are well-placed, precisely because there is a functional necessity that flows from the need to have interdependence. Exchanges between organizations, when of sufficient volume and frequency, are likely to lead to membership on the board. Banks are therefore members when loans become an important way of raising capital. The boards of regents of universities usually have an architect because they have been doing so much building and thus need advice as to which firms to employ.

Beyond this in nondomain areas, business organizations have created many trade associations, coalitions created to carry out joint programs vis-à-vis the government such as lobbying. Sometimes they conduct research programs or publish trade journals.

In health and welfare, coordination committees are increasingly being established. Those organizations with more professional active members and with a greater variety of occupations tend to be more involved in cooperative activities with other agencies (Aiken and Hage, 1968, Zeitz, 1976).

There is, therefore, a lot of evidence to support the hypotheses about when the power elites of organizations are likely to pursue strategies of domination and when they are likely to prefer strategies of interdependence. All of this research has been in the United States, but, as is indicated in the next chapter, it is typical in the USSR as well. This makes one wonder about the relevance of these hypotheses in such places as the Scandinavian countries, where consensus plays a vital role and competition is controlled, or in Japan and France where the government carefully regulates the course of events and oligopoly is encouraged. The latter two are especially interesting societies because of the predominance of a large well-educated group of generalists, and one would therefore expect more centralization than is true in the United States.

13.2.3. A Special Problem: Organizational
Exploitation and Corporate Crime

What is the definition of exploitation? One answer – and one that is too simple – would be the rate of earned surplus relative to the wage level. The difficulties with this approach are that these rates of return tend to be largely determined within a sector and are usually irrelevant in public people-processing organizations. If hospitals keep the wage rates of nurses very low one can say that they are exploiting a labor market situation, and yet it is difficult to speak about profits when in fact the organization may have deficits. For me, exploitation is not so much profits or rates of return – especially when socialist or public companies are included in the analysis – but instead a constellation of attitudes and behaviors upon the part of the dominant coalition where everything is done to maximize production volume regardless of the human costs involved. Thus it can exist in universities as well as in textile factories, in the USSR as well as in the United States.

It is too simplistic to say that the cause of the exploitation is the drive for profit. Power may be and indeed is just as powerful a motivator. The Nazi state pushed all organizations to excel, but in the name of the fatherland. The production quotas during the long drive to gain world power by the USSR are certainly as effective as any drive to be a millionaire. The real issue is the March and Simon assumption about maximization rather than satisfying. It is the drive to maximize any utility that creates the essential rationalization of exploitation. The central assumption is:

13.16 *The greater the dominant coaliton's emphasis on maximization of effectiveness, the greater the tendency to exploit.*

We are now prepared to predict when multinational corporations are most likely to be most exploitative. The answer is that when they are engaged in situations that require little task knowledge but large size, and elites have selected the strategy of growth, then the maximization of profit or prestige becomes paramount and we have our worst examples of exploitation. The copper companies in Chile or United Fruit in the Caribbean are illustrations. The oil companies are perhaps less exploitative, perhaps because they have had a larger amount of task knowledge which has led to a greater concern for derived goals, although they still share many of the same environmental characteristics.

Much different are the electrical companies, computer manufacturers, and chemical companies, although again there are differences among companies as well, depending upon how much their elites emphasize efficiency and growth. Although the evidence is at best fragmentary, the conduct of multinational corporations in the Third World appears to be quite different than in Europe. This stems less from the greater diligence of the governments in Europe, although this can be a factor, than from the quite different technologies involved as well as the scale of operations. Those in Europe tend to be technologically intensive with greater concerns about quality of product and continual innovation. But even here the hypothese would predict different comportments for Chrysler-Simca on the one hand and IBM on the other. In the Third World the companies have usually had low technological bases – as in mining – and have been concerned primarily with costs and growth. But, again there are many variations here as well. The conduct of Sears, Roebuck is quite different from the action of United Fruit in small Latin American countries during the 1920s and 1930s.

Also it is difficult to separate the impact of using more unskilled labor versus more skilled labor, which is part of the meaning of a more sophisticated technology. The more skilled labor in turn fights for a higher pay scale and also better working conditions. How much is the greater concern for human costs a function of enlightment on the part of the dominant coalition and how much is it caused by the militancy of the workers? Both themes are important and relevant to understanding how multinational corporations operate in the Industrial and Industrializing Worlds.

In addition to the environmental influences on the choice of goals and the relative importance of task knowledge and personnel size, there are some corollaries that reinforce these tendencies for organizations to be more or less concerned with domination. With greater personnel size, and especially with slow development in task-scope, the growth of the organization pushes it into being more centralized and from this comes a tendency to ignore the interests of the worker. The dominant coalition is small and far removed from the workers on the assembly line. We have already seen in the previous chapter how large size tends to be associated with low morale even when controlling for centralization. While much of the explanation may come from the deterioration of affective relationships, another part of the answer lies in the logic of large scale operations being concerned more with efficiency than human costs. This is the real problem, much more than the attempt to maximize profits.

What evidence is there for this? If one studies the history of American companies, one finds that most trusts developed in areas where the technological base was unsophisticated and yet the capital investment needs were great – steel, railroads, petroleum, glass, cement, and the like. It is also in these companies that one frequently finds the worst personnel practices and the least concern for the safety and welfare of the worker.

The recent payoffs of Lockeed and other American corporations engaged in business raise the issue of under what circumstances companies or perhaps more generally organizations engage in deliberate criminal acts such as price-fixing and the like. There are two levels that should be kept quite distinct. There are always bank tellers and accountants with their hands in the cash-box, physicians who practice unethical medicine, owners that burn their stores down, professors who steal ideas from students, and so forth. This is the level of white collar crime or individual felonies of one kind or another. It is quite different when management or administrators commit criminal acts in the name of an organization. It is this latter situation that is of more interest.

The practice of corporate crime is most likely in exactly the same situations that produce exploitation. The desperate competitive situation leads to desperate acts upon the part of the owners-managers. Perhaps the most interesting research on this problem has not been done in the United States but instead in the USSR (Berliner, 1957) where there are many examples not of price-fixing, which is done by the central government, but of the illegal exchanges of goods. Again, it is not a specialty of capitalism but instead of a macro environment that places great pressure on the dominant coalitions in organizations to expand production and to reduce costs. The quota and bonus systems are well calculated to have this impact. What is interesting is that both the USSR and the United States have this sytem, the former's being much more widespread.

Some people would argue that the USSR must do this because it is part of the world economy and this competition forces it to set quotas. In fact, it has not been part of the world economy and even today external trade is small and related to specific — and temporary — needs. The driving force is world power. Admittedly the enemy is capitalism, but the battle is not really an economic one.

Probably, although there is not enough evidence to be sure, the problem of price-fixing between companies or secret and illegal agreements on competitive bids with the government and the like are more likely to occur not in times of growth but instead during periods of stability or even general decline. Under these circumstances these illegal arrangements become methods of ensuring that each company survives. One finds price-fixing most relevant in the mining of raw materials, that is, in the same areas where cartels are most likely to be found.

Although we normally do not think about people-processing organizations and especially innovative ones as potentially exploitative, they can be. Typically the men who work for the President of the United States are asked to work long hours, staying away from their family but for small salaries. Indeed, among professionals and managers the single best test of exploitation is the number of hours worked per week over a period of several years. Very innovative organizations can have quite similar driving forces — perhaps a charismatic leader. The purity of the goal does not necessarily make it less exploitative.

In summary, the problem of exploitation and of criminal acts does not appear restricted to capitalism but does operate wherever there is likely to be a heavy emphasis on growth at all costs. Here not only do organizations attempt to dominate but they also try to exploit, are more likely to engage in criminal acts, and the like. It is more visible in economic organizations — not so much perhaps because of the profit motive but more because of the greater growth and efficiency concerns than in public organizations. But one has only to think about kickbacks between physicians and drug companies, about universities accepting funds in exchange for accepting certain students, about the relationship between organized crime and the police, to recognize that the problems of exploitation and of criminal acts by organizations also occur in the area of public administration. These were in general much more visible in the United States in the nineteenth century and are in the underdeveloped world today.

13.3. TRANSFORMATION OF NETWORKS AND MARKETS BY GROWTH AND DEVELOPMENT

In the previous chapter, the emphasis was on the transformation of the form of the organization by either the growth in task knowledge or the demand for the product. Organizations were perceived as passive agents. Here, the accent has been more on the visible hand of managers and the impact of organizations through their strategies of growth on both the market and the character of the competition. In other words, *how do organizations shape their environments?* While the accent is still on how task knowledge, demand, and the extent of control over organizations shape strategic choices, these choices restructure the market context, the extent of task knowledge, demand, and even the likelihood of some control being exerted.

The best way of appreciating how strategic choice does shape an environment is to see the role of an organization that pioneers a new technology and market strategy. If successful, it is emulated in various ways; this then shapes how the environment alters. Success is diffused! (See Figure 13.4.)

When IBM adopted the strategy of continual product replacement through generations of computers, it shaped the market in many ways. This prevented the growth of competition and meant that each of the competitors had to have an equally large – or even larger – commitment to research. Once one company or university or hospital adopts a continued emphasis or research as the way to grow, others are forced to go along. There is not much alternative, except niche creation vis-à-vis the giants that dominate.

Likewise the giants can be caught off guard by the development of new techniques that in turn can change the market context creating new competitors. Kodak ignored Land's camera. The office machines, and particularly Addressograph Multigraph, did not move into the new xerography technique exploited by Xerox. Obviously these new technologies can only flourish when the optimal size can be small, that is there is not a need for large capital investments.

The hypotheses about this are self-evident but worth stipulating so that the system of hypotheses comes full cycle:

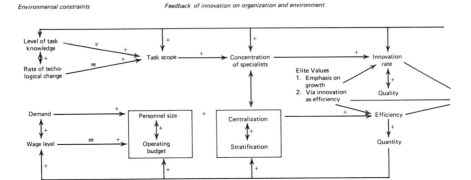

(a)

Figure 13.4   The transformation of the

13.17   The greater the emphasis on innovation by one organization in a specific market context, the more other organizations must match competition by their own emphasis.

13.18   The more that the set of organizations in a specific market context emphasizes innovation, the faster the growth in task knowledge.

Investment in R&D creates a never ending cycle of research, product development or improvement, leading to more investment in R&D. The impact on the growth in task knowledge is apparent but frequently lost to view. Most innovations occur in organizations and not in garages.

The choice of efficiency has exactly the same impact on the market context:

13.19   The greater the emphasis on cost by one organization in a specific market context, the more other organizations must match competition by their own emphasis.

13.20   The more that a set of organizations in a specific market context emphasizes efficiency, the greater the potential demand.

Constant price reductions can affect potential demand and increase it, just as innovation can lead to the recognition of the need for new products.

But neither quality nor price, neither an emphasis on innovation nor on efficiency can ultimately determine demands. Inherent in each product or

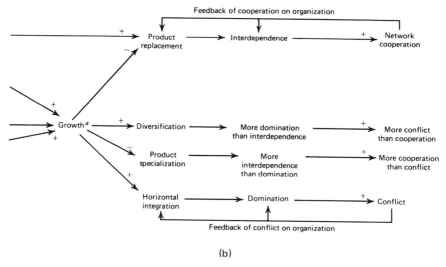

(b)

market and the larger environment.

service is not only product life but a potential demand. Organizational strategies can impact on this but it is still indeterminant to a certain extent. In the next chapter, we consider how societies affect demand.

The nature of the relationships between organizations also affect the shape of the market context. Again these hypotheses largely summarize what has already been said but are necessary to indicate how organizations shape their environments.

13.21 *The greater the emphasis on domination, through growth by efficiency, the more likely the market becomes dominated by a few large organizations who compete by all means possible.*

13.22 *The greater the emphasis on cooperation, through development by innovation, the more likely the market becomes dominated by networks of organizations who emphasize niche creation vis-à-vis each other.*

The first hypothesis is best viewed historically as the classic example of oligopoly. Previously the variables that affect this strategic choice were indicated. The second hypothesis is what has been extensively studied in the public sector but not so much in the private, although there are many illustrations.

Although one thinks of the growth of organizations in the nineteenth century (Chandler, 1977) in the examples already studied, one should not forget current illustrations – electric typewriters, large frame computers, pocket calculators, photo-copying, and the like. These are new technologies, but in which demand is also large. Quickly the markets become dominated by a few organizations locked in fierce competition. However, most of these organizations are more likely to be multi-organizations of the mixed mechanical-organic. Multi-organizations are more protected by having multiple divisions, each in a different market context. The consequence in the mixed breed is also a mix of strategies, cooperation in certain areas including sometimes research, and conflict or at least competition in other areas, especially sales and service.

Finally, one must recognize that excesses are noticed. Too ruthless pursuit of growth is likely to be checked by state regulation. The emergence of many American laws has occurred because of the truth of these previous hypotheses and a sense that limits had to be set on organizational behavior and the strategies of dominant coalitions.

13.4. CONCLUSIONS

In the previous chapter, the three variables task-scope, personnel size, and autonomy were seen as dictating the kind of organizational form. In this chapter, we have asked what determines these variables. The amount of knowledge affects task-scope and the duration of product life, and the amount of demand determines the personnel size and importance of efficiency or price. But knowledge also tends to fractionate demand into specialized needs and distinctive qualities. This is the main reason why task-scope and personnel size have almost no relationship with each other. Finally, organizational autonomy is affected by the availability of power.

The availability of these resources in the larger environment is not, however, the only factor that affects the choice of organizational form. Within limits the dominant coalitions can choose market strategies, which in turn are likely to affect the amount of knowledge and of demand as well as the nature of the competitive strategy. But as we have seen even these strategies tend to be fixed by the nature of the three resource variables residing in the environment – knowledge, demand, and power.

Choice is usually exercised at a particular historical moment in an industrial or public sector and then after that, all organizations with the same more or less throughput must continue to use the same strategy. They can choose a different strategy but then they are unlikely to remain effective. One exception is the strategy of niche creation for small companies or agencies in sectors dominated by giants.

We have synthesized the structural-functional and political-value perspectives by recognizing that the choice of strategy is dictated in part by knowledge and demand and in part by the values of the dominant coalition. But then these two perspectives have been combined with a cybernetic-adaptive and a conflict-critical one. The former indicates that if an incorrect strategy is selected then it must be changed or the organization will not survive. The latter focuses on the issue of why some organizations exploit and others do not.

Exploitation and corporate crime do exist but they are not necessarily a monopoly of capitalism. They are partially determined by environmental constraints. But a major problem remains in being able to provide a clear definition of exploitation, and until this is satisfactorily resolved, there is unlikely to be much real progress in the research. Similarly corporate crime is matched by collective crime in public administration and it needs to be studied as well.

Two different views of the environment have also been synthesized. On the one hand, there is the view of Burns and Stalker (1961) that it is the immediate technical-market context and on the other hand there are a number of inter-organizational relationships (Aiken and Hage, 1968; Turk, 1970 and 1973; Benson, 1975; Aldrich, 1979). Here the one is seen as impacting on the other. More specifically, the desire to dominate or cooperate — to avoid or form relationships — is again a function of the form of the organization, its environmental setting, and the values of the dominant coalition. Domination and cooperation have feedback effects on the nature of the market context, and the kind of organizational form.

We have previously stressed the transformation of organizational form. Now we can add the problem of the transformation of markets and of strategies. Parallel to the four forms are four kinds of markets and of strategies. It is worth repeating that discontinuous changes in knowledge, demand, or power produce the need for new forms and new strategies. The most likely source of change is the growth in knowledge which reduces demand, shortens product life, and expands task scope. In the next chapter the larger societal context is studied from this perspective.

Chapter Fourteen

Societal Constraints and the Evolution of Organizational Forms

Weber's interest in rational legal authority and bureaucracy centered on three questions, as we noted in Chapter 2: What forms are best for which functional performances? What consequences do these forms have for society? And, how does societal change favor particular forms and in what evolutionary sequence? The four major steady states with various subvarieties have been the focus of much of the book. How the environment affects the choice of forms began to emerge in the previous two chapters and especially in Figure 13.4. At various other points, the movement from one steady state to another has been analyzed as transformation — , the most basic process there is. We have yet to analyze at length the larger societal variables that produce transformation and most especially the evolution of forms.

Can we predict the organizational form of the future? Weber felt it would be rational-legal bureaucracy. In the previous chapter, we analyzed how environmental constraints shape the choice of organizational strategy, which in turn can affect the dynamic change from one steady state to another. An estimation of how these will change allows us to predict the most viable future distribution of organizations. In each society the environmental constraints are different. Therefore with the same set of hypotheses it is possible to predict quite different organizational forms. The end result may — in the long run — be the same but the pathways are quite different — the concept of equifinality applies.

Weber pondered what consequences bureaucracy might have for equality and democracy. He was optimistic on the first point and pessimistic on the second. I believe that Weber posed the problem in the wrong way. It might be better to ask how equality and democracy shape organizational forms than the other way around. The societal constraint is the more powerful influence even with the multinational corporation. This becomes particularly striking when one compares Scandinavia with the Anglo-Saxon countries or the Latin countries, to say nothing about Eastern Europe including the USSR. To shift to Asian countries makes the point even stronger. We have seen in Chapters 3 and 11 how Japanese organizations differ in some respects from others.

What differentiates these societies is the availability of a wide range of resources. In turn, these establish constraints on the kind of organizational choice that is available. It is here that the population model of organizations can be developed (Aldrich, 1979: Chapter 2). Beyond this, each country has a specific set of institutional patterns that are the substance of what we think of as the unique historical and sociological aspects of these societies. However critical these are, we are focusing only on the general resource situation rather than the specific institutional setting, not for lack of interest but for lack of space. The only book that comes close to really understanding this is Chandler's *The Visible Hand* (1977) and even it does not bring in other institutional factors that shaped the course of American organizations – and not just business firms. Indeed, the institutional analysis of the development of organizations within a specific nation-state has yet to be written.

Societies are incredibly complex. The number of variables that one could use to describe them is almost infinite. Ideally, one would like to have a relatively well worked out theory of society. But this would require another book, if not more (for the beginnings see Hage, 1972; Chapter 6). Here we shall focus on a few variables that impact on the major inputs – task scope and personnel size – and performances – innovation and efficiency – that have been so central in much of the analysis in the previous chapters. Beyond this, and especially because of their relevance in socialist and directed societies, we want to consider as well how much autonomy organizations are given and the nature of the coordination between them. The planned economy, while not popular in this country, is a well established fact in many others (Shoenfeld, 1965).

Parallel with these three sets of input performance variables are three major long-term processes in societies that are determining the pace, sequence, and final outcome of the evolution of organizational forms.

The modernization process is best viewed as the growth in knowledge, which leads to greater task scope and higher innovation rates (Lerner, 1958; Bell, 1973). Organizations become technological intensive and rely upon a high concentration of specialists. This is propelling us into post-industrial society and is non-reversible. The industrialization process is best viewed as the growth in demand for products and services, creating large scale organizations that are efficiently run (Chandler, 1977). Less familiar is the decentralization process which simultaneously results in greater autonomy and greater control. It is this process that sees at the same time the multi-organization and greater independence upon the part of the organizations within the larger structure.

Knowledge or technological intensity, like time, grows inexorably. In contrast, demand can wax and wane depending upon tastes, technological breakthroughs, and economic growth. Together these two resources represent major constraints within which organizations must work. They shape strategies and set limits on what form is most appropriate, as we have seen. But more critically if we can make predictions about what knowledge and demand will be like in the future, we can then predict what are likely to be the dominant organizational forms. The interplay between these forces is articulated within the societal distribution of power.

Since one variable – knowledge – keeps growing, then it logically follows that it dominates the system (Landes, 1969). This will strike readers raised in a political economy perspective as strange. The importance of power and wealth have long been appreciated. The importance of technology, especially in its relationship to the shape and form of organizations, has received much less attention.

14.1. SOCIETAL CONSTRAINTS AND THE EVOLUTION OF ORGANIZATIONAL FORMS

There are two different literatures relative to the development of nation states: one on modernization and political development (Lipset, 1960, Cutright, 1965; Lerner, 1958) and the other on economic development and industrialization (Adelman and Morris, 1973, Rostow, 1960). Although these two literatures are frequently confused and do indeed use some of the same variables in common, they describe quite different mechanisms of growth and development. Modernization occurs through the processes of mass education, rising communication, and the like. Industrialization occurs through the processes of capital formation and economic growth. They affect each other and there is a debate as to how much they are interrelated. Regardless, these two engines of societal change are in part affected by organizations and in part they determine or select the preferred proportions of organizational forms.

There are two central ideas that need constant reiteration. The first is that while organizations are the major motors of change, they are not the only ones. Whether families save or invest or spend their money affects capital formation and thus affects the rate of industrialization. Governments qua organizations can influence this but they and other organizations do not totally determine the rate of industrialization except in extreme cases, such as a totally planned socialist society like the USSR. Likewise families encourage or discourage children to strive to get more education which impacts on human capital formation and thus affects the rate of modernization. Again, governments qua organizations can influence this by limiting the number of places in schools or by special programs such as Operation Headstart, designed to increase the motivation of the individual, but they and other organizations do not totally determine the rate of modernization either. Thus, there is an interchange. Organizations, whether banks or schools, manufacturing firms or military forces, hospitals or research institutes affect rates of modernization and industrialization but they are not the only agents of action.

The second central idea is that all societies have all forms of organizations. What differs is the relative proportion of a particular kind and how this varies across time. Although some people have difficulty in understanding how one can describe a whole when the parts vary, the analytical problem is relatively simple. The key point is to recognize certain qualitative distinctions along the various continua of modernization and industrialization where the proportions shift enough that one can begin to speak about a significant change. Hypothetical ranges are indicated below but they should be considered as provisional.

14.1.1. Modernization and Organizational Forms

Modernization represents the developing knowledge base of a society. It has several critical components: the expansion of education, the growth in machine intensity, and the increase in the real income spent on research. The first component represents the growth in skills and the development of professional associations. The second reflects the use of machines. But the third is the creation of a never ending cycle of the production of knowledge, which in turn requires higher levels of education and more machines (Bell, 1973).

We might simply measure the quantity of PhDs. This provides a good aggregate indicator, which in some respects is important for predicting the full range of occupational specialties that can exist in a society. Another indicator is the average number of years of education completed, and the proportion of the 18–24 age group that is at the university level provides an estimate of the proportional effort made by a society to create an educated society. The range of differences between societies even today is enormous.

If one moves backwards in time, it was only in the previous century that even mass literacy occurred in a few countries, namely Scandinavia, Western Europe, and the Anglo-Saxon countries including the United States. Since then these countries have developed mass secondary educational systems and have begun to create a mass university system. Much of the discussion of post-industrial society (Bell, 1973) has focused on the importance of a society in which the majority have received a college education. The necessity of rethinking how society must be structured as this occurs has been one of the preoccupations of the futurists.

At what point one says there is a qualitative change in the level of modernization is difficult to say. My own preferences are for relatively broad ranges. When 50% of the population is literate, that seems important. When 50% have received a secondary education whether classical or vocational, whether formally in a school or informally in business, this seems like another critical stage because it means a sizeable pool of skilled labor. In general it has taken Western Europe about one century to move from the first to the second stage. If we also choose 50% who have received a college diploma or equivalent as the magic marker of post-industrial society when we have still not entered this era. Although since the 1960s the United States first achieved having 50% of the cohort 18-25 in higher education, roughly only one half of this group will complete their degree programs. The attrition rate is large but declining with time, as it did first in primary education and then in secondary. Nor does this say anything about the fact that a large proportion of higher education in the United States occurs in junior colleges where the content may be reflective of secondary education levels. Regardless, clearly the United States is approaching this threshold of 50% with a college diploma and will probably reach it prior to the end of this century.

Typically capital intensity is seen as a measure of industrialization and in one sense it is. But most capital is spent on equipment and it is this aspect that interests us. How important the growth in technology is for this is clearly reflected in Chandler (1977). Railroads, automobiles, planes, and the like generate enormous capital needs, primarily for the equipment needed to build the product or to provide the service. This is easy to see in the manufacturing sector but it is equally important in the universities, hospitals, and military organizations, all of which are now quite machine intensive. As we have seen, a technologically intensive sector requires constant updating of its machines.

Another way of distinguishing significant periods in the modernization of society is to examine the proportion of the GNP allocated to research of all kinds, whether academic, practical, military, product development, and the like. A very significant change probably occurs when one-tenth of one percent was allocated to R&D broadly defined. The next stage might be about 1%, which occurred just before or during the Second World War. When will ten percent be reached? Probably not until well into the 21st century.

Regardless of which crude indicators one uses and what arbitrary thresholds for qualitative distinctions, the importance of modernization can not be denied. It has two critical impacts relative to the constraints of the organization's environment.

Modernization impacts first of all on the inputs of the organization. It considerably broadens the task scope of the organization. *As noted in Chapter 12, growth in knowledge results in routine activities being replaced by machines and makes the remaining work activities more complex.* This requires a shift in the nature of the labor force, first from largely unskilled to skilled and then to professional/managerial (one could make further distinctions such as the relative importance of illiterate peasants as agricultural laborers versus literate unskilled labor, clerical skilled and craftsmen versus engineers, (semi-professionals and professionals). In this sense one can speak of a society growing more complex as its knowledge base grows. The work performed becomes more complex as machines replace first peasants, then unskilled laborers, then clerical workers, and so on.

But secondly the growth in the proportion of professional/managerial also means structural differentiation into a variety of occupational specialties. Complex tasks are handled by teams of specialists. Large masses of knowledge are broken into specialties, which are delimited but which can be mastered. This is, of course, another application of March and Simon's (1958) assumption of the limit to cognition. Since we can not know everything, we become the master of a certain body of knowledge. At the societal level this means that true occupational specialization, rather than what occurs on the assembly line, is a function of the growth in knowledge. The major exception remains in societies where the higher educational system places an emphasis on generalists rather than specialists, as in France and Japan.

The task scope of the organization is thus broadened by the influx of a wide variety of specialists who bring with them a wide variety of distinct technologies. But even prior to this is the impact of knowledge growth on how the members of organizations perceive tasks, an argument already made in Chapter 5. Knowledge growth means more complex and subtle perceptions of the environment and the recognition of new needs. The task becomes bigger at the same time it becomes more differentiated. More distinctions in kinds of clients/customers are perceived. This makes the task scope larger and so forth. The concentration of specialists increases simultaneously.

Modernization impacts also on the performances and outputs of the organization. *An educated, professionally oriented population is likely to prefer quality and to be more oriented towards change. This shift in consumer values away from price to quality has a large number of implications that have broad ramifications for organizations and their decision-makers.* It means that customers and clients want to be treated individually, with the accent on specialized needs and interests. Distinctive qualities as well as quality of product or service become critical. Likewise there is a greater interest in new products and services, a search for the latest, a faster movement into and out of fads and fashions. These hypotheses are perhaps quite self-evident but are worth making explicit because they indicate one of the ways in which societies are evolving and therefore environments are changing:

14.1 *The larger the knowledge base of the society, the larger the task scope of the average organization and the more emphasis on change and quality as goals.*

14.2 *The larger the task scope of the average organization and the greater the emphasis on change and quality as goals, the more the growth in the knowledge base of the society.*

This is the fundamental interchange between environment and organizations. Organizations produce knowledge in research institutes, socialize skills in schools, create new products and services in a wide variety of organizations, and so forth which in turn demand a more educated labor force.

The continual innovation in process technology means a steady movement in the aggregate towards automation, which reduces the needs for unskilled labor, as we have already noted. This knowledge may not be written in books – in fact it is most often written in patent law – but it is a critical aspect of a society. In turn, a professional labor force means a greater taste for and ability to create more knowledge in the form of innovation and in the search for quality. Perhaps the real issue is whether individuals can be isolated inventors as many were in the nineteenth century. The sheer complexity of the task of research in one area (Hagstrom, 1965) after another makes the individual inventor working in his garage more and more rare. It is now a team that creates and develops products and services. This was already true in the chemical industry in the late nineteenth century (Freeman, 1974). It was true of the invention of the airplane – there were only two Wright brothers but they had helpers. But increasingly it is the norm in most sectors of society.

If one accepts these two hypotheses, then it means that all societies are being pushed and propelled towards a never ending growth of knowledge and therefore towards even more complexity. This is especially true where 50% or more of their labor force have college diplomas (that is, at least 16 years of education) and where about 10% of the GNP is spent on research of all kinds, a situation as yet unreached. Organizations are being forced to expand their task scope, improve their quality and adopt an innovative strategy for survival.

Once one opens the Pandora's box of research, there is a never ending search for solutions. Each research problem or societal need solved generates two new ones. Each small incremental improvement in quality begets a greater recognition of how much mroe room for improvement there is. There is a never ending cycle of faster and faster product replacement as product lives continually diminish (Mansfield, 1968). This makes the organic-professional and the mixed mechanical-organic forms the most favored ones in post-industrial societies.

Organizations that do not innovate go out of business, at least in those areas where free market economies predominate. Although the United States does not like to admit it, in a number of industrial sectors, American companies have failed because they did not develop distinctive qualities that would make their products more desirable. The answer to this may be a question of design but it can also be and frequently is a technological problem, which is solved by research and development. If TV sets are to be made competitive, then either one develops an automated production process which reduces the price enough to compete even with cheap labor building them elsewhere, or else one differentiates the product enough so that one, in effect, can expect a certain demand. The solution to both problems is technological. An example of the former is pocket calculators and of the latter, IBM, which charges about 30% more for its products but can maintain this given the quality of product and of service. The continued success of Japanese and German firms is due to superior quality for which people are willing to pay more.

This leads to a very critical conclusion: *The more important the quality of the product or service, the more inelastic its price is, that is, price is unaffected by demand.* If the growth in mass higher education is leading towards a greater preference for quality, then it means that the markets are becoming less price elastic as well.

We can now predict the evolution of organizational forms in the United States. As more and more sectors, public and private, become technolog cally intensive, there will be a greater and greater movement towards the organic-professional and the mixed mechanical-organic.

The key idea here, that more educated people prefer distinctive qualities and more individualized products, and like change is perhaps the most controversial aspect of the ideas advanced above. It has a large number of implications, and perhaps most important it allows us to gradually predict the demise of price and therefore efficiency as *the* major performance. Weber built his model of evolution around the long-term supremacy of this performance. I am suggesting that in post-industrial society innovation is the most critical one. In part, this flows from shorter product lifes. In part, it flows from the adoption of innovative strategies by the competitors. But most fundamentally, it stems from the greater and greater emphasis on the production of knowledge in each society.

The more money spent on R&D, the faster the growth in knowledge and the more demand for even greater spending. Knowledge creates more problems than it solves. The fallout of new technologies such as in pollution, energy waste, and urban sprawls require more research to solve. The production of products can increase until the market is satiated, but we can never know too much. There is no end to the pursuit of knowledge. This production process is self-generating.

In underdeveloped societies – those in industrial and especially preindustrial stages – the traditional and mechanical forms are the preferred models. Here, where less than 50% of the labor force is literate and where less than one-tenth of 1% of the GNP is spent on research, one finds simple agriculture at best. Western and Northern Europe and the United States at the beginning of the nineteenth century, and a large share of the Third World even now are illustrations. The first real mechanical industries to emerge were the textile factories of England (Smelser, 1959). Not surprisingly we find that in many underdeveloped countries these tend to be the first to emerge as well. Indeed, again many of the balance of payment problems occur because of technology transfer to other societies and because the products can be built cheaper in other countries as long as they remain labor intensive.

The countries that have mass literacy and that are advancing towards a situation where half the labor force has some skill, which describes a large number of modernizing countries, have a considerable variety of organizational forms. Here one is likely to find sizeable numbers of all kinds, although traditional and mechanical types may still predominate. Certainly one will observe a greater differentiation in kinds within the institutional sector – different kinds of schools, factories, banks, police, welfare agencies, and the like.

The general variable, extent of knowledge base, or the indices such as the level of education and the research spent per capita, allow for an enormous variation between nations. Each society has a distinct and unique position and therefore is more likely to have more organizations with one form rather than another. The modernization process forces a transformation from a predominance of traditional to organic organizations, and from mechanical to mixed mechanical-organic. To a certain extent, insofar as specific public sectors and industrial sectors depicted in Chapters 8 and 13 tend to be characterized more by the degree of task scope than personnel size, it is possible to predict even somewhat the specific content of particular organizations.

Not only can societies be contrasted by the extent of their knowledge base but this may be done within specific areas. Much of the research effort of the United States, and even more of the USSR's is concentrated in industries that manufacture war equipment. In contrast, West Germany, which spends a higher proportion of its GNP on research than the United States, spends very little on military research. Likewise, although the USSR and the United States have high proportions of the population in college, the former concentrates on engineers and the latter more on PhDs and various professions. This, in turn, means different proportions of particular kinds of organizations as well as differences in the kinds of occupations. Also by looking at the production of PhDs and their areas of specialization makes for a number of specific predictions as well. This is perhaps most striking in the area of medicine where there has been an enormous expansion of both medical research and medical specialization. The consequence has been the development of extremely complex hospitals. The same is true in the areas of physics, chemistry, and biology.

14.1.2. Industrialization and Organizational Forms

The knowledge base is not the only societal resource. Another is the demand base of the country. This can be measured by the population and its per capita GNP or else by total GNP. Investments in capital formation lead to increasing industrial production and in turn to growth in per capita income, which generates demand that propels the expansion. Industrialization, the expanding wealth of society, is by far the more familiar process. The choice of significant ranges of development depends upon which aspect of industrialization one chooses to emphasize. One simple standard and crude measure is per capita income levels of $100, $1000, and $10,000. Sweden, Switzerland, and Norway have almost reached the third level of per capita wealth while the rest of Western Europe and the United States are not far behind.

Rising standards of living mean greater demand (Brown and Brown, 1966). The sheer size of the market is a function not only of wage level but of population size as well. While the world is moving towards the elimination of trade barriers and the integration of markets, it is still divided by national boundaries in many cases. The population size of the country has an enormous impact on the variety of organizational forms. Large markets mean large scale organizations – that is, more mechanical-bureaucratic and mixed mechanic-organic forms.

Although these boundaries are somewhat arbitrary, consider the difference between nations with a population of one million versus ten million versus hundred million. And consider even more the difference between a real GNP of ten billion dollars versus one hundred billion versus one trillion. These shifts in magnitudes alter considerably the possibilities for particular nations or societies to have certain kinds of outputs and forms of organizations. Contrast Cuba with China, or Switzerland with the United States. The average Swiss is richer than the average American but the aggregate wealth of the United States allows for much greater diversity.

Industrialization impacts also on the performances and outputs of the organization. A rich population base makes efficiency less important. Cost efficiency is the concern of an industrializing society but not of a post-industrial one. A comfortable standard of living means less cost consciousness upon the part of the consumer and concurrently a concern for convenience. The disposal society becomes the dominant living pattern (Toffler, 1970).

This in turn raises some interesting contradictions in the post-industrial society. Larger organizations are likely to become more cost conscious and yet if the environment is a rich one, this may not be what the consumers want. Thus organizations that continually grow in size may move beyond their optimal size, which in turn may be diminishing in any case if convenience is the larger concern. In one sense a concern for convenience is a concern for efficiency but of a very different kind. Building one service center in the middle of a large city and requiring people to wait in line reduces organizational costs enormously but clearly it wastes much client or customer time. The current trend towards outreach centers, suburban stores, many small clinics, branches of banks, university centers, and the like results from the desire upon the part of the population to conserve their time even if organizational efficiency declines. Note that as societies become richer this is not a real difficulty. Also, providing quality service may require fast service conveniently located. Individualized attention may be only possible in individualized units of large organizations or multi-organizations or even, for that matter, separate organizations. Small is beautiful! The hypothese are:

14.3 *The greater the demand base of the society, the larger the personnel size of the average organization and the greater the emphasis on efficiency as a goal.*

14.4 *The lower the cost, the greater the demand base.*

Just as organizations have an impact on the environment by building new products and developing new technologies, they also do so by having greater efficiency. The reduction in costs, usually as a consequence of mechanization, expands demand, which leads to greater personnel size and further economies of scale until some optimal size is achieved.

Chandler (1977) has documented the transformation of form from traditional to mechanical-bureaucratic steady states in a number of industries. In all cases, mechanization and coordination allowed for a reduction in cost, first in railroads, then in department stores, telegraph, telephone, steel manufacturing, meat packing, and so on.

We now have a tension. On the one hand reductions in cost increase demand, whereas preferences for individualized products and services reduce demand. Similarily, new technological breakthroughs suddenly can reduce demand. The impact of television on movie demand was quite sudden and almost catastrophic.

If the industrialization process were operating by itself, one would simply predict that larger and larger organizations would come to predominate everywhere. The top 500 multinational corporations would run the world. And i 1 the past century we have seen a remarkable concentration of economic power. This started in the nineteenth century with Singer Sewing Machine, followed quickly by Unilever, the American and British Tobacco Companies, the soap manufacturers, the chemical companies, elevator and electrical machine companies, and so forth.

But the modernization process puts some brakes on this push towards ever larger size. At this juncture, it is again worth repeating the distinction between multi-organization and organization. Some multinational corporations are the former and some the latter; some produce different products and some produce essentially one basic product. We are focusing on the growth of a single product line rather than the multi-organization. In fact, the limits to growth in particular products have led many companies to adopt the divisional structure and create the multi-organization.

The growth in demand, fueled by rising income levels, has a series of predictable consequences. It allows for the hiring of more personnel. But typically these are unskilled or semiskilled labor that work with machines, what Blauner (1964) would call machine tending. In turn, this allows for rationalization by means of better task specialization as in the assembly line or better coordination of the production process. Typically these are achieved by increased centralization and the use of formalized control procedures.

Essentially this was Marx's vision of the future but because so much attention has been paid to the inevitable revolution of the have-nots, little has focused on the growth of large scale firms that can drive prices down through better management. The growth in personnel size and capital investment pushes the organization into a more centralized form of power structure, with the use of rewards such as price rates as mechanisms of control.

This push towards greater production and larger economics of scale also creates the familiar booms and busts that one associates with free market economies. However, if in this kind of economic system there are increasing limits placed on growth in demand because of increasing preferences for individuated products and services, and where quality become more important than price, then there is a limit to overproduction. *The amplitude of the booms and busts is reduced because the potential demand is limited.* This is even more the case as the total economy is composed of a greater variety of products and services. Inherent in the diversity is a canceling of demand cycles. But this is a topic for another analysis.

Holding constant technological intensity or task knowledge, the expansion in demand leads to a push towards either the mechanical-bureaucratic form or the mixed mechanical-organic. How many of these organizations are strongly affected by both population base where international trade is restricted and per capita income? The distinctive quality of the United States was not that it industrialized first but that it industrialized fast with a large market and then went overseas as well. The consequence is that America developed many of the most famous mechanical-bureaucratic organizations because it had the advantage of very large demand bases.

One can see this time and time again. As income increases and product cost declines, there is a certain point where marginal elasticities start to operate. The reduction in price leads to a considerable expansion in demand, which in turn means a much greater ability for organizations to increase in personnel size. Demand, to a certain extent, determines how large organizations can become.

How far this growth can continue is a function, however, not only of demand but of technology. At some point, capacity to coordinate breaks down or there are reductions in the economy of scale and not just because of less efficiency. Lower morale, lower innovation and other performance costs may be more important. It is here that the limits proposition discussed in Chapter 2 plays a role. There are negative feedback effects due to size once optimal size has been passed. Admittedly it is quite difficult to predict optimal size but it is a useful concept.

The difference between industrial and post-industrial society is a difference between the importance of the mechanical-bureaucratic versus the mixed mechanical-organic. The nineteenth century in Western Europe and North America was dominated by the former and the middle twentieth century has seen the latter become much more important. The mechanical-bureaucratic form tends to product specialize, whether in sewing machines, foodstuffs, tobacco products, or the like. The mixed mechanical-organic form is a multi-organization and therefore much more stable and much less vulnerable to booms and busts. Products that die are replaced. Technological innovation is the strategy and it keeps various divisions of the organizations competitive.

Again, Weber built his model on the long-term role of efficiency. This is important where demand is a large determinant and strongly affected by price. But as demand decreases in size, then product innovation becomes a preferable strategy. Perhaps what so critically separates the preference for mechanical versus mixed mechanical-organic forms is product life. The mechanical organizations relied not only upon large demand but *long* term demand. As product life decreases, there is a powerful impact on size of demand. In fact, this is probably even more important than the sheer size of demand. Given short product lives, there is a considerable emphasis on avoiding large and fixed investments in plants and equipment.

Another obvious point about demand is that it can be increased by international trade. The logic of large organizations is to produce a product in one plant and ship it throughout the world. In the beginning this was the case with Singer and American Tobacco. But now preferences for individuated products push the multinational corporations to have plants in different countries, ones that can adapt to national preferences.

As international trade grows, all countries are gradually forced to industrialize. As companies in the postindustrial nations become technologically intensive, the Third World is forced to modernize. Thus the impact of these two forces of change is to transform organizations throughout the world and speed the pace of evolution everywhere.

A somewhat cursory classification of societies can be made by looking at the combination of knowledge base and demand base. In the United States we have an exceptionally large demand and also a complex knowledge base. Not unexpectedly, we find that mixed mechanical-organic form predominates. Among other predictions we would expect that there would be much more formalization in American organizations because of the larger size, given our reasoning.

Parallel with this mixed mechanical-organic organization preference as found in IBM., DuPont, General Electric, RCA. and the other organizations that are world famous, one also finds that all of them are really multi-organizations with a variety of technologies, some standardized products and some more individualized. The United States is the one country outside of Japan where the conglomerate is the dominant form of business organization. However, just the reverse tends to be true in the public sector, except for universities where again the multi-organization predominates. Here the long term decentralization of the political structure and the heavy ideological commitment to equality (Lipset, 1963) — which is not the same thing as saying either democracy or equality — have led to relatively small size school systems, health systems, and welfare systems in contrast to Western Europe, where more centralized delivery systems tend to predominate.

This does not mean that there is an absence of traditional, mechanical, and organic-professionals forms but only a strong push towards the mixed mechanical-organic variety. If we go back in time, the larger knowledge base of American society and the much larger demand base led to the development of mechanical organizations in the pure form of the assembly line (Chandler, 1977). The larger knowledge base also means that traditional industrial and mechanical industry tends to be different in the United States, with a greater concern for innovation than one might otherwise expect. But the reverse is equally true. The larger demand base also means that in large scale organizations there is less than one would expect. Indeed, the large demand base may have led to a number of American organizations, especially economic ones, being too large and therefore too centralized and formalized and correspondingly too rigid and nonadaptive.

There is an historical problem as well. For a long time, distance made American markets secure from international competition. As the cost of transportation and travel time diminishes, many American mechanical organizations are proving very inflexible and incapable of innovating. The car, shoe, steel, metallurgy, china, and electronic industries have been increasingly proving nonadaptive. While the complaint is usually low wages and foreign dumping, the truth of the matter is usually a lack of knowledge base, an unwillingness to automate that would result in greater productivity and lower prices.

The big question — and problem for the United States — is that large size may have produced a lack of adaptiveness, and especially in meeting foreign competition. Large firms are unwilling to develop markets that are small and yet these may be the large ones in the future. Thus many American companies have not invested in Africa because they consider the markets too small and risky. But the Japanese have invested. Large size organizations become unwilling to take risks.

A very different country is Israel. This is a country with a small internal demand base although its per capita GNP is not small, but for an underdeveloped country there is a relatively large knowledge base. As a consequence we would predict more decentralization than one would otherwise expect. The organic form tends to predominate even in areas that one might otherwise expect to be more traditional. The mechanical-bureaucratic and mixed mechanical-organic are therefore relatively rare. Another example is Sweden, which also has a small population base but is quite rich.

Britain, France, and Japan for different reasons have large demand and knowledge bases although not as large as those of the United States. The smaller size tends to reflect itself in a greater emphasis on smaller scale organizations, a higher preponderance of the organic and the traditional forms than one would find in the United States. When one makes exceptions for the kinds of educa- tion – generalist versus specialist – one also finds somewhat higher centralization than would be normally predicted. France, in particular, has relatively small firms. Many industries are dominated by (Ardagh, 1977) artisan operations more than by a true professional-organic model, another reason why centraliza- tion is somewhat higher. In the organizations that are large and correspond more to the mechanical or mechanical-organic mix, one tends to find more centraliza- tion because of the generalist tradition. The same is true for Japan. In France, one would predict a lower rate of innovation as a consequence.

Algeria, Nigeria, and Brazil are all countries that are industrializing rapidly, and in varying degrees modernizing as well. Although traditional organizations have predominated, one would expect to find increasingly the mechanical form. Brazil is now developing an automobile industry. Some of these countries have created multinational organizations, in textiles in particular.

This analysis is complicated by the presence of international trade, which changes the prospective demand base. However, many multinational corpora- tions do not trade as much as manufacture the products within market contexts (Vernon, 1971). General Motors builds cars in Australia. Unilever manufactures soap in the United States. Fiat constructs cars in the USSR. Coca-Cola bottles the drink almost everywhere except in India. Olivetti bought Underwood so it could manufacture typewriters within the American market. In general, multi- national corporations build plants in countries once the society industrializes enough to have its own competitive factories, which in turn is a function of the demand. Insofar as an organization produces a relatively unique product with special qualities it may not follow the pathway of the multinational corporation. French wine, Virginia ham, Mexican hats, and the like offer distinctive qualities. If so, then they may be shipped from one country to the next. This increased emphasis on quality in the countries with a large knowledge base has allowed a large number of societies to keep a particular sector of the traditional and mechanical industries if in fact they develop some distinctive quality.

Organizations concerned with quality are, as we argued in Chapter 13, more likely to be concerned with stability and less with growth. Most of the multi- national organizations are either mechanical or mixed mechanic-organic in form because their large size pushes them into growth strategies, which require pene- tration overseas. Services are less likely to be part of multinational corporations, although there are exceptions here as well, such as universities that locate branches overseas. Banks, hotels, and other commercial services have done this for some time. But in general, public administration does not export well. There are American hospitals overseas, and naturally the military takes its own with it, but these are the exceptions rather than the rule.

Even the underdeveloped countries are creating multinational corporations as they start to develop large scale, mechanical-bureaucratic forms, which in turn pursue growth strategies. Fourteen of the 500 largest multinationals are now owned and operated outside of Japan, the United States, Canada, and Western Europe. Increasingly, Korea, Algeria, and Brazil are proving that they have the capacity to compete on an international scale. If we assume that the modernization and industrialization process will continue, then we can argue that in all societies, the organic-professional and mixed mechanical-organic will increasingly predominate. Together these forces are making traditional organization and even mechanical organization in post-industrial societies more and more rare. When we examine organizations with these forms, we find that the relentless push of technology and of innovation is changing their steady states slowly but surely. Police departments are becoming professionalized. The food companies now invest in research to develop new food products. Since the advent of frozen foods, this industry is quite technologically intensive (Lawrence and Lorsch, 1965). The military services are largely electronic and weapon systems are exceedingly complex. The automobile companies are slowly automating with the introduction of robots. While these changes are occurring slowly, they appear irresistible.

In this context the resistance of people to machine society becomes ironic. Only as automation eliminates the routine work and as the computer handles individual needs, can man move away from the kinds of organizations – the mechanical-bureaucratic in particular – that treat him like a machine whether as a worker or as a customer. Those industries in the United States that have not automated or become more technologically intensive – placing more emphasis on R&D – or followed a strategy of innovation are going under one by one. While the cries of protectionism are heard everywhere, tariffs are only a short-term answer. Only innovation, both process and output, is the long-term solution.

But what of the developing world? First, the preference for qualities, individualized products, and the like means that increasingly the developed countries import a wide variety of craft products from the developing countries and not just primary materials. Second, when a developing country creates a new product that is technologically intensive, it has the opportunity of dominating the market. Third, as the modernization and industrialization processes proceed in the Third World, the organic-professional and mixed mechanic-organic will become the dominant forms there too.

While international trade has been traditionally dominated by questions of price, increasingly quality is becoming a more important factor. People will not give up their French fashions. German cars, or Japanese televisions almost regardless of the exchange rates because they have distinctive qualities. But increasingly this applies to a broad range of products produced in the Third World as well. Gradually and slowly they are penetrating various markets and especially those where taste is important. The large increase in tourism facilitates this whole process, but it too is a consequence of expansion in education. People with college degrees have a specific life style that puts a premium on travel, which in turn develops this sector in developing countries and leads to greater awareness of the Third World and its products.

The above discussion views societies as largely independent. In fact they are not. Most societies are part of a world economic system and many of them are also part of various political alignments. Just as the 1970s discovered the importance of interorganizational relationships so did the importance of economic and geo-political relationships between societies become an important focus in development (Wallerstein, 1974). We can not spell out all of the implications of this for organizational analysis, except to note that some of the deductions from this paradigm are different. These differences need to be noted, at least briefly.

Once societies are part of a world system then there are relationships between the economic core and the economic periphery. In the simplest situation is that the core imports raw materials and exports finished materials (Chirot, 1977). This slows down the rate of industrialization in the periphery. One can make the model more complex by noting that countries begin to develop within the periphery, they can start producing semi-finished products in a three-step production process. The core countries exchange the more technologically intentive products between them. As economic development occurs then there is an evolution in the nature of the products exchanged between core and periphery. The core economic powers keep producing the steadily more sophisticated products while the periphery and semi-periphery produce the less sophisticated. Since profits accrue to the more sophisticated products, then the core countries make more profit from this economic relationship.

There are also implications for modernization. As less sophisticated products and raw materials are the specialty of the pheriphery there is less need for mass education. Thus the labor force remains unskilled. The nature of this economic relationship can slow down or speed up the rate of modernization and of industrialization in the Third World. If multinational organizations maintain their mechanical-bureaucratic divisions in pheriphery countries and their organic-professional and mixed mechanic-organic divisions in the core countries then by definition the core countries will more quickly move into the post-industrial society phase and the process of evolution will be *retarded* in the pheriphery countries. There is some evidence that this is what is happening. Many mass produced products, which require the assembly-line and unskilled labor, are being produced in Third World countries by the multi-national corporations while they produce their high technologically intensive products in their home countries. Textiles, toy, and certain rubber products are all examples.

The logic of world systems thinking is to see the multinational corporation establishing a world wide division of labor that prevents or slows down the process of industrialization and of modernization whereas our above arguments on the role of education in the core economic countries leads to some opposite conclusions. Both forces are present and one will have to study which is more predominate and why in future research.

14.1.3. The Findings

Only recently have we begun to have some cross-national comparisons (Azumi et al., forthcoming; Hickson and Lammers, 1977). They indicate that, in general, there is considerable consistency in organizations in different countries but at the same time there are also some striking differences. Hickson and Lammers, in their classification of a large number of studies, noted that traditional organizations tend to predominate in the Third World, as we would expect given both the generally small knowledge and demand bases. Unfortunately, they did not have any information about China and India, which might have more mechanical organizations, as we have defined them.

In the United States, Western Germany, Britain, and Scandinavia, they found a preponderance of what they call the flexible bureaucracy. This probably reflects the mixed mechanical-organic organizations that are most likely to be studied and which are most visible. In the Latin countries, and as one would expect from Crozier's (1964) study, they were more likely to find what they called the classic bureaucracy. This is the mechanical organization. We would expect the task scope to be small and the size to be relatively large. Unfortunately, the number of cases studied in the Latin countries is fairly small. In particular, one of the studies classified is of local government in Belgium, rather than of organizations, raising questions about the level of analysis.

Unfortunately the pure professional-organic business firm as described by Burns and Stalker (1961) or exemplified in the plastics companies of Lawrence and Lorsch (1967 a and b) tends not to be studied as much as the larger companies that have figured in much of the other research. How misleading this can be is indicated in a recent news report (*New York Times,* 3 March 1979: Business) that much of the growth in exports for the United States during the past eight years occurred in many small companies that were technologically intensive and had distinctive products.

Hofstede (Hickson and Lammers, 1977), in a study of power distance and rule orientation in forty different countries, found that all four combinations existed. All the research was in a single multinational firm and therefore represents the same technology and, to a certain extent, size. The Scandinavian and Anglo-Saxon countries were most likely to have less power distance and less rule orientation – that is, to the organic pattern in this one corporation. In contrast, large moderately developed countries such as Greece, Spain, Turkey, Brazil, Argentina, Venezuela, Italy, Mexico, and so on were more likely to fit the mechanical pattern. Besides Italy, perhaps the most interesting exception in this category was France. But then since only one firm was involved, investments in various parts of the world may be creating differences in personnel size. The more traditional kinds of organizations, at least on these two variables, are in small and developing countries such as Hong Kong, Singapore, and the Phillippines. Some surprises are India and Japan.

Finally, there are few interesting cases with little power distance but a lot of rule orientation as in Israel, Austria, Switzerland, and Germany. If we take power distance as a measure of centralization, and rule orientation as a measure of formalization, then there is some evidence for the four forms even within the same firm. Unfortunately, we are not told whether the technology and the size is the same in each country. This would be a more direct test of the hypotheses. What is true for one multinational corporation is, however, not representative of all organizations or even all economic ones.

The nature of the modernization and industrialization processes are pushing organizations towards both bigger organizations and organizations with more task scope. Internally organizations are developing a greater concentration of specialists as a consequence of the development in task scope, and at the same time this is being reduced with growth in personnel size. There are pressures towards greater centralization with personnel growth and towards less centralization as the concentration of specialists increases. At various times these cross-pressures can erupt into conflict. These conflicts are increasingly managed by means of the coordination mechanisms discussed in Chapter 11.

14.2. THE STATE AND EVOLUTION OF FORMS

Neither the process of modernization nor that of industrialization occurs in a vacuum. The state in each society may take a powerful interest in how fast these processes occur and in what order. Increasingly the state attempts to control, to regulate, and to stimulate both processes. The role of the state must be at least briefly touched upon.

Essentially the state can approach organizations, whether public or private, in all sectors in two ways. First, it can radically reduce their autonomy, making them subservient to the state. Second, it can coordinate their activities for some common good. While these might appear to be the same thing, in fact they are not.

Autonomy is the amount of power the organization (or multi-organization) has to choose its goals and the means to achieve them. Clearly multinational corporations are very powerful and autonomous, frequently escaping regulation. One of the problems of a capitalist society is that the organizations may be given *too much* autonomy with all the abuses that can occur. However, it is not immediately clear whether there might not be situations of too little autonomy as well.

Coordination is a test of how much the organizations work together to control the general growth of the society and the achievement of various goals. Organizations may work as independent agents or they may form cartels. They may be directed in a formal plan or encouraged to cooperate in an informal arrangement. One finds that coordination and autonomy can exist together as in the cases of Japan and Sweden. In these countries, the major leaders of government, business, and labor make decisions together. These are consensual societies. At the same time and in somewhat contradictory ways, the specific organizations do have a large amount of autonomy relative to their strategies of market competition. Perhaps the key test of autonomy is whether or not the organization can set its own prices and pay scales, and choose whether innovation or efficiency will be its means for achieving either stability or growth. It is a separate and quite interesting analysis as to why these particular societies developed this particular combination. Furthermore, one suspects that this is a wave of the future, the achieving of the maximization of autonomy and at the same time the maximization of coordination, what the French would call *action concertée*.

The more typical societal arrangements are coordination combined with little autonomy as in most planned socialist economies of China, USSR and the Eastern bloc, and no coordination combined with a large amount of autonomy as in most unplanned capitalist economies of the United States, Britain, Western Germany, Canada, and the like. Actually, what is distinctive about many so called capitalist economies is that there are not only large mixtures of public and private ownership but various degrees of informal cooperation do occur (Aiken et al., 1975).

What makes this distinction between autonomy and coordination interesting is the very long-term process of increasing decentralization of power but at the same time increasing planning and cooperative behavior between organizations. Etzioni (1968) argued that we are moving towards the active society, which I interpret to mean towards a society in which more and more coordination occurs because of the desire to control the excesses of nineteenth century capitalism. The desires to achieve a *number* of social goals are too great and require concerted action.

What makes for an interesting study, and one that has not received any attention, is what some of the mechanisms are by which the state can control and direct but without stifling the policies and strategies of various organizations. Consider some of these cases. In France, there is a national plan, which represents the "*prévision*" or perceived growth of the society and stipulates the policies of the government relative to key priorities. As a consequence, organizations can make predictions about their environments and plan accordingly. Here, too, as in Israel, there are a number of publicly owned corporations such as SNCF (railroads), ORTF (radio and television), Renault (cars), La Manufacture des Tabacs (tobacco), but which are allowed a considerable amount of autonomy to make their own strategic decisions. Perhaps the most striking example of this is the banking area where there are three public owned banks but each is operated independently.

In contrast, in Britain the coal industry and the steel industry have each been operated as they are in the USSR — as giant corporations which, in turn, means large size, centralization, formalization, and correspondingly less attention to the needs of the consumer. The crucial issue is not whether the industry or the company is public or private owned but instead how the industrial sector is arranged. If the entire industry is organized as a mechanical organization, then all the problems described in the previous chapters flow. Efficiency may be greater unless, of course, optimal size has been passed, which is what one expects has happened in the coal and steel industries in Britain. One of the explanations for why public organizations in socialist societies have alienated workers, low innovation and a lack of consideration for their consumers, is precisely because they tend to be too large, having a monopoly over supply. Frequently, the size is too large, with therefore too much centralization. This is further compounded by the lack of autonomy. But giving autonomy to these organizations does not necessarily solve the problem. Instead, it may make it *worse* if in fact the iron law of oligarchy is operating.

Just as there are a number of quasi-capitalist societies that do not seem to fit into the American mold, there are also a number of quasi-socialist societies that do not fit into the Russian or Chinese pattern of planned economy. Yugoslavia has allowed some autonomy to organizations and does not enforce all firms into some comprehensive plan. In particular, competition between firms is allowed. Also interesting in these societies is the relative importance attached to industrialization versus modernization. A simple test is the proportion of GNP placed in capital formation — and especially in the economy — and the proportion placed in education and scientific research.

It is more difficult to find examples where there is little coordination and at the same time little organizational autonomy. These are probably most typical of fascist societies such as Italy and Germany prior to the Second World War, or authoritarian ones such as Spain and Portugal during the reign of Franco and Salazar respectively. Typically dictatorships have controlled prices and wages but not necessarily engaged in national plans. At the same time, these kinds of controls can provide a considerable amount of predictability that allows for individual organizations to pursue strategies. With the exception of the Third Reich, one is impressed how this combination of little coordination and little autonomy leads to a concern for ultra-stability and that the organizations pursue policies of stability rather than growth. These economies tend to be stagnant. Of course, what is cause and what is effect is difficult to say. In contrast, the combination of much coordination and much autonomy appears to lead to steady growth of the economy. Here, the predictability of the environment allows for a constant reinvestment and the pursuit of long term strategies (Shonfield, 1966).

One can apply these same variables to sectors other than the economy and in particular to the institutional realms of education and science, political (military, police, fire, courts, prisons, etc.), and health and welfare (hospitals, public health, welfare agencies, etc.). In these other areas there tends to be less autonomy. There may or may not be any coordination. In almost all societies the military is coordinated by the state, as are the police, courts, prisons, and other aspects of internal and external security. These are monopolies of the state and little competition is allowed. Wages are fixed, regulations promulgated, and the like. There are exceptions, such as the paramilitary organizations that were allowed to exist in the Weimar Republic. But the sheer rarity of this type of event indicates how much the state maintains its monopoly of force.

Much greater variety in autonomy and in coordination is found in education and science or in health and welfare. Both of these institutional sectors are coordinated in France and Sweden and to a lesser extent in Britain. Autonomy tends to be quite low as well. Teaching class time is fixed, wages are set, the purchase of hospital equipment is carefully controlled and the like. In contrast — again in the United States, Canada, and Western Germany — there is more autonomy and little coordination between states, provinces or *Länder*, even at the university level. Recently, Germany began to move in the direction of some coordination of higher education. It is interesting to observe that national coordination in public administration is least likely to occur in federated systems. What coordination there is occurs at the local government level and then more in education than in health.

It would take us somewhat afar to explain why there are these differences between these major institutional sectors. The major point is that while autonomy and coordination vary across institutional realms, these societies that have a characteristic pattern for one area tend to have comparable patterns for the other areas. There is a strain towards consistency across institutional sectors in a rank order even though there are differences between realms in the same society.

The impact of autonomy and of coordination on an organization is more likely to be on the choice of strategy and the nature of the interorganizational relationships rather than on the organizational system of variables per se. The hypothese are:

14.5 *The greater the coordination and the less the autonomy, the more likely the dominant coalition will choose a strategy of rapid growth through efficiency.*

14.6 *The greater the autonomy, the more likely the dominant coalition will choose a variety of strategies.*

14.7 *The less the coordination, the more likely the dominant coalition will emphasize competition as a form of conflict between organizations with the same goals.*

14.8   The less the coordination and the less the autonomy, the more likely the dominant coalition will choose a strategy of stability through efficiency.

Hypothesis 14.7 is almost a tautology because coordination implies the management of conflict. Typically organizations in coordinated societies are either given natural monopolies or else the elites agree among themselves on how the market will be divided up, which has the same consequence – the lowering of competition as a form of conflict.

It is more difficult to make predictions about the future changes in the extent of coordination and the extent of organizational autonomy. As organizations hire a more skilled and educated labor force, the members will fight for autonomy, and thus one strain with modernization is towards greater autonomy. However, the educated consumer will want his rights protected against the large and powerful organizations in which he works so there will be a countervailing tendency to limit the autonomy of organizations. One solution to this dilemma is coordination. This can prevent the worst excesses of a ruthless pursuit of profit, whether in a capitalist or socialist economy. Certainly, one sees increasing interest in national plans and other attempts at coordination in the United States (Aiken et al., 1975).

Thus, one might predict some convergence toward the combination of coordination and autonomy. Pure "socialist" societies such as the USSR and pure "capitalist" societies such as the United States will evolve though by different pathways. The United States will solve the problem by means of multi-organizations such as HEW, coalitions of organizations, and the like. The USSR will probably move in the direction of giving more autonomy slowly in specific areas such as wages, prices, and the like.

14.3.   ORGANIZATIONAL FORMS AND SOCIETAL PROBLEMS

Just as Weber worried about some of the excesses of bureaucracy, there are problems with the professional-organic and mixed mechanical-organic forms. While there are many desirable characteristics, such as a movement towards decentralization and greater equality, there are difficulties as well.

The major consequence of having a larger proportion of organizations that are professional-organic or mixed mechanical-organic in form, whether organized into multi-organizations or not, is the much greater emphasis on innovation and quality rather than stability and efficiency. But if so, then the necessity of continued emphasis on education becomes paramount. Managers and professionals must accept the idea of constant training (Hage, 1974), something which will be resisted.

How to establish continuing education programs, create professional control mechanisms, and motivate people to be concerned about their technological obsolescence are problems that are anything but easy to solve. The positive side of the coin is that changes in the social structure of organizations towards greater concentrations of specialists and more decentralization will help resolve some of these difficulties.

Another interesting consequence is a movement away from the formalism that concerned Weber. Standard rules don't work for the many individual cases that are recognized today. The real concern remains the opposite: will there be enough professional control and of the right kind?

Another danger in constant change and continual attempts to improve quality is the tendency to change too fast, causing an anomic condition (Durkheim, 1951) to occur. Rapid rates of automation can create unemployment. Sudden increases in the budgets of people-service organizations can result in great dislocations, as we have seen in the War on Poverty (Dewar, 1976) and the growth in American universities. The United States in particular – and for a variety of reasons – is subject to this tendency of too-rapid change rates. Although we are familiar with the booms and busts in the economy created by demand, now the danger is much more the rate of technological change, which can be either too fast or too slow. Explosions of knowledge can be as unsettling as loss of markets. One could make the case that this happened in medicine and is why we have problems in the health care system today.

The real adaptive problem is to manage growth in knowledge in a steady and measured way; to recognize that these processes can occur too rapidly as well as too slowly. Here coordination may supply some of the answer.

A constant problem will be the conflict engendered by the rising expectations created by mass college-educated publics. Not only do women want work and work with responsibility, but all will want a greater participation in power and greater equality of income and of status. The major arena of these contests will probably occur inside rather than outside organizations. The verity of the premises in Chapter 3 will be demonstrated by a series of many organizational conflicts during the course of the next few decades. And here Europe, except for Scandinavia, may find that it has the most difficult pathway ahead. The adaptiveness of the internal structure to these larger societal changes will not be easy.

In this sense, Weber's prediction about democracy and equality would appear to be correct. They are likely to become greater, but not because of bureaucracy as such but because of the continual conflicts within organizations, which, in turn, are generated by the modernization process.

Whereas conflict was not an element in Weber's model of bureaucracy, it does seem to be a critical component in both organic-professional and mixed mechanical-organic forms. The research results reviewed in Chapter 10 suggest that for the long term, conflict will increase in frequency but diminish in intensity, an insight of Durkheim's of almost a century ago (*La Division du Travail*, 1893). The management of conflict thus becomes a key attribute of managerial effectiveness.

More critical may be the growing role conflict. Kahn et al. (1964) have made clear the personal stress, tension, and role strain. The long-term trend seems to be for this kind of stress to grow. How individuals cope with this and the social conflict may become a crucial factor in their own satisfaction with work.

Organizations are bases of power, and who controls them controls the key actors in the larger society. Insofar as this control is shared widely, one can begin to speak about democracy with some greater assurance. Too often we think of Congress and of Parliament as proofs of the existence of democracy. They are only means to this end and in the final analysis it is how they respond to various interests, whether left or right, male or female, black or white, and so on. Their response depends not only on whether there are large organizations but also what these organizations demand. The values or goals of organizations and especially their concern for derived goals as we noted in Chapter 5 is a function of how widespread the participation is within them — whether workers, customs, or clients shape the strategic decisions. Responsiveness and social accountability are current themes and for good reason. Organizations have not been that socially conscious.

Here is where the dilemma between organizational autonomy and coordination may be most critical. On the one hand, organizations will try to maximize their autonomy. On the other hand they must be coordinated if the interests of the larger society are to be served.

So far the multinational corporations would appear to have escaped control. Their autonomy is a danger. But it appears likely that the same processes of modernization that are driving organizations toward cooperation are also driving various governments, which are also organizations, to work together to control organizations. The current steel agreements are only the beginning and actually not the first step in the continual development of even more complex arrangements that are setting limits on the autonomy of organizations and preventing their worse abuses. This process is likely to continue.

To solve the dilemma of how to maintain both autonomy and cooperation, competitors must learn to work together in even more complex arrangements. This again is not likely to occur automatically but must be in part mandated by legislation and in part facilitated by various inducements such as joint funding (Aiken et al., 1975). When the danger is very great, then cooperation is likely to occur voluntarily — as in the North Atlantic Treaty Organization, which is the cooperation of armies. But without perceived dangers then cooperation needs some force to propel it.

And this is probably the single biggest concern confronting societies in the future. If they do not learn ways of cooperating, of preventing competition from becoming unbridled, then complex problems are unlikely to be solved. Worse yet, the logic of growth leads to all the various difficulties that we have observed at various points in this book – alienation of workers (Chapter 9), centralization (Chapter 12), conflict (Chapter 11), indifference to larger societal problems or derived goals (Chapter 5), maladaptation to changing circumstances (Chapter 8), and so forth. The more that organizational elites become concerned about growth at any price, the more that these difficulties are likely to flow. At the other extreme, however, if organizations are not given any autonomy and are forced to coordinate everything, we have many of the same problems – alienation of workers and centralization, cynicism or fatalism rather than conflict, little innovation and again an indifference to larger societal problems.

The modern debate between capitalism and socialism – the two choices of the totally free market and the totally planned economy – would not appear to be satisfactory. There is too much autonomy and not enough interorganizational cooperation in the first instance and too little autonomy and too much cooperation in the second instance. This would appear to be the great unresolved problem of the latter part of the twentieth century: to find a better way of handling the dilemma of organizational autonomy and interorganizational cooperation. The multi-organization is one potential solution but it may not be the best.

Coordination is necessary – can it be achieved, especially across national boundaries? Post-industrial societies such as the United States, Japan, and Western Europe exist in a single world. The thesis of the world economy is a popular one. Not just a single economy but more importantly a largely single but highly differentiated public with access to the same information. There is single set of sciences and of arts, of youth cultures and of aged populations, of welfare needs and of life expectancies. The increasing number of meetings of the leaders of the post-industrialized world are a sign that the policies in various ways must become increasingly integrated as well. Actions of one nation can be counterproductive if not followed by another. The energy crisis is only the most dramatic example.

The problems for the industrial and traditional societies are different but comparable. In part, they engender the greater need for cooperation between organizations in the post-industrial societies. Weber worried about the dangers of plutocracy. The greater danger today is the gap between the rich nations that are post-industrial and the Third World. This is a problem which will not be solved if the logic of growth is pursued to its ultimate extreme in the post-industrial countries. For it is organizations that tax, that produce and sell goods, that set prices and profit ratios, and the like. And it is governments that must learn to cooperate to solve international inflation and unemployment, crop surpluses and energy deficiencies, and so on. The groups that control these organizations will control their policies on these matters.

Finally, we end with an essentially optimistic note, for I am by nature an optimist. If more education, the modernization process, does produce a greater concern for innovation and for quality, a greater awareness of a more complex world and of social need, then we have yet to witness the true revolution that can occur. The development of mass college education took twenty years to unfold in the post-industrial societies. The United States did not reach 50% of the relevant age cohort, 18–24, until the late 1960s. And one can seriously question the relevant quality of the education received. However, in just this twenty years, the proportion tripled. Most of these educated people are still in their twenties or early thirties. They will not be in command of organizations for another twenty-five years, when they are in their forties or fifties. Thus, the real impact should be occurring towards the end of this century. What world will they produce? We shall have to wait and see. As this occurs, we can test the predictions that have been made.

Appendix A

Premises

3A Occupational or other interest groups want the same rank in power, prestige, pay, and privileges as they have in training and skill.

3B The greater the proportion of members who have low rank, the more important will be hierarchical levels and social characteristics as the basis of interest group formation.

3C The greater the proportion of members who have high rank, the more important will be occupation and value preferences as the basis of interest group formation.

3D The more similar the occupational activities, value preferences, rank level, and social characteristics of the interest groups, the more likely they are to form a coalition.

4A The dominant coalition will try to reduce risk as much as possible.

5A The greater the diversity of interest groups represented in the dominant coalition, the more complex and varied the choice of priorities will be.

5B The general values and personality characteristics of individuals remain relatively stable across time.

5C To survive, organizations must maintain a minimum level of innovation, efficiency and morale, and a balance between quality and quantity.

5D The more that innovation and quality are emphasized, the more difficult it is to maintain a minimum level of quantity and efficiency, and vice versa.

6A The greater the equality of rank on skill, power, pay, and privilege, the greater the amount of change implemented.

6B The greater the diversity of knowledge, the greater the amount of change implemented.

8A The greater the resource base, the greater the capacity for information feedback and the more likely that eventually the right action is selected.

9A   Individuals attempt to maximize benefits and reduce costs.

9B   Organizations attempt to maximize benefits and reduce costs.

9C   All individuals consider as benefits interesting work, job autonomy, salary equity, and social integration, and as costs monotonous work, close supervision, insecure employment, and social isolation.

9D   The more that the control mechanism indicates a basic trust, the more likely it will be accepted.

11A   All organizations need coordination and control.

11B   There are two basic mechanisms for achieving coordination and control: programing with an emphasis on sanctions, and feedback with an emphasis on socialization.

11C   The greater the diversity of organizational structure, the greater the emphasis on coordination and control by means of feedback and socialization.

11D   The greater the difference in rank in the organizational structure, the greater the emphasis on coordination and control by means of programing and sanctions.

12A   The greater the knowledge input, the greater the diversity of social structure.

12B   The greater the number of resources other than knowledge, the more likely these are to be concentrated in the hands of an elite.

13A   Given the lack of choice of the most appropriate strategy for controlling the environment, the next closest one in the typology of strategies will be selected.

Appendix B

Hypotheses

3. 1 The greater the concentration of highly trained and skilled specialists, the greater the decentralization of power in strategic decision and vice-versa.

3. 2 The greater the concentration of highly trained and skilled specialists, the greater the destratification of pay and prestige and vice-versa.

3. 3 The greater the concentration of highly trained and skilled specialists, the greater the equality of rights and responsibilities and vice-versa.

3. 4 The greater the centralization of power in strategic decisions, the greater the stratification of pay and prestige and vice-versa.

3. 5 The greater the centralization of power in strategic decisions, the lower the equality of rights and responsibilities and vice-versa.

3. 6 The greater the stratification of pay and of prestige, the lesser the equality of rights and responsibilities and vice-versa.

4. 1 The higher the risk, the more likely the trajectory will follow a network pattern.

4. 2 The lower the risk, the more likely the trajectory will follow a hierarchical pattern.

4. 3 As the number of decision-issues increases the variety of origins increases and therefore the variety of trajectories and the emergence of the network pattern.

4. 4 As the number of decision-issues of the same kind increases, the low risk decisions are delegated and routinized, reducing the variety of trajectories and encouraging the emergence of a hierarchical pattern.

4. 5 The greater the concentration of specialists, the greater the number of decision-issues and number of issues of the same kind.

4. 6 The greater the concentration of specialists, the greater the amount of information search and the amount of deliberate delay.

4. 7   The greater the decentralization, the greater the joint creation, delegation, and routinization of the decision-making process.

4. 8   The greater the centralization, the greater the discussion and the greater the negotiation.

5. 1   The greater the centralization, the more likely the dominant coalition will choose the objectives of quanity and low cost with little emphasis on innovation, and demonstrate effectiveness in this way.

5. 2   If the organization is polycentralized, then the dominant coalition is more likely to choose the objectives of quality and moderate cost with little emphasis on innovation, and demonstrate effectiveness in this way.

5. 3   If the organization is mixed centralized-decentralized, the dominant coalition is more likely to choose the objectives of quantity and moderate low cost with some emphasis on innovation, and demonstrate effectiveness in this way.

5. 4   The greater the concentration of specialists, if they are professionals, the more likely the dominant coalition will choose the objectives of quality and of innovation.

5. 5   The greater the value of particularism in the dominant coalition, the more they will choose quality as an objective.

5. 6   The greater the value of the external environment in the dominant coalition, the more they will choose innovation as an objective.

5. 7   Given the values of universalism and a focus on the external environment in the dominant coalition, they will choose a combination of quantity-quality and moderate innovation.

5. 8   Given the values of particularism and a focus on the internal-organization in the dominant coalition, they will choose a combination of quality with little innovation.

5. 9   The greater the professionalism of the dominant coalition, the more likely it is to emphasize particularistic rather than universalistic values.

5.10   The greater the cosmopolitanism of the dominant coalition, the greater the emphasis on external rather than internal focus.

5.11   The greater the professionalism in the dominant coalition, the more likely they will choose quality as an objective.

5.12   The greater the cosmopolitanism in the dominant coalition, the more likely they will choose innovation as an objective.

5.13   Given non-professional values and cosmopolitanism in the dominant coalition, they will choose a combination of quantity-quality and moderate innovation as objectives.

5.14   Given professional values and localism in the dominant coalition, they will choose a combination of quality and little innovation as objectives.

5.15 If the dominant coalition overemphasizes some objectives of the organization, it creates ineffectiveness in others and is replaced.

5.16 If the standards of effectiveness change, then the dominant coalition will be evaluated as ineffective and be replaced.

5.17 The larger the size of the dominant coalition, the more it will attempt to achieve a balance in its emphasis in objectives.

5.18 The less visible the effectiveness of the organization, the less change in the dominant coalition.

5.19 When a new dominant coalition emerges, it will tend to emphasize the opposite objectives of the previous elite.

6. 1 The greater the concentration of highly trained and skilled specialists, the greater the rate of output innovation.

6. 2 The greater the stratification of pay and prestige, the less the rate of output innovation.

6. 3 The greater the centralization of power in strategic decisions, the less the rate of output innovation.

6. 4 The greater the normative equality of rights and responsibilities, the greater the rate of output innovation.

6. 5 The greater the concentration of highly trained and skilled specialists, the greater the rate of process innovation.

6. 6 The greater the centralization of power in strategic decisions, the less the rate of process innovation.

6. 7 The greater the stratification of pay and prestige, the less the rate of process innovation.

6. 8 The greater the quality of rights and responsibilities, the greater the rate of process innovation.

6. 9 The greater the emphasis placed on the objective of innovation by the power elite, the greater the innovation rate.

6.10 The more committed the dominant coalition is to the introduction of change and the greater the concentration of specialists, the more likely there is to be a radical innovation.

6.11 The higher the standards of performance relative to outputs, the more likely the dominant coalition will be open to radical innovations.

6.12 The greater the sharing of work decisions among peers with the same skill and expertise, and the greater the creativity.

6.13 There is a curvilinear relationship between the sharing of work decisions among peers with the same skill and expertise and individual creativity that is a function of the number of people who participate in the sharing of the work decisions.

6.14 The greater the diversity of activities performed by the individual, the greater his creativity.

6.15 The greater the diversity of perspectives entertained by the individual or by his work group, the greater his or their creativity.

6.16 There is a curvilinear relationship between the diversity of activities performed by the individual and the individual's creativity.

6.17 There is a curvilinear relationship between the diversity of perspectives entertained by the individual or by his work group and the individual's creativity.

7. 1 The greater the ease of measurement, the more frequent the measurement and the greater the variety of measures, then the greater the frequency with which performance gaps are detected.

7. 2 The more frequent the measurement and the more frequently that performance gaps are detected, the smaller the extent of the performance gap.

7. 3 The more severe the standard and the longer the time span, the greater the extent of the performance gap detected.

7. 4 The greater the extent of the performance gap and the longer the time span, the greater the number of performances on which gaps are detected.

7. 5 The greater the number of performances on which gaps are detected and the greater the extent of the performance gap, the more likely the choice of a radical innovation.

7. 6 The more radical the innovation, the greater the need for new personnel, funds, and technologies.

7. 7 The more new technology, personnel and specialties, the greater the behavior change of the membership.

7. 8 The more new occupational specialties and the job autonomy of the innovators, the greater the change in power and status of particular positions.

7. 9 The more behavior change in positions and relationships, the more role conflict.

7.10 The more change in the power and status of particular positions, the greater the power and status conflict.

7.11 The more role, power, and status conflict, the less the job autonomy of the innovators.

7.12 The greater the consensus about the performance gap, the less the role, power, and status conflict.

7.13 The greater the consensus about the performance gap, the less the extent of conflict, and the extent of costs and the more the extent of benefits perceived, the more likely the decision to institutionalize the innovation.

7.14 The greater the consensus about the performance gap, the greater the duration of the time span for experimentation.

7.15 The greater the cost of the innovation, the greater the duration of the time span and the extent of costs perceived.

7.16 The greater the measurability of benefits and of costs, the greater the number of benefits and of costs perceived and the more likely the decision to institutionalize the innovation.

7.17 The more centralized the organization, the more that the dominant coalition will resist radical change because of their vested interests.

7.18 The more stratified the organization, the more that the dominant coalition will resist radical change because of their vested interests.

7.19 The less the normative equality of the organization, the more that the dominant coalition will resist radical change because of their vested interests.

7.20 The deeper the crisis facing the organization, the less the dominant coalition will resist radical change because of their vested interests.

7.21 The greater the experience with role behavior change in the past, the less members resist radical change.

7.22 The greater the experience with different perspectives, paradigms, schools of thought, and so on, the less members will resist radical change.

7.23 The greater their experience with different cultures, languages and social groups, and so on, the less members will resist radical change.

7.24 The sharper the increase in the rate of change, the greater the resistance to any change.

7.25 The more standardized is the work-flow or throughput, the more important are losses of status and of power.

7.26 The more professionalized is the work-flow or throughput, the more important are gains of improved job performance, and especially as regards quality.

7.27 The more standardized the work-flow or throughput, the more important are the costs of efficiency and of production.

7.28 The more professionalized is the work-flow or throughput, the more important are benefits of quality and of improved organizational prestige.

8. 1 The longer the period of success with one form, the more difficult it is to transform the system.

8. 2 The greater the concentration of specialists, the greater the amount of information and the better its quality.

8. 3 The greater the degree of centralization, the less the amount of information and the poorer its quality.

8. 4 The greater the elite value placed on long term planning, the greater the demands for information, both quantity and quality.

8. 5 The higher the standards of performance of the elites, the more likely they are to see the need for a large change.

9. 1 The greater the concentration of specialists, the greater the average interest in work and the less the monotony and routineness.

9. 2 The greater the centralization, the less the feelings of job autonomy and the greater the sense of close supervision.

9. 3 The greater the stratification, the greater the salary inequalities and the greater the employment insecurity.

9. 4 The greater the normative equality, the greater the privilege equity and the greater the sense of doing responsible work.

9. 5 The greater the concentration of specialists, the greater the job satisfaction.

9. 6 The greater the centralization, the less the job satisfaction.

9. 7 The greater the stratification, the less the satisfaction with salary.

9. 8 The greater the normative equality, the more the satisfaction with privileges and responsibilities.

9. 9 The greater the task visibility, the lower the morale.

9.10 The greater the formalization, if it does not restrict job autonomy, the higher the morale.

9.11 The higher the level of communication, the greater the morale.

10. 1 The greater the degree of differentiation or of complexity, the greater the degree of conflict.

10. 2 The greater the participation of the membership in decisions, the greater the degree of conflict.

10. 3 The greater the emphasis on rules, the greater the degree of conflict.

10. 4 The greater the discrepancy between the extent of the concentration of specialists and the predicted level of decentralization, the greater the conflict and the less the consensus.

10. 5 The greater the discrepancy between the extent of the concentration of specialists and the predicted level of destratification, the greater the conflict and the less the consensus.

10. 6 The greater the discrepancy between the extent of the concentration of specialists and the predicted level of normative equality, the greater the conflict and the less the consensus.

10. 7 The greater the discrepancy between the extent of the concentration of specialists and the predicted level of emphasis on the goal of quality versus quantity, the greater the conflict and the less the consensus.

10. 8   The greater the discrepancy between the extent of the concentration of specialists and the predicted level of emphasis on the goal of change versus stability, the greater the conflict and the less the consensus.

10. 9   The greater the concentration of specialists, the greater the variety of occupations, the larger the size of the role-set, and the greater the involvement of the role partners and therefore the greater the role conflict.

10.10   The greater the centralization and the stratification (that is, the difference in powers and rewards), the less the role conflict.

11. 1   The greater the concentration of specialists, the greater the volume of unscheduled and scheduled communications.

11. 2   The greater the concentration of specialists, the greater the volume of vertical and of horizontal unscheduled communication.

11. 3   The greater the concentration of specialists, the greater the emphasis on training and education.

11. 4   The greater the concentration of specialists, the greater the emphasis on peer approval and attitude conformity.

11. 5   The greater the degree of centralization, the greater the degree of formalization.

11. 6   The greater the degree of stratification, the greater the degree of formalization.

11. 7   The greater the degree of normative equality, the less the degree of formalization.

11. 8   The greater the degree of centralization, the greater the use of rewards and punishments and the more grades in the reward system there will be.

11. 9   The greater the degree of stratification, the greater the use of rewards and punishments and the more grades in the reward system there will be.

11.10   The greater the degree of normative equality, the less the use of rewards and punishment and the more grades there will be.

11.11   The greater the degree of centralization, the greater the task visibility.

11.12   The greater the degree of stratification, the greater the task visibility.

11.13   The greater the degree of normative equality, the less the task visibility.

11.14   Given a moderate level in the concentration of specialists – where the specialists are craftsmen – and centralization, then the vertical communication is both upward and downward and within and between departments.

11.15   Given a moderate level in the concentration of specialists – where specialists are craftsmen – and centralization, there is little horizontal communication and what occurs is at the bottom of the hierarchy relative to the throughput.

11.16   Given a moderate level in the concentration of specialists – where the specialists are craftsmen — and centralization, then control is via a mixture of rewards with artisan socialization with peer approval being important.

11.17 Given a moderate level in the concentration of specialists — where the specialists are craftsmen — and centralization, there is little scheduled communication and little formalization but instead a reliance on customs.

11.18 Given a moderate level in the concentration of specialists — where the specialists are engineers — and centralization, then vertical communication is both up and down but within departments and not between.

11.19 Given a moderate level in the concentration of specialists — where the specialists are engineers — and centralization, then there is horizontal communication usually at the top echelons and within particular departments.

11.20 Given a moderate level in the concentration of specialists — where the specialists are engineers — and centralization, then there is a lot of scheduled communication and of formalization but again primarily in particular departments.

11.21 Given a moderate level in the concentration of specialists — where the specialists are engineers — and centralization, control is via a mixture of rewards and of professional socialization and where peer approval is only somewhat important.

12. 1 The greater the task scope, the greater the concentration of specialists.

12. 2 The greater the task scope, the greater the number of interest groups.

12. 3 The greater the task scope, the more likely the coalition will be unstable.

12. 4 The greater the task scope, the more likely the basis of the coalition will be occupations and values — that is, preferences about organizational performances and utilities.

12. 5 The greater the task scope, the greater the number of decision-issues.

12. 6 The greater the personnel size, the greater the centralization.

12. 7 The greater the personnel size, the greater the stratification.

12. 8 The greater the personnel size, the less the normative equality.

12. 9 The greater the organizational autonomy, the greater the centralization.

12.10 The greater the organizational autonomy, the greater the stratification.

12.11 The greater the organizational autonomy, the less normative equality.

12.12 Given simple tasks, with many exceptions, and if the size of the work force is small, then the most efficient arrangement is low mechanization with a pooled work-flow housed in a moderately flat structure.

12.13 Given simple tasks, as the number of exceptions decreases and the size of the work force increases, then it becomes easier to mechanize and arrange the personnel sequentially, housed in a tall structure.

12.14 Given complex tasks, as the number of exceptions decreases and as the size of the work force increases, then one must automate and have very high production continuity, with personnel arranged reciprocally and housed in a tall structure but with many departments.

12.15 Given complex tasks, as the number of exceptions increases and as the size of the work force decreases, then automation is impossible, and the most efficient arrangement is a team housed in a flat structure having many departments.

12.16 The greater the task scope, the greater the communication volume.

12.17 The greater the personnel size, the greater the emphasis on formalization and task visibility.

12.18 Given small task scope and personnel size, there is an emphasis on vertical communication both up and down.

12.19 Given large task scope and personnel size, there is an emphasis on horizontal communication at the top.

13. 1 The greater the technical knowledge, the more likely the demand is to be specialized and limited in scope.

13. 2 The greater the technical knowledge, the greater the diversity of work and therefore the larger the task scope.

13. 3 The greater the growth rate in technical knowledge, the shorter the product life.

13. 4 The greater the growth rate in technical knowledge, the faster the needed response rate.

13. 5 The greater the potential demand, the greater the average personnel size.

13. 6 The less the predictability of potential demand, the smaller the average personnel size.

13. 7 The greater the potential demand, the greater the importance of efficiency.

13. 8 The greater the available power, the greater the organizational autonomy.

13. 9 The larger the average size of the organization, the greater the potential for growth, the less the level of task knowledge, and the less the growth in this, the greater the emphasis on efficiency and growth, and therefore the more the dominant coalition will attempt to dominate its environment and eliminate competitors.

13.10 The smaller the average size of the organization, the less the potential for growth, the higher the level of task knowledge and the less the growth in this, the greater the emphasis on innovation and quality, and therefore the more the dominant coalition will attempt to achieve equality and accept competitors.

13.11 The more that the dominant coalition emphasizes efficiency and growth, the more likely it is to attempt to dominate its environment and to eliminate its competitors.

13.12 The more that the dominant coalition emphasizes innovation and quality, the more likely it is to attempt to achieve equality and live with competitors.

13.13 The fewer the number of competitors there are and the larger they are, the more likely that a dominant coalition will choose a policy of domination.

13.14 The greater the degree of conflict in interorganizational relationships, the more likely the dominant coalition will choose a policy of domination and vice versa.

13.15 The greater the degree of cooperation in interorganizational relationships, the more likely the dominant coalition will choose a policy of interdependence and vice versa.

13.16 The greater the dominant coalition's emphasis on maximization of effectiveness, the greater the tendency to exploit.

13.17 The greater the emphasis on innovation by one organization in a specific market context, the more other organizations must match competition by their own emphasis.

13.18 The more that the set of organizations in a specific market context emphasizes innovation, the faster the growth in task knowledge.

13.19 The greater the emphasis on cost by one organization in a specific market context, the more other organizations must match competition by their own emphasis.

13.20 The more that a set of organizations in a specific market context emphasizes efficiency, the greater the potential demand.

13.21 The greater the emphasis on domination, through growth by efficiency, the more likely the market becomes dominated by a few large organizations who compete by all means possible.

13.22 The greater the emphasis on cooperation, through development by innovation, the more likely the market becomes dominated by networks of organizations who emphasize niche creation vis-à-vis each other.

14. 1 The larger the knowledge base of the society, the larger the task-scope of the average organization and the more emphasis on change and quality as goals.

14. 2 The larger the task-scope of the average organization and the greater the emphasis on change and quality as goals, the more the growth in the knowledge base of the society.

14. 3 The greater the demand base of the society, the larger the personnel size of the average organization and the greater the emphasis on efficiency as a goal.

14. 4   The lower the cost, the greater the demand base.

14. 5   The greater the coordination and the less the autonomy, the more likely the dominant coalition will choose a strategy of rapid growth through efficiency.

14. 6   The greater the autonomy, the more likely the dominant coalition will choose a variety of strategies.

14. 7   The less the coordination, the more likely the dominant coalition will emphasize competition as a form of conflict between organizations with the same goals.

14. 8   The less the coordination and the less the autonomy, the more likely the dominant coalition will choose a strategy of stability through efficiency.

Bibliography

Abell, Peter, 1971. *Model Building in Sociology.* New York: Schocken.

—— (Ed.), 1975. *Organizations as Bargaining and Influence Systems.* London: Heineman.

Abernathy, William, 1978. *The Productivity Dilemma: Roadblock to Innovation in the Automobile Industry.* Baltimore: Johns Hopkins University Press.

Adams, Walter, 1970. "Competition, Monopoly, and Planning," in Maurice Zeitlin (Ed.), *American Society Inc.* Chicago: Markham.

Adelman, Irman, and Cynthia Morris, 1973. *Economic Growth and Social Equality in Developing Countries.* Stanford: Stanford University Press.

Aiken, Michael, and Jerald Hage, 1966. "Organizational Alienation: A Comparative Analysis." *American Sociological Review, 31* (August): 497–507.

——, 1968. "Organizational Interdependence and Intra-organizational Structure." *American Sociological Review, 33* (December): 912–930.

——, 1971. "The Organic Organization and Innovation." *Sociology, 5* (January): 63–82.

Aiken, Michael, et al., 1975. *Coordinating Human Services.* San Francisco: Jossey-Bass.

Albrow, M. C., 1964. "The Sociology of Organizations." *British Journal of Sociology, 15* (December): 350–57.

Aldrich, Howard E., 1972. "Technology and Organizational Structure: A Reexamination of the Findings of the Aston Group." *Administrative Science Quarterly, 17* (March): 26–43.

——, 1976a. "Resource Dependence and Interorganizational Relations Between Local Employment Service Offices and Social Services Sector Organizations." *Administration and Society, 7* (February): 419–54.

——, 1976b. "An Interorganizational Dependency Perspective on Relations Between the Employment Service and the Organization Set," in R. Kilman, L. Pondy, and D. Slevin (Eds.), *The Management of Organization Design,* Vol. II. New York: Elsevier North-Holland.

——, 1978. "Centralization Versus Decentralization in the Design of Human Service Delivery Systems: A Response to Gouldner's Lament," in R. Sarri and Y. Hasenfeld (Eds.), *Issues in Service Delivery in Human Service Organizations.* New York: Columbia University Press.

——, 1979. *Organizations and Environments.* Englewood Cliffs, N.J.: Prentice-Hall.

Aldrich, Howard E., and Diane Herker, 1977. "Boundary Spanning Roles and Organization Structure." *Academy of Management Review, 2* (April): 217–30.

Aldrich, Howard E., and Jeffrey Pfeffer, 1976. "Environments of Organizations," in Alex Inkeles, James Coleman, and Neil Smelser, (Eds.), *Annual Review of Sociology,* Vol. 2. Palo Alto, Calif.: Annual Review, pp. 79–105.

Alutto, Joseph A., and James A. Belasco, 1972. "A Typology for Participation in Organizational Decision Making." *Administrative Science Quarterly, 17* (March): 117–125.

Anderson, Perry, 1974a. *Lineages of the Absolutist State.* New York: Humanities.

Ardagh, John, 1977. *Modern France in Transition.* (3rd ed.) London: Penguin.

Argyris, Chris, 1972. *The Applicability of Organizational Sociology.* London: Cambridge University Press.

Ashby, Eric, 1956. *An Introduction to Cybernetics.* New York: Wiley.

Azumi, Koya, and Jerald Hage (eds.), 1972. *Organizational Systems.* Lexington, Mass.:

Bacharach, Samuel, and Michael Aiken, 1976. "Structural and Process Constraints of Influence in Organizations: A Level Specific Analysis." *Administrative Science Quarterly, 21* (December): 623–642.

Bain, Joe, 1956. *Barriers to New Competition: Their Character and Consequences in Manufacturing Industries.* Cambridge, Mass.: Harvard University Press.

Baldridge, J. Victor, 1971. *Power and Conflict in the University.* New York: Wiley.

Baldridge, J. Victor, and Robert A. Rurnham, 1975. "Organizational Innovation: Individual, Organizational, and Environmental Impacts." *Administrative Science Quarterly, 20* (June): 165–167.

Bales, Robert F., 1950. *Interaction Process Analysis.* Cambridge, Mass.: Addison-Wesley.

Barnard, Chester I., 1946. "Functions and Pathologies of Status Systems in Formal Organizations," In William Foote Whyte (Ed.), *Industry and Society.* New York: McGraw-Hill.

Bannister, E. Michael, 1970. Multiorganization *Human Relations, 23* (October): 405–431.

Becker, Selwyn W., and Gerald Gordon, 1966. "An Entrepreneurial Theory of Formal Organizations – Part I: Patterns of Formal Organizations." *Administrative Science Quarterly, 11* (December): 315–344.

Becker, Selwyn W., and Duncan Neuhauser, 1975. *The Efficient Organization.* New York: Elsevier.

Bell, David, 1973. *Post-Industrial Society.* New York: Free Press.

Ben-David, Joseph, 1958. "The Professional Role of the Physician in Bureaucratized Medicine: A Study of Role Conflict." *Human Relations, 2*: 901–911.

Benson, J. Kenneth, 1975. "The Interorganizational Network as a Political Economy." *Administrative Science Quarterly, 20* (June): 229–49.

——, 1977. "Organizations: A Dialetical View." *Administrative Science Quarterly, 22* (March): 1–21.

Berliner, Joseph S., 1957. *Factory and Manager in the USSR.* Cambridge, Mass.: Harvard University Press.

Biggart, Nicole, "Uncreative-Destructive Process of Organizational Change: The Case of the Post Office." *Administrative Science Quarterly, 22,* (September): 410–426.

Blalock, Herbert M., 1969. *Theory Construction: From Verbal to Mathematical Models.* Englewood Cliffs, N.J.: Prentice-Hall.

—— (Ed), 1971. *Causal Models in the Social Sciences.* Chicago: Aldine-Atherton.

Blalock, Herbert M., and Ann Blalock, 1968. *Methodology in Social Research.* New York: McGraw-Hill.

Blau, Peter M, 1955. *The Dynamics of Bureaucracy.* Chicago: University of Chicago Press.

——, 1963. *The Dynamics of Bureaucracy: A Study of Interpersonal Relations in Two Government Agencies.* Chicago: University of Chicago Press.

——, 1968. "The Hierarchy of Authority in Organization." *American Journal of Sociology,* 73 (January): 453–467.

——, 1970a. "A Formal Theory of Differentiation in Organizations." *American Sociological Review, 35* (April): 210–218.

——, 1970b. "Decentralization in Bureaucracies," in Mayer N. Zald (Ed.), *Power in Organizations.* Nashville, Tenn.: Vanderbilt University Press.

——, 1972. "Interdependence and Hierarchy in Organizations." *Social Science Research, 1* (April): 1–24.

——, 1973. *The Organization of Academic Work.* New York: Wiley-Interscience.

Blau, Peter M., and Richard A. Schoenherr, 1971. *The Structure of Organizations.* New York: Basic Books.

Blau, Peter M., and W. Richard Scott, 1962. *Formal Organizations: A Comparative Approach.* San Francisco: Chandler.

Blau, Peter M., Wolf V. Heydebrand, and Robert E. Stauffer, 1966. "The Structure of Small Bureaucracies." *American Sociological Review, 31* (April): 179–191.

Blau, Peter M., Cecilia McHugh Falbe, William McKinley, and Phelps K. Tracy, 1976. "Technology and Organization in Manufacturing." *Administrative Science Quarterly, 21* (March): 20–40.

Blauner, Robert, 1964. *Alienation and Freedom: The Factory Worker and His Industry.* Chicago: University of Chicago Press.

Boldand, Walter R., 1973. "Size, External Relations and the Distribution of Power: A Study of Colleges and Universities," in Wolf V. Heydebrand, (Ed.), *Comparative Organizations.* Englewood Cliffs, N.J.: Prentice-Hall, pp. 428–440.

Bohrnstedt, George W., 1969. "Observations on the Measurement of Change," in E. Borgatta (Ed.), *Sociological Methodology.* San Francisco: Jossey-Bass, pp. 113–136.

Bradford, Leland P., J. R. Gibb, and K. D. Benne (Eds.), 1964. *T-Group Theory and Laboratory Method: Innovation and Re-education.* New York: Wiley.

Braverman, Harry, 1974. *Labor and Monopoly Capital.* New York: Monthly Review.

Brenner, Robert, 1977. "The Origins of Capitalist Development: A Critique of Neo-Smithian Marxism." *New Left Review, 104* (July-August): 25–90.

Brewer, John, 1971. "Flow of Communications, Expert Qualifications, and Organizational Authority Structures." *American Sociological Review, 36* (June): 475–484.

Brinkerhoff, Merlin B., and Phillip Kunz, 1972. *Complex Organizations and Their Environments.* Dubuque, Iowa: Wm. C. Brown.

Brown, Ernest, and P. Browne, 1968. *A Century of Pay.* London: MacMillan.

Brown, Richard H., 1978. "Bureaucracy as Praxis: Toward a Political Phenomenology." *Administrative Science Quarterly, 23* (September): 365–382.

Bucher, Rue, 1970. "Social Process and Power in a Medical Study," in Mayer Zald (Ed.), *Power in Organizations.* Nashville, Tenn.: Vanderbilt University Press, pp. 3–48.

Buckley, Walter, 1967. *Sociology and Modern Systems Theory.* Englewood Cliffs, N.J.: Prentice-Hall.

——, 1968. *Modern System Research for the Behavioral Sciences.* Chicago: Aldine.

Bunge, Mario, 1958. *Causality.* Cambridge, Mass: Harvard University Press.

Burchard, Waldo, 1954. "Role Conflict of Military Chaplains." *American Sociological Review, 19* (August): 528–535.

Burns, Thomas, and G. M. Stalker, 1961. *The Management of Innovation.* London: Travistock.

Cadwallader, Mervyn, 1959. "The Cybernetic Analysis of Change in Complex Organizations." *American Journal of Sociology, 6* (September): 154–158.

Campbell, Donald, and Julian Stanley, 1963. *Experimental and Quasi-Experimental Designs by Research.* Chicago: Rand McNally.

Campbell, John P, 1977. "On the Nature of Organizational Effectiveness," in P. Goodman and J. Pennings (Eds.), *New Perspectives on Organizational Effectiveness.* San Francisco: Jossey Bass, pp. 13–55.

Campbell, John P., M. D. Dunnette, E. E. Lawler, III, and K. E. Weick, Jr., 1970. *Managerial Behavior, Performance, and Effectiveness,* New York: McGraw-Hill.

Cangelosi, Vincent E., and William R. Dill, 1965. "Organizational Learning: Observations toward a Theory." *Administrative Science Quarterly, 10* (September): 175–203.

Caplow, Theodore, 1954. *The Sociology of Work.* Minneapolis: University of Minnesota.

——, 1964. *Principles of Organization.* New York: Harcourt Brace & World.

Caplow, Theodore, and Reece J. McGee, 1958. *The Academic Marketplace.* New York: Basic Books.

Carey, Raymond, 1972. "Correlates of Satisfaction in the Priesthood." *Administrative Science Quarterly, 17* (June): 185–195.

Caves, Richard, 1972. *American Industry: Structure, Conduct, and Performance.* Englewood Cliffs, N.J.: Prentice-Hall.

Champion, Dean, 1975. *The Sociology of Organizations.* New York: McGraw-Hill.

Champion, Dean J., and H. Betterton, 1974. "On Organizational Size and Administrative Ratios: A Critical Examination of General and Specialized Hospitals." *Pacific Sociological Review, 17* (January): 98–107.

Chandler, Alfred D., 1962. *Strategy and Structure: Chapters in the History of Industrial Enterprise.* Cambridge, Mass.: MIT Press.

——, 1977. *The Visible Hand.* Cambridge, Mass.: Harvard University Press.

Child, John, 1972a. "Organizational Structure, Environment and Performance: The Role of Strategic Choice." *Sociology, 6* (January): 2–22.

——, 1972b. "Organization Structure and Strategies of Control: A Replication of the Aston Studies." *Administrative Science Quarterly, 17* (June): 163–177.

——, 1973a. "Parkinson's Progress: Accounting for the Number of Specialists in Organizations." *Administrative Science Quarterly, 18* (September): 328–348.

——, 1973b. "Predicting and Understanding Organization Structure." *Administrative Science Quarterly, 18* (June): 168–185.

——, 1973c. "Strategies of Control and Organizational Behavior." *Administrative Science Quarterly, 18* (March): 1–17.

——, 1976. "Participation, Organization, and Social Cohesion." *Human Relations, 29* (May): 429–51.

——, 1977. *Organization: A Guide to Problems and Practice.* London: Harper & Row.

Child, John, and Roger Mansfield, 1972. "Technology, Size and Organization Structure." *Sociology, 6* (September): 369–393.

Child, John, 1977. in Malcolm Warner (Ed.), *Choice and Constraint.* Lexington, Mass: Lexington Books.

Chirot, Daniel, 1977. *Social Change in the Twentieth Century.* Harcourt Brace Jovanovich,

Clegg, Stewart, 1975. *Power, Rule, and Domination.* London: Routledge and Kegan Paul.

Clegg, Stewart, and D. Dunkerley (Eds.), 1977. *Critical Issues in Organizations.* London: Routledge and Kegan Paul.

Coch, Lester, and J. R. P. French, 1948. "Overcoming Resistance to Change." *Human Relations, 1* (August): 512-533.

Coe, Rodney M. (Ed.), (August) 1970. *Planned Change in the Hospital: Case Studies of Organizational Innovation.* New York: Praeger.

Cohn, Steve, and Romaine Turyn, n.d. "Organizational Structure, Decision Making Pro-Procedures and the Adoption of Innovations." Unpublished paper, University of Maine.

Coleman, James S., 1974. *Power and the Structure of Society.* New York: Norton.

Collins, Randall, 1975. *Conflict Sociology.* New York: Academic.

Comstock, Donald, and W. Richard Scott, 1977. "Technology and the Structure of Subanits: Distinguishing individual and Workgroup Effects." *Administrative Science Quarterly, 22* (June): 177-202.

Conway, James, 1976. "Test of Linearity between Teachers' Participation in Decision Making and Their Perceptions of Their Schools As Organizations." *Administrative Science Quarterly, 21* (March): 130-139.

Cortez, Dan, 1974. "How Polaroid Bet Its Future on the SX-70." *Fortune, 89* (January): 82-87.

——, 1974. "The Two Faces of Xerox." *Fortune, 90* (September): 116-121.

Corwin, Ronald G., 1969. "Patterns of Organizational Conflict." *Administrative Science Quarterly, 14* (December): 507-521.

——, 1970. *Militant Professionalism: A Study of Organizational Conflict in High Schools.* New York: Appleton-Century-Crofts.

——, 1972. "Strategies for Organizational Innovation: An Empirical Comparison." *American Sociological Review, 37* (August): 441-454.

——, 1973. *Reform and Organizational Survival: The Teacher Corps as an Instrument of Educational Change.* New York: Wiley.

Coser, Lewis A., 1956. *The Functions of Social Conflict.* London: Free Press.

Costner, Herbert, and Robert Leik, 1900. "Deductions from Axiomatic Theory," in H. Blalock (Ed.) *Causal Models in the Social Sciences.* Chicago: Aldine, pp. 49-72.

Cremin, Lawrence Arthur, 1961. *The Transformation of the School: Progressivism in American Education.* New York: Knopf.

Crozier, Michael, 1964. *The Bureaucratic Phenomenon.* Chicago: University of Chicago Press.

——, 1972. "The Relationship Between Micro and Macrosociology." *Human Relations, 25* (July): 239-251.

Crozier, Michael, and E. Friedberg, 1977. *L'Acteur et le systeme.* Paris: Editions du Seuil.

Cummings, Larry L., and Aly M. ElSalmi, 1970. "The Impact of Role Diversity, Job Level, and Organizational Size on Managerial Satisfaction." *Administrative Science Quarterly, 15* (March): 1-11.

Cutright, Phillips, 1963. "National Political Development," *American Sociological Review, 28* (April): 253-264.

Cutright, Phillips, 1965. "Political Structure, Economic Development and National Social Security Programs," *American Journal of Sociology, 70* (March): 537–550.

Cyert, Richard M., and James G. March, 1963. *A Behavioral Theory of the Firm.* Englewood Cliffs, N.J.: Prentice-Hall.

Dachler, H. Peter, and Berhard Wilpert, 1978. "Conceptual Dimensions and Boundaries of Participation in Organizations: A Critical Evaluation." *Administrative Science Quarterly, 23* (March): 1–39.

Daft, Richard, and Selwyn Becher, 1978. *Innovation in Organizations: Innovation Adoption in School Organization.* New York: Elsevier.

Dalton, Melville, 1950. "Conflicts Between Staff and Line Managerial Officers." *American Sociological Review, 15* (June): 342–351.

Darkenwald, Gordon G., Jr., 1971. "Organizational Conflict in Colleges and Universities." *Administrative Science Quarterly, 16* (December): 407–412.

Davis, James A., 1963. "Structural Balance, Mechanical Solidarity, and Interpersonal Relations." *American Journal of Sociology, 68* (January): 444–462.

Davis, Otto, M. H. Dempster, and Aaron Wildavsky, 1966. "A Theory of the Budgeting Process," *American Political Science Review, 60* (September): 529–547.

Delbecq, Andre L., 1968. "How Informal Organization Evolves: Interpersonal Choice and Subgroup Formation." *Business Perspectives,* (Spring): 17–21.

Dewar, Robert, 1976. *Shifts Toward More Mechanistic Styles of Social Coordination and Control As Consequences of Growth and Technological Innovation.* Unpublished doctoral dissertation, University of Wisconsin.

Dewar, Robert, and Jerald Hage, 1978. "Size, Technology, Complexity, and Structural Differentiation: Toward A Theoretical Synthesis." *Administrative Science Quarterly, 23* (March): 111–136.

Donaldson, Lex, John Child, and Howard Aldrich, 1975. "The Aston Findings on Centralization: Further Discussion." *Administrative Science Quarterly, 20* (September): 453–460.

Donaldson, Lex, and Derek Pugh, 1977. in Malcolm Warner (Ed.), *Choice and Constraint.* Lexington, Mass.: Lexington Books.

Dornbursh, Sanford, and W. Richard Scott, 1975. *Evaluation and the Exerciser of Authority.* San Francisco: Jossey-Bass.

DuBick, Michael, 1978. "The Organizational Structure of Newspapers in Relation to their Metropolitan Environment." *Administrative Science Quarterly, 23* (September): 418–433.

Duncan, Robert B., 1972. "Characteristics of Organizational Environments and Perceived Environmental Uncertainty." *Administrative Science Quarterly, 17* (September): 313–327.

——, 1973. "Multiple Decision-Making Structures in Adapting to Environmental Uncertainty." *Human Relations, 26*: 273–291.

Durkheim, Emile, 1933. *The Division of Labor in Society.* New York: MacMillan.

Easterlin, Richard, 1968. *Population, Labor Force, and Long Swings in Economic Growth.* New York: Columbia.

Emery, Fred and Einar Thorsrud, 1964. *Form and Content in Industrial Democracy.* OSLO: Oslo University Press.

——, 1976. *Democracy At Work: The Report of the Norwegian Industrial Democracy Program.* Canberra: The Australian National University, mimeograph.

Emery, Fred, Julius Marek, and E. L. Trist, 1965. "The Causal Texture of Organizational Environments." *Human Relations, 18* (February): 21–32.

Engel, Gloria V, 1969. "The Effect of Bureaucracy on the Professional Autonomy of Physicians." *Journal of Health and Social Behavior, 10* (March): 30–41.

——, 1970. "Professional Autonomy and Bureaucratic Organization." *Administrative Science Quarterly, 15* (March): 12–21.

Etzioni, Amitai, 1960. "Two Approaches to Organizational Analysis: A Critique and A Suggestion." *Administrative Science Quarterly, 5* (September): 257–278.

——, 1961a. *A Comparative Analysis of Complex Organizations.* New York: Free Press.

——, 1961b. *Complex Organizations.* New York: Holt.

——, 1964. *Modern Organizations.* Englewood Cliffs, N.J.: Prentice-Hall.

——, 1965. "Dual Leadership in Complex Organizations." *American Sociological Review, 30* (October): 688–698.

——, 1968. *The Active Society.* New York: Free Press.

——, 1969. *The Semiprofessions and Their Organization.* New York: Free Press.

——, 1975. *A Comparative Analysis of Complex Organizations.* New York: Free Press.

Evan, William, 1966. "The Organizational Set: Toward A Theory of Interorganizational Relations," in James D. Thompson (Ed.), *Approaches to Organizational Design.* Pittsburgh: University of Pittsburgh Press, pp. 173–192.

——, 1972. "An Organization-Set Model of Interorganizational Relations," in M. Tuite, M. Radnor, and R. Chisholm (Eds.), *Interorganizational Decision-Making.* Chicago: Aldine, pp. 181–200.

——, 1976. *Organization Theory.* New York: Wiley.

Evers, Frederick, Joe Bohlen, and Richard Warren, 1976. "The Relationships of Selected Size and Structure Indicators in Economic Organizations." *Administrative Science Quarterly, 21* (June): 326–342.

Faunce, William A, 1958. "Automation in the Automobile Industry: Some Consequences for In-Plant Social Structure." *American Sociological Review, 23* (June): 401–407.

Feldmox, Julian, and Herschel Kanter, 1965. "Organizational Decision-Making," in James G. March (Ed.), *Handbook of Organization.* Chicago: Rand McNally, pp.

Feuer, Lewis, 1969. *Marx and Engels: Basic Writings on Politics and Philosophy.* Garden City, N.Y.: Anchor.

Fiedler, Fred E., 1967. *A Theory of Leadership Effectiveness.* New York: McGraw-Hill.

——, 1972. "The Effects of Leadership Training and Experience: A Contigency Model Explanation." *Administrative Science Quarterly, 17* (December): 453–70.

Flamant, Maurice, and Jeanne Singer-Kere, 1970. *Modern Economic Crisis and Recessions.* New York: Harper & Row.

Forrester, Jay W, 1961. *Industrial Dynamics.* New York: Wiley.

Fournet, Glenn, P., M. K. Distefano, and M. W. Pryer, 1966. "Job Satisfaction: Issues and Problems." *Personnel Psychology, 19* (Summer): 165–183.

Francis, Arthur, 1977. "Families, Firms, and Finance Capital." Unpublished paper, Nuffield College, Oxford.

Freeman, Christopher, 1974. *The Industrial Economics of Innovation.* London: Penguin.

Freeman, John, 1973. "Environment, Technology and the Administrative Intensity of Manufacturing Organizations," *American Sociological Review, 38* (December): 750–63.

——, 1975. "The Unit Problem in Organization." Paper presented at the annual meeting of the American Sociological Association.

——, 1978. "Effects of the Choice of the Unit of Analysis on Organizational Research," in Marshall Meyer, et al., (Eds.), *Studies on Environment and Organizations.* San Francisco: Jossey-Bass.

——, 1979. "Going to the Well: School District Administrative Intensity and Environmental Constraint." *Administrative Science Quarterly, 24* (March): 119–133.

Freeman, John, and Michael T. Hannan, 1975. "Growth and Decline Processes in Organizations." *American Sociological Review, 40* (April): 215–28.

French, John R. P., Jr., and B. Raven, 1959. "The Bases of Social Power." Ann Arbor, Mich.: Institute for Social Research.

Friedson, Eliot (Ed.), 1963. *The Hospital in Modern Society.* New York: Free Press.

Fullan, Michael, 1970. "Industrial Technology and Worker Integration in the Organization." *American Sociological Review, 35* (December): 1028–1039.

Fulton, Robert L., 1961. "The Clergyman and the Funeral Director: A Study of Role Conflict." *Social Forces, 39* (May): 317–323.

Gamson, William, and Norman Scotch, 1964. "Scapegoating in Baseball." *American Journal of Sociology, 70* (July): 69–76.

Georgopoulos, Basil S., and Floyd C. Mann, 1962. *The Community General Hospital.* New York: Macmillan.

Georgopoulos, Basil S., and A. S. Tannenbaum, 1957. "Study of Organizational Effectiveness." *American Sociological Review, 22* (August): 534–540.

Gerth, Hans H., and C. Wright Mills, 1946. *From Max Weber: Essays in Sociology.* New York: Oxford University Press.

Getzels, Jacob W., and E. G. Guba, 1954. "Role, Role Conflict, and Effectiveness: An Empirical Study." *American Sociological Review, 19* (April): 164–175.

Getzels, Jacob, and Phillip W. Jackson, 1968. *Creativity and Intelligence: Explorations with Gifted Children.* New York: Wiley.

Gibbs, Jack, 1972. *Sociological Theory Construction.* Hinsdale, Ill.: Dryden.

Gilman, Daniel Coit, 1906. *The Launching of A University, and other Papers: A Sheaf of Remembrances.* New York: Dodd, Mead.

Glisson, Charles, 1978. "Dependence of Technological Routinization on Structural Variables in Human Service Organizations," *Administrative Science Quarterly, 23* (September): 383–395.

Goffman, Erving, 1961. "On the Characteristics of Total Institutions," in D. R. Cressey (Ed.), *The Prison.* New York: Holt, Rinehart, & Winston, pp. 15–67.

Goldman, Paul, and Donald Van Houten, 1977. "Managerial Strategies and the Worker: A Marxist Analysis of Bureaucracy." *The Sociological Quarterly, 18* (Winter): 108–125.

Goodman, Paul, and Johannes Pennings, 1977. *New Perspectives on Organizational Effectiveness.* San Francisco: Jossey-Bass.

Gordon, Gerald, Christian Tanon, and Edward Mooise, 1975. "Decision-Making Criteria and Organization Performance," mimeograph, Cornell University.

Gordon, Gerald et al., 1972. "Organizational Structure and Hospital Adaptation to Environmental Demands." Paper presented at the University of North Carolina Health Services Research Center Symposium on Innovation, Chapel Hill, North Carolina.

Gouldner, Alvin W., 1954a. *Patterns of Industrial Bureaucracy.* New York: Free Press.

——, 1954b. *Wildcat Strike.* Yellow Springs, Ohio: Antioch Press.

——, 1957. "Cosmopolitans and Locals: Toward An Analysis of Latent Social Roles." *Administrative Science Quarterly, 2* (September): 281–306.

——, 1958. "Cosmopolitans and Locals: Toward An Analysis of Latent Social Roles." *Administrative Science Quarterly, 2* (December): 444–480.

——, 1959. "Organizational Analysis," in Robert K. Merton et al. (Eds.), *Sociology Today.* New York: Basic Books.

——, 1960. "The Norm of Reciprocity." *American Sociological Review, 25* (April): 161–178.

Granick, David, 1960. *The Red Executive: A Study of the Organization Man in Russian Industry.* New York: Columbia.

Greenblatt, Morris, R. H. York, and Esther Brown, 1955. *From Custodial to Therapeutic Patient Care in Mental Hospital.* New York: Russell Sage.

Greenspan, Alan, and Arthur Okum, 1977. "Debate: How to Stop Inflation." *Fortune, 95* (April): 116–120.

Greiner, Larry E., 1967. "Patterns of Organizational Change." *Harvard Business Review, 45* (May-June): 119–130.

Gross, Neal, Ward Mason and Alexander McEachern, 1958. *Explorations in Role Analysis.*

Grusky, Oscar, 1960. "Administrative Succession in Formal Organizations." *Social Forces, 39* (December): 104–115.

——, 1963. "Managerial Succession and Organizational Effectiveness." *American Journal of Sociology, 69* (July): 21–31.

——, 1969. "Succession with an Ally." *Administrative Science Quarterly, 14* (June): 155–70.

Gullahorn, John T., 1956. "Measuring Role Conflict." *American Journal of Sociology, 61* (November): 299–303.

Gurr, Ted, 1970. *Why Men Rebel.* Princeton, N.J.: Princeton University Press.

Hage, Jerald, 1965. "An Axiomatic Theory of Organizations." *Administrative Science Quarterly, 10* (December): 289–320.

——, 1966. "Rejoinder." *Administrative Science Quarterly, 11* (June): 141–146.

Hage, Jerald, 1972. *Techniques and Problems of Theory Construction in Sociology.* New York: Wiley-Interscience.

Hage, Jerald, 1974. *Communication and Organizational Control: Cybernetics in Health and Welfare Settings.* New York: Wiley-Interscience.

Hage, Jerald, 1975. "Frontier Problems in Organizational Theory." Paper presented at the national meetings of the American Sociological Association.

Hage, Jerald and Michael Aiken, 1967a. "Program Change and Organizational Properties: A Comparative Analysis." *American Journal of Sociology, 72* (March): 503–519.

——, 1967b. "Relationship of Centralization to Other Structural Properties." *Administrative Science Quarterly, 12* (June): 72–91.

——, 1969. "Routine, Technology, Social Structure, and Organizational Goals." *Administrative Science Quarterly, 14* (September): 366–377.

——, 1970. *Social Change in Complex Organizations.* New York: Random House.

——, 1972. "Organizational Conflict and Consensus." Paper presented at the annual meetings of the American Sociological Association.

Hage, Jerald, and Robert Dewar, 1973. "Elite Values Versus Organizational Structure in Predicting Innovation." *Administrative Science Quarterly, 18* (September): 279–290.

Hage, Jerald, and Robert Hanneman, n.d. "Longitudinal Test of an Axiomatic Theory." Unpublished paper, University of Wisconsin.

Hage, Jerald, and J. Rogers Hollingsworth, 1977. "The First Steps Toward the Integration of Social Theory and Social Policy." *Annals of the American Academy of Political and Social Science, 434* (November): 1–23.

Hage, Jerald, and Gerald Marwell, 1968. "Toward the Development of an Empirically Based Theory of Role Relationships." *Sociometry,* (June): 200–212.

Hage, Jerald, Michael Aiken, and Cora Bagley Marrett, 1971. "Organization Structure and Communication." *American Sociological Review. 36* (October): 860–871.

Hagerman, Ronald Louis, (1968) "A Test of Hage's Axiomatic Theory of Organizational A-daptiveness in a State System of Junior Colleges" unpublished masters thesis, Southern Illinois University.

Hagstrom, Warren O., 1965. *The Scientific Community.* New York: Basic Books.

Hall, Richard H., 1962. "Intraorganizational Structural Variation: Application of the Bureaucratic Model." *Administrative Science Quarterly, 7* (December): 295–308.

Hall, Richard H., 1963a. "Bureaucracy in Small Organizations." *Sociology and Social Research, 48* (October): 38–46.

——, 1963b. "The Concept of Bureaucracy: An Empirical Assessment." *American Journal of Sociology, 69* (July): 32–40.

——, 1967. "Some Organizational Considerations in the Professional-Organizational Relationship." *Administrative Science Quarterly, 12* (September): 461–478.

——, 1968. "Professionalization and Bureaucratization." *American Sociological Review, 33* (February): 92–104.

——, 1972. *The Formal Organization.* New York: Basic Books.

——, 1977. *Organization Structure and Process* (2nd ed.). Englewood Cliffs, N.J.: Prentice-Hall.

Hall, Richard, J. E. Haas, and N. J. Johnson, 1967. "Organizational Size, Complexity, and Formalization." *American Sociological Review, 32* (December): 903–912.

Hall, Richard H., J. Eugene Haas, and Norman J. Johnson, 1967. "Examination of the Blau-Scott and Etzioni Typologies." *Administrative Science Quarterly, 12* (June): 118–139.

Hannan, Michael, and John Freeman, 1977. "Obstacles to Comparative Studies," in P. Goodman and J. Pennings (Eds.), *New Perspectives on Organizational Effectiveness.* San Francisco: Jossey-Bass, pp. 106–131.

Hannan, Michael, and Alice Young, 1974. "Estimation in Panel Models: Results on Pooling Cross-Sections and Time Series." Technical Report, Laboratory for Social Research Stanford.

Hannan, Michael, John Freeman, and John Meyer, 1976. "Specification of Models for Organizational Effectiveness." *American Sociological Review, 41* (February): 136–143.

Hannan, Michael, Alice Young, and F. Nielsen, 1975. "Specification Bias Analysis of the Effects of Grouping of Observations in Multiple Regression Models." Paper presented at annual meeting of the American Educational Research Association.

Hanneman, Robert, 1974. "The Distribution of Defense Contract Awards among Major Contractors 1956-1987: a Comparison of Competing Explanations." Unpublished master's thesis, University of Wisconsin.

Hanneman, Robert, 1979. "Inequality and Development in Britain, France and Germany Unpublished doctral dissertation, University of Wisconsin.

Hare, Paul, Edgar Borgotta, and Robert F. Bales, 1955. *Small Groups.* New York: Knopf.

Hedberg, Bol. T., Paul Nystrom, and William Starbuck, 1976. "Camping on Seesaws: Perspectives for a Self-Designing Organization." *Administrative Science Quarterly, 21* (March): 41–65.

Heise, David, 1970. "Causal Inference from Panel Data" in E. Borgotta (Ed.), *Sociological Methodology.* San Francisco: Jossey-Bass, pp. 3–27.

Heise, David, 1975. *Causal Analysis.* New York: Wiley.

Heise, David R., and George W. Bornstedt, 1970. "Validity, Invalidity, and Reliability," in E. Borgatta (Ed.), *Sociological Methodology.* San Francisco: Jossey-Bass, pp. 104–129.

Helmich, Donald, and Warren Brown, 1972. "Successor Type and Organizational Change in the Corporate Enterprise." *Administrative Science Quarterly, 17* (September): 371–81.

Hernes, Gudmund, 1976. "Structural Change in Social Processes," *American Journal of Sociology, 82* (November): 513–47.

Heydebrand, Wolf V., 1973a. *Comparative Organizations.* Englewood Cliffs, N.J.: Prentice-Hall.

——, 1973b. *Hospital Bureaucracy: A Comparative Study of Organizations.* New York: Dunellen.

——, 1977. "Organizational Contradictions in Public Bureaucracies: Toward A Marxian Theory of Organizations." *The Sociological Quarterly, 18* (Winter): 83–107.

Heydebrand, Wolf and J. J. Noell, 1973. "Task Structure and Innovation in Professional Organizations" in W. Heydebrand (Ed.), *Comparative Organizations,* pp. 294–322.

Hibbs, Douglas Jr., 1973. *Mass Political Violence: A Cross-National Causal Analysis.* New York: Wiley-Interscience.

Hickson, D. J., 1966. "Convergence in Organizational Theory." *Administrative Science Quarterly, 11* (September): 224–237.

Hickson, D. J., D. S. Pugh, and D. C. Pheysey, 1969. "Operations Technology and Organization Structure: An Empirical Reappraisal." *Administrative Science Quarterly, 14* (September): 378–397.

Hickson, D. J., C. R. Hinings, C. A. Lee, R. E. Schneck, and J. M. Pennings, 1971. "A Strategic Contingencies Theory of Intraorganizational Power." *Administrative Science Quarterly, 16* (June): 216–229.

Hills, Frederick, and Thomas Mohoney, 1979. "University Budgets and Organizational Decision-Making." *Administrative Science Quarterly, 23* (September): 454–465.

Hinings, C. R., D. J. Hickson, J. M. Pennings, and R. E. Schneck, 1974. "Structural Conditions of Intraorganizational Power." *Administrative Science Quarterly, 19* (March): 22–44.

Hirsch, Paul, 1972. "Processing Fads and Fashions: An Organization Set Analysis of Cultural Industry Systems." *American Journal of Sociology, 77* (January): 639–59.

——, 1975a. "Organizational Analysis and Industrial Sociology: An Instance of Cultural Lag." *American Sociologist, 10* (February): 3–12.

——, 1975b. "Organizational Effectiveness and the Institutional Environment." *Administrative Science Quarterly, 20* (September): 327–44.

Hirschman, Albert O., 1970. *Exit, Voice, and Loyalty: Responses to Decline in Firms, Organizations, and the State.* Cambridge, Mass.: Harvard University Press, 1970.

Hofstadter, Richard, 1955. *The Age of Reform: From Bryan to F.D.R.* New York: Knopf.

Hofsteole, G., and M. S. Kassens (Eds.), 1976. *European Contributions to Organization Theory.* Amsterdam: Van Gorcuno.

Holdoway, Edward, John Newberry, David Hickson, and R. Retter Heron, 1975. "Dimensions of Organization in Complex Societies: The Educational Sector." *Administrative Science Quarterly, 20* (March): 30–58.

Homans, George, 1950. *Human Group.* New York: Harcourt & Brace.

——, 1961. *Social Behavior: Its Elementary Forms.* New York: Harcourt Brace & World.

——, 1967. *The Nature of Social Science.* New York: Harcourt Brace & World.

Humnson, Norman, Patrick Doreian, and Klaus Teuter, 1975. "A Structural Control Model of Organizational Change," *American Sociological Review, 40* (December): 813–824.

Hyman, Richard, 1972. *Strikes.* London, Fontana.

Hyre, Kary, 1970. "An Exploration of Some of the Implications of Varied Mobility Patterns in Formal Organizations." Unpublished masters thesis, University of Wisconsin.

James, Henry, 1930. *Charles W. Eliot,* 2 vols. New York: Houghton Mifflin.

Kahn, Robert, et al., 1964. *Organizational Stress: Studies in Role Conflict and Ambiguity.* New York: Wiley.

Kallenberg, Arne, 1977. "Work Values and Job Rewards: A Theory of Job Satisfaction." *American Sociological Review, 42* (February): 124–143.

Kaluzny, Arnold, James Veney, and John Gentry 1974. "Innovations of Health Services: pitals and Health Departments." *Milbank Memorial Fund Quarterly, 52* (Winter): 51–82.

Kaluzny, Arnold, James Veney, and John Gentry, 1972. "Innovation of Health Services: A Comparative Study of Hospitals and Health Departments. Paper presented at the University of North Carolina Health Services Research Center Symposium on Innovation, Chapel Hill, North Carolina.

Karpik, Lucien, 1972a. "Le Capitalisme Technologique," *Sociologie du travail, 13* (January-March): 2–34.

——, 1972b. "Les Politiques et les logics d'action de la grande entreprise industrielle," *Sociologie du travail, 13* (April-June): 82–105.

Katz, Daniel, and Robert L. Kahn, 1966. *The Social Psychology of Organizations.* New York: Wiley.

Kerr, Clark, and Abraham Siegel, 1954. "The Interindustry Propensity to Strike: An International Comparison," in A. Kornhauser et al. (Eds.), *Industrial Conflict.* New York: McGraw-Hill, pp. 189–212.

Kervasdoué, Jean de, 1973. *Efficiency and Adoption of Innovations in Formal Organizations.* Unpublished doctoral dissertation, Cornell University.

Khandwalla, Pradip, 1972. "Environment and Its Impact on the Organization." *International Studies of Management and Organization, 2* (Fall): 297–313.

——, 1977. *The Design of Organizations.* New York: Harcourt Brace Jovanovich.

Kimberly, John, 1976. "Organizational Size and the Structuralist Perspective: A Review, Critique, and Proposal." *Administrative Science Quarterly, 21* (December): 571–97.

Klonglan, Gerald, Richard Warren, Judy Winkelpleck, and Steven Paulson, 1976. "Interorganizational Measurement in the Social Services Sector: Differences by Hierarchical Level." *Administrative Science Quarterly,* vol. 21 (December): 675–687.

Knight, Kenneth, 1967. "A Descriptive Model of the Intra-Firm Innovation Process." *Journal of Business, 40* (October): 478–496.

Knowles, K. G. J. C., 1954. "Strike Proneness and Its Determinants." *American Journal of Sociology, 60* (November): 213–229.

Kover, Andrew, 1963. "Reorganization in an Advertising Agency: A Case Study of Decrease in Integration." *Human Organization, 22* (Winter): 252–259.

Kochran, Thomas, Larry Cummins, and George Huber, 1974. "Determinants of Interorganizational Conflict in Collective Bargaining in the Public Sector." *Administrative Science Quarterly, 20* (March): 10–23.

Kuznets, Simon, 1967. *Secular Movements in Production and Prices.* New York: A. M. Kelley.

Lammers, Cornelius, J., 1967. "Power and Participation in Decision Making in Formal Organizations." *American Journal of Sociology, 73* (September); 201–216.

——, 1969. "Strikes and Mutinies: A Comparative Study of Organizational Conflicts between Rulers and Ruled." *Administrative Science Quarterly, 14* (December): 558–572.

——, 1977. "The Contributions of Organizational Sociology." Paper presented at the Third Colloquim of EGOs, Germany.

——, 1978. "The Comparative Study of Organizations," in R. H. Turner, J. Coleman, and R. Fox (Eds.), *Annual Review of Sociology,* Vol 4. Palo Alto, Ca: Annual Reviews, pp. 485–510.

Lammers, Cornelius, and David J. Hickson (Eds.), 1978. *Organizations Alike and Unalike.* London: Routledge and Kegan Paul.

Landes, David, 1969. *The Unbound Prometheus: Technological Change and Industrial Development in Western Europe from 1750 to the Present.* Cambridge, Eng.: Cambridge University Press.

Lawrence, Paul R., and Jay W. Lorsch, 1967a. "Differentiation and Integration in Complex Organizations." *Administrative Science Quarterly, 12* (June): 1–47.

——, 1967b. *Organization and Environment: Managing Differentiation and Integration.* Cambridge, Mass.: Harvard Graduate School of Business Administration.

Lefton, Mark, and William R. Rosengren, 1966. "Organizations and Clients: Lateral and Longitudinal Dimensions." *American Sociological Review, 31* (December): 802–810.

Leifer, Richard, and George Huber, 1977. "Relations Among Perceived Environmental Uncertainty, Organization Structure, and Boundary-Spanning Behavior." *Administrative Science Quarterly, 22* (June): 235–247.

Lenski, Gerhard E., and Jean Lenski, 1974. *Human Societies: A Macro Level Introduction to Sociology.* New York: McGraw-Hill.

Leontif, Wassily, 1966. *Input-Output Economics.* New York: Oxford University Press.

Lerner, Daniel, 1958. *The Passing of Traditional Society.* New York: Free Press.

Levine, Sol, and Paul White, 1961. "Exchange and Interorganizational Relationships." *Administrative Science Quarterly,* vol. (March): 583–601.

Lieberson, Stanley, and James F. O'Connor, 1972. "Leadership and Organizational Performance: A Study of Large Corporations." *American Sociological Review, 37* (April): 117–30.

Lipset, Seymour Martin, 1950. *Agrarian Socialism.* Berkeley: University of California Press.

——, 1960. *Political Man.* Garden City, N.Y.: Doubleday.

——, 1963. *The First New Nation.* New York: Basic Books.

Lipset, Seymour Martin, Martin A. Trow, and James S. Coleman, 1956. *Union Democracy.* Glencoe, Ill.: Free Press.

Litwak, Eugene, 1961. "Models of Bureaucracy which Permit Conflict." *American Journal of Sociology, 67* (September): 177–184.

——, 1968. "Technological Innovation and Theoretical Functions of Primary Groups and Bureaucratic Structures." *American Journal of Sociology, 73* (January): 468–481.

Lorsch, Jay W., 1965. *Product Innovation and Organization.* New York: Macmillan.

Lorsch, Jay W., and Paul R. Lawrence, 1965. "Organizing for Product Innovation." Harvard Business Review, 43 (January-February): 109–122.

Lourenco, Susan, and John Glidewell, 1975. "A Dialectical Analysis of Organizational Conflict." *Administrative Science Quarterly, 20* (December): 489–508.

Lynch, Beverly, 1974. "An Empirical Assessment of Perrow's Technology Construct." *Administrative Science Quarterly, 19* (September): 338–357.

McCleery, Richard H., 1957. *Policy Change in Prison Management.* East Lansing: Government Research Bureau, Michigan State University.

McEwen, William J., 1956. "Position Conflict and Professional Orientation in a Research Organization." *Administrative Science Quarterly, 1* (September): 208–224.

McGregor, Douglas, 1960. *The Human Side of Enterprise.* New York: McGraw-Hill.

McNeil, Kenneth, 1978. "Understanding Organization Power: Building on the Weberian Legacy." *Administrative Science Quarterly, 23* (March): 65–90.

Mahoney, Thomas A., and William Weitzel, 1969. "Managerial Models of Organizational Effectiveness." *Administrative Science Quarterly, 14* (September): 357–365.

Maniha, John K., and Charles Perrow, 1965. "The Reluctant Organization and the Aggressive Environment." *Administrative Science Quarterly, 10* (September): 238–57.

Mann, Floyd C., and Richard Hoffman *Social Change in Power Plants.* New York: Holt.

Mann, Floyde C., and Lawrence K. Williams, 1960. "Observations on the Dynamics of a Change to Electronic Data Processing Equipment." *Administrative Science Quarterly, 5* (September): 217–256.

Mansfield, Edwin, 1968. *The Economics of Technological Change.* (New York: Norton.

Mansfield, Roger, 1973. "Bureaucracy and Centralization: An Examination of Organizational Structure." *Administrative Science Quarterly, 18* (December): 477–488.

March, James G. (Ed.), 1965. *The Handbook of Organizations.* Chicago: Rand McNally.

March, James G., and Herbert A. Simon, 1958. *Organizations.* New York: Wiley.

Maris, Robin, 1964. *Economic Theory of Managerial Capitalism.* New York: Free Press.

Martin, Linda G., 1976. "How Beatrice Foods Sneaked Up on $5 Billion." *Fortune, 91* (April): 119–131.

Marwell, Gerald, and Jerald Hage, 1970. "The Organization of Role-Relationships: A Systematic Description." *American Sociological Review, 35* (October): 884–900.

Marx, Karl, 1967. *Capital,* Vol. II. Moscow: Progress.

Marx, Karl, and Frederick Engels, 1969. "Manifesto of the Communist Party" in Lewis Feuer (Ed.), *Marx and Engels: Basic Writings on Politics and Philosophy.* Garden City, N.Y.: Anchor.

Maslow, Abraham, 1954. *Motivation and Personality.* New York: Harper & Row.

Mayntz, Renate, 1964. "The Study of Organizations: A Trend Report and Bibliography." *Current Sociology, 13* (3): 95–156.

May, Rollo, 1969. *Love and Will.* New York: Norton.

Meadows, Donella M., D. L. Meadows, J. Randers, and W. W. Behrens, III, 1972. *Limits to Growth.* New York: Universe.

Mechanic, David, 1962. "Sources of Power and Lower Participants in Complex Organizations." *Administrative Science Quarterly, 7* (December): 349–364.

Melcher, Arlyn, 1975. *Structure and Process of Organizations: A Systems Approach.* Englewood Cliffs, N.J.: Prentice-Hall.

Melio, Nancy, 1971. "Health Care Organizations and Innovation." *Journal of Health and Social Behavior, 12* (June): 163–173.

Merton, Robert K., 1957. *Social Theory and Social Structure.* Glencoe, Ill.: Free Press.

Meyer, John, John Boli-Bennett, and Chris Chase-Dunn, 1975. "Convergence and Divergence in Development," in *Annual Review of Sociology,* Vol. I, A. Inkeles (Ed.), Palo Alto, Calif.: Annual Review, pp. 223–460.

Meyer, Marshall W., 1968a. "Automation and Bureaucratic Structure." *American Journal of Sociology, 74* (November): 256–264.

——, 1968b. "Expertness and the Span of Control." *American Sociological Review, 33* (December): 944–950.

——, 1968c. "Two Authority Structures of Bureaucratic Organizations." *Administrative Science Quarterly, 13* (September): 211–229.

——, 1972a. *Bureaucratic Structure and Authority: Coordination and Control in 254 Government Agencies.* New York: Harper & Row.

——, 1972b. "Size and the Structure of Organizations: A Causal Analysis." *American Sociological Review, 37* (August): 434–441.

——, 1975. "Organizational Domains." *American Sociological Review, 40* (October): 599–615.

Michels, Robert, 1962. *Political Parties.* Glencoe, Ill.: Free Press.

Miller, James G., 1975a. "The Nature of Living Systems." *Behavioral Science, 20* (November: 343–365.

——, 1975b. "Living Systems: The Society." *Behavioral Science, 20* (November): 366–535.

Mills C. Wright, 1957. *The Power Elite.* New York: Oxford University Press.

Mintzberg, Henry, 1973. "Strategy-Making in Three Modes." *California Management Review, 16* (Winter): 44–53.

——, 1978. "Patterns in Strategy Formation." *Management Science, 934–948.*

——, 1979. *The Structuring of Organizations.* Englewood Cliffs, N.J.: Prentice-Hall.

Mintzberg, Henry, D. Raisinghani, and A. Théoret, 1976. "The Structure of 'Unstructured' Decision Processes." *Administrative Science Quarterly, 21* (June): 246–275.

Moch, Michael, 1976. "Structure and Organizational Resource Allocation." *Administrative Science Quarterly, 21* (December): 661–74.

Moch, Michael, and Edward Morse, 1977. "Size Centralization and Organizational Adoption of Innovations." *American Sociological Review, 92* (October): 716–25.

Mohr, Lawrence, 1971. "Organizational Technology and Organizational Structure." *Administrative Science Quarterly,* vol. (December): 444–459

Morin, Piere, 1976. *Le Developement des organizations* (2nd ed.). Paris: Dunod.

Morse, Nancy C., 1953. *Satisfaction in the White Collar Job.* Ann Arbor: Survey Research Center, University of Michigan.

Mouzelis, Nicos P., 1967. *Organization and Bureaucracy.* London: Routledge.

Mulder, Mark, 1976. in Hofstede and Kasseml (Eds.), *European Contributions to Organization Theory.*

Mulder, Mark, and Henke Wilke, 1970. "Participation and Power Equalization." *Organizational Behavior and Human Performance, 5* (September): 430–48.

Nagel, Ernst, 1961. *The Structure of Science.* New York: Harcourt Brace & World.

Negandhi, Anant (Ed.), 1971. *Organizational Theory in an Interorganizational Perspective* Kent, Ohio: Kent State University.

——, 1975. *Interorganizational Theory.* Kent, Ohio: Kent State University.

Normann, Richard, 1971. "Organizational Innovativeness: Product Variation and Reorientation." *Administrative Science Quarterly, 16* (June): 203–215.

O'Connor, James, 1973. *The Fiscal Crisis of the State.* New York: St. Martin's.

O'Hanlon, Thomas, 1975. "Swinging Cats Among Conglomerate Dogs." *Fortune, 91* (June): 114–119.

Ouchi, William, 1977. "Relationship Between Organizational Structure and Organizational Control." *Administrative Science Quarterly, 22* (March): 95–113.

Ouchi, William, and Jerry Johnson, 1978. "Types of Organizational Control and Relationship to Emotional Well Being." *Administrative Science Quarterly, 23* (June): 293–317.

Palumbo, Dennis, J., 1969. "Power and Role Specificity in Organizational Theory." *Public Administration Review, 29* (May-June): 237–248.

Parsons, Talcott, 1951. *The Social System.* Glencoe, Ill.: Free Press.

——, 1956a. "Suggestions for a Sociological Approach to the Theory of Organizations." *Administrative Science Quarterly, 1* (June): 63–85.

——, 1956b. "Suggestions for a Sociological Approach to the Theory of Organization – II." *Administrative Science Quarterly, 1* (September): 225–239.

——, 1966. *Societies: Evolutionary and Comparative Perspectives.* Englewood Cliffs, N.J.: Prentice-Hall.

Parsons, Talcott, and Neil Smelser, 1956. *Economy and Society.* Glencoe, Ill.: Free Press.

Parsons, Talcott, Robert Bales, and Ed Shils, 1953. *Working Papers in the Theory of Action.* New York: Free Press.

Patton, Michael, 1972. "Structure and Diffusion of Open Education: A Theoretical Perspective and an Empirical Assessment." Unpublished doctoral dissertation, University of Wisconsin.

Paulson, Steven K., 1974. "Causal Analysis of Interorganizational Relations: An Axiomatic Theory Revised." *Administrative Science Quarterly, 19* (September): 319–337.

Payne, P. L., 1967. "The Emergence of the Large-Scale Company in Great Britain, 1870–1914," *Economic History Review, 20* (December): 519–42.

Peabody, Robert L., 1962. "Perceptions of Organizational Authority: A Comparative Analysis." *Administrative Science Quarterly, 6* (December): 463–482.

——, 1964. *Organizational Authority.* New York: Atherton.

Pelz, Donald C., and Frank M. Andrews, 1966. *Scientists in Organizations: Productive Climates of Research and Development.* New York: Wiley.

Pennings, Johannes, 1973. "Measures of Organizational Structure: A Methodological Note." *American Journal of Sociology, 79* (November): 686–704.

——, 1975. "The Relevance of the Structural-Contingency Model for Organizational Effectiveness," *Administrative Science Quarterly, 20* (September): 393–410.

——, 1976. "Dimensions of Organizational Influence and Their Effectiveness Correlates." *Administrative Science Quarterly, 21* (December): 688–699.

Perrow, Charles, 1961a. "The Analysis of Goals in Complex Organizations." *American Sociological Review, 26* (December): 854–866.

——, 1961b. "Organizational Prestige: Some Functions and Dysfunctions." *American Journal of Sociology, 66* (January): 335–341.

——, 1963. "Goals and Power Structures: A Historical Case Study," in Eliot Freidson (Ed.), *The Hospital in Modern Society.* New York: Free Press, pp. 112–146.

——, 1965. "Hospitals, Technology, Goals and Structure," in James March (Ed.), *Handbook of Organizations.* Chicago: Rand McNally, pp.

——, 1967. "A Framework for the Comparative Analysis of Organizations." *American Sociological Review, 32* (April): 194–209.

——, 1968. "Organizational Goals," in *International Encyclopedia of the Social Sciences* (Rev. ed.). New York: Macmillan.

——, 1970a. "Departmental Power and Perspective in Industrial Firms," in Mayer Zald (Ed.), *Power in Organizations.* Nashville, Tenn.: Vanderbilt University Press, pp. 49–89.

——, 1970b. *Organizational Analysis: A Sociological View.* Belmont, Cal.: Wadsworth.

——, 1972. *Complex Organizations: A Critical Essay.* Glenview, Ill.: Scott, Foresman.

Pettigrew, Andrew, 1972. "Information Control as a Power Resource." *Sociology, 6* (May): 186–204.

Peyrefitte, Roger Alain, 1977. *Le Mal francais.* Paris: Plon.

Pfeffer, Jeffrey, 1972b. "Size and Composition of Corporate Boards of Directors," *Administrative Science Quarterly, 17* (September): 382–94.

——, 1977a. *"Power and Resource Allocation in Organizations,"* in B. Staw and G. Salancik (Eds.), *New Directions in Organizational Behavior.* Chicago: St. Clair, pp. 235–65.

——, 1977b. "Usefulness of the Concept" in P. Goodman and J. Pennings (Eds.), *New Perspectives on Organizational Effectiveness.* San Francisco: Jossey-Bass, pp. 132–145.

Pfeffer, Jeffrey, and Husein Leblebici, 1973a. "The Effect of Competition on Some Dimensions of Organizational Structure," *Social Forces, 52* (December): 268–79.

Pfeffer, Jeffrey, and Husein Leblebici, 1973. "Executive Recruitment and the Development of Interfirm Organizations," *Administrative Science Quarterly, 18* (December): 4457–4461.

Pfeffer, Jeffrey, and Philip Nowak, 1976. "Joint Ventures and Interorganizational Dependence," *Administrative Science Quarterly, 21* (September): 398–418.

Pfeffer, Jeffrey, and Gerald Salancik, 1974. "Organizational Decision Making As A Political Process: The Case of a University Budget." *Administrative Science Quarterly, 19* (June): 135–51.

——, 1978. *The External Control of Organizations.* New York: Harper & Row.

Pheysey, Diana C., Roy L. Payne, and Derek S. Pugh, 1971. "Influence of Structure at Organizational and Group Levels." *Administrative Science Quarterly, 16* (March): 61–73.

Pinder, Craig, and Larry Moore, 1979. "The Resurrection of Taxonomy to Aid the Development of Middle Range Theories of Organizational Behavior," *Administrative Science Quarterly, 24* (March) 99–118.

Pondy, Louis, 1967. "Organizational Conflict: Concepts and Models." *Administrative Science Quarterly, 12* (September): 296-320.

——, 1969a. "Effects of Size, Complexity, and Ownership on Administrative Intensity." *Administrative Science Quarterly, 14* (March): 47-61.

——, 1969b. "Varieties of Organizational Conflict." *Administrative Science Quarterly, 14* (September): 499-506.

——, 1970. "Toward A Theory of Internal Resource Allocation," in M. Zald (Ed.), *Power in Organizations.* Nashville, Tenn.: Vanderbilt, University Press, pp. 270-311.

Presthus, Robert, 1961. "Weberian vs Welfare Bureaucracy in Traditional Society," *Administrative Science Quarterly, 6* (June): 1-24.

Price, James L. 1968. *Organizational Effectiveness: An Inventory of Propositions.* Homewood, Ill.: Irwin.

——, 1972. *Handbook of Organizational Measurement.* Lexington, Mass.: Heath.

——, 1977. *A Study of Organizational Turnover.* Ames, Iowa: University of Iowa Press.

Pugh, D. S., 1969. "An Empirical Taxonomy of Structures of Work Organizations." *Administrative Science Quarterly, 14* (March): 115-126.

Pugh, D. S., D. J. Hickson, C. R. Hinings, K. M. MacDonald, C. Turner, and T. Lupton, 1963. "A Conceptual Scheme for Organizational Analysis." *Administrative Science Quarterly, 8* (December): 289-316.

Pugh, D. S., D. J. Hickson, C. R. Hinings, and C. Turner, 1968. "Dimensions of Organization Structure." *Administrative Science Quarterly 13* (June): 65-105.

——, 1969. "The Context of Organization Structure." *Administrative Science Quarterly, 14* (March): 91-114.

Pugh, D. S., D. J. Hickson, and C. R. Hinings, 1969. "An Empirical Taxonomy of Structures of Work Organizations." *Administrative Science Quarterly 14* (March): 115-125.

Quinney, Richard (Ed.), 1979. *Capitalist Society: Readings for A Critical Sociology.* Homewood, Ill.: Dorsey.

Rasner, M., B. Kavcic, A. S. Tannenbaum, M. Vianello, and G. Weiser, 1973. "Worker Participation and Influence in Five Countries." *Industrial Relations, 12* (May): 200-212.

Rice, George H., Jr., and Dean W. Bishoprick, 1971. *Conceptual Models of Organization.* New York: Appleton-Century-Crofts.

Ritzer, George, 1976. *Sociology: A Multiple Paradigm Science.* Boston: Allyn & Bacon.

Ritzer, George, and Harrison M. Trice, 1969. *An Occupation in Conflict: A Study of a Personnel Manager.* Ithaca, N.Y.: State School of Industrial and Labor Relations, Cornell University.

Rizzo, John R., Robert J. House, and Sidney I. Lirtzman, 1970. "Role Conflict and Ambiguity in Complex Organizations." *Administrative Science Quarterly, 15* (June): 150-163.

Robertson, Wyndham, 1976. "Merck Strains to Keep the Pots Aboiling." *Fortune, 93* (March): 134-139.

Roethlisberger, Fritz J., and William J. Dickson, 1939. *Management and the Worker.* Cambridge, Mass.: Harvard University Press.

Rogers, Everett, 1962. *Diffusion of Innovations.* New York: Free Press.

Ronken, Harriet O., and P. R. Lawrence, 1952. *Administering Change: A Case Study of Human Relations in a Factory.* Boston: Harvard Graduate School of Business Administration.

Rosen, R. A. Hudson, 1970. "Foreman Role Conflict: An Expression of Contradictions in Organizational Goals." *Industrial and Labor Relations Review, 23* (July): 541–552.

Rosenberg, Hans, 1958. *Bureaucracy, Aristocracy and Autocracy: the Prussian Experience 1660–1815.* Boston: Beacon.

Rosengren, William R., 1967. "Structure, Policy, and Style: Strategies of Organizational Control." *Administrative Science Quarterly, 12* (June): 140–164.

Rosengren, William R., and Mark Lefton, 1970. *Organizations and Clients.* Columbus, Ohio: Merrill.

Rosner, Martin M., 1968. "Economic Determinants of Organizational Innovation." *Administrative Science Quarterly, 13* (March): 614–625.

Ross, Ian C., and A. Zander, 1957. "Need Satisfactions and Employee Turnover." *Personnel Psychology, 10* (Autumn): 327–338.

Rostow, Walt Whitman, 1948. *British Economy of the Nineteenth Century.* Oxford: Clarendon.

——, 1960. *The Stages of Economic Growth.* Cambridge, Eng.: Cambridge University Press.

Rousseau, Denise, 1978. "Characteristics of Departments, Positions and Individuals: Contexts for Attitudes and Behavior." *Administrative Science Quarterly, 23* (December): 521–540.

Rushing, William A., 1966. "Organizational Rules and Surveillance: Propositions in Comparative Organizational Analysis." *Administrative Science Quarterly, 10* (March): 423–443.

——, 1969. "Organizational Size, Rules and Surveillance," in J. A. Litterer (Ed.), *Organizations: Structure and Behavior.* New York: Wiley, pp.

Satow, Roberta Lynn, 1975. "Value-Rational Authority and Professional Organizations: Weber's Missing Type." *Administrative Science Quarterly, 20* (1975): 526–531.

Scherer, Frederick, 1970. *Industrial Market Structure and Economic Performance.* Chicago: Rand McNally.

Schmidt, Stuart, and Thomas Kochon, 1972. "Conflict: Toward Conceptual Clarity." *Administrative Science Quarterly, 17* (September): 371–81.

——, 1977. "Interorganizational Relationships: Patterns and Motivations." *Administrative Science Quarterly, 22* (June): 220–234.

Scott, W. Richard, 1975. "Organizational Structure." in A. Inkeles, J. Coleman, and N. Smelser (Eds.), *Annual Review of Sociology,* Vol. 1 Palo Alto, Cal.: Annual Review, pp. 1–20.

Scott, W. Richard, et al., 1967. "Organizational Evaluation and Authority." *Administrative Science Quarterly, 12* (June): 93–117.

Seashore, Stanley E, and E. Yuchtman, 1967. "Factorial Analysis of Organizational Performance." *Administrative Science Quarterly, 12* (December): 377–395.

Seashore, Stanley E., and Bowers, David G., 1963. *Changing the Structure and Functioning of an Organization.* Ann Arbor, Mich.: Institute for Social Research.

Selznick, Philip, 1949. *TVA and Grass Roots: A Study in the Sociology of Formal Organizations.* Berkeley: University of California Press.

Sharp, Margaret, 1973. *The State, the Enterprise, the Individual.* New York: Wiley.

Shonfield, Andrew, 1965. *Modern Capitalism: the Changing Balance of Public and Private*

Power. New York: Oxford.

Sills, David L., 1957. *The Volunteers, Means and Ends in a National Organization.* Glencoe, Ill.: Free Press.

Simmel, Georg, 1955. *Conflict.* New York: Free Press.

Simmons, Roberta G., 1968. "The Role Conflict of the First-Line Supervisor: An Experimental Study." *American Journal of Sociology, 73* (January): 482–495.

Simon, H. A., 1964. "On the Concept of Organizational Goal." *Administrative Science Quarterly, 9* (June): 1–22.

Smelser, Neil, 1959. *Social Change in the Industrial Revolution: An Application of Theory to the Lancashire Cotton Industry.* Chicago: University of Chicago Press.

Smelser, Neil, 1963. *Theory of Collective Behavior.* Glencoe, Ill.: Free Press.

Smith, Clagett G., 1966. "Comparative Analysis of Some Conditions and Consequences of Intraorganizational Conflict." *Administrative Science Quarterly, 11* (March): 504–529.

Starbuck, William, and John Derthen, 1973. "Designing Adaptive Organizations." *Journal of Business Policy, 3*: 21–28.

Steers, Richard, 1975. "Problems in the Measurement of Organizational Effectiveness." *Administrative Science Quarterly, 20* (December): 546–58.

Stinchcombe, Arthur, 1965. "Age and Structure of Organizations," in James G. March (Ed.), *The Handbook of Organizations.* Racine, Wisc.: Rand McNally.

Stoddard, Ellwyn R., 1962. "Tactics of Lateral Relationship: The Purchasing Agent." *Administrative Science Quarterly, 7* (September): 161–186.

Stogdill, Ralph M., 1971. "Dimensions of Organization Theory," in James D. Thompson and Victor Vroom (Eds.). *Organizational Design and Research.* Pittsburgh: University of Pittsburgh Press, pp. 1–56.

Strauss, Anselm, L. Schatzman, D. Erlich, R. Bucher, and M. Sabshin, 1963. "The Hospital and its Negotiated Order," in E. Freidson (Ed.), *The Hospital in Modern Society.* New York: Free Press, pp. 147–169.

Street, D., R. D. Vinter, and C. Perrow, 1966. *Organization for Treatment.* New York: Free Press.

Stymne, Bengt, 1968. "Interdepartmental Communication and Intraorganizational Strain." *Acta Sociologica, 11*: 82–100.

Tannenbaum, Arnold S., 1968. *Control in Organizations.* New York: McGraw-Hill.

——, et al., 1974. *Hierarchy in Organizations.* San Francisco: Jossey-Bass.

Taub, Richard P., 1969. *Bureaucrats Under Stress.* Berkeley: University of California Press.

Taylor, James C., 1971. "Some Effects of Technology in Organizational Change." *Human Relations, 24* (April): 105–123.

Terreberry, Shirley, 1968. "Evolution of Organizational Environments." *Administrative Science Quarterly, 12* (March): 590–613.

Thompson, James D., 1967. *Organizations in Action.* New York: McGraw-Hill.

——, 1971. *Approaches to Organizational Design.* Pittsburgh: University of Pittsburgh Press.

Thompson, James D., and W. J. McEven, 1958. "Organizational Goals and Environment: Goal Setting as an Interaction Process." *American Sociological Review, 23* (February): 23–31.

Thompson, Victor A., 1961a. "Hierarchy, Specialization, and Organizational Conflict." *Administrative Science Quarterly, 5* (March): 485–521.

——, 1961b. *Modern Organization.* New York: Knopf.

——, 1965. "Bureaucracy and Innovation." *Administrative Science Quarterly, 10*: 1–20.

——, 1969. *Bureaucracy and Innovation.* Tuscaloosa, Ala.: University of Alabama Press.

Toffler, Alvin, 1970. *Future Shock.* New York: Random House.

Tosi, Henry, Ramon Aldag, and Ronald Storey, 1973. "On the Measurement of the Environment: An Assessment of the Lawrence and Lorsch Environmental Subscale." *Administrative Science Quarterly, 18* (March): 27–36.

Tracy, Phelps, and Kaya Azumi, 1976. "Determinants of Administrative Control: A Test of A Theory with Japanese Factories." *American Sociological Review, 41* (February): 80–94.

Trussel. Ray, et al., 1960. *The Teamsters Study.* New York: Columbia School of Public Health.

Turk, Herman, 1970. "The Interorganizational Networks in Urban Society: Initial Perspectives and Comparative Research." *American Sociological Review, 35* (February): 1–9.

——, 1973. "Comparative Urban Structure from an Interorganizational Perspective." *Administrative Science Quarterly, 18* (March): 37–55.

——, 1977. *Organizations in Modern Life.* San Francisco: Jossey-Bass.

Turner, Arthur N., 1955. "Interaction and Sentiment in the Foreman-Worker Relationship." *Human Organization, 14* (Spring): 10–16.

Tushman, Michael, 1979. "Work Characteristics and Submit Communicative Structure: A Contingency Analysis." *Administrative Science Quarterly, 24* (March): 82–98.

Uttal, Bro, 1977. "How Ray McDonald's Growth Theory Created IBM's Toughest Competitor." *Fortune, 95* (January): 94–105.

Utterback, James, 1971. "The Process of Technological Innovation Within the Firm." *Academy of Management Journal, 14* (March): 75–88.

Vanderwicken, Peter, 1974. "P&G's Secret Ingredient." *Fortune, 90* (July): 75–79.

Van de Venn, Andrew, André Delbecq, and Richard Koenig, 1976. "Determinants of Coordination: Modes Within Organizations." *American Sociological Review, 41* (April): 322–238.

Vernon, Raymond, 1971. *Sovereignty At Bay.* New York: Basic Books.

Walker, Charles R., 1950. "The Problem of the Repetitive Job." *Harvard Business Review, 28* (May): 54–58.

——, 1957. *Toward the Automatic Factory: A Case Study of Men and Machines.* New Haven, Conn.: Yale University Press.

Walton, Richard E., and John N. Dutton, 1969. "The Management of Interdepartment Conflict: A Model and Review." *Administrative Science Quarterly, 14* (March): 73–90.

Walton, Richard E., John N. Dutton, and Thomas P. Cafferty, 1969. "Organizational Context and Interdepartmental Conflict." *Administrative Science Quarterly, 14* (December): 522–543.

Warner, Malcolm (Ed.), 1977. *Choice and Constraint.* London: Halsted.

Warner, W. Keith, and Eugene A. Havens, 1967. "Goal Displacement and the Intangibility of Organizational Goals." *Administrative Science Quarterly, 12* (March): 539–555.

Warren, Donald I., 1968. "Power, Visibility, and Conformity in Formal Organizations." *American Sociological Review, 33* (December): 951–970.

——, 1969. "The Effects of Power Bases and Peer Groups on Conformity in Formal Organizations." *Administrative Science Quarterly, 14* (December): 544–557.

Ways, Max, 1974. "Business Faces Growing Pressure to Behave Better." *Fortune, 89* (May): 193–195.

Weber, Max, 1946. "Bureaucracy," in H. H. Gerth and C. Wright Mills (Eds.), *From Max Weber: Essays in Sociology.* New York: Oxford University Press.

——, 1947. *The Theory of Social and Economic Organization.* New York: Oxford University Press.

Weick, Karl, 1976. "Educational Organizations as Loosely Coupled Systems." *Administrative Science Quarterly, 21* (March): 1–19.

Weisbrod, Burton, 1964. *External Benefits of Public Education.* Princeton, N.J.: Industrial Relations.

Weiss, Robert S., 1956. *Processes of Organization.* Ann Arbor, Mich.: Institute for Social Research.

Whisler, Thomas L., 1964. "Measuring Centralization of Control in Business Organizations," in W. W. Cooper et al. (Eds.), *New Perspectives in Organization Research.* New York: Wiley, pp. 314–333.

White, Harrison, 1961. "Management Conflict and Sociometric Structure." *American Journal of Sociology, 67* (September): 185–199.

——, 1970. *Chains of Opportunity: System Models of Mobility in Organizations.* Cambridge, Mass.: Harvard University Press.

Wildavsky, Aaron B., 1975. *Budgeting: A Comparative Theory of the Budgeting Process.* Boston: Little, Brown.

Wildavsky, Aaron B., and Arthur Hammond, 1965. "Comprehensive vs. Incremental Budgeting in the Department of Agriculture." *Administrative Science Quarterly, 10* (December): 321–346.

Wilson, James Q., 1966. "Innovation in Organizations: Notes Toward A Theory," in James D. Thompson (Ed.), *Approaches to Organizational Design.* Pittsburgh: University of Pittsburgh Press, pp. 193–218.

Woodward, Joan, 1965. *Industrial Organizations: Theory and Practice.* Oxford: Oxford University Press.

Zald, Mayer N., 1963. "Comparative Analysis of Measurement of Organizational Goals: The Case of Correctional Institutions for Delinquents." *Sociological Quarterly, 4* (Summer): 206–230.

——, 1967. "Urban Differentiation, Characteristics of Boards of Directors, and Organizational Effectiveness." *American Journal of Sociology, 73* (November): 261–272.

——. (ed.) 1970. *Power in Organizations.* Nashville, Tenn.: Vanderbilt University Press.

Zaltman, Gerald, and Robert Duncan, 1977. *Strategies for Planned Change.* New York: Wiley.

Zaltman, Gerald, Robert Duncan, and Jonny Holbek, 1973. *Innovations and Organizations.* New York: Wiley.

Zeitlin, Maurice, 1970. *American Society, Inc.* Chicago: Markham.

——, 1974. "Corporate Ownership and Control: The Large Corporation and the Capitalist Class." *American Journal of Sociology, 79* (March): 1073–1119.

Zeitz, Gerald, 1976. *Boundary-Spanning, Power and Control in Professional Human Service Organizations.* Unpublished doctoral dissertation, University of Wisconsin.

Zetterberg, Hans, 1963. *An Theory and Verification on Sociology.* Totowa, N.J.: Bed-
minster.

Zey-Ferrell, Mary, 1979. *Dimensions of Organizations: Environment, Context, Structure,
Process, and Performance.* Santa Monica, Cal.: Goodyear.

Name Index

Abell, Peter, 5, 109, 118
Abernathy, William, 7, 162, 174, 380, 386, 393, 417
Addams, Jane, 158
Addressograph Multigraph Co., 463
Adelman, Irman, 470
Administrative Science Quarterly, 321
Aiken, Michael, 3, 5, 7, 8, 9, 12, 13, 16, 17, 42, 63, 65, 66, 69, 70, 73, 74, 75, 77, 78, 84, 85, 97, 98, 102, 103, 105, 107, 114, 140, 141, 162, 163, 165, 170, 172, 173, 176, 177, 178, 181, 182, 183, 189, 192, 193, 198, 207, 208, 210, 213, 215, 218, 225, 252, 258, 263, 287, 299, 307, 309, 311, 312, 313, 334, 335, 337, 340, 351, 353, 363, 364, 366, 368, 372, 380, 381, 388, 397, 401, 409, 410, 411, 412, 413, 414, 415, 418, 419, 424, 452, 456, 458, 467, 487, 490, 492
Albrow, M. C., 23
Aldrich, Howard E., 3, 7, 8, 12, 16, 70, 96, 136, 199, 258, 271, 277, 364, 381, 386, 387, 396, 403, 418, 420, 424, 434, 440, 441, 445, 446, 459, 467, 469
Algeria, 482, 483
Allutto, Joseph A., 58, 99, 301
American Medical Association, 229
American Motor Corp., 112, 434
American Telephone and Telegraph (AT&T), 190
American Tobacco Co., 445, 454, 478, 480
Andrews, Frank, 199, 200, 204, 205

Anglo-Saxon countries, 94, 469, 471
Anheuser Busch Co., 445
Anthropology, 450
Ardagh, John, 59, 83
Argentina, 485
Argyro, Chris, 100, 101, 104
Armour Food Co., 277, 445
Ashby, Eric, 247, 273, 351, 432
Aston, University of, 66, 70, 84, 269, 365, 396, 399, 411
Atlantic and Pacific Tea Co., 435, 453
Australia, 482
Austria, 486
Avery, Swell, 277
Azumi, Koya, 3, 7, 10, 12, 63, 69, 72, 87, 102, 258, 269, 311, 363, 381, 399, 408, 411, 413, 415

Bacharach, Samuel, 9, 13, 84, 85, 102, 105, 372
Baldridge, J. Victor, 2, 8, 33
Bales, Robert F., 122, 136, 150, 153, 157, 202, 209, 251, 271
Bannister, E. Michael, 10
Barnard, Chester I., 34, 35, 37, 38, 41, 43, 167, 230, 354
Barton, Allen, 35
Beatrice Food Co., 434
Becker, Selwyn W., 7, 155, 162, 163, 167, 172, 173, 174, 176, 182, 183, 185, 191, 198, 220, 258, 426
Belasco, James A., 58, 99, 301
Belgium, 84, 307, 372, 485

Bell, David, 30, 46, 99, 191, 214, 216, 217, 280, 469, 471
Benson, J. Kenneth, 2, 3, 8, 10, 33, 67, 144, 467
Berliner, Joseph S., 27, 259, 462
Beyer, Janice, 167
Bidwell, Charles, 10
Biggart, Nicole, 250, 277
Blalock, Herbert M., 5, 39, 41, 43, 45
Blau, Peter M., 3, 4, 5, 17, 23, 25, 28, 54, 63, 66, 68, 69, 71, 72, 73, 74, 75, 80, 96, 98, 100, 104, 107, 115, 116, 124, 127, 128, 143, 173, 179, 181, 182, 185, 214, 280, 311, 354, 358, 380, 381, 391, 394, 395, 400, 402, 403, 404, 405, 409, 411, 440
Blauner, Robert, 11, 20, 54, 257, 300, 303, 316, 317, 318, 327, 343, 382, 402, 404, 409, 478
Bohlen, Joseph, 69
Bohrnstedt, George W., 6, 41, 79
Borden Food Co., 445
Borgotta, Edward J., Jr., 202
Bowers, David G., 25, 166, 250, 306
Brazil, 482, 483, 485
Brinkerhoff, Merlin B., 3
Britain, 58, 69, 244, 266, 275, 285, 307, 339, 435, 481, 485, 487, 488, 489
British army, 275
British Motors, 445
British Tobacco Co., 478
Brown, Ernest, 2, 10, 14, 155, 196, 207, 217, 221, 224, 254, 287
Bucher, Rue, 67, 124, 128
Buckley, Walter, 2, 46, 79, 82, 273, 369
Bunge, Mario, 14
Burns, Thomas, 1, 2, 15, 16, 24, 28, 29, 30, 31, 32, 33, 34, 35, 36, 38, 39, 42, 43, 46, 47, 49, 55, 60, 86, 87, 118, 119, 136, 137, 140, 157, 164, 165, 168, 170, 242, 250, 255, 263, 269, 281, 286, 327, 346, 357, 411, 422, 423, 445, 467, 485
Burns-Stalher model, 242

Cadwallder, Mervyn, 272
Cafferty, Thomas P., 329
California Packing, Del Monte, 445
Campbell, Donald, 80, 136
Campbell, John P., 131, 132, 134, 136

Campbell's Soup Co., 445
Canada, 71, 90, 483, 487, 489
Caplow, Theodore, 24, 62, 86, 131, 154, 155, 230, 249, 256, 271, 286, 294, 301, 309, 315, 326, 348, 353, 385, 456, 457
Cangelosi, Vincent E., 2, 272
Catholic agencies, 184, 231, 433, 447
Caves, Richard, 445
CBS, 437
Centre Nationale de Recherche Scientifique, 448
Champron, Dean, 56, 68
Chandler, Alfred D., 7, 10, 11, 30, 44, 64, 73, 96, 110, 147, 148, 150, 173, 174, 188, 189, 192, 199, 220, 231, 252, 270, 272, 276, 277, 283, 407, 412, 413, 416, 418, 424, 430, 432, 434, 435, 437, 441, 444, 445, 446, 453, 465, 469, 472, 478, 480
Child, John, 2, 3, 8, 17, 66, 68, 70, 102, 103, 143, 173, 248, 269, 364, 369, 379, 381, 411, 423
Chile, 460
China, 477, 485, 487, 488
Chirot, Daniel, 484
Chrysler Corp., 171, 384, 461
Civil Service, 71, 309
Civil War, 238
Clegg, Stewart, 2, 17
Coca-Cola, 445
Coch, Lester, 44, 54, 128, 165, 166, 199, 240
Cohn, Steve, 176
Coleman, James S., 9, 54, 60, 86, 93, 118, 119
Collins, Randall, 17
Columbia University, 190, 192, 383, 457
Comstock, Donald, 9, 13, 412
Concorde, 168, 237
Consumer's Guide, 257
Consumer's Union, 100
Control Data, 434
Conway, James, 58, 61, 99, 107, 301
Corfom, 112, 115, 168, 228, 244
Corvair, 195
Corwin, Ronald G., 2, 8, 186, 321, 322, 323, 325, 334, 335, 336, 344, 347
Coser, Lewis A., 295, 332
Costner, Herbert, 39, 43

Cremin, Lawrence Arthur, 112, 175, 218, 223, 227
Crozier, Michael, 2, 3, 23, 56, 87, 104, 114, 115, 263, 446, 485
Cuba, 477
Cummings, Larry, 130, 140
Cutright, Phillips, 470
Cyert, Richard, 2, 8, 16, 57, 77, 83, 90, 173, 389, 390

Dachler, H. Peter, 53
Daft, Richard, 7, 162, 163, 167, 172, 173, 174, 176, 182, 183, 185, 191, 197, 220
Dalton, Melville, 39, 76, 329, 335
Darkenwald, Gordon G., Jr., 321
Davis, Otto, 55, 93
de Kervasdoué, Jean, 177
Delbecq, Andre L., 3, 8, 20, 98, 361, 370, 372, 380, 383, 402, 404, 405, 410, 412, 413, 437
Dempster, M. H., 55
Dewar, Robert, 3, 7, 63, 65, 69, 102, 162, 172, 186, 187, 194, 232, 234, 252, 368, 380, 388, 395, 397, 399, 403, 418, 491
Dewey, John, 218
Diamond Match Co., 445
Dickson, William J., 315
Dill, William R., 2, 272
Donaldson, Lex, 70, 151, 396
Dornbusch, Stanley, 26
Dow Chemical, 394, 448
Duncan, Robert, 7, 16, 39, 110, 136, 161, 162, 165, 170, 188, 193, 198, 207, 209, 210, 212, 217, 218, 229, 240, 438
Dunkerly, D., 2, 17
Dunn & Bradstreet, 348
Du Pont, 10, 11, 112, 115, 173, 175, 190, 192, 220, 231, 244, 252, 276, 277, 431, 437, 480
Durkheim, Emile, 191, 315, 335, 344, 388, 491, 492
Dutton, John N., 329

Easterlin, Richard, 197
Edsel, 228
Einstein, Albert, 168
Eliot, Charles, 158, 242-243
Emery, Fred, 54, 199, 286, 316, 317
Engels, Gloria, 29, 54, 60, 79, 146, 304, 311
England, 244, 382, 475

Etzioni, Amitai, 1, 2, 15, 16, 86, 98, 100, 119, 130, 352, 353, 354, 357, 358, 359, 362, 375, 487
Europe, 202, 433, 435, 445, 493
Eirropean Group of Sociologists, 3
Evan, William, 3, 251
Evers, Frederick, 69
Exxon Corp., 434

Faunce, William A., 68
Feuer, Lewis, 304
Fiat, 482
Fielder, Fred, 131, 150, 152
Fisk, James, 272
Flamant, Maurice, 197
Ford, Henry, 276, 406, 416, 445
Ford Motor Company, 58, 112, 146, 192, 196, 198, 220, 436, 447, 453, 459
Forrester, Jay W., 2
Fournet, Glenn P., 58
France, 65, 67, 73, 224, 263, 266, 275, 277, 318, 342, 433, 435, 440, 448, 451, 455, 459, 473, 481, 482, 486, 489
Freeman, John, 3, 4, 7, 42, 43, 131, 162, 164, 165, 169, 170, 174, 189, 192, 218, 381, 447, 474
French, John, 44, 54, 102, 106, 165, 166, 199, 240, 266, 343, 433, 446, 482, 483, 487
Fullan, Michael, 300

Gamson, William, 133
General Dynamics, 394
General Electric, 146, 190, 192, 277, 448, 480
General Foods, 190
General Motors, 9-10, 11, 146, 172, 175, 190, 195, 252, 277, 383, 437, 448, 482
Gentry, John, 186
Georgopoulos, Basil S., 16
Germany, 57, 238, 435, 475, 483, 486, 488, 489
Gerth, Hans H., 15, 25, 36, 61
Getzels, Jacob W., 213
Gibbs, Jack, 5
Gilman, Daniel Coit, 158, 219, 245
Glidewell, John, 8
Glisson, Charles, 412
Goffman, Erving, 258, 402, 405
Goldman, Paul, 2, 11, 131, 136, 140, 153

Goodwill Rehabilitation, 172
Gordon, Gerald, 7, 96, 155, 162, 172, 176,
    177, 214, 426
Gouldner, Alvin W., 23, 25, 28, 35, 37, 42,
    143, 147, 150, 367
Grace, W. R. Company, 434
Grandes Ecoles, 277
Granick, David, 27
Greece, 485
Greenblatt, Morris, 161, 207, 221, 224,
    287
Gross, Neal, 224, 324, 344, 347, 348
Grusky, Oscar, 3, 131, 132, 133, 150
Gurr, Ted, 322

Haas, J. E., 29
Hage, Jerald, 1, 2, 3, 4, 5, 7, 10, 12, 13, 15,
    16, 17, 23, 24, 25, 34, 35, 36, 37, 40, 42,
    43, 45, 46, 47, 48, 55, 56, 63, 65, 66, 68,
    69, 70, 73, 74, 75, 76, 77, 78, 80, 96, 98,
    102, 103, 107, 114, 137, 140, 141, 146,
    148, 162, 163, 164, 165, 167, 170, 172,
    173, 176, 177, 178, 181, 182, 183, 186,
    187, 189, 192, 193, 194, 195, 198, 202,
    207, 208, 210, 211, 213, 215, 218, 223,
    224, 225, 226, 230, 232, 233, 236, 241,
    245, 252, 253, 263, 269, 271, 281, 287,
    288, 299, 309, 311, 312, 313, 334, 335,
    337, 338, 340, 344, 350, 351, 353, 357,
    359, 360, 363, 364, 365, 366, 368, 380,
    388, 395, 396, 397, 399, 400, 401, 403,
    409, 410, 411, 412, 413, 414, 415, 418,
    419, 440, 452, 456, 458, 459, 467, 469,
    490
Hagstrom, Warren, 8, 474
Hall, Richard, 1, 2, 3, 6, 24, 29, 41, 54, 58,
    61, 83, 84, 130, 147, 148, 150, 180, 220,
    271, 311, 345, 363, 365, 381, 403
Hammond, Phillip, 55
Hannan, Michael, 4, 6, 41, 42, 43, 131
Hanneman, Robert, 440, 482
Harlan County, 321, 456
Harvard University, 58, 113, 190, 192,
    242-243, 274, 348, 454, 457
Havens, Eugene A., 130
Headstart, Operation of, 238, 285, 470
Health, Education & Welfare, Department of,
    10, 180, 196, 442
Hedberg, Robert T., 2, 10, 33
Heinz, 445

Heise, David, 5, 6, 41
Helmich, Donald, 196, 217
Herker, Diane, 3
Hernes, Gudmund, 60
Heron, R. Retter, 63, 71, 72
Hewett-Packard, 190
Heydebrand, Wolf, 3, 17, 63, 69, 179, 182,
    391
Hibbs, Douglas, Jr., 322
Hickson, D. J., 3, 4, 8, 10, 13, 32, 53, 56,
    63, 71, 72, 83, 84, 87, 88, 89, 109, 124,
    174, 281, 346, 365, 380, 381, 383, 402,
    404, 405, 408, 409, 425, 485
Hills, Frederick, 2, 8, 61
Hinlings, C. R., 83, 88, 90, 281, 365
Hirsch, Paul, 3, 13
Hirschman, Albert O., 7, 293, 295, 308,
    322, 323, 325, 349, 356
Hirschman model, 294
Hoffman, Richard, 68, 211, 224, 231, 233,
    236, 318, 409
Hofstadter, Richard, 285
Holbeq, Jonny, 7, 16, 110, 161, 162, 165,
    170, 188, 193, 198, 207, 209, 210, 212,
    217, 218, 229, 240
Hollingsworth, J. Rogers, 146
Homans, George, 5, 12, 13, 234, 271, 315,
    318
Hong Kong, 485
Hotpoint, 237
Howard Johnsons, 435
Huber, George, 3, 130, 140
Hyman, Richard, 58, 321

IBM, 110, 111, 122, 190, 192, 431, 437,
    439, 449, 453, 461, 463, 475, 480
I. G. Farben, 445, 448
Imperial Chemical, 445, 448
Imperial Tobacco, 445
India, 482, 485, 486
Institute of Health, 10
Israel, 481, 486
Italy, 342, 485, 488
Ivy League, 253, 457

Jackson, Phillip W., 213
James, Henry, 242
Japan, 69, 72, 83, 92, 275, 300, 311, 316,
    434, 442, 445, 459, 473, 475, 480, 481,
    482, 483, 486

Jewish agencies, 433, 447
Johns Hopkins University, 190, 219, 245
Johnson, Jerry, 29, 73, 300, 316

Kahn, Robert, 2, 10, 11, 25, 162, 164,
    224, 248, 250, 257, 324, 327, 347, 357,
    379, 391, 492
Kalmar, 318
Kaluzny, Arnold, 7, 162, 172, 174, 185,
    186, 188, 192, 193, 232
Karpik, Lucien, 2, 8, 65, 93, 143, 245,
    449, 456
Kasarda, John, 10
Katz, Daniel, 2, 10, 11, 25, 162, 164, 248,
    250, 257, 357, 379, 391
Khandwalla, Pradip, 114, 130, 258
Kimberly, John, 3, 163, 380, 384, 435
Klonglan, Gerald, 458
Knight, Kenneth, 189, 192, 193, 194,
    198, 212, 217
Kodak, 445, 463
Koenig, Richard, 3, 8, 369, 370, 372, 380,
    402, 403, 404, 405, 412, 413, 437
Korea, 483
Korvettes, 435
Kover, Andrew, 91, 288
Kunz, Phillip, 3
Kuznets, Simon, 154

La Manufacture des Tabacs, 487
Land, 158
Lammers, Cornelius, 1, 2, 8, 53, 54, 87, 322,
    339, 340, 343, 425, 485
Land camera, 463
Landes, David, 470
Latin America, 202, 293, 461, 485
Lawler, Edward, 107
Lawrence, Paul R., 2, 3, 8, 9, 16, 33, 92,
    114, 121, 141, 153, 168, 183, 223, 232,
    245, 263, 265, 266, 269, 313, 325, 329,
    335, 344, 345, 348, 349, 350, 352, 353,
    355, 362, 366, 380, 381, 385, 409, 416,
    423, 437, 438, 483, 485
Lefton, Mark, 382, 395
Leifer, Richard, 3
Leik, Robert, 39, 43
Lenski, Gerhard E., 92
Lerner, Daniel, 469, 470
Lever Brothers, 278
Levine, Sol, 452

Libby's, 445
Lipset, Martin, 86, 470, 481
Lipset, Seymour, 9
Litwak, Eugene, 24
Lockeed Corp., 461
Look, 277
Lorsch, Jay W., 2, 3, 8, 9, 16, 33, 92, 114,
    121, 141, 153, 183, 232, 263, 265, 266,
    269, 313, 325, 329, 335, 345, 348, 349,
    350, 352, 353, 355, 362, 366, 380, 381,
    385, 409, 416, 423, 437, 438, 483, 485
Lourenco, Susan, 8
Lutheran agencies, 447

McCleery, Richard H., 77, 207, 211, 221,
    225, 226, 236, 241, 243, 245, 288, 366
McDonald's, 416
McEachern, Alexander, 224, 324, 344
McEven, W. J., 130
McGee, Reece J., 86, 348, 456, 457
McGregor, Douglas, 262
McNeil, Kenneth, 2, 15, 17, 29, 110
Mahoney, Thomas A., 2, 8, 61, 131, 132, 136
Maniha, John K., 432
Mann, Floyd C., 16, 68, 211, 223, 224,
    225, 231, 233, 236, 318, 386, 409
Mansfield, Edwin, 162, 164, 165, 254, 434,
    439, 474
March, James G., 1, 2, 6, 7, 8, 16, 23, 32,
    35, 57, 62, 63, 77, 83, 84, 90, 110, 114,
    116, 118, 122, 130, 140, 167, 173, 188,
    195, 215, 218, 272, 293, 294, 298, 300,
    323, 352, 353, 376, 388, 389, 390, 426,
    429, 454, 473
Marek, Julius, 286
Maris, Robin, 57, 234
Martin, Linda G., 283, 434
Marwell, Gerald, 13
Marx, Karl, 29, 60, 79, 143, 146, 191, 300,
    304, 343, 393, 454, 478
Maryland, 86
Maslow, Abraham, 199, 319
Mason, Ward, 224, 324, 344
Matra, 440
Mayntz, Renate, 23
Meadows, Donella M., 433
Mechanic, David, 101, 324
Merton, Robert K., 12, 23, 25, 28, 35,
    42, 46, 147, 148, 164, 184, 323, 324,
    341, 344, 346, 348, 354

Mexico, 485
Meyer, John, 3, 63, 74, 381, 391, 394, 400, 403, 404, 423
MGM, 449
Michels, Robert, 202
Michigan, 100, 253
Miller, James G., 2, 18, 20, 109, 212, 316
Mills, C. Wright, 15, 25, 36, 61, 94
Ministry of Education, 266, 275, 448
Ministry of Health, 244, 275, 432
Mintzberg, Henry, 3, 8, 70, 130, 244, 272, 276, 305, 394, 407, 424, 425, 435, 438, 441
Mobil Oil Corp., 434, 453
Moch, Michael, 71, 172, 176, 179
Model T, 276, 406, 445
Mohr, Lawrence, 388
Montgomery Ward, 73, 277, 434, 446, 453
Morin, Piere, 299, 317, 318
Morris, Cynthia, 470
Morrison, Sammuel, 113
Morse, Nancy C., 96
Mouzelis, Nicos P., 2
Mulder, Mark, 53, 58, 99

Nader, Ralph, 53
Nader's Raiders, 100, 237, 253
Nagel, Ernst, 35
National Biscuit Co., 445
National Polio Foundation, 435
NCR, 252, 262, 436
Nebraska, 205
Nestle, 445
Neuhauser, Duncan, 155, 258, 426
Newberry, John, 63, 71, 72
New School of Social Research, 205
New York, City of, 112, 257
Nigeria, 482
Nobel Prize, 200
Noell, J. J., 179-182
North America, 86, 480
Northern Europe, 475
Norway, 317, 477
Nowak, Phillip, 459
Nystrom, Paul, 2, 18, 33

Office of Economic Opportunity, 245
Office of Education, 10
O'Hanlon, Thomas, 434

Olivetti, 482
ORTF, 487
Ouchi, William, 3, 73, 300, 316

Packard Motor Co., 281, 287, 434
Palumbo, Dennis, 67, 74, 76, 83, 84, 104, 172, 179, 181, 732
Paris, 88
Parsons, Talcott, 7, 16, 25, 28, 35, 36, 39, 44, 136, 143, 144, 153, 157, 209, 214, 249, 353, 375, 379, 388, 459
Patton, Michael, 175, 205, 224, 225
Paulson, Steven K., 69, 70, 365, 381, 399, 411, 412, 415, 458
Payne, P. L., 107
Peabody, Robert L., 106
Pelz, Donald C., 199, 200, 204, 205
Pennings, Johannes, 57, 66, 131, 136, 141, 153, 307, 309, 382
Pennsylvania, 53
Perrow, Charles, 1, 2, 9, 11, 17, 20, 23, 53, 64, 83, 86, 92, 96, 102, 130, 131, 134, 135, 136, 137, 138, 139, 140, 141, 143, 144, 145, 147, 216, 220, 253, 266, 287, 352, 353, 355, 357, 380, 381, 382, 387, 402, 403, 404, 405, 432, 435, 437
Peru, 53
Pettigrew, Andrew, 33, 109
Peugot, 445
Peyrefitte, Roger Alain, 59, 73, 83, 277
Pfeffer, Jeffery, 3, 7, 16, 17, 89, 90, 96, 131, 453, 459
Philco, 65, 220, 453
Phillippines, 486
Pillsbury Flour, 445
Plymouth, 171
Polaroid, 190, 276, 278, 393, 439
Pondy, Louis, 321, 322, 326
Portugal, 488
Prethus, Robert, 259
Price, James L., 1, 3, 15, 17, 23, 34, 44, 54, 63, 65, 66, 106, 130, 131, 132, 134, 137, 138, 140, 173, 213, 294, 295, 306, 308, 309, 311, 313, 316, 321, 348, 353, 357, 358, 362
Proctor and Gamble, 431, 445
Progressive era, 285
Proposition 13, 251
Public Health Service, 448
Puerto Rico, 183

Pugh, D. S., 16, 23, 29, 36, 63, 66, 70, 151, 173, 364, 365, 381, 385, 395, 396, 415

Quaker Oats, 445
Quinney, Richard, 4, 7, 17, 67

Raisinghani, Henry D., 131, 272
Rasner, M., 99
Raven, Eugene, 102, 106
R.C.A., 95, 190, 431, 480
Remington-Rand, 110
Renault, 440, 487
Rensselaer Institute of Technology, 190, 238
Reynolds Tobacco, 437
Ritzer, George, 9, 14
Robertson, Wyndham, 439
Rogers, Everett, 184, 188, 193, 208, 232, 233
Ronken, Harriet O., 168, 223, 245, 344
Rosenberg, Hans, 34
Rosengren, William R., 205, 382, 395
Rostow, Walt Whitman, 470
Rousseau, Denise, 9, 107, 298, 308

Salancik, Gerald, 16, 89, 90
Santa Barbara, 244
Saturday Evening Post, 277
Scandinavia, 318, 469, 471, 485, 491
Schmidt, Stuart, 321, 322, 323, 326, 453
Schoenherr, Richard A., 3, 63, 66, 71, 72, 75, 115, 116, 173, 381, 391, 400, 404, 411
Schonfield, Andrew, 254, 275, 469, 488
Scotch, 133
Scott, W. Richard, 9, 13, 26, 28, 54, 68, 100, 107, 124, 132, 311, 354, 369, 402, 412
Sears and Roebuck, 10, 73, 446, 461
Seashore, Stanley E., 25, 131, 132, 134, 138, 153, 166, 250, 306
Seeman, Mebin, 8
Selznik, Philip, 17, 25, 134, 150, 152, 387
Shepard, John, 210, 217, 319
Shils, David L., 136, 153, 209
Sills, David L., 435
Simca, 440, 461
Simmel, Georg, 91, 169, 315, 326, 335
Simon, H. A., 1, 2, 6, 8, 23, 32, 35, 62, 63, 110, 114, 116, 118, 130, 152, 155, 167, 188, 195, 215, 218, 272, 293, 294, 298,

300, 323, 352, 353, 376, 388, 426, 429, 454, 473
Singer-kére, Jeanne, 197
Singer Sewing Machines, 435, 436, 445, 454, 478, 480
Smelser, Neil, 209, 214, 327, 475
Smith, Clagett G., 307, 321
SNCF, 194, 487
Social and Rehabilitation Services (Dept. of), 10
Social Security Administration, 10. 432
Spain, 485, 488
Stalker, G. M., 1, 2, 15, 16, 24, 28, 29, 30, 31, 32, 33, 34, 35, 36, 38, 39, 42, 43, 46, 47, 48, 55, 60, 84, 87, 118, 119, 136, 137, 140, 157, 164, 165, 168, 170, 250, 255, 263, 269, 281, 286, 327, 346, 357, 411, 422, 423, 445, 467, 485
Standard Oil Corp., 437, 445, 454
Stanley, Julian, 80
Starbuck, William, 2, 18, 33
Steers, Richard, 131, 134
Stinchcombe, Arthur, 418, 444
Strauss, Anselm, 60
Street, D., 405, 435
Sweden, 57, 317, 477, 487, 489
Switzerland, 477, 486

Tannebaum, Arnold S., 3, 16, 18, 25, 44, 53, 56, 58, 61, 65, 66, 77, 84, 138, 201, 250, 305, 307, 329
Tanon, Christian, 96
Taylor, James C., 99, 262, 272
Teacher Corps, 186
Teamster, 112, 229
Terreberry, Shirley, 286, 423, 439
Texaco, 426
Texas Instruments, 188, 190, 276
Textron, 449
Théorêt, A., 131, 272
Third Reich, 488
Third World, 259, 480, 483, 484, 485, 493
Thompson, James, 3, 7, 11, 17, 64, 114, 130, 133, 143, 220, 257, 272, 293, 352, 353, 355, 363, 369, 370, 380, 382, 391, 394, 402, 432, 433, 445, 457
Thompson, Victor, 38, 41, 43, 73, 335, 353, 388
Thorsrud, Einar, 54, 199, 316, 317
Time, 184

Toffler, Alvin, 231, 233, 254, 418, 477
Tracy, Phelps, 3, 102, 407, 413, 415
Trice, Harrisen, 167
Trist, E. L., 286
Trow, Martin A., 9, 86
Trussel, Ray, 112, 229
Turk, Herman, 3, 13, 424, 467
Turkey, 485
Turner, Arthur N., 315

UCLA, 244
Underwood, 482
Unilever Ltd. (British), 278, 431, 445, 478
United Fruit, 460, 461
United Fund, 433
United Soviet Socialist Republic, 58, 67,
   136, 238, 254, 259, 455, 459, 460, 462,
   469, 470, 476, 482, 487, 488, 490
United States, 57, 69, 70, 72, 92, 112, 133,
   176, 202, 219, 234, 238, 244, 245, 253,
   254, 266, 274, 275, 277, 285, 293, 307,
   312, 339, 340, 341, 342, 372, 433, 437,
   442, 447, 451, 455, 458, 459, 460, 462,
   471, 472, 475, 477, 479, 480, 481, 482,
   483, 485, 487, 489, 490, 492, 494
United States Army, 275, 277, 384, 453
United States Navy, 219, 384
Universal Studios, 434
University of California, 58, 100, 190, 244,
   253, 277
University of Chicago, 190
University of Illinois, 90
University of Wisconsin, 112, 223, 226-
   227, 293, 432
U. S. Post Office, 277, 281
U. S. Rubber, 453
U. S. Steel, 190, 193, 198, 252, 287, 436,
   437, 446
Uttal, BRO, 276, 283, 434
Utterback, James, 7, 173, 174, 177, 190,
   393, 448

Van de Ven, Andrew, 3, 8, 20, 98, 369,
   372, 380, 383, 402, 403, 404, 405, 412,
   413, 437
Vanderwicker, Peter, 431
VanHouten, Donald, 17
Veney, James, 186
Venezuela, 485
Vernon, Raymond, 8, 17, 453, 482

Veterans Administration, 10, 266, 406
Vietnam War, 133, 275
Vinter, P., 405
Vinter, R. D., 435
Virginia, 482
The Visible Hand (Chandler's), 416
Volkswagen, 430
Volvo, 175, 317, 318

Walker, Charles R., 68, 225, 231, 233, 236,
   257, 316, 318, 386, 409
Wallerstein, Immanuel, 484
Walton, Richard E., 8, 325, 329, 348
Warner, Malcolm, 3, 17, 130, 143, 248,
   269, 382, 423
War on Poverty, 13, 180, 184, 245, 252,
   253, 285, 334, 491
Warren, Donald L., 69, 102, 106, 353, 359,
   375, 458
Ways, Max, 280
Weber, Max, 15, 23, 24, 25, 26, 27, 28, 29,
   32, 35, 36, 37, 39, 41, 42, 43, 45, 46, 48,
   54, 106, 107, 130, 191, 219, 230, 235,
   250, 256, 262, 272, 277, 279, 411, 445,
   480, 490, 491
Weick, Karl, 2, 18
Weimar Republic, 489
Weisbrod, Burton, 257
Weitzel, William, 131, 132, 136
Welpert, Bernhard, 53
Western Electric, 315
Western Europe, 92, 275, 293, 442, 470,
   475, 477, 480, 481, 483
Western Germany, 485, 487, 489
Western Union, 445, 446
Westinghouse, 190, 448
Whisler, Thomas L., 67, 76
White Harrison, 133, 150, 323, 452
White Tower, 416
Wildausky, Aaron B., 55, 114
Wilke, Henke, 99
Williams, Lawrence C., 223, 224, 225, 231,
   233, 386
Wilson, James Q., 167, 173, 445
Winkelpleck, Judy, 458
Wisconsin, 100
Woodward, Joan, 2, 11, 64, 87, 161, 174,
   220, 231, 257, 269, 281, 287, 380, 382,
   386, 402, 404, 405, 409, 438
World War I, 220, 252

World War II, 112, 113, 254, 255, 262, 278, 434, 472, 488

Xerox, 190, 276, 278, 393, 439, 449, 463

Yale, 190, 192, 457
Young, Alice, 6, 41
Yuchtman, E., 131, 132, 134, 136, 153
Yugoslavia, 57, 488

Zald, Mayer N., 2, 3, 8, 17, 132, 381, 394
Zaltman, Gerald, 7, 16, 110, 161, 162, 165, 170, 188, 193, 194, 198, 207, 209, 210, 212, 217, 218, 229, 240
Zeitlin, Maurice, 7, 17, 94, 459
Zeitz, Gerald, 102, 103, 105, 373, 374, 458, 459
Zetterberg, Hans, 37
Zey-Farrell, Mary, 1, 3, 6, 54, 63, 271, 365, 380, 411

Subject Index

Absenteeism, 316, 318, 350
Activities, *see* Tasks
Adaptiveness:
  and change, 6, 164, 247-248, 491
  definition of, 248, 260-263
  and environment, 250
  and forms, 263-270
  process of, 7, 21, 249, 272-281, 367-368
  of structure, 79-80, 262
  theory of, 274-284
  and transformation, 164, 262, 267, 286-289
Adjustment:
  equilibrium, problem of, 257
  process of, 249-250, 256-260, 284
  and production functions, 256-257
Alienation, 16, 18, 19, 143, 300, 302, 305
  see also Morale
Analytical paradigms, *see* Paradigms
Anomie, 341
Attitudes, 144, 302-308, 313
  versus behavior, 298
Authority:
  hierarchy of, *see* Hierarchy, authority
  kinds of, 28, 106
  levels of, 66, 403-407
  limits on, 26
  and qualifications, technical, 28

rational-legal, 2, 23, 24-25
  traditional, 264
Automation, 174, 231, 236, 257, 287, 318-319, 385, 407
  and technology, 401, 404-405, 417, 481, 483
Autonomy, organizational:
  assumption of, 253, 452-453, 492
  and centralization, 61, 393-394
  changes in, 380
  and coordination, inter-organizational, 486-490, 492-493
  definition of, 387
  limits to, 8, 441-442, 452
  power, as input of, 257-259, 379, 381, 382, 387
  professional, *see* Job autonomy
Axiomatic theory, 34-36

Behavior, 324
  change of, 211, 221-225, 233
  see also Job autonomy
Boards;
  and crises, 95-96, 97, 156, 283-284
  innovation and radical, 217-219
  kinds of, 96
  power of, 94-98, 132, 156, 187, 247, 278, 394
  and succession, 151, 156, 247

Boards (Cont'd)
and worker representation, 57, 97-98, 303
  see also Elites
Boundary, organizational:
and measurement, 175, 182, 384
as problem, 9-10, 406
throughput, and similarity of, 10-11, 265-266, 409
  see also Throughputs
Budget, operating, 55, 385, 387, 393, 440
and size, personnel, 173, 385, 440
Bureaucracy, size and personnel, 385, 440
critique of, 28-29, 490
and efficiency, 26-29, 32, 444, 480
and innovation, 42, 43, 51
theory of, 2, 24-29, 36-37, 39, 122, 468-469
  see also Mechanical form

Capital, 257, 260-261, 472
Capitalism, 454, 487, 493
Cartels, 7, 443, 451, 462, 487
Centralization:
and autonomy organizational, 61, 393-394
causes of, 82-83, 263-269, 387-388, 396-401, 411-412, 418, 479
changes in, 45, 77, 131, 161, 239-240
and communication, 24, 42, 360-362, 365, 371-372
and complexity, 39-40, 59
and concentration of specialists, 59, 69-74, 76-82, 86, 264-265, 337-339, 419, 486
and conflict internal, 76, 223, 328-329, 330-331, 334-339, 346-347
and control social, 8, 42, 360-364, 366, 419
definition of, 42, 65-66
and effectiveness, types of, 137-138, 141-142, 264
and efficiency, 36-37, 40, 141, 264
and feedback, 280-281, 351-352
and formalization, 36, 37, 40-42, 141, 360-367, 411-412, 419
and innovation, rate of, 40, 42, 169, 184, 187, 193-194
and job autonomy, 100-107, 225, 267, 311
and leader of importance, 158

and morale, 40-42, 302-304
and production, volume of, 36, 40, 143, 264
and professional activity, 77-80, 127
and size personnel, 390-391, 396-401, 411-412, 479
and stratification, 40, 43, 59, 73, 76-77, 80-82, 264
as strategy for overcoming resistance to change, 239-245
and task scope, 396, 412, 418
and task visibility, 419
and technology, 387-388
tendency towards, 82, 341
and values, 184-185
and vested interests, 230-231
Change:
and adaptation, 164, 247-248, 491
capacity for, 229, 231-234
in centralization, 45, 77, 131, 161, 239-240
  see also Power, structure of
and coalition, dominant, 242, 248, 270, 283-284, 367-368
and conflict, 19, 164, 168, 220-226, 288, 289
in demand, 259-260, 380-382
discontinuity in, 250, 379-380, 393
and elites, 167, 217, 226, 231, 236, 242, 248, 270, 283-284, 286, 367-368
as environmental condition, 152, 154, 157, 197-199, 250, 252-254, 286-287, 333-334, 418
and equilibrium, problem of, 164, 242, 249-270, 418-420
of form, *see* Transformation
in goals, 162-163
incrementalism of, 162, 274
and knowledge, diversity of, 167-168, 385-386, 388-389, 438, 469-470
no stability, 253-254
and organization quo system, 161, 207, 260
and performance gap, 276-279
of power, structure of, 7, 154, 211, 221, 223
and rank, of equality, 166-167
resistances to, 19, 164, 208, 221-226, 229-239
and resources, 211, 218-219, 274-275

Change (Cont'd)
  speed of, 233, 239, 240, 252-254, 419-
    420, 491
  stages in, 1, 16, 208-229
  see also Adaptiveness
Charismatic leader, 28-29, 195, 219, 240,
    245, 277
  see also Leadership
Choice:
  and constraints, 150, 424, 442-452
  and environment, 283, 423
  of exit versus voice, 8, 293-295
  kinds of, 423, 426-442
  and size optimal, 7, 424
  strategic, 3, 19, 248, 273, 423, 426-
    430
  of structure, 7, 423
Clients:
  as input, 370, 395
  as interest group, 100
  and resistance to change, 237-239
  tastes of, 251
  variety of, 370, 389, 395
  see also Customers
Coalition, dominant:
  acceptance of, 128-129
  basis of, 4, 19, 91-92, 138
  causes of break-down in, 93, 109, 122-
    123, 129, 152, 197, 279, 288
  and change, 167, 217, 226, 231, 236,
    242, 248, 270, 283-284, 286,
    367-368
  and crises, 221, 224, 230-231
  and decision-making, 121, 146
  definition of, 186-187
  and effectiveness, 152-155, 207, 232
  and efficiency, 153-154, 300
  and ideology, 143-144
  and interest groups, diversity of, 138
  and leadership, 150-152
  and objectives, organizational, 130-131,
    138, 144, 149, 152-155, 249
  in political-value paradigm, 13, 16, 90-91
  professionalism of, 147-149
  size of, 167, 230, 354, 394
  stability of, 19, 54-55, 91, 93-94, 121,
    389
  succession of, 150-155, 158, 219, 415
  theory of, 54-55, 90-94, 143-149, 191-
    194, 230-231, 460-461

  and transformation, 415
  and values, 91-92, 143-149, 154-157,
    184-187, 193-194, 206, 283-284,
    415, 455-456
  see also Centralization; Elites; Power,
    structure of
Communication:
  and centralization, 24, 42, 360-362, 365,
    371-372
  and concentration of specialists, 360, 362,
    365-367
  and control, social, 31, 353, 365
  and formalization, 365-366, 412-413
  kinds of, 32, 199, 356-357, 360, 370-372
  in mechanical form, 31-32, 355-356
  and morale, 311, 313
  networks of, 24, 31, 356-357
  in organic form, 31-32, 356-357
  and size, personnel, 408-410
  and task-scope, 408-412
Competition, 413, 415, 423, 449, 453,
    464-466
  in public sector, 455, 457, 465
Complexity, 3, 39-40, 59, 328, 365
  and concentration of specialists, 63, 70
  definition of, 39
  and innovation, 40, 176-183, 186-187
Consumers, *see* Customers
Concentration of specialists:
  and causal ordering, 76-78, 80-82
  and centralization, 59, 69-74, 76-82, 86,
    264-265, 337-339, 419, 486
  and communication, 360-362, 365-366
  and complexity, 63, 70
  and conflict, 330-331
  definition of, 63-65
  and effectiveness, types of, 139, 140-142,
    264
  and feedback, 279-281
  and innovation:
    radical, 183-194
    rate of, 169
  and interest groups, 93-94, 138, 167,
    173, 330
  and leader, importance of, 158
  and morale, 302-304
  and occupation, kinds of, 263-265
  and professionalism, 73-74, 148-158,
    180-183, 186-187, 474-475
  and size, personnel, 381-382

Concentration of specialists (Cont'd)
  see also Structural differentiation
  stability of, 77-78
  coalition, 94
  and stratification, 59, 73-74, 76-78,
    80-82
  and structural differentiation, 74-75,
    388-389
  and task scope, 389, 396-400, 413, 418
  and technological change, 281, 381-382
Conflict, internal, or meso, 13, 38
  causes of, 38-39, 62-63, 76, 221-226
  and centralization, 76, 223, 328-329,
    330-331, 334-339, 346-347
  and change, 19, 164, 168, 220-226,
    288, 289
  and coalition theory, 90-93
  and complexity, 328
  and concentration of specialists, 330-
    331, 334-339, 344-345
  definition of, 223, 321-328
  in decision-making, 118, 120-122
  as disequilibrium, 62-63, 288, 323,
    331, 419
  kinds of, 221, 223, 322, 324
  management of, 4, 19, 335, 492
  and morale, 337-338
  and normative equality, 330-331
  and power, micro, 45, 54, 56, 60, 76-
    77, 80, 132, 168, 221, 223, 257,
    280
  as resistance to change, 19, 164, 208,
    221, 229-239
  role, 19, 224-225, 322, 344-349, 492
  and rules, 328-329
  and size, personnel, 347-348
  and stratification, 330-331, 334
  violent, 8, 169, 339-343, 350
Conflict, inter-organizational or macro,
    455-458
Conflict-critical, paradigm of, 2, 424
  concepts in, 18-19, 247-248
  definition of, 17
  and environment, 8, 17, 343
  and power, 144, 147, 329, 343
  premise in, 108
  vis-a-vis other paradigms, 17-18, 45,
    66-67, 146, 300
Conformity, 16, 19, 33, 356, 359, 374-
    375

  and compliance, 16, 106-107
    see also Control, social
Consensus, 16, 19, 236, 321, 327, 328
Constraints:
  environmental, 141, 423, 424, 425,
    470-485
  kinds, 437-442, 443, 451-452
  on leaders, 150
Contingency, theory of:
  departments, 88
  effectiveness, 153
  leadership, 131, 150-152
  organizations, 41, 380-381
Control:
  social, or meso:
    and centralization, 8, 42, 360-364,
      366
    and communication, 31, 353, 365
    and innovation, 419
    mechanisms of, 311, 351-355
    in mechanical form, 31
    and morale, 310-314, 317-318
    organic form, 31
    problems of, 4, 367-369
    and rank, 351-355
    self-, 264, 352
    and structure, social, 3, 351-355, 360-
      367
    typology of, 355-359
  span of, 381, 403
Co-operation:
  internal, or meso, *see* Teamwork
  inter-organizational, or macro, 455-456
Coordination:
  internal or meso, 3, 13
    mechanisms of, 19, 351-355
    and rank, 351-355
    and structure, social, 3, 351-355, 360-
      367
    typology, 355-359
  inter-organizational, or macro, 486-490,
    492-493
Coping, effectiveness of:
  and coalitions, dominant, 207,
    232
  theory of, 87-90, 280
Cosmopolitanism, 147-148, 184-185, 194-
    195
Cost-benefit analysis, 36, 257, 298-301,
    304

Costs, 226, 299
  human versus material, 7, 44, 254, 293-
    295, 312-313, 317, 460
  individual, 235, 299-300, 315, 347
  of innovation, 188
Creativity, 13, 199-205
Crime, corporate, 4, 7, 19, 461-462
Crises:
  causes of, 153-155, 212-213, 214-217,
    249-250, 251-252, 256, 260, 261,
    289
  and coalition, dominant, 217, 221, 224,
    230-231
  and innovation:
    radical, 194-195, 197, 212, 214-217,
      231, 243
    rate of, 198
  kinds of, 248-271, 289, 379
  responses to, 249-271, 285
Customers, 100, 427
  needs of, 238-239, 379, 429, 430, 434,
    465, 483
  and participation, 53-55, 137, 286
  resistance to change, 154, 237-239
  tastes of, 250-251, 265, 386, 419, 446
  see also Clients
Cybernetic-adaptive paradigm, 467
  abstractness of, 2, 18, 271
  concepts in, 18-20, 245-246, 260-262,
    273, 289, 351, 379
  lack of theory in, 273
  and performance gap, 194-195, 246,
    271, 368
  vis-a-vis other paradigms, 2, 18-20, 245-
    246, 273-274

Decision:
  high- risk, 16, 55, 109-115, 124-129
    and coalition, dominant, 114-115, 129-
      130
    definition of, 110-114
    trajectory of, 118-120, 122-123
  low-risk, 16, 19, 140
    and creativity, 199-204
    definition of, 110-114
    delegation of, 66, 71-72, 115, 120, 123,
      129, 381, 391-392
    difference from high-risk, 55, 109-110
    frequency of, 54-55, 110-111, 119-
      120

  and power, structure of, 123, 124
  routinization of, 120, 123-124, 127,
    129 .
  and sharing of power, 124, 128-129
  and trading of votes in, 55, 117-118,
    119-120
  trajectory of, 119-120
  nonroutine, see Decision, high risk
  routine, see Decisions, low risk
  strategic:
    and centralization, 59-60, 65-66, 86,
      128
    definition of, 53-54, 57
    see also Centralization; Coalition
  work, 54, 57, 128-129
    and job autonomy, 87-88, 101, 102,
      104
    see also Job autonomy
Decision-making, process of, 4, 21, 54-55
  and centralization, 125, 127-128, 129,
    184, 193
  and coalition, dominant, 117, 121, 146,
    390
  and concentration of specialists, 125-
    127, 129
  conflict in, 19, 117, 121-122, 124,
    239
  and decision-issues, number of, 120,
    126, 390
  delay in, 117, 118, 127
  delegation in, 117, 127, 391-392
  discussion, 116, 117, 120-121, 128,
    184, 239
  duration of, 117
  hierarchical pattern of, 119, 129
    see also Hierarchy, authority
  and high risk decisions, 118, 119, 120-
    124
  information search in, 116-119, 127
  and interest groups, 90-91, 120-121
  joint creation, 117-118, 119, 127, 168
  negotiation in, 54, 118, 128
  network pattern, 119, 129
  objectives of, 117, 119, 122, 129
  participation in, 117, 193, 264
  routinization of, 117, 127
  stability of, 120, 124
  and structure, social, 124-129
  trading of votes in, 55, 117-118, 119-
    120

Decision-making (Cont'd)
and values, 146
Democracy, 285, 468, 491, 492
industrial, 53, 61-62, 98-100, 481, 492
Demand, 286, 379-380
changes in, 259-260, 380-382
as constraint, 429, 446-447
and growth, 413-415, 430-431, 440
predictability of, 440
and size, personnel, 440, 444-446, 447-
449, 466, 478
and transformation, 270, 380
Departments:
and coalition theory, 84-85, 90-94
discontinuity between, 85-86, 265
number of:
and interdependence, 353, 403
and structural differentiation, 74-75,
381, 403
and structure, social, 74-75, 181-182
relative power of, 4, 13, 56, 83, 85-86
and uncertainty theory, 84, 87-90
Design, organizational, 2, 75, 250, 268,
271, 274, 407
typology of, 403-413
Development, *see* Growth
Differentiation, *see* Structural
differentiation
Directorships, *see* Boards
Discipline, worker, 26-28, 37, 42
see also Control, social
Disequilibrium, 28, 180
and conflict, 62-63, 288, 323, 331
and equilibrium, 164, 247, 288-289
and growth, 419
and innovation, radical, 212-217
kinds of, 19, 62-63, 248-271
and system functioning, 207, 269, 288,
367-369, 418
see also Crises; Equilibrium
Dissatisfaction, of members, 8, 68, 298-
309
see also Morale
Division of labor, *see* Structural differentiation
Domain, organizational, 423, 457
see also Objectives, organizational
Dominant coalition, *see* Coalition, dominant
Domination, 18, 19, 424, 452-460
Dysfunctions, 28-29, 32, 35

as crises, 251-255
in mechanical form, 43, 255
as mechanisms of change, 43, 132
in organic form, 43, 255
rules as, 28, 32, 367-368
see also Performances

Effectiveness:
and coalition, dominant, 150-155
contingency of, 153
definition of, 135-136
and efficiency, 44, 135-136, 212-213
and innovation, rate of, 135-136
and leadership, 150-151
and morale, 44, 153, 212-213
and objectives, organizational, 131-132,
133-143, 152, 154, 155-158
and power, structure of, 137-138, 154,
264
as prestige, 57-58, 135, 212
and production, volume of, 44, 460
as profit, 135, 153, 212
problems with, 131, 152-153
quality versus quantity, 135-136, 153,
212-213, 252-253, 330, 427
and survival, organizational, 153-154
types of, 135, 137-138, 141-142, 150,
251-256, 264
Efficiency, productivity:
in bureaucracy, 26, 28, 29, 32, 444,
480
and centralization, 36-37, 40, 141, 264
and coalition, dominant, 153-154, 300
definition of, 36
and demand, 440-441
and formalization, 37, 40
and innovation, rate of, 35-36, 40, 44,
153-154, 251-252, 419
and morale, 40, 45, 57, 254, 293, 300,
319-320, 419
and turnover, 300
Effort:
collective, 295-297
individual, 102
Elasticity, marginal, 258, 430, 440, 475,
479
Elites:
and boards, 94-95
and change, 167, 217, 226, 231, 236, 242,
248, 270, 283-284, 286, 367-368

Elites (Cont'd)
complacency of, 155
control of, 122, 130
as inner circle, 394
and objectives, organizational, 156
and perception of customer need, 139
and power, concentration, 286, 390-393
replacement of, 158, 284
size of, 354
values of, 132, 165, 183, 184-187, 455-
456
see also Coalition, dominant
Employment, 299
Energy, 19, 251
Entropy, 19, 286
Environment, 7
assumptions about, 250, 380
changes in, 152, 154, 157, 250, 252,
253, 286-287, 333-334, 418
in conflict-critical, 8, 17, 343
control of, 422
constraints of, 423, 424, 425, 437-442,
443, 451-452
in cybernetic-adaptive, 3, 379
definition of, 12
dimensions of, 424-425, 442
and equilibrium, 286, 418
evolution of, 286-287, 473-475, 480,
484
exchanges of, 7, 379, 420, 422, 453,
474
and form, organizational, 286-287, 353
kinds of, 444-451
and objectives, organizational, 157
predictability of, 250, 282
and resources, 274-275, 380-381
responses to, 148, 444-452
stability of, 30, 34, 96, 250, 424
and system openness, 39-44, 79, 248
task, 381
turbulence in, 96, 214, 287, 424, 439
typology of, 443-452
uncertainty of, 424, 441
Equality, 60-61, 166, 225, 304, 481
Equifinality, 19, 248, 415, 468
definition of, 417
openness to, 41
and transformation, 415-420
Equilibrium:
and change, 164, 248, 249-270, 418-420

and conflict, 331, 419
definition of, 249, 270-271
and dysequilibrium, 164, 247, 288-
289
of environment, 286, 418
of inputs and performances, 256-260,
284
moving, 9, 156, 179
of objectives, organizational, 156, 157,
249-250, 251-256
in performances, 251-256
as processes, 21, 249-250
of structure:
and performances, 263-270, 288
social, 60, 62, 79-82
see also Disequilibrium
Evaluation, 26, 203, 209-210, 212-217,
351
Evolution:
of environment, 286-287, 473-475,
480, 484
of organizational forms, 28-29, 43, 45,
416, 418, 475, 480, 484
as strategy for change, 239-244
and traditional forms, 265-266, 475
Exchange:
with environment, 7, 379, 420, 422,
453, 474
between organizations, 459
theory of, 234-236
Expertise, 88
see also Professional training
Exploitation, 18, 19, 254, 342, 424, 454,
460-463
and mechanical organizations, 94, 460-
463

Feedback, information and centralization,
280-281
and control, 212-217, 351-352
difficulty in getting, 212-213, 381
and planning, 282-283
quality of, 212-217, 273-274, 279-
280
quantity of, 212-217, 273-274, 279-
281
and resources, 275-276
Form, organizational, 20
and adaptiveness, 261-262
changes in, 267, 270

Form (Cont'd)
contradictions in, 154, 155, 158, 247
and dysfunctions, 48, 263, 490-494
and environment, 29, 48-49, 262, 286-287, 428-429, 442-452
evolution of, 450, 468, 470-485, 486-490
and innovation, radical, 211
kinds of, 24, 30-33, 262-270, 355-362, 401-410, 428-429
and performance, 29, 48, 263-264
of power, 85-87, 263-265
and process, 20, 34, 272-286
transformation of, *see* Transformation
Formalization:
and centralization, 36, 37, 40, 42, 360-367, 411-412, 419
and communication, 412-413
and concentration of specialists, 360-367
and decisions, delegation of, 120, 123, 124, 127, 129
definition of, 36
and efficiency, 36-37, 40
and morale, 40, 42, 311-314
and normative equality, 68, 360
and size, personnel, 408-413
and stratification, 40, 360-367
Futurology, 275

Gemeinschaft, 315
Goals, 6, 19, 27, 30, 130, 341
changes in, 161, 162-163
and coalitions, dominant, 152
definition of, 130, 158
derived, 92, 143
individual, 32, 130
and objectives, organizational, 130, 155
and values, 92, 143-149
see also Objectives, organizational
Group, peer, 175, 201-202, 316-320, 324, 356-358
Growth, of organizations, 4, 7, 19
and demand, 413-415, 429-430
as dejective, 136, 427-430
and inter-organizational relations, 455
optimal, size, 424
processes of, 413-420

and regulation, 466
speed of, 259-260, 278

Hierarchy, authority, 24
acceptance of, 128
as basis for interest group formation, 91-92
dual, 85-86, 266-267
levels in, number of, 66, 403-407
and power:
board, 94-99, 156, 187, 278, 394
departmental, 85-86
lower echelons, 88-89
and specialization, 28
Human relations:
and change, 164-165
sharing of power in, 128, 166
as technique, 18, 138, 164, 240
see also Participation in decision-making

Ideology, 143-145
Implementation, 209-210, 220-226
Industrial democracy, 53, 61-62, 98-100
Industrialization, 92, 469, 470, 476-486
Industrial-military complex, 17
Information feedback, *see* Feedback
Initiation, 209-210, 217-220
Innovation:
periods of, 197-199
properties of, 188-192
radical, 4, 19, 188-191
and centralization, 193
and concentration of specialists, 183-194
and conflict, 207-208, 332
and cost, 190
and crises, 194-195, 197, 212, 214-217, 231, 243
definition of, 164, 191
and divisibility, 190
and form, 211, 287
and innovation rate, 164, 174-175
measurement of, 192-193
and organizations, new, 189
and performance, standards of, 195, 213-217
and power structure, 211

Innovation (Cont'd)
 rarity of, 189-190, 193, 207,
  228
 and risk, 188, 190
 stages of, 207-229
 and technology, 188-190, 191-192,
  218-219, 220-225
 rate of:
  and centralization, 40, 42, 169, 176-
   184, 187, 193-194
  and coalition, dominant, 149
  and complexity, 40, 177, 179-180,
   182-183
  and concentration of specialists, 169,
   176-177, 264, 397-398, 414, 416
  and conflict, 191, 207
  and control, 419
  definition of, 161-163, 170, 171, 177-
   178
  and demand, 431
  and efficiency, 35-36, 44, 153-154,
   251-252, 419
  and inter-organizational relations,
   455
  kinds of, 162-164
  and morale, 40, 252, 367, 419
  and normative equality, 169
  in organic form, 16, 31-33
  and resources, slack, 173, 177
  and size, personnel, 173, 182, 190,
   245
  and stratification, 38, 40, 169
  and task scope, 413, 414-415, 416,
   418, 474-475
  and values, 149
Inputs, 10
 clients as, 370, 379
 control of, 89
 innovation in radical, 224
 knowledge as, 257, 379, 383-386, 389,
  404, 438-439
 labor as, 257, 386
 and outputs, 249, 256-260, 284, 419
 power as, 257-258, 379, 382, 387
Institutionalization:
 of form, 255, 277-279
 of innovation, 211, 226-229
 of power structure, 123, 277
Integration, social:
 horizontal, 74-75, 342-349

 social, 296, 299, 315-316, 318-319,
  420
  see also Interaction, social
 vertical, 74-75
 see also Structural differentiation
Interaction, social, 319, 354, 402
 see also Integration, social
Interdependence:
 of organizations, *see* Inter-organizational
  relations
 work-flow, 353, 403
Interest groups, 8, 57
 bases of, 91, 94
 and conflict theory, 90-91, 229-230
 measurement problems, 91
 number of, 91, 94, 138, 389-390
 rank of, 58, 91-92, 166, 330
 representation of, 53-54, 98-100, 442
 and specialists, 138, 167, 173, 330
Interests:
 class, 212, 300, 333
 difference from values, 47, 133
 of middle class, 146-147
 self, 48, 57-58, 169, 333
 vested, 15, 19, 166-167, 227-228, 240
 of worker, 461
 of working class, 146-147
Inter-organizational relations, 3, 424, 452-
  460, 467, 489-490

Job autonomy, 13, 19, 54, 57, 299, 317
 and centralization, 87-88, 100-107, 225,
  267, 311
 and concentration of specialists, 105
 and decision sharing, 200-201
 and decisions of work, 87-88, 101, 102,
  104
 definition of, 102-103
 and formalization, 102, 371, 373-374
 and job codification, 102, 371-373
 and supervision, 102, 311-313
Job codification, 363-364
 and formalization, 363-364
 and job autonomy, 102, 371-373
Job enlargement, 316-320
Job enrichment, 316-320
Job satisfaction, 293
 and centralization, 305-308
 and concentration of specialists, 305-
  307

Job satisfaction (Cont'd)
and conflict, 294-295
and innovation, 367-368
measurement of, 297-298
and morale, 295-296
and stratification, 305-308
and turnover, 294-295
see also Morale
Job titles, 71-72, 391, 403

Knowledge:
diversity in, 168, 170, 180, 196, 389,
389, 438
growth in, 385-386, 388, 469-470
as input, 257, 379, 383-386, 389, 404,
438-439
limits to, 167, 272-273
measures of, 180
and modernization, 469-471
in production function, 257
as resource, 275-276, 381, 383
and structural differentiation, 30-31, 47-
48, 180, 381
and task scope, 382-383, 386, 388-390,
438-439
and task or technical, 303, 438-440
442-452, 455, 466, 469
and technology, 214, 380, 385-386,
439
see also Professional activity;
Professional training

Labor force:
education of, 270
kinds of, 43, 385
and morale, 294-295, 309
size of, 257-259, 260-261
skill, level of, *see* Skill, level of
and technology, 385-386, 407
Leaders, 150-151, 158, 256, 284
charismatic, 195, 219, 240, 245, 277
see also Coalition, dominant; Elites;
Leadership
Leadership, 131, 150
and coalition, dominant, 150-152
definition of, 152
and succession, 4, 132-133, 150, 256
Legitimacy:
of occupational specialties, 280
of organization, 278, 379

Loyalty, 293-295, 309, 320, 350

Machines, 471
kinds of, 382
and labor, 257-259, 385-386, 388
and technology, 382-383, 400, 402, 403-
407
see also Automation; Throughputs
Marginal utility, 45, 258, 262
Market, 30, 34, 235-236, 253-260,
414
and changes in coalition, 93
new, 431-432
share of, 423, 429-430
specialization of, 427-429, 438-439
strategies of, 428-437, 443-451, 466
Marx, 62, 302, 454, 479
neo-, 2
Marxist, theory of, 53, 59, 60, 62, 302,
343, 454, 479
neo-, 212, 300
Mechanical form:
and adaptiveness, 281
communication in, 31-32, 356-357
control in, 351-355, 356, 359
and environment, 30-32, 444-446
and feedback, 279, 355-356
and innovation, 37, 42-43, 157, 264
power structure in, 82-83, 85-86
structure, social in, 57-58, 261, 264
Mechanic-organic form:
control, social, 355-356
coordination, 355-356, 361-362
and environment, 447-449
and innovation, 264-266
power structure in, 85-86, 265-266
structure, social, 264-265
Mergers, 134, 453
Middle class, 321, 430
upward, 73, 321
Modernization, 92, 99, 469, 470-476
Morale, 16, 165
and centralization, 42, 302-304
and communication, 311, 313
and concentration of specialists, 302-
303
and control, 310-314, 317-318
definition of, 295-296
and effectiveness, 44, 153, 212-
312

Morale (Cont'd)
and efficiency, 40, 45, 57, 254, 293, 300, 319-320, 419
and formalization, 40, 42, 311-314
and innovation, rate of, 40, 252, 367, 419
as motivation to participate, 1, 35, 153, 293
and normative-equality, 302-305
and participation in decision-making, 47, 138
and productivity, *see* Efficiency
and rules, 28, 32, 311-313, 367-368
and size, personnel, 419
and stratification, 38, 40, 42, 303-304
and supervision, 311
and task visibility, 419
and turnover, 19, 293-294, 308-309
Motivation, 39, 65
to participate, 1, 35, 153, 293
to work, 38, 293, 296-297, 354
Multi-organization, 10-11, 265-266, 383

Needs:
customer, 191, 238-239, 379, 429, 430, 434, 465, 483
lack of concern for, 19, 259
worker, 199, 297, 301, 305, 319-320
see also Demand
Neo-marxism, *see* Marxism
Normative equality, 67-68, 169, 302-305
and formalization, 68, 360
as power strategy, 89-90
and size, 391
and vested interests, 230

Objectives, organizational:
and coalition, dominant, 130-131, 138, 144, 149, 152-155
definition of, 133-134
and effectiveness, 131-132, 133-143, 152, 154, 155-158
equilibrium of, 156, 157, 249-250, 251-256
and goals, 130, 144, 155
human versus material costs, 7, 44, 254, 293-295, 312-313, 317, 427-428
innovation:
versus efficiency, 427-428
radical, as 194-195

rate of, 187
quantity versus quality, 145, 149, 252-253, 330, 427-428
and values, general, 144-145
see also Goals
Occupation:
and change, 48, 70, 167-168, 219-220
and concentration of specialists, 263-264
and coping, 87-90, 92, 280
creation of, 76-77, 219-220, 270, 388-389
power of, 7, 91, 104, 259, 349
Offices, 26-27, 30, 32
Oligarchy, law of, 202
Oligopoly, 7, 444-446
Orders, 106-107
Organic form, 16, 30-34, 263-264
and adaptiveness, 281
communication in, 31-32, 356-357
and control, 356-357
and coordination, 356-357
dysfunctions of, 43, 157
and innovation, 170
of power, 82-83, 85-86
and structure, social, 57-59, 263-264
and strategy for change, 242, 244
trend towards, 99
Organization:
boundaries, of, 10-11, 12, 17, 265-266, 384, 409
change of, 9, 161, 207
definition of, 249, 257, 265
and group, 268
as input-output systems, 162, 249, 257, 265-266, 379
and multi-organization, 10-11, 265-266, 383, 480
new, 189, 244-245, 432
set, 251, 287
and survival, assumption of, 262, 272
and technology, 418-419
Organization-set, 3
Outputs, 10
changes in, 162, 163
imbalances between, 249, 251-256
structure and, 249, 260-270
in innovation, radical, 224
measurement, problems of, 155, 257

Paradigms, 1, 14-20
  see also Conflict-critical; Cybernetic-
    adaptive; Political-value;
    Structural-functionalism
Participation in decision-making:
  and acceptance of power structure, 124,
    128, 263-264
  as compromise, 60-61
  and conflict, 138-139, 328-329
  of customers, 53-55, 137, 286
  and morale, 57, 138
  in peer group, 200-204
  as process, 117, 193, 264
  and productivity, 57, 138
  of workers, 6, 53-55, 61-62, 98-100,
    263-264, 284-285, 316-317,
    491
Particularism, 144-145, 148
Pay, 58-60, 67-68
Performances, organizational, 15
  and equilibrium, problem of, 155, 164,
    248, 249-270, 284, 418, 420
  gap in, 209-210, 214, 224-225, 227-
    228, 263, 283
  measurement of, 155
  and stable steady-states, 255, 256
  and standards of, 195, 213-217, 255,
    260, 283, 426
  and structure, 25-28, 30-33, 34-46, 136-
    145, 262-270, 273
Personality, 323
  of innovators, 217-219
  of leaders, 152, 156-157
Phenomenology, 9-10, 13, 18, 48, 326
Planning, 254, 274-275
Political economy, 2, 17
Political-value, 466-467
  and analytical level, 8, 17
  concepts in, 16-17, 19, 133
  definition of, 16, 184
  and innovation, 184-185
  and leadership, 132-133
  as paradigm, 2, 57-58, 143, 389
  premise in, 16, 184, 456
  vis-a-vis other paradigms, 16-17, 66-67,
    77, 143, 184, 205, 273
Politic process, in organizations, 33, 57-58,
    279, 394
Position, 13, 27, 324
Power:

micro:
  and decision-making, 54-55, 60-61
  definition of, 54-56
  demands for, 76
  departmental, 85-86
  occupational, 257
  sharing of, 60-61, 76-77, 166, 240,
    329
  struggles of, 45, 54, 60, 76-77, 80,
    132, 168, 221, 257, 280
  as zero-sum game, 55-56, 77
organizational, see Autonomy
processes of, see Decision-making;
    Succession
structure of, 7, 54, 67, 76-77, 164,
    211
  acceptance of, 124, 128, 263-264,
    266-267, 329
  causes of, 82-83, 263-269
  change in, 7, 154, 211, 221, 223
  and effectiveness, types of, 137-138,
    154, 264
  equilibrium in, 62, 67
  institutionalization of, 123, 277
  premise, 57-59, 60-62, 82-83, 166-167,
    330, 351-355
  and process of decision-making, 123,
    124
  stability of, 129, 329
  transformation of, 122, 211, 223
  types of, 84-87, 108, 263-267
  see also Centralization; Hierarchy,
    authority
Powerlessness, 107, 300
Predictability:
  of environment, 250, 275, 282
Prestige, 57-58, 135, 212
Priviledge, 57-58, 68
Processes:
  absence of theories about, 4, 207
  of change, 131
  and form, 20, 207, 286-289
  kinds of, 21, 109, 133, 249-250, 379
  production as, 10-11, 171, 401-410
  of stability, 131
  see also Decision-making; Innovation;
    Succession; Throughputs
Production:
  continuity of, 403-407, 417
  functions, 257-260

Production (Cont'd)
  as quantity versus quality, 35, 460
  volume of, 35-36, 44, 460
Productivity, *see* Efficiency
Products:
  availability of, 12
  changes in, 253, 278, 286
  differentiation in, 173, 174, 432, 443,
    453
  examples of, 112-113
  life of, 439, 448, 465, 474-475, 480
  mix of, 162, 383, 386
  replacement of, 432, 434-435, 443,
    449-451
  see also Services; Task scope
Profession, *see* Occupations
Professional activity, *see* Professionalism
Professionalism, 73-74, 105
  and centralization, 73-74, 77-79, 127
  and innovation, 149, 180, 186-187
Professional training, 26-27
  and centralization, 73-74
  and complexity, world view, 148
  and innovation, 179, 181, 182-183,
    186-187
  and job autonomy, 105
  and values, 148-158, 474-475
  of work-flow, 235
Profit, 135, 153, 212
Promotion, 27, 38, 150-151

Qualifications, technical, 26-27, 28, 33,
    38-39
  maximization of, 147, 300, 454-456
  see also Skills, level of
Quality:
  objective of, 145, 149, 283
  and professionalization of work-flow,
    235
  versus quantity, 135-136, 153, 212-213,
    252-253, 330, 427
Quantity:
  object of, 145
  versus quality, 135-136, 153, 212-213,
    252-253, 330, 427
  and standardization of work-flow, 235

Rank, 58, 69
  and basis of coalition, dominant, 92-93,
    389

  and change, 166-167, 170
  and control, social, 351-355
  and coordination, 351-355
  and equality, 58, 108
  and morale, 294
  premises about, 57-59, 60-62, 82-83,
    108, 161-167, 330, 351-355
  see also Centralization; Normative
    equality; Stratification
Rationality, 13, 48
  assumption of, 272
Recruitment, 158, 242, 244, 284
Regulation of organizations, 55, 93, 280-
    382, 387, 423, 433
Relations, social, 315
Resistance to change, 164
  causes of, 19, 208, 221, 229-239
  of coalition, dominant, 99, 229, 490
  and crisis, 224
  of customers, 227, 237-238
  definition of, 223
  in implementation stage, 220-226
Resources, 7
  availability of, 7-8, 219, 258, 288, 380,
    415, 419, 440, 447, 452, 466
  and change, 211, 218-219, 274-276
  competition for, 12, 413, 415, 423,
    449, 453, 464-466
  concentration of, 391-393
  controllers of, 154, 255
  dependence on, 453
  and feedback, information, 275-276
  slack, 173, 177, 190, 192-193, 219,
    274-276, 447
Responsibilities, 68, 491
  and morale, 299, 491
  as power strategy, 89-90
Revolution, 282
  as strategy of change, 239-244
Rewards, 352, 375
  regularity of, 188
Risk:
  amount of, 115
  in decision-making, 110-114
  examples of, 112-113
  and innovation, 186, 188, 193
  and number of decisions, 115
  and power, 89-90
  premise about, 115
Role conflict, *see* Conflict, internal

Role-relationships, 13
Role-set, 344-346
Role specialization, 70, 280
Routinization:
    of decisions, 120, 123-124, 127, 129,
        394
    as stage, in change process, 209-210,
        226-229
    of work, 293, 302-303, 385-396
    see also Work-flow, standardization of
Rules, 25, 26, 28, 328-329, 369
    as dysfunctions, 28, 32, 367-368
    and morale, 28, 32, 311-313, 367-
        368
    and visibility, 362-364, 370-373

Sanctions, 351, 358-359, 375
Satisfaction:
    expressive, 299-300, 306-308, 367,
        419
    job, see Job satisfaction
Scale, economics of, 407, 440, 478
    and demand, 440, 449
Self-selection, 231
Services, 12, 253
    see also Products
Size:
    budget, see Budget, operating
    optimal, 386, 442-452, 479
        and choice, 386, 424
        and technology, 386, 436, 446
    personnel, 3, 16, 41
        and adaptiveness, 479, 481
        and centralization, 381, 390-391,
            396-401, 411-412
        and choice, 7, 424
        of coalition, dominant, 230, 354,
            394
        and communication, 408-410
        and concentration of specialists, 381-
            382
        see also Structural differentiation
        and conflict, 347-348
        definition of, 384
        and demand, 440, 444-446, 447-449,
            466, 479
        and formalization, 408-413
        and innovation, 173, 182, 183, 190,
            245
        and inter-organizational relations, 455

    and minimal level of, 10, 69-
        70
    and morale, 419
    and normative equality, 391
    and stratification, 391
    and structural differentiation, 30-31,
        44, 63, 74-75, 180, 182, 355,
        381
    and task-scope, 400, 403-410
    and task visibility, 413
    vis-a-vis technology, 3, 380
Size, plant, 12
Skills:
    centrality of, 87-89
    level of, 407
        and authority, 58, 66
        and concentration of specialists, 63-64,
            75
        and coping, 89-90
        and distribution of rank, 58-60
        as input, 257-260, 261
        and job autonomy, 58
        and morale, 303
        and rank, desire for, 58, 62, 76-77
        see also Concentration of specialists
Social class, 27, 343
    and demand, 447
    and values, 146
Social control, see Control, social
Social distance, 354
Socialism, 62
Socialization, 175, 351-353, 357-358
    to change, 231-232
Social organization, see Organization
Social structure, see Structure, social
Society:
    capitalist, 172, 212, 259, 487, 490,
        493
    as context, 7, 469, 490
    consensual, 487
    coordination of, 12
    developing, 7, 259, 475, 480, 483, 484,
        485, 493
    Fascist, 488
    industrial, 99, 479-480, 493
    post-industrial, 30, 46, 191, 334, 469,
        471, 472, 475, 477, 479, 493
    socialist, 469, 470, 487, 490, 493
    values of, 59
Specialists, 62

Specialists (Cont'd)
distribution of, 61
as generalists, 72-73, 83
and power, 58-60, 128, 280
Stability, 77, 170, 253-254
of coalition, dominant, 19, 54-55, 91, 93,
121
of power structure, 129, 329
Standardization:
of jobs, *see* Job codification
of work-flow, 235, 352-353, 354-355,
356-357, 412
see also Throughputs
Standards, 352
of performance, 195, 213-217, 255-256,
260, 283, 426
Status-pyramid, *see* Stratification
Status-sets, 326
Steering, process of, 249, 251-256,
285
Stragetic choice, 3, 19, 423, 426-430
see also Choice
Strategies, 3
of environment, control over, 19, 424,
432-437
market, 170, 389, 428-437, 451, 466
to overcome resistance to change, 208-
239, 245
Stratification:
and centralization, 40, 43, 59, 73, 76-79,
80-82, 264
and complexity, 40, 59
and concentration of specialists, 59,
73-74, 80-82
definition of, 37, 67-68, 73-74
and formalization, 40, 360-367
and innovation, rate of, 38, 40, 169
and mobility, 73, 321
and morale, 38, 40, 42, 303-304
and production, volume, 38, 40, 42,
303-304
and professional, 73, 78-79
and size, personnel, 391
and structural differentiation, 74-75
and vested interests, 230
Strikes, 58, 255, 321, 333, 339-343
Structural differentiation, 30, 31, 44,
63, 74-75, 180, 182, 355,
381
definition of, 388

Structural-functionalism, paradigm of, 2,
466-467
concepts in, 15-19, 209
definition of, 15
examples of, 24-50
functions in, 2, 5, 35, 44, 153, 209,
297
as paradigm, 15-16, 143
premise in, 16, 23-24, 35, 44-45, 135,
153
and values, 143
vis-a-vis other paradigms, 1-2, 15-20,
45, 205, 273, 300
weaknesses in, 16, 324-325
and Weber, 2, 15, 23
Structure, social, 7, 19, 25, 76, 423
causes of, 2-3, 30-31
and control, social, 3, 351-355, 360-
367
and departments, 74-75, 181-182
diversity in, 389, 390
equilibirum in, 62, 79-82
and processes, 124-129
in structural-functionalism, 2
and values, 147
see also Ccntralization; Concentration
of specialists; Normative equality;
Stratification
Succession, 3, 6, 131
causes of, 152-155, 283-284
and leadership, 6, 132-133, 150
and performance, 152-155, 256, 283
as process, 21, 133
and innovation, radical, 231
survival, of organization, 152, 274
and transformation, 279
Supervision, 26, 28, 32, 39, 223, 299, 364
close, 102, 301-302, 311-313
routineness of, 293, 303
see also Hierarchy, authority
System:
and adaptiveness, 260-262
change of, 207, 260
and environment, 379
and equilibrium, 207, 269, 288, 367-269, 418
forms of, 263-266, 268-269, 355-362,
401-410, 428-429
openness of, 39-44, 79, 136, 248
steady-states in, 255-256, 258, 261, 264,
271, 355-359, 405, 406-407, 428

System (Cont'd)
survival, assumption of, 35, 44, 262, 425

Tasks, 32
complexity of, 303, 319, 354-369, 370-
372, 403-407, 437, 472-473
interdependence of, 353, 370
scope of, 55, 363
specialization of, 388, 412, 416, 456
variety of, 203-204, 319, 353
visibility of, 311-313, 359, 360, 402,
413, 419
work-flow, *see* Work-flow
Task scope:
and centralization, 396, 412, 418
change in, 40
and coalition, stability of, 389
and communication, 408-412
and concentration of specialists, 389,
396-400, 413, 418
and decisions, number of, 390
definition of, 383
and innovation rate, 413, 414-415, 416,
418, 474-475
and interest groups, number of, 389
and knowledge, 382-383, 386, 388-390,
438-439
and modernization, 472
and size, personnel, 400, 403-410
and technology, 382-383, 386, 388-390,
413, 437, 473
and values, 390
Teamwork:
and innovation, 168
tension in, 297
in work groups, 317-319
Technological breakthroughs, 281, 416,
431-432, 447-448
and changes in coalition, 93
definition of, 111, 191, 386, 441
and environmental change, 386
examples of, 161-162, 174, 190, 218
and innovative periods, 198
and mechanization, 441
and performance gap, 192-193
problem in measuring, 192-193
and resistance, 120, 223-225
see also Innovation, radical
Technology, 3, 16, 41

automation of, 236, 257, 287, 318-
319, 385, 401, 404-405, 417
and centralism, 387-388
change in, 161-162, 250, 286, 382-383,
388-390
see also Technological breakthroughs
and choice, 7
and concentration of specialists, 281,
381-382
and context, 30, 34, 381
definition of, 382-383
kinds of, 11, 382-383
and information, 279-280, 381
and innovation, 188-190, 191-192, 218-
219, 220-225
and labor-force, 385-386, 407
and organizations, new, 418-419
and production, 174, 369, 386
and risk-taking, 110-112, 120
and routine work, 55, 231, 380, 385-
386, 387-388, 402, 403-407
and task scope, 382-383, 386, 388-390,
413, 437
and transformation, 270
vis-a-vis size, 3, 380, 381, 396-401, 403-413
see also Task Scope; Throughputs
Theories:
of adaptiveness, 274-275
of autonomy, 394, 442, 465
axiomatic, 34-36
of bureaucracy, 2, 24-29, 36-37, 39
of coalitions, 54-55, 90-94, 143-149,
191-194, 230-231, 460-461
of conflict, 229-237, 330-334, 454-458
of control, 311-312, 351-362, 405-
410, 454-458
of coordination, 351-362
of coping, 87-90, 280
of creativity, 199-204
of decision-making, high risk, 110-116,
119-129
of effectiveness, 137-143, 195-196
of effort, collective, 298-305
of innovation:
radical, 191-197, 212-229
rate of, 165-170
mechanical versus organic, 29-34
of morale, 298-305, 311-312
of resistance to change, 229-237, 274-285

Theories (Cont'd)
of role-sets, 344-346
of size, 390-393, 405-410, 440-441,
    454-458, 465
of structure, 57-63, 330, 351-362, 387-
    394
of succession, 150-157
of technology, 389-390, 405-410, 438-
    440, 444-452, 465
of turnover, 294-295
of values, 143-149, 184-187
Third World, *see* Society, developing
Throughputs, 402-413
and boundaries of organization, 10-12,
    20, 265-266, 424, 453
and change, 172, 218, 270
and form, 211, 264, 287
as hurdle, 174
and innovation, process of, 162, 217-
    220, 223, 224, 240
as technology, 10, 20, 171, 175, 277,
    402
typology of, 403-407
Time, 102, 188, 216
Traditional form, 263-264
and change, 232, 264
and control, 356, 361-362
and coordination, 356
environment of, 446-447
of power structures, 85-86, 264
structure, 263-265
Transformation:
causes of, 157, 207, 246, 247, 270,
    286-289, 333-334, 380, 393,
    413-420, 463-466, 470-485,
    486-490
definition of, 109, 262
difficulty in, 207, 255, 279, 281-282,
    288, 417
and forms, viable, 263-270
kinds of, 267, 393, 413-420, 478-479
and other processes, 109
of power structure, 122, 211, 223
process of, 287-289, 367-269, 393,
    418-420
Tuberculosis, sanitariums, 435, 447,
    450
Turnover, 13, 350
and change, 7, 256
and morale, 213, 294, 308-309, 318

Uncertainty, 3
and communication, 353
coping with, 3
and departmental power, 83, 87-90, 126
of environment, 441
and information search, 116
and programming, 353
theory of, 56, 114, 369
Unions, 118
leaders of, 57, 58, 321, 335, 342, 343,
    456
Universalism, 144-146
Utility, marginal, *see* Marginal utility

Values:
anti-change, 282
and centralization, 184-185
differences from interests, 133
and dominant coalition, 91-92, 143-149,
    154-157, 184-187, 206, 283-284,
    415, 455-456
and goals, 92, 143-149
and innovation, 184-187
of leaders, 151-152
and objectives, organization, 145-147
    185
planning, 282-283
pro-change, 184-187, 206
and professionalism, 147-148
and structure, social, 143, 147
typology of, 144-145
Vested interests, 15, 19
and change, 43, 166-167, 227-228, 240,
    244
and work-flow standardization, 229,
    230-231
Visibility:
of performance, 155, 212-217, 226, 228
of task, 311-313, 359, 369, 402, 413,
    419

Wert-rationality, 48
Work:
dimensions of, 425
routine, 231, 380, 385-386, 387-388,
    402, 403-407
Worker, participation, 6, 53-55, 61-62,
    98-100, 263-264, 284-285, 316-
    317, 491
Work-flow, task, 161

Work-flow (Cont'd)
  centrality of, 88
  kinds of, 139, 234-237, 370, 380, 402,
    403-410
  professionalization of, 235
  standardization of, 229, 230-231, 235,
    352-353, 354-355, 356-357, 412

  and technology, 380-381, 401-
    402
  see also Throughputs
Workforce, 257
Working class, *see* Social class

Zweck-rationality, 48